Castles in Medieval Society

Castles in Medieval Society

*Fortresses in England, France,
and Ireland in the
Central Middle Ages*

CHARLES L. H. COULSON

OXFORD
UNIVERSITY PRESS

OXFORD

UNIVERSITY PRESS

Great Clarendon Street, Oxford OX2 6DP

Oxford University Press is a department of the University of Oxford.
It furthers the University's objective of excellence in research, scholarship,
and education by publishing worldwide in

Oxford New York

Auckland Bangkok Buenos Aires Cape Town Chennai
Dar es Salaam Delhi Hong Kong Istanbul Karachi Kolkata
Kuala Lumpur Madrid Melbourne Mexico City Mumbai Nairobi
São Paulo Shanghai Taipei Tokyo Toronto

Oxford is a registered trade mark of Oxford University Press
in the UK and in certain other countries

Published in the United States
by Oxford University Press Inc., New York

First published 2003
First published in paperback 2004

British Library Cataloguing in Publication Data

Data available

Library of Congress Cataloging in Publication Data

Coulson, Charles.
Castles in medieval society: fortresses in England, France, and Ireland in the central
Middle Ages/Charles L.H. Coulson.
p. cm.
Includes bibliographical references (p.) and index.
1. Castles—England. 2. Fortification—England—History—To 1500. 3.
Fortification—Ireland—History—To 1500. 4. Fortification—France—History—To 1500. 5.
England—Social conditions—1066-1485. 6. France—Social conditions—987-1515. 7.
Social History—Medieval, 500-1500. 8. Ireland—History—1172-1603. 9. Castles—Ireland.
10. Castles—France. I. Title.
DA660.C635 2003   355.7'094'0902—dc21   2002028261
ISBN 0-19-820824-3
ISBN 0-19-927363-4 (Pbk.)

1 3 5 7 9 10 8 6 4 2

Typeset in Minion by
Cambrian Typesetters, Frimley, Surrey

Printed in Great Britain
on acid-free paper by
Biddles Ltd,
King's Lynn, Norfolk

To H.O.H.C., whose challenge—'What is the use of castles, when they always surrendered if besieged for long enough?', I have taken so long to meet—

And

To R.C. ('Otto') Smail, who said of some of these ideas in their original form (1970), 'this must be investigated very carefully; very carefully indeed': and who wrote 'the college clock has struck three and you will be closeted with your examiners. The exigencies of the moment mean that you will not be aware of it—but I am sitting here willing you on with all the power at my command' (1972).

Acknowledgements

A book long in gestation acquires many debts. Those who are not responsible for the blemishes which remain include the late R. Allen Brown (my research supervisor in 1965–72), Christopher Brooke, Dick (C. N.) Johns, J. G. Edwards and Otto (R. C.) Smail, my first mentor in castellology. To Professor C. H. Lawrence, to my thesis examiners Maurice Keen and Robin du Boulay, and to Michael Thompson, who all read earlier versions in whole or part, I record my gratitude. For encouragement over many years I am grateful also to Marjorie Chibnall, my once and continual teacher, and similarly to Michel de Boüard, Pierre Héliot, Anthony Emery, Arnold Taylor, Edmund King, Derek Renn, John Blair, Alf Smyth, Philip Dixon, and to Howard Colvin whose counsel and friendship have been most generous. I have benefited also from discussions with Eric Fernie, John Kenyon, Katharine Keats-Rohan, Susan Reynolds, David Crouch, Robert Liddiard, Matthew Strickland, John Goodall, Pamela Marshall, Jean Mesqui, Marie-Pierre Baudry, and especially with Ann Williams, David Roffe, David Dumville, Vivien Brown, and from the fellowship of the annual Anglo-Norman Studies Conference at Battle. Membership of the Castle Studies Group has also brought many advantages. My colleague Richard Eales at the University of Kent has been a generous friend and advisor for many years. To him, to Malcolm Barber, to Michael Jones, and to Michael Prestwich I owe many suggestions for improving the final version of this book. Terry Barry has identified some Irish castles for me. The editorial support at the Oxford University Press, especially of the History Commissioning Editor Ruth Parr, of the copy editor Jeff New, and comments by the Referees to whom it was submitted and the typing of Sally Hewett have been no less important. Where illumination has failed me the fact will be obvious but none of these are responsible. No one has done more to sustain such illumination as I possess than my wife Anne.

Nonington
Easter 2002

Contents

Introduction

Castles are not an obscure subject.[1] Of all the monuments of medieval European civilization they are probably the most familiar, rivalled only by the parish churches and great cathedrals. They may well be the most popular form of amateur history. How they are perceived has coloured ideas of medieval society, aristocratic culture, faith, and strife, permeating them all with images of dungeons, battering-rams, and boiling oil. There ought to be an extensive literature, authoritative as well as accessible, to serve (and to guide) this interest; but the historical context in Britain has not achieved popular recognition. This neglect (less marked in France or Germany) is largely due to the prevailing modernist culture legitimated by the amateur and professional military strategist in numerous guises. Documentary historians have, in the past, compliantly tended to regard 'fortification' as an arcane technology relevant mainly to warfare.[2] Archaeologists have been somewhat less prone to military determinism, with their triple rationale of warfare, society, and religion ('cult objects'). Art history, in Britain, has begun to move towards a more holistic schema of development which no longer conceives of an evolution dependent upon tactical 'improvements'.[3] Conversely, the gap between what is now the accepted academic view and the public perception is constantly widened by the pastiche medievalism of the visual media (in all shades from 'Robin Hood' to fantasy of the Tolkien variety), nourished like the popular literature by a blood-and-guts view as alien to the mature society of the middle ages as it is to its architecture. The picturesque is an authentic original element and must be accommodated, but not in the form of sado-romanticism. Idealism has not been imposed by historians and moralists. Humane values, though prone to exaggeration, do properly belong. Their importance is seen in the neglected medieval laws and customs governing the tenure and building of castles, to look no further.[4]

Much of what has gone wrong is both due to and expressed by the crushing imbalance in published writings, academic almost as much as popular, between emphasis on the brutal technology and the space given to social, aesthetic, and cultural aspects.[5] Fortresses were only occasionally caught up in war, but

[1] For what follows see Coulson, 'Cultural Realities and Reappraisals in English Castle-study', with bibliography; also Introduction, Liddiard (ed.), *Anglo Norman Castles*. My thanks are due to Dr Liddiard for allowing sight of this prior to publication.

[2] Cf. M. Prestwich, 'English Castles in the Reign of Edward II', 159–78.

[3] e.g. Heslop, 'Orford Castle, Nostalgia and Sophisticated Living', 36–58. Fernie, *Architecture of Norman England*—'there were very few purely military buildings in Norman England' (p. 49).

[4] Surveyed in Coulson, 'Rendability and Castellation in Medieval France', 59–67.

[5] But see e.g. Platt, *The Castle in Medieval England and Wales*, esp. chs. 7, 8, 'castles of chivalry'.

constantly were central to the ordinary life of all classes: of the nobility and gentry, of widows and heiresses, of prelates and clergy, of peasantry and townspeople alike, to whose interaction with castles this book is devoted. Correcting this perspective has required much of the first half to be concerned with seeing how we have arrived at the familiar scenarios of the castle-books since current traditions began in the early twentieth century.

The tendency to militaristic *idée fixe* is made worse by the peculiarly English error, reinforced by historical accident, of supposing that 'the castle' was, and could only be, the sort of exclusive lordly residence not (in truth) introduced by 'the Normans' but spectacularly multiplied by them in Britain in the demonstrative style of all their buildings.[6] As a study of 'keeps' shows, defence was but one, and seldom the primary factor, even in the Conquest process. The whole cultural and socio-political context is essential. To turn to the European background is to be convinced of the fact. In France fortresses of every possible kind were 'castles', be they entire ancient towns, newer ecclesiastical precincts, great territorial *capita*, and lesser castellated mansions, descending in scale down to ephemeral earthworks and campaign-forts (some British 'castles' of 1066–*c*.1100 fall into this category); reducing even to mere crenellated platforms on ships and to architectural elements like battlements: all of which were called or styled *castrum* and *castellum* by contemporaries.[7] The only satisfactory term to cover this diversity is that which they themselves most used: *fortalicium* ('fortress', but also 'element' and 'sign' of fortification). It meant always the symbolism of aristocratic armed power, incidentally only the physical 'strength' (nugatory unless manned) for forcible resistance to an enemy. Castles were not truly anticipations of premodern 'military architecture'. The original vocabulary is treated in detail in the first half of this book. It offers new insights for England and Ireland derived, in no small part, from associating Britain with the provinces of France with which links were so intimate during that central medieval period which runs from the later eleventh to the late fourteenth century, the era 'covered' by this book.

Historical authenticity has been scarcer even than the social dimension in the very large popular literature. General architectural surveys predominate, ample at least in illustration. Categorization and an arbitrary structural scheme of evolution of 'castles', taken as a select few from the broad class of 'noble defended residence', by separating those held to be 'military' have misrepresented and suppressed the medieval phenomenon of the fortress. Here, instead, by quoting excerpts of texts as fully as may be helpful and in translation, chiefly of 'records' covering a wide spectrum, and by addressing themes rather than limited periods or regions, authenticity has been put first. This is primarily an institutional not an architectural study, seeking to go back to the documentary basics. Some 'ground-

---

[6] Cf. Armitage, *Early Norman Castles* with A. Williams, ' "A Bell-house and a Burh-geat": Lordly Residences in England before the Norman Conquest', 221–40; Coulson, 'Peaceable Power in English Castles', 71–97.

[7] For all this see below Part I, Ch. 2, sec. 1. Coulson, e.g. 'Castellation in Champagne in the Thirteenth Century', esp. 349–56; also '*Seignorial Fortresses*', index.

clearing' accordingly accompanies textual exposition in the first half, mingling the modern consciousness of 'the castle' with the medieval realities.[8] Parts III and IV are thus able to turn from argument to pure illustration of the social realities of castles, among which symbolism was always important.[9]

Too often castle-study has operated in a historical vacuum. Instead of examining the structure in the light of the builder's career, social position, and political aims, or of the family history of ownership, sometimes even without considering properly the state of the local peace, a scenario of constant pressing danger has tended to be assumed but is seldom proved.[10] 'Medieval' is equated with 'anarchic'. Monographs, particularly the former Ancient Monuments guides, and rare general works of scholarship, most notably *The History of the King's Works*, have not altered the violent and murderous fixations of popular castellology.[11] Indeed, recent popularizations have accentuated them. In a recent survey of English publications since *c.*1970, selected with an eye to saner thinking, seventy-five books are listed, but nearly all for no more than hints of innovation.[12] Among more academic papers and articles questioning is stronger and more direct, as is to be expected. A few among a select eighty of these articles published in the last twenty years take castle-study substantially forward. The narrowly 'military' approach is the bugbear identified in an incisive review article by David Stocker, published in 1992.[13] Stocker sees even one of the most flexible of recent writers as 'still proposing an underlying military imperative',[14] and as no more than 'emerging from the shadows of the armchair-strategic view'.[15] Tradition has insisted that non-defensive elements were signs of 'decline'. Thus 'early' castles must necessarily be more 'military' and later ones more 'residential'. The ingrained but largely imaginary scenario from 'impregnable' fortress to country house is part of this well-nigh universal view.

Not until 1983, when David King's unevenly comprehensive archaeological gazetteer with historical source-notes eventually appeared, were the English and Welsh 'military' sites presented as a whole and the printed texts initially searched.[16] Even limited by the conventional definition of 'the castle' as 'a private

---

[8] Dixon, e.g. 'The Donjon of Knaresborough: The Castle As Theatre', 121–39; with Lott, 'The Courtyard and the Tower: Contexts and Symbols in the Development of Late-medieval Great Houses', 93–101; with Marshall, 'The Great Tower of Hedingham: A Reassessment', 16–23.

[9] Coulson, 'Structural Symbolism in Medieval Castle-architecture', 73–90; also, 'Some Analysis of the Castle of Bodiam, East Sussex', 51–107.

[10] e.g. Coulson, 'Battlements and the Bourgeoisie: Municipal Status and the Apparatus of Urban Defence in Later-medieval England', 119–75; Emery, *Greater Medieval Houses*, vols. 1 and 2.

[11] Brown *et al.*, *King's Works*, vols. 1 and 2, and Plans; Marshall and Samuels, *Guardian of the Trent: The Story of Newark Castle* (pp. 34, 42), refer to gaols as *oubliettes* and assume that the bishop of Lincoln's prisoners (including clergy) were thrown down into them.

[12] Coulson, 'Cultural Realities', bibliography.

[13] Stocker, 'The Shadow of the General's Armchair', 415–20; cf. M. Thompson, 'The Military Interpretation of Castles', 493–545.

[14] M. Thompson, *Decline of the Castle*, and *Rise of the Castle*. [15] Pounds, *The Medieval Castle*.

[16] D. King, *Castellarium Anglicanum*. Cf. Beeler, *Warfare in England 1066–1189*, Appendix A; Renn, *Norman Castles*, gazetteer. On numerical estimates see Eales's important 'Royal Power and Castles in Norman England', 49–78.

fortified residence of king or noble',[17] those seats judged by King to be 'seriously fortified' (assessed by scale, siting, nomenclature, and details) total well over a thousand in England and Wales (not the hundred or so untypical major examples of tradition[18]). King's purview, moreover, as reiterated in 1988, required 'military structures' to be starkly distinguishable from 'domestic' and ('not-seriously-fortified') 'rejects'.[19] His survey put English castle-study paradoxically on a new quantitative footing whose qualitative implications have still to be digested. Taken as a whole, the visible archaeology now demands a reassessment which must bring in economic, political, and social circumstances. Very creditably walled towns are not, as is usual, excluded by David King, and minor sites (the overwhelming majority) get due attention—but as forts, not as gentry-seats. Sheer number and enormous diversity compel new thinking.

Wider perspectives are needed. Turning to France, whence so much (but far from everything) came, and especially to its charter-material, can be very illuminating. The long-extended substantial pedigree and more diversified forms of Continental fortresses help to correct the 'private' and 'fortress-home' conceptual straitjacket.[20] Only by discarding or greatly broadening such ideas can fortresses be given their proper place in medieval society. The French castle-literature inevitably also tends to militarism, but less strongly and differently. Thinking (recently) in terms of the *demeure seigneuriale* and of the *habitat rural noble* dilutes the defensive fixation. But the *château* (still more the misconceived neologism *château fort*) is still a construct too narrow for the authentic castle. The German *Schloss*, *Burg*, or *Festung* is more diversified and truer to its original. In general, following their different experience, the word 'fortress' and variants are understood across the Channel more sensitively to mean an architectural specimen of the militant aristocratic ('feudal') culture.[21] It is a more social concept but one still tinged with the ideas satirized by Sellar and Yeatman—otherwise 'feudal anarchy' and *guerre privée*, not so prevalent in England.[22] But irrespectively, military history still tends to view castles everywhere doctrinally as elements in some scheme of 'national defence'.

The military tendency (derived essentially from war since Napoleon, heightened by 1914–18 and 1939–45) might be less strong had popular theorists been exposed to countervailing material of the kind this book provides.[23] Documents

---

[17] Brown, 'A List of Castles 1154–1216', 249–80, collates 327 'castle' source-references.

[18] Toy, *Castles of Great Britain*, indexes about 175 English and Welsh.

[19] D. King, *The Castle*, e.g. 1–3, is 'interpretative' not historical.

[20] e.g. Mesqui, *Châteaux et enceintes*. Coulson, ' "National" Requisitioning For "Public" Use of "Private" Castles in Pre-Nation State France', in *Medieval Europeans*, ch. 7 .

[21] e.g. Meirion-Jones and Jones (eds.), *Manorial Domestic Buildings*; Mummenhof, *Schlösser und Herrensitze in Westfalen*.

[22] Sellar and Yeatman, *1066 and All That*, 17 ('the feutile system'), 29–30. Coulson, 'The Castles of the Anarchy', in *Anarchy of King Stephen*, ch. 2; and sequel, 'The French Matrix of the Castle-provisions of the Chester–Leicester *Conventio*', 65–86.

[23] But see e.g. McNeill, *English Heritage Book of Castles* esp. chs. 1, 3. Cf. Hughes, 'Medieval Firepower', 31–43.

for a social history of fortresses are abundant. The remains of the dwellings to
which banks, walls, and towers were the shell or carapace are found almost everywhere; but despite important work by P. A. Faulkner in the 1960s, the domestic
imperative is only beginning to be appreciated.[24] Attempts in the 'life in the castle'
vein have catered chiefly for children, aimed to interest girls, and boys too young
to demand 'murder-holes', 'flanking fire', and strategy-speak.[25] Castle-study has
been curiously arrested in its adolescence, in English especially. This frozen
immaturity, in all but particular areas, is not the fault of the pioneers. George T.
Clark's architectural papers, republished with a much-criticized but valiant
historical introduction as *Medieval Military Architecture in England* (1884),
combined a civil engineer's expertise with documentary awareness and acute
architectural sensitivity. Ella Armitage's pioneering (but polemical) institutional,
archaeological, and source-based book *The Early Norman Castles of the British
Isles* (1912) was far in advance of its time.[26] Castellology has had significantly few
female exponents.[27] Also in 1912 appeared A. Hamilton Thompson's *Military
Architecture in England During the Middle Ages*, the fruit of wide-ranging and deep
knowledge, despite its title essentially cultural in sympathy, as thorough for its
date architecturally as historically.[28] These three solid and original books were
marred by little more than applying unthinkingly the strategic, imperial, and
soldierly ideas of late-Victorian Britain to an era which was almost utterly
different.

    This wrong turn was not quite inevitable: an alternative tradition might well
have sprung from the aristocratic ethos which contemporary plutocracy and
political power made visible everywhere in the Victorian country house. It could
so easily have happened, in England as abroad, that the continuities of the *château*
and the *Schloss* from medieval to early- and later-modern times should have
prevailed.[29] They do in Sir James Mackenzie's anecdotal compilation *The Castles
of England, their Story and Structure* (1897); as also in T. MacGibbon and D. Ross's
*The Castellated and Domestic Architecture of Scotland from the Twelfth to the
Eighteenth Century*, five elegant volumes of socio-architectural continuum
(published 1887–92). T. Hudson Turner and his continuator (and employer) J. H.
Parker, the Oxford antiquarian and publisher, reflected the same culture but
confined their four volumes (somewhat nominally) to *Some Account of Domestic
Architecture in England*, and covered the whole era from 1066 to Henry VIII

---

[24] Coulson, 'Cultural Realities', 179–80.
[25] e.g. Earnshaw, *Discovering Castles*; Davison, *Looking at a Castle*; Oakshott, *A Knight and his
Castle*; also Burke, *Life in the Castle in Medieval England*; cf. Kenyon, *Medieval Fortifications*, part 2
(artefactual).
[26] Armitage, *Early Norman Castles*. She and Round ('Castles of the Conquest') savaged Clark's,
Medieval Military Architecture, insisting that castles in England were a new subject and that the
Normans began it, (see I, ch. 2, below).
[27] Also, Turner, *Town Defences*.
[28] A. H. Thompson, *Military Architecture*.
[29] e.g. such a coverage as Gebelin, *The Châteaux of France*, trans. Hart, from the tenth to the nineteenth centuries, is rare for England.

(1851–9). Harold Leask's *Irish Castles and Castellated Houses* (1951) is a late but brief exemplar.[30] The logic faded away thereafter of treating most 'castles' as medieval country-houses, to be revived only recently; and incipient understanding of their widely varying 'defensive' panoply as really dual-purpose, also symbolizing the noble lifestyle, went too. There is much sociological perception in architect-historian Hugh Braun's *The English Castle* (1936) and in the distinguished work of Arnold Taylor, but in Sidney Toy (1953, 1955) and Stewart Cruden (1960) it tends to be submerged.[31] The respected work of the medievalist R. Allen Brown (1954, 1976) joined lifestyle to militarism with rare historical authority, but in him the soldierly view still predominated.[32] Dissenting from it, as we do, is not just an attribute of belonging to the post-war generation: the current reappraisal depends upon a fresh perception of the truth derived from going back to the basics.

In France also, but more variably, it became the rule to keep aesthetics and all metaphysics out of *castellologie*, confining them to 'domestic' but especially to church architecture.[33] These compartments were devised early on. Thus Arcisse de Caumont, truly 'fondateur de la science archéologique en France' (Larousse), divided his seminal *Abécédaire* into 'Ère Gallo-Romain', 'Architecture Religieuse', and 'Architectures Civile et Militaire'.[34] In Germany the more diffuse 'country-house' literature reflects modern landlordism as well as faithfulness to archaeological diversity since the Carolingian *Palast* era.[35] By contrast, in France the 1789 Revolution made almost everything before then *féodal* (a term as condemnatory as our vernacular pejorative 'medieval'), unpatriotic as well as outmoded (even barbaric); whereas in Germany emergent pan-German Romantic nationalism, manifested politically in 1848, 1870, and 1933–45, defined German identity medievally in terms of *Reich* and *Ritterzeit* (and even of the *Raubritter* and 'robber-baron'). In Britain, the overthrow of King Charles I in the Civil War and the demolitions of royalist places ordered by Parliament made castles, like Cavaliers, 'wrong but wromantic', if not dangerous then sinister—admirable only as rational applications of strategic ruthlessness. How different castellology might have been but for this wrong turning is illustrated in France by Eugène Emmanuel Viollet-le-Duc (1814–79), best known as architect-restorer to Napoleon III at Carcassonne and Pierrefonds, but also of churches like Notre-Dame de Paris and elsewhere. Although imbued with the pervasive militarism of his century he

[30] J. Mackenzie, *Castles of England*; MacGibbon and Ross, *Castellated and Domestic Architecture of Scotland*; Parker, *Domestic Architecture*, appending percipiently (iii. 401–22) a 'List of licences to crenellate from the patent rolls', see Coulson, 'Freedom to Crenellate by Licence: An Historiographical Revision', 86–137. Leask, *Irish Castles and Castellated Houses*.
[31] Toy, *Castles of Great Britain*, and *Fortification*; Cruden, *Scottish Castle*; Braun, *English Castle*; Taylor e.g. in Brown *et al.*, *King's Works*, i. 293–422.
[32] Brown, e.g. *English Medieval Castles* (repr. Woodbridge 2001) and *English Castles* (repr. London 2002); bibliography of his writings by V. Brown in *Studies in Medieval History Presented to R. Allen Brown*, 353–7.
[33] Coulson, 'Structural Symbolism' (1979); also, 'Hierarchism in Conventual Crenellation, 69–100.
[34] De Caumont, *Abécédaire*.
[35] Discussed in Thompson, *Rise of the Castle*, 18–27.

expressed original artistic and spiritual insights, dedicating his *Essai sur l'architecture militaire au moyen âge* (1854) to Prosper Mérimée, inspector-general of historical monuments as well as novelist. Viollet-le-Duc's architectural scholarship was combined with originality as an engineer, but subsequent changes of taste away from the style of imaginative but careful reconstruction, practised in Britain most notably by William Burges at Castell Coch, Glamorgan (compare his additions at Cardiff), rather marooned Viollet-le-Duc, so that his vision lost some academic respectability.[36] Symptomatically, the Victorian 'sham-castles' even of so scholarly a designer and 'restorer' as Anthony Salvin have also been left in disfavour.[37]

It would be both unwise and impossible to ignore these influences. The present work adopts some of this Romantic pedigree but seeks to put the brutalism imposed on the period in truer perspective. Instead of presenting referenced generalities it employs case-studies, preferring examples and detail in context, taking warfare as no more than one part of the social tapestry. 'Violence' must be kept in proportion. The book is document- not architecture-based, expounding topically collated sources and minimizing argument from secondary works. The Continental literature is vast and (like so much else) can only be sampled. Matters of detail are pursued (if 'the devil is in the detail', so is the spirit), but particulars given are representative and an effort has been made always to relate *minutiae* to the central theme of the social relationships of the lay aristocracy, *bourgeoisie*, clergy, and peasantry to the fortress in all the variety of its forms. Above all, the aim has been to make a fresh start, avoiding the traditional constructs and shibboleths of the literature of 'castles'. It runs a risk to go directly to the sources, trusting that they will appeal to sophisticated palates jaded by all levels of *table d'hôte* fare, as well as be accessible to the newcomer to the subject. But this method is (incidentally, as it happens) a style now in vogue.

The method, in fact, is by no means new. Feeling himself embroiled in conflict (between his own scholarly but rather severe Anglican view of the middle ages and that of Roman Catholic apologetics), G. G. Coulton went to his document-index 'with damnable iteration'.[38] The present writer agrees with him that the period speaks best through its own documents, and shares some of his temperamental earnestness; but this book, while serious, hopes to be no more polemical or disjointed than the mode of analysis and presentation dictates. By drawing upon the accessible printed *extenso* records and summary translated *calendars*, which have their own (less obvious) difficulties but require somewhat less interpretation than the very large body of chronicle material, the aim is to provide a series of

---

[36] Pevsner, *Pioneers of Modern Design*, 136–8. Viollet-le-Duc's *Essai sur l'architecture militaire* was drawn from his *Dictionnaire de l'architecture française*. More cultural still is his complementary *Dictionnaire du mobilier français*.

[37] Girouard, *The Victorian Country House*, 157–63, 273–90 (also his *The Return to Camelot*, on romantic medievalism, and *Life in the French Country House*): cf. Viollet-le-Duc on the (vanished) donjon of Coucy, *Dictionnaire de l'architecture française*, iv. 74–84.

[38] e.g. Coulton, *Ten Medieval Studies*; also *Life in the Middle Ages*; and also *Fourscore Years: An Autobiography*, ch. 33.

signposts for the general reader who needs a corrective supplement to orthodox books of castle-study and wishes to pursue it in greater depth. It is hoped also to equip the teacher with a source-book which may contribute to bridging the gap between 'history' and 'archaeology'.[39] The full Index of Persons, Places, and Subjects, it is hoped, will offer some compensation for the sacrifice of chronological and geographical order entailed by analysis by topics. Some loss of differentiation between periods and regions is harder to remedy. Chronological leaps and modern analogies are partly inevitable, partly deliberate. Specialists naturally work in terms of evolution and change—but this book is concerned with the basic continuities which make the middle ages a peculiar and fascinating period. Any such approach to an enormously various and constantly evolving era incurs great risks, some of which cannot be minimized. Some irritation may be provoked—but the risks will be justified if something of the peculiar medieval European thought-world, too readily ignored by the modernisms (technical and 'strategic') to which 'castle study' is particularly prone, emerges as a result.

The basic vocabulary, direct idiom, elementary syntax, and natural-sense word-order of the texts translated or adapted here are respected, so far as comprehension allows, in the author's translations and adaptations. Given the importance of the original terminology of fortification (if the loose vocabulary, contrasting with modern technical jargon, can be so described), the original words are quoted wherever it matters. Given the quantity and quality of the photographs which are the chief merit of a large proportion of the recent books on castles, in this book they are entirely omitted. The most photogenic sites are often the least typical. Moreover, if one good picture is worth pages of text, perhaps one good and full document may be better than either. By drawing upon a restricted but representative sample of printed, not manuscript, record collections (see the Bibliography), it has been possible to comb them thoroughly, instead of picking snippets perhaps more widely but according to a preconceived set of ideas. Accordingly, this book provides a basis for wider search, particularly the local research which can best advance the subject. Using documents which are in only a few cases the result of modern selection (being almost all from complete original archives) does produce a miscellany—but it helps to ensure that original sources, not modern preoccupations, have set the agenda. Some focused passages of revisionist argument occur in Parts I and II, but they deal with issues too important to be fudged. It is hoped that readers unfamiliar with my journal articles will be relieved of the need to look them up—and that those who know them will forgive any reiteration.

In order to be sensitive and to achieve as far as possible an accurate insight, without too intrusive an effort at interpretation, most of the texts are given quite fully (often including the revealing verbal rind), or alternatively in long excerpts or extended interpolated summaries. Without even touching the mass of manu-

---

[39] Mathieu, 'New Methods on Old Castles', 115–42; cf. Mortet and Deschamps (eds.), *Recueil de textes.*

script material in British (still more in French) archives, local and national, much case-detail has still had to be excluded, or relegated to the footnotes. It is one of the attractive qualities of the period that universal human problems (e.g. reconciling poverty with protection, power with justice, and government with God) are so prominent and persistent. Another indigenous element is the individuality and personal nature of the obligations of society, not so much impersonal and abstract citizenship as man to man, vassal to lord, and the king to all his subjects.[40] The female dimension (Part IV) and the role of children were essential to these relationships, through which, both major and minor, runs the linking thread of common principles. Binoculars are as necessary as the microscope—but keeping both in focus is not easy as we attempt to show that the records can be as vivid as the physical remains of the castles, cathedrals, parish churches, and houses themselves, when all are seen in their proper and mundane peaceable social environment.

With these intentions, the ideal of footnotes confined to bare references is not only unattainable but actually undesirable. As Professor Brown remarked (1969), footnotes 'cite the authority for statements made and they also lead all those who wish to follow into the deep woods, green pastures and rewarding byways which lie on either side of the motorway of the text'.[41] Getting off motorways, even for the newcomer, need not entail a map, boots, four-wheel-drive vehicle—or whatever are their academic equivalents.

The organization of this book also requires explanation. Texts have been put together according to a combination of theme, geographical region, and period— but themes, announced in the frequent section headings, receive priority. It has seemed best to set aside tradition and let topics be dictated by the evident concerns of particular classes and social groupings, relating them to those functions of fortresses which are clearly evident from the sources. Since many popular castle-books presume an overriding, largely autonomous, architectural evolution (even taking this alone as constituting a 'history of the castle'), to provide a supplementary study such as this requires emphasis not on structural changes but, instead, must highlight the substantial institutional and sociological continuities. Much remained but little changed along with the castellated noble residence, and the walled-town which was its patrician, *bourgeois* equivalent, well into the sixteenth and seventeenth centuries, in France especially. It is true that fortresses were especially characteristic of the European middle ages, but there was not much about them, even architecturally, which was exclusively medieval; and, in truth, very little which was peculiarly 'feudal'.[42]

Such demythologizing can necessarily have little respect for the literary and

---

[40] e.g. Powicke, *Military Obligation*. Poole, *Obligations of Society*, stands just outside the large 'military institutions' *genre* of scholarship.

[41] Brown, *Normans and the Norman Conquest*, p. ix.

[42] See 'fortification'-type books, e.g. Toy, *The Strongholds of India* and *The Fortified Cities of India*; Hogg, *Fortress: A History of Military Defence*, also *The History of Forts and Castles*; Forde-Johnston, *Castles and Fortifications*; Kightly, *Strongholds of the Realm*; Muir, *Castles and Strongholds*, etc.

media industry devoted to the charisma of 'the castle' of convention—but historical truth will gain. How much richer the broader cultural understanding can be
may be seen by considering in the round the familiar but little-known example of
Bodiam Castle in Sussex, built after 1385 by Sir Edward Dallingridge chiefly to
proclaim his leadership of the local gentry, out of pride, not fear.[43] To see Bodiam
as it really was does not make the concept of 'the castle' disappear, but rather
expands it to its proper dimensions, comprehending all the myriad castellated
buildings of lords, ecclesiastics, burgesses, and even of the rural community.
Fortification was the predominant aristocratic style to which all classes, whether
as subjects or as proprietors, conformed in various ways and to varying degrees.

[43] Coulson, 'Bodiam Castle' (1992); summary, 'Bodiam Castle: Truth and Tradition', 3–15; Saul,
'Bodiam Castle', 16–21. Goodall, 'The Englishman's Castle Was His Home', and 'The Battle for
Bodiam Castle'.

PART I

Castles: Ancient, Various, and Sociable

Introduction

How castles are perceived and what they actually were is crucial to this first Part. An account of the evolution of the popular image cannot be attempted here. It would begin, perhaps, with the colourful denunciations by monastic chroniclers such as Abbot Suger of Saint Denis and our own 'Peterborough E', the Anglo-Saxon Chronicle continuator, famous for his distortion of the role of castles in King Stephen's reign.[1] The *romans* of Chrétien de Troyes, Girart de Roussillon, and others would be examined for the chivalric and domestic *ambiance* of the fortress. Manuscript illuminations and paintings, like the detailed but poetic illustrations of the monthly labours of the peasants and *divertissements* of the nobility in the Chantilly Museum devotional 'Hours' of Jean, duc de Berry, would supply authentic insights.[2] Froissart and other chroniclers would amplify 'chivalry' while showing fortresses as the setting of deeds of arms as well as of dalliance, hunting, jousting, and menial agriculture. This mosaic picture, co-ordinated with archaeology, would reveal how far the image of castles has been altered since. An essentially medieval style of noble building could be shown continuing, not much modified, in 'Renaissance' mansions,[3] courtly pageants, and masques;[4] and reflected by such topographers as John Leland,[5] William Camden, and Daniel Lysons; and pictorially by S. and N. Buck, in the earlier eighteenth century. Such a survey would show how Victorian tastes for romantic fiction and fantasy, expressed and gratified in literature by such as Thomas Gray, Horace Walpole, Byron, Walter Scott, Mrs Radcliffe, and Harrison Ainsworth, contributed their morbid, macabre, and sadistic ingredients to the popular militarism of nineteenth-century nationalism, which reverberates down to the present.[6] The stages would also emerge by which the soldier, amateur and professional, infiltrated and, particularly in England (with its parliamentary dislike of fortifications at home,

---

[1] E. King, *Anarchy of King Stephen*, 1; and ch. 2 of Coulson, 'Castles of the Anarchy'; also id., 'French Matrix', *passim*.

[2] e.g. *Flowering of the Middle Ages*, Evans (ed.), pp. 134, 139; Meiss, *Painting of Jean de Berry*, pls. 419–24 (foreground cropped); McNeill, *Castles*, pl. 1, pp. 109–13. Heslop and Grlic, *Twelfth-Century Castles and the Architecture of Romance* (forthcoming, *pers. comm.* Sandy Heslop).

[3] Apparent, even in England; e.g. Howard, *The Early Tudor Country House*.

[4] e.g. A. Young, *Tudor and Jacobean Tournaments*, esp. illustrations.

[5] *Leland's Itinerary*, Smith (ed.); Thompson, *Decline of the Castle*, 171–8, collates castle references.

[6] e.g. Brown, 'Some observations on the Tower of London', 106–7, on 'the national scandal . . . of the presentation . . . of the monument to the public. Any innocent visitor . . . will be led to suppose that this royal and noble castle, if not actually built by Henry VIII for the purpose, has always existed solely for the incarceration, torture and eventual execution on the block of as many distinguished political prisoners as possible . . .' etc. (There has been some improvement since; re-flooding of the moat is currently in question). Clark, *The Gothic Revival*, e.g. on Thomas Gray, pp. 33–42.

but jingoistic advocacy of them abroad), actually subverted the image of the fortress, with the historians' connivance, by the end of the nineteenth century.[7] All this must be taken as read.[8] Exploring these avenues would be no mere excursion but an emancipation from the powerful constraints of received thinking.

The unique English experience of the Norman Conquest peculiarly reinforced the illusion of 'castles' as at once garrison-forts holding down a subject populace, but also as 'private', and consequently dangerous to public order and to monarchy. The notion is shown to be false when tested against the architectural and later realities of royal English sanctioning of fortification, continuously from the accession of King John to after the death of Elizabeth I in 1603.[9] Each propertied class (nobles, ecclesiastics, burgesses) had its own fortresses, but their proliferation is no proof of 'feudal anarchy' in England or in France.[10] Notions not only of 'bad barons' and irresponsible nobles but also of patriotic kings are out of date. Moreover, castles were too diversified in type and in ownership to be used to demonstrate the obvious and manifold evils of a class-divided society.[11] They were not so much more oppressive than the post-medieval 'country-house'. In rulers' hands they greatly strengthened government at all levels and gave some security (accompanied by exploitation) to the labouring poor in town and country. But at whatever degree of noble or property-owning society, castles separated privileged secular and ecclesiastical 'haves' from the less privileged or unprivileged 'have-nots'.[12] These are the issues to be tackled in Part I.

[7] e.g. Grose, *Military Antiquities* (1812), i. 350–93; ii. 1–8; Clarke, *Fortification* (1890); Capt. Thuillier, RE, *The Principles of Land Defence* (1902); Capt. Straith, (professor of fortification at the Hon. East India Coy.'s military seminary, Addiscombe), *A Treatise on Fortification* (1836).

[8] Discussion and bibliography in Coulson, 'Cultural Realities'.

[9] Coulson, 'Freedom to Crenellate' and 'Sanctioning of Fortresses in France', 38–104; and id., 'Peaceable Power', esp. 92–7.

[10] Aubenas, 'Les Châteaux-forts', 548–86. Nuanced synthesis of recent work, tending to this view, Dunbabin, *France in the Making*, 40–3, 143–50, etc.

[11] e.g. Kaeuper, *War, Justice and Public Order* (Oxford 1988) on 'private fortification' (pp. 211–25) and 'private war' (pp. 225–65). See Part III below.

[12] The conventional perspective is centrist e.g. Southern, *Making of the Middle Ages*, ch. 2, 'The bonds of society', including the formation of the county of Anjou; Eales, 'Royal Power and Castles', 49–78 and 'Castles and Politics in England, 1215–24', 23–43; also Coulson, 'Fortress Policy', 13–38.

1

A Fresh Look at Early Castles

Before those institutions became established which are thought of as medieval (and more loosely as 'feudal'), fortresses were already ancient. To speak of 'fortresses and society' is, indeed, a truism. As soon as wealth for survival was accumulated, notably harvested grain and domesticated animals, demarcation and defence were required. In the Mesopotamian city states of the Fertile Crescent, in Egypt, and in China, large populations were concentrated on townships surrounded by towered walls, battlemented and imposing, the massive gates fronted by intricately redoubled barriers which symbolized the power of the priest-king. The peaceable and egalitarian civilization of the Indus Valley differed but little. If the archaeology were evidence too overwhelming almost to contemplate, the bas-reliefs commemorating the victories of the monarchs of Assyria and of Egypt, and the historical books of the Jewish Old Testament, would be adequate demonstration of the place of fortresses in Ancient civilization.[13]

In the harsher northern regions remnants of prehistoric settlements are correspondingly poor and sparse. Even those of mediterranean Europe, and Greek fortifications of megalithic masonry, contrast sharply with the earthworks of the north.[14] Until the Bronze Age scarcely any equivalence existed. Viewed from the opposite direction, since the early modern period, the roles of western Europe and ancient East have been reversed. Civilization, as the industrialized world understands it, is European. But it is relatively very young there. Consequently, the Ancient communities can seem startlingly ahead of their time, be it in bureaucratic administration, in sanitation, or in 'defence'. Their fortification, to go no further, nevertheless does not imply any Staff College or Woolwich Academy, nor their infrastructure. For appreciating how natural fortresses were to normal Ancient and medieval societies (and how various) a long perspective is essential.

The Roman Empire which collapsed in the West during the fifth century left behind, among much else, a state-system of *castella* (army-forts increasingly 'medieval' in appearance) and the relics of municipal life on the Ancient scale within walled cities, generally known, in Gaul as in Britain, as *castra*.[15] In England

---

[13] e.g. Yadin, *The Art of Warfare in Biblical Lands*; Tuulse, *Castles of the Western World*, 7–21; Tracy (ed.), *The Urban Enceinte in Global Perspective*.

[14] e.g. Hogg, *Hill-Forts of Britain*; Allcroft, *Earthwork of England*; Winter, *Greek Fortifications*; A. Lawrence, *Greek Aims in Fortification*.

[15] e.g. Hanfmann, *Roman Art*, pl. 46 (reconstruction of the *castellum* of Deutz), pp. 81 etc.; Johnson, *Roman Forts of the Saxon Shore*, with 'continental comparison', pp. 43–95.

the many 'chester' place-names (*caer* in Wales) testify to a tradition adopted by the Anglo-Saxon boroughs (*burhs*), some of them (like Dover) styled *castrum*. After the Conquest, Orderic Vitalis' comment (*c*.1125) on 'the extreme fewness in England of the works which the Gauls call castles (*castella*)', has helped to give the impression that the Normans (as in France the *seigneur féodal*) actually invented, not an adaptation of a commonplace domestic form (English or Carolingian), but an entirely new species of fortress. Surely intentionally, because insular Anglo-Saxon England possessed only its relatively few walled boroughs (many of them established in Wessex by King Alfred to resist the Danes) and much older hill-forts, Orderic was not so specific. As an Englishman by birth but Norman by later upbringing, and as a monk of Saint-Evroul, the militant accoutrements of the thegn's homestead, with 'burh-gate and bell-house', to him were different enough from lordly fashion in Normandy, his adopted home, not to be 'castles'; and it saved face to make this his explanation for the second total English defeat of the century.[16] The matter will be further discussed.

1. Fortresses in Transition

A conspectus as broad as Orderic's, and extending beyond Europe, is necessary.[17] East and West had remained in touch. The Graeco-Roman Empire in Asia Minor and the Balkans had cities fortified in traditional Near-Eastern style, befitting their dignity,[18] like Antioch, Nicaea, and Constantinople itself, with triple walls unequalled in magnificence in the West, even by the eleventh-century Avila or later-thirteenth-century Carcassonne and Conway.[19] Byzantine farmsteads, notably in the frontier *limes* of North Africa, housing small communities, have been revealed, also fortified as elsewhere.[20] It has been a recent modern fashion to insist that in addition to the 'private fortified residence' criterion a 'feudal' environment is required for a place to qualify as a 'castle'.[21] The Franks or 'Latins' on the First Crusade (1096–9) indifferently called the forts, walled towns, and villages they encountered 'castles', just as to St Jerome in his Latin Vulgate Bible translation towns were *castra*. The Crusaders found in the East a society in which fortifying was, as in their homelands, as much art as necessity; but on a scale astounding even to Raymond of Toulouse, whose province had many Roman arenas, theatres, temples, aqueducts, and town walls. Emperor Alexis Commenus'

[16] By Swein and Cnut (Canute), 991–1016.

[17] Chibnall, 'Orderic Vitalis on Castles', 43–56, shows Orderic's vocabulary (esp. pp. 53–4). His comment on the fewness of 'castles' in England in 1066 carries some uncertain extra weight in that it may be derived from William of Poitiers (p. 47); *Orderic Vitalis*, Chibnall (ed.), ii. 218; also on 'castle' words, i. 244–386; ii. p.xxxvi. See ch. 2 below.

[18] As did peaceful Pompeii with its 7 gates in AD 79 (Toy, *Fortification*, 32–3). Grant, *Cities of Vesuvius*, index.

[19] Van Millingen, *Byzantine Constantinople*, elevation and section, p. 106, reproduced Runciman, *Fall of Constantinople*, 90, cf. ibid. 88 (map).

[20] Diehl, *L'Afrique byzantine*; MacMullen, *Soldier and Civilian*, on the militarization of society.

[21] Chiefly by Brown, below ch. 2; Davison, *The Observers' Book of Castles*, e.g. 11, 14, is conventional.

daughter, the Princess Anna, vividly recorded the courtly Greeks' reaction to the northern 'barbarians'. West–East contacts were long established but the flow of influence was very much *de haut en bas*, from South-East to North-West. Certainly, regarding fortification the Byzantines had little to learn. Frankish ambition and piety combined perhaps with a Byzantine appeal for mercenaries, backed by the papacy, produced a stark confrontation of cultures. There could hardly have been a Norman not ashamed at the poor timber halls and stockaded earth banks which at home had acquired the proud Romanesque style of *castrum*.[22]

T. E. Lawrence, in an undergraduate thesis in 1910, while at Jesus College, Oxford, did something to correct the military-developmental approach by showing the Franks' indifference in their own castles in the Holy Land to Byzantine and Armenian example.[23] Just as in post-Conquest England so also in the new principality of Antioch, in the short-lived Frankish county of Edessa, and in the kingdom of Jerusalem as a whole, the early Crusader castles had as much cultural style about them as 'military science'.[24] Neglecting the aesthetic, artistic, symbolic, and demonstrative elements in the design of fortresses while properly emphasizing those same elements in the churches built by the same masons and for the same patrons, is unbalanced. It has led, among other oddities, to the notion that the 'history of castles' consists in an arbitrary and imagined progression from walls without 'flanking' to those with towers; from defence conducted only from the parapet to walls with looped mural-galleries; from castles with 'keeps' to those without, and with single walls to the 'integrated concentric' fortress—and so forth. All of this, within an overarching schema of decline towards the late medieval era, is supposed to be driven, like some modern arms-race, almost solely by the possibility of being attacked. A milieu of constant danger is conjured up while the cultural environment (including the drive of aesthetic and technical emulation constant in building) is thought to influence only 'domestic' and 'religious' architecture. One symptom of this is that very few writers in English have studied the whole field.[25]

Byzantium was part of that early milieu, despite profound differences.

[22] *The Alexiad*, trans. Sewter, 308–31; Mayer, *The Crusaders*, 46–50; Haskins, *The Normans in European History*, chs. 7, 8. The 1091 *Consuetudines et Justicie*, cl. 4, are often cited to support an earthwork monopoly of 'the castle': Haskins, *Norman Institutions*, 282.

[23] T. E. Lawrence, *Crusader Castles*: but to say 'there is not a trace of anything Byzantine in the ordinary French castle or in any English one: while there are evident signs that all that was good in Crusading architecture came from France or Italy' (p. 56) goes too far.

[24] R. C. Smail, *The Crusaders*, ch. 4 (esp. pp. 94–5). Sahyun 'is a warning against simple generalizations' (p.106); also *Crusading Warfare (1097–1193)*, 1–21 (determinedly criticizing military theorists); 204–15 ('military functions' of castles; not 'strategic' but as local bases and refuges); 215–44 (developmental theories criticized). More recently, see Müller-Wiener, *Castles of the Crusaders*; Kennedy, *Crusader Castles*; Pringle, 'Crusader Castles: The First Generation', 14–25: cf., Deschamps, *Les Châteaux des croisés en Terre Sainte*, i. 3–57; ii. *passim*.

[25] Fernie, *Architecture of Norman England*, p. ix. King, *The Castle*, esp. ch. 4; Brown, *English Medieval Castles*, ch. 4. In 1247 Henry III wanted the *nobilitas* and absence of 'defects' of refortified Dover castle to be shown off to a 'French' visitor, Coulson, 'Structural Symbolism', 75.

Politically the ideas, and some of the practice, of the old Roman centralized state were still preserved. Provinces centered on proudly walled capital cities under appointed governors, military districts ('themes') under local commanders, and an almost deified emperor with the attributes of an Oriental despot as well as of a Christian king, had (so far as they had ever existed there) long vanished in the West. With them had gone the state-controlled and paid army which could make any sort of reality of some 'strategic network' of fortresses.[26] *Castra* and *castella* were 'civilianized', no longer barracks of professionals but becoming more than ever multi-purpose. In wartime they might defend and help to gain territory by supporting campaigns—but distinctions between 'field-army' and 'garrisons' often go too far, even in the Crusader States. Among the military functions of castles (a varying fraction of their whole *raison d'être*), that of protecting refugees from 'the open country' has been neglected.[27] This the walled town had most space for. Conspicuously large baileys to many of the chief Norman castles (at Coldred and Walmer, Kent; Kilpeck, Herefordshire; and elsewhere enclosing the parish church), sometimes incorporating the village or *burgus* ('bourg') or a monastery, clearly served not defence as such but lordly prestige.[28] Imposing as it was, the stone 'great-tower' was scarce in England, little commoner in France (and unknown in Ireland) until the later-twelfth century. It was essentially a compact, fireproof, turriform mansion, evolved from the upper-hall house, more convenient (but also restrictively more expensive) than the ringwork house or the mound- or *motte*-based noble dwelling. Defence dominated the design of neither form.[29]

Privatization of nearly all the functions of government is to us the essential characteristic of what came to be called 'feudalism'. In England, the compact kingdom of Wessex more than others reacted as a unit to the era of Scandinavian invasions, but in Europe they disrupted and accelerated the disintegration of the Carolingian state in the ninth and tenth centuries.[30] Frontier barricades of the sort which the rich and populous Roman Empire had been able to build and man in north Britain, along the Rhine and the Danube, and later in south-eastern England by the chain of *castella* of 'the Saxon Shore', were no longer possible. Instead, the protection of the rural populace in the fragments of Carolingian Gaul devolved upon increasingly hereditary local officials—in the late-Roman walled towns upon the bishops very frequently. 'Regular' forces had dwindled to re-

---

[26] Oman, *Art of War*, i. 171–228, is somewhat idealized; G. Webster, *The Roman Imperial Army*, ch. 2. 'Strategic' ideas are pervasive, e.g. Beeler, *Warfare in England*, esp. 51–7.

[27] Assertions of an 'offensive' role are numerous, but see Painter, *Feudalism and Liberty*, 129–30; Smail, *Crusading Warfare*, 204–15; Coulson, 'Seignorial Fortresses', ii, Index 'military functions of fortresses'. C. Marshall, *Warfare in the Latin East*, chs. 3, 6. Moore, 'Anglo-Norman Garrisons', 205–59 (valuable tabulated data).

[28] Pounds, 'The Chapel in the Castle', 12–20; Beresford, *New Towns*, 125–9, 334–5; M. Thompson, 'Associated Monasteries and Castles', 305–21.

[29] Coulson, 'Cultural Realities' and 'Peaceable Power' for discussion and references.

[30] Hill and Rumble (eds.) *Defence of Wessex*; Hollister, *Anglo-Saxon Military Institutions*, 140–4; Smyth, *King Alfred the Great*, 135–44, on Alfred's fortifications and their Carolingian affinities; Reuter, 'The Making of England and Germany', in *Medieval Europeans*, ch. 3.

emerge eventually as small personal retinues, the armed companions of the new territorial lords—but the past was not lost. Much had survived in the provinces of mediterranean Gaul, in Spain, and Lombardy south of the Alps, remoulding invaders who came to take over, not in the long term to destroy. In northern Gaul, romanized Germany west of the Rhine and the region south of the Danube, in what was to become the Low Countries, and similarly in Britain, the stamp of Rome was somewhat less durable. There too, nevertheless, the Roman Church represented her ideals of public organization (in somewhat more humane form), her discipline, learning, art, and language.[31] The 'Donation of Constantine' as a document was a medieval forgery, but (as forged titles often did) it reflected fact.

In the new dispensation, the idea remained that defence was a public duty and that the keeping and creating of fortresses was publicly accountable. The case regarding fortifying has been forcefully introduced by Robert Aubenas (1938);[32] regarding the conditional tenure of fortresses, particularly under 'rendability', together with the question of authorization, it remains to be established.[33] These political and institutional matters can only be touched upon here.

2. The Carolingian Response To Invasion

With these social determinants in mind and setting aside English stereotypes of the typical 'Norman Conquest approach', it is time to narrow the focus to the 'France' of the subtitle and to the Carolingian kings. 'France' must be used as a geographical expression since it did not correspond to modern France until the end of the fifteenth century, if not later. Gallic national unity is an illusion more powerful even than the myth of 'Normanity'.[34] The provinces east of the Rhône–Saône belonged to the Germanic 'empire', and the present French frontiers with Italy (created after 1860), Germany, and Belgium (set up in 1830) are the result of gains and losses as late as 1860 (Savoy and Nice) and 1870–1918 (Alsace-Lorraine). Throughout the early period, *Francia* essentially meant the north-central Parisian plain and the Seine basin (but excluding Normandy). Part of Flanders and Hainaut, outside modern France, was a fief of the Capetian kings, but the remainder of modern Belgium and most of 'Holland' were nominally imperial and culturally strongly Germanic.

Under the impact of internal disintegration and of external attacks by the

---

[31] Reynolds, *Fiefs and Vassals*, pts. 4, 5 and 6; cf. e.g. Dawson, *Making of Europe*, pt. 3; and Oakley, *Crucial Centuries*, pt. 1. Finó, *Forteresses*, ch. 2 ('l'aube des temps féodaux'), is a typical gloss. Dunbabin, *France in the Making*, chs. 3, 4.

[32] Aubenas, 'Les Châteaux-forts', in 1938, combated the 'anarchy' view with a wealth of chronicle citations. It is now in retreat. Coulson, 'Fortresses in Late-Carolingian France', 29–36.

[33] Coulson e.g. 'Rendability and Castellation' (1973), summarizing 'Seignorial Fortresses' (1972); also id., 'Castellation in Champagne', 'Fortress Policy' (1984) and 'French Matrix' (1995); for revisions of the restrictive theory of 'licences' see also id., 'Structural Symbolism' (1979: England and France); 'Hierarchism in Conventual Crenellation' (1982) and 'Freedom to Crenellate' (1994 England); 'Sanctioning of Fortresses in France' (1998).

[34] Myth is quite unashamed in popular culture, e.g. Uderzo and Goscinny, *Le Tour de Gaule d'Astérix*. Beaune, *The Birth of an Ideology*.

Norsemen (*Normands* to the French) penetrating far up the fine navigable river-systems (particularly the Somme, Seine, and Loire), the Carolingian Empire which Charlemagne had left to his son Louis in 814 began more visibly to dissolve into its component unities.[35] New compromises between local power and public authority had to be forged; between individual strength and social responsibility; between the emerging new castle-holding class and the former proprietors, especially the Carolingian counts, bishops, and abbots.[36] The new 'castles' naturally tended to be smaller than the old ones; but to label the older 'communal' and the newer 'private' ('personal' also will not do), as the traditional view of this era as *les temps des usurpations* has required, falsifies a complex reality. It was collapse not defeat, conversion not subversion. Lordship was a public office. The evolution of the horsed aristocrat who might also fight as 'cavalry' occurred very slowly (it was arguably still incomplete by the time of Hastings); and when the 'knight' can be said confidently to have emerged is very debatable, but certainly much later.[37] The concept of 'the feudal knight', in fact, is almost as dubious as is 'the feudal castle'. At least the technical proficiency of the horsed warrior is not in doubt: described by Anna Comnena as 'irresistible'; and acclaimed by an Arab chronicler, also at the time of the First Crusade, who averred that a charging Frank 'would make a hole through the walls of Babylon'.[38] The new aristocracy were not usurpers: had they not been ready to evolve to fill the ecological void, it would have been necessary to have invented them. Circumstances, in all probability, did just that.

Accusations of 'brigandage' are commonly made against those new to power by the established.[39] King Charles II, nicknamed 'the Bald', in the year 864 at Pîtres (Pistes) issued the celebrated appeal to his subjects, attempting still to resist changes which were inexorable:

We exhort you to remain firm in your fidelity and as the dear liegemen of God and of ourselves to be ever ready, if it happen that we have need, each and every one of you immediately our messenger arrives or as soon as our necessity becomes known to you, to serve God and ourselves in arms against the pagans or against others whoever they may be, or to do whatever may promote the common advantage and most surely be to our assistance. And it is our will and express instruction that whoever, in these late times, may have estab-

---

[35] Smyth, *King Alfred*, 141–4. The 'edict of Quierzy' (877) was prophetic of Charles the Bald; *MGH*, II, ii, *Capitularia* ii, 355–61. Dunbabin, *France in the Making*, pp. vii, xxv, 3 (Map, Treaty of Verdun, 843), *et passim*.

[36] Aubenas, 'Les Châteaux-forts', *passim*, combating the romantic illusion that France then 'se hérisse de châteaux', which ideas 'ne résistent pas à une critique objective'.

[37] Gillingham, 'Thegns and Knights', 129–53; also ibid. 155–78, 179–200, 201–20. Extensive literature, e.g. Barber, 'When Is a Knight Not a Knight?'; Boulton, 'Classic Knighthood as Nobiliary Dignity', 1–18, 41–100. Between the Bayeux Tapestry (c.1080) and the First Crusade (e.g. *Alexiad*, n. 22 above) much development of heavy cavalry occurred: *Bayeux Tapestry*, Stenton (ed.), 11 *et passim*; Bloch, *Feudal Society*, 288–99, pls. vi, vii; militarily, Hollister, *Military Organization*, ch. 3; Powicke, *Military Obligation*, ch. 5.

[38] Smail, *Crusading Warfare*, 106–15.

[39] Ecclesiastics gave castles a particularly bad press, Coulson, 'Castles of the Anarchy', 72, 75–6, and 'French Matrix', 75–6.

lished castles, fortifications, or palisaded earthworks (*castella et firmitates et haias*) without our authorization shall have all such fortifications destroyed by the beginning of August, since the near-dwellers and those who live round about them suffer therefrom much loss and inconvenience. And the forts which the makers refuse to destroy those the royal counts, in whose counties they may be, shall destroy, informing us in due course of anyone who proves recalcitrant. And let those counts who neglect to fulfil this order be well assured that as was wont to be specified in the capitularies of our predecessors, disobedient counts we will arraign and to their counties appoint others who are willing and able to obey our mandate.[40]

Appointed officials were increasingly eluding royal control and tending to become hereditary magnates. Powers of government were slipping from the king's hands, whether by delegation or passivity is a question of interpretation very largely. Lordship and governance had to be exercised on the spot. Organized protection for lives and chattels was needed at the enemy targets rather than exhortation invoking Christian obedience to the anointed king. The monasteries, we know, were quick to respond to the danger from the extensive ravages of coastal and riverborne piracy.[41] The reaction of prominent laymen is much less documented. The greater continuity of cathedral and abbey administrations, coupled with the close co-operation between Court and Church, ensured that charters were readily granted to ecclesiastics and that many more have survived, as copies, abstracts in chronicles and cartularies, or even as original parchments. The clue to what lay magnates were doing lies in Charles's allusion to the local impact of these spontaneously created defences. Such forts, of permanent or temporary structure, were unauthorized but mainly objectionable for the exactions which they imposed nearby. What apparently was happening was that new de facto 'castellaries' were already being set up, fragmenting the old estates, challenging their authority, and diverting their revenues.[42]

These *castellaria*, as they later developed, were often extensive administrative circumscriptions, to which each castle was the head-place or *caput* and safe place of resort for the rural population to guard and supply.[43] In Anglo-Saxon England there was a similar system developed (in Wessex and beyond) to protect the populace from the Danes.[44] In return for protection, the refugees owed to the lord

---

[40] *Recueil Général*, Jordan *et al.* (eds.), i. 79–82; cf. A Thompson, *Military Architecture*, 32, 35, 55, etc.

[41] Coulson, 'Fortresses in late-Carolingian France'. Grants of new, less endangered sites abound; e.g. *Recueil Charles II*, i. 91–3 (844), among the earliest. *Recueil Louis IV*, 3–5, shows the monks of Vézelay (*dép.* Yonne) made a *castellum* of their precinct instead (936).

[42] n. 200 below and text. 'Châtellenie' (*castellarium, castellaria*, etc.) is ubiquitous in the records but confined by English historians to the sense of 'military district dependent on a castle', e.g. Stenton, *First Century*, 192–4, 293 (index 'castlery'); Beeler, *Warfare in England*, 8, 207, 286–9 concurs; cf. Bloch, *Feudal Society*, 394–407; Dunbabin, *France in the Making*, index 'castellanies'.

[43] The register of Count Henri le Libéral, of Champagne (1156–81) defined the castellary (often *castrum/castellum*) of Provins (*dép.* Seine-et-Marne) as extending 'from the paved road to *Aliotrum* wood, thence to Jouy wood, and from there to the Seine'; Jubainville, *Histoire de Champagne*, ii. p. vii.

[44] n. 30 above. Reconstructive essay, Bachrach, 'The Tower at Langeais, 992–994', 47–62 (n. 302 below). The thesis of a modernistic medieval rationality is common, especially in war, e.g. Rogers, 'Edward III and the Dialectics of Strategy', esp. 83–5.

of the fortress labour services for the upkeep of the defences, sometimes the duty of guarding them, and often also other payments in cash or kind. Such local agreements were generally beneficial to the otherwise defenceless peasantry, but they cut across men's loyalties to the Crown and caused them to look elsewhere for protection.

From Catalonia in northern Spain, where the Christians faced Moslem Saracens, not equally 'pagan' Scandinavian raiders, comes an example of the reshaping which society was undergoing. Borell II, who was count of Barcelona from 954 to 992, fortunately thought it well in 986 to record the arrangements which had been made by his grandfather, Count Wilfred 'the Hairy', for the fortress of Cardona very late in the ninth century. Dwelling-towers had already appeared to accompany ditched enclosures.[45] The document, abbreviated a little in translation from the clear but crude Latin of its period, runs as follows:

Precept of Count Borell for the security of the castle (*castrum*) of Cardona, made before Easter in the 986th year from the Crucifixion of our Lord Jesus Christ and in the first year of the co-regency of King Louis [V, of France], son of Lothar, under his great and imperial authority and by the Divine mercy . . .—I Borell, by the Grace of God count and marquis, do ordain, guarantee, and concede in the castle called Cardona and its appurtenances to all its inhabitants and to their posterity and progeny whatever material possessions they now have there, so that from this present day forward they may hold these and enjoy them undisturbed, securely and contentedly for ever, without being harmed or harassed by anybody. For when my grandfather Wilfred, count and marquis of such esteemed memory, first constructed and built that castle of Cardona and set its bounds, he by his precept, word, and record ordained that all the people who should come to stay there as inhabitants, as also those who might flee to it with their goods and decide to settle there, should enjoy their goods lawfully and quietly in perpetuity. And he promised to protect and defend such men from any wrongs done to them, punishing those responsible, and doing them justice in all circumstances . . . And these undertakings my brother Miro, count and marquis, has confirmed. And I Borell, jointly with my sons Raymond and Ermengarde, binding ourselves and all our descendants, have stablished and fully confirmed them and do hereby order it to be observed that from this present day and moment henceforward, every man who wishes to live there or desires to settle there within this place and its circumscription shall hold and possess everything which he had originally, has now, or which is legally his, wherever it may be, in lawful quietude under our protection. And for all this, you [the settlers, etc.] shall do to us exclusive service, making no payments of dues or taxes to any other lord except to Holy Church, and you shall do the stipulated works (*opera*) on the castle, namely on its tower (*turris*), walls, and superstructures, and digging to deepen the ditches (*valles*) for one day in each week, for your souls' salvation as also for resisting the pagans and evil Christians. Should occasion arise that you are in dire peril (*mayor necessitas*), all of you shall, without any coercion, labour on strengthening (*emparabitis*) the fortifications as may seem to you most expedient. For the entire responsibility of defending yourselves against your enemies then rests on you.

---

[45] Southern, *Making of the Middle Ages*, 120. The genealogy shows Borell had an uncle, who died *c.*927, and a cousin (d. 984), both named Miro, but not the brother mentioned. Dunbabin, *France in the Making*, 40–3, citing Coulson, 'Fortresses in Late-Carolingian France', 36.

... [Provisions covering litigation between inhabitants in the count's court, etc.]—This memorandum or precept or confirmation or judicial acknowledgment has been made so that nobody should dare to infringe or alter it, or through negligence disturb it henceforth and in future.[46]

By contract, lordship and dependence here are being constituted, with the intending subjects requesting a powerful man's protection, which he gives both by applying the laws by which they shall live and by providing, with their co-operation, the walled fortress and castellary where they can dwell in safety or within easy reach of it. Their submission would later be known technically as 'commendation'.[47]

It was normal to date charters by the king's regnal year and Count Borell accordingly acknowledged the notional authority of the last of the French Carolingians, who was ousted in 987 by Hugh Capet. Formerly duke of *Francia*, the heartland of France around Paris, Hugh's direct male descendants of the Capetian dynasty were to rule France down to 1328 in marvellous unbroken succession. These kings were in course of time to reconstruct (virtually to re-invent) the power of the monarchy, in part by exploiting the centralization inherent in lordship.[48] Their rights over the fortresses held of them in direct fief played a crucial part in this process but have been almost entirely neglected.[49] French historians have tended to blame 'feudal anarchy' rather than foreign assault or internal collapse for the passing of the more celebrated than substantial glories of the Carolingian Empire and monarchy. The new lords and their castles have been cast as the chief villains: according to Marcel Garaud (1953), 'la construction des châteaux et l'action du régime féodal ruinèrent l'organisation Carolingienne'. So, inevitably, the evidence (and it is considerable) that fortresses remained (and new ones became) socially responsible has tended to be disregarded.[50] The fashion for regarding 'feudalism' as an agent and symptom of political disintegration, and monarchy conversely (not always satisfactorily distinguished from lordship) as the sole force for political construction, still lingers on. R. Allen Brown may have made too much of his 'no castles without feudalism' circular argument, but his

[46] *Amplissima Collectio*, Martène and Durand (eds.), i. 336–40; now repr. in *Cartas de Población y Franguicia de Cataluña*, J. M. Font Rills (ed.), 3 vols. (Barcelona 1969–83: ref. due to T. N. Bisson). The works are: *ipsa opera ad ipso* [sic] *castro, id est turrem* [sic] *et muros et supersitos, et valles in profundum ad fodiendum ipsa* [sic] *septimana diem unum*. The word *emparare*, like *firmare*, meant as much 'to munition' as 'to build fortifications'.

[47] Ganshof, *Feudalism*, 5–9; synonymous with homage *per* Reynolds, *Fiefs and Vassals*, 18–19.

[48] Despite Fawtier, *Capetian Kings of France*, the process was not ineluctable; cf. Petit-Dutaillis, *Feudal Monarchy*. Dunbabin, *France in the Making*, brings a non-statist perspective.

[49] Cf. Coulson, 'National Requisitioning', generally relating 'national' to feudal factors; also 'Fortress-policy', down to 1204; and, for 1204–c.1226, 'The Impact of Bouvines', 71–80; also, 'Valois Powers Over Fortresses', 147–60; fortress-law was still basic, see also my 'Community and Fortress-Politics in France', 80–108; question surveyed generally in Coulson, 'Seignorial Fortresses', esp. 88–148, 307–58.

[50] Garaud, 'La Construction des châteaux', 54–78 (p. 54). Also Kaeuper, *War, Justice and Public Order*, 211–65, attempting to reconcile 'French' tradition with reappraisals down to 1988, but omitting Aubenas, 'Les Châteaux-forts'.

remark (to an Anglo-Continental gathering) that 'feudalism, properly under-stood, is a force for order not disorder', helps balance. 'Feudalism', Brown declared, 'is a social discipline working towards integration and not disintegra-tion; it is [*sic*] a curb upon the would-be over-mighty subject; and it greatly adds to, and does not detract from, the powers of rulers, especially when . . . they are able to retain also substantial fragments of ancient and pre-feudal sovereignty.'[51] The facile equation of 'feudal' with 'chaotic' is outmoded: 'feudalism' (broadly construed) was an alternative system of order. The control of fortresses, chiefly their use rather than their construction (which has received disproportionate emphasis), fulfils both of Brown's conditions: it was monarchical in ultimate origin but tenurial in implementation. Thus local lordships exercised the primary economic, judicial, and military authority over the peasant order of society under the new dispensation. The castellary became a normal unit of government, and magnates who became barons and *châtelains* in the evolving hereditary nobility truly were the associates, and 'companions' (*comites* or 'counts') of the king. They were his (junior) partners in the business of ruling, and their fortresses were places of public resort in war as habitually in peace. Several of the great princely families in France were descended from Carolingian officials. Although they had long ceased to be dismissable holders of Crown offices they were not the 'bad barons' of caricature.[52]

3. Castles and Social Reconstruction

Undoubtedly, for the underdog, this new social structure was as usual harshly exploitative, as the harshness of the times frequently entailed. It was the natural outcome of poverty, exacerbated by the more conspicuous inability of the later Carolingians to protect all those whom they regarded as their subjects. The Emperor Charles 'the Fat' was displaced in 887 as sole ruler of France in part because of his ineffectiveness against the Norsemen. His supplanter, the Capetian King Eudes (887–98), was not much better. The political philosophy modelled on that of the semi-deified Roman emperors, which is so clearly reflected in the preambles of charters, was irrelevant to the realities of sparse population, poor communications and trade, scanty revenues in kind as much as in cash, and a society in many ways sadly altered.[53] The future lay with the territorial lord who could rule the land, monopolize the productive labourer, and, despite aggressive opportunism, carry forward the search for a more stable and secure society.[54] But

---

[51] Brown, 'Genesis of English Castles', 1–14, and 'An Historian's Approach', 131–48 (p. 5 quoted).

[52] e.g. E. King, 'Stephen and the Anglo-Norman Aristocracy', 180–94. On the 'French' nobility, *La Noblesse au moyen-âge, XIe-XVe siècles*, Contamine (ed.), contains valuable material, esp. ch. 3. Higounet, 'En Bordelais "principes castella tenentes" '. Also, Richard, 'Châteaux, châtelains et vassaux', 433–47.

[53] Previté-Orton, *The Shorter Cambridge Medieval History*, i. 342–60. Eleventh-century society and economies achieved some revival, M. Barber, *Two Cities*, chs. 2, 3 (with many valuable text-excerpts).

[54] e.g. Fulk Nerra in Anjou, Southern, *Making of the Middle Ages*, 83–9, *et passim*. Dunbabin, *France in the Making*, chs. 4, 8.

the example of the past did not by any means fail to mould that future, for the family of Charlemagne, who had sought to revive something of the Roman Empire in the West, was successful not least in that they left as their legacy the doctrine (enshrined in fortress-law) that power was a public trust. In the responsibility of magnates for the defence of the whole community of the realm, and this predominantly by means of fortresses of all kinds,[55] the sub-Roman or Romanesque tradition was as deeply imprinted politically as it was architecturally and in all other forms of art.

Change was sometimes accomplished more co-operatively than might be thought.[56] If the administrator on the spot was, not unsurprisingly, best informed about the needs of local defence and often obliged to take the initiative to meet them, the Crown and the Church soon became eager to approve, sanction, and assist the process. Another text from the Carolingian realms shows how. It is dated 926, from the archives of the abbey of St Maximin at Trier, an imperial city on the River Moselle still famous for its magnificently ostentatious Roman gateway (the *c*.300 AD *Porta Nigra*).[57] Addressed to 'all in the Catholic Christian Church', it retrospectively relates that three nobles named Franco, Norpold, and Hubert 'had, each man, diligently searched for places of safety where some sort of fortification (*aliquid firmitatis*) might be made against the attacks of the heathen, who had depopulated [*sic*] almost the entire Belgic kingdom of Gaul'. A suitable site (*castrum*) was eventually discovered 'on the bank of a river . . . defended on all sides by steep cliffs, which land belonged to the abbey at Trier'. The Abbot and Count Gilbert, lord (*senior*) of the enterprising trio, agreed to accept other lands in exchange for the site and the parties solemnly recorded the transaction at the abbey, in the presence of a representative of King Henry 'the Fowler' who appended his official seal as a witness, together with twenty-four other notables. Naming them committed them to support the pact, as the custom was. At the end, for greater security, is written: 'should there be anyone (which we do not believe possible) who shall attempt to upset this exchange, he shall incur the wrath of God and of his saints, and pay a [specified] penalty to the king's treasury.'[58]

---

[55] The polemical record (*c*.1022–8) of Hugh de Lusignan's dealings with Duke William of Aquitaine is illuminating in many ways; Martindale, 'Conventum inter Guillelmum Aquitanorum Comes [*sic*] et Hugonem Chiliarchum', 528–48; also Beech *et al.*, *Le Conventum*; fortress-aspects interpreted Coulson, 'French Matrix', 76–80. Part II, n. 367 below.

[56] Brian Davison (*Observer's Book of Castles*, 11) takes the anti-romantic reaction too far: 'even now castles are often seen as symbols of an age of romance, suggesting chivalry and glory. In reality [*sic*] they bear witness to an age of violence, reminding us of rebellion and repression . . . we should not lament their passing.' Brice, *Forts and Fortresses* (Oxford 1990), 'the definitive visual account of the science of fortification' (pp. 38–69 on 'the medieval world'), in similar vein (p. 4 frontispiece) sees his subjects as 'in life, awesome. In ruin, romantic. In legend, eternal. In purpose, death. Never forget that this architecture is designed to kill people . . . remember them', etc. Ervynck sees them as 'Top Predators of the Feudal System'.

[57] Both 'heavily ornamented' and 'truly a defensive gateway . . . with portcullis', Fletcher, *A History of Architecture*, 216 (drawing), 224.

[58] *Amplissima Collectio*, i. 280–1.

In a second document, Franco and Norpold only precisely detail the lands they ceded to the abbey in return for joint ownership of the 'hill or rock suitable for making a fortification (*munitio*)' and for lands to provide the necessary supporting territory. The act was done in the cathedral of Trier with the archbishop present. Insecurity echoes still in the concluding sentence, warning that, 'if anyone dares to contest this transaction let him submit to due process of law'.[59] Damnation, royal ire, and monetary penalty often combine in these enforcement clauses to give what security was possible. It was a formula commonly adopted by the growing Peace of God movement to repress law-breaking and violence.[60]

This *castrum* near Trier was evidently a natural fortress, capable of being strengthened artificially without difficulty. Just as isolated hilltops might from their use as places of safety be called 'castles', without man-made defences, so also topographical terms for such sites were occasional synonyms for 'fortress'. In southern France *puy* ('peak') and *roche* (in Italy *rocca*) are common in this sense. The thirteenth-century fortified new-town or *bastide* of Puymirol in the Agenais was latinized as *Grande Castrum*. The ancient psalmist's 'the Lord is my rock and my fortress . . . and my high tower' shows the same association.[61] It often illuminates contemporary ideas of what constituted a fortification (see Ch. 2 below). Refuge-fortresses of this kind frequently developed into towns in their own right, particularly if situated close to a river and generally suitable for trade and settlement. But the problem of promoting and endowing existing towns was not so easily solved. As with established religious communities, their status and security meant they often had to be walled, wholly or in part. Their separate jurisdictional identity, privacy, and the need to police traffic at the entries, all required walls for everyday convenience—apart from occasions of danger of attack attracted by wealth much greater than that of the peasant, less mobile, and more concentrated. With sufficient warning, cattle and even harvested crops could be moved out of harm's way behind fortress walls. Food in carts, or on the hoof, provided sustenance for the refugees until the danger was past, the gates could be opened, and the devastated countryside be reoccupied and its fragile dwellings of wattle, mud, and thatch rebuilt. Stone walls resistant to the fire and to the sword of the invader were both secure and dignified. The walled towns were the vitals of early medieval (as they had been of Roman) civilization; country-dwellers of the *pagus* were rustics and pagans, desert-dwellers and heathen beyond its urban pale. So town authorities were always conscious of their dignity and eager to exaggerate danger when parading their patriotic schemes for walling.[62]

---

[59] *Amplissima Collectio*, 282. Count-Abbot Gilbert, as lay-protector, 'ordered' the whole transaction.

[60] Barber, *Two Cities*, 35–6, 121–2; Debord, e.g. 'The Castellan Revolution and the Peace of God in Aquitaine', 125–64.

[61] Psalm 18: 21, etc.; *Rôles Gascons*, ii. 213–14.

[62] Meulemeester, 'Les *Castra* Carolingiens comme élément de développement urbain', 95–119. Pirenne, *Economic and Social History*, 53–6, emphasized the institutional spin-off of defence. A. Thompson, *Military Architecture*, 21–34, put defence needs first; but Coulson, 'Battlements and the Bourgeoisie', sees town walls as mostly by-products of municipal aggrandizement.

In 911 Charles III was obliged to surrender formally the rich Channel province which became Normandy to Rollo and his piratical following.[63] The same year he accorded this 'diploma' or charter to Bishop Stephen of Cambrai (*dép.* Nord):

In the name of the Holy and Indivisible Trinity: we Charles, by mediation of the Divine clemency king of the Franks, mindful of our duty to promote the well-being of the realm entrusted to our care and following the practice of our predecessors—have received the petition of Counts Garnier and Thierry on behalf of our faithful subject, the reverend Bishop Stephen. From it we have learned that among the hereditary endowments of his church of St Crispin, sometime pontiff [legendary] of the Holy Roman see, he has a town (*villa*) called Lestorf [now a hamlet in Namur, Belgium] which is situated on the River Sarie, exposed to many kinds of dangers, as much from barbarian attacks as from internecine disasters. The demands of these calamitous times, the petitioners have argued, should be met by strengthening the place with a fortification (*castellum*), by conferring on the town a periodical market and power to mint coins, and by placing it under our secure and perpetual kingly immunity and protection. These requests, our faithful and most respected subject Létard, count of the district (*pagus Indensis*), for the love of God and of his regard for Bishop Stephen, has endorsed. Accordingly we hereby order, and do corroborate this our precept with might unconquerable, that the site of the town shall indeed in perpetuity be fortified (*munimen castelli possideat*) and have market and mint, perennially protected by our royal shield. No duke, count, justiciary, or other judge shall henceforth presume to enter it, whether to try lawsuits or to require from anyone sworn mutual pledges for keeping the peace. Such powers, and all others, to our regal status belonging, we do grant to the bishop and to his successors in title freely to exercise to their own advantage . . .[64]

If this were taken as no more than an early royal 'licence to fortify', most of its significance would be lost. The royal self-image in style, title, and ecclesiastically drafted propaganda serves only to emphasize the puny reality behind the monarchical theory. Licences were already more a matter of acknowledging lordship and of honouring the recipient than of serving any regulatory function. They were used not to waive any prohibition but to affirm the lord–vassal relationship.[65] King Charles 'the Simple' had little alternative but to concede graciously what had previously been settled between his powerful and now virtually immovable local governors. Despite the grandiloquent verbiage, his power was becoming less important than that of the local magnate, but the aura of royal authority conferred prestige and might smooth out practical obstacles. Even the fiction of monarchy shrank with each such alienation of revenues. The peace-keeping

---

[63] Douglas, *William the Conqueror*, 16–17.

[64] *Recueil Charles III*, 150–2. Charles styles himself *rex Francorum* and *vir illustris*, possibly interpolated although the editors regard the charter as 'original'. Its penal clause is particularly emphatic (see ibid., Introduction, p. lxix). Of the fine for infraction 'of 30 pounds of the purest gold', 20 are payable to the bishop, only 10 to the royal fisc. Coulson, 'Fortresses in Late-Carolingian France', 35.

[65] Coulson, 'Fortress-policy', 15–20 and references; also 'Sanctioning of Fortresses in France', *passim*. Although in England few licences (post-1199) were not royal, the same was true: Historiography in Coulson, 'Freedom to Crenellate By Licence', 89–103. Also id., 'Castles of the Anarchy', 75–8, 86–90, on the 'adulterine castle' myth.

system of mutual accountability, whereby men bound themselves in groups to be answerable for any misdeeds by another member of the coterie, has appeared already and is put under the local lord's supervision.[66] Ecclesiastical 'immunity', here given to Lestorf, is another very characteristic feature of life which emerged early. The association with fortification is typical. Regalian franchises, both lay and clerical, frequently exercised wide powers passed over to them by the Crown. Plenary exemption from royal jurisdiction, often total in effect, was particularly complete for ecclesiastical properties and almost invariably applied to the precincts of cathedral churches and monasteries, where no outsider was to intrude, even on the king's business.[67] This realistic delegation of public author-ity severely modified the structures of centralized statehood but did not destroy them. Fortresses were already, and continued to be, at the sharp end of the compromise which adjusted 'privatized' (but still 'public') power to the realities of the medieval polity. It will only seem remarkable how great were the resultant inroads upon the freedoms of the diffuse castle-holding class if the misguided eighteenth-century equation of 'anarchic' with 'feudal' and 'medieval' is allowed to persist—and if we continue to regard castles as brutalized architecture in the service of a rapacious nobility.[68] The contrast has surely been exaggerated between French 'disintegration' and the kingship of England, where the Norman kings took over a strong functioning monarchy, but where class divisions were scarcely less stark. Such is the strong implication of fortress-law and practice in both regions of Europe.[69] It is corroborated by the historiographical, literary, and terminological implications reviewed in the next two chapters, which demon-strate that between the modern and post-romantic concept of 'the castle', which has too long prevailed, and the very diffuse and elusive medieval reality a great gulf lies.

[66] Bloch, *Feudal Society*, 271, 420; cf. Stenton, *First Century*, 141–2.
[67] Bloch, *Feudal Society*, 104; cf. Cam, *Liberties and Communities*, 100–3 and 'franchises' (index).
[68] It is odd e.g. to deny that regalian jurisdictions (in England) were not properly 'feudal' (i.e. appertaining to the fief) as does Helen Cam, *Liberties and Communities*, 205–22 (pp. 207–8); nn. 165, 201 below. Susan Reynolds, *Fiefs and Vassals* (index), eschews 'feudalism' entirely.
[69] For a cautious defence of 'baronial' proprieties see Coulson, 'French Matrix', 66, 72, 75, 80, 85–6.

2

Variety Violated: Some Conceptual Problems

Until the conflict between the diffuse reality and the narrow perception is resolved the centrality of castles (in all their manifestations) to society as a whole will remain obscured. The 'military' straitjacket falsifies them. Viewing them as adjuncts to the chivalric lifestyle is better, but still insufficient. Allen Brown, in 1976, associated himself with the view that 'castles, like other good things in life, spread socially *de haut en bas*', being initially, 'in the late ninth and tenth centuries . . . confined to the greatest lords'.[70] Without question the castellated and fortified style of building was aristocratic, and undoubtedly it spread early and fully as widely as the noble ethos itself.[71] The *bourgeois* were to acquire their communal castles and castellated town-halls.[72] Even the peasantry had such refuge-forts as the earlier-fourteenth-century Jerbourg promontory castle on the Isle of Guernsey and also Grosnez on Jersey.[73] During the Hundred Years War in France, converted ('incastellated') churches served rural refugees.[74] The whole population was affected, directly or indirectly. Structurally, of course, fortresses were highly diversified.[75] What is less obvious is the fact (and the conclusions which must be

---

[70] Brown, *English Castles*, 26: socially aware, justly assessing 'symbolism', but still mechanistic in ascribing structural change to fear of attack. The real drive was undoubtedly aesthetic-technical emulation, as with all aristocratic architecture: e.g. Gimpel, *Cathedral Builders*, ch. 3, etc; du Colombier, *Chantiers des Cathédrales*, ch. 2, etc. Wide purview in Platt, *The Castle*, chs. 1–6, but propounding a largely military interpretation of the earlier castles.

[71] Cf. Eales, 'Royal Power and Castles', 56–62, tracing a pattern of post-Conquest explosion, with later 12th-century contraction 'of the castle-owning class'. Fixot, 'Les Fortifications de terre et la naissance de la féodalité dans le Cinglais' (Normandy), 61–6, shows how early was the 'knightly' proliferation. De Boüard, 'Les Petites Enceintes circulaires d'origine médiévale en Normandie', 21–36, illustrates how 'manorial', even 'domestic', were the results on the ground (amply confirmed for England and Wales by King, *Castellarium Anglicanum*).

[72] Pounds, *The Medieval Castle* considers only (Norman) castles in towns (pp. 92–6). E. English, 'Urban Castles in Medieval Siena', 175–98, shows deep sociological insight. See also Coulson, 'Battlements and the Bourgeoisie', *passim*.

[73] King, *Castellarium Anglicanum*, 'English Islands'.

[74] e.g. M. Jones, 'War and Fourteenth Century France', 103–20. Also Bécet, 'Les Fortifications de Chablis', 7–30. Despite Bonde, *Fortress-Churches of Languedoc*, 35–40, etc., 'fortified churches' were only '*incastellatae*' if they were to the clergy illicitly munitioned.

[75] Architectural and institutional type mattered little in actual warfare e.g. Jones, 'War and Fourteenth Century France', 108–10; Coulson, 'Seignorial Fortresses', ch. 4, 2(a). Bates, *Border Holds*, 12–20, 22–4, transcribes 1415 and 1509 Border-defence surveys of 'castles and fortalices', listing their tenants.

drawn from it) that nearly all the forms, from the Gallo-Roman cathedral city of the fifth century[76] to the gun-forts, built to the order of Henry VIII at the end of his reign (1538–47) along the south and south-east coast of England,[77] were known to contemporaries as *castra* or *castella*. Roman legionary marching-camps and stations had, of course, been 'castles' also.[78] But the problems of nomenclature addressed in this and the next chapter go far beyond semantics. They are so fundamental as to require more particular reference and fuller notes than elsewhere in the book.

1. The Modern Construct of 'The Castle'

How it came about that a segment of castellated architecture (highly significant though it is) eventually monopolized the term 'castle' itself,[79] is a matter not of medieval development essentially but of modern historiography.[80] In England, it chiefly derives from historians' views of the Norman Conquest; in France, from their interpretation of the collapse of the Carolingian monarchy in the later ninth and tenth centuries in terms of a new phenomenon of *la féodalité*.[81] From the notion (inherently suspect) of a positively revolutionary new sort of castle, in English perspective flowed the belief that castles themselves were entirely new and peculiarly 'feudal', not 'communal' in any way but 'private'.[82] The pre-Conquest era, with its 'united monarchy' and boroughs fortified 'for all the people', exerted natural (if dubious) influence; but national pride seized upon Orderic's excuse

[76] Bachrach, 'Early Medieval Fortifications', 531–69, strains to justify modern classification by examining mainly 10th–11th-century literary allusions (esp. pp. 531–4) but presents much (including architectural) data on post-Roman 'fortifications' (precincts, urban citadels, town *castra*, early stone towers, etc.). The early-medieval 'French' perspective is invaluable (ref. due to R. Eales). For a comparable list from chronicles of early *turres* in NW France, see Castles Studies Group *Newsletter* 15, 16; nn. 99, 113, 289–93, 302 below. Baudry, *Fortifications des Plantagenêts en Poitou*, 21–4.

[77] Plus considerable (vanished) works at Hull, Shelby, *John Rogers*, 24–34, 'comparing closely with Walmer, Sandown, Hurst and St Mawes "castles" ' (pp. 139–42). The finest is Deal. Whether these were 'real castles' is a vexed question, e.g. Brown, *English Castles*, 128; Pounds, *The Medieval Castle*, 299–300 (for both they are 'forts');Toy, *Castles* (pp. 265–6) equivocated.

[78] e.g. Webster, *Roman Imperial Army*, ch. 4, 'camps and forts'; also Johnson, *Roman Forts of the Saxon Shore*. The classical 'marching camp' meaning survived for siege-camps, e.g. Henry III in 1253 *in castris apud Benauges* (*dép.* Gironde), *Rôles Gascons*, i. 273; J. Gardelles. *Châteaux du sud-ouest*, 96–8.

[79] Harvey, *Castles and Walled Towns*, 1, refers to 'the Norman invaders' introduction of castles in our [*sic*] sense of the word'; but applying 'castle' to any other structure. Sir Charles Oman's *Castles*, 1–5, put down to chroniclers' failure to recognize 'a new phenomenon' (below). Brian O'Neil's *Castles*, 1, denounced this laxity in relation to any pre-1066 (or post-1485) 'private fortress', whether by topographers, cartographers, popular usage, or by medievals themselves. To Brown, *English Castles*, 43–6, walled towns styled 'castles' were 'exceptions of that best sort which prove the rule' (p. 43).

[80] Cf. E. Brown, 'The Tyranny of a Construct'. Counihan, 'Ella Armitage, Castle Studies Pioneer' and 'Mottes, Norman or Not', adopts her subject's beliefs. In general, Briggs, *Saxons, Normans and Victorians*, 3–26, *et passim*.

[81] e.g. Calmette, *Le Monde féodal*, 165–74; specimen of a vast genre.

[82] e.g. Armitage to Harold Sands (letter, 7 July 1907), about 'forming a small syndicate of persons . . . who are thoroughly interested in castles, and who are aware how new the subject really is' (quoted Counihan, 'Ella Armitage', 52).

blaming the English defeat on lack of castles and magnified sympathetically the prowess of the Normans. Psychological compensation has boosted both Normans and 'castles', mostly in conjunction. Retrospection clinched the image of triumphant military technology, up-to-date cavalry beating obsolete infantry, and of awesome 'castles'. What was in good measure accidental in 1066 has taken on the guise of the inevitable. The trend grew in force. Since defence of the nation became a governmental monopoly, to a large extent, in Tudor England,[83] and in France from the end of the reign of Louis XI (1461–83),[84] despite renewed disunity during the 'Wars of Religion' (c.1562–94) and under Louis XIII (1610–43), fortified noble residences, long styled 'castles' and *châteaux* more by virtue of status than from being 'seriously fortified', because now distinct from State forts were thought of as 'private' in contrast. The concept was then put back into the *époque féodale*, apparently plausibly. Structural specialization required by the technology of artillery defence with cannon made the royal forts, like late-fifteenth-century (Aragonese) Salses in Roussillon, or the Henrician castles, such as Sandown, Deal, and Walmer ('the castles that keep the Downs'), seemingly even more different.[85] Castle-books usually cut off here: books on 'fortification' tend to start earlier and end much later, with military logic. An incidental effect of this shift has been to make 'stately homes', nobles' palaces, and gentry-houses seem to be less 'public' than they really had been—whereas most medieval 'castles' had been the country mansions of their era (a fact increasingly being recognized). Like the seventeenth- and eighteenth-century 'power-house', castles were places of public resort.[86] The early Stuart parliamentarian lawyer Sir Edward Coke made 'the castle' into a symbol of personal independence. His dictum that 'the house of every one is to him as his castle and fortress' enshrined the fallacy in proverb. William Pitt the Elder, a century later, adopted the same libertarian image. Castles to them were 'a good thing', standing for sturdy resistance to the 'tyranny' of the State. In France the demolition of castles by Henri IV and Richelieu to punish 'arrogant' nobles and 'overmighty subjects' set up an opposite perception, an alternative attitude which has generally proved much stronger. The same trend in England drew force from the similarly vindictive 'slighting' of fortresses (150, including Corfe, Lichfield Cathedral Close, and no fewer than thirty-eight town walls) by the English Parliament after

---

[83] Reflected in the 1534 Treasons Act, reserving royal fortresses, 'ships, ordnance, artillery or other munitions or fortifications of war': Elton (ed.), *The Tudor Constitution*, 61–3 (p. 62 cited).

[84] Contamine, *Guerre, état et société*, traces 'les débuts de l'armée d'ancien régime' back to 1445 (ch. 10) and earlier.

[85] Hogg, *Forts and Castles*, 104–9. An early 16th-century watercolour of the original (1497–) castle of Salses, reproduced by Finó, *Forteresses*, 426 ('da fortaleza de Salssas'), shows that 'seignorial' features (115 foot high *donjon*; *échaugettes*, etc.) were combined with an array of elements beloved by the war-gamer, here also practical. The *donjon* has 'une silhouette fort semblable à celle d'autres donjons espagnols de l'époque', not in any war zone; Weissmüller, *Castles from the Heart of Spain*, *passim*.

[86] Girouard, *Life in the English Country House*, esp. ch. 1; *Life in the French Country House*, ch. 1.

1642. These events perpetuated castles' rebellious, anti-social, and anarchic image.[87] To the *feudiste* and lawyer-historian Denis de Salvaing, nobles' fortresses were simply 'grains of sand and gall-stones in the bowels of the State' (1668). Coke had agreed.[88] That both of them, members of the *Noblesse de Robe*, were venal partisans of aristocratic privilege is the least oddity of the curious historiography of castles.

The chief reasoned and quite recent reflection in English of this pervasive doctrinal inheritance is that of R. Allen Brown. To him 'castles' were military and 'feudal' in equal measure.[89] Writing in 1954, he differentiated 'this particular type of fortress . . . which we instinctively and rightly associate with the Middle Ages . . . from earlier and later military works', principally by its 'private and residential character'.[90] So Anglo-Saxon *burhs* and Roman fortifications were 'communal'. In 1969 Brown dealt cursorily with the other sort of *burh*, not the Alfredian walled town-of-refuge but the noble thegn's homestead,[91] which (to him) though 'private' enough was not 'seriously fortified'; and, if (militarily) fortified was not a castle because, having no tenure of land by knights in fief, the Anglo-Saxons had no feudalism; and castles had to be 'feudal' to be castles.[92] Later, citing the support of Ella Armitage's *Early Norman Castles* (1912), with supplementary sophistries, seemed to Brown no longer adequate. Armitage's review of early vocabulary[93] he corrected in one significant particular: she had asserted that the 'word *castel* appears for the first time in the Anglo Saxon Chronicle' in connection with the earthworks thrown up by the 'Norman favourites' of Edward the Confessor. Brown pointed out that Dover in the Anglo-Saxon Chronicle for 1051

[87] Thompson, *Decline of the Castle*, 179–85; (cf. Coulson, 'Fourteenth-Century Castles', *passim*; also id., 'Some Analysis of Bodiam', 83–4 *et passim*; 'Cultural Realities', *passim*.). Enaud, *Les Châteaux-forts*, 84–5 (Josselin), 226 (Cinq-Mars-la-Pile), etc.

[88] Salvaing, *De l'usage des fiefs*, 289, cf. 271–2; *per* Coke (*upon Littleton*, bk. 1, cap. 1 sect. i f), 'no subject can build a castle or house of strength imbattelled etc. or other fortress defensible . . . without the licenses of the King, for the danger which might ensue, if every man at his pleasure might do it'. This doctrine was tradition but fiction.

[89] Preface, n. 32. What follows is to be read in the light of Harper-Bill, 'R. Allen Brown, A Personal Appreciation'.

[90] Brown, *English Medieval Castles*, 17; ch. 8 ('The Castle in Peace') and ch. 9 ('The Castle in General'), recast in 1976 (*English Castles*), are notably aware sociologically.

[91] Williams, ' "A Bell-house and a Burh-geat" ', stressing continuities of lordship, including ostentatiously 'fortified' residences. Also Coulson, 'Peaceable Power', 96.

[92] nn. 37, 51 above; cf. Davison, 'The Origins of the Castle in England' and his 'reply' to Brown, 'An Historian's Approach'. Saunders *et al.* presented the results of 'Five Castle Excavations'. Debate put in some perspective by Coad, 'Medieval Fortifications', 215–27. Coad comments (p. 217): 'if as seems evident from . . . Sulgrave and Goltho . . . individual Saxons fortified their residences, the physical distinction between the burgh . . . and the castle . . . perhaps separated by no more than two or three years, may well be small.' Richardson had agreed, review of *King's Works* (1965). Everson's doubts on the dating at Goltho require attention, 'Goltho and Bullington'. Cogent (if 'military') documented summary, B. English 'Towns, Mottes and Ringworks of the Conquest', 45–62.

[93] Armitage, *Early Norman Castles*, 23–4, 138–44, 383–4; App. D. 'The words "castrum" and "castellum" '. Her teleology surfaces e.g. in praising Flodoard for having 'the right sense . . . not far from his mind'. Polemic and the aim (1907) to 'supersede Clark', *Medieval Military Architecture*, vitiate an otherwise distinguished pioneering work.

was called *castelle*.[94] Had Continental influence (and Latin) been as strong in Alfred's reign (871–99), it must be added, his fortified towns would have been *castra* like those built in Germany by King Henry 'the Fowler' (919–36), perhaps influenced by the English *burhs*.[95] The Norman sources' use of *castrum* and *castellum* for pre-Conquest Dover Brown explained away as showing that these words 'had not yet hardened into their technical meaning of castle'. The sclerosis, in reality, is ours. Brown thought with Armitage that at Dover this castle was only the *burh* (or *burgh*) occupying the Iron Age earthworks, where the Saxon St Mary in Castro church survives surrounded by the late-twelfth and thirteenth-century ramparts.[96]

Armitage's conclusion, like Brown's, was that contemporary Continental vocabulary (but for chroniclers' slipshod language) corresponded to 'the castle' in England as it happened to be after 1066 and as seen in 'Conquest' retrospection and in 'military' rationalization.[97] Their back-to-front approach is typically English, not European, as the Belgian scholar J. F. Verbruggen demonstrates. He affirmed (in 1950) the identical use of *castrum* and *castellum*, continuing well after the end of the thirteenth century, to mean indifferently a *château-fort* or a walled town (the place-name evidence on this point is overwhelming[98]). Verbruggen denied that by the eleventh century *castrum* was becoming a technical term for 'a private fortified residence'. Having reviewed other styles in currency (e.g. *castiau*, *munitio*, *municipium*, *oppidum*, *firmitas*), vernacular as well as Latin, he concluded: 'these examples are characteristic of the medieval writer (*clerc*). They show how cautiously one must proceed to discern their different meanings. In general one must not jump to the conclusion that either a castle (*château*) or a fortified town is in question just relying on the latin word.'[99] Writing about Poitou in the eleventh and twelfth centuries, Sidney Painter reached the same verdict.[100] Some greater precision is apparent in the later middle ages, as we shall

[94] Brown, 'An Historian's Approach', 40, n. 43 ('1151' in error, cf. 'Genesis of English Castles', 10).
[95] Thompson, *Rise of the Castle*, 19; the medieval-type ambivalence of German terminology, Thompson regrets (p. 13), for having removed 'the boundaries so clear [*sic*] in English and French', leading 'to much confusion of thought'. Anderson, *Castles of Europe*, 40; cf. conventional definition (p. 17).
[96] First suggested to be Iron Age by G. T. Clark; see Renn, 'The Avranches Traverse at Dover Castle', 79. In 1970 the 2nd-century forts of the Roman fleet-base were discovered on the western margin of the vanished harbour-basin below, 'between the hills' (another *castrum*); Philp, *Roman Forts at Dover*, 1–2, 91–3, 97–9, etc.
[97] Renn applies an important behavioural insight linking late pre-Conquest 'display openings' in church towers with several early-Norman castle-towers, 'Burhgeat and Gonfanon', 178–98. On the military ineptitude of 'keeps' and 'proto-keeps' see Coulson, 'Cultural Realities', 180–8, and 'Peaceable Power', 71–7, 81–91.
[98] e.g. Mesqui, 'Crécy-en-Brie', esp. 18–19, 44–5. Also Coulson, 'Castellation in Champagne', 352–6.
[99] Verbruggen, 'Le Sens des mots *castrum*, *castellum*'. His evidential base is slender, but *pace* Bachrach, 'Early Medieval Fortifications', 535–6, he is not *parti-pris*. Cf. Mesqui, 'Crécy-en-Brie', 44–5, n. 2, on the 'terminology' of fortifications in Adémar de Chabannes (d. 1034). Also editorial notes on *castrum, munitio, castellum, civitas, villa, urbs*, in *Peter of les-Vaux-de-Cernay*, W. Sibly and M. Sibly (eds.).
[100] Painter, 'Castellans of the Plain of Poitou', *Feudalism and Liberty*, 24–5. On the refuge-function of castles and much else see ibid., ch. 11, 'English Castles in the Early Middle Ages', 129–30. Hollyman,

see, but there is no expression at any time remotely as restrictive as 'private fortified residence'. This invention should be added to the tyrannical construct of
'feudalism' exposed recently by Peggy Brown.

Using old words for new forms of familiar phenomena does not, of course,
necessarily deny their novelty. But to insist literal-mindedly that both word and
phenomenon were new goes too far. Despite the authentic style, Brown asserted
that the *castrum* of Dover 'was not a castle at all but the Old English borough
occupying the whole area enclosed by the former Iron Age earthworks'. This
township is now represented only by St Mary in Castro. Being styled *burh* in 1048
and *castrum* or *castellum* in connection with events in 1051, 1064, and 1066,[101]
Dover by its size and enduring character demonstrates Verbruggen's point. It was
emphatically 'communal'. To fuss and refine upon language too inexact to be
treated as 'technical terminology' would lack sense of proportion: but the drift of
that original language (as the second part of this chapter shows) is consistent.
Where it is not neutral or ambiguous it lends no support whatever to the (tautologous) 'castles must be Norman and feudal' case; nor, certainly, does it more
than slightly modify it: but the language does reopen an artificially mutilated and
truncated subject. It remains true, of course, that fortresses, by whatever name, are
not known to have been involved in the English resistance after Hastings, to any
extent;[102] nor (which is more surprising) had any been involved in the 'political
crisis and near civil war', in Brown's words, of 1051–2;[103] nor on other occasions
since the Danish invasions (including that of Cnut).[104] The investigated archaeology is also mute, its silence equally enigmatic. With the exception of the
Alfredian and Mercian *burhs*, the physical traces on the ground of Anglo-Saxon
'fortifications' are numerically paltry so far, and (given, not least, the cost of excavation) are likely to remain so. But new understanding of what a personal fortress
was, coupled with the significant evidence at a handful of sites of thegns' residential *burhs* with their lordly 'burh-gate and bell-house', an increasing number of
which are known to be overlaid and obliterated by Norman works, demands
reconsideration.[105]

Two quite distinct questions have become obscured in the polemical wake of

---

Vocabulaire féodal, leaves out *castrum* and *castellum*. Except for British sources, the *Revised Medieval
Latin Word-List*, Latham (ed.) is unhelpful, cf. Ch. du Cange, *Glossarium*, e.g. i: *affossare, alatoria,
archeria, balista, barbacana, belfredus*, etc.

[101] Brown, *English Castles*, 44–6 (with full refs.). Thompson, *Military Architecture* (1912), pp. 35–8,
also follows Round, *Feudal England* (1895), 249–53; and *Geoffrey de Mandeville*, App. O, pp. 328–46,
'Tower and Castle' (see below).

[102] Stenton, *Anglo-Saxon England*, 591–2, 597–8, on resistance at Roman-walled Exeter and the
natural fastness of Ely. Gillingham, 'William the Bastard at War', 147, 153, 155–6, 159. Williams, *English
and the Norman Conquest*, ch. 2 *et passim*.

[103] Brown, 'An Historian's Approach', 140.

[104] As Armitage, *Early Norman Castles* (pp. 11–79), conscientiously pointed out, insisting on the
novelty of Continental 'private' fortification as well, despite severer linguistic contradiction (esp. p.
70). Bennett, 'Wace on Warfare', 234, blaming lack of castles for Swein's success, echoing Orderic.

[105] nn. 91, 92 above. Coulson, 'Peaceable Power', n. 119, lists known Anglo-Saxon sites beneath
castles—Carisbrooke and Haughley should be added.

J. H. Round's aggressive refutation in 1902[106] of the suggestion of G. T. Clark (1884) that some 'mottes' might be Danish or Anglo-Saxon castles ('doubly absurd', says Brown). The issue of post-Conquest 'continuity' remains vexed. Reliance on the fact that fortresses were militarily insignificant in the record of the last Anglo-Saxon period was an effect of the imbalance of castle-studies. It does not mean that they were socially negligible. Their number and importance rivalled 'castles'. In the second place, what chance there might have been of a properly complex definition, sensitive to the records and to the archaeology, fell victim to 'Normanism' and to militarism, both set on proving that 'proper castles' everywhere, as the chosen instruments of the conquering race, must be 'seriously fortified, private, noble residences'[107](all dubious premisses, with early 'keeps' most conspicuously). By then extending to later castles and exporting the exaggerated domestic 'continuity' controversy, which acted upon indigenous French *anarchie féodale* doctrines, the social, 'civilian', and public significance of fortresses at large, not just in Britain, was obfuscated.[108]

No general bibliographical review would be appropriate here, but the effect of the J. H. Round doctrine also upon Alexander Hamilton Thompson, whose book on castles, like that of Armitage, appeared in 1912, is illuminating. While obliged to accept that in Domesday Book (1087–90) *castrum Harundel*, for instance, was Arundel town, Thompson (as many since have done) exaggerated Orderic Vitalis' excuse (made about sixty years after the event) that the 'extreme fewness' (*paucissimae*) in England of 'the *munitiones* which the Gauls call *castella*' had contributed to the warlike Saxons' defeat, making out of it a considered refutation of G. T. Clark's then fashionable open-minded but wrongly focused ideas of Saxon castles. Actually even boroughs fell within the scope of the Gallic 'castle'. In England defensible towns were, indeed, quite few; but Thompson sought to prove Orderic's exactitude by arguing that he was referring to the four or five *casteles* put up (three, probably, in remote Herefordshire, another in Essex) by Edward the Confessor's Norman protégés in 1051–2. (Orderic did not say there were none). Brown spells out this argument with his usual vigour.[109] Although, certainly,

[106] Round, 'Castles of the Conquest', 313–40; via his (anonymous) review of Clark's *Medieval Military Architecture* (esp. i. 20–33). He pursued his vendetta with Freeman (e.g. diatribe in *Feudal England*, index), but at that time considered Clark's theory about mottes 'highly probable' (p. 31), though not fully substantiated (pp. 43–4 etc). See nn. 175, 176 below.

[107] Round, in 1894, was still cautious about 'what we may term "private castles" ' (review of Clark, 43–4). Armitage 'carried the contention a stage further' with support also from St. J. Hope (e.g. 'English Fortresses and Castles of the Tenth and Eleventh Centuries'). By 1912 this 'proposition [was] . . . generally adopted by the best English archaeologists' (*Early Norman Castles*, pp. vii–ix), including A. Thompson, but e.g. ch. 3 of his *Military Architecture* is warily titled 'The English Castle after the Conquest'.

[108] The academic battleground of 'Anglo-Saxon feudalism' (or 'proto'-feudalism), e.g. Round, *Feudal England*, John, *Land Tenure in Early England*, esp. 140–61, and Brown, *Origins of English Feudalism*, etc., is peripheral here. The older French consensus, now crumbling, is shown by e.g. Luchaire, *Louis VI, le Gros* (1890), pp. lxv–lxxxv, on *nobles brigands*, etc; also Petit-Dutaillis, *Feudal Monarchy*, 376; on the popular level, identically, by e.g. Hergé, *Le Sceptre d'Ottokar*, 21, on 'Syldavie'. Also Garaud and Calmette (nn. 50, 81 above), cf Aubenas, 'Les Châteaux-forts'.

[109] Thompson, *Military Architecture*, 37, n. 2—'it does not follow [*sic*] that the name was applied to

Anglo-Saxon lordly seats (the once-numerous thegns' *burhs*, structurally houses, within ring-works) shared all or most of the normal functions of the Norman 'castle', in features (e.g. no 'motte') Orderic would have known them to be both distinct from some contemporary north-west French fashion and perhaps, on average (the issue remains unclear), less defensible. But towns (as the word *burh* implies) had been designed and provided with guard and repair services for just such a purpose.[110] The 'communal'–'private' argument generated by Clark's (uncharacteristic) lack of caution in calling mottes 'English castle-mounds' has concealed the obvious fact that Orderic meant that *any* fortifications were few. By the standards especially of *c.*1125 this was reasonable. Had the boroughs' condition and military organization after the death of Harold and his brothers allowed them to be defended as were the fortified city of Exeter and the natural fastness of Ely (held by Charles Kingsley's heroic patriot Hereward the Wake), then the final collapse of English resistance after 1069–71 would have needed less special pleading from a British-born Norman monk. In fact, it is very doubtful whether 'castles' would have made much difference.

   A strong antidote to all these symptoms of insularity is provided by exposure to European (especially French) documents and to the recently assembled and vast *corpus* of (provisionally) identified in King's *Castellarium Anglicanum* 'castle'-sites, and, now, to awareness of the current reappraisals in English castle-study; but its effect depends on some open-mindedness.[111] Because Allen Brown's 1976 'new edition' of his 1954 book (now *English Castles*) is doctrinally forthright, both widely known and well documented, direct criticism is as unavoidable as it is regretted.[112] It will be brief and confined to the crucial first part of his first chapter on 'Continental Origins', added to meet the challenge of new work.[113]

the town before the Conquest' (naturally not.); Brown, *English Castles*, 40, 43, etc; Chibnall, 'Orderic Vitalis on Castles', 47, quoted n. 111 below. The passage, perhaps interpolated, for late 1067 to early 1071 'is based on the now-lost final section of William of Poitiers': Eales, 'Royal Power and Castles', 59, n. 44. Roffe, *Domesday: The Inquest and the Book*, separates the two stages.

   [110] Armitage, *Early Norman Castles*, 14–6, 26–7, mentions 5 *burhs* built or restored by Alfred, 30 by Ethelfleda (Mercia), 18 by Edward the Elder; cf. Radford, 'Later Pre-Conquest Boroughs'; Smyth, *King Alfred*, 135–44; Hollister, *Anglo-Saxon Military Institutions*, 140–4. Cf. Coad (n. 92 above), quoted. The Fyrd was equally irrelevant in 1066–71.

   [111] Cf. Pounds, *The Medieval Castle*, begins with the Orderic quotation, p. 3: 'Munitiones enim quas castella Galli nuncupant Anglicis provinciis paucissimae fuerant, et ob hoc Angli licet bellicosi fuerant et audaces ad resistendum tamen inimicis extiterant debiliores', and takes it traditionally but is comprehensive in scope, particularly geographically (e.g. pp. 54–71) and 'baronially' (e.g. pp. 130–51); occasionally radical: e.g. p. 224: 'a castle replaced the thegn's burh, in very many instances . . .' Also, the parish church was often nearby, 'a few' were within the bailey itself (one—unsatisfactory—example, p. 223). Pounds makes no (acknowledged) use of King, *Castellarium Anglicanum* (1983).

   [112] Repr. 1954, version 2001 by Boydell Press; 1976 by Phoenix Press forthcoming (*pers. comm.* V. Brown). Professor Brown, then Reader in History at King's College, London, was the author's research supervisor in 1965–72, a relationship at that time, and until his premature death by liver cancer in February 1989, warily cordial. Academic appreciation, especially of his early work, Coulson, 'Peaceable Power'.

   [113] Including Coulson, 'Seignorial Fortresses' (1972) and 'Rendability and Castellation' (1973). Brown, *English Castles*, 14–28, reflects a virtual *tabula rasa*. Cf., among the admirable insights of Pierre Héliot, his disquisition 'Les Résidences princières'. On Carolingian counts' widespread use of late-Roman town-citadels as capital residences, see Bachrach, 'Early Medieval Fortifications', 540, 543–6 (e.g. Poitiers, Bordeaux, Saintes, Nantes, Angoulême).

Campaigning still against the 'loose usage' which allows Iron Age and Roman fortresses to be 'castles' and unfortified houses to be *châteaux*, and reasserting that 'the true nature of the castle proper' as French and a Norman importation in 1066 had been established (as though for all time) by Armitage's *Early Norman Castles*, Brown sets proper 'castles' apart from all other 'forms of fortification'. Because (to him and to many) the diagnostic union of perfect noble house with perfect military fort was broken, as he sees it, from the early sixteenth century (and so 'Deal, Walmer, Camber and the rest are not castles'), and since castles can only be 'medieval' or 'more meaningfully feudal', there can for Brown be no castles at any other time or place.[114] Furthermore, 'we are dealing exclusively with the residences of the great'. Naturally, the richest built the largest castles. By definition, these were an unrepresentative minority, excluding the lesser nobility and the religious and urban corporations.[115] As artificial limits such criteria are convenient and quite conventional. The mischief has been done by making populist fallacy academically respectable. Brown argues that contemporary vocabulary is a 'terminology' which vindicates an essentially modern attitude, insisting that it corresponds to the linguistic, institutional, social, and structural realities. In so doing he has not served well his proclaimed task as a teacher of 'cancelling errors and unravelling erroneous hypotheses'.[116] It is unfortunate that initial hypothesis has been hardened by the passage of time.

In English analysis it was once useful (but intellectually slovenly) to distinguish the new 'Norman'[117] castles as 'private' (because intended supposedly to keep the natives out; although the fact that most were also 'non-royal' was as much in historians' minds), and to set them apart from the more-than-a-century-old boroughs and other works meant 'for all the folk'.[118] All fortifications, after all, served a public, greater or smaller, according to their capacity directly or indirectly. It is as odd a view of the original language as it is of the medieval polity, no less than (regarding the previous era) to insist that all Roman *castella*, Anglo-Saxon *burhs* (both manorial and walled towns) together with their counterparts in France, the Carolingian state-seats and public-defence works, were castles only in name. Combining this with an outmoded 'feudal' and 'non-feudal' polarity compels Brown to such assertions (echoing T. E. Lawrence) as that, the 'western

---

[114] Likewise Brown, *Architecture of Castles*, 7–16, more succinctly.

[115] Cf. Coulson, 'Hierarchism in Conventual Crenellation' and 'Battlements and the Bourgeoisie'. Brown also excludes all but a few of the very numerous minor (seignorial) sites, the majority catalogued by King, *Castellarium Anglicanum* (see i. 49); grand total 1,492 (including some by traditional nomenclature). Wilkinson, *Castles of England*, correctively puts name-style first; n. 124 below.

[116] Brown, 'An Historian's Approach', 132–3.

[117] On the validity of *normannitas*, R. Davis, *The Normans and their Myth*, esp. 105–6 on the large non-Norman element in William's army, 'perhaps a fifth or sixth of the whole'; see precision studies of Keats-Rohan, e.g. 'Bretons and Normans' and 'English Landholders 1066–1220'.

[118] The pious purpose of Ethelfleda, King Alfred's daughter, founding the *burh* of Worcester (Brown, *English Castles*, 15), has been as overstretched in traditional interpretation as Orderic's dictum. Conversely, underrating the refuge-role of castles has led to exaggerating their 'offensive' function, even when, as rarely, fully 'garrisoned', e.g. Gen. J. Hackett, in Anderson, *Castles of Europe*, 12–13 (Foreword).

Crusaders also took the castle to their crusading states in Outremer', as though fortifications were unknown to the Byzantines and to the Seldjuk Turks. In England, the seignorial castles of the Norman settlement were as much part of the enterprise as the castles which William I had built, causing 'poor men to be hard oppressed'[119] (by labour-services which vindicated the new authorities). Neither type surely was so anti-social for so long that its subject peasantry was not governed and occasionally protected through it, as well as exploited. The frequency noted of very large bailey enclosures, later often contracted or abandoned (rationalized as due to the cost of walling them in stone), as well as township (*burgus*) enclosures, churches, and even monasteries closely associated with Norman castles, suggests different ideas.[120] Despite admitting some very large 'castles' and some very small 'communal fortifications', Brown maintains that they were utterly distinct. This orthodoxy, which he inherited but augmented, has caused much confusion. Among many others less erudite, it perplexed the editor of the chronicle of the First Crusade, the Norman *Gesta Francorum*. Noting that 'the word *castrum*, which I have translated "castle" can also mean a little walled town', Professor Hill in 1962 'assumed' that, being the eleventh century 'and such castles as Caernarvon as yet unbuilt . . . the small fortified towns of the East would have looked to the [anonymous Norman] Author rather like the "motte and bailey" castles with which he was familiar'.[121] Normans, of all people, had a much wider perspective. How an earlier generation of scholarship attempted to reconcile the J. H. Round and English conception with the plain reality of the texts (especially, but not solely, the early ones) Sir Charles Oman illustrates (1926).[122] Having complacently propounded his own version of the 'private fortified residence' definition, 'guided by commonsense and logic only', he remarks that 'mistranslation' has confused 'medieval monastic chroniclers and modern historians' alike.[123] John Wycliffe in the late fourteenth century, Oman says, wrongly 'understood *castella* to mean "litil towns" ', since at the time of the latin Vulgate Bible (early fifth century) '*castellum* was being used in a very vague sense, as was also *castrum*'. Wycliffe naturally, but perversely to Oman, used both to mean populated places, small and great, whether regularly fortified or not. Oman also castigated Jerome's Vulgate itself. Jerome, he says, 'blundered' in latinizing the Greek for a 'mere village' into *castellum*, thus trapping 'unskilled latinists in the

---

[119] *Anglo Saxon Chronicle* E (trans. Tucker), full epitaph quoted Douglas, *William the Conqueror*, 373. See Part II, n. 101 below.

[120] Beresford, *New Towns*, 125–9, 334–5; 9 castle-names for *bastides* in Gascony are listed (p. 659); Puymirol is another (p. 666), etc. New Buckenham, Castle Rising (Norfolk), Sleaford (Lincs.), Devizes (Wilts.), Newark (Notts.), and Saffron Walden (Essex) are some notable early cases: Coulson, 'Castles of the Anarchy', 83–7.

[121] Hill (ed.), *Gesta Francorum*, pp. xviii, 10, 22. Siege-castles were also *castra*; e.g. Le Maho, 'Fortifications de Siège', 181–7; Speight, 'Castle-Warfare in the *Gesta Stephani*'.

[122] Oman, *Castles*, 4–5.

[123] Citing the author of the *Cursor Mundi*, c.1300 AD, 'stating that Bethany was the castle of Lazarus, Martha and Mary . . . No doubt he conceived them as a feudal family, with a portcullis and coat of arms'. Quite possibly so, given the lack of time-sense, etc.; but *castellum* still did not exclusively mean our 'castle'.

later Middle Ages when the feudal castle had become a familiar phenomenon'. The Roundian takeover of 'castles' allowed no second thought. In Carolingian France and Anglo-Saxon England, Oman does admit, *castellum* continued to mean 'an inhabited place, not always a small one' (especially once-Roman cities), as witness Egbert of Kent and Offa of Mercia styling Rochester a *castellum*; likewise, says Oman, contemporary Mâcon and Vitry were so styled. So far so good: of course the word (still classically vague) was applied to the 'new phenomenon . . . the stronghold of the feudal lord', from the tenth century onwards. Oman regrets the inconvenience that 'no new word was coined . . . but both chroniclers and clerks drawing up charters preferred to use the old terms'. Their failure to mark what was allegedly so novel Oman ascribes to pure linguistic conservatism: 'not only *castellum* but *arx, munitio, turris*, all words old and familiar with no necessary connection with the feudal castle' continued in use, as he notes. What is truly remarkable is not the continuity of such classical vocabulary but the linguistic larceny which induces Oman to condemn all these contemporary usages as 'equally delusive to readers in later ages', as though Round and Armitage could not have erred. That the multifarious traditional early vocabulary merely absorbed whatever was new (and in France, unlike England, it impinged gradually) would have been thought completely natural but for the Round–Freeman-Clark controversy. Some of the protagonists of this spurious 'castle-revolution' accept as Oman does that 'during the tenth and eleventh centuries . . . it is impossible to discover, except from the context, whether a writer is speaking of a *castellum* of the sort that St Jerome or Charlemagne knew, or of one of the new royal or baronial strongholds'. The truth is deeper still. In fact this supposed 'transitional period', during which Brown believed usage hardened into modern precision, was very prolonged, nor was 'the old sense . . . forgotten', despite Oman. It continued in the popular European usage of 'castle', *château, kastel, castello,* or *castillo* which never coincided with the originally academic and modern 'baronial stronghold' construct. Traditional nomenclature survived also, in Britain, where it might not be looked for: in the originally early-nineteenth-century maps of the Ordnance Survey.[124]

These facts, interpretations, and questionable inferences, fifty years after Sir Charles Oman wrote, were to be taken considerably further, especially the last. Brushing aside the typological overlap between large 'castles' and small walled towns (and numerous other non-structural complexities), Brown defended in 1976 the very subjective criterion of 'serious fortification' and, though giving some place to the importance of lordly symbolism (as in the *donjon* tower), did not grasp the crucial interaction between status and its expression in fortified features.

---

[124] Wilkinson, *Castles of England*, original not only in providing a selective gazetteer from which the following statistics of local nomenclature (mostly *per* OS maps) can be compiled: out of 216 'castle' sites (cf. approx. 680 medieval), 40 are Iron Age (a few only reused); 15 are Roman; 16 are wholly new Tudor and Stuart castellated mansions: of 112 post-1650 'castles', 67 are largely 18th- and 19th-century, 45 are old rebuilt. No fewer than 33 'castles' are Tudor and Stuart rebuilds of medieval. These figures could be multiplied by adding the Anglo-Saxon *chester/caster* and the Celtic *caer* names, denoting (mostly walled) Roman sites. Many native *bury*, etc. places also belong.

Brown's (adopted) concept of some 'hybrid or half-way category' (e.g. alleging *domus defensabilis* to be equivalent to 'fortified manor-house') is as unsound in actual nomenclature as it is architecturally implausible. Not 'the degree of fortification made one's house a castle', but the wealth and rank of its lord or community and (as it might be) the prestige and antiquity of the site.[125] By giving first place to rank (dynastic or personal, collective as with a city or religious order, or that belonging to the *caput* by its importance on the tenurial map), and by treating the 'military' attributes (though often highly sophisticated) as ancillary to hierarchy, the many contradictions created by simplistic architectural exposition can be resolved.[126] Unfortunately, Brown's just appreciation of the aristocratic nature of 'castles' (*recte* of fortification per se) insufficiently balanced his preoccupation with the violent aspects of nobility. War he continued to regard as omnipresent and fundamental. On this he gave less ground in 1976 than he did regarding his previously absolute rejection of any 'communal' element in 'castles'. Acknowledging arguments put forward in 1972, he accepted that 'the "private" nature' of a fortress was 'obviously limited', if it was built and held by delegated public authority (signalized frequently by being handed over on demand under rendability); and further because it 'could be and was regarded as standing for the defence as well as the control of its neighbourhood'.[127] It agreed with Brown's 'constructive' view of 'feudalism' to reject 'the castellated free-for-all still implied in some text-books', that is, what may be dubbed the 'feudal anarchy' school which still flourishes in the popular media. But conceding that lordly castles housed often very large retinues (albeit smaller than in an Iron Age fortress, Roman camp, or medieval fortified town or city) did not lessen the general conviction so clearly expressed by Allen Brown that 'the (medieval) castle' was a species utterly distinct, not to be assimilated (as the 'fortification' books do) to earlier Scottish brochs,[128] to earlier and coeval Irish raths and ringworks, to Carolingian manses, or to (in his words) 'the burghs of Old English thegns' or to 'the innumerable "homestead moats" of England' (some licensed to be crenellated, many styled 'castle', and still more listed as castles in David King's catalogue).[129] None of these, Brown sweepingly

[125] Brown, *English Castles*, 16–18. H. Le Patourel, 'Fortified and Semi-Fortified Manor Houses', pursues structural classification and political tradition at the expense of historical reality—Coulson, 'Freedom to Crenellate by Licence', 135–6.

[126] The quality and quantity of such work is rich in France. Exemplary instances are Mesqui and Ribéra-Pervillé, 'Les Châteaux de Louis d'Orléans', and Mesqui, 'Le Château de Crépy-en-Valois': also Mesqui, 'Maisons, maisons fortes ou châteaux', 185–214 (also n. 98 above). See also Jones *et al.*, 'Seigneurial Domestic Buildings of Brittany'; the grander houses are castellated (e.g. figs. 7, 9, 12).

[127] Brown, *English Castles*, 18, n. 12.

[128] Cf. Cruden, *Scottish Castle*, ch. 1, 'The Earliest Castles', 1–6.

[129] King, *Castellarium Anglicanum*, *passim*; Forde-Johnston, *Castles and Fortifications*, 35–43 ('Duns'); cf. the anecdotal but cultural de Breffny, *Castles of Ireland*; Thompson, *Rise of the Castle*, ch. 2, 'Germany', esp. 13–21. Moated sites admit of few generalizations, see Platt, *Medieval England*, 111–15 *et passim* for context, e.g. to *Moated Sites Research Group, Reports* 1–13 (1973–86), continued by *Medieval Settlement Research Group, Reports* since 1986 (National Monuments Record, London). Coulson, *Castles and Crenellating* (in preparation), will focus, with full illustration, on the noble fortified style.

asserted, were 'seriously fortified', but are to be attributed instead to 'normal domestic security' (not defined) or alternatively to 'military aggression or lordly pretension'.[130] Ambition, or even bellicosity, are not so dismissively to be periodized or confined to 'the great'. In conclusion, taking his stand not on 'any divine law' but on 'sheer historical fact', Brown summed up his position with this tautologous, circular redundancy: 'the castle as we know it is the product of feudalism', originating in the ninth and tenth centuries 'with the establishment of feudal society', spreading with the Crusades to the Near East, 'and declining as a viable institution in any given country when . . . society ceases in any meaningful sense to be feudal'.[131] Forceful expression only serves to display the shallowness of these ideas. The rest of Brown's first chapter (1976) exaggerates the 'defensive' drive of early 'castles' (of 'keeps' especially, despite consistent structural evidence), offering no historical scenario in justification. Elaborating such old views in the way this does reduces them very effectively to absurdity. It is less necessary to examine here his 'Origins', with an eye to the Norman Conquest (in his chapter 2), of great towers ('donjons'), earthworks, and 'mottes'. False definition is the basic problem, one crucial in so many ways to the purpose of this present book. In Brown it is taken further than anywhere else. It may have provoked a reciprocal intolerance, reminiscent perhaps of John Horace Round, to whom we must return. He it was who established the orthodoxy prevailing, as Brown disarmingly put it in 1976, 'when I and the world were young'.

Where Brown deals historically with the castle as the scene of the aristocratic lifestyle, few of these criticisms apply. Allen Brown has done more than any recent writer to add a historical vision to the popular pursuit of castle-study by his books and castle guides, and to reconcile the two. He managed that rare combination of documentary expertise (sometime an assistant keeper at the Public Record Office) with architectural awareness (although not archaeological sympathy).[132] He undertook his task with missionary zeal and energy. If intolerant of ideological deviation, his didacticism was softened by great personal charm and generosity. Perhaps his most important contribution has been to assert the centrality of castles in medieval history.

[130] The traditional attempt (e.g. Brown, *English Castles*, 17) to justify earthwork and generalize 'castle' criteria based on the *Consuetudines et Justicie* text of 1091 (Haskins, *Norman Institutions*, p. 282, cl. 4) is no longer tenable in the light of Coulson, e.g. 'Freedom to Crenellate by Licence', 93, 100–2 *et passim*, discussed below (n. 240 and text).

[131] He seems to think this occurred only in the early Tudor period in England. Brown, *English Castles*, 19–20, cf. ch. 8, 'The Castle in Peace'; same message in his *Dover Castle* and *Rochester Castle* Official Guidebooks, pp. 3–4 and 5–6.

[132] Few present at Burlington House when he delivered the address published in 1970 as 'An Historian's Approach' will have forgotten his combative rejection of archaeological free-thinking. He himself conducted several seasons of excavation at Boughrood Castle, co. Radnor, but justly acknowledged Dr Arnold Taylor as 'my master' in architectural analysis (*pers. comm.*).

2. Some Contrasts With the Sources

By way of broaching the less ideologically committed and more digressive theme of the social involvement of fortresses (that is, of castles in all their diversity) throughout the period, we may turn to the contrasting atmosphere of the best of French *castellologie*. Jean Mesqui's work is distinguished not least in advancing from local architectural and documentary research towards generalization. How he treats terminology respects complex facts. His long article of 1981 devoted to the castle-township of Crécy-en-Brie and its architectural context of the western part of the county of Champagne is exemplary. From an examination of the counts' late-twelfth- and thirteenth-century lists of vassals, the fief rolls, he concluded (as, simultaneously, did the author) that 'there is absolutely no descriptive element in their terms of *domus fortis*, *fortericia* or *fortitudo*, *castellum* or *castrum*, nor do they correspond to defensive strength'.[133] In particular, Mesqui avers, 'castle' was a term of status, 'denoting places which were centres to administrative and judicial districts called *châtellenies*', being only as structurally dignified as their lords, for a wide variety of causes, thought desirable. These *capita* of castellaries (in Britain also) were great tenurial nuclei, *centres juridiques*, having kinship with the 'strong-houses' of the numerous minor nobles which, by comparison only, might be termed *fortifications privées* were it not that their own lesser functions were also public as well as dynastic. The words *fortitudo* and *fortericia* mean rather 'fortification' and 'fortifying', says Mesqui, than fortress in the modern sense of 'stronghold'. Implicit here (which in the texts is often explicit) is that appearance, impact, symbolism, pride, ostentation, and power *tout court* were as basic to 'fortification' as were utilitarian concepts such as accommodation and defensibility. At Crécy-en-Brie extreme interpretative care was needed since the *agglomération* comprised a 'communal' core *castellum* progressively expanded by the later thirteenth century into a conventional 'castle' with an inner *bourg* and an outer town (*le marché*).[134]

The nomenclature of the components of the *agglomération fortifiée* of Crécy fittingly introduces the great variety of 'castle' usages. To sample them is no pedantic exercise in linguistics, but an essential preliminary since the process reveals the great diversity of functions and structures. It shows that all classes of society were affected, not just the nobility. The familiar type of castle of English (and many French) castle-books is naturally prominent; not as distinct as in tradition and far from isolated, but still recognizable for all that contemporaries had no special word for it. The simplicities of the modern English stereotype accord better with our much shorter insular acquaintance than they do with the

---

[133] nn. 98, 126 above. Mesqui, 'Crécy-en-Brie', 44–5 (n. 2). Coulson, 'Castellation in Champagne', 349–56 (paper delivered Durham, Sept. 1980). An older exemplar of the more 'art-historical' style of the *archéologue*, on Boulogne, etc., is Héliot's admirable 'Châteaux de plan polygonal', 41–59. England had several contemporary (earlier 13th-century) examples, notably Bolingbroke (Lincs.): M. Thompson, 'Origins of Bolingbroke Castle', 152–6, etc.

[134] Mesqui, 'Crécy-en-Brie', 21 (map-plan).

Continental European experience of fortresses; but French complexities apply also to, and illuminate, Anglo-Norman England and English Ireland. To switch from one 'country' to another is to move within regions of the same civilization.[135] Regretfully, lack of space and time have excluded Iberia, the Italian peninsula, Germany, the Low Countries, and wider Europe, which the task of restoring the subject of castles in society to its full and proper scope would otherwise bring in.

Because the impress of all things Roman affected both France and England (though unequally, and Ireland not directly at all), it will be useful to remember this first. As we have seen, the stations of the Roman legions by the early fifth century had so frequently developed into towns in Britain and Gaul with the waning of the distinction between soldier and civilian that *castrum* came to mean very generally a (fortified) settlement.[136] Although late-Roman towns in most regions of Britain fared much worse in the invasion era than they did particularly in southern Gaul, the place-name 'caster' in all its forms often preserved the popular association. Indeed, remarkably few major Roman settlements were not 'Chester' or 'Bury' to the Anglo-Saxons.[137] From the second century AD many rather smaller and stronger forts or *castella* had been erected as frontier defence-bases. The British forts of the 'Saxon Shore', protecting south-east coast ports, are well known, though the earlier Channel Fleet base at Dover possessed bastioned walls in imperial style. As the field-army lost its former superiority in discipline and armament over the barbarians, even before the third century, the legions' and auxiliaries' declining manpower required defensible bases, although, as their grand gateways show, there was more to it than that. These castles were built and apparently used in more medieval fashion as patrolling bases, prestigious barracks and supply depots, and for refuge for army detachments, often composed of auxiliary light cavalry. Unlike the marching-camps, intended only to prevent surprise attack in enemy territory, or the permanent stations, which were arsenals, headquarters, and recruiting and training centres, these *castella* are believed to have been chiefly meant to be locally maintained in very much the same way as coeval and later fortified towns, and often came to be similarly populated. They were novel in style—symbols of authority as well as utilitarian forts. Towers were built at quite close intervals, not recessed but projecting systematically from the outer face of the wall ('curtain' in the eighteenth-century-derived jargon) for maximum visual impact and, if need be, to provide flanking defence by archery, slingshot, and by 'catapults' (*ballistae*) apparently sometimes mounted on turntables.[138] They differed somewhat from the old *castra*, which

---

[135] e.g. M. Barber, *Two Cities*, with topical breadth and much use of source-quotation.

[136] This 'civilianization' of the legions began early: MacMullen, *Soldier and Civilian*, pp. v–vi; chs. 1, 2, 4, 7 *et passim*; figs. A–H; also G. Watson, *Roman Soldier*, ch. 6: and case-studies, e.g. Higham and Jones, 'Frontier Forts and Farmers', and D. Mason, 'Roman Site at Heronbridge'.

[137] Cameron, *English Place Names*, 35–6, 54–5, 58, 110–16, 130, 154–5, 214; Stenton, *Anglo-Saxon England*, 744–7 and end map; Butler, 'Late-Roman Town Walls in Gaul'. Motives of defence and prestige compared by Wacher, 'Romano-British Town Defences'.

[138] At Burgh castle (Suffolk) the projecting bastions, 'flat-topped with circular sinkings in the middle . . . probably to be connected with the mounting of ballistae', were added to the primitive-type

were larger and initially of earth and timber, which had small sentry-box turrets, usually rectilinear and projecting only internally, rounded corners, and thin walls backed by earthen embankments, intended to afford accommodation for entire armies.[139] This spuriously modern world vanished, albeit gradually. What followed developed from the local circumstances, without grand strategy, of the sub-Roman world.[140]

With the fall of Rome in the West, standing state armies and their whole support apparatus became economically unsustainable and disappeared. Roman devices of fortification continued to be known (but their technology was largely ignored), being familiar from the substantial surviving monuments: in England, Portchester, Pevensey, and Burgh (briefly) became medieval castles, but not Lympne, Dover, Richborough, or Reculver. Five of these, plus Bradwell in Essex, became early Christian church sites.[141] New conditions (especially economic) restricted eye-catching refinements of masonry, irrespective of military value. Social and economic factors modified the *castrum* in some of its new forms, while the old continued: but the medieval inheritance of 'castle' irreducibly carried with it the idea of an authoritative official establishment.[142] The most immediate application was thus not to lordly forts but to fortified towns which, though private corporations of a sort, were the most capacious and collective fortresses known to the medieval world. The castle-look, in its various regional guises,[143] denoted

rounded angles when the walls were 7–8 feet high (guide leaflet anon. n.d.; personally verified); Marsden, *Greek and Roman Artillery*, esp. ch. 6 'Artillery and Fortifications'; Toy, *Castles of Great Britain*, 8–23, etc. The *castellum* architectural design, signifying authority, was adopted for enormous Arab Near-Eastern palaces and caravanserais, e.g. Qasr al-Hair, Mshatta, Qasr at Tuba, Ukhaidir, Tshan; Cresswell, *Early Muslim Architecture*, 113–15, 119–22 (unusually but tellingly sceptical on 'defence'), 125, 134–7, 192–203.

[139] e.g. Richmond, 'Roman Timber Building', 15–26; Ward, *Romano-British Buildings*, chs. 1–3, deal with 'fortifications'.

[140] Cf. A. Lawrence's military determinism (*Greek Aims in Fortification*, e.g. 419–29) and Oman's dismissive vision of post-Roman muddle, e.g. *Art of War*, i. 41–2. Vindicating alleged medieval military modernism may be no less misguided, e.g. Lt.-Col. Burne, *The Crécy War*, 10–12. Corrective works can share the same beliefs e.g. Hewitt, *Organization of War*, pp. vii–viii *et passim*; Contamine, *Guerre, état et societé*, pp. v–vi *et passim*.

[141] King, *The Castle*, 90, admits: 'the [English] castle-builders of the 11th. and early 12th. centuries knew, or could very easily have found out, a lot more about military science than they cared for or needed to use'; cf. Smail, *The Crusaders*, 94.

[142] Mints proclaimed municipal status in Aethelstan's England (*c*.894–940) and in Charles the Bald's France (823–77), where 'of over 80' mint-towns, 'about half are *civitates*, representing practically every see in *Francia* proper. The next most numerous category is *castra* or *castella*, other sites fortified since Roman days . . . the privileged religious houses'. The 'presumably unfortified *vicus* has become rare'. In England mint-towns are *civitas* or *urbs*, mostly 'ancient tribal capitals . . . with Roman walls and a bishop'. Others 'qualify by virtue of their walls' (e.g. Chichester, Exeter, Leicester). 'In France *civitas* meant the capital site and, in particular, its walls, a royal possession for the defence of the realm, possibly subinfeudated, but far from free and hardly less dependent than the *castrum*': quoted from Rigold, 'Presidential Address', 101–3, 106.

[143] e.g. Lambert of Ardres's famous timber tower on the motte of *c*.1117; description translated Brown, *English Castles*, 36; likewise Durham's, Armitage, *Early Norman Castles*, 148; also at La Cour Marigny (*dép.* Loiret, *c*.1000–95), cf. the bishop of Auxerre's eulogized castle-palaces at Varzy and Noyers (*dép.* Yonne); Mortet, *Recueil*, i. 10–11, 98–101; nn. 256 ff. below.

authority and consequently noble rank, official or assumed.[144] In the Edict of
Pîtres (Pistes) of 864, as we have noted, 'castle' meant some kind of newly erected
fort, *castella* being almost synonymous with the all-inclusive *firmitates* and *haias*
(literally 'hedges'). But places of dignity were honoured as 'castles', like the
Carolingian royal palace at Compiègne in 877, fortified monastic precinct walls at
Saint-Denis (898), at Compiègne again (917), and at Tours (918). All the same,
examination of the wording of the charters shows clearly that in each of these
typical instances the term is used to distinguish from within the actual curtilage
wall from the rest of the enclosed conventual buildings (similarly at Lestorf town,
as we have seen). Otherwise, the *castrum castellum* was usually the entire walled
area considered as an entity. At Lestorf in Namur the curtilage is meant: here 'the
castle' of the town consisted of walls to be added to enclose part at least of the
small urban site. In all this ambiguity regarding the architecture, symbolism
remained the consistent element—so much so that *castrum* or *castellum* need not
imply even part of a whole fortified complex of whatever size. The sense of 'castellated features' is even to be found. Later but typically, at Rochechouart (*dép.*
Haute-Vienne) in 1262, *castrum* meant the town and its wall, as well as ostentatious embellishment of such a seignorially pretentious kind as to challenge the
monopoly of the *vicomte*.[145] Similarly but more technically, 'castles' were, of
course, until Henry VIII's time, the timber battlemented structures erected on the
prows and poops of ships commandeered for sea battles. Miniature model castles
are also found. Edward I's children had two of these perennial toys. Edward III
caused 'a canvas castle' to be taken from Wigmore castle (Salop) to Woodstock
Palace in 1341. Only these last conform to our idea of 'castles'.[146] There was truly
no 'hardening' of this diversity of meanings into technical terms. The core meaning continued to be a place in the noble fortified style, of whatever size or quality.

Just how multifarious were the post-Conquest castles of England and Wales is
widely reflected.[147] Making of them a special class ignores the lack of standardization.

[144] For the *castellum de Compendio*, formerly *palatium* (*dép.* Oise), 'begun' in 877, and the *castellum
Sancti Dionysii*, see *MGH* ii (*Capitularia Regum Francorum*), 360. The castle-precinct at Saint-Denis
(*dép.* Seine), destroyed in the 885–6 Norse siege of Paris, was rebuilt by 898 as 'castellum . . . a novo
constructum' (*Recueil Charles III*, 16–17). By 917 Compiègne abbey had a precinct *castellum* with *propugnacula*, and St Martin's abbey at Tours (*dép.* Indre-et-Loire) in 918 had a 'castrum quod est circa
monasterium' (ibid. 202–6, 225–7).

[145] Coulson, 'Sanctioning of Fortresses in France' discusses. *Correspondence A. de Poitiers*, i. 415–17:
'. . . que domus est sita in castro de Rupecavardi . . . vico publico intermedio a parte anteriori, et a
posteriori jungitur muro castri.' This wallside building was to be 'absque fausatis [gables], tonellis,
turribus et castro [*sic*]'.

[146] Brooks, *English Naval Forces*, 13–14. Taylor, 'Military Architecture', i. 98, n. 1; Alfonso had a
castellettum of wood (1279); Edward of Caernarvon's *castellum*, mainly wooden, made by his cook, cost
44s. 6d. and was displayed in Westminster Hall at Margaret's wedding in 1290 (alas! No picture
survives): *CCR 1339–41*, 608: Discussed, Binski, 'The Painted Chamber at Westminster', 74–5.

[147] *Orderic Vitalis*, Chibnall (ed.), computer-aided Index, i. 244–386, including castle-vocabulary,
delineates its early 12th-century Norman linguistic diversity; summarized Chibnall, 'Orderic on
Castles', e.g. 53–4; also Yver, 'Les Châteaux-forts en Normandie', 28–115. Literature summarized, B.
English, 'towns, mottes and ringworks' *passim*, arguing that the Conqueror's own castles were
(initially) extempore, small, and hasty ringworks.

The quite Herculean work of D. J. C. (David) King, summed up in 1988, is basic.[148] His paper 'Ringworks of England and Wales', published in 1969 with Leslie Alcock, showed that smallish sub-circular enclosures were very numerous, some possibly pre-Conquest. In 'The Field Archaeology of Mottes' (1972), King's figures indicate a heavy preponderance of 'Motte and Bailey' castles, but all forms of earthwork were employed, together with a very few masonry structures. Though generally small in area, many of them possessed outer enclosures or 'baileys' of the sort which (elsewhere) might be supposed to be for refugees and cattle. These usually slightly embanked enclosures, demarcated not defended, are often of far greater size than would have been needed by the household retinues alone of the new Norman lords, and many were soon abandoned.[149] Sometimes an estate church or dependent township occupies them, or was meant to. Taken with the unequivocal evidence of the early stone towers, 'keeps', and 'proto-keeps', it is clear that the same propagandist gigantism prevailed here as in the enormous new Norman cathedrals and abbey churches (also both public and private), demonstratively and boastfully dwarfing their Anglo-Saxon predecessors (such as Canterbury, Durham, Winchester, Peterborough, Romsey, St Albans).[150] Enlarged conventual communities seldom explain this *folie de grandeur*. Even the more modest 'manorial' seats, castles, and *mansa maneriorum* to small fiefs, which are the great majority, outshone and would have successfully overawed the dependant peasants of many previous thegn's *burhs*, even such as Sulgrave, Earls Barton (Northants.) or Goltho (Lincs.) Enormous attached parks and hunting chases modified the very landscape.[151] For the present purpose, the size-differentiation of noble rank matters much less than that castles came in all sizes and to very many specifications.

To enumerate the various sorts of habitations and sites styled 'castle' and the like in the medieval records of Britain and France is to run through the full range of medieval architecture.[152] The Carolingian fortified religious curtilage-castle has

---

[148] King, *The Castle*, chs. 6, 7, 'The Primitive English Castle', 'Earthwork', and 'Stone'. His thumbnail descriptions in *Castellarium Anglicanum* give nearly full weight to the great uncelebrated majority.

[149] D. King and Alcock, 'Ringworks of England and Wales'; based on field-survey and very rare excavations 'ringworks', total 204–48, mottes (more identifiable) 720; 'other early castles', 141; 'total existing castles' 1,580 (pp. 124–5, including *addenda*). Omissions are sites judged too slight or too 'domestic' (King, *The Castle*, ch. 1) to be 'military', rejecting manors, ecclesiastical precincts, etc. Also e.g. D. King, 'The Field Archaeology of Mottes'. On the prestige element, and on churches in baileys, see Pounds, *The Medieval Castle*, 18–19, 24.

[150] Coulson, 'Peaceable Power', on 'keeps', including Dover, Chilham, Orford, Castle Acre, Eynsford, Trim, Castle Rising, Middleham, Walmer, Hedingham, Rochester, Norwich, Canterbury, London, Pevensey, and Bramber. Anglo-Saxon prosperity financed the Norman building-mania, e.g. Morris, *Cathedrals and Abbeys*, 185–94.

[151] e.g. Everson *et al.*, *Ludgershall Castle*, ch. 5; Liddiard, 'Castle Rising', 169–86. Davison, 'Sulgrave, Northamptonshire'; G. Beresford, 'Goltho Manor' (for dating cf. Everson, 'Goltho and Bullington', 93–9); Williams, 'Burh-geat', *passim*; also Renn's important 'Burhgeat and Gonfanon', esp. 178–86.

[152] French scholars tend to quote the *castrum/castellum* when in doubt while continuing to think of 'castles' (new style) (e.g. Gardelles, *Les châteaux du sud-ouest*); or to use titles as broad as Ritter's *Châteaux, donjons et places fortes*; or to be ambivalent, trying to reconcile modern and medieval usage: Duby, *France 987–1460*, 56–7 etc.

been sufficiently dealt with for the present.[153] The same sense is found in a charter of William the Conqueror relating to a 'castle', apparently a palisaded 'ringwork', built by him in 1067 'around the church of Saint-Jacques-de-Beuvron' (*dép.* Manche, near Avranches) on the Norman frontier, to establish it against the count of Brittany.[154] At least as importantly, he founded there a new lordship, a castellary endowed with a circumscription or *banlieue* having jurisdiction of crimes of bloodshed, and right of toll and market, to set the tenant up on the feudal map. Near the opposite end of the spectrum, similar to naval fore- and after-castles on ships, were the 'wooden castles' consisting of planks and components of timber turrets which, as on other occasions, were prepared in 1170 for the invasion of Ireland.[155] Prefabricated palisading and turrets (*bretasches*) for crowning temporary entrenchments similarly, after 1066 in England and (later) in Wales, equipped 'fieldworks' and tentative lordly seats, many of which achieved permanence.[156] More utilitarian than majestic, such mere kits of parts were still 'castles'.

When an actual dwelling is meant (as it normally is), it could just be a site distinguished by nature, as shown by the *castrum* converted in the early tenth century into a refuge-fortress near Trier in Germany, largely by tenurial, not structural, change.[157] More distantly, an entirely unfortified house, occupied by armed force and defended in arms, might be tantamount to a castle; how it was used mattered quite as much as the sort of building it was: in 1373, at Barton on Humber, one of the citizens made an affray and, with other malefactors, 'went into his house and held it as a castle for one day and would not surrender to the constables, until the commonalty of the town arose and took him by force' (in the words of the *calendar* translation). This 'castle' was real also by virtue of usurped authority. Similarly in 1375, a manor-house of the abbot of Dorchester at Huntercombe was 'held as a fortress' in the course of a similar

[153] Licensed English precincts (58) discussed in Coulson, 'Hierarchism in Conventual Crenellation' and *The Castles of Communities* (in preparation). M. Thompson, *Cloister, Abbot and Precinct,* cf. 103–26 (with acknowledgement).

[154] *Regesta,* i. 2, 66. This castle, with its 'leuga cum sanguine et teloneo' (cf. the vast ' "Lowry" or castlery' of Tonbridge, Kent: Pounds, *The Medieval Castle,* 50–1) developed into a *prévôté,* farmed for £100 p.a.; Powicke, *Loss of Normandy,* 76; marked as 'S. Jacobus', Stapelton map (endpaper). William compensated the monks of Fleury (St-Benoît) sur Loire and of Mont-Saint-Michel for their losses. Similarly, in 1153, the future Henry II set up Robert FitzHarding at Berkeley (Gloucs.) by building him a castle: *Regesta,* iii., no. 309; Coulson 'Castles of the Anarchy', 89–90.

[155] *CD Ireland,* i. 2, 4. Two *castella lignea* from Lancaster cost £14. 11s.; from Carlisle 'three wooden towers and 700 planks' cost £7. 3s. 3d. See Higham, 'Timber Castles: A Reassessment', emphasizing their longevity; also Higham and Barker, *Timber Castles,* 348–9. Vocabulary (including *castel*), 361–3; Bennett, 'Wace on Warfare', 234.

[156] e.g. in 1238, carpenters making two wooden *castell* cost £18. 14s. 7d.; transported to Chester castle (cost £5), where stacked and roofed over (cost 12s.). These two dismantled 'castles', called *bretaschias,* were apparently used to refortify the old earthwork castle site at Rhuddlan (Flintshire) in 1241, costing 25s. in transport and 62s. for extra timber for repairs; plus £20 labour and transport for two new ones: *CLibR* i. 348, 382–3; ii. 69–70, 102 (1242, with details of ropes, nails, mallets, pegs, lard, grease, mattocks, shovels, cranes, ladders, and provisions). On Anglo-Welsh friction see Powicke, *Henry III and the Lord Edward,* 630–6.

[157] nn. 58, 59 above.

disturbance.[158] Instances of church buildings being forcibly occupied occur at times of lawlessness, the word used to describe the act of lay usurpation often being 'incastellation', or conversion into a castle.[159] Buildings which might anachronistically be called 'civilian' did not so much physically become 'military' by adaptation but existentially by use. The modern naval establishment 'HMS *Ganges*' was (and is) no ship, but is military none the less. The whole differentiated medieval castle-phenomenon thus ranges all the way from kits of parts to the psychological and metaphysical concept, prominent in literature and in the visual arts.[160] Buildings displaying the lordly attributes of 'fortification' range from the 'strong' to the merely powerful. Frequently they conveyed the message of authority (like the 'keep' conjecturally ascribed to William Rufus at Norwich) without being defensive at all.[161]

Because the physical debris remains, backed by an overweening mythology, understanding of the whole conceptual, social, and institutional context has suffered. Even at the technological level, siegecraft, which has left little physical record, tends to be underrated in assessing the military value of so many supposedly 'impregnable' fortresses. Since essentially sieges were warfare in which buildings were centrally involved, the part played by the architecture varied from the ancillary to the merely incidental.[162] No fortress, however expensively constructed, could passively defend itself, after all. Proud as Richard Coeur de Lion was in 1198 of his new Château Gaillard, on the Seine above Rouen—even, it is said, claiming it could be defended were its walls made only of butter (a boast disproved in 1204)—manpower alone made it more than an empty shell, militarily purposeless.[163] Castles' normal existence was administrative, the office and

---

[158] *CPR, 1370–74*, 303–4; *1374–77*, 220. Use of 'military' language, deliberately exaggerating the heinousness of breaches of the peace, is also habitual: e.g. in 1319 Edward II's bailiff of Scarborough was 'besieged in his house by certain disturbers of the peace of the town', who had also seized the castle (*CPR, 1317–21*, 264). In 1350 Colchester was subjected to forcible harassment by 'siege' (i.e. lying in wait) and entry of the suburbs, continued with a 'siege for a quarter of a year by ambushes far and near around the town', etc. In 1364 the ringleader was pardoned (*CPR, 1364–7*, 54–6).

[159] Coulson, 'Seignorial Fortresses', Index 'incastellation'; Chibnall, 'Orderic on Castles', 52–3; *ecclesie . . . incastellate* (1225), *Layettes*, ii. 63–4. In 1212 Simon de Montfort (the Elder), for the peace of his Albigensian conquests (and to confound the Cathars), declared: 'ecclesias a laicis incastellari prohibemus . . . et incastellatas dirui praecipimus': *Thesaurus Novus*, Martène and Durand (eds.), i. cols. 831–8. Church council declarations of 1041, 1042–3, 1054, 1065, 1123, 1209 make clear the nature of 'incastellation'—excerpted Bonde, *Fortress Churches of Languedoc*, 211–6.

[160] e.g. van Emden, 'The Castle in French Literature'; Whitaker, 'Otherworld Castles'; Dean, 'Early Fortified Houses': A. Mackenzie, 'Castles in Manuscript Painting'; and Gaines, 'Malory's Castles'.

[161] On Norwich see Heslop. Reconsiderations by Philip Dixon, Pamela Marshall, and Paul Drury pending (e.g. *Castle Studies Group Newsletter* 15, 24–6). In general see Coulson, 'Peaceable Power', 'Structural Symbolism', 'Hierarchism in Conventual Crenellation', and case-study, 'Some Analysis of Bodiam', esp. 51–4, 66, 83–4, 92–3, 99–107. The disciplined art-historical approach has great value, cf. Tuulse, *Castles of the Western World* (facile *Kunstgeschichte*). See Coulson, 'Cultural Realities', *passim*. Aldred, *Castles and Cathedrals: the Architecture of Power*, gives a sketch; Steane, *Archaeology of Monarchy* and *Archaeology of Power*, are more thorough.

[162] Bradbury, *Medieval Siege*, combines narrative with treatment of the crucial circumstantial factors; Duffy, *Siege Warfare 1494–1660*.

[163] But see Gillingham, 'Richard I and the Science of War', 194–207. A. Thompson tried to explain e.g. Caerfilly's being 'almost without a history' as successful deterrence: 'a castle like Caerfilly' (*sic*:

home of the skeleton residential staff. Their everyday manorial routine (common to all estate centres, at all periods) consisted of court sessions, festivals with the lord in residence with his 'riding household', rent-receiving, and mundane house-keeping. The fact that fortification was occasionally vindicated by violence does not mean that war determined castle-design.[164]

3. Castellaries Were Also 'Castles'

How it was that the cataclysm of the Norman Conquest has been thought to require that there could only be one sort of castle—'private', 'seriously fortified', and not 'communal', has been considered. To what extent (if at all) any individual noble or collective corporation (religious house, chartered or franchised borough) had 'private' attributes (and their residences likewise correspondingly[165]) is a question which raises large issues. Here we need note only that 'castle', meaning 'town', is particularly frequently met with in the case of new 'frontier' settlements (the *bastides*) and is common especially in southern France. In Britain after the Conquest this usage is (unsurprisingly) rare. English boroughs were seldom latinized as *castra*, although in the records of the Crown the coupling of 'fortresses and towns', 'castles and closed towns' and the like, quite indifferently, is as habitual in England as in France.[166] The cases of Dover and of Arundel have been noted. In 1101 a grant of 'the city and tower and castle and all the fortifications of Colchester' is standard phraseology for a whole urban complex. In 1201 we find *burgenses nostri de castello* of Launceston (Cornwall), but *castellum* here means as much the castle-dependencies or castellary as the walled town itself.[167] The danger, even in England, of assuming that 'castle' and town were terminologically distinct is shown by Old Sarum. The Norman episcopal palace-castle, adjacent to the

half-a-dozen at most in Britain) 'did not put an end to local warfare: it merely warned an enemy off a forbidden track' (*Military Architecture*, 274, 287).

[164] St. J. Hope, *Windsor Castle*, and Hearsey, *The Tower*, represent opposite poles of socio-architectural anecdotalism. Social historians must prefer Girouard, e.g. *English Country House*, ch. 2, 'The Medieval Household'; or Labarge, *A Baronial Household*, esp. ch. 1, 'The Castle as a Home'; also Altschul, *The Clares, 1217–1314*, 122–34, on the political role of Caerfilly castle in 1267–74.

[165] e.g. Richard, 'Châteaux, châtelains et vassaux', on the advent of the *neuf-château*, sometimes with names of the 'newcastle' type (Châteauneuf, Castelnau, Châtillon), by the Ferté and Fère ('*firmitas*) element, and by the eulogistic e.g. Beauvoir, Clermont, Beaumont, Montfort, Roquetaillade, etc. The 'homes of the military class' (Denholm-Young, *Country Gentry*, 34–40; cf. Coulson, 'Freedom to Crenellate by Licence', 109–11) were no more 'private' than their owners, as e.g. Cam, *The Hundred*, 55 ff. shows.

[166] Standard collective phrases are *citee, chastel ou bourg* (1341); 'chastialx, abbeis, priories, citees, villes et burghs viz toutes les forteresces tout envyron la terre d'Engleterre assis sur la costere' (1369); and 'castles and towns closed and fortified' (1370): *Rot Parl*, ii. 129, 300 (petitions for due guarding); *CCR, 1369–74*, 61. Coulson, 'Battlements and the Bourgeoisie', *passim*. Pirenne, *Medieval Europe*, 54, on urban 'murage' taxes *ad opus castri* (no date). As *capita* the phrase *omnia alia loca et fortitudines* is typical (1245, Pyrenees); *Layettes*, v. 161.

[167] *Regesta*, ii. 15; *Rot Chart*, 93a. At York (1321) the *fortalicia* of the city was its walls and ditches. *Castellaria* was 'used to describe an honor with a capital castle at its name-place, but often meant no more than the appurtenances, land, services etc. owed to the castle'; Brown, 'English Castles 1154–1216', 182–91, 249–55.

cathedral complex, all within the Iron Age hill-fort, concentric with it but much smaller, appears to be as neat a contrast as could be wished: but in 1227 the clergy's petition to Henry III to sanction their move to New Salisbury, by the Avon, from their cathedral precinct in the borough, spoke of the *translatio de castro nostro Sarisbirs*. The whole still-communal fort-town was 'the castle'.[168]

Repercussions of the Norman Conquest debate distorted the English perception yet further. By supposed contrast with what went before, 'castles' were seen not only as forts (contradicting the palatial grandeur and relative defencelessness exemplified in such great tower 'keeps' as at London, Colchester, Canterbury, and Norwich) and by mistaken analogy regarded as 'private'—they were also, by assumed but unverified association with an exaggeratedly military process of takeover, taken to be technological structures more than social and administrative institutions. Close parallels with the simultaneous ecclesiastical rebuilding were ignored.[169] It compensated for the collapse of Anglo-Saxon rule which, despite a sophisticated system of field army (*fyrd*) and garrison service and its advanced military institutions was shamefully swift and complete, for historian-apologists to see 'the Normans' as super-soldiers in the style of Victorian imperialists.[170] Armitage explaining mottes as refuges from 'a hostile peasantry' typically blended militarism with strong latent Saxon patriotism, believing 'no Norman land-holder' to be 'safe in his usurped estates without the shelter of a castle'. In fact, the population was largely docile and inert. Admiration for the Normans exaggerated their castles' novelty and supposed a modernistic, centrally directed scheme of castle-implantation, doubly dubious.[171] Associated with the (exaggerated) superiority of their cavalry over 'old-fashioned' infantry, the military view of castles was a substantial comfort to late- and post-Victorian pride.[172]

When in 1892 John Horace Round wrote his discursive biography *Geoffrey de Mandeville* (using the evil deeds of that classic villain of Stephen's reign to take some anti-Gallican and nationalistic revenge),[173] the modern English doctrine of castles was still in formation and not yet tyrannical.[174] In an appendix to his 1892

---

[168] Contrast alleged by Brown e.g. Brown *et al.*, *Castles*, 10–11; same usage in 1304, 1317, 1331: *Rot Parl*, i. 174; *CCW* i. 470–1; *CPR, 1330–34*, 82, 234.

[169] Fernie, *Architecture of Norman England*, 19–26, cf. Beeler, *Warfare in England*, esp. 8, 38, 43–4, 49–57. B. English, 'Towns, Mottes and Ringworks', deals only with King William's own campaign castles in the towns. Williams, *English and the Norman Conquest*, ch. 1, describes the initial settlement prior to the revolts, and the scattered resistance of 1068–70 (ch. 2); n. 102 above.

[170] Brown, *Normans and Norman Conquest*, 5, n. 11 quotes Thomas Carlyle's famous condemnation of 'Saxon' inertia.

[171] Armitage, *Early Norman Castles*, esp. 7, 85, 378; followed e.g. by Pounds, *The Medieval Castle*, 27–31; cf. Eales, 'Royal Power and Castles', 63–6; Coulson, 'Castles of the Anarchy', 72–3, 75, 79–80, 88–90, and 'Freedom to Crenellate by Licence', 88–90, 93–109.

[172] Oman, *Art of War*, i. ch. 7 is classic; cf. e.g. Bennett, 'Warhorse Reconsidered', 19–40 and caption to plate 3a, p. 24; Bayeux Tapestry, showing 'the English shieldwall . . . Such a dense formation of armoured footmen was impenetrable to cavalry'.

[173] Hollister, 'The Aristocracy', *Anarchy of King Stephen*, ch. 1, revises 'Round's portrait of the so-called "turbulent baronage" of Stephen's so-called anarchy in the light of recent scholarship' (p. 37). New studies by Edmund King, David Crouch, and Donald Matthew.

[174] Introduction, nn. 34, 36; above nn. 80, 101, 106, 107.

book, Round dwelt upon the coupling of *turris* and *castellum* in both Mathilda's
and Stephen's grants to Geoffrey of the citadel of London (and its wide appurtenances), making out of the phrase a complete explanation of how it was that so
new a phenomenon as 'the castle' was believed to be had yet received no special
name. Having reviewed eight references, seven British and one Norman, to 'tower
and castle', and similarly 'castle and mote' (motte), castigating *en passant* G. T.
Clark's 'great work on our castles' (for a reasonable but subsequently disproved
theory about Gloucester's vanished great tower[175]), Round presented his *trou-
vaille*: this phrase, he announced, was 'a transition form' reflecting 'the essential
fact that there went to the making of the medieval "castle" two distinct factors
... the Roman *castrum* or *castellum* and the medieval "motte" or "tour" '. The
'castle' was 'the fortified enclosure' component, and this element Round
(wrongly) supposed had rapidly and early taken over, so that the 'tower' survived
only for the chief castle at London, everywhere else 'castle' ousting 'tower'.

Archaeologically and linguistically impossible though it is, this ingenious
idea is still notable: Round as yet accepted a substantial continuity; he understood
that 'castle' (very often) meant 'enclosure'; he, so far, had not evolved the
'communal–private' stick[176] wherewith to beat Clark's (and indirectly, Freeman's)
belief in possible pre-Conquest 'castles'—but he was apparently unaware that
castrum/castellum often meant not the *caput* (let alone narrowly its structure) but
the appurtenances and castellary, a sense which agrees with six of his eight
instances of 'tower/motte and castle' and is precluded by none.[177] This is of great
importance. Metaphysically (of little interest to Round), the tower or the motte
signified lordship and contained the lord's residence or its most conspicuous part;
whereas the 'castle' represented the lordship and territory. Such combinations of
a precise with a general term in an umbrella phrase are common. With castles it
is these wider attributes which most need to be disinterred from the debris of
controversy and restored to the light.

[175] Reviewing Clark in 1894, Round (pp. 27–8) justly recognized the previous state of ignorance and
fantasy (Clark 'had to make his own bricks'), but his resentment of Clark's reputation (e.g. 'Tower and
Castle', 346, n. 3), though he used his data, and Round's animosity towards Freeman (Clark's dedi-
catee of *Medieval Military Architecture*), are regrettable ('Tower and Castle', 330, 334, n. 3, 336–7,
339–40, 342–6), especially for one who apparently did his archaeology looking out of train windows,
or at second hand. In 1902 ('Castles of the Conquest') he cites Clark's data to refute Freeman as often
as is consistent with rejecting Clark's idea of Anglo-Saxon mottes (pp. 313–40 *et passim*) as reused by
the Normans (pp. 319, 323), but he still believed some could be pre-1066 (p. 333).

[176] A dichotomy gelling in 1902 ('Castles of the Conquest', 334); developed by Armitage in 1900–12
(*Early Norman Castles*, p. vii, etc.). Round in 1902 (pp. 315–16, 321–2) also denounced Oman for
endorsing Clark in his first (1898) edn., cf. *Art of War*, ii. 12, n. i ('some of Clark's theories are out of
date') and Christison, *Early Fortifications in Scotland*. Round approved of Mrs Armitage's work, with
characteristic reservations ('Castles of the Conquest', 332–3). He was not aware of 'ringworks'; she was
very equivocal (p. 313); cf. D. King, *The Castle*, 42–3, 57–8.

[177] The *castellum de Wigornia* [Worcester] *cum mota* (probably); the *motam Hereford cum toto castello*
(surely) included the castellary; at Colchester it is superfluous (*turrim et castellum et omnes ejusdem civi-
tatis firmitates cum omnibus quae ad illam pertinent*); at Gloucester (*custodiam turris Gloc cum toto
castello*), since the castle-enclosure was indivisible, *castellum* comprised the (necessary) revenues (and
territory). The reference to Caen is structural and irrelevant; those to Dublin, Carlisle, and Appleby
(*temp.* Hen. II) *chastel et tur*, and *dongun* indicate inclusive lordship-units ('Castle and Tower', 328–31).

Round (and Clark still more so) had to contend with the Victorians' anachronistic expectation of a castle as a towerlike building of masonry. Just how erroneous architectural chronology then was is now hard to believe. Creating an orthodoxy of mere earthworks was a notable triumph.[178] Consequently, Round accepted more readily than did his followers (e.g. Oman) the early chroniclers' styling of towns such as the former *civitas* of Rochester and the *burh* of Wareham (Dorset) as *castella*, because this illustrated his 'true meaning' of 'fortified enclosure' (*burh* in English). But to him, as to them, it was equally 'obvious that there could be no "castle" at Wareham in 876'. And he was just as scornful as Oman of the 'confused' translation of the Greek for 'village' as *castel* in the *c.*1000 English Gospels.[179] This, he asserted (with startling assurance) was 'a misunderstanding'; without considering whose. The definition he adopted (if he did not invent it), and successfully perpetuated, is essential to the view of 1066–70 as a conquest rather than a colonial takeover. Its partner is the French 'feudal anarchy' view (with the role it ascribes to castles) of what is seen as the collapse of the Carolingian state by usurpation.[180] Round's premiss was that 'a new and distinct type of fortress [was] the outcome of a different state of society'—here lie the seeds of the 'communal–private' dichotomy. Such an alleged sociological shift, its dating no less than its nature, remains extremely elusive on both sides of the Channel.[181] This, the feudal hypothesis, as it may be called, is as insecure a foundation as is the bogus 'terminology'. Faced with a contemporary vocabulary which was still less amenable than he thought, and with the adverse or at best equivocal evidence of archaeology, of which he and his contemporaries were almost wholly ignorant, Round's implicit belief that 'the old English state' had been radically different required that Norman castles (together with their Netherlandish, Norman, Breton, and other antecedents) must be correspondingly new. His proof of this proposition (like that of R. Allen Brown) is chiefly instinctual. Preferring not to argue any further that the 'keep' (tower or motte) was the new element (carefully avoiding labelling either as 'private' or 'feudal'), Round's

[178] Mackenzie, *Castles of England* (1897), belongs to the old school, e.g. he labels sites without masonry as 'non-existent', at the end of each county section. Round himself (p. 331, n. 3) was struck that *castellum* 'is even applied by Giraldus Cambrensis to the turf entrenchment thrown up by Arnulf de Montgomery at Pembroke'. The earliest conquest 'castles' were campaign 'fieldworks' of this type, i.e. ringworks not more laborious motte-and-bailey: English, 'Towns, Mottes and Ringworks'.

[179] Oman, *Castles*, 4–5, duly chastened by Round ('Castles of the Conquest', 315–16, 321–2). Round cannot avoid praising Freeman for translating *castellum* ('1051') at Dover as 'town'; and disagreeing with Skeat and with Oliphant (p. 332) that *castel* was 'no English name' (cf. Eales, 'Royal Power and Castles', 53).

[180] Aubenas, 'Les Châteaux-forts', nn. 10, 32, 36, 81, 108, etc above; Coulson, 'Sanctioning of Fortresses in France'. The 'Conventum inter Guillelmum Aquitanorum Comes [*sic*] et Hugonem Chiliarchum', dated 1022–8, supplies an authentic corrective (n. 55 above).

[181] Brown, *English Castles*, 19–24, discusses 'the problem of terminology which bedevils the task of the historian of the origins of feudalism', but wrote confidently of 'these events and developments which produced the castle as an integral part of the new feudal society' (p. 22). The 'first feudal age' of Marc Bloch (*Feudal Society*, 61–71 *et passim*) is an unduly neat schema, *per* Reynolds, *Fiefs and Vassals*, e.g. 3–14 on 'The historiography of feudalism', and 38–45 on the origins of nobility in France; see list of works cited there.

essay then takes a variety of texts (especially Robert de Torigny) as support of 'the more probable explanation' (of why *castellum/castrum* prevailed in site names over *turris*), namely that 'the older of the two factors may have given its name to the whole'.[182] It is a shallow foundation for such a monument. The linguistics do not support these 'new' castles—and contradict the belief that only these were 'true castles'.

The separate allusions to 'tower' and 'castle' adduced by Round, whether at Arques (near Dieppe), Rouen, London, or at Torigny (and whether the word *turris* or *arx*, as in Orderic, is used), when disentangled from his side-swipes at G. T. Clark and E. A. Freeman, prove nothing more than the architectural dominance of the 'great tower' over the few early Norman castles which possessed one—whether original or added later matters little.[183] These texts cannot establish any such general definition as Round advanced. References to 'the tower' (as also at Bristol, Rochester, and Gloucester) indicated either where a charter was given or a prisoner housed;[184] or, where the whole 'body of the castle' (i.e. the castle proper) was intended, as at the Tower of London, it was pure synecdoche, representing the whole by its most significant part. Round's argument goes nowhere— unless to reveal the faulty evolution of future dogma.

Seemingly abandoning his conceit, Round devotes the second half of his 'Tower and Castle' essay in the *Geoffrey de Mandeville* appendix to discussing the dates of the *turres* of Rochester, Newcastle, and (at length) Arques (not visited). His case comes to little more than asserting that 'the distinction between a *castellum* and a *turris* . . . has not . . . hitherto been realized'. The interpretative 'revolution in Norman military architecture' which Round trumpeted, relying on his dialectical semantics to substantiate imagination, has made less impact than his legacy in fathering an orthodoxy of 'private', 'military', largely earthwork 'castles' of 'feudal' (even narrowly Norman) invention, which has oppressively prevailed for a century.[185]

Perhaps most to be regretted, for its long-term effect, has been Round's surprisingly exclusive focus on the structure of 'the castle'. Because in both Britain and France 'castle' to contemporaries frequently meant the administrative lordship, a form of words continued to be needed to indicate precisely whether the fortress proper or its dependencies was intended. Some English examples are in

---

[182] Expressly 'my theory' (p. 333); extensive digressions pp. 334–7. Comparison truly shows the achievement of Armitage (1912), whose archaeological demonstration especially makes what sense can be made of the Round thesis, *Early Norman Castles*, esp. 63–79, 94–250.

[183] See for Britain, Renn, *Norman Castles*; for France, e.g. Châtelain, 'Essai de typologie des donjons romans quadrangulaires de la France de l'Ouest', *Château-Gaillard*, 6 (1973), 43–57.

[184] e.g. the disgraced justiciar, Hubert de Burgh, was kept in 1233 under parole in the *dunjo* of Devizes castle (a palatial 'shell-keep' of some kind on the motte; Renn, *Norman Castles*, 163–4); although 'the said castle outside the keep' was to be 'open to the king and his men', knights Henry III sent 'to enter the castle' were denied admission (*CPR, 1232–47*, 19–20). Their mandate was *ad morandum in ballio castri*, excluding the keep; *Close Rolls, 1231–34*, 238.

[185] 'Castle and Tower', 343. Armitage, *Early Norman Castles*, consolidated all of Round's ground, with substantial additions, and an equal anti-Clark rancour. A. Thompson (*Military Architecture*, 1912) was also a convert, but less aggressively.

order: an 'inquisition *post mortem*' on the late Roger de Clifford (a formal inventory of his tenures for fiscal purposes), compiled in 1327, gives financial details relating to the 'castles' of Appleby, Brougham (Westmorland), and Skipton in Craven (Yorks.), in each case for 'the castle within the walls and without the walls', a constant phrase in the Rolls.[186] Since the revenues of the lordship were collected at, and its unity expressed by, the administrative centre, it was natural to refer to the lands and *caput* collectively as 'the castle'. Similarly, the word *manerium* meant equally 'manor-house' and 'manor', so the residence was frequently distinguished as *mansum manerii* or 'manor place'.[187] Even in seventeenth-century France, although *château* had survived as a common town name, the emphasis had become strongly proprietorial in the sense of 'noble mansion', so the learned lawyer Denis de Salvaing felt it necessary to recall the original breadth of meaning to his noble clientele.[188] The *château*, he made clear, was a parcel of territorial, jurisdictional, and lucrative elements together constituting an economic and lordly unit of local government. That English examples from the thirteenth and fourteenth centuries show no exclusivity narrowing to the modern country-mansion sense of *château* is, therefore, hardly surprising. What to an Irish eighteenth-century gentleman under the English Ascendancy would be signified by 'The Castle' (i.e. the Dublin administration) was not so far from the medieval meaning. Thus, in 1285 the mansion of the castle of Hornby (Lancs.) was 'the body of the castle', likewise at Eardisley (Herefs., 1278), Leeds (Kent, 1314), and Elmley (Worcs., 1321); at Banbury (Lincs., 1322) and Berkeley (Gloucs., 1326) similarly.[189] Accordingly, when alleged 'waste' was investigated in 1327, regarding 'the castle of Warwick since it came into the king's hands by reason of the minority of the heir of Guy de Beauchamp', the commissioners were told to assess (any) damage done by the royal keepers 'in the lands, houses, walls and buildings of the castle, and in the mills, parks, woods, and stews belonging thereto'.[190] Richard's Castle (Salop), famous foundation of the 1050s, is described in an inquisition *post mortem* of 1361 as comprising a pasture with two parks and the rest of 'the

---

[186] *CIPM* vii. 41–2. Roger also had Pendragon (alias Mallerstang) and *Burgh under Staynesmore* castles (Brough, built within the Roman fort of Verterae), both Westmorland.

[187] e.g. In 'Licences to Crenellate from the Patent Rolls', partial list in Turner and Parker, *Domestic Architecture*, iii. 402–22.

[188] Salvaing, *De l'usage des fiefs*, 271: 'quant au mot *castrum*, nos ancêtres l'ont employé non seulement pour signifier la maison seigneuriale, mais aussi toutes les dépendances que nous appellons mandement.'

[189] Viz. *corpus castri*: *CCR, 1279–88*, 314 ('the castle of Hornby with appurtenances, except the body of the same'); *CPR, 1272–81*, 162–3, 272 (Eardisley; confiscated for two weeks to punish contemptuous refusal of a royal writ: cf. draconian contemporary Capetian reactions, Coulson, 'Community and Fortress-Politics in France', 82–5, 87–8, 107–8); *CPR, 1313–17*, 152 (Leeds, Kent: the 'body of the castle' comprised 'the houses, towers and bridges, and the head of the pond', i.e. the mill-house and sluice-dam); *CCR, 1318–23*, 311 (Elmley: inventory to be made of arms and stores, with 'safe keeping'); *CPR, 1321–4*, 46 (Banbury: manned in 1322 Lancaster crisis); *CPR, 1324–7*, 327 (Berkeley: to be guarded and manned to help Edward II fleeing into Wales).

[190] *CPR, 1324–7*, 352 (Mortimer and Isabella regime); Earl Guy died in 1315, leaving Thomas aged 2; Sanders, *English Baronies*, 76. For the grand works begun by Earl Thomas, see R. K. Morris, 'The Architecture of the Earls of Warwick', 161–79.

manor'.[191] Taken by itself, the castle-proper (in modern parlance), like the imposing capital-seat of the de Roos at Helmsley (Yorks.) in 1352, might be reported as 'worth nothing within the walls'. In fact £5 a year was required at Helmsley to maintain 'the walls of the said castle, the houses, and buildings now existing within the same'. The jurors were mindful that 'there should be in the castle of Helmsley a constable for the keeping of the same' (paid 3d. per day and a robe annually), together with a parker and a paling-maker to maintain the park fences.[192]

The record calendars (Close, Patent, Fine, etc.) show that such skeleton staffs and care-and-maintenance budgets were the commonplace norm. 'Garrisons' were rare. Stewardship prevails. Lyonshall 'castle' (Herefs.) was worth at least £40 a year in 1326, meaning the whole parcel of revenues receivable at the mansion.[193] Castle Troggy (Mons.) in 1306 had 'a tower newly built' with 'a messuage, 130 acres of arable, 100 acres waste [uncultivated], 7 acres pasture, and a grove of little oaks, all pertaining to the same tower'.[194] The ancient and imposing Bigod seat at Framlingham (Suffolk) was better endowed but fiscally subordinate: 'the manor . . . including a castle', was the not-uncommon formula of the inquisition.[195] 'Custody' or 'keeping' had a range of meanings—but when guarding was needed (in the modern sense) it might be confined to the capital fortress, as with Dublin and Wexford in Ireland in 1335–7, whose 'bodies' (here the demesne lands) alone were farmed out at rent.[196] But normally it was vital not to sever the fortress from any of the local resources upon which its existence depended. At Prudhoe (Northumb.), pleading Scottish incursions across the Cheviot moors, a partition giving away dower lands 'without which it cannot be maintained' was bitterly objected to by Gilbert de Umfraville in 1331, just come of age.[197] He won; but the

[191] CIPM xi. 180–1; Brown, English Castles, 43–4.
[192] CIPM x. 32–5; Toy, Castles, 111; Pickering (Yorks.), in 1361, likewise: CIPM x. 92–116 (late of Henry of Lancaster).
[193] CFR, 1319–27, 95, 382. John de Felton might lose Lyonshall (and its status) for the £40 in land elsewhere, at the king's will.
[194] CIPM iv. 290–310, on Roger Bigod, earl of Norfolk. Bungay is 'the castle with its procinctus' ('castellary' rather than 'precincts'); Chepstow (Mons.) is 'Strugoil . . . the castle with the borough and other members' of 'the whole honour of the castle of Strugoil' to which Troggy (see King, Castellarium Anglicanum, Mons.) belonged; including Irish castles, etc.
[195] e.g. Balliol's Fotheringhay (Northants.) in 1290: 'the manor with its castle', adding 'there is no profit from the castle on account of the great charge from the costs of the walls, houses and others within the same'; CD Scotland, ii. 100–1. Also see CIPM vii. 371–9; viii. 117–27 (Ireland); ix. 44 (Stamford, Lincs.; 'including a ruinous castle', 1347); x. 104 (Newcastle under Lyme, 'castle and town', 1361). Frequently coupled as 'castle and manor' for comprehensiveness, e.g. Oakham (Rutl.), 1347 ('including a walled castle and a manor house built within the castle, a fishpond . . .', etc.) CIPM ix. 59–60; Wood, English Medieval House, 38–9, 71, 123, 129, 137, 294, 296, 345.
[196] CPR, 1334–8, 123, 320, 349. Dublin castle was the more important administrative centre.
[197] CIPM vii. 284–7. The 'bare body' of Prudhoe (west of Newcastle) had gone to Gilbert as heir in his two-thirds. The jurors upheld his view, saying lands worth an extra 54s. 8d. p.a. were needed for its sustenance 'in time of peace'. Trouble with Roger Mauduit, Gilbert's new stepfather, lay behind the appeal (CCR, 1323–7, 399; Sanders, English Baronies, 73), but Prudhoe park had been worth 100s. p.a. 'before the devastation of the Scots', now only 5s. p.a. See Brown, 'English Castles, 1154–1216', 182–91. Pevensey (Sussex) was, however, kept separate from the honour for much of the period 1066–1266; K. Thompson, 'Rape of Pevensey', passim.

principle that 'bodies of castles have not been usually divided and assigned in dower',[198] was expressly upheld the same year in the case of Blaenllyfni and of Bwlch-y-Dinas castles (Brecknock). Castles-proper were put in dower, and their accommodation and facilities were partitioned like manor-houses, all the same.[199]

The territoriality of castles has been neglected in yet another way—English writers since Round have shared his reluctance to acknowledge the umbilical attachment of the *châtellenie*, unless as a sort of military zone. The anglicism in vogue has been 'castlery',[200] representing *castellaria*, a variant of *castellania* with its cognate *castellanus* (*châtelain*). Confining 'castlery' to the great castle-centred estates or *honors* is another recent English tradition. Castellaries (the form adopted in this book) consisted normally of anything from an extensive *territoire banal* such as the *leuga* of Tonbridge (akin to such a religious Liberty as around Ely) down to the 'home-farm' and park of humbler castles such as John de Segrave's Bretby (Derby.) and Caludon (War.).[201] These, too, had their dependent fiefs; miniaturized '*honors*', perhaps, but no more 'military' than Tonbridge castle and town's Lowry whose 'primary purpose' Norman Pounds 'assumes . . . was the defence of Tonbridge castle' (1991). If this was originally so then it did not last long—in fact, as Professor Pounds accepts, 'the specific obligations of its inhabitants are not known'. Moreover, as he notes, '*castellaria* . . . was deceptive. It not unusually meant . . . a baronial honour.' Castle-guard is a further complication: aware that the realities of defence depended considerably more on personnel (and how paid for, in feudal 'kind' or cash) than on inanimate architecture, military apologists have done their best to construct a national (or, at least, a local) system out of the distinctly scanty evidence for services of guard.[202] Some brief consideration is

[198] *CCR, 1330–3*, 232, 263, 403–5. The widow had been endowed on marriage with 'a third of the castles . . . with the honour'. Assignment ordered in May was redefined in October 1331, as 'a third of the value of the bodies . . . and a third of the honour'. A very detailed partition (Nov. 1331) set out her portion in land, plus a third of the revenues receivable at the two castles, including use of the franchisal prison in Blaenllyfni. The ambiguity of 'castle' had even deceived the Chancery, responding to the routine request for dower to be assigned.

[199] See Part IV below.

[200] n. 42 above; Stenton, *First Century*, 192–4, citing those of Dudley, Tutbury (Staffs.), Eye (Suffolk), Berkhamstead (Herts.), Pontefract, Richmond (Yorks.), Nottingham, Bramber, Hastings, Pevensey (Sussex).

[201] *CIPM* vi. 428–9; omitting Bretby as a castle. Caludon is a '*forclettum* surrounded by water'. Dumbreck, 'The Lowry of Tonbridge', 138–47, and Ward, 'The Lowry of Tonbridge and the Lands of the Clare Family'. Dumbreck's diagram reproduced in Pounds, *The Medieval Castle*, 50. Cam, *Hundred Rolls*, 55–8 (general), 206–9 (including Bury St Edmunds' liberty) etc. Much also relevant in essays reprinted as Cam, *Law-Finders*, chs. 1, 2.

[202] Summarized King, *The Castle*, ch. 2. More substantially, with maps, etc., Pounds, *The Medieval Castle*, 33–53. Moore, 'Anglo-Norman Garrisons', 209–10. Earlier Stenton (1932) found only nine named English 'castleries' (n. 200 above), plus three other castles receiving guard. Work by Round (1902), Ballard (1910), and Painter (1935), D. King combines with his (admittedly random) searches to produce (an unreferenced) list of 86 English and Welsh instances, plus six further 'castleries' (unnamed). King justly notes the 'numerous gaps', insufficiency of numbers and of rates of commutation, and lapsing of 'tenure by castle-guard into a curious sort of rentcharge'. Suppe, 'The Garrisoning of Oswestry', surveys the actual 'peace' and 'war' staffing during the wardship of 1160–75. His 'Persistence of Castle-Guard' seeks to generalize this incident. See also Brown, 'English Castles 1154–1216', ch. 3, 'Royal Garrisons', esp. pp. 112–35 ('Castle-Guard'); and pp. 135–48 ('Sergeanty Tenures

needed of the bearing of this problem upon how the castle impinged upon its territorial dependents.[203] Sir Frank Stenton's trenchant doctrine still prevails (1947). It is tinged with the familiar strain of hypothesis.

Stenton started from the conventional belief that the new rash of 'castles' in England after 1066 (institutionally and tenurially far less novel) sustained not so much a landed settlement and governmental takeover at the top as a military conquest.[204] Lack of opportunity and seeming absence of need to master the vast archaeology obstructed progress. Focusing away from economic and social factors on the ground distracted attention from the lordly functions of castles and of the previous *burhs* alike—while the anarchy theory ('baronial revolt') prolonged the military scenario. It fitted the dogmatic separation of architectures 'domestic', 'religious', and 'military' to believe, with Stenton, that 'the conditions of feudal society demanded the continual presence of knights in the castles of the eleventh and early twelfth centuries'.[205] The note of hypothesis pervading this whole genre sounds in his view that what might be implied by the two mid-twelfth-century Welsh border castle-guard pacts he cites actually constituted 'normal conditions of life' which 'must have been much the same everywhere'. It is a slender basis for such a large superstructure. Not 'garrisoning', by the same reasoning, but rather suit of court, the formal attendance of enfeoffed former household knights of the retinue with, in 'war', some (usually token) reinforcement of the castle-household, would objectively be more likely and more 'normal'. Making good the correspondingly quite large gaps in the early evidence for knight-service 'in the field' has required Stenton (and others) to gloss over the uncomfortably speculative view that while 'little is known of the method by which . . . [castle-guard] was organized . . . the evidence suggests that a rotation of duty was originally established among the knights of an honour', later commuted into (very notional) money-payments 'when the private castle lost its first [*sic*] military

and Miscellaneous Services'). Much valuable data also in ch. 8 ('Baronial Castles and the Crown'). Review, Coulson, 'Peaceable Power', esp. 77–81.

[203] Knightly work-services at Launceston: bratticing one battlement (1307), 'preparing a crenel' (1313), are among curiosities (*CIPM* iv. 277; v. 211), both for the fief of Efford, Cornwall (Coulson, 'Fourteenth Century Castles', 149–50). Purely recognitory, non-utilitarian, services shed an undervalued light e.g. *CIPM* xiv. 92 (1375); xv. 191–2, 212–14. Sergeanties can be so specific as to be (deliberately) memorable but almost non-exercizable, e.g. *CIPM* vi. 356 (1325); vii. 256 (1331); xiv. 4–5 (1374).

[204] Architectural refutation, Coulson, 'Peaceable Power'. An unknown proportion of the 1,000-plus castles built 1066–*c*.1200 (the 1066–1100 total will be the bulk, but cannot be typologically quantified: see careful estimates by Eales, 'Royal Power and Castles', 54–8), were probably abandoned early and were either ephemeral 'fieldworks' or failed lordship-seats during the initial land-scramble (e.g. Hawcock's Mount, west of Shrewsbury: Pounds, *The Medieval Castle*, 38). Solid data are unobtainable. Thinking of the ruler as 'inspector-general of fortifications' (King, *The Castle*, 6, 174), and of a national strategy, persists at all levels (e.g. Beeler, *Warfare in England*, 8, 37–8, 43–4, 49–57, 159–60, etc.) but has lost credibility: Morillo, *Warfare Anglo-Norman*, 85–8. Eales's review balances royal *dirigisme* with baronial and sub-baronial initiative (pp. 63–9).

[205] Stenton, *First Century*, 190, 199. Art history is beginning to reassemble the *disjecta membra* of medieval architecture, e.g. Gem, 'An Early Church of the Knights Templars'; Gardner, 'Influence of Castle-Building'; Heslop, 'Orford'; see Coulson, 'Cultural Realities', bibliography.

importance'.²⁰⁶ This centrist conviction (at its extreme in the absurdity that with Henry II's 'nationalized' fortifying 'the baronial castle had become an anachronism'²⁰⁷) Stenton balances with his usual cultural insight (which the French records endorse) that 'the baronial castle' (but sub-baronial also) 'was the expression of ideas which underlay the social custom of the whole French-speaking [*rectius* 'aristocratic'] world'. What is supposed to have happened in Stephen's 'anarchic' reign misrepresents the English picture, just as *anarchie féodale* does the French.²⁰⁸

Stenton was understandably puzzled (and disappointed) that the *castellaria*, by his definition 'the district organized feudally for the defence of a particular castle', (if so vital) should be 'so rarely mentioned in English records'. It goes, as we have seen, largely by other names and under a different (largely economic) guise which was either below the then visible social horizon, or was too indistinct from the normal *honor* and lesser lordly aggregation of demesnes and fiefs to be discernible in such terms. In order to establish the credibility of Stenton's 'castlery' vested with military castle-services as a general phenomenon, its distinctive existence 'as a territory rather than a mere group of fees' (and more) must be made out. Richmond's Yorkshire Domesday castellary (*castellatus*) is not very convincingly offered. It was not coextensive with fiefs owing castle-guard and was quite exceptional, like Dover and a very few other dispersed castle-guard lordship-affinities. The handful of other examples—in Sussex (Hastings, Lewes, plus Bramber and Pevensey); in the Welsh March (Caerleon, Richard's Castle, Ewias Harold, Clifford, Montgomery); Dudley (explicitly a *castellaria* in Domesday); Pontefract and possibly Tutbury—are singularly few by comparison with the host of major *capita* and the multitude (now known) of lesser ones, whatever allowance be made for poor documentation.²⁰⁹ Garrisoning, there is no doubt, was an occasion not an institution. Only in special circumstances did it become institutionalized.

But this issue is subsidiary. What matters here is that just as the castles must be

---

²⁰⁶ M. Prestwich, 'The Garrisoning of English Medieval Castles', gives a balanced summary; cf. the officers'-mess ideology reflected e.g. by M. Powicke (*Military Obligation*, 26): 'the Norman Conquest, by its very nature, ushered in a new era in military history. The fact of conquest by a large army of volunteer warriors . . . led in the first place to a reliance on their future military service . . .' If so, its organization was suspiciously unsystematic, despite voluminous apologetic, cf. Holt, 'Introduction of Knight Service'. The vast literature of 'military institutions' has neglected social aspects very largely and the non-military sphere almost entirely; cf. Crouch, *Image of Aristocracy*, esp. chs. 8, 9, 10.

²⁰⁷ Stenton, *First Century*, 192–3, and n. 1 ('temporary importance of baronial castles in the reign of Richard I'); cf. Brown, 'List of Castles', 253, on the confiscations and 'demolitions' culminating in the brief repossession (under rendability) of 'all castles in England' (1176), despite which 'the private castle survived as triumphantly after 1176 as before'; after 1214 'showing a marked resilience' (p. 256): see Part II, Ch. 3, sec. 2 below.

²⁰⁸ Coulson, 'Castles of the Anarchy', and 'French Matrix', *passim*; also 'Freedom to Crenellate', 86–112; Aubenas, 'Les Châteaux-forts', *passim*, shows how.

²⁰⁹ Pounds, *The Medieval Castle*, 33–5, adds Chichester and Arundel. Of these capital castles, Hastings and Bramber were soon obsolete structurally; Arundel and Lewes were modestly modernized but mattered as honorial seats mainly; Chichester was an ex-Roman *civitas*; Pevensey alone was thoroughly refortified, c.1250. Stenton, *First Century*, 193–4. James Tait preferred 'castellany' for the Sussex Rapes (ibid. 193 n. 2).

reassessed so must the special sense imposed on *castellaria*. Stenton accepts that 'before the end of the twelfth century, the word was . . . less restricted', and came to mean 'the whole complex of fees which contributed to the maintenance of a . . . castle'. It would be more satisfactory to take it as normal much earlier, as Stenton does for Eye and Berkhamstead, namely that a *castellaria* was a castle-centered fiefdom—but also to recognize the lowly status and modest structure of the great majority of 'castles of the Conquest'.

Norman Pounds's book, for all its conventional 'military' tone, implies some scepticism on tenurial manning, although he does not query the misappropriation of the medieval *castellaria*.[210] Having reviewed the foregoing and other cases, Pounds remarks that otherwise, 'castleries in the strict sense [*sic*] are largely absent from lowland England'. Large blocks of territory were certainly less common there (as he notes), compared with France; but the issue is basically artificial. In their 'civil' administration castle-lordships differed little (if at all) from ordinary larger 'manors'—obviously so, since whether the *caput* was a castle was a matter of mere repute very often. A handful of castles with guard-services (never very practical, ephemeral except fiscally, and possibly only experimental) are overwhelmed by the multitude without. In compiling his 'social history', Pounds has valuably moved the emphasis towards the mere gentry with their sometimes miniaturized (but still lordly) castellaries, bringing archaeological reality to bear.[211] The fortress was as inseparable from its 'estate' (in every sense) as any country-house which was no mere house in the country.[212]

It will be useful to conclude this chapter by considering certain other common terms, notably the significant divergence between the modern and medieval understanding of 'fortress'. *Fortalicium* is a still more elusive word than *castrum/castellum*. Whereas 'castle' by extension occasionally meant 'a component, unit, or feature of fortification', this is a regular meaning of *fortalicium* (*forteritia*, *forcellettum*, etc.), in addition to 'fortress' in the modern sense. As 'fortress' it was a near-synonym of 'castle', possessing the same seignorial aura, rarely if ever suggestive, unlike the modern (Walter Scott) 'fortalice' or 'fortlet', of a structural diminutive.[213] Thus, the *fortalicia* of York city (1312) meant generally

[210] Pounds, *The Medieval Castle*, 50–1. On some recent writers of the 'military architecture' school dismissed (on archaeological grounds) by Stocker (English Heritage), see 'The General's Armchair', 415–20; Coulson, 'Cultural Realities', *passim*.

[211] Pounds, *The Medieval Castle*, 9–11, 18–22, 59–68, 102–6, 130–52, 184–221, etc.

[212] e.g. Brandon castle (War.), burned *c*.1265, was still 'the castle with its members' in 1309 (*CIPM* v. 95–6). Newark (Lincs.), confiscated in 1322–3 as 'the castle', included 'the issues'; synonymous with 'the manor', and with 'the castle and honour of Newark' (*CFR, 1319–27*, 90, 98, 196). At Bamburgh (Northumb.) a smith held land by sergeanty for 'making the ironwork of the ploughs *castelli de Bamburg* . . . by ancient enfeoffment' (1212); still so in 1372, when there were three ploughs: *Book of Fees*, i. 204; *CIPM* xiii. 172. For other notable castle-sergeanties, *Book of Fees*, i. 120, 247, 281; ii. 1254, 1364, 1391.

[213] e.g. seizure ordered in 1324 of the absent and hostile Queen Isabella's 'castles, fortalices, lands and other places', and safe-keeping of the bodies of the said castles and of the said fortalices, lands and places'; later, specifically 'reserving for the king's ordinance the keeping of the bodies of the castles': *CFR, 1319–27*, 300–2; *CCR, 1323–7*, 223; *Rymer's Foedera* ii. i (London 1816), 569. The phrase 'little castle',

its boundary curtilage of wall, towers, and ditch.[214] The distinction here between 'castle' (the bailey) and 'tower' (Clifford's Tower, on the early motte) was still, of course, necessary when, in 1334, the sheriff of York was authorized to repair 'the paling about the king's tower of York, and between it and the castle there'.[215] As misleadingly (but quite consistently) rendered in the calendars, timber repairs were sanctioned (1322) to 'the houses and fortalices (i.e. *fortalicia*-'fortifications') within the castle' of Newport (Mons.), this being one of 'the castles and fortlets' (*sic*) formerly of the great Clare lordship of Glamorgan.[216] It is clear that *fortalicium* was not a diminutive: it might seem that the early-thirteenth-century square moat known as Kirtling Towers (Cambs.) was a lesser place styled accordingly *forcelettum* in 1336; but in 1309 the inquisition reported 'the manor' as 'including a certain castle', late of Robert de Tany.[217] Stogursey (Stoke Courcy, Som.), despite its size and being the Hundred centre, was in the same fashion a *forcellettum*,[218] whereas ancient Egremont (Cumb.) was both 'castle' and 'fortress' in the dower assignment of 1322, made to Thomas de Multon's widow.[219] To the businesslike functionary (the escheator south of Trent) who allocated the lands, the imposing 'mount' castle was simply 'the chief messuage of the manor'.

This quality, practical, objective, and everyday, frequently occurs. At Castle Carlton (Lincs.), the administrative as well as the residential function of this early motte castle with two baileys was emphasized in 1308 and again in 1369 by referring to the whole site as 'the capital messuage'.[220] Inquisitions *post mortem* were descriptive financial surveys, not 'strategic appreciations', of course: but it is striking how predominant was this accountant's approach, even in Ireland and in the

like 'old castle' (*CIPM* iii. 298), even 'good castle' (Caerfilly, but also Neath, 1296; *CIPM* iii. 244–5), is occasional, but still vague; e.g. Mitford (Northumb.) is both 'the castle, worth £14 yearly' and 'the little castle' (*sic*: a motte with two baileys, etc.); *CIPM* v. 171–2; cf. vi. 323.

[214] *CCR, 1318–23*, 350. As noted above.
[215] *CCR, 1333–7*, 284; such 'orders' as calendared are frequently warrants obtained by the 'recipient' to secure payment or other privilege (Coulson, 'Battlements and the Bourgeoisie', 120 *et passim*); Brown *et al.*, *King's Works*, i. 116; ii. 889–93.
[216] *Fortalicia/fortalitia* are habitually translated 'fortalice' or 'fortlet' in the Calendars. *CCR, 1318–23*, 440, 624.
[217] King, *Castellarium Anglicanum, sub.* Cambs.; *CIPM* v. 101–2. Moor End (Northants.), consistently 'castle' in magnatial occupation ('more a habitation than a fortress'—King), was licensed to be crenellated as a 'fortalice' with a park in 1347: *CCR, 1346–49*, 222; *CFR, 1445–52*, 239. These questions will be addressed in Coulson, *Castles and Crenellating* (in preparation). The French *forceletz* occurs as 'fortresses' in the Irish petitions of 1342, largely printed *CCR, 1341–43*, 508–16.
[218] *CIPM* v. 73; probably to distinguish it from 'the manor with its members'; Ellesmere 'fortalice' (Salop) was also a major castle and a Hundred court seat, *CCR, 1349–54*, 111; cf. Cam, *The Hundred*, 277–9, and *Liberties and Communities*, 70.
[219] *CCR, 1318–23*, 566–7; Part IV below. In 1338 John de Multon's eldest sister received the whole castle-proper; *CFR, 1337–47*, 79–81; *CIPM* vi. 198–201, on Th. de Multon. Tattershall (Lincs., see Tipping, *Tattershall Castle*, chs. 1 and 2, pp. 210–11, and end-plan) was *castellum* in 1298, 'castle and manor' in 1306, and *forcelettum* in 1329, which in this instance included the appurtenances (*CIPM* iii. 372–5; iv. 259; vii. 172–3).
[220] *CIPM* v. 27–8; *CCR, 1369–74*, 204–6 (a detailed partition in dower). Castle Donington (Leics.; another inverted territorial name) in 1361 was 'the manor . . . including a castle in place of the chief messuage'. Thomas de Holland, late earl of Kent, also had Cottingham and Bossal ('Buttercrambe') castles (Yorks.), noted as 'manors' only (*CIPM* x. 552–4).

English marches.[221] In the case of magnificent, lake-girt Kenilworth (War.), which sustained the longest of the rare English sieges (June–December 1266), it seems almost disrespectful to comment tersely—'the custody of the castle exceeds the revenues by 100s. at least, besides repairs.'[222] It was one of Edmund of Lancaster's seats on his death in 1296. Another was Pickering (Yorks.), recorded as 'out of repair' (*debile*), a chaplain in the castle costing £3 a year and Edmund's old nurse £1, both charged to the revenues. Edmund's comital seats at Lancaster ('a capital messuage, *viz* the castle . . .') and at Derby ('including the site of an old castle where there is usually a capital messuage surrounded by dykes') sound scarcely impressive even as residences. Their glory was ancient but physically vestigial. Tutbury was better, having 'a castle well-built, with close, lands, rents etc. . . . including a preserve'.[223] This is the language of the estate agent or steward. Its domination of the unselected, ordinary records can only be appreciated by reading them *in extenso* even if, less laboriously, in calendar form.

Very often, as we have noted, the rank of the proprietor, not the quality of his castellated residence, determined which places were called 'castles'.[224] Style, renown, and antiquity mattered most, not structural definition by degree of fortification. The correlation of that degree with rank and wealth was erratic. To say of Haverhill (Suffolk), as David King does, 'a poor moat with nothing but the name of castle', violates medieval etiquette so often preserved in site names. 'The manor of the castle', with nearby Clare, had belonged to the great Gilbert de Clare, earl of Gloucester and Hertford, founder of Caerfilly (stunning, but merely 'a castle good and well-provisioned with a preserve . . . two mills', etc.).[225] Status once acquired by a site tended to become vested in it, along with the services of its dependants. Bedford castle, with shell and tower 'keep' and two baileys, including the upper part of its immense motte, was razed by Henry III to commemorate punishing the contempt committed there by Fawkes de Bréauté, after the great siege of 1224.[226] In 1311–12 it was still known as 'the site of the castle' (*situm castri*)—not 'the place where it had once been' but, as at Barton Segrave (1321, Northants.) and Boarstall (1348, Bucks.: 'the site of the manor within the moat'), rather the centre still of its lordly and administrative circumscription and

[221] The modern outlook finds this natural from the character e.g. of Oakham castle (Rutl.) already mentioned: *CIPM* ix. 59–60; x. 523–30 (1360, still more 'domestic'); but notably much the same in Irish inquisitions, see *CIPM* iv. 231, 304–7 (1306), 328–30 (1307), etc. (Part III, Ch. 2, sec. 1 below).

[222] *CIPM* iii. 288–9, listing the (water-)mill, dams, meadows, moor, park, rents, judicial revenues, etc; on the siege, Powicke, *Henry III and the Lord Edward*, 506, 518, 531, 538–9.

[223] *CIPM* iii. 291–301. The full valuations ('extents') are seldom calendared. Tutbury (as usual) shrugged off its punitive dismantling by Henry II in 1175 after the Young King's rebellion of 1173–4, Brown, *List of Castles*, 232, 279.

[224] e.g. Moor End (n. 217 above); Coulson, 'Some Analysis of Bodiam', 96–8, and 'Freedom to Crenellate', 132–6. Inquisitions valuably reflect local juries' language; e.g. ancient Burton in Lonsdale (Yorks.) was *le Motehall* and *Castilhowe* (*CIPM* xii. 384–5, on John de Mowbray). Lordly proprietors liked calling their residences 'castle' as much as many a Victorian *nouveau riche*.

[225] *CIPM* iii. 234–51, King, *Castellarium Anglicanum*, *sub* Suffolk; analysis of surviving popular nomenclature in Wilkinson, *Castles of England* (n. 124 above).

[226] William de Beauchamp obtained some relaxation for the *caput* of his barony; *Rot Litt Claus*, i. 632; Sanders, *English Baronies*, 10–12; Bradbury, *Medieval Siege*, 140–1. Baker, 'Bedford Castle'.

seat of the Beauchamp barony of Bedford, despite loss of donjon, motte, and crenellations, leaving only a residence behind.[227] Structural and moral humiliation also befell Skipsea (Yorks.), destroyed in 1221 and temporarily abandoned, but in 1350 it was still 'the castle'. Cash payments in lieu of castle-guard services ('ward') were still being made there.[228] Barnstaple (Devon), in 1273/4, still had 'a place called the castle', although it had been officially destroyed. A walled dwelling on the motte comprised 'hall, chamber, kitchen, and other houses' which were 'almost built'. In 1326 Barnstaple manor was recorded as including 'a ruinous castle and a court of the tenants', so the barony still functioned regardless.[229] By contrast, at Drogheda (co. Meath), 'lately called Castelblathagh', the *situm* was indeed the 'site' or place on which the castle and town were built. But 'seat' not 'site' is the usual meaning.[230] When the sense 'vacant plot formerly occupied (by a castle)' is intended, confusion is generally explicitly avoided, as it is by the phrase *locum ubi castellum quondam fuit*, the expression adopted for Richard de Granville's castle-seat in 1207. The monks of Neath abbey (Glam.) acquired both site (in the modern sense) and Granville's lands, which together constituted his modest *castellaria*.[231]

Medieval nomenclature (the word connotes rank), whether popular or learned, was clear continually over many centuries, for all that it lacked terminological precision. Public place-names, like people's associations with and memories of castle-sites (as inquisitions bear witness), were hard to efface. The fact we have exemplified that *castrum/castellum* was, among other characteristics, an inclusive territorial concept with the normal (loose) sense of 'castellary', context not contrary, demonstrates the error of elevating 'the castle' into an icon. The enormously various nature of castles on the ground agrees. The medieval reality, of course, lacks most of the artificial aura, some of the soldierly glamour, and all of the bogus precision of its modern image. But although fuzzy and diffuse, the

---

[227] *CIPM* v. 199–200; vi. 186–8. The round keep, mined in the siege, was removed, the revetted ditches filled up, the outer bailey 'levelled to the ground', but the 'lesser bailey' wall, cut down to half its height (more difficult than total destruction by undermining), was, though without symbolic battlements, to be coped as a curtilage wall to Beauchamp's baronial *mansiones*. He also obtained some remission of derogation for the reduced motte, which he could wall but not crenellate (n. 226 above). Barton Segrave, licensed to be crenellated 1310; 'castle' still, 1406 (*CPR, 1307–13*, 303; *CFR, 1405–13*, 30. *CFR, 1347–56*, 81). Boarstall, 'houses', etc. detailed *CCR, 1346–49*, 445–6.

[228] *CIM* iii. 18–20; *caput* of Burstwick barony until 1221 (Sanders, *English Baronies*, 24 n. 7). 'Destruction' even of buildings (still less so of earthworks) was rarely as thorough as at Bedford. Feudal services, etc. and the castellary in any case were almost indestructible. King, *Castellarium Anglicanum*, sub Yorks.

[229] Partitioned after 1213; Sanders, *English Baronies*, 104–5; *CIPM* ii. 56–7; vi. 448, held with appurtenances 'as a whole barony'. Two chantries survived also 'in the castle'. Its equivocal state began in 1228 when Henry de Tracey's Torrington was razed as 'unlicensed', but at Barnstaple the walls were to be reduced to 10 feet (as at Bedford) to enclose 'his buildings and *mansio*' as a *firmitudo murorum* (*Close Rolls, 1227–31*, 69–70).

[230] *CCR, 1343–6*, 627, in 1345 recalling the original foundation (*c*.1228); 25 marks p.a. rent still payable by the Crown (to Joan de Mortimer, countess of March).

[231] Clark, *Cartae*, i. 56–8. Granville, founder of Neath abbey (1130), had a castle somewhere west of the River Neath. His castellary extended to the Tawe: Knowles and Hadcock, *Medieval Religious Houses*, 113, 122; *Glamorgan County History*, iii. Pugh (ed.), 23.

genuine article has all the durable strength of authenticity. Reinstating it against the prevailing 'Robin Hood' image may not be more difficult than substituting grassy mounds and enigmatic earthworks for the 'cloud-capped towers' (but not 'the gorgeous palaces') of earlier romance which the Round–Armitage revolution accomplished nearly a century ago. The truth was not necessarily prosaic, however—an authentic romantic vision of castles did exist, as will be shown.

3

Some Social Relations of 'Castles and Fortresses'

The testimony of the documents is, then, very far from the confident declarations of what constituted a castle (more usually 'the castle') which are the opening ritual of innumerable castle-books.[232] What the less numerous 'fortification' books gain by breadth they lose by an even greater obsession with 'defence'. To contemporaries what mattered was clearly not this type of thinking at all. Of the array of technical words of modern castellology, derived mostly from the seventeenth century and later gunpowder era and celebrated in countless 'glossaries of terms', there is scant sign (see Index, 'Terminology'). Place-styles, moreover, had as much to do with rank as with structures as such. 'Fortification' was always an architectural 'manner', seldom if ever purely utilitarian.[233] It was a major genre in what is becoming known as 'the architecture of power'. Actual medieval buildings defy arbitrary classifications invented to sustain ideological positions. Knepp (Sussex), for instance, declassified by David King ('a low platform with counterscarp bank; some remains of masonry; always very much of a hunting-lodge, and seldom called a castle') nevertheless was a castle in fact as well as in name and had fortress-character as late as 1368. The unimpressionable compilers of the inquisition on John de Mowbray mention, 'Knappe: . . . includes a messuage *ad modum forceletti*, a park with deer . . .', etc.[234] With little exaggeration, the Irish city of Waterford, a mere seven acres in extent, was described in 1375 as 'like a little castle' by burgesses hoping for royal support and commercial privileges. The image here

---

[232] Expanded to an assertive manifesto by D. King, *The Castle*, 1–14: castles cannot be 'corporate habitations' and must be 'seriously fortified', although many were far from grand, etc. He defends the 'military' approach against 'the contemporary fashion to dwell on the castle's peaceful functions, which is a healthy reaction against the totally military view. Nevertheless castles need to be considered in military terms . . . war is what they were meant for' (p. 5). Cf. Watson, 'Expression of Power', 59–77.

[233] e.g. Tibbers, co. Dumfries (Cruden, *Scottish Castle*, 72, 75), despite the stresses of 1298–1302, was both 'castle' and 'house'; Selkirk, Lochmaben, and Linlithgow were alternatively 'peel', 'fortress', and 'castle': *CDScotland* ii. 257, 291, 327–8, 331–2, 340, 396, 468, 483 (1302–6). Conversely, castle features such as crenellation, moats, drawbridges, gatehouses, etc. were ubiquitous at 'manors', including large royal ones: e.g. *CLibR* ii. 218; iii. 244–5, 248, 332, 372 (Woodstock, 1244, 1249, 1251; Kingscliffe, 1249; Havering, 1251).

[234] *CIPM* xii. 385. The jurors reported this at Steyning nearby. For the castellated manor-houses at Shenley (Bucks.), Conington (Hants), Mulbarton, Brundall ,and Ketteringham (Norfolk), see *CIPM* x. 385 (1359); xii. 58–9 (1365); 337–8 (1370).

is of the beleaguered outpost of Englishry, 'little' by self-deprecating humility.[235]
The militant concept to which they appealed was universal but requires careful
handling—it does not translate into modern strategy-speak. Architectural
features had their own rules. When John de Sutton of Holderness was arraigned
in 1352 for building a castle at Swine (Yorks., *alias* Branceholme), an occasion
notable for being virtually the sole case to be found of officious or jealous interference, he not only denied that his 'houses' there, 'strengthened with tiles and
mortar', were any such 'castle, crenellated and battlemented' as had been alleged,
but (as though to show criteria were venal as well as subjective) forthwith and
without difficulty obtained a licence to crenellate, and a pardon for good
measure.[236] He was denying undue social pretension while also covering himself
in case of future local jealousy.

    It is because a far broader and looser sense of the 'castle' operated in the medieval
sphere, whether the period be early, middle, or late, that the social interactions of
fortresses were so diffuse and pervasive. These elusive connotations, corrections,
and resonances are explored in this chapter. It is done with no little resignation.
Although as a tool of analysis, even as a hypothesis, the modern construct of 'the
castle' carries with it too many false associations to continue to be useful, its dominance of the modern popular mind is not likely to change. The 'battering-rams and
boiling-oil' view of the middle ages will continue to slander the period. It satisfies
psychological need and will not easily be replaced.[237] Scholarship has not modified
the popular image of 'feudal' (of *féodal* still less, perhaps) or even of 'medieval',
words both still current in virtually the Enlightenment sense of 'barbaric'.[238] But
conversely, the rediscovery of what castles were to medieval people is all the more
important as a result. Castles are probably, with 'knights', the dominant popular
impression of the period. That Tussauds, of Chamber of Horrors fame, for a time
took over Warwick castle is the problem (but also the opportunity) in a nutshell.
Perhaps Disney World is a sign of hope that a more authentic romanticism may
become acceptable. If chivalry rather than Snow White can dethrone war, truth will
benefit. Without this possibility the present task would scarcely be worth attempting. As it is, the records and the archaeology allow no option—and modern French
usage is quite sympathetic.[239]

---

[235] *CPR, 1374–77*, 145; on bourgeois hyperbole see Coulson, 'Battlements and the Bourgeoisie',
passim; *CDIreland*, i. 226–7 (1227); Bradley, *Walled Towns in Ireland*, 12–14.

[236] *CPR, 1350–54*, 218; Coulson, 'Freedom to Crenellate', *passim*.

[237] Popular imagery (often sadistic) is particularly clear in cartoons, e.g. Gary Larson, *The Far Side
Gallery 2*, 15, 26, 34, 38, 57, 63, 65, 76, 98. Animal fat was used, e.g. to burn the props in the mine under
the NE angle of Rochester keep in 1215; *R Litt Claus* i. 238b. Burning oil was dropped to destroy wooden
siege-works, but not from the spyholes (conventionally *meutrières*) in gate-passage vaults, where it
would harm the defenders more. For mineral oil thrown by trebuchets and mangonels see Partington,
Greek Fire, esp. 1–41; Bradbury, *Medieval Siege*, index 'Greek Fire', etc.; Viollet-le-Duc, *Dictionnaire de
l'architecture*, art. 'Siège'. Alleged use of molten lead is one of many typical projections of modern
psychosis (e.g. *Sunday Telegraph*, 18 July 1999, pp. 22–3).

[238] e.g. Mackrell, *'Feudalism' in Eighteenth Century France*, 1–16, etc. Reynolds, *Fiefs and Vassals*,
3–13, etc.

[239] The breadth of even late-medieval nomenclature is reflected throughout by Contamine, *Guerre*,

1. Earthwork and Ashlar: Policing, Hierarchy, and Aesthetics

The historical text particularly relied upon to support the Anglocentric view of aboriginal castles as primarily (or even exclusively) quite small ('private') works of earth and timber, is the famous clause 4 of the 1091 *Consuetudines et Justicie*.[240] Taking their tone from ecclesiastical denunciations of castles used against the Church, historians have supposed that the dukes of Normandy, and the kings of England, restrictively licensed castle-building on a systematic basis.[241] Clause 4 seemed to justify this view, as it sets out a definition of what minimum standard constituted a fortification. Precision rarely attempted—acts of violence and illicit armed assembly were the real problem. For structures of earth and timber with few diagnostic features definition was especially difficult, but their existence was incontrovertible. Disorder in the duchy after the Conqueror's death highlighted the need to distinguish the by-no-means trivial but entirely normal fenced ditches and boundary banks of farmsteads from works so built and located as to facilitate use by armed men to disrupt the peace, by deterring all but resolute counter-measures on the part of the ruler, including the baronial authorities. It was also important to define serious intrusions upon the tenurial and jurisdictional map (before they usurped permanent status) in such a way as to set them apart from established castles sanctioned by long-user, law, and custom, most of which in Normandy also consisted of crude earth and timber. The occupants of extempore lairs could just as well usurp lordship, collect revenues, and acquire 'rights'. Those which relied not on works at all but on mere inaccessibility and on natural defensibility, needing no artifice to make them troublesome centres for armed forays, would have to be covered as well. It is these provisions which are most revealing. Clause 4 was, then, the (abortive) solution devised during a pause in their civil war by the sons of William the Conqueror, to pacify the duchy of Normandy after four turbulent years of lawlessness following their father's death.[242] William Rufus, king of England, and Duke Robert of Normandy, his ineffective elder brother, looked back to the harsh order of William the Bastard's later years to declare what had then been, as they alleged, the practice in a wide range of local-government matters. Fortifying was but one out of fourteen clauses (by modern paragraphing) devoted to it:

état et société, but p. 5 and n. 14 tend to interpret late wartime restrictions (1416, 1426, 1437, 1444) on public subvention for fortress-defence as universal structural criteria of what was de facto a *forteresse*. The aim was to limit aid to places best capable of protecting refugees. The *moustier fort*, some abbeys, and other forts might be militarily unsatisfactory in such extreme conditions.

[240] Haskins, *Norman Institutions*, 282 (4); nn. 22, 130 above. Conventional view: Dunbabin, *France in the Making*, 199–201 (p. 200).

[241] e.g. Thompson, *Military Architecture*, 89–90, 102, as 'an edict of the council of Lillebonne' of 1080; redated Haskins, *Norman Institutions*, 277–8, to July 1091, 'the only year in the July of which (Robert and Rufus) were in Normandy and in friendly relations', partitioning the duchy (provisionally). Consequences of redating not assessed by Pounds, *The Medieval Castle*, 26–9. Cf. Eales, 'Royal Power and Castles', 71–3; Coulson, 'Rendability and Castellation', 59; also 'Freedom to Crenellate', 93, 101–2, and 'Castles of the Anarchy', 72–3; also 'French Matrix', 74.

[242] But Haskins, *Norman Institutions*, 277–81, and D. Bates, *Normandy Before 1066*, 162–6, accord the whole document general and impartial authority as a retrospective declaration of Norman laws.

Nobody in Normandy was permitted to make earth-works (*fossatum*) in the *terra plana* unless such that the dug spoil could be thrown directly up from the bottom [onto the bank] without standing on any kind of step (*scabellum*). And nobody was allowed to erect a palisade there, unless it formed a single line (*una regula*) and that without projections and parapet-walks (*sine propugnaculis et alatoriis*). Nor might anyone make a stronghold (*fortitudo*) upon any promontory or island (*rupe vel insula*), or create a new castle-lordship (*castellum*) in Normandy. Nobody in Normandy was permitted to deny [use of] the fortress of his castellary (*fortitudinem castelli sui vetare*) to the lord duke of Normandy, if he desired to have it in his hand.[243]

The passage forms one brief section of a comprehensive statement of the 'most necessary' of the rights, once claimed in Normandy by the Conqueror, which Rufus and Robert, but not their younger brother Count Henry, sought to reassert. The last sentence refers (in standard form) to existing and lawful fortresses, distinguished as *castella*, which the duke was entitled to requisition whenever necessary under the familiar governmental power of rendability vested in the direct overlord throughout the provinces of France, inherited in the duchy as elsewhere from Carolingian times. *Reddibilitas* and the sanctioning of fortresses were part of early medieval civilization.[244]

Like Orderic Vitalis' excuse for the English defeat, that 'what the Gauls call castles were very few in England', the 1091 *Consuetudines* item appeared to chime so exactly with the British experience of 'Norman castles' that it was taken to be an exact specification of 'the castle'. By that simplistic reasoning the seemingly redundant prohibition of new 'castles' should have made the rest superfluous. Ella Armitage thought the document dated to 1080 (Council of Lillebonne, to whose record the manuscript became collated), giving it the authority of the Conqueror.[245] Redated (by C. H. Haskins) to during the civil war in the duchy, and regarded, as we have done, as directed against the sort of 'very nasty fortlets' (*munitiunculas pessimas*) complained of as a symptom of disorder in England during Stephen's reign (1135–54);[246] and seen not as a 'ban' declaring general principle but as a reassurance offered to established baronial and sub-baronial jurisdictions by whose consent any new lordship (castellar or otherwise) had normally

[243] *Terra plana* may mean 'land without fortresses' (as e.g. *Layettes*, i., 105, of 1175) or simply 'plain', in distinction to the *rupis vel insula*. Here *propugnaculum* must mean a timber brattice (*bretaschia*) or projection (cf. n. 263 below); elsewhere 'outworks' when associated with *fossa* (*Recueil Charles III*, 205, of 917) but vaguer when with *turris*: Brussel, *Nouvel Examen*, i. 313–14, of 1080–96. It is vague in literary use, e.g. Chibnall, 'Orderic on Castles', 54. Castellary for *castrum/castellum* in both occurrences makes best sense here. *Fortitudo* (twice) is figurative as well as physical, but 'fortress-proper' is a usual sense, in this context.

[244] Part II, below. Coulson, 'National Requisitioning', for overview. Haskins (*Norman Institutions*, 278) was unaware of the generality of this frequently used ducal right. Background to 1091 in Poole, *Domesday Book to Magna Carta*, 104–8; also Yver, 'Les Châteaux-forts en Normandie', 60–5. Yver implies ducal licensing of castle-building but without explicit statement or evidence (pp. 50, 53, 55, 60–1, 76, 80–1, 101, 105). He tends to deny *ex hypothesi* that franchisal *châtellenies* (and *avoueries*) could exist in Normandy (p. 76).

[245] Armitage, *Early Norman Castles*, 377–8. She also misconceived the *c.*1115 *Leges Henrici Primi* allusion to *castellacio trium scannorum* (Coulson, 'Freedom to Crenellate', 100–2).

[246] *Gervase of Canterbury*, i. 160; Coulson, 'Castles of the Anarchy', 60 *et passim*.

to be created, the *Consuetudines* clause makes contemporary sense. Contemporary 'bans' were not prohibitions as such but were intended to submit major new castles to local consent. Such documents used terms such as *turris* (stone or timber 'donjons' enmotted or free-standing) as well as the cover-all *castrum/castellum*.[247] In the *Consuetudines*, *castellum* is used distinctively of 'proper castles', naturally as an afterthought. Notably this receives less prominence than is given to the more important principle which is recalled of the rendering of established forts. The structural prescription in Clause 4 permitted low ring-works. It defined neither what a 'castle' was (post-Conquest castles in Britain fell below as well as above these criteria) nor some cut-off point of official interest, but attempted simply to strike at the visible symptoms of lawlessness, namely the upstart occupation of natural fastnesses and erecting irregular field-works. The 'incastellation' of churches, often mentioned by chroniclers such as Orderic,[248] may have been regarded as covered but was probably left out deliberately, so as not to intrude upon episcopal jurisdiction. Clearing up the debris of discord was (as we shall see) a normal feature of pacifications (ineffective in 1091). The vagueness of *castrum/castellum* created difficulties.

Writing of the 'small, circular enclosures' of Normandy, Michel de Boüard typically considered that they came below the 'one-throw-of-earth-from-ditch-to-bank' rule, restricting profiles to a height of 10 feet or less. 'Such excavations', he deduced, 'were not considered to be military', but were classed with those surrounding most *maisons rurales*, to protect them against *les animaux carnassiers et les rôdeurs*.[249] Wolves and robbers may not have been so finely discriminating. Much depended on the unspecified height and character of the palisade, and much more always depended on manning. The weakest link in the argument that 'military' works were structurally distinct is the vast grey area disclosed by archaeology.[250] Small castles were 'knightly' (just as the *burh* was thegnly in pre-Conquest England), and still smaller establishments belonged to a lower class: but all were in various ways demonstrative, their character depending upon the size of the labour force which could be coerced to build them—and so on the rank and means of their possessor.[251] Manorial curtilages acting as property boundaries, as fences protecting man and

---

[247] e.g. *Recueil Philippe I*, 315–17 (1092), regarding a (stone) *turris* (destroyed by mining) and *munitiones* which had encroached on Compiègne abbey (*dép*. Oise). Philip put under ban (i.e. created a licensing franchise, as the gloss confirms) any intrusive *turrim aut munitionem sive domum defensabilem*. In 1080–96 the count of Blois, to protect his lordship, forbade any *turris vel propugnacula* (perhaps 'battlements') at the bishop's palace, Brussel, *Nouvel Examen*, i. 313–14. See Coulson, 'Seignorial Fortresses', App. C. 'Regional and Particular Bans on Fortification in France'.

[248] Chibnall, 'Orderic Vitalis on Castles', 48, 52–3, *et passim* on warfare in Normandy *c*.1087–1108, 1138–42.

[249] de Boüard, 'Les Petites enceintes circulaires', 21–35; conventional treatment of the *Consuetudines et Justicie*, 32; map-diagram of 27 sites of enclosures of internal diameter of 65–163 feet.

[250] e.g. Brown, *English Castles*, 48–9: arguing from the truism that 'there is a difference between one's garden fence and the walls of Caernarvon castle', betrays the underlying absurdity of this position (Eales, 'Royal Power and Castles', 52–3).

[251] As in pre-Conquest England, Williams, 'A Bell-House and a Burh-Geat', 225. A social-rank explanation proposed also (Normandy) by Fixot, 'Les Fortifications de terre'. On Poitevin castellaries

beast from wolves and casual human marauders, were everywhere. The demarcation of territory (parks especially) was often by substantial earthen banks, akin to early linear 'dykes', hedged or palisaded along the top. Even when elementary defences to gentry-seats and farmsteads could be dispensed with, still the symbolic separateness of ditch, bank, and moat, setting apart the manor and dependent buildings from the great open fields, was retained. Numerous manorial 'extents' (descriptive valuations) and dower and co-heiress partitions show that the manor-place, or (more grandly) the 'capital messuage', consisted of the 'houses within the moat', severed in dignity from the *basse cour*, often a mere farmyard.[252] Irreducibly, virtually all were farm-houses, grand or small. In France especially, inner and outer courts might be adorned by turrets, seignorial dovecote, gatehouse, and show of castellation; but these features were just richer versions of the primitive *gentilhommière*.[253] Their overt militancy might vary with period, rank, and place but their symbolism did not. In the more sophisticated thirteenth century, as late as 1268 in the county of Nevers in north-central France, any palisaded earthwork was still regarded as legally constitut-ing a fortification.[254] And in Normandy, possession of a *mota* similarly conferred rights on its lord to the labour services of his peasantry for the repair of a type of fortress and noble seat never socially outmoded.[255] Although the opportunities for expressive architecture were greatly enlarged by building in masonry, they were once equally exploited especially by the timber *donjons* of the eleventh and earlier twelfth century. One such 'tower-house' (*domus lignea turris*) at La Cour-Marigny (*dép.* Loiret), built by Aubry, a leading noble *castri Castellionis* (i.e. of the resort of Châtillon-sur-Loing), had an upper-floor dwelling and dormitory floored with wood-blocks, and a cellar below for storage of provisions.[256]

see Hajdu, 'Castles, Castellans in Poitou'; socio-military as well as political, the analysis is backed by detailed appendices. The psychological-symbolic also matters, e.g. Samson, 'Knowledge, Constraint and Power'.

[252] n. 129 above. Major English examples of the very numerous but underrated castles of 'manorial type' are Bampton (licensed 1315, Oxon.) of Aymer de Valence, Coulson, 'Specimens of Freedom', 8–9, and Somerton (licensed 1281, Lincs.) of Anthony Bek.

[253] e.g. Binney, 'Château d'Olhain', 174–8; a late and refined example. Others, preserved by rural conservativeness, are Cherveux, Toury, Pontivy, La Brède: Énaud, *Les Châteaux-forts*, 30, 59, 86, 100. Coulson, 'Castellation in Champagne', 349–56.

[254] *Les Olim*, i. 719–20. By virtue of having an ancient 'palacium a giant, quod est fortalicium secun-dum usus et consuetudines patrie', the prior of La Charité-sur-Loire (*dép.* Nièvre) was upheld by the parlement in the right to fortify anew at Aubigny-sur-Loire in the same lordship; inaccurately calen-dared in *Actes du Parlement*, ser. i, i, 113. Du Cange, *Glossarium*, under *glandis*. *Les Plessis* names and those with *Mote* are diagnostic: Laurent, *L'Atlas des château-forts* is selective.

[255] *Jugements de l'Echiquier*, Delisle (ed.), 256 (1210), xx, ii, 238–432: viz. 'judicatum est quod homines Rogeri Caperon, qui manent in feodo suo lorice, debent reparare motam suam apud Bonam Villetam.' Conversely, his hauberk-fief status obliged them to make him a *mota* if he lacked one (*et facere de novo nisi aliqua esset*, or *si aliqua ibi non esset*). Other similar verdicts, ibid. 324 (1223), 392 (1240); on water-mill rights, ibid. 283–4. As late as 1469, a *Belle Mote* near Saint-Bénoît-sur-Loire (*dép.* Loiret) justified licence by Louis XI to refortify, granted to Baudes Meurin, his secretary: *Ordonnances*, xvii, 219 (quoted Part III, Ch. 1, sec. 4 below).

[256] Brown, *English Castles*, 36, Armitage, *Early Norman Castles*, 89–90, translate *in extenso* Lambert of Ardres's description of *c.*1117 of Arnold of Ardres's timber tower-house; summarized Thompson, *Military Architecture*, p.256; text, Mortet, *Recueil*, i. 181–2 ('*c.*1060'). *Lambert of Ardres*, 160–1. Other valuable passages on building are pp. 59, 74, 106–7, 111–12, 115–16, 117, 142.

For dignity and authority as well as durability, stonework was of course supreme.[257] In prosperous parts of France great patrons enjoyed it very early on. In the south, on the Mediterranean, the eleventh-century bishops of Maguelone (*dép*. Hérault) 'caused their cathedral and precinct to be grandly (*solemniter*) adorned with towers, walls and all necessary offices and other fortifications (*fort-alitia*)'.[258] Similarly the works of Hugh de Noyers, bishop of Auxerre (1183–1206) in north-central France, are celebrated with relish, particularly their eloquent fortifications, which always proclaimed lordship, ancient authority, and temporal power.[259] Bishop Hugh's buildings were the noble castle of Varzy (*dép*. Nièvre), his palace at Sainte-Eugénie with 'solid walls, towers and outworks' (*propugnac-ulis*), whose inner keep (*presidium*) boasted 'towers, fortifications and advanced defences of impregnable strength', surrounded by wide, spring-filled ditches.[260] These moats were not only 'no small augmentation of the fortifications', but, 'by reason of the multitude of fish they provided, by the mills the bishop built there, and other profitable assets, they greatly improved the entire establishment (*totique municipio*)'. This aesthetic of embattled comfort, a taste beloved by an aristocracy glorying in its own splendour, was not so much 'military' or 'religious' as seignorial, emblematic, and hierarchical.[261] We need a new or recalibrated vocabulary to grasp it. Architecturally its style could not be more different from the 'civilian' Roman, early Carolingian, or, for that matter, from the early modern classical revival mansion—and yet the evocative spirit was much the same. Architectural nobility took its militant form directly from the warlike manner of life of noble patrons[262]—just as did the ostentatiously pacific 'Palladian' classical style from its different ethos. Power of old had tended to assume a façade of archi-tectural bellicosity, overt or restrained as taste dictated. Bishop Hugh of Auxerre built only palaces (*domus episcopales*) at his seats (*domus*) of Toucy and Cosne (both *castra episcopalia*), but at 'his patrimonial noble castle of Noyers' (*dép*.

[257] Admired in England, even in Northumbria, since the time of Bede (d. 735) as 'in the Roman manner', Clapham, *English Romanesque Architecture*, i. 41, 60. Only in 15th-century England did brick become more fashionable: Thompson, *Decline of the Castle*, ch. 5 ('A Martial Face'). Prestwich, 'Castle-Building', 28–61.

[258] Mortet, *Recueil*, i. 87–91 (p. 90), paid for out of pious donations; text dated '1030–1063/90'.

[259] Mortet, *Recueil*, i. 96–101. Ailred (1110–66), abbot of Rievaulx (Yorks.), significantly allegorized the elements of keep, ditch, and wall, typical of contemporary castles, in a sermon on the Assumption of the Virgin; quoted Thompson, *Rise of the Castle*, 181. Miller, *Bishop's Palace*.

[260] On the standard literary formulae see van Emden, 'The Castle in French Literature', esp. 4–5; on *chastel* for 'small town' (p. 2); literary 'impregnability', tunnels, food reserves (pp. 6–7, 20–2); siege allusions (pp. 8–11); references to large exterior windows (p. 12); postern gates 'treachery' stories (pp. 14–20). These are the important genre context.

[261] Gerald of Wales's description (later-12th-cent.) of his family's castle of Manorbier (Pembs.) and Iolo Goch's eulogy (14th. cent.) of Criccieth (Caerns.) are notable Welsh examples: quoted Brown, *English Castles*, 201, 203; Johns, *Criccieth Castle* guide, 4, 35, n. 1; Part II, n. 139 below.

[262] e.g. the *nobilitas* 'without defect' of rebuilt Dover castle which Henry III in 1247 instructed to be 'shown off' to the count of Saint-Pôl. Even 'undefended' houses had turrets, or at least crenellated screen-parapets, seldom (unless low-class 'vernacular') no castellated element whatever: Wood, *English Medieval House*, chs. 11, 12, *et passim*; Thompson, *Decline of the Castle*, ch. 4; Viollet-le-Duc, *Dictionnaire de l'architecture*, arts. 'Maison', 'Palais', 'Crénau', etc.; for Brittany and north-west France see nn. 21 (Introduction), 126 above.

Yonne) he spared no effort to improve the *munitio municipii*, be it on walling the lower *burgus*,[263] or on ditching the already 'impregnably sited' *castrum* and adding higher and thicker walls around the hilltop keep (*presidium* and *turris*). His precautions nominally against missile 'engines',[264] and to ensure that 'enemies be shut off from the keep by multiple obstacles and barriers', indicate (as very commonly) an inventive ingenuity, suggested perhaps (if the eulogy is not fanciful) by Frontinus' *Strategems* or Vegetius' *De re militari*. Such learning (and its display) was as fashionable as skill in warfare or practical poliorcetics.[265] The one merged constantly into the other. For everyday living at Noyers, Bishop Hugh had built outside the verge (*septa*) of the chief keep (*presidii principalis*) a *palatium magne nobilitatis*, 'which to it was no slight fortification' (*sic*). He lived magnificently as his rank required, ingeniously constructing several 'underground tunnels from the wine cellar beneath the chief keep into the lower palace' for their secret provisioning, together with a piped water-supply and also piped wine, both facilities meant, we are told, 'for defence in the greatest security'.[266] This revelling in defensive parade is very characteristic. Guard-chambers stocked with weapons and lodgings for knights were also provided, not in constant expectation of attack but to ensure that the bishop was nobly attended, and that only those people the lord wished to see could reach him. The regulation of access to the lord's presence transcends period and is a constant feature of 'domestic' planning. Places of common and public resort, such as the Baptistery, were outside the upper enclosure. All these works, we are assured by the panegyrist, were much admired and served both the 'utility' of the Church and 'the needs of the poor'. Aristocratic ethos, not only to modern eyes, frequently clashed with ideals of Apostolic poverty.[267]

---

[263] '[Projecting] from its wall [-top] he fixed robust *propugnacula*' (i.e. hourds: Viollet-le-Duc, *Dictionnaire de l'architecture*, art. 'Hourd') 'made from very solid timbers'; Mortet, *Recueil*, i. 109–11 (p. 99 quoted).

[264] The *situm machinis erigendis accommodum . . . in cacumine montis* he countered by thickening and raising the new existing wall, building another within *in capite ejus turrim*, with deeper exterior ditches with *antemuralia* (counterscarp fencing), and by constructing 'from immense beams' a covering to ward off 'whatever missiles the enemy might hurl down with engines' (*tormenta jaculatoria*): see Viollet-le-Duc, *Dictionnaire de l'architecture*, art. 'Engin'. For modern trials see Payne-Gallwey, *The Crossbow*, pt. 4. D. King, 'The Trébuchet', 457–70.

[265] e.g. consulted (allegedly) by Geoffrey of Anjou (1149/51) before assaulting Montreuil Bellay castle; Mortet, *Recueil*, i. 96–8, nn. 7, 3, 1; ii. 80–3. Numerous editions and MSS show the fashion for Vegetius. Alexander Neckham (1157–1217), while condemning architectural quasi-military extravagance, offered detailed advice on how to build and besiege: Mortet *Recueil*, ii. 179–82. Saphet, in Syria, as rebuilt by the Templars (1240–60), was magnificent as well as strong, with fertile environs 'blessed by God with the fat of the land', with 12 mills, etc.: ibid. 261–4 (detailed).

[266] Mackenzie, *Castles of England*, retails many anecdotes of 'secret' tunnels. This troglodytic fascination deserves extended treatment. Lord Hastings's upgraded Ashby (Leics., 1462–80) had a tunnel 50 feet long, linking the Lord's Tower to the kitchen: Jones, *Ashby de la Zouche Castle* guide, end-plan.

[267] e.g. Dixon, 'Control of Access to the Lord', 47–57. Mortet, *Recueil*, i. 100–1. Peter the Cantor (1187–97) inveighed against lofty, turretted palaces, with *propugnacula*, as due to 'lust for building . . . out of the tears and plundering of the poor . . . granges castellated as an eternal witness of avarice', etc.; invective in the style of St Bernard (cf. the deterministic militarism of Berman, 'Fortified Monastic Granges'). Ostentation was the target e.g. of Hugh de Fouilloi, *c*.1153, condemning those who 'convert to other lordship monasteries which are, as it were, the castles of God' (*quasi castra Domini*): Mortet, *Recueil*, ii. 91–4.

Such typical adulatory descriptions reveal fortifications in a truer light. Facile modern distinctions between 'functional' and 'decorative', 'serious fortification' and 'sham', and so on, serve only the demarcations of modern specialisms. 'Weak' castellation still conspicuously affirmed noble status; and thoroughly defensible buildings did so too, the reality of their strength and cost showing their lord's power and wealth, in addition to deterring any physical confrontation. French ecclesiastical precincts, as in England (but often more grandly), were walled, ditched, and towered as befitted their dignity and renown.[268] The intrusions of other lords, lay nobles particularly, were polemically denounced: such as 'the most nefarious tower', built near the priory of Celle-en-Brie (*dép.* Seine-et-Marne) which the mother-house of Marmoutier (near Tours) first bought out and then 'caused to be destroyed, the whole thing, in wood and in stone'.[269] From clerical invective against such intrusions castles have derived most of their bad publicity and sinister reputation.[270] Occasionally, in a severe prophetic spirit, ecclesiastics might denounce the extravagances of castle-building, as by Alexander Neckam of St Albans deploring 'man's vain ostentation in superfluous architectural ornament'. In his late-twelfth-century treatise *De naturis rerum* he inveighs (in an age of many English stone towers to both churches and castles) against 'towers erected to threaten the stars, overtopping the peaks of Parnassus, but to no use'.[271] No explicit defence was offered to such accusations—but surviving buildings and pictures are very eloquent. One text, less puritan and more typical, is the rhapsody on a tower once by the sea near the major port-town of La Rochelle (*dép.* Charente-Maritime). It was written not later than 1130 by Richard de Poitiers:

And to thee, O maritime tower, built strongly upwards with projections (*propugnaculis*), the sons of the stranger will come; but covered with shame and ignominy one and all, they shall flee to their own land! You shall have no fear of their threats (*minas*) but shall boldly

[268] Andres abbey, by Boulogne, *c.*1164, had its churchyard (*cimiterium*) walled in stone; but the main sanction against encroachment was the abbatial anathema. Saint-Hubert-d'Ardenne abbey (Luxembourg) received an enclosure 'in honour of the church of St Giles' (*c.*1065–70), comprising 'a stone wall and crown (*corona*) of eight towers'; Mortet, *Recueil*, i. 191–3, 387–94 (p. 389). Also Coulson, 'Hierarchism in Conventual Crenellation', on 58 English religious houses with licences to crenellate and their context.

[269] Mortet, *Recueil*, i. 324–6 (1177–87), after recital of the 'improvement' (1104–24) of Marmoutier itself (*dép.* Indre-et-Loire) and its 'munitioning with walls round about'. The common label 'fortified church' is misleading.

[270] Coulson, 'Freedom to Crenellate', 86–90, 98–9, 110 on castle-phobia; also 'Fortress-Policy', 16–20, 'Castles of the Anarchy', 75–8, 88, 90–2, and 'French Matrix', 66, 69, 72, 75–6, 81, 85–6, on doctrine and details. Peace of God and related decretals often pilloried castle-building, incastellation of churches, and activities based upon *castra/castella*, e.g. Mortet, *Recueil*, i. 113–15 (1041), 115–16 (*c.*1065), 116–17 (1042/3), 152–3 (1054), 250–1 (1080), 364 (1123).

[271] nn. 265, 267 above; cf. Girouard, *Victorian Country House*, 157–8, uncharacteristically astray on Peckforton (Cheshire, 1844–50): 'Salvin realized that genuine castles were intended primarily for use, not effect . . . no higher than . . . defence made necessary . . . long, low, sober and businesslike'; contrast e.g. Meiss, *Painting in the Time of Jean de Berry*, pl. 16, 18, 19, 171, 183, 185–8, 194, 197, 419–25, etc.

hold up your countenance to the North. Stand on your guard-duty and take your stance upon your fortification (*munitionem*) summoning, if need be, your allies coadjutory (*conlaterales*) to come to your aid with their forces! [272]

A canon of Châlons (*dép.* Marne), Gui de Bazoches, allowed himself a more personal pleasure: pride in having a castle in the family (structurally obsolescent though it was) and noble *Champenois* connections belonging. He lovingly refers (*c.*1172) to his dynastic stronghold as 'rising, girded with ramparts set with timber towers, hanging on the smoothly swelling hill tending towards the South, at whose foot, clothed with verdure and woods on both sides, flows the River Aube'.[273] It is an idyllic picture long anticipating the landscape art of Claude Le Lorrain (1600–82). Gerald of Wales's Manorbier castle (Pembs.), in his almost caressing late-twelfth-century description, is bathed in the same calm and peaceful light.

Lambert of Ardres's account (1181) of the round stone *domus* built by Count Baldwin II of Guines at his comital seat near Boulogne (*dép.* Pas-de-Calais) shows a more technical and less scenic appreciation; but one still emphatically aesthetic.[274] Upon the motte (*dunjo*), in superior 'squared' stone (i.e. ashlar, not rubble), 'he built and suspended it high in the atmosphere' (*aere*). Lambert makes its flat timber leaded roof with 'pinnacles' and superb view sound a wonder of delight. It was a Daedalus' maze within of passages and chambers, 'with a chapel like Solomon's' (i.e. circular) at the entry, and around the building (*oppidum*) a *firmitas* of a stone wall. The gateways Baldwin 'strengthened and decorated' with 'warlike towers and devices' (*machinamentis*). Elsewhere, at Tournehem, Baldwin possessed an old *turris*, also filled with 'labyrinthine' apartments, whose 'rough workmanship' he had improved conformably to late-twelfth-century taste. Having noted that the (ground-floor) entry-passage was defended by a portcullis (*cataractas*), Lambert, less soberly, then plunges into a lurid story of 'terrible prisons for keeping (and to speak more truly, for despoiling) wretched beings, in the bowels of the earth, dragging out a terrified existence . . . [eating] the bread of affliction'. Nineteenth-century novelists (and historians) took great note: such purple passages are the part of the genre of particularly clerical invective whose understanding presents considerable difficulties.[275] To insist that imprisonment

---

[272] Mortet, *Recueil*, i. 387. In similar vein, as late as 1603–10, is *Macbeth's* 'Our castle's strength will laugh a siege to scorn' (V. v); cf. Duncan's and Banquo's contrasting praise of Dunsinane, also typical (I. vi). Viollet-le-Duc, *Dictionnaire de l'architecture*, art. 'Pinnacle'.

[273] Mortet, *Recueil*, i. 126–7; 'topographically accurate' on Rumigny (*dép.* Ardennes, *arr.* Rocroi), which belonged to Gui's uncle (*c.*1172), archdeacon of Laon. See Coulson, 'Castellation in Champagne', for tenurial context. Styled *castellum/castrum* in 1204/5, when 'jurable and rendable'; but only 'liege for the castle and appurtenances of the new fief', in *c.*1200/1 (Coulson, 'Seignorial Fortresses', App. A, 3a, b, c). Cf. Manorbier, Part II, n. 139 and text.

[274] Arts Council Catalogue, *The Art of Claude Lorrain*, pls. 4, 5, 7, 10, 14, 20, 21, 29, 32, 36. Mortet, *Recueil*, ii. 141–4. Jean de Colmieu's famous description of Merckem motte, Flanders, equivocally styled *munitio quedam quam castrum vel municipium dicere possumus* (also *arx*, and *villa*), views it as an example of a local aristocratic style (*ante* 1130): Mortet, *Recueil*, i. 312–14; *Lambert of Ardres*, 111, 112.

[275] Preface, n. 11 and n. 270 above. The Peterborough E manuscript of the *Anglo Saxon Chronicle* for 1137, 'but written in the 1150s', probably an elaboration of William of Malmesbury's diatribe against

was not a normal medieval punishment (unlike execution or even mutilation), but only detention preparatory to trial, and that individuals incarcerated in the long term were generally of higher rank, kept for ransom or to avoid political problems (like Robert of Normandy, 1105–34), who were expected to be treated honourably, can do little to deflect the craving (medieval as well as modern) for atrocity. Yet cells for keeping prisoners pending trial (and in episcopal castles to impose clerical discipline) were common and necessary in castles as an aspect of their normal role as court-houses. By English eighteenth- and early-nineteenth-century standards (to look no further), surviving ground-floor (seldom basement) chambers, with outward-opening, heavily barred doors, ventilation and light apertures (exteriorly mere slits, as for storerooms and cellars), provided not uncommonly with latrines, were relatively humane. The *oubliettes*, as a means of slow execution, expected by readers of Mrs Radcliffe, Byron, Dickens, and Edgar Allan Poe, among modern horror-romantics, and ineradicably embedded in popular mythology, are very hard to find; but popular dungeon-mentality still continues to dominate the presentation of monuments.[276] 'Market forces' make history conform to public prejudice even on clearer issues than this. Not wholly false but basically morbid, even sadistic, in motivation, the whole 'dungeon'-fixation has its place (however marginal) in authentic contemporary perception, as Lambert of Ardres on Tournehem demonstrates. But the tower-complex he goes on to describe was also apparently a sports-centre and fish-farm.

Returning to the open air, Lambert mentions some compounds outside the 'tower' of Tournehem for boxing matches and athletics, mentioning Baldwin's *propugnacula* (here 'outworks') and 'very strong ditches', and his walling of the adjacent town. Lambert then expatiates on that frequent and lucrative accompaniment of mansions, a large fish-pond made by damming the river 'full of great fishes'. Moats offer a revealing insight into the ambivalence of 'fortification': fish-farming and scenic quality chiefly motivated what incidentally looked 'strong' and might be defensive in the event of attack, especially by mine tunnels. Conveying power allied with comfort was the focus uniting this ambivalent double-purpose. Many motives coalesced in castle-building, and moats more obviously than other elements in castellated architecture combined them.[277] They establish a link, moreover, with 'water-features' as an element in the later

Bishop Roger's motte castle put into Malmesbury abbey precincts, E. King, Introduction, *Anarchy of King Stephen*, 1 (abbreviated translation). But see *William of Malmesbury: Historia Novella*, King (ed.), p. xcvi. For overview see R. Pugh, *Imprisonment in Medieval England*.

[276] e.g. Pounds, *The Medieval Castle*, 99–100, 202; Toy, *Castles*, 254, mentions prisons at Skenfrith, Conway, Warwick, Warkworth, Dalhousie, and Crichton. Episcopal Llawhaden had a 'considerable permanent prison' (King, *The Castle*, 5) partly for clergy discipline. Pevensey, *caput* of its rape, had 'basement' (not subterranean) cells in the gatehouse. Bellamy, *Crime and Public Order*, 162–98. Viollet-le-Duc, *Dictionnaire de l'architecture*, arts. 'Oubliettes', 'Prison'. Brown, 'English Castles, 1154–1216', 238–43, and n. 6 above.

[277] Coulson, 'Some Analysis of Bodiam', 55, fig. 2, 83–9, 103. Summary note, Leslie, 'English Landscape Garden', 3–15. Recognized as an enduring type in Germany, e.g. Mummenhof, *Wasserburgen in Westfalen*; Wildeman, *Rheinische Wasserburgen*. C. Taylor, 'Medieval Ornamental Landscapes', 38–55, assembles known English cases at castles (including Caerfilly, p. 53).

landscape-architecture of the country-house. Bodiam castle (Sussex: 1385–92) and many earlier mansions are now recognized as having had them. When (which is seldom) moats are deep and defensibly dammed, their 'strength' is more than visual (e.g. Kenilworth, War.; Caerfilly, Glam.), adding a military dimension to the economic and scenic qualities of lakes (e.g. Leeds, Kent, with corn-mill) and of demarcating water-filled ditches, of fish-stews and preserves. These, like attached parks, church, town, dovecot, and the rest were, above all, attributes of aristocracy.[278] In the 'Deeds of the Bishops of Auxerre' (prelates badly infected with what Peter the Cantor called 'building mania') we are told that Bishop William (1207–20), lacking 'only a sufficient residence' at Meung-sur-Loire (*dép.* Loiret), built there 'an episcopal castle of great nobility, a palace with towers and *propugnacula*' (here 'pinnacles'?). Two bridges across the Loire and the rebuilding of his cathedral were no less works of self-advertisement combined with piety of the sort praised by contemporaries less censorious than St Bernard of Clairvaux.[279] Bishop Gui, who enjoyed another facilitatingly long 'pontificate' (1247–69), was able to embellish the palace hall at Auxerre with 'crystal-clear glass windows', a two-storey chapel, and a more prosaic 'double chamber' (latrine block) serving both storeys of the hall, adorned with visually pleasing 'turrets'. Where the palace had previously been open and unenclosed, by the riverside of the Yonne, Gui built 'new and strong walls, with a gateway and battlements (*propugnaculis*) of costly workmanship most beautiful to behold'.[280]

Flatulent literary texts of this kind and self-indulgent building are not peculiarly ecclesiastical.[281] Lay nobles acquired equally refined tastes. It may be difficult to see relatively crude earthworks in this same cultural light (masonry ruins are also often deceptively crude and brutal), but elaborate towers crowning mottes, turrets (*bretasches*) to the crenellated palisading, and much ornamental carpentry, presented originally a far less sombre and utilitarian appearance. By reinstating in the mind's eye the whole vanished timber component, which excavation has

---

[278] Salvaing, *De l'Usage des Fiefs*, ch. 63, 'Des Etangs': frontier Dauphiné law had few restrictions, unlike Anjou and Touraine. Fresh fish was needed for the late-medieval 146 'jours maigres' a year and for noble consumption: Dyer, 'Consumption of Freshwater Fish'. On noble dovecots, Salvaing, ch. 43; Viollet-le-Duc, *Dictionnaire de l'architecture*, art. 'Colombier'; Pounds, *The Medieval Castle*, 105–6, appreciates the domesticity but denies the castle quality of 'moated sites' (n. 129 above).

[279] n. 267 above: *libido aedificandi* and *morbus aedificandi*: Mortet, *Recueil*, ii. 202–9. The early Cistercian statutes forbade even stone bell-towers (1157), rules against *nimis grandia et sumptuosa aedificia* being renewed in 1240. But 'strong and secure prisons' were ordered (1229) both for discipline and exercise of jurisdictional franchises: *Thesaurus Novus*, iv. cols. 1350–1 (3); 1246–51 (16); 1371–4 (3, 4). The violent resistance in 1212 to the abbot of Cluny by the monks of La Charité-sur-Loire, with complicity of the count of Nevers, shows the potential of such towered precincts: *Recueil Cluny*, vi. 5–9.

[280] Mortet, *Recueil*, ii. 206; 'camera dupplicis . . . cum jucunde visionis turricula decenti situatas' [*sic*]. The earlier *turris* '(great-)tower or 'keep' begins to be differentiated by *turriculum*' (mural) tower, or turret. By this date *propugnaculum* may be more confidently translated 'battlements'.

[281] e.g. Count William of Nevers's celebration of his sumptuous refounding of St Stephen's abbey (*dép.* Nièvre) with 'a high and strong' *muri clausura*, three 'beautiful and conspicuous towers', etc., and corresponding endowment with lordly powers, in 1097: *Recueil Cluny*, v. 67–74. Ecclesiastical documents have naturally survived best.

facilitated at Hen Domen, by Montgomery (Salop), the artistic-defensive detail as well as the gigantism still visible of great English mottes (e.g. Thetford, and Haughley, Suffolk), of towers, and of bailey enclosures, at the greatest magnatial (and royal) castles, can be properly evaluated. Close parallels are provided by the cathedrals and great churches. To do so it is necessary to revise perceptions of 'early castles' in the light of the still-evident artistic sophistication of the twelfth-century castle-palaces such as Old Sarum, Farnham, Newark, and Winchester (Wolvesey). Surviving ornate early 'keeps' correctively help, notably the White Tower, London; Colchester and Hedingham, Essex; Castle Rising and Norwich, Norfolk; Canterbury and Rochester, Kent; by showing what rich and ambitious patrons could achieve when time and money were plentiful. These stupendous residences show the same aesthetic of powerful grandeur as later ones. Very tellingly, they and others were very evidently meant to be imposing, not to be defended. Extended, gently rising, processional ramped entrances with bypass access for menial attendants, large windows, complete absence of defensive bow-loops (all still true of Dover 'keep', 1176–89), and many other features show that oppressive but peaceable power was their message to an abject population. Making people labour on castle-works (anciently *burh-bot*), especially in the towns, rubbed in the new rulers' power as well as displaying their enormous ambition.[282]

2. Architectural Eulogy and Noble Ambition

The works celebrated among the 'Deeds of the Bishops of Auxerre' echo the spirit and tone of English architecture and panegyric even during the 'anarchy' of Stephen's reign. How castles were regarded by Bishop Roger of Salisbury (1102–39) and his clan coincided with the view of the biographer of Bishop Hugh (1183–1206), or of Bishop Gui.[283] Prelates as magnates revelled in ostentatious power. Scientifically up-to-date, artistically, technologically, and also militarily vying with their peers, abbots, priors, bishops, and lay patrons built ever-higher ceiling vaults, loftier towers, and ever-larger traceried windows in the great churches and palaces with great halls, kitchens, and noble suites of apartments. The drive for 'more height, more light' in churches was relatively simple, visible, and uncomplicated: not so the various types of castellated building which expressed the more plainly materialistic realities of power and wealth. Whether

---

[282] References etc. in Coulson, 'Peaceable Power'; Kenyon, *Medieval Fortifications*, analyses recent British excavations (with bibliography); also Higham, Barker, *Timber Castles*, e.g. 144–6 for Iolo Goch's poem on Sycherth (*c.*1390). Prior Lawrence's poetic description (n. 143 above) of earthwork Durham castle is a rare survival: Armitage, *Early Norman Castles*, 148, conjecturing that its tower's 'galleries' were hourds; cf. Brown, *English Castles*, 34, 35–6, 226 (53) and 'The Architecture', Stenton (ed.), *The Bayeux Tapestry*, 76–87. Borgund is an exemplar: Ahrens, 'An English Origin for Norwegian Stave Churches?', fig. I.

[283] T. Heslop, 'Orford'; also *Norwich Castle Keep*; Coulson, 'Castles of the Anarchy', 81–6, and 'Cultural Realities'. Stalley, 'Buildings Erected by Roger, Bishop of Salisbury', 1–27, 317–19. E. King, *Anarchy of King Stephen*, 16–17, on Roger and his nephews, Alexander of Lincoln (builder of Newark) and Nigel of Ely.

symbolism came out on top (as more consistently occurred in the later middle ages), leaving sometimes a mere semblance of physical defensibility—or was subordinate, so that utilitarian resistance seemingly prevailed (as in borderlands, and contested territory), so that a barely adorned self-evident strength of structure predominated, with an 'active defence' by crenels, loops, machicolation, and so on, did not alter the architectural programme—all such different permutations of ingredients were noble-style 'fortification'. The labels 'serious' and 'sham' are travesty, not analysis. Real 'strength' and allusive defence possessed equal prestige, and were scarcely differentiated. Thus when Bishop Gui of Auxerre at Régennes (*dép*. Yonne) 'constructed' (here 'rebuilt') 'a very noble small dwelling (*habitaculum*)' it still had the due panoply of *muros*, *fortericiam*, *fossata*, *propugnacula*, and *turres*. Next to the entry 'a tower of hewn stone most strong and of exceptional size, which they call "the portal", contained numerous dwellings within and in the thickness of its walls'.[284] Within the walls of the fortress (*fortaricie*) were stables, the improved episcopal hall, and a two-storey chamber-block adjacent to it. The residence of Régennes had been upgraded. As much pride was taken in making the domestic apartments 'more beautiful than customary' as in providing 'on the other hand (*ex alio vero parte*)' the accoutrements of 'defence' which were the alter ego of noble architecture. At Régennes they included 'the necessary covered-ways (*appendicia*) for the manning (*munitio*) of the walls'. The place satisfied the contemporary noble criterion of powerful outward militancy which denoted a castle; whereas, by contrast, Beauretour ('a place with much fish in connected ponds'), though not devoid of seignoralia, was styled *receptaculum*.[285] The episcopal castle of Varzy, magnificently rebuilt by Bishop Hugh, Gui restored after a serious fire, making 'the walls and *propugnacula*, better than before', as well as their roofs and skyline, enhancing the place with dwellings and fortifications alike. At Villechaud on the Loire, Bishop Gui had vindicated in the king's court his right to build a castle against objections by the count of Nevers. It stood low but was suitably conspicuous from afar. The *fortericia*, contentious symbol of higher lordship and for that reason resented by Nevers, was less important in this case to the chronicler than the 'double hall and chapel of exquisite nobility, fit for a king's habitation'; less noted than the wine-cellars, so excavated in the rock below as to remain cool even in high summer; or the stables and 'masonry barn of immense capacity', themselves enclosed by lesser outer walls. The 'vineyard of choice vines' planted nearby is also proudly mentioned.[286]

---

[284] Mortet, *Recueil* ii, 207–9. This 'château . . . maison de plaisance des évêques d'Auxerre, fut démoli pendant la Révolution' (ed.). 'Keep' towers often reflect this evidently admired 'cellular' construction of chambers within exaggeratedly 'thick' walls, e.g. Dover (1180–9).

[285] But *receptaculum* and *receptum* were also synonyms for 'fortress'; e.g. in the 1095 Peace of God decretals for Touraine, *receptacula vel munitiones* were mostly towns: *Thesaurus Novus*, iv. cols. 121–4 (12). The two *receptacula idonea* in Poitou awarded by the 1174 treaty of Henry II, after the Young King's revolt, to Richard were guaranteed innocuous like fortresses and in the popular version called *castella*: text, *Recueil Henri II*, ii. 19, 21. In Saintonge in 1201 the *receptum de Bruolio* was specifically defined as the castle *de barbacanis* (outworks) *infra*: *Layettes*, v. no. 131.

[286] Mortet, *Recueil*, ii. 207–9; 208, n. 4, states that Gui made good his right to fortify in the king's

Rarely in such architectural eulogies is any mechanism or motive suggested other than the glorification of the patron and of his standing—which is normal.[287] Cowering in fear was ignoble; outfacing danger had 'style'. In fact dangers (actual or potential), let alone the counter-measures geared to developments in siegecraft such as preoccupy the 'strategy-speak' of modern analysis, are seldom even implied. Likewise, such motives as are cautiously inferable from over 500 English licences to crenellate (1200–c.1578) strikingly coincide with those of post-medieval mansion-building; the more so when the licence was associated more or less closely with building projects. Appeals to danger were standard and can, in the vast majority of cases, be shown to be mere parading of pretended public service. Towns, especially, hid behind this screen. The actual occasions for building were almost universal.[288] We are wrong to set 'castles' apart. Lip-service to defence as a public good perfunctorily cloaked motives of aggrandizement. Explicit avowal is not to be expected, but the 'Celebration of the Province of Tours' (c.1210) comes quite close. Having reviewed the rivers and towns of the archdiocese, 'which give increase of honour, beauty, decorum, and strength (fortitudinis) to the metropolitan city' (Tours, dép. Indre-et-Loire), the eulogy descants upon the city itself in flowery language which tempts sympathetic imitation. Its site is 'incomparable, warding off the approach of enemies'; its bridges are 'of great breadth and solidity (firmitatis)'. Châteauneuf town is portrayed likewise, with houses so grand that 'almost all are turretted, with sky-scraping pinnacles (propugnacula)'. Tours cathedral had been thrice burned, we are told, once by the (tenth-century) Normans, 'with the entire city (cum toto castro; una cum castro)'. In 1175 'the whole castle' was again burned, but the shrine-church of St Martin of Tours was unharmed. Presumably these (and other early) burnings are mentioned as testimony to the city's resilient majesty, alluding incidentally to its seaward vulnerability on the Loire, a situation not at all difficult of enemy access. Poetic licence, in all these texts, is the price of conceptual truth and of spiritual accuracy. Consequently such panegyrics deserve great weight. Much of our blinded sight is due to preferring historical 'models' (especially of conflict) insensitive to the insights of art history—and to the surviving architectural record.[289]

---

court: issues discussed in Coulson, 'Sanctioning of Fortresses in France'. The text typically emphasizes wall-tops ('muros et propugnacula munitiones castri in suis cacuminibus pro majori parte dirupta vel collapsa egregie reparavit'), here implying hourding or bratticing. For propugnacula and great 'unmilitary' exposed roofs see Viollet-le-Duc, Dictionnaire de l'architecture, arts 'Charpente', 'Couverture'.

[287] e.g. the terms of Edward I's licence for Lichfield cathedral close (Staffs., 1299) and the king's defence of Walter Langton's building, writing to Boniface VIII in 1303: CPR, 1292–1301, 409; CCR, 1302–7, 81–2; Foedera i. ii, p. 956; Coulson, 'Hierarchism in Conventual Crenellation', 77–9. Important summary, Cherry, 'Imago Castelli', 83–90.

[288] e.g. inheriting, dynastic ambition, political prominence, position in local affairs, wealth, etc.; Girouard, Victorian Country House, esp. 393–427, over 30 case-studies; Coulson, 'Freedom to Crenellate', passim; to be discussed in my Castles and Crenellating.

[289] Territoriality offers better explanations than the conflict model. Mortet, Recueil, ii. 211–13. See Bachrach, 'Early Medieval Fortifications', 547: table of 13 lesser urbes (Poitiers 104 acres, down to Périgueux 12 acres), 569, fig. 11 (plan-diagram). On urban panegyric in Italy, Zancani, 'Lombardy in the Middle Ages', 219–24.

To turn back from southern and central France to Britain makes a contrast that is more apparent than real. The sometimes obsessive English and north-west French preoccupation with earthworks as castles par excellence is not due to a different original 'military' culture but to historical accident. Peculiar Conquest and late-Carolingian historical experiences, slanted by technological and political fixations, have produced a view of castles which is not the rounded perception of contemporaries. It is also geographically unbalanced, biased towards the North, unrepresentative even of France as a whole. The published *Colloques* of the Société Française d'Archéologie are corrective. Bernard Bachrach's compilation of data of names and site-details for Anjou, Touraine, Poitou, Limousin, Aquitaine, Périgord, and beyond is a valuable succinct demonstration of these provinces' comparatively rich late-Roman and early medieval patrimony of *castra/castella*. Most English–Continental comparisons are made with relatively upstart and deprived Normandy.[290] Great masonry complexes (justly '*agglomérations castrales*') were normal in France south of the Loire, in the Midi as well as in the south-west. Their sheer number, wealth, antiquity, and size correct the Anglo-Norman perspective.[291] Those styled *castrum* by Adémar de Chabannes (988–1034) in his *Chronicon*, Bachrach reckons as totalling twenty-six. Under a seemingly personal purism which led him to shun the chroniclers' vogue for what H. W. Fowler called 'elegant variation', Adémar chose to distinguish *castra* from *castella*, *burgi*, *munitiones*, and even from *firmitates*. In principle they are late-Roman, 'Gallo-Roman', and early-medieval walled towns, many with tenth- and eleventh-century stone great-towers as citadels, sometimes divided into *vieux château* and *neuf château*. Others, like Montignac and Gençay, were major comital centres. Few at this period (especially in idiosyncratic Languedoc) were at all compatible in the size and type of their populations with the modern idea of 'the castle'.[292] Direct and indirect evidence of towers of masonry (prestigious but only comparatively fire-resistant) is plentiful. Very many are earlier than the well-known 'keeps' of Fulk Nerra of Anjou (987–1040), some sites having been abandoned early and few excavated. Anglocentric notions that 'castles' were invented in Normandy (Doué-la-Fontaine is a favourite) or in the provinces of the north-west (or even refined during the very Norman settlement of England), or that

[290] Bachrach, 'Early Medieval Fortifications', *passim*; endowing Adémar de Chabannes's 'terminology' with archaeological precision seems forced (pp. 531–4; n. 99 above); Debord, '*Castrum* et *Castellum* chez A. de Chabannes', 97–113. But criticisms of Jean Richard's modernistic classification ('Châteaux, châtelains et vassaux', 433–47), echoing Héliot, are justified. Richard, like Gardelles (*Les Châteaux du sud-ouest*, 7–9, 13), neglects original vocabulary. Cf. Yver, 'Les Châteaux forts en Normandie', esp. 33–42, 'Avant Guillaume le Conquérant'. Baudry, *Fortifications des Plantagenêts en Poitou*, provides an impressive alternative comparison, no less relevant to England.

[291] Bachrach, 'Early Medieval Fortifications', 536–49; Aubenas, 'Les Châteaux-forts', 548–86. Post-Roman continuity was a reality in the south especially, in the north-west much less, in England almost legendary: Dunbabin, *France in the Making*, e.g. 169–79 (Toulouse, Aquitaine).

[292] Bachrach, 'Early Medieval Fortifications', 549–59; the case of Blois (p. 554) highlights the difficulty of making name coincide with site-type. Others vary greatly viz. Loudun, Argenton-sur-Creuse, Melle, Brosse, Blaye (p. 554; a late-Roman *castellum* called *castrum* by Adémar). For Gençay in the 1022–8 *Conventum*, see Coulson, 'French Matrix', 77–80.

they evolved in some nebulous fashion with 'feudalism', however defined and dated, confront a reality in the French provinces of the south-west and south (and elsewhere) going back to Charlemagne and before, whether they be styled *castra*, *castella*, or otherwise in Adémar's *Chronicon* and in other early-medieval narrative sources.[293]

Both of these aspects, the later-twelfth- and earlier-thirteenth-century literary image and the buildings of the sub-Roman or 'Gallo-roman' era, ('Romanesque' in art is now more narrowly defined), help to clarify what the castle was to medieval people and delineate its full scope.[294] A wider chronological and political range of reference will now help to draw these various strands together for the whole of the period until the early fifteenth century which is 'covered' by this book.

Returning to the minimalist earthwork-type castle, we find that they aroused lordly interest, as in the Norman *Consuetudines et Justicie* (and in the Anglo-Norman *Leges Henrici Primi* of *c*.1115), for example, also in Champagne. Their legal status was enshrined in the custom of the Nivernais (1268). That intrusive castles must not challenge the establishment was the rule. His wariness of competition from the Capetian magnate, Count Robert of Dreux, brother of Louis VII (1137–80), led Count Palatine Henri le Libéral of Champagne-Brie to restrict Robert's ditching of the *domus* of Savigny. In Champagne Robert was a vassal and had to behave with due subordination, whatever his wealth and lineage. In 1160/1 he and Count Henri agreed that the rampart of Savigny, begun with 'a ditch of two casts', should be completed with a submissive single cast of earth from ditch-bottom to bank-top, and there was to be no palisade (*briteschia*) along the crest. Humble as this was (more so than the Norman 1091 criteria which allowed palisading), Count Henri insured further against Robert's pretensions by making the place (*domus* still) rendable to him in case of war: it must be handed over to Henri on demand; averting any conceivable hostile use of course, but primarily to make acknowledgement on demand that the fief was held from Champagne. Constant provision for war can be deceptive. Robert's rank, however, was recognized in that Henri expressly and reciprocally promised to respect while in his hands 'in good faith, the said house, fish-ponds (*stagna*) and corn-mills', and to return them as soon as war ended 'stocked (*munita*) as they had been when handed over'. This obligation was usually taken for granted. Perhaps to avoid awkwardness, the fief of Savigny was transferred in 1167 to the lordship of the bishop of Beauvais, by agreement.[295]

---

[293] Attempts, here and elsewhere, to antedate 'castle' ('private fortified residence') to fit early 'terminology' and to make it coincide with 'la naissance de la féodalité' are unconvincing: Bachrach, 'Early Medieval Fortifications', 559–60, 565–9: five of the *castra* were later 9th-century, built (as refuges) against the Vikings. Neither Doué-la-Fontaine (Brown, *English Castles*, 23–5), nor Langeais, nor even Mayenne (*Castle Studies Group Newsletter*, 10, p. 41; Fernie, *Architecture of Norman England*, 55) has any claim to be 'the earliest castle in W. Europe'.

[294] Even in England, the normal image was administrative, as in Edward I's post-1274 inquiry (e.g. Cambridgeshire 1278–9) into tenures in *omnibus aliis will[is] et hamelettis ut in castris, forcelettis, feod[is] militum, terris*, etc.: text, *Rot. Hund.* ii. 356a; also similarly 430b, 497b, 514a, 517a.

[295] Brussel, *Nouvel Examen*, i. 381, n. a, 382, n. b. In 1176 Count Henri similarly limited a *domus firma*

The question has been considered elsewhere, and is throughout this book, how the conventions and practice of sanctioning new and rebuilt fortresses and of handing them over, or 'rendering' them on the lord's requisition, affirmed tenurial bonds, even when strained, and made fortresses accountable to the superior and ruler. Their originally clericalist anti-social image, despite these rules, and the reasons for rejecting it are the concern of Part II. Castles and fortresses were truly 'for all the folk', and their public profile reflected it. Neglect of rendability (since Du Cange in 1668) is itself in large part due to ignoring that fact.

Pacts for fortifying, whether treaties as at Savigny or formal grants of licence *de haut en bas*, are a rich vein of information about the conspicuous, symbolic and significant recognition-features of fortification.[296] Status-acknowledgement and conformity to rank in the local hierarchy by due genuflexion on the part of the subordinate feudatory, and watchful concern by the dominant lord against any fragmentation of his territory and infringement of his authority by the creation of any new castle and castellary without his consent and conditions (frequently rendability in 'war' and on demand), were safeguards implemented normally by due legal process, according to familiar custom, without force or violence.[297] Force could not establish legitimacy. At the visceral level of conflict-avoiding symbolic acts, dominance-recognition, and territorial marking, lordly relationships generally obeyed a formal code which conditioned and complemented their fortresses' seignorial display. Demonstrations of brute architectural strength were rare, not merely because turning fortification towards full attack-deterrence was highly expensive.[298] Throughout the period, lords and their vassals, particularly if of lower rank, tended to be more interested in the symbols of strength. Any more would take them out of their class and usually beyond their means. Metaphysics matter deeply.[299] Too fundamentalist an approach leads to the crude and subjective categorizing of fortifications into artificial grades between 'strong', 'seriously fortified', and 'sham'; in truth, as has been argued, no fortification, however decorative, was spurious. Contemporaries were naturally more discerning.[300] With

in Marsangis town (*dép.* Marne) to a house *planam et absque muro, cum fosseo unius jacture*: Jubainville, *Histoire de Champagne*, iii. 465–6. A Dreux–Champagne pact in 1206–7 allowed La Fère-en-Tardenois (*dép.* Aisne: Héliot, 'Châteaux de plan polygonal', 52–3) to be built in return for a ban at Torcy and in the border: Brussel, *Nouvel Examen*, i. 386–7. Many Champagne licences 1160–1262 were of this type: Coulson, 'Seignorial Fortresses', App. B (4).

[296] Coulson, 'Structural Symbolism', *passim*; also 'Castellation in Champagne', 357–8, and 'Freedom to Crenellate', 96–7, etc.; and 'Seignorial Fortresses', Index, 'Criteria of Fortification', for refs.

[297] Fully discussed Coulson, 'Sanctioning of Fortresses', *passim*. Background, Martindale, 'His Special Friend', 21–57.

[298] e.g. the stupendous octagonal late-14th-century *donjon* of Largöet-à-Elven (Brittany, *dép.* Morbihan), taller even than vanished Coucy (177 feet), at 185 feet from its ditch: Enaud, *Les Châteaux-forts*, 87, 104, both exemplary triumphs of *orgueil* and of high-rise dwelling.

[299] e.g. Coulson, 'Hierarchism in Conventual Crenellation', and 'Some Analysis of Bodiam', *passim*; Dixon and Lott, 'Courtyard and Tower', 93–101; (English) bibliography in Coulson, 'Cultural Realities', 204–7.

[300] Some 'military' features (e.g. arrow- and crossbow-loops, battlements, machicolation, draw-bridges), nominally 'anti-personnel' in function, achieved visual impact at less cost than massive elements: cf. discussion by Mesqui and Ribéra-Pervillé of 'Les Châteaux de Louis d'Orléans', esp.

earthwork, the volume of spoil laboriously moved to create large ramparts, tall mottes, and extensive baileys spoke unambiguously for itself of large resources of authority, subject manpower, and money, although the timber-works now vanished were doubtless no less eloquent. Masonry gave durability and greater artistic scope to such detailed features as the cut stone permitted, elegant mouldings and enhanced battlements. Ashlar was best, not rubble masonry, and always had greatest prestige, in England since Bede's day, and when resources permitted it came to dominate earth and timber when in combination. Craftsmen cost even more than massed gangs, which in England became less available as exemptions from *operationes castellorum* multiplied.[301] Bernard Bachrach has shown, with permissible speculation, how great an outlay of all kinds of resources the construction of the hall-*donjon* of Langeais (992–4) in Anjou must represent.[302] Ditches, moats, and banks, of course, were never superseded, but notably in the English royal licences to crenellate (England and Gascony) from King John's reign onwards, recognition-features concentrated on masonry elements such as mural towers, stone mortared walls, and on battlements ('crenels') constantly, sometimes mentioning drawbridges, but archery loops and moats very seldom. In England, crenellation was adopted as the diagnostic symbol of fortification from the later thirteenth century. These elements are ambivalent in that their cost and practicality depended on their massiveness. Battlements ranged from the solid to the low and flimsy. How 'strong' they were was entirely at the builder's discretion. Licence covered major fortification on the same basis as the normal embellishment of manor-houses.[303] Licences and, in France, pacts for fortification generally ignore defensibility. Their unconcern emphasizes that it is quite mistaken to select 'military architecture' as 'genuine fortification'. In totality, the social functions of fortresses in everyday operation vastly outweigh the much exaggerated military role of the few in emergencies. Nor was the licensing of fortification in England other than perfunctory. Anyone with Court access who paid the nominal 'writ of course' fee was licensed. In France it was lordly in essence and not reluctant in normal circumstances. An overlord with the right to give permission was generally very ready to demonstrate his right by doing so, whereas his vassal

321–3, denying that they (and others) belong truly to 'l'architecture militaire' but rather to 'l'architecture civile'. This pursues classification unduly far.

[301] Edwards, 'Edward I's Castle-Building in Wales', 15–81, esp. tabular analyses, 55–6. In general, Salzman, *Building in England*, esp. ch. 4, 'Wages'; Knoop and Jones, *Medieval Mason*, chs. 4, 5; and pp. 235–9, 'Statistics of masons' wages and of prices'.

[302] Bachrach, 'The Tower at Langeais'. This tends to technological assimilation (occasionally extreme), a strong trait of the historiographical reaction against earlier romanticism (n. 44 above). The cost–benefit analysis, summarized on pp. 53–4, is perhaps unduly narrow: cf. Gimpel, *The Medieval Machine*, esp. 237–52, for an explicit thesis of medieval-modern parallelism. On the palatial character of early 'keeps' see Coulson, 'Cultural Realities' (in general), 'Peaceable Power' (detail).

[303] Summary, Emery, *Greater Medieval Houses*, i. 174–80. A significant extreme is the 1292 licence of William de Beauchamp, earl of Warwick, to 'build and crenellate a wall of stone and lime around a garden' (*viridarium*), within the *mansum* or castle of Hanslope (Castlethorpe, Bucks.): *CPR*, *1281–92*, 497: Parker, *Domestic Architecture*, iii. 403. In France, a garden wall with seignorially pretentious turrets at Couilly, near Meaux, caused friction in 1253: *Layettes*, iii. 192 (below).

was no less eager to receive the accolade of nobility conferred thereby on his family residence. A charter or letter patent itself conferred recognition and legitimacy.

Many manor-places in England were styled 'castle', by their owners or by popular acclaim, after being licensed, irrespective of the sort of 'crenellation' consequently added: sometimes, indeed, when no building at all seems to have been done. But there was no rule about it. A licence did not of itself confer the title 'castle', even informally. In 1338 William Heron obtained licence '. . . to crenellate his dwelling-place of his manor of Ford, Co. Northumberland'. Not satisfied, he applied for and got a formal charter in 1340 in unique terms granting 'that he may hold his manor-house of Forde, which is enclosed with a high embattled wall, by the name of a castle . . . without impediment . . . for the defence of those parts against the attacks of the Scots'. It evidently conformed to the castle image in both respects. Heron's grant was by charter, not patent, since a parcel of lordly rights, also seignorially expressive but lucrative as well, came with it. It is one of a significant group of mainly charter licences, beginning with Kirkoswald (Cumb.) in 1201. Although the danger from the Scots at Ford was more than justificatory verbiage, the enhancement of Heron's status among his local peers was the object of the exercise.[304] The factors involved were sociological, variously expressed from the great magnate, who less often had to prove his status, down to mere gentry who eagerly did so, and town oligarchs likewise.

In 1261 permission was obtained from Henry III for the addition of a palisade to the earthwork at Old Basing in Hampshire. Many licences, both English and French, were issued for works militarily so insignificant that prestige and perhaps repressing neighbours' jealousy are the chief plausible reasons.[305] Even in closely governed England, 'enforcement' in any form was non-existent. That a measure of military affectation, and a modicum of actual defensibility, were considered appropriate to a gentleman's residence is apparent in this order sent to his seneschal of Gascony and to all concerned by Edward I in 1281:

Touching what Amanieu de Loubens, donzel (*domicellus*), has told us about his intention to construct a house or manor for his residence, without any major or undue fortification (*sine magno et indebito fortalicio*), in the lands which he holds of us directly in our provostry of la Réole [*dép.* Gironde]—we gather that he has been unjustifiably hindered from doing so by you, our seneschal, and by your deputies; so we have accordingly ordained that the place where the work has been commenced shall be inspected to find out what kind of fortification (*cujusmodi fortalicium*) he wishes to make there and if and how it might affect our interests or those of others, now or in the future . . . And we have, in the meantime, granted permission to Amanieu that he may complete the house with its dependencies as now begun in timber (*domum ligneam erectam cum suis appendiciis*) so far as relates to the enclosure (*clausura*) of earth or timbers and to the roofing with tiles, together with other intramural operations, but not involving any further curtilage, palisading, or

---

[304] *CPR, 1338–40*, 114; *1343–5*, 409; *CChR* iv. 468–9.
[305] *CPR, 1258–66*, 172: in general see Coulson, 'Freedom to Crenellate' and 'Battlements and the Bourgeoisie', for demand-led licensing.

defensive devices, such as a drawbridge (*palis et ingenio et ponte levadicio*), rather greater ditches or other works characteristic of major fortification.[306]

Amanieu had to build according to his rank if the jealousies of his fellows and superiors were not to be aroused. Greater lords, barons especially, fortified and issued their own licences in the duchy as elsewhere. A 'donzel' was truly a 'lordling'—but one whom his duke would wish to encourage as his own vassal and supporter.

3. Some Incidentals of the Castle Image

The progressive elaboration of 'defences' was naturally matched by the terminology of licences. Their precise formulae, in Britain and France, chart a lengthening vocabulary of features but add little in principle to the examples already mentioned. The aim was to include all that was most expressive of lordship, not omitting new fashions. But a castle was defined by the use made of it as well as by the structural features it incorporated. In this final section we accordingly illustrate some of the implications of this fact. Foremost, castles were economic units. Thus, in 1222 Count Henry V of Grandpré acknowledged that his overlord Thibaut IV, count Palatine of Champagne and Brie, 'has handed over to me Château-Porcien [*dép.* Ardennes], namely the fortress and the revenues'.[307] When a grantor wished to sever the almost indissoluble bond between fortress and castellary it had to be done very explicitly. Count Raymond V of Toulouse in 1177 sanctioned all the future landed acquisitions (in 'mortmain') throughout his wide dominions by the knightly Order of St John of Jerusalem, but excluded 'the capital places of castellaries (*capitibus castellorum*) which I decree reserved to myself'.[308] By this expression towns (usually walled) were included. So far towns have been mentioned only incidentally, but examples are numerous and specific, both early and late, of these 'castles of communities', in Hamilton Thompson's apt phrase, being in all respects 'proper castles'.[309] The early Cistercian monks avoided sites for their monasteries located 'in cities, fortified places (*castris*), or towns'. Essentially the walling of towns and of religious establishments performed the basic function of setting apart a distinct 'peculiar' and jurisdictional area— separating and, if need arose, protecting the permanent inhabitants, and those

---

[306] Viz. *augmentacione fossatorum et aliis operibus magni fortalicii: Rôles Gascons*, ii. 125. For a slightly less ostentatiously militant but comparable English dwelling of c.1180–1236, see G. Beresford, 'The Medieval Manor of Penhallam', 90–145, esp. figs. 25–7, 35; also Martin, 'Glottenham'. The 'lawlessness' rationale prevails, in both discussions.

[307] *Layettes*, i. 54–8: *forteressiam scilicet et proventus cum omnibus pertinentiis ejusdem castri.*

[308] Ibid. 113. Raymond also reserved *justiciis et expeditionis vel exercitus gratia mandamento*, i.e. judicial and military rights attached to the castle-territories.

[309] Thompson used it apologetically, *Military Architecture*, p. viii. Comparison of texts with sites is often necessary (e.g. Mesqui, 'Crécy-en-Brie', 17–23, ' "Le Château" '). Early instances of textual clarity in Mortet, *Recueil*, i. are 113, Amboise (1040–60); 111–12; Vendôme (post-1040–post-1060); 250, on Normandy *ecclesie in civitatibus, vel castellis, vel burgis* (1080); 351–2, La Roche Canillac (1114); 375–7, Bruges (1127). Others collated Coulson, 'Seignorial Fortresses', Index 'Terminology'.

who took refuge within their walls on occasion. It was much the same as with the fortified lordly establishment whose population in peacetime might also be quite large if the lord was in residence. Towns were frequently employed as major administrative centres for the receipt of revenues and the holding of courts,[310] but this governmental role primarily belonged to the lord's personal seat, his town citadel, or to his estate centres in the country where the community of his household and his fiscal and secretarial personnel were housed, and where his tenantry periodically assembled at the great church feasts and on judicial and fiscal occasions. The 'banquets' of popular romance were but one of the uses of the great hall. This was the daily life of the fortress—the scratching of quill pens on parchment in the great hall and in the chancery behind the screen in the chapel, was much more commonly to be heard than the tramp of armed men on the battlements.

Of all the physical elements, the 'great tower', 'donjon', or (in newspeak) the 'keep' most symbolized dominion, lordship, and seignorial authority and lasted the longest, in France especially but also in Spain. Late in the year 1203, and shortly before he lost the duchy of Normandy to the victorious King Philip *Auguste*, John of England made a routine grant of 100 acres of land in return for due service and 'for delivering to us annually at our tower of Rouen, fifty capons (*capones*) in full satisfaction therefor' (or, presumably, their cash equivalent). The ancient 'great tower' of Rouen castle was deliberately destroyed and replaced by one of his own typical cylindrical towers after the conquest by King Philip, in order to supplant an object of Norman loyalties. The result is that it is now pictorially known only from its representations in the Bayeux 'Tapestry', late in the Conqueror's reign. This 'tower' was the capital centre or nexus of all the tenures of Normandy.[311] It was always desirable to have such a focus for a host of non-military reasons. The lack of a proper *caput* in Quercy, in 1290 recently regained by Edward I from Philip IV of France by treaty, in right of the Plantagenet duchy of Gascony, caused Edward to write to his seneschal in those parts to remedy the deficiency:

As we have learned for certain that we have no possessions of our own (*proprietales*), or hardly any, in our land of Quercy . . . especially at places suitable for our seneschals and bailiffs to hold judicial sessions (*assisas*) as is right and fitting (*ut deceret*) and to exercise other rights of justice, capital and minor (*altam et bassam*)—we order and instruct you to set about buying a good castle or fortress (*castellare seu fortalicium*), by the advice of our

---

[310] Knowles, *Monastic Order*, 314, as 'cities, fortified places or villages'. Urban *banlieues* were jurisdictional castellaries e.g. Carpentras (*dép.* Vaucluse, 1155) *Layettes*, i. 74–5: 1155; Corbie (*dép.* Somme, 1180), *Ordonnances*, xi. 216–30; and in the county of Ponthieu (*dép.* Somme), viz. Abbeville (1184), Crécy (1194), Noyelles-sur-Mer (1195), Waben, Marquenterre (1199), Ponthoile (1201), Doullens (1202), etc: ibid. iv. 53–9; *Recueil Ponthieu*, 198–200, 202–4, 227–9, 230–2, 236–40, 433–5.

[311] Round, *Geoffrey de Mandeville*, 334–6; built by Duke Richard I (942–96); Brown, *Bayeux Tapestry* (ed. Stenton), p. 81; *Rot Chart*, 113b, 11 Nov. 1203; next day, a land-grant for an annual cash payment *ad turrim Rothomagensem* (ibid. 113a). Philip II habitually and certainly deliberately built circular *donjons* in his conquests and elsewhere, characteristically French as to Ritter, *Châteaux, donjons et places fortes*, 55–7 (Louvre, Paris; Dourdan, Chinon, Gisors, Rouen, Falaise, Vernon, Laon, etc.).

special clerk, Master Stephen de Lafitte, together with a site suitable for a new town (*bastide*) to be founded nearby . . .[312]

A court-house customarily had a gaol. The form in which a common medieval word for the castle 'keep', its *donjo*, has come down to us shows the notoriety of its use as a prison. Gaols often used castle-sites (e.g. Cambridge, Hertford, Canterbury). Originally such a hall as the Salle de L'Echiquier at Caen, or the great halls surviving in the castles of Winchester and Oakham (Rutland) and Westminster Palace were also court-houses and, on occasion, dormitories. Norman Pounds has surveyed the English castles which were the offices, treasuries, and gaols of county sheriffs, many of them always unsuited to any other purpose.[313] 'Unfortified' halls might suffice (and often did), but lacked the lordly atmosphere particularly desirable in frontier Quercy. Fortification, like the *fasces* of the Roman lictors, being a mark of judicial franchise denoted penal power. Some castles had little else to boast. Lincoln castle in the later middle ages is one of many instances. In 1344 the government of Edward III ordered a report to be made on its condition, the reason given in the king's writ being that 'the buildings there are at the present time so much out of repair that there is great reason to fear the escape of prisoners from the gaol'.[314] Franchisal prisons were necessarily not much less numerous than castles where courts were held. Their administrative role, not any 'strength', was the chief reason. They were, in fact, often insecure to judge from the frequency of references to escapes in the Chancery Rolls. Dilapidation is often blamed, but the actual cause was probably as much the normal scanty skeleton staff of resident officials (caretakers not 'guards') in all but a few castles, except when the lord was in residence (and the greater his rank the longer his absences as a rule), combined with an undoubted element of collusion and corruption.

Significantly, castles were burgled no less it seems than 'manor-houses' in England.[315] They were not police stations, although their association with the law

[312] *Rôles Gascons*, ii. 554. For the Gascon forms *castel, castellare, castéra, castet* see Gardelles *Les Châteaux du sud-ouest*, Index; *castillon/châtillon* is universal. On economic-seignorial penetration in the SW by new *bastides* see Coulson, 'Community and Fortress-Politics in France', 92–3, 103–7; and Part III, Ch. 2, sec. 3 below.

[313] M. de Boüard, 'La Salle dite de l'Echiquier, au château de Caen', attempting to assimilate it to the upper-hall pattern; C.J. Blair, 'Hall and Chamber'; Brown *et al.*, *King's Works*, ii. 856–61; Pounds, *The Medieval Castle*, 91–6: 'the banqueting halls' of popular imagery. Sheriffs' seals featured castles: Cherry, 'Imago Castelli', 87.

[314] *CPR, 1343–5*, 388. Competition in prestige with the cathedral complex left the comital seat in the shade: *CCR, 1330–3*, 255; Coulson, 'Hierarchism in Conventual Crenellation', 76–7, 98 (22), Part IV; cf. King, *The Castle*, 29: same military preoccupation in Brown *et al.*, *King's Works*, ii. 766–7, recognizing that Odiham (Hants) was built by King John as a park hunting-lodge ('por lui deporter') and as 'a convenient resting-place on the way from Windsor to Winchester', but emphasizing the (fortuitous) 'military value' of its (slightly fragile) octagonal keep (ibid. i .76), 'demonstrated in 1216' by 'its garrison of 3 knights and 10 sergeants' refusing to surrender to Louis le Lion for over a week. Often-cited Civil War sieges (e.g. Basing, Corfe, Donnington) are still less conclusive, given variable extraneous circumstances.

[315] e.g. Somerton (Lincs.), stocked with wine to receive the captive Jean *le Bon*, in 1359; Clinton's Maxstoke (War.) in 1357, and Kiriel's Westenhanger (Kent) in 1382: *CPR, 1354–8*, 651; *1358–61*, 221; *1381–5*, 133, 319.

in their role as centres of jurisdiction, royal or franchisal, lasted a very long time. In England, many castellated Victorian county prisons and court-rooms descended directly from the county-town castle (often in the same building, as at Lincoln and Lancaster). Many more were built in castle-style. Sitting in judgement was so attached to seignory that if there was no castle, the place where the courts of the lordship were held, even if no more than under a tree, like many Hundred courts, or in a field plot, was the substitute. Thus in 1433, in the frontier French province of the Dauphiné, the officials of the Dauphin 'king of Bourges' Charles VII, going around the capital sites of the *honor* of Clermont to take ceremonial possession before accepting the heir, finding at Le Passage 'no sort of castle (*alicujus castri*) or house appurtenant to the lordship of that place', made do with the court-site, 'where also forfeited goods are sold by auction', situated near the churchyard. The *maison forte* built there by 1344 had already disappeared, but not its associations. On that plot they planted, 'on a long pole, a banner painted with the Delphinal arms'. The idea was to show that judicial power had briefly reverted: similarly, under rendability the ceremony of placing the lord's banner (and of shouting his war-cry) was normally performed at the summit of the chief tower of the capital castle.[316]

Court-houses, assembly-rooms, prisons, noble residences, estate offices—the peaceful functions of castles outweighed all others. They were not barracks (compare Roman forts with parade grounds nearby) nor drill-halls. Justice could only be done to everything that went on in them by drawing extensively on literary and narrative sources, in addition to records in the narrow sense. For all purposes of lordship, fortification was a customary (but not invariable) accessory of fashion. Even as safe-deposits for valuables, fortresses were rather less often used than religious houses, which regularly had treasuries and strongrooms for devotional gold- and silverware, seldom unattended. Where there was a regular need it might be otherwise: in south-west England, in 1263, Henry III ordered a special castle to be set up to protect the valuable metals extracted from the royal tin-mines in Devon.[317] This was to be 'a good and strong building, with a tower (*turris*) of stone in which the treasure, metals, and tools for the workings of the mine may be deposited, and our mine-workers be able to dwell'. In addition, the custodians of the mine were expressly told 'to wall and fortify' this 'house' or *domus*. The word *domus* is a significantly ambivalent term constantly encountered especially in France (e.g. Champagne fief rolls), which often denoted what was a lesser fortress. Burglary was a real danger, so Henry III's 'convenience and

---

[316] Salvaing, *De l'Usage des Fiefs*, 83–8; for Le Passage, see Andru, Colardelle, Moyne, Verdel. 'Les Châteaux de Clermont', 33. As performed elsewhere, e.g. at five Astarac county castles (*dép.* Gers, 1244); at two Turenne viscounty castles (*dép.* Lot, 1263): *Layettes*, ii. 543–4, 539–40; *Foedera*, i, i, 425–6.

[317] *Close Rolls, 1261–4*, 227–8; Jolliffe, 'The Chamber and the Castle Treasures Under King John', 117–42; Brown, 'English Castles, 1154–1216', 209–32, also on prisons, 233–43. Parker, *Domestic Architecture*, ii. 193 and plates, of late-13th-century treasury of Merton College, Oxford. St Lawrence Hospital, Westminster, had a (licensed) jewel tower: *CPR, 1377–81*, 325; *1385–9*, 215 (description). In 1340 20,000 sacks of Edward III's tax-in-kind wool were divided between Sleaford castle (bishop of Lincoln), Caythorpe castle (lady de Burgh), and St Katharines priory, Lincoln: *CCR, 1339–41*, 531–2.

security' were seriously at risk, countered by this appropriately turriform royal lordly outpost, which was works' depot, lodging, and safe-deposit all rolled into one.[318] Similarly in 1204, the castle of Dublin was rebuilt by order of King John expressly to be a treasury and administrative centre for his outlying dominion of Ireland, in which he took particular interest. Dublin castle needed all the attributes of a power-advertising fortress to assert the king's new title of *Dominus Hibernie*. Emphatic features were indicated, including 'good ditches and strong walls', a donjon (*turris*) which was to be built before the *castellum et baluum* (*sic*) and dependencies (*percunctoria*). There was, as usual, more to this mandate than the mailed fist. David King, a convinced militarist, truly declared that 'neither for housing the upper class nor for local administration and estate management were the defences of a castle remotely necessary'. It is indeed most significant that, in his words, it was 'only in the feudal ages that it . . . was thought worthwhile to employ them in such civilian connections'. Throughout the period, in fact, it is almost impossible to find any purely 'civilian' (noble and non-vernacular) residence without some 'fortified' allusion, however faint—for example, courtyards, curtilage-gateways, parapets, moats, or tower-elements. In France this leitmotif is very eloquent of the unique fortified manner of architecture in medieval society.[319] In the case of Dublin, the castle-constable, like the constable of Bordeaux, capital of Gascony, was the treasurer of 'the land'. Probably the initiative to build had come from the justiciar (viceroy) pleading the lack of somewhere adequate to keep the king's treasure (not cash only, but vital administrative rolls and memoranda as well). In fact there was already a castle there, but King John, perhaps to assert his power as Normandy slipped from his grasp, agreed that a *fortelicia* 'would be very useful to us, for this as for many other purposes'. Dublin deserved the dignity of a *castellum* and one which was to be *quam fortissimum poteritis* and to be located, in fortress-style, where the justiciar judged best 'for the governance of the city, and for defending it should the need arise'.[320] Because the citizens of Dublin were legally obliged, as was normal, to maintain their walls and ditches, the king in an afterthought next day (doubtless also prompted) sent an order to them 'to fortify their town'. It was all part of the manifestation of royal power in Ireland for local administrative reasons, though it was done at a moment of grave

---

[318] Saunders, 'Lydford Castle, Devon', 123–86; excavation revealed 'a purpose-built gaol', rebuilt 'towards the middle of the 13th. century'. A mound was (atavistically) piled up around the base to enmotte the tower which also had a bailey. As the Stannaries prison it was in use until the 18th century.
[319] *Rot Litt Claus* i, 6b, 45b. King, *Castellarium Anglicanum*, i. p.xvi. Pounds, 'Lostwithiel', 203–17, and pl. 53–4, shows how this initially late-13th-century Stannary gaol, courthouse, tin-foundry, etc., showed its rank chiefly by size (especially of the hall), not by castellation (1734 Buck engraving, pl. 53a). Parker, *Glossary*, 5th. edn., pp. 67–8, acknowledged the 'ornamental' use of 'battlements' (but denied it in France). Frankl, *Gothic Architecture*, 246, remarks: 'There is, as yet, no terminology for the styles of military architecture, and this is a subject to which more thought could profitably be devoted.' As he sees it, 'some forms are taken as adornment from military architecture, especially battlements'.
[320] *Ad urbem justicandam et si opus fuerit defendendam* (only once seriously threatened, by Edward Bruce in 1316). Dublin castle's Storehouse Tower may have been the keep. The SE tower is large (diam. 56 feet), also cylindrical with very thick walls: Leask, *Irish Castles*, 53–4. Manning, 'Dublin Castle', 119–22.

(but remote) political crisis in the 'Angevin Empire'. Such mandates are seldom transparent: the order may well have been asked for to strengthen the justiciar's leverage with the citizens.

The stress put on the way in which fortifications manifested lordly power does not detract from the fact that force was its ultimate sanction and that fortresses might facilitate, if need be, resistance to forcible challenge. The castle was the embodiment and instrument of the territorial lord's power: but so also were his mill (*moulin banal*), his church, barns, and gallows, all of which might be allusively 'fortified'. When a tenant died his *caput* figured crucially when his feudal superior took back his land before the heir did homage and received his inheritance. In England the (royal) escheator's procedure was both formal and thorough. Only afterwards, when his subordination had been signalized, was the heir ceremonially invested with his fiefs by the overlord. The *caput* of the fief in England was treated merely as the chief site of the property. In France, however, very usually if the *caput* was a fortress (by name, repute, or style of building) it was specially and ceremonially taken back into the superior's possession to demonstrate his unique control, namely (as often expressed) *in signum reddibilitatis, dominiique directi et superioritatis*. This is how it was phrased in the detailed record of 1433, relating to the Dauphiné in eastern France adjoining alpine Savoy.[321]

On behalf of King Charles VII, the governor of the province delegated to the Castellan of La Tour-du-Pin the task of visiting each chief place of the component fiefs making up the *honor* of the lately deceased Viscount Aymer of Clermont. He was directed 'to implant and to affix at each place and castle, namely on the donjons (*in Donjonis*) and on the higher and more conspicuous (*magis apparenti*) points thereof 'the royal dauphin's banner, which was there to remain for three days in signification of his 'repossession (*reddibilitas*), overlordship, and superiority'. The Castellan went accordingly to the first castle, that of Virieu (*dép.* Isère), dating possibly from 1034 and *chef-lieu de châtellenie* since at least 1107, and 'put a banner on its donjon, namely on the great round tower on the east side of the castle', and caused the act to be officially witnessed and recorded by a notary. The same day he did likewise at Paladru, also recorded in 1107 and still styled 'castle', although the lordship seat had long been transferred to Montferrat. There he fixed a banner 'atop a certain tower over the gateway on the west side', indicating that it had no proper 'keep'. Given the present ruinous state of these castles, these details are archaeologically valuable. The same day he went to the castle of Montferrat, successor by the early fourteenth century to Paladru, and there he placed another banner with due solemnity 'on the summit of the donjon on the west side of the castle'. His next call was to Le Passage where, as noted, there was

---

[321] Salvaing, *De L'Usage des Fiefs*, 83–8, printed *extenso* in Andru *et al.*, 'Les Châteaux de Clermont', 28–31, 33, etc. For rendering *pro bono dominio* see Coulson, 'Seignorial Fortresses', Index 'Recognitory Rendering'. Banner-placing, handing over of keys, actual evacuation by the castellan, and entry by the lord's men 'in great force or small' were some of the features (at 'castles' and towns almost indifferently). An overall survey of rendability, jurability and cognate fortress-customs is projected.

no surviving castle or seignorial building, but the functions of lordship were still attached to the place where they were exercised, in the field by the churchyard. Castles were quite often 'ghosts' in this way, spiritually outlasting their material 'bodies': or, to be more exact, institutionally still alive but structurally decrepit.

Despite thrice-repeated and loudly proclaimed summons at the next *caput*, this time a fortress with dependent *bastide*, now La Bâtie-Divisin (in 1433 *castrum*; *maison forte* in a homage of 1317), the Castellan of La Tour-du-Pin found the gate shut, the custodian refusing him 'the opening up of the castle' because he said he held it for the heir of Jean de Clermont. He denied, moreover, that the fief of *Castrum Bastidae* was held from the late viscount, directly or in sub-fief, claiming it as a direct rendable tenure (*per se de feudo reddibili et directo*) from the king-dauphin. On this account, the custodian 'would not permit any pennons or delphinal banners to be placed'—being, as he argued, a separate fief in its own right. No threat of a fine could procure access to place a banner atop the 'great tower'; procedure was punctilious: refusal of entry was a necessary legal step, not a violent discourtesy, ceremoniously performed so as not to prejudice the stance. It was five days later that the castellan-commissioner concluded his task by visiting the town of La Tour-du-Pin at Hauterive and entering the last of the castles of the viscounty (*videlicet ad castrum dicti loci*). There, the record from the delphinal archives at Grenoble relates, he placed a banner 'on the summit of the great square tower on the east' to be displayed there for the customary three days. Thus the feudal proprieties were duly observed, and the overlord's rights ceremoniously demonstrated with their draconian principle that all land came from the lord and that all castles were peculiarly his.[322] With typical late-medieval punctilio the proceedings, embodied in memoranda (*notas*) by those who had perambulated the Barony of Clermont, were engrossed (written out in full) by public notary and deposited in the treasury at Grenoble.

Ceremony tended to grow more elaborate over time, but all this was characteristic of the permanent principle. At the very centres of seignorial pride, the gesture of humble submission and surrender emphasized that fortresses were not only, like ordinary property, conditionally held from a superior who stood for the wider demands of the public interest, but were subject also to fortress-customs which put special constraints upon construction, tenure, and succession. Fiefs were the overlord's to give and, in certain restricted circumstances, to take back. Fortresses were lawfully his to use when he had need of them, and the vassal could not gainsay his right. Aimeri de Thouars, lord of Luçon (*dép.* Vendée) in Poitou, under severe French pressure at the time, expressed this convention in 1230 to Henry III of England. Their relationship was understood by both as a permanent one of mutual duty, activated by, but not conditional upon, warlike emergency. When the young Louis IX had withdrawn, Luçon

---

[322] The liege homage allegedly done to Charles VII as dauphin by the late lord could not be impugned, 'on which account, the custodian *nullos penuncellos sive bannerias delphinales ... supra ipsum castrum apponi permitteret*'. To have allowed it would have derogated his master's status of tenant-in-chief and created a precedent—fears constantly present in medieval legalism.

castle was left 'totally destroyed by the enemy', with much damage to Aimeri's lands. Expecting further French attack, he requested King Henry, as a vassal ready faithfully to serve his lord to his power, 'to afford to me and to my castles, being yours also, such subvention as may redound to my advantage and be mutually to our honour, yours and mine'. The fortresses of the lands of Luçon were lawfully and properly as fully at the lord king of England's disposal as Aimeri himself: as he put it, expecting help as of right from his lord, 'ego vester sum, et dicta castra mea vestro servitio sunt parata'.[323] Feudal custom, not *force majeure* or *raison d'état*, made this understanding, however it may have been observed, a matter of honour.

4. Conclusions: Part I—Castles 'For All The Folk'

How nobles, not moderns, saw castles is the heart of the matters dealt with in this chapter and whole first half of this book. Because all propertied classes were imbued with the chivalric ethos, which might be described as noble without necessarily being altruistic or considerate to non-nobles, not only the lay aristocracy (Part III, chs. 1, 2 below) and women (Part IV) but also the higher clergy were affected, as also were the *bourgeoisie* to a lesser extent. The peasant community was differently touched (Part III, ch. 3). Each was a part of the whole social body of the medieval castle. Castles were 'for all the folk', as very much more than occasional refuges.[324] The verdict of the archaeology is as clear as is that of the representative documents. If what they reveal might seem here to 'have little to do with castles' as hitherto familiar, especially to English readers, it is not due to any pursuit of mere originality (desirable though that might be in this subject). Rather, it follows from seeing what a balanced sample of the mainstream evidence has to say. The aim of this and the following Part is to do the preliminary job of clearing away some of the remaining obstructions, especially those due to historical constructs and to anachronistic militarism, while introducing the authentic language and some of the spirit and historical context of the early-medieval reception and modification of its inheritance of fortresses.

The attractive but delusive simplicities of the war-gaming view of fortresses the author began to discard, by reluctant and progressive reappraisal, over thirty years ago. Since then more than twenty academic articles have sought to put in its place a comprehensive set of alternative vignettes. On a lighter note, as a companion to the fieldwork of examining and photographing castles in England, Wales, and France, a large-scale model of 'the ideal (military) castle', was started at that time. Since then it has changed, evolving in the 'non-military' aspects

---

[323] *Royal Letters*, W. Shirley (ed.), i. 386. Phrases like 'total destruction', even when not special pleading, often mean no more than laying land waste. See also ibid. 25–6, 49–50, 93, 125–6, 155–6, 185–6, 231, 302–3, 383–4, 386–7, 388 for similar appeals in 1219–31; see Part II, Ch. 3, sec. 1, etc. below. Baudry, *Fortifications des Plantagenêts en Poitou*, 307–8.

[324] n. 118 above. Misused to support the facile 'communal' (Anglo-Saxon)/'private' (Norman) antithesis of historiographical convention.

which constitute advanced castle-study. The process of architectural research this model has required has given innumerable insights and lines of enquiry. These and other investigations, and the articles publishing their results, are the foundation of this book.

PART II

Castles and the Public Interest

Introduction

The 'wrong but wromantic' atmosphere clings persistently to the medieval fortress especially in popular writing. It would be complacent (if convenient) to ignore altogether the bad press and to limit discussion to castles' important colourful aspects, objective as well as imputed. To sit in judgement upon this or any other major social institution involves modern perceptions and a maze of connected paths. But medieval opinions as well as modern attitudes have made the utility, neutrality, or (perhaps) the iniquity of 'private fortresses' as adjuncts to 'baronial tyranny' (in reality, the kings' castles were little different) into matters central to the purpose of this book. If fortresses had been an alien implant in the body politic, as traditional views of 'old English' society and of the Norman Conquest might imply, and truly chief instruments of oppression by an irresponsible warring minority, as the *anarchie féodale* scenario holds, then their importance would be chiefly technical and their impact largely negative. This being far from the truth, some attempt must be made to investigate how contemporaries at large regarded them—not only their owners and users. It will then be possible to reassess their moral standing as part of medieval civilization.

To do so, some shibboleths must suffer. First, it is necessary to set aside entirely (or to receive with caution) the pious notion that kings patriotically implemented the public good in their 'castle-policy'. Their own interests might point that way, but not necessarily more so than those of the great magnates. Royalism, clerical (medieval) or Whig (modern), is an obstruction. Secondly, the magnificent modern construct of 'the castle' shrinks, perhaps disconcertingly, when put back into context. Its substantive social role does not live up to the castle-enthusiast's expectations—although it reveals fortresses as far more important, but also rather elusive. Boyish imaginings and techno-history will be disappointed. Even militarily, castles have been greatly exaggerated—perhaps along with warfare itself. Even within the present limits of evidence, of period and of place, fortresses are a paradoxically complex subject; and to what extent they served the public interest is a question not easily answered—beyond affirming that the verdict deducible from a variety of English (with some French) record sources is favourable in the sense that little apparently adverse evidence stands up. Unfortunately, the most vociferous or best-recorded original opinion, that of emulous churchmen, is hostile (unless as proprietors, as we have seen) but is of little objective value. Burgesses' condemnations of neighbouring castles also attract a heavy rate of discount. Because Christian ideals laid such stress on public utility, on benefit to the whole of society, it is important not to reject references to that standard as mere lip-service: to do so would be to throw out the baby with the bathwater.

These problems are addressed in the three following chapters. Fortresses were but one attribute of a lawfully armed aristocracy. Noble arms-bearing took numerous ancillary forms (Chapter 1). How it was reconciled with peacekeeping spotlights the legitimacy of fortifying and holding castles. It will be shown that these commonplace activities were in no essential fashion inimical to peacekeeping: castellans were themselves policemen—but strains broke out during the English civil war of King John's reign and its aftermath (1215–c.1226), as also, most notoriously, during 'the Anarchy' of 1139–53 and afterwards (Chapter 2).

Those unduly influential episodes are compared with the Angevin record, notably of Henry II, and with measures taken by Edward I after 1274. Some illuminating cases of exemplary and punitive 'official' destruction of fortifications (truly 'slighting', that is 'humiliating', as in England in 1642–60) provide us with comparisons, as do the preventive restrictions adopted in the Plantagenet–Capetian truces of 1160–1200, and in some later treaties with the Scots. What clearly emerges is the contemporary respect for correct conduct between vassal and lord. In this, the elusive sense of the public interest had its place (Chapter 3). Evidence is direct as well as inferential. The substantial (but neglected) practices of both formalized and pragmatic co-operation by fortress-holders with their lords (including the king) stand in corrective contrast with images of irresponsibility. Rendability, and all it implies, imposes a drastic and all-pervasive reappraisal of the relationship of seignorial and communal fortresses to the medieval polity at large. No liability could be more demanding than the commandeering of castle-homes. Virtually every aspect of this book has been informed by it. Compulsory handover is corroborated by the equally compelling evidence supplied by the English and 'French' practices of 'licensing', authorizing, or more broadly sanctioning the creation of all sorts of new fortresses and occasionally the updating of old ones.[1] This material, in contrast with rendability, has not so much been ignored as misrepresented to support notions of mistrustful central government policing to 'control' 'dangerous' 'private castles'. Very large bodies of chiefly charter material modify received views of the role of fortresses at large in the social interactions of deeply class-divided societies, English, Irish, and Welsh, as well as in the regions of the kingdom of France.[2] What they combine to affirm is that a much greater harmony of political aims prevailed than has been supposed between those in immediate possession of fortresses and their feudal superiors, including the king.

To assert that castles were built and used under conventions broadly imbued with a sense of social responsibility, in England especially strong though mostly unwritten and ad hoc, does not go at all too far. Many exemplary documents of 'licensing' and of 'rendability' occur throughout this book. It is hoped subsequently to analyse a larger sample of both closely related customs in a more narrowly focused way than would be appropriate here.

---

[1] See Bibliography, 'Coulson', for specific infrastructure. The frequency of reference to the author's own work is regretted but unavoidable.

[2] The general concept of 'class' remains useful: e.g. Duby, *France, 787–1460*, pt. ii; Hay, *Europe in the Fourteenth and Fifteenth Centuries*, pp. iii and iv.

In this second Part ideas, not chronology, are again put first, avoiding intrusive periodization or regionalization. The 'class-system' is naturally fundamental. It was as obvious and seemed as divinely ordained as to the Victorian hymn-writer, that 'the rich man in his castle' coexisted with 'the poor man at his gate'. It may have been Tudor state propaganda which proclaimed Henry VIII in 1533 to be ruler of 'a body politic, compact of all sorts and degrees of people divided in terms and by names of spirituality and temporality', which social groups were bound to him 'to bear next to God a natural and humble obedience'. But the Act of Appeals expressed an enduring commonplace.[3] Class provides this study with many of its thematic divisions.

Class conflict is briefly discussed before, at the end of Part II (Chapter 3, section 4), introducing the town-fortresses of the *bourgeoisie* (another topic calling for more detailed examination), and broaching an aspect of noble castles in France during the Hundred Years War when their subordination to 'national' defence went a few steps further. Importantly, it was even then incomplete and some of the relatively minor innovations proved to be short-lived. In many ways the sub-medieval period (the *époque féodale*) did indeed last until 1789.

---

[3] Elton, *Tudor Constitution*, no. 177 (p. 344).

1

Noble Military 'Liberties', Ethos and Ethics

How it can be compatible with an orderly society to exalt the civilian possession of weapons is a constant perplexity to Europeans contemplating the United States. But the Second Amendment, for all its apparent incongruity, is true to an earlier political conception: one with affinities to medieval circumstances. It is anachronistic statist thinking to regard fortresses as the medieval equivalents of modern military 'plant', neglecting their wide social diffusion, their complex and ambivalent character, and the differences I have illustrated.[4] This mentality constantly taints the 'private castle' with the slur of illicit violence.[5] That fortresses were a basic ingredient of the medieval polity, not an instrument of civil war waged by an anti-social minority, appears more fully by considering the medieval 'arms ban'. It was so pervasive that I take it first. Ideologically the colonial American view (of 1789)[6] that self-defence with private arms and armies ('a well regulated militia') conduced not to anarchy but 'to the security of a free State', is proximate to the medieval noble liberties of *guerra*, of fortifying, and of arms-bearing.[7] Good regulation, of course, is essential. Noble liberties were symptoms not of the imagined 'state of nature' free-for-all parodied so aptly by Sellar and Yeatman as 'the banorial rites of carnage and wreckage', but mark a society in which no man (unless, possibly, the cleric) was a civilian. But whether, by modern standards, it could be described simply as 'organized for war' must be questioned.[8]

---

[4] Militaristic popularization may be exemplified by a sometime custodian at Beaumaris castle (Anglesey) explaining to the author (*c.*1960) the purpose of the fireplaces set in the inner faces of the curtains (serving vanished hall, chamber, etc.) as being to send up a 'smokescreen to confuse besiegers in time of war'.

[5] Even Painter, having stressed its consensual elements, declared, 'as a political system pure feudalism was little removed from anarchy': *Feudalism and Liberty*, 7.

[6] Morrison, Commager, *The Growth of the American Republic*, vol. i, Appendix, pp. 297–8 (Bill of Rights only). Traditional elaborations analysed in Bellesiles, 'Origins of Gun Culture' and *Lethal Imagination*.

[7] Modern belief that only state violence can be legitimate distorts perceptions of all these aspects; cf. Kaeuper, *War, Justice and Public Order*, ch. 2; also ch. 1, 'Medieval Violence' and ch. 3.3, 'Private War'. Ideal and actuality sensitively balanced in his Introduction to *Violence in Medieval Society*.

[8] Sellar and Yeatman, *1066 And All That*, p. 29; cf. Smail, *Crusading Warfare*, p. v.

1. Weaponry and Architecture

The large arms-bearing class was, in fact, far more, and much else, than a triumphalist 'gun lobby'. Hunting, however ('the image of war without its guilt, and only five-and-twenty percent of its danger', as R. S. Surtees's Jorrocks nicely put it), does offer some useful analogies. War-gaming and the ritualized warfare of chivalry also have distant affinities: but the gulf is still wide. What makes medieval society so different was that its social stratification was partly (but conspicuously) articulated by war-type practices. Hierarchy was exceptionally military in nature. The ruling class was not so much an officer-cadre to some general military reserve, as rather an association of club or regimental type with associate grades of membership, shading off to the subordinate masses.[9] It would take the parallel unduly far to liken castellated buildings to (say) Territorial Army drill-halls or, conversely, to golf clubhouses—analogies, in fact, are hard to find. To the noble castellated residence, of course, the Stuart, Georgian, and Victorian country-house is the closest social parallel. Tudor monarchy and 'Renaissance' made little impact on the sub-medieval continuities of the aristocratic panorama.[10]

Self-defence was as prominent in medieval Europe as it was in colonial North America. The direct lord was bound to give to his tenants-in-fief and other dependants proper support, failing which they were theoretically entitled to transfer their allegiance to another lord willing and able to protect them. In default of protection, war-damage compensation was payable.[11] Lapse of time made no difference: the abbey of Sordes in Gascony (*dép.* Landes) had to wait until 1280 to be fully recompensed by Edward I for losses incurred in the 1252–4 revolt against Henry III's lieutenant in the duchy, Simon de Montfort.[12] It was a particularly pious act:

Since the lord King Henry our father, of celebrated memory was sometime indebted to our beloved in Christ the abbot of Sordes ... for damages he once suffered in the war of Gascony (*guerra Vasconie*), of which part ... has been repaid to him—We, wishing to show him special favour, have granted him a further 50 marks by gift to be spent on walling (*ad clausuram*) the town of Sordes.

---

[9] Cf. Prestwich, *Armies and Warfare*, esp. chs. 2, 9. Barber's conspectus (*Two Cities*, 25): 'the cement which held this [social structure] together was Christian belief' (ch. 2, *passim*) puts technology in its due place.

[10] Crouch, *Image of Aristocracy*, chs. 6–9 (including hunting, pp. 305–10) covers much of it.

[11] Montferrand and Le Gard castles near Bordeaux, probably razed by 'the French' during their occupation of the city and part of the duchy in 1294–1303, waited over 10 years. Edward II (1313) ordered assessment of compensation for this and other war-damage, and payment (*Rôles Gascons*, iv. 270–1, 275; Gardelles, *Les Châteaux du sud-ouest*, 154; site only; razed by citizens, 1591). Even in the emergency after 1356, clearances around town walls caused claims for compensation: Timbal, *La Guerre de Cent Ans*, 184–200 (with documents). This included ordinary encumbrances, e.g. buildings in the ditches of Cherbourg (*dép.* Manche); licensed to be rebuilt in 1314: *Registres du Trésor*, i. 445.

[12] *Rôles Gascons*, ii. 96: *in centum marcis* (? *libris*—to reconcile the amounts stated). Sordes is near the *vicomté* of Béarn; garrisoned for Edward II against Charles IV in 1323 (Gardelles, *Les Châteaux du sud-ouest*, 35). Bémont, *Rôles Gascons, Supplément*, pp. lxiii–lxx, on the 'war' of 1252–4.

Good lordship required that the social contract be morally as well as legally binding, towards the clergy especially. Protection was not so much a civic right of the
defenceless as an ethical duty of the strong.[13] It was in addition, of course, an
economic and political necessity if the vulnerable agricultural cycle, in particular,
was not to be disrupted, imperilling the subsistence of the entire community as
well as the position of the wealthy. Protection and compensation which, after
Robert Bruce's victory at Bannockburn in 1314, often took the form of tax-
remission in northern England, were developed areas of medieval custom and of
subjects' expectations in consequence.[14]

Striking a pragmatic balance between peacekeeping and respect for the right
and practice of weapon-ownership, at all levels of society, required that arms kept
compulsorily for defence-service should be publicly displayed only by 'the military class'.[15] The nobility, knighthood and gentry, bore weapons and defensive
armour (under varying restrictions) by the privilege of their order. In exactly the
same way, their residences customarily bore the marks of defence such as battlements, arrow-slits, towers, and the like. Just as the liberty of arms-bearing was an
appurtenance of rank, so also the architectural features of fortification habitually
denoted the aristocrat. But whereas townspeople displayed pride in their wealth
and status with castle-like 'defences', with turreted *hôtels de ville* and castellated
town-houses, when venturing abroad even rich merchants were well advised to
make no show of force.[16] Their independence might have to be satisfied by an
unpretentious measure of security—thus in 1289, Edward I, as duke of Gascony at
Condom (*dép.* Gers), permitted three merchants from Lucca in Tuscany, who had
petitioned that they were staying at Bordeaux and believed themselves to be in
danger, to have such arms as they should choose but to bear them 'covertly and
secretly . . . for the protection and defence of their lives and persons', anywhere in
the duchy. Steel caps inside bonnets and brigandines (medieval 'bullet-proof
vests') were common.[17] Given the touchiness of the Gascon nobility regarding any
sort of pretension by the lower orders, it was natural to stipulate that this permission (granted under Edward's duty 'to provide for the safety and protection of the
inhabitants of our said land') should not give rise to 'any misdeeds or complaint'.

---

[13] e.g. Poole, *Obligations of Society*, 1–11; cf. Dawson, *Making of Europe*, 19–37, 203–18, etc. (including 'feudal anarchy'); cf. Locke, *Two Treatises* (1691), 346–8; J. J. Rousseau (1762), e.g. Introduction by
E. Barker to *The Social Contract*. Strickland, *War and Chivalry*, for review of the issues 1066–1217.

[14] e.g. *CCR, 1318–23*, 233 (1320); *CPR, 1313–17*, 240–1 (1314), 257 (1315). Duties owed by rulers have
been relatively neglected.

[15] Denholm-Young, *Country Gentry*, 34; Prestwich, *Armies and Warfare*, ch. 3 (esp. 75–81). On the
1181 Assize of Arms (Henry II) and sequels, e.g. Powicke, *Military Obligation*, 54–6, 82–3, 119–21
('distraining' knighthood on £20 freeholders from 1224), but excluding unfree serfs: Poole, *Obligations
of Society*, 33–4; also on 1205 'communes', Tait, *English Borough*, 221, 253. In 1333 knighthood was
imposed on holders for three years of £40 in land or rent (*CCR, 1333–7*, 93). Text of 1285 Statute of
Winchester, Stubbs's *Select Charters*, 464–9.

[16] Cf. their architecture, Coulson, 'Battlements and the Bourgeoisie'.

[17] *Rôles Gascons*, ii. 450; the terms (*arma deferre, delacio armorum, portacio armorum*) are the same
as for nobles. For appropriate 'arms' see Viollet-le-Duc, *Dictionnaire du mobilier*, arts. 'Brigandine',
'Gambison', 'Hoqueton', 'Jacque', etc.

It was understood that the Italians would have their proper attendants—but when Philip VI's court of the parlement issued a similar warrant to a native merchant of Toulouse in 1347 he was limited to a following of two men, also to be armed discreetly, and to a period of one year only. He had claimed that 'his capital enemies lay in wait to kill him, by day and by night'.[18] Philip's officials applied no such restrictions in 1349 to Pierre Guérot, with up to five companions whom he might recruit, he fearing attack (he said) by the emulous squire (*écuyer*) Lancelot de Francières. It may well be that Pierre doubted his own entitlement to bear adequate weapons, but his desire to put himself so punctiliously in the right may have been anticipatory.[19] Rather stricter policing is evidenced in contemporary England. We find, in 1328, during the period of widespread disturbance after the fall of Edward II (1326–7), two Norwich merchants 'privately' arrested (not by royal officers) for travelling armed to Reading fair (Berks.). They were exonerated since 'they wore no armour except two single (*simplicibus*) aketons . . . by reason of the dangers of the road and not for committing evil'.[20] A padded jerkin of some kind was also the pretext for the arrest of a priest in 1331, this time by Edward III's household marshals. Being armed 'within the king's verge' (in proximity to his household) was an especial offence.[21] It is a very telling fact that such trivia (contrasting with the misdeeds of gentry gangs) received notice when fortifying in France and in England was only (and rarely) restricted and for lordly, not security, reasons. It was a natural corollary of noble arms-bearing, both of them attributes proper to the diverse levels of aristocracy, like hunting, deer-parks, and warrens.[22]

For a man of gentle birth and landed status to advertise his power to protect his household, manorial curtilage, and agricultural accessories by whatever degree of fortification sufficiently reflected his position and deterred infringement was to make conspicuous his right of self-defence and complied with the fashion of his class. But his first instinct normally was to go to law.[23] Fortification is easily (even instinctively) misunderstood. Aesthetic style, by contrast, in British later-seventeenth- and eighteenth-century country mansions of the Palladian and Classical era sufficiently proclaims itself, since colonnaded porticos, pedimented windows, urns, statuary, and suchlike are patently little more than a (derivative Graeco-Roman) pastiche, affecting proportions perhaps, but essentially dignifying the Jacobean, Carolean, Queen Anne, or Georgian residential box and its appurtenances. Unlike

[18] *Actes du Parlement*, ser. ii, ii, 201 (French calendar).

[19] Ibid. 301. On poor royal French peacekeeping, Vale, *Origins of the Hundred Years' War*, 112–13 ('private war'). But 'late-medieval England was known throughout Europe for its high rate of crime', Bellamy, *Crime and Public Order*, 3.

[20] *CCR, 1327–30*, 314: held by the bailiffs of the liberty of Reading abbey.

[21] *CCR, 1330–33*, 243 (May 1331: Mortimer was overthrown by the *coup d'état* at Nottingham castle on 19 Oct. 1330).

[22] 'The hunt was the normal outdoor pastime of the medieval nobility'—Hohler, 'Court life in peace and war', 147 (caption); Crouch, *Image of Aristocracy*, 305–10. C. Taylor, 'Medieval Ornamental Landscapes'; Lasdun, *English Park*, esp. ch. 2.

[23] Examples of *oyer et terminer* descriptions of assaults on precincts and manor houses, Coulson, 'Conventual Crenellation', 84–91.

the *château style*, so long-lived in France,[24] the architectural features and also the
overall layout in Classicism are not dual-purpose (although landscaping and parks
were common to both and had no military affectations). The motifs are purely
'civilian', far simpler in ethos than the almost all-pervasive 'fortified' manner of
medieval noble architecture which covered the enormous span of building types
from the predominantly physically defensive (but still symbolic) mass of a Krak
des Chevaliers[25] (Syria; later twelfth to later thirteenth century) to such late and
purely allusive castles as Faulkebourne (Essex; licensed 1439) and Thornbury
(Glos.; licensed 1510).[26] Superficially simple, the actual duality of 'fortification'
requires no less architectural analysis than has been lavished on churches. One
obstacle is that the allusive, retrospective historicism of early-modern (Tudor) and
later post-Palladian (Stuart) pre-Gothic Revival architecture appeals so obviously
to artistic nostalgia, making castles, by contrast, seem to be 'functional' and utilitarian. Because castles sprang from late-Roman legionary and municipal *castra* and
castella, they appeared to owe more to Mars than to Minerva, an impression
doubly reinforced—first, by the popular view that they must have developed
primarily to deal with 'medieval' violence and lawlessness; and secondly, by the
propensity of medievalists, reacting against romantic idealization of 'chivalry', to
emphasize the ruthlessness of war and of lesser violence.[27] In fact, as we have seen,
castles' parentage was far more complex. It may, indeed, be wrong to seek a
medieval militarism of familiar type. The expression of public authority and legitimate power was much more important than actual warfare in castles' gestation
and development. Post-medieval noble building makes fewer intellectual
demands. Additionally, the modern virtual state monopoly of weapons (so that,
for example, 'taking the law into your own hands' is condemned), combined with
nation-state ideology and a public mind which no longer tolerates aristocratic,
military, judicial, or even political power, distances us enormously from the era of
castles. Put more simply, reducing 'castles' to adjuncts of some imagined medieval
war machine, or in nobles' hands to instruments of organized or illicit violence
('private war'), becomes less seductive once their roles, ceremonial, governmental,
institutional, and social, are given their due prominence.[28]

   Militant architecture and weaponry of all kinds, protective or potentially
aggressive, for the reasons outlined have much in common as icons of rank and
power. But whereas fortifying itself was rarely an act of force and did not ordi-
narily endanger the peace or jeopardize the public interest, the unrestrained use
of weapons might well do both. Building was always an aristocratic hobby, but

---

[24] Girouard, *French Country House*—late English exemplar at Waddesdon Manor, Bucks.
[25] Molin, 'Non-Military Functions of Crusader Fortifications', 367–88. Pringle, *Secular Buildings
Crusader Kingdom* (including Gazetteer); Ellenblum, *Frankish Settlement*.
[26] Thompson, *Decline of the Castle*, 60, 62–3, 91–2.
[27] Especially in English: Coulson, 'Cultural Realities', bibliography. On the 'form follows function'
debate, Worsley, Castles Studies Group *Newsletter* 12, 43–5 (from the *Daily Telegraph*).
[28] Harold Perkin, *Origins of Modern English Society*, esp. chs. 6, 7. Cf. tendency to read back modern
military ideas, Ayton, Introduction, *Medieval Military Revolution*.

playing at war could be dangerous to society. Delegating law-enforcement risked abuse. Fortresses were quite often involved—as is to be expected, since they were residences of the participants and (like stone buildings, such as churches) might give protection and impunity to combatants, be it momentary and incidental or solid and enduring.[29] New castles were peacefully sanctioned by local seignorial authority, with or (more often) without royal involvement in France, most often with it in England (most clearly after c.1200);[30] but preventing the associated noble liberty of arms-bearing from wreaking the havoc occasionally caused by large-scale state-sponsored violence called for constant vigilance. A review of the large and intricate 'law-and-order' literature would be of marginal relevance here,[31] but contrary to the popular perception that fortifying was a lawless activity causally associated with the 'robber baron', castle-building properly belongs to the hierarchical ambitions and interactions of seignorial politics. Technological enthusiasts have colonized the void left in the past by academics. Architectural historians have been slow to respond. Technical determinism cannot account for the strong chivalric (indeed sporting) element evident even in systematic warfare.[32] It was this spirit to which fortifications primarily responded. Charting them on a local map with 'strategy' in mind, in the belief that some modern logic would be vindicated, reducing what was a chronological palimpsest due to the accidents of tenurial impact to a Staff College schema, would have amused a contemporary.[33] Economic geography, as well as pride and status, noble and *bourgeois*, was in play. Fortification was determined by personal factors far more than by planning or by geography.

The picture with personal weapons (most men carried a knife or dagger) was more complicated: whereas a knight's accoutrements, notably his heavy horses, were increasingly (from the later thirteenth century) beyond the means of even the quite affluent gentry, missile-weapons were deadly. The long-range and powerful crossbow, and later in England the cheap and nasty longbow, were much less expensive and more lethal than the earliest handguns.[34] Rationing of

[29] But Vale, *Origins of the Hundred Years War*, 114–18 *et alibi* sees violence as the prime mover of fortifying in Gascony; also 'The War in Aquitaine', and 'Seigneurial Fortification and Private War in Gascony'. Cf. Coulson, 'Sanctioning of Fortresses in France', for alternative consensual and territorial model.

[30] Coulson, 'Freedom to Crenellate', *passim*; cf. R. R. Davies, *March of Wales*, 70 ff.

[31] Summary Kaeuper, *War, Justice and Public Order*; also ch. 3 (1) 'Tournaments'; (2) 'Private Fortification' (combining for France Coulson, 'Seignorial Fortresses', with G. Fournier, *Le Château*).

[32] e.g. Walter Manny's expedition in 1338: R. Barber, *Knight and Chivalry*, p. 44, and chs. 10–12. ('Chivalry in Action'). Strickland discerns a blend of 'honour' and savagery in 'Conduct in Edward I's Campaigns in Scotland'—e.g. 'The reportage of atrocity is essentially formulaic, spiced with salacious features' (p. 45).

[33] Caveats in Smail, *Crusading Warfare*, e.g. 3–12, 205–6 (reacting excessively against *Kriegsgeschichte*); but Contamine, *War in the Middle Ages*, maps e.g. p. 221. Overall defence planning in the Holy Land may be discerned in fortifying by the military orders; see M. Barber, 'Frontier Warfare, 1178–79', 15 *et passim*.

[34] Hardy, 'The Longbow' (esp. 161–2) is not immune to legend. Few 'arrow slits' were usable by other than crossbows: Jones and Renn, 'Military Effectiveness of Arrowloops'. Study is lacking of this favourite weapon, *temp.* Richard I and John, cf. Payne-Gallway, *The Crossbow*.

weapons by cost, as practised later with firearms and cannon, accordingly did not work. With any sort of building, by contrast, cost was decisive. Fortifying was, in short, an activity mostly incidental to lawlessness and peripheral to peacekeeping. To this I will return (Ch. 2).

2. The Aura and the Abuse of Arms

The interaction of weaponry and architecture was largely indirect—on the social plane. The spirit of the arms-bearing class was basic. In the borderlands of Gascony, for instance, vendetta and legitimate defence might be almost indistinguishable. A quasi-national interest might additionally confuse them.[35] In 1270 Daurde de Baras, tenant in Quercy of King Louis's brother Alphonse de Poitiers, alleged that 'the men of the king of England and of the bishop of Cahors [separately] are daily invading his land, [attacking] his people and the subjects (*homines*) of his *castrum* of Larnagol [*dép*. Lot, near Figeac]'.[36] He had made a similar complaint the previous year. The remedy he obtained from the count of Poitiers (since 1249, also of Toulouse) was an order to the French seneschal of Agen and Cahors to allow him to use arms if necessary to defend his interests, with waiver so that 'he shall not be arraigned for contempt of the arms-ban; and, so that if he is, it shall not be implemented: provided always that he do not go beyond this [limit] by bearing arms in ways not permitted'.[37] This licence by Alphonse, granted in his council (parlement) of April–May 1270 at Toulouse, immediately offended Bertrand de Cadillac, who protested that Daurde 'was his capital enemy and had obtained the dispensation to do him evil'. He demanded a similar licence in order to retaliate. Alphonse's lawyers wavered: self-defence was a right not to be denied if the lord had failed to protect; Bertrand was first refused, but the seneschal was to be instructed to tell Daurde to stop—which was then cancelled and a more even-handed order to prohibit both from bearing arms to do the other mischief was sent out instead.[38]

To the extent that fortifying exercised this right of self-defence, restricting it would have been unjust if not unlawful, as well as impracticable. It is clear that an attempt by Philip IV in 1311–12 to make cognizance of infraction of the arms' ban (*facta armorum*) into a royal monopoly, thus depriving the greater franchisees, which Edward II's parliament more circumspectly pronounced in 1313,[39] could not generally override do-it-yourself protection, retaliation, and pre-emptive (or

---

[35] But local patriotisms predominated: Coulson, 'Community and Fortress-Politics in France', 80–2, 95–7, 102–3.

[36] *Enquêtes A. de Poitiers*, 312–13.

[37] 'Et non fiat contra ipsum condampnatio armorum in tali casu, et si facta fuerit non levetur; proviso tamen ne in portatione armorum non excedat in aliis casibus non permissis.'

[38] *Enquêtes A. de Poitiers*, 338–9: cf. 1269 order to help Baras defend himself if properly his tenant for the fief in contention (*Correspondence A. de Poitiers*, ii. 161).

[39] *CPR, 1313–17*, 26; text (*Foedera*, ii, i, 232) of mandate to the Exchequer expresses it obliquely: 'que homme reigne sans tote force et saunz armes bien et peisiblement al honour de nous et a la pays de nous et de nostre roiaume,' reserving cases of breach to the king's court.

quite gratuitous) aggression. Philip's judicial council (parlement) in 1311 had instructed the seneschal of Toulouse to order the count of Comminges (in the Pyrenees, a dependency of the counts of Foix), together with 'other barons of the region (pays)', to desist from hearing in their courts offences against the ban on bearing arms, which was now claimed to be a peculiarly royal power.[40] Exemptions to reconcile regality with armed individualism were necessarily numerous. Even allowing for the fact that a *ban* was not a prohibition but a lordly inhibition of so wide a range of activities as to be truly commonplace or *banal*, contemporary verdicts by the royal parlement, the Parisian chief tribunal and executive council, were partisan, vague, and hesitant where they might have been expected to be firm, objective, and practical. In 1313 the prior of Cambon successfully petitioned against a fine imposed by the seneschal of Carcassonne. It appears that in his dwelling within the precinct (*enceinte*) of La Grasse abbey (*dép.* Aude)—that is, within the monastic inner liberty—the prior had assembled twelve named *consorts* in arms, for his own protection as he claimed. The seneschal, based in the magnificently refortified royal city-fortress and power-centre of Carcassonne, had clearly been unduly officious. The previous year the Crown lawyers, seeking always to extend royal jurisdiction, had overreached themselves, forbidding even the wearing of swords except only when making a journey.[41] It was more realistic to sanction self-defence quite explicitly, as indicated by a further instance in 1316 relating to the wild region of Auvergne, when two brothers 'with their appropriate suite (*decenti comitiva*)' were licensed to pursue in arms five named outlaws (*bannis du royaume*) who had murdered the brothers' father. Even local senechals' imposition of fines for offences against the peace and assembly in arms were regularly appealed against.[42] Arms and petitions often went together. Officials' zeal was not always for the public peace; nor were their actions always impartial.

All grades of society were expected to own weapons and accoutrements, ranging from peasant arms to the full knightly panoply. Only their use was theoretically regulated.[43] Observing this required fine, often unreal, distinctions to be made between possession and public display or use. What was never in question was the armed (and castellated) persona of the noble. The lavish expenditure and pride exemplified at the summit of the social pyramid, by Edward, prince of Wales, victor at Poitiers (1356), in and upon his warhorses (many individually named), and by his concern for their breeding and management, permeated the whole aristocracy, from great nobles to mere gentry.[44] Valuation lists, initially

[40] *Actes du Parlement*, i, ii, 82; but encroachment on the ducal arms-ban in Gascony was unlawful: Coulson, 'Community and Fortress-Politics in France', 96–7; Vale, *Origins of the Hundred Years War*, 113, n. 302, on *c.*1310 petition.

[41] *Actes du Parlement*, i, ii, 100, 107 (calendar). Implementation delegated to franchisees, here (1312) the bishop of Orléans regarding his clergy. Shennan, *Parlement of Paris*, chs. 1–3.

[42] *Actes du Parlement*, i, ii, 191, 626.

[43] n. 338, above. In France non-noble field service was rare after 1337: Contamine, *Guerre, état et société*, 746, 'Obligations Militaires', except for *guet et garde* (Part III, ch. 3, secs. 3, 4 below).

[44] *Black Prince*, iv. 15, 34, 56, 66, 113, 290, etc.; Hewitt *Organisation of War*, 87–8; Given-Wilson, *English Nobility*, esp. 2–11.

made so that mounted combatants might be compensated by the Crown for horses lost on campaign, underline the correlation of price with rank (just as with modern ministerial limousines). Household officials were similarly awarded robes. Military efficiency, though not irrelevant, was subsidiary. 'Honour' (to them) or 'prestige' (to us) was a heavy burden to some poor or unpractised 'rustic knights', but 'arms' were a cherished privilege to many. *Arma* were heraldic bearings as well as weapons, as social differentiation increased. The 'profession of arms', like heraldry ('coat armour') and fortification, connoted nobility.[45] The widespread impounding of weapons resorted to at a number of towns by Philip V in the disturbances of 1317 could only be applied to the *menu peuple*, ostensibly to ensure that they could not sell or pledge their weapons and armour—which would be needed if they were summoned to serve as footmen.[46] Individuals of lesser origins who were 'professional soldiers', in the sense of making a career out of the practice and rewards of arms, might acquire quasi-nobility; but any association with military affairs, however indirect, conferred honour and social power.[47] Town authorities, vested with basic borough franchises, cherished along with their walls and gates their control of the communal urban arsenal of weapons and their right to call the townsmen to arms on their own authority, or when authorized. In the charter of rights conceded in 1254 by the bishop of Limoges to his township of Saint-Junien (*dép.* Haute-Vienne), the *custodia armorum villae* is one of the duties and distinctions of the *consuls*, along with other 'military duties' such as calling out and leading the militia (*exercitus*), fortifying the walls, collecting tolls at the gates, 'and doing all similar things which appertain to the splendour (*ad ornatum*) of the town'.[48] This socialized arms-worthiness, whether in urban microcosm or at large, was truly organic and institutional. It certainly had military corpuscles in its bloodstream, but 'militarized', in the sense of dominated by soldiery and by organized hostilities, it was not.

Medieval civilization, therefore, was warlike in a sense—but the degree is easily exaggerated: other cultural elements deeply imbued the warfare. Not the least illumination available from studying the evidence of the whole social fortress phenomenon is to realize how little fortification depended on war—and how much it was part of architecture as an art (Part I, Ch. 3). The often violent social milieu paradoxically emphasizes the underlying pacifism of the architectural panorama. If 'law and order' were analysed from this standpoint alone the results would surprise. That we do not experience brutalism in the buildings, if preconceptions are set aside, but rather the gamut from quasi-baroque grandeur to

---

[45] e.g. *per* Ayton, 'the characteristic mark of chivalric status, the warhorse, was now usually a spectator from the baggage park', given the predominance of archery in battle *temp.* Edward III: 'Knights, Esquires and Military Service', 82 *et passim*. On 'the peerage of soldiers' Keen, *Laws of War*, 254–7.

[46] *Registres du Trésor*, ii. 266–7: a notably cautious procedure including northern *châteaux et villes qui sont sièges de châtellenies ou de vicomtés royaux* (calendar).

[47] An older French assessment is Perroy, *Hundred Years War*, 44–5, 126, 163, 303–4.

[48] *Amplissima Collectio*, i. 1320–3; Part IV, Ch. 3, secs. 2, 3 below.

proto-rococo dilettantism, refutes the 'rape and pillage' approach.[49] Perhaps such measures as permitting (in February 1235) the abbot of Holmcultram in border Cumberland 'to have sergeants furnished with bows and arrows until Christmas to protect their granges and the bodies of the brethren dwelling therein' should not be taken as showing how far short reality came, but rather the ambitious standard of weapons-control attempted.[50] Precautions against disorder during noble assemblies seldom went so far as, at the 1336 Westminster parliament, to 'forbid all persons ... from wearing jacks, plates, habergeons, swords, long knives, or other armour or arms in the city of London and suburbs, in the palace of Westminster, or in any place between the city and palace, by land or by water'. The prior of Coventry, for his protection, had been specially exempted but was nonetheless attacked. Display was the offence, not possession of 'offensive weapons', crimes of violence apart. Knives were ordinary wear (as still in formal Scottish dress), for use at table and otherwise. Any 'unnatural' death had in England to be adjudicated by the coroner. Numinous regality as much as security traditionally caused arms-bearing 'within the king's verge', in technical proximity (often quite remote) to the royal Court and household, wherever lodged, to be punished with great severity. Magnate households were armed but were not armed camps.[51] Their members were not effete intellectuals (compare a modern rugby football team), but neither were they thugs. In 1343 the unpopular archbishop of Canterbury John de Stratford, who had been treasurer, chancellor, and 'principal councillor' to Edward III, received permission to do what was abnormal in 'taking in his company as many armed men and others as shall be necessary for his protection' when he was travelling to Canterbury. In 1340 he had quarrelled bitterly with the king over war finance, but was reconciled with him by 1343. The cathedral prior received the same indulgence.[52]

Tension arose in that weapons' accessibility aggravated quarrels; but publicly carrying and wearing them (but not normally in England being horsed and armed with banners displayed) was, with certain restrictions, a right of the privileged marking the public authority vested in any person of rank or office. Accordingly, fortification was rationed implicitly by rank and cost, rarely otherwise. Thus also the profession of arms conferred a de facto ennoblement. Of all arms the sword, though not the most lethal, was the most honourable and symbolic, figuring still

---

[49] e.g. Heslop, 'Orford', 36–7, 47–55; and *Norwich Castle Keep* (dating and interior under reconsideration), *passim*; also e.g. Dixon and Marshall, 'The Great Tower', 431: 'time and again buildings have been interpreted according to what has been expected rather than what is there.' See also Coulson, 'Some Analysis of Bodiam', esp. 54–66, and 'Cultural Realities', 201, Bibliography.

[50] *CPR, 1232–47*, 93, 116; renewed for two years, Aug. 1235; again anywhere not within forest jurisdiction ('covert'). 'Marauding Scots' (Parker, *Domestic Architecture*, ii. 22), lairing in Inglewood, were a problem after c.1314.

[51] *CPR, 1334–8*, 283. Cf. p. 256 (Apr. 1336), showing that the bishop of Ely owned large stocks of high-technology weapons (80 crossbows and three springalds, given to Edward III). Maitland, *Constitutional History*, 107. Woolgar, *The Great Household*, 67 (1448 Caister Inventory, items 24, 41).

[52] *CPR, 1343–5*, 115, With 'special protection' for both (so that any hostility to them was as though to the king); reciting their petition that 'diverse threats have been uttered by evil disposed persons and plots formed'. McKisack, *Fourteenth Century*, 153–4, 159–79, etc.

today at coronations and borne before the lord mayor of London.[53] In 1328 the
party of Queen Isabella and Roger Mortimer, having overthrown Edward II, in the
young king's name nervously instructed the mayor and sheriffs of London 'to
prohibit by proclamation in the City the bearing of arms, and to arrest and
imprison offenders until further order, sergeants-at-arms of the king, Queen
Isabella and yeoman of earls and barons excepted'.[54] Their status, symbolized by
arms (the sword especially), was sacrosanct. Shortly beforehand, the usurper
Mortimer (calling himself 'the king's kingsman') jointly with an adherent had
caused the subservient Chancery to award them licence 'to go armed with armed
men', despite the Statute of Northampton.[55] The corresponding architectural
displays of nobility and power were commonplace among the 'inns' and town-
houses of the City. Several of them had already been and were later to be dignified
by licences to crenellate. Edmund of Lancaster had apparently started the fashion
with his palace in Fleet Street, formerly of Count Peter of Savoy whose name the
site preserves, licensed in 1293. The wealthy Cahorsin pepperer, William Servat,
followed in 1305, adding battlements and a turret to the gateway to the forecourt of
his house in Bucklersbury; and in 1341 John de Pulteney of Penshurst (Kent) and
Cheveley (Cambs.), alderman and mayor, did likewise at his majestic house in
Candlewick Street, later grand enough to be occupied by the Black Prince.[56]
Attendants, officials, and retinues, large or modest, made up the complementary
human environment of great personages, graduated in size and type according to
the wealth and rank of each. Sumptuous hospitality, generally offered to all-
comers, was expected of them; but after the disastrous harvest and near famine of
1315–16, Edward II was moved to check such ostentatious consumption to avoid
both offence and disturbance. As rendered in the modern calendar (from the original French), the sheriff of each county, in market-places and public assemblies
where accustomed, was instructed to have proclamation made:

limiting the number of courses at the tables of lords and forbidding minstrels to go to the
houses of great lords beyond the number of three or four a day, unless requested to do so
by the lord; or to go to the houses of the smaller people at all unless requested to do so; and
ordering them to be satisfied with the meat and drink, and with the reward (*curtasie*) that
the lord may give them of his free will, without demanding aught else; and forbidding
messengers or couriers to come into the house unless they carry their lord's mail, or bear
a message to the lord of the house; and forbidding archers to come unless specially
requested.[57]

[53] Poole, *Obligations of Society*, 33–4; Oakshott, *The Archaeology of Weapons*, 90–2, 200–1; Crouch, *Image of Aristocracy*, 190–8.
[54] *CPR, 1327–30*, 355. Magnates had a bare sword borne before them. Also *CCR, 1447–54*, 182.
[55] *CPR, 1327–30*, 322, 336; McKisack, *Fourteenth Century*, 201, 203.
[56] Schofield, *Medieval London Houses*, gazetteer *et passim*; Coulson, 'Freedom to Crenellate', 120, and 'Battlements and the Bourgeoisie', 194 *et passim* for context of aspiration; *CPR, 1292–1301*, 30; 1301–7, 379; 1340–3, 331.
[57] *CCR, 1313–18*, 306: exemplar to the sheriffs of London. Lavish building attracted no such inhib-ition. Prestwich, *The Three Edwards*, 142. Woolgar, *The Great Household*, 21–9; ' "minstrel" encom-passed all entertainers' (p. 28).

The principle that every person should observe his or her proper station was balanced by dutiful charity and 'courtesy' by the rich and powerful. This ideal, not some medieval 'gun law', was the convention which chiefly restrained weaponry. The very detailed hierarchy of dress and costume laid down by the 'Sumptuary Law' of 1363 covered all degrees from agricultural servants to squires, knights, great merchants, and king's clerks.[58] The only other emblem of status mentioned concerned hunting with hawks. Directions were given how to advertise an escaped falcon *que soit perdu de son Seigneur*. Only if the finder were *gentile homme d'estat d'avoir Faucoun* could he keep, let alone hunt with, such a noble bird of prey; if a lowly *simple home* he had to give it up, if unclaimed within four months, to the county sheriff, receiving only his due expenses.[59] The re-enactment of these rules in 1402 restricted cloth of gold, velvet, ermine, and gowns touching the ground to men of knight-banneret's rank and above, with the significant exception 'saving always that *gentz d'armes*, when armed, may wear such clothing as they please'.[60] Belts and daggers, as an often highly ornate fashion-accessory (similarly 'harness of silver' or inlaid plate armour) were restricted, but with that theoretical and consensual latitude common to much medieval 'legislation', to men owning goods worth £200 or landed income of £20 per annum, a tenth of the level prescribed at this time to be regarded as of knightly rank. Significantly also, these rules arose not from royal fiat but, as usual, from petitions by 'the Commons in Parliament', behind whom stood the magnates of the land. The problem alleged was people apeing the great and getting above their station.[61] Similar conventional grades of society, mildly adjusted to the facts of wealth, were detailed in the resented 1379 Poll Tax categories (dukes paid £6. 13s. 4d.; graduated down to the basic 4d. for each adult). Though not a flat rate, it bore heavily on the poor, contributing to the 1381 Peasants' Revolt.

Being seemingly patriotically over-armed was unacceptable if it contravened courtly etiquette. Social imperatives prevailed over military. Thus, status-jealous elements in the 1389 parliament complained that, although by statute all men were bound to be armed and arrayed in defence of the realm 'according to their estate', 'there be many who equip themselves with arms beyond (*plus avant*) what their rank demands; and many have arms of greater value than the whole residue of their possessions'. They pointed particularly at people in potential danger, namely those 'living on the sea-coast, on the Marches of Scotland, and

---

[58] Regarded as a governmental ploy to make knighthood more attractive; M. Powicke, *Military Obligations*, 172–3, although the 1379 move to restrict some clothes to knights with £40 p.a. was a (failed) Commons' initiative, successful in 1479. Cf. Baldwin, *Sumptuary Legislation, passim*; *Rot Parl*, ii. 278–82; iii. 66; v. 504–6.

[59] Additional rules for 'falcons, laner, or laneret, austour or other falcon': *Rot Parl*, ii. 282b, penal incarceration prescribed (two years) plus paying the falcon's value, for 'any thief or concealer'.

[60] *Quant ils sount armez* (i.e. in military array, literally 'on parade': *Rot Parl*, iii. 506 (76); v. (1463/4), 504–6 (iv). An attempt in 1379 to tighten up the £40 p.a. cloth grades ('fur, cloth or ribbon of gold, cloth of silk'; also jewellery—*perree* ie. *pierrerie*) was rebuffed: ibid. iii. 66 (55).

[61] As late as 1482 the dress, etc. rules were kept in adapted form, *inter alia* restricting masculine display to lords: *Rot Parl*, vi. 220–1 (1).

other marches'.[62] The social impropriety was not all: because so much wealth had
been invested in body armour (horses and weapons are not directly mentioned),
detailed as comprising 'plates, habergeons, bacinettes [inner or sole helmets],
aventails [mail neck-guards], gloves of plates, actons, palettes, protective jacks,
and other armours', such items as these were being seized by parish priests to get
paid their due burial fees when the owners died. To judge from the response of
Richard II's regency council, the implied harm to Border and coastal defence
caused the inner circle of courtiers as little concern as did the latent anticlerical-
ism or the equally fashionable emulation in arms encouraged by over forty years
of the French war.[63] At a time of worsening fortunes and even threats or raids, this
is to be noted. Lesser gentry and aspiring freeholders, rather below the social level
of the knightly and sub-knightly county membership of the Commons, were the
offenders, to judge from the type of armour mentioned.[64]

Fortresses were entirely a product of this militant noble milieu. Those who had
the governance believed it to be quite as vital to preserve the social structure as to
defend the peace or even the land itself.[65] Class prevailed, not the Utilitarians'
concept of commonwealth as 'the greatest good of the greatest number'.
Fortresses served primarily the privileged nobles, prelates, and upper bourgeoisie;
the urban populace less directly, and the rural majority more remotely still,
though effectually as refuges in case of war. Although all able-bodied 'fencible
men, from 16 to 60', were potentially liable to serve in the levée en masse, such
fellowship of arms, equally for technical as for socio-economic causes and particularly in France, increasingly excluded the peasants, jacques and roturiers, whether
serfs or euphemistically menu peuple and simples hommes. But if we must abandon, for England or for France, the anachronistic image of whole nations unitedly
at war,[66] to regard the smaller constituent 'companies', based on the regional,
family and tenurial affinities of the great nobles, as perversions of some corporate
ideal ('bastard feudalism') goes too far. Although large numbers of retainers, in
fourteenth- and fifteenth-century France and England, wearing their lord's badge
and receiving his 'livery' of food and clothing (and 'maintenance' in various
guises), could endanger the peace, they were socially quite as natural as 'private
fortresses' and as noble arms-bearing.[67] How this latter endured in full vigour is

---

[62] Rot Parl, iii. 57–8 (14); 82 (xi, 36). Self-prescribed social control explained such rules, not
'national service'. Fortifying in the north reached further down the ranks of gentility; Emery, Greater
Medieval Houses, i. passim.

[63] To the plea that all arms should go to the executors or heirs en defens du Roialme (routine pretext
for privilege: Coulson, 'Battlements and the Bourgeoisie', passim), the reply was: 'Let it be done as duly
and formerly.'

[64] e.g. Edwards, 'Personnel of the Commons', i. 150–67; and now the History of Parliament volumes,
e.g. Raskell et al. (eds.), The House of Commons, 1386–1421, detailed biographies. See weapons
prescribed to each sub-knightly class by wealth in 1285, Stubbs's Select Charters, 466 (vi). Illustrated in
Edge and Paddock, Arms and Armour of the Medieval Knight, ch. 4.

[65] For urban aspects see Coulson, 'Battlements and the Bourgeoisie'.

[66] A tendency naturally strongest in studies of the Hundred Years War (nn. 91–2 below); cf. K.
Fowler, Age of Plantagenet and Valois, esp. ch. 2, 'The Protagonists'.

[67] Lewis, 'Organisation of Indentured Retainers', is the classic e.g. 200–12. Hicks, Bastard
Feudalism, esp. ch. 4. Lewis, Later Medieval France, e.g. 101–10.

shown by the laws of Charles VI (1380–1422). His advisors saw no inconsistency with preservation of the peace, perceiving no incompatibility between privatized power (judicial or military) and public order.[68] The literature of civil violence concerns fortresses only to the extent that they manifested aristocratic military force in general. W. Douglas Simpson, in the 1930s and 1940s, tried to show that internal security had some effect on castle planning, but succeeded only in drawing attention to the increasing degree of segregation within large houses of the lord from his *familia* of relatives and closer dependants drawn from his wider connections and 'affinity'.[69] Great 'households', in their barely differentiated 'civilian' and 'military' guises, were smaller versions of the king's own entourage and court.[70] In some form they long outlasted the middle ages, through the early-modern period, and even endured into the era of industrialization, persisting into the period overshadowed by the First World War. In recovering the world to which castles belonged, it is useful to recall how recent is the disappearance of what Harold Perkin has called 'the old society', architecturally perpetuated by 'the country-house'. Mark Girouard has done much to illuminate a way of life which made domestic servants a major category of employment still in late-Victorian Britain, and which sustained and multiplied landed estates with their parklands and capital mansions in almost true sub-medieval style.[71] The 'house of the castle' (*domus castelli*), increasingly integrated (in England by the later fourteenth century) with the walls, had essentially the same elements as the Jacobean and later mansion. The great hall with detached kitchen, buttery, pantry, and screens passage at the 'lower end', facing the dais, oriel window, and high table at the 'upper' end, with attached lord's chamber (-block) and lower end apartments, the courtyard plan and turreted gatehouses, all with crenellated parapets, reflect a socio-political reality of remarkable longevity.[72] What the castellated mansion continued to proclaim, the landscaped setting also still echoed.[73] It may in royalist ideology have become true by 1649 that 'subject and sovereign are clean different things', in the words of Charles I from the scaffold, but the medieval monarch and 'prince' had coadjutors in the nobility who were his partners in government as of right. Fortresses were of the woof and weft of this seamless socio-political

[68] Typical measures 1410–11 (Charles VI), *Recueil Général*, vii. 243, 244–8, 251: n. 74 below.

[69] Simpson, 'Bastard Feudalism and the Later Castles'; nn. 93, 130, 230 below. Thesis criticized Cruden, *Scottish Castle*, 87–90; Coulson, 'Some Analysis of Bodiam', 64–6 (p. 64, n. 21 refs.); e.g. Faulkner, 'Domestic Planning', and 'Castle-Planning'. Cultural view, Coulson, 'Fourteenth-Century Castles', e.g. 142–7 (Maxstoke).

[70] Crouch, *Image of Aristocracy*, ch. 9; Given-Wilson, *English Nobility*, 87–103; Woolgar, *The Great Household*, 8–20.

[71] Perkin, *Origins of Modern English Society*, pp. 143, 418, ch. 2. In Wood, *English Medieval House*, the sociology tends to be submerged by the architectural detail.

[72] Brown, 'English Castles, 1154–1216', ch. 1, on *Domus in Castello*; also Thompson, *Decline of the Castle*, chs. 4, 5, 7; Howard, *Early Tudor Country House*, ch. 2, illustrations *passim*.

[73] Coulson, 'Bodiam Castle: Truth and Tradition', esp. 7 (RCHME Plan); Everson, 'Bodiam Castle and Designed Landscape', 79–84 (with further suggested sites, p. 83; updated C. Taylor, 'Medieval Ornamental Landscapes'); also Mowl and Earnshaw, *The Lodge as Prelude to the Country House*; Curtis (ed.), *Monumental Follies*, county gazetteer.

fabric—along with both the aura and, no less, the abuses of the aristocratic power expressed by arms.

3. 'Adventures', 'Feats of Arms', and Fortresses

Accordingly, just as hunting, arms-bearing, estate management, and fortifications were the proper occupations and adornments of medieval aristocracy, so also was the mimic warfare of tournaments and jousting—as was war itself, a hobby which might have dire consequences for society when it overflowed. The umbilical link between weapons and heraldry, being a warrior and being noble (characteristic of, but not unique to, this period), was expressed in microcosm by the permission granted in 1411 by the militarily and politically ineffectual Charles VI of France to the ushers (*huissiers*) or doorkeepers of the king's hall entitling them 'to bear arms like nobles' when off duty. They were a non-menial, but lowly, class of royal domestics.[74]

Jousts illustrate other concomitants of the same thought-world to which fortifications belong. As both a soldierly and chivalric profession, frequent warlike exercise and collective association were necessary to the knighthood (in the broad sense) in order to develop skills of horsemanship and dexterity and to foster group identity. The large literature on various aspects of this reflects their sociological, technological, and romantic appeal.[75] Assemblies were sometimes termed 'Round Tables', symptomatic of the widespread Arthurian cult. The new orders of knighthood set up by European princes in the fourteenth century promoted the movement, so organized tournaments combined social junketing with the more courtly individual encounters using blunted and special equipment (so that tournament armour gradually diverged from 'field armour'). Nearly complete warlike realism was obtained in the *mêlée* or mock battle between groups of combatants on occasion. Such displays of martial prowess sometimes degenerated into veritable battles in miniature which threatened to spread beyond the 'lists' and the authority of the marshal, risking extraneous faction-fighting. But danger to the peace (that to victims' souls was frequently urged by the Church) seems rarely to have been highly rated. More often objections were due to interference with a greater event elsewhere, perhaps with a rulers' 'national' war, or to nervousness on the part of individual rulers, such as Henry III and Richard II, or to political tensions. One example of many in the last decade of Edward II's faltering reign is the proclamation ordered to be made by all the sheriffs of England in February 1320, in this instance not only prohibiting 'tourneying' without royal licence but also 'forbidding any armourer to prepare, complete, or sell any arms for exercising such feats of arms, or to take to send them to any place, until further order'.[76] After the king's flight to South Wales to take (unavailing) refuge with

---

[74] *Recueil Général*, vii. 251; n. 391 above.
[75] e.g. Barber and Barker, *Tournaments*, with original MS illustrations; Buttin, 'La Lance et l'arrêt de cuirasse'; Prestwich, *Armies and Warfare*, 217–31; also Duby, *France, 987–1460*, 156, 181, 193, 199 (episodic comment).   [76] *CCR, 1318–23*, 224.

Hugh Despenser and in his castles of Caerfilly and Neath (January 1327), similar nervousness produced from the Isabella and Mortimer 'regency' an order to the sheriff of Norfolk and Suffolk (March 1327), 'to forbid any earl, baron or man at arms from tourneying, making bourds [tilting], or jousts, seeking adventures or doing other feats of arms without the king's special [specific] licence', arresting offenders' persons and equipment and reporting their names.[77]

Comparisons with France show somewhat different but generic practices. Since warfare itself was 'nationalized' as royal war in England to a degree barely reached (for good and for ill) in France by the end of the fifteenth century (Italian wars, 1495), permissive governmental supervision of noble military freedoms in general was correspondingly looser across the Channel. Similarly, the formalized licensing of fortification in France was essentially franchisal, not almost wholly royal as in England.[78] Surveillance of military liberties was also more akin to the erratic and diversified 'arms-ban' primarily exercised by the greater feudatories (including the king) than it was to 'policing'. Increasing but episodic supervision from Paris is exemplified by Philip IV's ratification of the right of those barons of Auvergne who exercised capital jurisdiction (*haute justice*) 'to bear arms, even on another's lands, for the purpose of governing (*justicier*, as calendared) their lands and fiefs' (1304). A region of strong 'liberties', Auvergne's noble freedoms were exempted from King Philip's centralization in return for a voluntary subsidy.[79] It looks like an abdication of state power on the king's part, but this was normal *laisser-faire* policy. In February 1339 when, as he hoped, on the point of seizing the remnant of the Plantagenet duchy of Gascony from Edward III, a similar but more extensive charter of noble privileges was issued by King Philip VI, hoping to appease those who had identified their own interests with nominal English rule hitherto.[80] It was certainly an act of political expediency (and of some cynicism, given the Capetian and now Valois record hitherto in Gascony and elsewhere[81]), but it does show what was traditionally acceptable and considered normal. To Bernard Ezi, lord of Albret, and to his momentary adherents, Philip granted, *inter alia*, that:

they may when they consider it expedient declare (*indicare*), prosecute, and continue wars between themselves, discontinuing them for the duration of any royal war . . . They may also bear arms and use them according to what we shall more fully ascertain was formerly the custom of the Aquitanians in the time when the king of England held [*sic*] the duchy.

[77] *CCR, 1327–30*, 47; also ibid. 407 (Aug. 1328), 413 (Oct.), 544 (May 1329), etc.
[78] Coulson, 'Freedom to Crenellate', cf. 'Sanctioning of Fortresses in France' (also examines prohibitions). By Continental standards, England's licensing was that of a great franchise (e.g. Coulson, 'Castellation in Champagne', 356–8, 'Seignorial Fortresses', App. B, 4; also Gascony, 1214–1317, App. B, 3). It was similarly non-restrictive, almost apolitical, and honorific to applicants.
[79] *Recueil Général*, ii. 817.
[80] Ibid. iv. 380–2 as '1331'; cf. Vale, *Origins of the Hundred Years War*, 113 (p. 199); *Ordonances*, ii. 61–3. Philip VI ratified the treaty by his lieutenant, King John of Bohemia (killed when blind at Crécy, 1346), previously employed 1332, 1337 (Contamine, *Guerre, état et société*, 50–1).
[81] Coulson, 'Community and Fortress-Politics in France', esp. 107–8. Labarge, *Gascony 1214–1453*, 102–24.

We grant in addition to the barons and nobles of the duchy that the castles, fortresses, or other such places (*loca*) of the lord d'Albret and of the other nobles whosoever, wherever they may be and whatever their legal position (*status*), they being obedient to us and to our successors, shall not be damaged (*derimantur*) in whole or in part, nor taken away, nor transferred from the lordship, control (*subjectione*), or fief (*ressorts*) of their present or future lords, unless it be with the consent of those concerned; or unless demolition or forfeiture be due by previous sentence for crimes and wrongs under written law (*de jure scripto*) or according to the accepted custom ruling where the place is located, according as it may variously prescribe.

Regarding their style of life, potential defectors to the Valois party were also reassured (with whatever credibility experience allowed) that royal officials would not interfere with the nobles' courts of justice, unless by way of appeals—a crucial reservation: it was chiefly by exploiting to (and beyond) the limit the king's right to hear appeals as superior or overlord that Plantagenet ducal powers and territory had been clipped. Castles were at the nub of this: by arbitrary confiscation and the penal or even vindictive damaging of fortresses (here—*castra, fortalitia aut loca alia*), kings since Philip III (1270–85) had taken to previously novel lengths the principle traditionally expressed by rendability (and otherwise) that fortresses were subordinate to public priorities. They had targeted castles so to evoke respect (and fear) from obstreperous lords and whole regions.[82] The qualified but clearly defined military and jurisdictional freedoms of nobles which normally obtained were, for instance, recognized in a not dissimilar *pancarte* to the nobles of the eastern marcher province of the Dauphiné in 1349, by Humbert, the last non-royal dauphin. Fortresses again figured importantly. Humbert's designated successor Charles, as king (Charles V, 1364–80) accepted and perpetuated the entire detailed constitution in 1367. The viscounts of Turenne upon the north-east frontier of Gascony were among many others who enjoyed similar franchises as of right.[83] The similarities with England are more important than the differences, for our purposes. What were quite comparable powers and outlook on the part of the great and lesser English nobles were to such an extent modified by the precocious monarchial tradition in England, by the realm's much smaller size and population, and by greater centralization of government (despite the more 'continental' situation obtaining in the Scottish March and in Ireland[84]), that contrasts can slip out of proportion when viewed in too Anglocentric a way. 'Parliamentary' views of English constitutional development during the Plantagenet–Valois conflict of 1337–1453 beg many questions, but 'France' acquired a standing army and a quasi-absolutism by the end, ruling over the whole 'kingdom' and a country not much less large than modern France once the Burgundian challenge had been defeated (1477). Given these two (somewhat opposite) transformations, to focus upon the essential broad social similarities,

---

[82] Coulson, 'Valois Powers Over Fortresses', 150–9; Louis VII (1137–80) and Philip II (1180–1223) had been more scrupulous, unlike King John of England, Coulson, 'Fortress-Policy', esp. 33, 36.

[83] *Ordonnances*, v. 34–56; vi. 522–6 (1280–8, confirmation of 1378).

[84] Tom McNeill's *Castles in Ireland* is a valuable assertion of the social determinants.

which are the area in which fortresses lived, breathed, and had their being, cannot avoid cutting across boundaries of time and geography, as well as of thought. Our own prejudices are part of the problem. The pre-war and draft/conscription generation in Britain (but not in the United States) is fading, and with it the tendency to classify fortresses as belonging to the department of war. 'Law and order' is also encumbered with present-day values.[85] By comparison with the quasi-universal community of aristocratic culture throughout medieval (western) 'Europe', the modern criterion of the 'public interest', by which judgements in retrospect have to be made, is a hard taskmaster. Tournaments bring several of these issues together.

In a sense tournaments were a noble 'free-for-all', 'wrong but wromantic' since sometimes lethal—one of those diagnostic 'military' freedoms, which despite their apparent excesses were readily sanctioned by the kings of France and England. That they were not so much tolerated as taken as natural exposes the falsity of regarding them (like 'private castles') as nervously controlled and licensed spasms of chivalric barbarity. That the differences between the English and French treatment of tournaments were so slight is one demonstration of this point. So is the proximity of tournaments and war. King Philip IV, at the time of the 1296–7 Anglo-French war over his partial but peremptory seizure of the duchy of Gascony (1294–1303), promulgated the rule (November 1296) in his court of the parlement:

> ... for the common advantage (*utilitas*) and needs (*necessitas*) of his realm, that for the duration of a royal war there shall be no other war waged in the realm; and should, perchance, any war have been commenced (*mota*) already between anyone, then it shall by truces or pacts, valid for one year, be discontinued in accordance with the customs of the locality, renewing the truces on expiry as may be needed until the king's war has been concluded.[86]

Guerra, although I have conventionally translated it as 'war', had normally very little in common with modern, all-out, national hostilities. The term 'feud' ('vendetta' is still worse) is almost equally inapt, and 'private war' is tendentious. The legitimate conflicts Philip IV wished to interrupt were distractions of effort, like tournaments. 'National' war was different essentially because it was royal war. Philip the Fair's contest with Edward I, brought to a head by the endemic rivalries between sailors of Normandy and of the Cinque Ports, caused pressure to be put by the French on Gascony. Edward then used the commercial leverage of English supplies of raw wool, on which the great towns' manufacturing largely depended, to exert influence on (French) Flanders. Economic, diplomatic, and political measures then escalated into war with an initially consensual invasion of Gascony. Ultimately this led to the spasmodic hostilities of the 'Hundred Years War' after 1337.[87] Concentrating the forces he might summon to meet Edward I's

---

[85] Barber, *Two Cities*, esp. i. 2 and iv. shows the culture-gulf.
[86] *Les Olim*, ii. 405.
[87] e.g. Vale, *Origins of the Hundred Years War*, ch. 2, 'Anglo-French Civilization'.

defiance[88] also required Philip to interfere temporarily in trials by battle (*gagia duelli*), and to refer such cases to the royal or feudatories' courts, as appropriate, to be pursued *via ordinaria* without (as it was thought) the option of testing God's intervention. King Philip also ordained that 'warhorses (*equi armorum*) or weapons shall not be seized for debts'; and moreover that, 'during the king's war, no tournaments, jousts or cavalcades (*equitaciones*) should be held'. There was no intention to stop knightly exercises, whether their warlike or their purely social elements predominated. Both aspects were equally present in a permissive exemption obtained from Edward III in January 1345. It heralded a chivalric prelude to Edward's no less chivalric but far more deadly engagement the following year:

... at the request of the knights of the county of Lincoln, licence to Henry de Lancaster, earl of Derby, whom they have elected for life to be captain for this purpose and other captains to be chosen after him, to hold jousts at Lincoln on Monday in every Whitsun week, whether or not it be in time of war and irrespective of any forbidding of arms-bearing in the realm in time of peace; provided always that if the king on the said feast have any assembly elsewhere within the realm, by reason of a round table, jousts or other deeds of arms, the jousts at Lincoln shall not be held but the captain shall appoint another day for them within one month.[89]

Edward Plantagenet was already a renowned captain, with youthful experience against the Scots.[90] His cousin, Henry of Lancaster, was shortly after to win dazzling successes evicting the Valois forces from western Gascony,[91] and in 1346–7 there followed his own victory at Crécy-en-Ponthieu and the capture of Calais, which events together transformed the position of the English underdog. But all that is familiar—perhaps too familiar. If this book avoids glamorous epic and 'blood and guts' history, what Philippe Contamine has called *l'histoire batailles*, it is partly because even when anachronism is resisted and insight is deepened by studying the social and administrative infrastructure, military history still harks back to the same self-serving soldierly view of warfare as a universal engine of civilization. Among much other distortion, it has caused medieval fortresses to be gravely misrepresented.[92] Max Weber's cynical defini-

[88] A notional temporary handover, closely akin to rendability, was to have symbolized Philip's lordship of the duchy, purging 'contempts' by Edward I including alleged refusal to deliver Gascon fortresses to Philip's summons (*Thesaurus Novus*, i. 1249–52 of 1293). Nine years' partial French occupation ensued: *Rôles Gascons*, iii. pp. cxvi–clxxxii (Bémont). F. Powicke, *Thirteenth Century*, 665–6; Vale, *Origins of the Hundred Years War*, ch. 6.
[89] *CPR, 1343–5*, 379 (translation slightly adapted). Similarly, Edington, 'Tournament in Medieval Scotland', 46–62.
[90] Nicholson, *Edward III and the Scots*. 'Unmilitary' kings, notably Henry III and Richard II, were less confident.
[91] e.g. Burne, *Crécy War*, 100–13; cf. Curry, *Hundred Years War*, 61; Lodge, *Gascony 1214–1453*, 125–34, on Henry of Grosmont's 1345–50 campaigns and character.
[92] Contamine, *Guerre, état et société*, p. vi *et passim*. Succinctly put by Michael Howard: 'Whether one likes it or not, war has played for better or for worse a fundamental part in the whole process of historical change': quoted Allmand, *Hundred Years War*, 172. Hewitt, *Organization of War*, pp. vii–viii,

tion of the state as 'the agency which holds a monopoly of legitimate violence in the area under its control' fashionably exalts the influence of warfare. Medieval war was a frequently grim and destructive aristocratic game which has been allowed to taint fortresses.[93] If they are to be defended (section 4 below), it must be on more authentic grounds. But it may finally be noted that state control of war came very late: in England not until the later Tudors. In France it was effectively delayed by royal minority and civil war until the ministry of Cardinal Richelieu (1624–42). State control over the behaviour of nationals on the high seas came later still. Medieval mutual reprisal and licensed privateering (if not outright piracy), under 'letters of marque and reprisal', persisted beyond coastal waters until the early nineteenth century.[94] John Locke, in 1691, while lauding the triumphs of Reason, had to admit that sovereign rulers were, towards each other, 'in a state of nature'.[95] However makeshift and fallible the rules, it is permissible to argue that overlordship and the Church had already equipped medieval Christendom with political ethics and arbitral mechanisms such as have only recently been excelled. Medieval agonizing over the ideals of the Just War and the moral lessons of church mural paintings of the Last Judgement spring to mind.[96] It is fashionable to be cynical in this area, to see chivalry as sublimated thuggery, the Crusades as racist brutality, and the religious vocation as sham. But only if private fortification and its remote relative 'private war' are seen under colour-corrected light can their social impact be objectively assessed.

4. Castles: Innocent or Guilty?

Having now overhauled the appropriate criteria, it is possible to examine further what reality may lie behind the ambivalent suspicion, academic as well as popular, directed against 'castles'. Monarchism is partly responsible. The Stuart lawyer and eventually Chief Justice, Edward Coke, thought that unlicensed fortifying would endanger society. In Denis de Salvaing's already modern perspective (1668), *châteaux* were 'gallstones in the bowels of the state'—definitely anti-social. He not less unjustly, and in the monarchist spirit already strong in the writings of

---

was cautious. Battle injuries and mortality (e.g. Visby, 1361; Towton, 1461—cases of excavated mass-graves) should not so impress moderns: Gillingham, *Wars of the Roses*, 42–4, 133–5; Contamine, *War in the Middle Ages*, 257–9, pl. 10.

[93] Coulson, 'Cultural Realities', *passim*, bibliography. McNeill, *Castles in Ireland*, 52–5, 75–7, 104–117, is cautious over military determinism; cf. Simpson, 'Tower Houses of Scotland', 229–42; Ramm *et al.*, *Shielings and Bastles*, for socio-economic analysis. Aesthetic case summarized in Coulson, 'Structural Symbolism'.

[94] e.g. Marcus, *A Naval History of England*, ii. Index 'Privateers'. Hinsley, *Power and the Pursuit of Peace*, 282–3.

[95] Locke, *Two Treatises*, 294.

[96] e.g. Keen, *Laws of War*, 63–188; Runciman, *History of the Crusades*, i. 83–92. On 'Dooms', e.g. Rickert, *Painting in Britain*, 186, 188–9; Boase, 'King Death', 204–44 (esp. p. 228); Caiger-Smith, *English Medieval Mural Paintings*, pls. xii, xvi, xviii, xix, etc. Some impartiality marked arbitrations, e.g. by Louis IX for Henry III in 1264, Treharne, 'The Mise of Amiens', 223–39; by Edward I over the Scottish succession, F. Powicke, *Thirteenth Century*, 598–608.

other early modern *feudistes*, said of *la guerre privée* that 'the lords of fiefs . . . no longer exercise the power which they formerly arrogated to themselves (*s'attribuoient*) to make war by their own authority'.[97] But facing both ways with one foot in the records of the past at Grenoble, Salvaing was aware that fortresses had been rendable to the lord (not to the king as such) by his feudal right; that the lucrative building of seignorially expressive dovecots (*colombiers*) involved the *seigneur haut-justicer* in some provinces. He believed rightly, in part, that whereas *maisons fortes* were legitimated by the right of self-defence, any more elaborate fortifications required licence from the high-justice overlord. But he was in no doubt that because weathercocks (*giroüetes*) 'do not arouse any jealousy in the lord', pretentious though they were, they did not require his licence. This last point he deduces, with lawyerly retrospection, from a verdict by the parlement of Paris in February 1659, sentencing 'some burgesses of Lyon (*dép*. Rhône) to have the battlements and loops (*meutrières*) of their houses within the jurisdiction (*justice*) of Montagny demolished at once', on demand of the baron suing in right of his heiress-wife.[98] Such assertions of the social superiority of *noblesse* provided the antiquarian lawyers of the *ancien régime* with ambitious clients and lucrative consultancies. Their interest records what remained of medieval aristocratic privilege once most of the functions of government (including war, but not 'justice') had been yielded to or taken over by the Crown.[99] In England under Charles I a nearly final takeover was accomplished by the Long Parliament, but to the disadvantage of the Crown. A more drastic change occurred in France in August 1789, commonly regarded as the end of the *époque féodale*. Thereafter the perception of the role of military force and judicial power (but compare the modern English JP) which had been wielded by nobles in contravention of the new image of the 'private citizen' steadily darkened. How the castle-image then fared, influenced deeply but equivocally by the late-eighteenth- and nineteenth-century Romantic Movement (e.g. by the 'Gothic novels') explains many of today's assumptions. It deserves full and separate treatment. What cannot be omitted is some flavour of the original and contemporary literature of castle-phobia.

That fortresses were hostile to the public interest is, in part, a tradition surviving from a minor but well-publicized medieval literary genre, chiefly ecclesiastical in origin. The most influential 'English' specimen is without question the entry for 1137 in the Peterborough continuation of the Anglo-Saxon Chronicle, written with some kind of hindsight nearly twenty years later by a monk of that once-major Anglo-Saxon abbey. It was, in fact, one specimen of a literary genre

---

[97] Salvaing, *De l'Usage des Fiefs*, 83, 289; similarly Brussel, *Nouvel Examen*, i. 140–4. Reynolds, *Fiefs and Vassals*, 1–14 *et passim*, strips away historiographical accretions but has little on fortress-customs (eg. pp. 170–1, 261, 242). It is optimistic to disregard as now rare the view of 'the whole middle ages as dominated by unruly barons and knights who made war on each other and tyrannized over hapless peasants from their castles' (ibid. p.476); cf. Duby, *France 987–1460*, 55–90 (esp. p. 87). The caricature is far from dead, even academically.

[98] Salvaing, *De L'Usage des Fiefs*, i. 265–74; nn. Part I, 88, 188, 278 above. Valuable (like Brussel) historiographically and for many lost documentary excerpts.

[99] Valuable insights afforded by Mackrell, *'Feudalism' in Eighteenth Century France*, esp. 53–69.

particularly closely related to a passage in William of Malmesbury's *Historia Novella* in which William generalized his indignation at the motte castle thrown up within the abbey precincts at Malmesbury, albeit by the local bishop, Roger of Salisbury, during the civil war of the reign of King Stephen. Worcester Cathedral close also suffered an intruded motte. William, writing at the time, moderated his language a little—'there were in England as many lords, or rather tyrants, as there were lords of castles, each claiming to protect but in fact exploiting the surrounding area'.[100] Such underdog views are quite usual. Usurpation undoubtedly occurred during 'The Anarchy' of 1139–53, but such stories were blown up by the monk of the ancient Saxon abbey into perhaps the best-known of all English atrocity tales:

Every great man built himself a castle and held it against the king; and they filled the whole land with these castles. They cruelly oppressed the wretched men of the land with castle-works. When the castles were made, they filled them with devils and evil men. Then they took those men who they imagined had any property, both by night and by day, peasant men and women, and put them in prison for their gold and silver, and tortured them with unutterable torture; for never were martyrs so tortured as they were . . . [lurid details omitted] . . . Many thousands they killed with hunger. I neither can nor may tell all the wounds or all the tortures which they inflicted on wretched men in this land; and this lasted the nineteen winters while Stephen was king; and ever it was worse and worse. They laid imposts on the towns continually, and called it *censerie* [or *tenserie*]. When the wretched men had no more to give, they robbed and burned all the towns, so that you might well go a day's journey and never find a man sitting in a town or the land tilled.[101]

'God and his angels slept' is the familiar epitome. How bad things actually were, where and when (not everywhere or all the time); how much should be discounted for interested exaggeration, and for pious martyrology, and how much for 'creative' retrospection—matters less for our purpose than that hatred of castles and their possessors existed and was easily played upon. Local memories of Geoffrey of Mandeville are a likely ingredient. Certainly, allegations that as many as 1,115 new castles were built (about thirty-five are known to have been), and that they were termed 'adulterine' because they were 'unlicensed', as has been generally supposed (when it was merely a term of abuse, no licensing 'system' then existing), are no more or less than later castro-phobic fantasy.[102]

[100] E. King, *Anarchy of King Stephen*, 1–2 (Introduction). John of Worcester told a similar tale in the late 1130s, also possibly influencing William of Malmesbury, probably embellished by Peterborough *Anglo-Saxon Chronicle*, E version (Part I n. 275 above).

[101] Clark (ed.), *The Peterborough Chronicle, sub* 1137. D'Auvergne's, *The English Castles*, 4, 10–11, exemplifies popular but serious comment, still traditional, e.g. Pounds, *The Medieval Castle*, 29–30. Cool reappraisal, White, *Restoration and Reform*, 1193–65.

[102] Coulson, 'Castles of the Anarchy', esp. 75–6, 'Freedom to Crenellate'; 98–9 *et passim*. Specific reassessments: White, 'Continuity in Government'; Blackburn, 'Coinage and Currency'; Hollister on 'baronial responsibility' in 'The Aristocracy'; and Holt, 'The Treaty of Winchester'; King (ed.), *Anarchy of King Stephen*, chs. 4, 5, 1, 9. On the supposed 'anarchic feudalism' of the 1148/53 Chester-Leicester *conventio* in context, see Coulson, 'French Matrix'.

Reactivating the pre-Conquest obligation of *burh-baut*[103] (as *operationes castellorum*), in response to local disturbances and organized campaigns, was no doubt doubly unpopular when peasants cultivating clergy land were affected (as Peterborough's may well have been). Such labour, as after 1066, was 'cruel oppression'. Urban prosperity and trade were patchily affected by 'The Anarchy', but the bedrock complaint echoes the Anglo-Saxon Chronicle's epitaph on William the Conqueror, who 'had castles built, and poor men hard oppressed' (1087).[104] Castles, more than the wholesale and grandiose rebuilding of cathedrals, abbeys (Peterborough itself notably), and other great churches, trumpeted a shameful and alien takeover, still alive in popular memory, and revived the continuing shock of harsh and exploitative domination. Castles, be they royal or seignorial, could hardly have been popular, except to 'the Normans'. In the form experienced after 1066 they were somewhat 'un-English', as Orderic had said.

Castle-phobia, then, derived from the victim-view, from modern statism, and from propaganda. The sort of abuses of local power (castle-based or not) which any abeyance of higher governance permitted, tends to be known only when it was in the interest of the literate and privileged to advertise or record it. Ecclesiastics when jealously defending their own interests adopted a different tone as themselves the proud proprietors of castles (Part I, Ch.3 above). Any modern judgement, having the majority in mind as well as the elite, cannot light-heartedly salute 'castles' as 'one of the good things in life' (especially under the narrow definition).[105] But to go to the other extreme would be no less unbalanced. Fortresses, whether familial, royal, corporate (urban or ecclesiastical), or just ephemeral, were prominent facts of a life which for the poor was often grim. When fortresses are pilloried in the records, the axe being ground was not the cause of social equality or, necessarily, the greater local good. So the reasons for the demolition in 1151 of the castle of Montreuil-Bellay in Anjou (*dép.* Maine et Loire) by Count Geoffrey Plantagenet, father of Henry, duke of Normandy and future king of England (1154–89), require caution. Gerald de Bellay may not have been quite the classic 'robber baron' of romance, medieval or modern. Orderic had cast Robert of Bellême in that role. But by this charter Count Geoffrey (1129–51) was parading his actions as the pious hero of 'order':[106]

In the name of the Holy and Indivisible Trinity, whence all good doth proceed: I Geoffrey, son of King Fulk of Jerusalem, and by the Grace of God[107] count of Anjou, do hereby recall

---

[103] With bridge-repair and army (*fyrd*) service composing the *trimoda necessitas* attached to land-tenure: Hollister, *Anglo-Saxon Military Institutions*, 59–63.

[104] n. 119 above. Purser, 'William FitzOsbern', e.g. 136, n. 17 on *Anglo-Saxon Chronicle* resentment at his castle-work demands as regent during William I's absence.

[105] Brown, *English Castles*, 26.

[106] *Recueil Henri II*, 23–5; also *Regesta*, iii. 6–7 (1151): 'relative à l'abolition des mauvaises coutumes établies . . . par Giraud Berlai' (Delisle's gloss-heading). Chibnall, 'Orderic Vitalis on Castles', 43, 46–8, 52, 53–4, 56; affirmative in tone. General Anjou context 1108–80, Dunbabin, *France in the Making*, 333–40.

[107] In 1272 Philip III objected to the count of Foix using this traditional comital style: cf. Langlois, *Philippe III*, 190. Even the minor count (Geoffrey) of Perche used it in the late 12th century: K. Thompson, 'The Counts of Perche', cat. nos. 148, 150 (pp. 192–3)—ref. acknowledged.

to the memory of those who shall come after me (*successorum meorum*) so that they shall not pass into oblivion the events here following, which I have caused to be recorded in writing—Let everyone, present and future, know that by reason of the faithlessness and insufferable savagery (*infidelitatem et intolerabilem sevitiam*) of Gerald de Bellay inflicted by him on all the churches subject to his power and cruelly vented on their possessions, I have with the aid of God besieged and at great expense, with the very greatest and most prolonged labours, wholly destroyed the fortifications (*menia*) of the castle and totally uprooted its great-tower (*turrem*) and the entirety of its buildings.

Gerald had not prudently removed himself in good time ('Gerald, and those who were with him there, I hold captive'), with the result that his surrender and defeat were as complete as his humiliation.[108]

Only in legend were fortresses arrogantly 'impregnable', even the most costly. Destroying heavy masonry by 'mining' beneath the foundations, as was quickly done in 1215 by King John to the keep of Rochester (Kent), was a special skill, as devastating to occupied as to undefended buildings.[109] Blockade was tedious but relatively inexpensive. Long sieges (three years at Montreuil-Bellay) were not diminished in the telling. Accounts can give mistaken notions of some advantage of defence over attack.[110] Buildings were always vulnerable. Geoffrey's strong word *eradicavi* indicates mining, not the longer process of pulling down with ropes and tackle.[111] King Philip I, not the most energetic of the slothful early Capetians, in exemplary fashion destroyed by mining the rogue tower built within the precinct of Compiègne abbey (*dép.* Oise) in 1092.[112] Even a rock-based castle as magnificent as Crusader Krak des Chevaliers (Syria) had its outer enceinte penetrated in this way (1271) and soon after surrendered.[113] No fortress-commander could risk attack unnecessarily nor 'laugh a siege to scorn' (*Macbeth*).[114] The Hospitallers lost Marqab, near the Mediterranean coast, to the Sultan Kelaoun in 1285, after eight days of tunnelling through rock beneath an outer bastion and eventually under the truly great 'tower' itself.[115] Long and active assaults were

[108] 'On the whole it is uncommon to find the lord of a castle besieged in it . . .': Brown, *English Castles*, 186. In August 1216 King John allowed John Marshal not to stay in Worcester castle as constable if Prince Louis should besiege it; similarly Walter de Lacy at Hereford: *Rot Litt Pat.* 194a. Bradbury, *Medieval Siege*, 72, 85–6, 278; Index 'Mining', etc.

[109] The famous 40 pigs were carcasses, 'of the fattest and least good to eat' (*Rot Litt Claus*, i. 238b) not animal torches (Painter, *King John*, 363).

[110] n. 269 below. The traditional tenet that defence ('strength' of fortifications) enjoyed an ascendancy over siegecraft prior to chemical artillery (cannon) drastically underrates earlier technology: e.g. Thompson, *Military Architecture*, ch. 4; Brown, *English Medieval Castles*, ch.7; Pounds, *The Medieval Castle*, 106–13; Bradbury, *Medieval Siege*, ch. 9. The human factor and structural weakness always mattered.

[111] But King John certainly exaggeratedly used *funditus prosternere* etc. (Ch. 3, sec. 1 below).

[112] *Recueil Philippe* I, 315–17; *fecimus predictam turrim penitus . . . fundotenus suffodere* (but a verbose, ecclesiastically composed, polemical text with 'literary' influence).

[113] Detailed account, D. King, 'The Taking of Le Krak des Chevaliers in 1271', 83–92.

[114] But e.g. Warren, *Henry II*, 39.

[115] C. Marshall, *Warfare in the Latin East*, 233; and 241–8, on 'The effectiveness of sieges' (with tabulated detail).

highly expensive[116]—that of Castle Bytham (Lincs.) in 1221 cost at least £500[117]—
but even the strongest and most resolutely defended place would succumb if
attacked with sufficient time, determination, and equipment.[118] The risky decision
to resist was not lightly taken and involved many factors. To attack a first-class
fortress was a serious commitment of resources and prestige but, in consequence,
any rebel against authority faced death without ransom. Pre-emptive or purely
punitive demolitions, as notably by Henry II (below), were more likely, quickly
effective and usually quite cheap.[119] Fawkes de Bréauté, in 1224, suffered for seizing a royal judge and immuring him within the Beauchamps' castle of Bedford of
which he had custody. For this flagrant contempt of the young Henry III, the king
took and—very exceptionally—almost totally obliterated it as a condign example,
at a minimum recorded cost of well over £1,400.[120] Fawkes, the former loyal
servant of King John, to whom he owed his entire wealth and position, had
prudently left the place under the command of his brother, who had refused every
opportunity to surrender. Fawkes was thus able to negotiate his own banishment,
escaping the capital sentence inflicted on his luckless brother and on eighty
members of the foolhardy garrison. The moral was clear: last-ditch resistance,
even with such an expensively updated baronial castle as Bedford, incurred
normally unthinkable penalties. Instances of such resistance (for which castles
were seldom designed) were thus extremely rare. Public authority was not easily
defied. Although castles had assisted the expansion, for instance, of the Angevin
state, they were potential liabilities and costly assets.[121] This was the further
message of Geoffrey Plantagenet's charter of 1151, which might seem to slur all
'baronial' castles. Geoffrey had his piety, as well as his power, to proclaim. Having
recounted the fall of Montreuil-Bellay, the propaganda opportunity was not to be
missed (with becoming modesty):

Now, having thus vigorously acted, and acknowledging that it was not by my own but by
God's might that Gerald was defeated; I hereby establish, having taken counsel, that all the
customs and exactions which Gerald and his forbears have usurped within the ecclesiastical obedientary of Méron [by Saumur, near Montreuil-Bellay] shall be wholly quashed. I
grant further that the lordship of Méron shall be quit of all dues, as Geoffrey 'Greymantle',

[116] Hence clemency rewarded early surrender and severity punished obduracy: Bradbury, *Medieval Siege*, index.
[117] Expenses on the Close Roll (*Rot Litt Claus*, i. 449b, 450, 454b, 453–4, 457a) alone total £498 (arms £47; wages £129 included). G. Fowler, 'Munitions in 1224', 117–32.
[118] The Mortimer terms to Caerfilly (Glam., S. Wales) first refused, then had to accord pardon to Hugh Despenser III in 1326–7: *CPR, 1324–7*, 341, 344; *1327–30*, 10, 12–13, 18, 37–9.
[119] Brown, 'List of Castles', *passim*.
[120] Carpenter, *Minority of Henry III*, 365–70. Costs on the Close Roll alone, including £51 for arms, but only £12 wages, etc. (*Rot Litt Claus*, i. 606a–612a, 613a–618b; ii. 4a, 7–8, 10b, 27b, 65a, 109b, 139a, etc.). Baker, 'Bedford Castle', 15–22; cf. e.g. £500 spent 1247–50 on the Blackgate, Newcastle: Brown *et al., King's Works*, ii. 747; Brown, *English Castles*, 191–4; Bradbury, *Medieval Siege*, 140–1.
[121] Southern, *Making of the Middle Ages*, 80–90, on Geoffrey Greymantle (958–87), and Fulk the Black (*Nerra*, 987–1040), still locally celebrated as a great castle-builder (13 at least were claimed as 'built' by him). On the deterrent effect of the fall of Bedford and of Kenilworth long afterwards see M. Prestwich, 'The Garrisoning of English Medieval Castles', 198.

our predecessor [958–87] once granted, reserving to the comital court only cases of homicide, rape and arson. . . . All this have I done for the welfare of my soul (and others'). Should any heir of mine, or anyone else, infringe this grant, may he incur the Divine wrath. Done in the chapter[-house] of Saint-Aubin, in the presence of the abbot and of the bishops of Normandy and of Anjou.

Geoffrey (traditionally 'Plantagenet' for his badge, the gorse-like 'lowly broom') had conquered Normandy by 1144, during King Stephen's conflict with Angevin partisans in England, and had passed the title of duke to Henry, his son by Mathilda, as grandson of Henry I. Geoffrey, otherwise nicknamed le Bel, was the 'mere count' who had married Queen Mathilda, styled 'the Empress' as widow of the Emperor Henry V. He was no doubt keen to vindicate his position, in part by razing Montreuil-Bellay as a gesture to the Church, although it seems to have been a long-established castellary. Indeed, the castle was subsequently rebuilt.[122] The legalities, along with clerically inspired stories of Gerald's 'savagery', matter less than the display of righteous and 'enlightened', Church-blessed comital authority.

How seriously atrocity stories in general should be taken is, with castles, an acute and an unusually pervasive problem, one compounded by sado-romanticism. Our subconscious images, exemplified by the novelists' picture of the terrible 'Reginald Front-de-Boeuf' in his castle of Torquilstone (*Ivanhoe*), or of 'the butcher of la Brohinière' in Conan Doyle's *Sir Nigel*, tend to be disowned by the sober scholarship of medieval technicality.[123] 'Atrocity' is so tinged with propaganda as to be hard to handle. It remains strong in popular culture. Although intellectualized into the background, it persists in the 'dungeon' resonances of the video and theme park. Without taking either medieval polemic or modern romanticism too literally, some of the milder forms of this genre describe events which could have happened, although much was probably fantasy then, just as it is now. A hint, unfortunately no more, reminiscent of Edgar Allan Poe's horror stories, occurs in the prosaic proceedings of the parlement of Paris for 1255 under Louis IX. It is an order from this body, the royal executive and jurisdictional council, following complaint that the lord of Montréal (*dép.*Yonne) in Burgundy had imprisoned several priests and also gravely maltreated them. Reportedly, he had even 'caused a certain priest to be consumed by flies (*muscis comedi*)'. Previously, the royal council had responded (with strict propriety since Montréal was said to be a ducal fief) by requesting the duke of Burgundy to use his lordly right 'to place such keepers in the castle as should avert such behaviour there in the future'. The councillors had also put it to the duke that, in the circumstances,

---

[122] Finó, *Fortresses*, 17 (with the flourish of Geoffrey consulting Vegetius for guidance in conducting the siege); Mesqui, *Châteaux-forts*, 252–3. Chibnall, 'Normandy', 93.
[123] Contrast e.g. William Golding's novel *The Spire* with Fitchen, *Construction of Gothic Cathedrals*. Socio-ideological studies least evade the problem e.g. Cohn, *Pursuit of the Millenium*; Barber *Two Cities*, 168–92, 'Popular Religion and Heresy'; Ladurie, *Montaillou*. Bradbury, *Medieval Siege*, index 'Atrocities'; Brown, 'Observations on the Tower of London', 106–7; Gillingham, *Richard the Lionheart*, 4. Plessis-lès-Tours in Scott's *Quentin Durward* differs completely from the pacific reality.

he would be within his rights to pay for these caretakers 'from the revenues of the said castle and castellary'. Because dues were mostly payable at the *caput*, this would be convenient, but under rendability putting in troops was at the cost of the lord of the fief, not the castellan, as was any extra-normal provisioning.[124] Circumstances at Montréal were exceptional, but the position of the delinquent vassal, whom the duke had neither restrained nor summoned to court to defend himself, was not to be jeopardized. Saint Louis accordingly sent to Montréal the local bishop (Auxerre) together with the royal castellan of Noyon (*dép.* Oise) to intercede directly. The latter (deliberately) was a connection by marriage of the culprit. His authority and relationship enabled him to be trusted to satisfy both ecclesiastical indignation (often dressed up in lurid language) and the family interests, while tactfully minimizing the intrusion upon the duke of Burgundy's jurisdiction.[125] The matter, even discounting the voracious flies, was delicate: since no case had come before the ducal court, there could be no appeal from it to Paris to give the Crown lawful cognizance. The incident in this record is an isolated though notable one—it contrasts with increasing direct and harsh royal intervention markedly stepped up from the accession of Philip IV (1285).[126]

Kings, unlike 'barons', are seldom accused of abusing their power. It may be observed that the humane conscience of the powerful has seldom been a sufficient restraint, even when the Christian ethic has been more effectively implemented than it was in the middle ages. In much of England for much of the time that sanction tended to be efficacious. Rulers as well as prelates were so eager to exploit any available moral high ground that allegations of flagrant misconduct need to be cautiously salted, as Lewis Warren showed regarding Roger of Wendover's slandering of King John.[127] The propaganda associated with Henry I's expulsion of Robert of Bellême from his earldom of Shrewsbury in 1102 makes truth diffi-cult to disentangle. In his Norman lands in France, Robert subsequently became one of the archetypal tyrannical and sadistic castle-lords of tradition. His English fortresses (Arundel, Bridgenorth, Shrewsbury, Tickhill), it is worth noting, were of little use to him against the king's brief and ruthless campaign. Politically isolated in advance, Robert was easy, if not fair, game. Tom Paine's view (*c.*1790) that 'one honest man is worth all the crowned ruffians living' may go too far, but anti-royal and anti-social acts should be distinguished. Kings could do wrong, despite A. L. Poole. 'Robert de Bellême', he wrote in 1955, 'the finest military architect of the day', was 'typical of the Norman baron at his worst . . . whose ingenious barbarities were proverbial'.[128] It is a lame truism that harsh times bred

---

[124] *Actes du Parlement*, i, i, 5 (cursory calendar); *Les Olim*, i. 438 (partial text). Locally declared for Auxonne *villa cum castro* (*dép.* Côte-d'Or), 1197: *Layettes*, i. 193–4. Explicitly *c.*1283 by *Beaumanoir*, 351–2.

[125] Richard, 'Châteaux, châtelains et vassaux' wrongly ascribes rendability to the 12th-century asser-tion of ducal power. It is already developed by 1024–8, Coulson, 'French Matrix', 79–81.

[126] Coulson, 'Valois Powers over Fortresses', 152–9; also 'Community and Fortress-Politics in France', 82–4, 86–9.   [127] Warren, *King John*, 11–16.

[128] Poole, *Domesday Book to Magna Carta*, 105–6, 112, 117–19; Hollister, 'Campaign of 1102 Against Robert of Bellême', 193–202; for Orderic's condemnation, Chibnall, 'Orderic Vitalis on Castles', 45, 48, 49, 52. Bridgenorth keep was probably mined by Henry II, surviving in ruins to show the king's power.

hard men; but it is slipshod thinking to tar fortresses with the same brush, as guilty by association. Castles of all kinds were residences, not torture-chambers. Their possessors' opportunities were vast and often not conducive to moderation. The evil lay in the socio-political structure, most of it dictated by economic circumstances, however much alleviated by the Christian ideals represented by an often corrupted Church.

There is little cause to suppose that France was materially worse. That 'barons' were always properly 'controlled' in England, by contrast, is patriotic gloss.[129] One item of contrary evidence made its way on to the Patent Roll in 1311 concerning the remarkable behaviour of John de Somery, who powerfully added to Dudley Castle (Staffs.).[130] In the abbreviated calendar translation of the appointment of a commission to enquire into accusations made by William de Bereford, chief justice of Common Pleas, it is stated that John:

has obtained such mastery in the county of Stafford that no one can obtain law or justice therein: that he has made himself more than a king there; that no one can dwell there unless he buys protection from him either by money or by assisting him in building his castles; and that he attacks people in their own houses with the intention of killing them, unless they make fine for his protection.

Significantly, John himself obtained the inquiry, doubtless exaggerating the defamation he alleged against de Bereford 'and others' so as to make it easier to refute. A month later proceedings were revoked by Edward II's council without explanation.[131] Mostly later English evidence of 'noble brigandage' complements this picture of a racketeering castellan, but de Somery apparently cleared himself—and the usual polemical discount should be applied. Earl Warenne threw his weight about at Lewes in 1266–72, but fortresses were inert instruments. If a problem at all, they were the least of the repercussions of any power-devolved aristocracy exercising extensive military, fiscal, judicial, and other governmental functions. Castles' conspicuousness has attracted mythology like no other aspect of noble privilege. Some cautious advocacy is offered in this and the next Part (e.g. Part III, Ch.3) to adjust the usual castle-image—politically negative, technologically neutral (but amoral), and socially detrimental—to accord better with the probabilities. The moral aspect of castles does deserve consideration. Obviously, the more virile virtues in society were, not unnaturally, accompanied by some of

---

[129] Extreme version, Poole, *Domesday Book to Magna Carta*, 150; on Geoffrey de Mandeville, 147; ch. 5 *passim*.

[130] Simpson, 'Castles of Dudley and Ashby-de-la-Zouche', wrote (p. 151) that de Somery is 'the authentic picture of a baronial thug, of the type that was to become increasingly common . . .'; theme moderated in Stones, 'The Folvilles of Ashby-Folville, Leicestershire', 117–36. Dudley tower-house on the early motte has been extensively excavated: 'Medieval Britain', *Med Arch*, 29 (1985), 203–5 (Plan); 30 (1986), 172; 31 (1987), 166–7; 32 (1988), 286.

[131] *CPR, 1307–13*, 369. The site was sensitive in 1218 and in 1262: Coulson, 'Freedom to Crenellate', 130. Earl Warenne over-asserted his rights at Lewes castle *c.*1266–72: (*Rot Hund*, ii. 201a, 209a, 210a, 213b), imposing murage on knights fees to wall Lewes town and claiming free warren in all his barony. He persecuted Robert Aguilon (thrice licensed to crenellate Perching in consequence), imprisoning him and others (*CPR, 1258–66*, 307, 381; *1266–72*, 189).

the virile vices; but the rich and powerful knew well and often pondered the force-ful parable of the beggar and the rich man ('Dives and Lazarus'). Role-reversal in the afterlife is a frequent theme. That parable was a favourite subject of Henry III for mural paintings.[132] He was not alone in taking to heart the duty of almsgiving which wealth imposed. Ecclesiastical poor relief, especially at monastery gates, also complied. Such ethical teachings and practice beneficially moderated social relations and fostered such social harmony as was compatible with severe inequal-ity. The labour of the peasant was his appointed lot in his earthly existence, with mostly slight chance of improving it. The economic servitude of the urban poor was little better, sometimes worse.[133] But protection was their due in return, and equality in the Day of Judgement was God's promise—even to the extent of reversing the fortunes suffered, or enjoyed, in life (as, famously, in Dante's *Inferno*).[134]

Ideals are a less fashionable subject than analysis (part-realistic, part-cynical) of the practices which often disregarded them. A case which accords with this sceptical genre of 'realism',[135] highlighting a monastic attitude to serfdom which was far from Christian, came to the parlement of Paris in 1334. The monks of Cîteaux itself in Burgundy, mother-house of the once-great reforming order of Cistercians, had vindictively pursued a man who had formerly been their serf but became free as a citizen of a royal town. They resorted to having him assaulted and imprisoned.[136] He had flaunted his prosperity and new status as a king's burgess by adding a dovecot and a small tower to his house, properly attributes of gentle birth and symbols of his social 'arrival'. In revenge the monks' servants had attacked, pillaged, and wrecked the buildings. Fortunately for him it was a matter of royal pride to uphold the acquired rank of the king's protégé—so the abbey was formally punished when he sued in Philip VI's court. An incident at Waltham Abbey, Essex, in 1366, has similar overtones.[137]

'Castles' as symbols of higher status, though usually no more than castellated *maisons seigneuriales* for the gentry and knightly class, differed only in degree of pretension and potential defensibility from the Cluny ex-serf's country *manoir*.[138] Their normal peaceful existence as country seats, embellished with the militant noble display celebrated in panegyric (Part I, Ch.3), was remote from horror, brutality, and the clash of arms. This was how Gerald of Wales, in the mid-twelfth century, liked to recall his family castle of Manorbier in Pembrokeshire. The scenic aspect of a multifaceted institution cannot be recalled too often:

---

[132] Brown *et al. King's Works*, i. 128; ii. 950; Luke 16: 19–31.

[133] Hilton, *English and French Towns*, 61–3, 134–41 (comparisons); Schofield, Vince, *Medieval Towns*, 211 (archaeology).

[134] Boase, 'King Death', esp. 204, 228, pls. 51, 233.

[135] Coulton, *Ten Medieval Studies*, Prefaces (1906, 1915), against Roman Catholic and other false apologetics; cf. Tawney, *Religion and the Rise of Capitalism*, i (esp. 67–74); also the (underappreciated) rigorous scepticism of monarchical rectitude in Jolliffe, *Angevin Kingship*, e.g. 343–50.

[136] *Actes du Parlement*, ii, i, 98.

[137] Coulson, 'Hierarchism in Conventual Crenellation', 81; n. 335 below.

[138] e.g. Mesqui, 'Maisons, maisons-fortes ou châteaux', *passim*; Coulson, 'Castellation in Champagne', esp. 350–6.

The castle called Maenor Pyrr . . . is distant about three miles from Penbroch. It is excellently well defended by turrets and bulwarks, and is situated on the summit of a hill, extending on the western side towards the sea-port, having on the north and south a fine fishpond hard by its walls, as conspicuous for its grand appearance as for the depth of its waters. On the same side is a beautiful orchard, bounded by a vineyard and elsewhere by a wood, remarkable for its projecting rocks and by the height of its hazel trees. On the right hand side of the promontory, between the castle and the church, by the site of a very large lake with a mill, there flows down the valley a rivulet of never-failing water, where the sand-dunes are piled up by the violence of the winds. Over to the west the Severn Sea, bending its course towards Ireland, enters an incurving bay at some distance from the castle.[139]

Giraldus Cambrensis describes his beloved Manorbier, as R. Allen Brown says, 'in terms reminiscent of a modern advertisement for a gentleman's country seat—which indeed in a contemporary sense it was'.[140] But not, it must be added, in any narrow sense: 'castles' were normally as public in lodging extended households and as open to visitors as any 'stately home' in its original heyday. All were on show. The chronicler-courtier, Norman-Welsh by birth, dwells on the castle-landscape with as delicate an appreciation as any manuscript illumination or any late-medieval ('Renaissance') artist. Even so early, and in South Wales still in Anglo-Welsh contention,[141] Manorbier like so many castles has 'little or no military history'.[142] The serene aristocratic atmosphere of the pages of *Country Life* magazine fits it much better than any soldierly image of a 'strategic network of fortresses'. The depth and scope of this ambivalent dual personality breaks apart modern categorization. For good and for ill, castles were an integral feature of the noble and larger society which produced them, participating as much in its economic and cultural life as, albeit marginally overall, in its military activities. In so far as these activities were 'innocent', fortresses were certainly not guilty.

[139] *Giraldi Cambrensis Opera*, Brewer *et al.* (eds.), i, *De Rebus a se Gestis*, 21. Langland, *Piers Plowman*, had a darker vision than *Sir Gawain* or Joachim du Bellay; excerpts, Evans, *Flowering of the Middle Ages*, 12, 134, 316.

[140] Brown, *English Medieval Castles*, 177.

[141] Davies, 'March of Wales', 41–61 (esp. 45–6, 48, 55, 58, 60).

[142] D. King, *Castellarium Anglicanum*, *sub*. Pembs. Different perspective, J. A. Green, *Aristocracy of Norman England*, 172–93.

Peacekeeping at Home and Abroad

Since fortifying, like the 'arms-ban', operated as a noble perquisite, the restraining hand of the 'public interest' must be pursued also in other directions than 'military activities'. Political as well as social motives were involved. Royal and magnatial concerns loomed large. In continuing to enquire whether, to what extent, and how militant individualism was channelled in ways compatible with notions of morality, good governance, and of civilization there is risk. Modern analogies may distort. Cynicism in the guise of realism is an easy way out—but it is clear that in the middle ages public spirit was expected to provide a large part of the solution. Not so much because sense of duty fell short, but because of centralizing ambitions, the role of the Crown (also of the great feudatories, especially in France) necessarily expanded; but centralism was obviously greater in England, albeit from a more 'advanced' state already in 1066. Castles supply a certain perspective on these wider questions—as well as perhaps undue scope for moralizing.

1. Fortifying and 'Purprestures', 1217–c.1274

The contrast, for instance, is especially strong between the direct intervention by Henry III's regency government (1216–28) and the situation in Nevers, Auxerre, and Tonnerre, in north-east central France, disclosed by the 1235 peacekeeping edict of Count Gui of Nevers. He, conjointly with the Countess Mahaud (in the fragment of the text which survives), confined their prohibition of illicit violence to the demolishing or burning of 'houses' (*domus*), 'excluding from this statute all fortresses (*forterescie*)'. The count shared with his magnates (*principes terre*) the jurisdiction of offences against such lesser seignorial buildings (peasant dwellings were not intended)—but he and the nobles he took into counsel before issuing the edict did agree to enforce a common banishment of any convicted offender who rejected an award of damages made against him in the seignorial court. That house-destruction (jealousy is a likely cause) was also a 'civil wrong' is shown by the proviso that the victim had to give consent before the outlaw could be allowed to return.[143] In Britain also, nobles of castle-holding status were

---

[143] *Layettes*, iii. 289–90. Next to royal demesne, once part of the duchy of Burgundy: Duby, *France 843–1460*, 215 (map). Banishment argued to be 'not an admission of weakness' of law, but due process: Summerson, 'Structure of Law Enforcement', 313–27.

public authorities in their own right—but theirs was a more junior partnership in government.

Public law in England, even during the pacification following the civil war between King John's party and the rebel, French-supported barons, reached further. In May 1217 the royalists had triumphed in the confused mêlée or 'Fair' of Lincoln, fought largely within the city walls and around the castle, which was the second Battle of Lincoln.[144] In the reissue that year of Magna Carta a new section dealing with fortifying was added at the end by the regent, William Marshal, to help consolidate the peace, just won but still precarious. Castle-building as such was not put in the dock (the fact deserves emphasis)—indeed, licensing was complimentary and recognitory in nature, as we have seen, not at all the precaution of watchful government that has been supposed.[145] Licences 'to crenellate' in England had tentatively begun with the implementation of Chancery reforms at John's accession (notably the enrolling of copies or abstracts of documents issued), but licensing was in no sense a 'system', still less one of 'rationing'. Recipients were self-selecting, applying if the honour or convenience to them justified the trouble and (modest) expense.[146] Accordingly, the presumption was by 1217 very clear that fortifying done as an act of war differed radically from the continual peacetime process of repairing and improving castles and founding new ones. Even association with actual violence of whatever sort tainted a wholly lawful noble activity (as building has been at all periods). What now mattered to the Marshal's government, in ostensible theory—and it was applied with latitude—was fortifying done in wartime. This created a presumption of illegality. The new Magna Carta clause (no. 47) stated:

We have established also, by the common council of our whole realm, that all adulterine castles (*castra adulterina*), namely those which have been constructed or rebuilt (*reaedificata*) from the commencement (*a principio*) of the war moved between the Lord John, our father, and his barons of England, shall at once be demolished (*diruantur*).[147]

Such works of war (actually very few), potentially implicated with unlawful force by the abeyance since September 1215 of the king's peace, were prima facie also irregular—or at least the doctrine to that effect strengthened the Marshal's hand against surviving pockets of disaffection.[148] The old Stephanic word *adulterinus*, coined by clerical invective and originally meaning little more than 'misbegotten' or 'improper', had acquired some official standing, but it was still ambiguous and

---

[144] Powicke, *Henry III and the Lord Edward*, 12, 736–9 (sketch), cf. Oman, *Art of War*, i. 412–19. Castle also indirectly involved in the first battle of Lincoln (1141—Stephen captured).

[145] On imagined licensing 1066–*c*.1189 see Coulson, 'Castles of the Anarchy', 79–80, 86–90; also Eales, 'Royal Power and Castles', esp. 69–74. For revision of historiographical doctrine see Coulson, 'Freedom to Crenellate', and for urban applications, 'Battlements and the Bourgeoisie'; for 'religious', see id., 'Hierarchism in Conventual Crenellation'.

[146] Summarized, Emery, *Greater Medieval Houses*, i. 174–80. Finó, *Fortresses*, 72–4, 461 ('droit de fortification' *sic*); cf. Coulson, 'Sanctioning of Fortresses in France'.

[147] *Stubbs's Select Charters*, 292–303 (June 1215); 336–9 (amended after John's death); 341–4 (p. 344, cl. 47). Carpenter, *Minority of Henry III*, 21–7, 50, 60–3, 74, 142 (Magna Carta). See also below.

[148] e.g. Painter, *King John*, 348–77.

not a legal term.[149] As the text shows expressly, 'adulterine' did not mean 'unlicensed'. Since the point has been much confused, in the belief that 'private' fortresses were guilty until proved innocent (specifically, that only royal licence could regularize their presumed irregularity), some further clarification is needed.

Globally, the building of fortifications was subject only to appropriate genuflection to the lord of the fief. There was apparently no prohibition in law, British or Continental. Apart from tenurial propriety, a more general rationale applied: it was a cardinal principle of law that an act of violence should not create *de jure* right—however frequently in practice accomplished fact may have eventually been accepted. Regularizing wartime fortification was consequently a normal feature of treaties of pacification; and encroachments on lands and rights had similarly to be at least notionally rectified in order to restore the *status quo ante bellum*. War was an intrusion into normality (though it might also be legitimate), like any *indebita novitas* lacking precedent. This prevalent idea was often expressed by the term *purpresture*. In England the question was a separate topic of inquiry in Edward I's great inquisition initiated in 1274—item 13 out of fifty-one in the formal questionnaire sent out to each locality.[150] The 'purprestures' reported under oath by the jurors empanelled in each township and rural administrative district, eventually copied out and condensed into the Hundred Rolls, are in great part minutely technical and often voluminous. Civil wrongs were incidental. Offences by royal officials had much attention, but encroachments on the king's, not on others', rights are asked about. Many originated in the 'time of war' between the conflicts of Northampton and Evesham (1264–5) and during its aftermath, but it was a general start-of-reign clear-up. Numerous minor trespasses, such as building upon 'royal' (i.e. public) streets and sites in towns, are detailed. With striking nonchalance one Northamptonshire panel mentioned among other derelictions which were alleged against Berengar le Moine, an overambitious minor knightly tenant of Ramsey abbey[151] (Hunts.), (namely failing to pay, or withdrawing, a 20 shilling rent and missing two Hundred Court attendances in 1272–3) the fact that he had: 'constructed a castle (*castrum*) at Barnwell ten years past; and in the village he holds a weekly market for one day and a fair every year; and for five years past he has held an assize of bread and ale, by what warrant they know not.'[152] Berengar's aspirations exceeded his grasp; but this complete, if minor, seignorial package, with elegant little castle to match (with double cross-slot crossbow loops, impressive but poorly designed), together with a sort of weights-and-measures inspectorate (receiving the fines for infraction) standing as

[149] Ecclesiastical invective perhaps coined by Abbot Suger of Saint-Denis (*c.*1081–1151): Coulson, 'Castles of the Anarchy', 75–6. On the almost ritualistic involvement of castles shown by one chronicler, Speight, 'Castle Warfare in the *Gesta Stephani*', 269–74.

[150] *Rot Hund*, i. 13–14; with translation, Cam, *The Hundred*, 248–57 (pp. 250–1), *et passim*. Prestwich, *Edward I*, 92–8.

[151] In 1275 he owed £120 to the Jews; bought out by Ramsey in 1276; 'pensioned off' with Chatteris manor for life: E. King, 'The Abbot of Peterborough as Landlord', 33–5 (due to Edmund King).

[152] *Rot Hund*, ii. 7b.

a token but eloquent share of public authority, was but nominally anti-social.[153] Such perquisites were lucrative as well as prestigious. Nothing whatever was done about the new castle.[154] Under the item 'of sheriffs taking bribes', the Norfolk jurors had a great deal more to say about William Belet's *castellum* at Marham. This and Barnwell are the only such cases in the Hundred Rolls. Belet, in contrast, had punctiliously had his inconspicuous 'moat' at Marham licensed to be crenellated (as a *domus*) in June 1271, but the resultant castle (owing its title, as so often, to the licence and to the tenant's status[155]) was associated by the jurors in 1272–3 with extortion, though by the sheriff's sergeants, not by Belet. A man arrested at Swaffham Fair apparently paid them 6 shillings not to be put in the prison at the castle. Trifling as this was, it formed part of an extraordinary orchestrated chorus of sustained vilification.[156] Among the 'purprestures' within the Hundred, said the local worthies: 'William Belet has constructed and erected a certain castle at Marham, injurious (*in prejudicium*) to the king, to his castle of Norwich [35 miles east] and to the entire country (*patria*), in that should war arise—may it not!— the king's enemies could take refuge there and ravage the whole country and the adjacent religious houses.' This is arrant nonsense. A franchisal ('private') gaol at Marham, 8 miles west of Swaffham, could well have been used entirely legitimately (without official venality) to discipline miscreants at the fair. The only surprise is Belet's complicity—and that his modest ditched castle possessed a prison worth the name[157]—but the insinuation is all of a piece with that fantasy about Norwich and invasion, which even in *c.*1337–45 or *c.*1369–88, when the French war went badly, would still have been highly implausible here.[158] Ecclesiastical machination is to be inferred: Castle Acre Priory is 3 miles north of Swaffham.[159] The clergy were practised in embroidering the public good.

They, or those whom they influenced, then tried again, giving evidence on the questionnaire item 'Liberties granted which impede the general operation of law (*communam justitiam*)':

---

[153] Not 'slighted' but respectfully quarried for stone for the adjacent early 17th-century manor house: plan and plate, Toy, *Castles*, 133, 142, 154. Barnwell priory took no action, seemingly (cf. Marham) and the whole follow-up was lax: Sutherland, *Quo Warranto Proceedings*, e.g. 96–8, 118, 123, 136–44. Licences to crenellate Sheffield (1270), Aberystwyth town (1277), Braybrooke (1304), Bletsoe (1327–*CPR*, 1266–72, 447; 1301–7, 207; 1327–30, 130; *CChR*, 1257–1300, 206) were formally paraded (not 'tested') in 1278–81, 1329, 1330–1, 1344: *Quo Warranto*, 75b, 187a, 573b–575b, 817a–818a.

[154] In 1340 the escheator's officious seizure of 'the manor' for acquisition by Ramsey without (mortmain) licence was overruled by the king's council: *CCR, 1339–41*, 347–8.

[155] *CPR, 1266–72*, 540: 'to William Belet and [exceptionally] his heirs.' It was a single knight's fief, of his wife's lands, paying 10s. p.a. for 'guard' of Dover. Henry III's gift to him of 20,000 'slates' (*sclattorum*; i.e. stone roofing slabs: Salzman, *Building in England*, 232–3), delivered to repair Boarstall (Bucks.), showed exceptional favour: *CLibR, 1267–72*, 179. Non-ecclesiastical recipients are rare.

[156] *Rot Hund*, i. 436b, 458a, 519b. Corruption at Sheffield castle prison was by the lord's seneschal selling freedom to indicted criminals: ibid. 110a.

[157] On 'private jails' e.g. Cam, *The Hundred*, 74, 213, 235; 'private' gallows and (in England supervised) hangings, 128–9, 177–8, 209, 213, 235.

[158] Town authorities rivalled ecclesiastics in the inflation and manipulation of 'invasion scares'. Coulson, 'Battlements and the Bourgeoisie', esp. 121, 124, 136, 141, 144–6, 155–6, 162. Petition-speak was a special genre.

[159] Historical-architectural overview, Butler and Given-Wilson, *Medieval Monasteries*, 183–6.

They say that William Belet has raised a certain castle at Marham, as has been deposed else-where ... which is damaging (*ad nocumentum*) to the counties of Norfolk, Suffolk, Cambridge, and Huntingdon, and greatly to the peril of the lord king and his heirs, both with regard to the Isle of Ely [35 miles SSW], where the king's enemies lately laired-up (*se receptaverunt*); and to the town of [King's] Lynn [13 miles NNW] which has always adhered loyally to the king; as also by reason of many other dangers more fully set out in the inquiry depositions (*inquisitione*).[160]

Wild exaggeration was common currency, but tension ran high. Not long after-wards an armed affray occurred at Marham itself. In July 1276 Thomas de Walsoken (by Wisbech, 14 miles W) was pardoned the 'outlawry published against him for assaulting the castle of William Belet at Marham', having proved his alibi, being out of England at the time.[161] He sounds like a scapegoat. Whatever the fears left by the aftermath of the Barons' War, following the fall of Kenilworth castle in December 1266 (after a siege of six months), and by the occupation until the summer of 1267 by some of the Disinherited rebels of the natural fortress of Ely,[162] the trivial site-works at Marham Castle[163] merited no such tantrums. Belet himself was peaceable and insignificant. His 'homestead moat' (as sites of this order are called in the older volumes of the Victoria County History) would not be heavily manned. Nevertheless it aroused a co-ordinated local and clerical campaign, backed by the burgesses of Lynn who, in favour-seeking style, paraded their public spirit. The *castellum* these cohorts denounced (and attacked) is described in an inquisition of 1308, on the death of Belet's widow, as no more than 'a capital messuage' to its miniscule home farm (in 1315 another inquisition put this at 119 acres of arable, etc.).[164] It was far from easy to cast Marham in the stan-dard 'villain' role of ecclesiastical invective, customarily modelled on those many biblical kings denounced by Temple chroniclers for 'doing evil in the sight of the Lord'—but the clergy coalition did its best. In the long term such smears have been remarkably successful. At Marham ulterior motives are obvious: Belet's site closely adjoined the Cistercian nunnery of Marham priory and other religious establishments. There was a Gilbertine priory north of Shouldham, just over a mile away (WNW), and another house slightly further to the NNW.[165] These will

---

[160] *Rot Hund*, i. 521a. Inquiry was procured: *CIM*, *1219–1307*, 329, no. 1089; but in vain: cf. King, *Castellarium Anglicanum*, 309 (unduly credulous). Courtesy of E. Rose, CAO Norfolk, in sending copies of county records (Feb. 1989) acknowledged.

[161] *CPR*, *1272–81*, 152–3: not a 'gentleman' to go abroad; perhaps a sailor, very possibly randomly suspected of being one of a band from Bishop's Lynn. On Lynn's slow emancipation see Coulson, 'Battlements and the Bourgeoisie', 182–3.

[162] e.g. Prestwich, *Edward I*, 56–9.

[163] A small sub-rectangular earthwork 'moat' at grid ref. TF 7053–0956: Leah *et al.*, 'Earthworks at Hills and Holes, Marham', 506–11 (ref. due to R. Liddiard).

[164] *CIPM* v. nos. 14, 600. ('120 acres arable, 5 acres pasture, 60s. rent of assize; held of the king in chief for 1 knight's fee', 1308). Belet was long dead. Ralph Bigod, her son and heir by a subsequent marriage, was then 'aged 50 and more'.

[165] OS Maps 124, 125 (King's Lynn; Fakenham); Knowles and Hadcock, *Religious Houses*, 272, 275, 194, 196; also Westacre (Augustinian, 6 miles NE), ibid. 179; and the great Cluniac priory of Castle Acre (8½ miles ENE of Marham moat), 96, 98–9.

be the 'adjacent religious houses' which the hostile jury ('packed', as was not unusual) had asserted, in the revealing verbiage of clerical invective, might be 'ravaged', together (for good measure) with the whole country within a 30-mile radius. Some of this tract of country lay within the notional *districtus* of Norwich, thus justifying dragging in its castle. This is authentic 'rape and pillage' stuff—but still bogus.

In fact, it is likely that William Belet in 1271 may have anticipated difficulties from the Cistercians. Showing access to influence was one reason for getting a licence. Desiring to set his stamp upon his wife's property, now held jointly, he took advantage of his state of royal favour (shown by an exceptional gift, of 'slates' for his main house at Boarstall) to get a licence just in case. Caution was needed, since Marham priory had been incorporated into the powerful family of Waverley abbey (Surrey) in 1252, soon after the nunnery at Marham was founded (1249). Henry III's formal sanction of fortifying at Marham gave no protection—it may indeed have had the opposite effect: challenging not only the nuns nearby but provoking the dominance of a religious consortium in the region drawing also on King's Lynn, where the bishop of Norwich shared lordship. Thus the implied royal ratification of Belet's possession and self-aggrandisement (evidently lawful, whence the indirect attack) raised an ecclesiastical whirlwind unique in the Hundred Rolls. Henry III had been weak in his last years. Edward was overseas, so nothing was done to uphold Belet's right. Initially ineffective, clerical pressure in the end triumphed: in 1385 'the manor called *Beletes* in Marham' (family name-tags often celebrated emergent individuals or long tenure), which had since been enlarged to comprise 160 acres of land, 40 acres of meadow and 10 shillings of rent (all yielding a mere 40 shillings a year), was acquired by the abbess and nuns on the death of the widowed dowager.[166] The miniature castle-fief would not henceforth challenge the ecclesiastical hegemony of the area, thanks to relentless (and unscrupulous) pressure. Very many noble seats, comprising the vast majority of 'castles' in England and France, were of this dignified but lowly sort which imposed on little more than the ground they occupied.[167] 'Purprestures' of this order existed largely in the minds of their competitors.

Prejudice against 'private' castles, that is, those of the whole seignorial type, has been very enduring, against all logic, when it did not cloak self-interest, as at Marham. To contemporaries, in England or France, who it was who held the castle and where it was sited mattered more than exactly what sort of structure it was, with few exceptions.[168] For sure, less partial proponents of the public interest than ecclesiastical aristocrats defending their privileges would have more

---

[166] *CPR, 1385–89*, 46: left for life to Mathilda, widow of John de Denham, with pious reversion to Marham priory: noted as not held in-chief (*sic*).

[167] The 'lesser castle' phenomenon has been accommodated by the style 'strong house': e.g. Bur (ed.), *La Maison forte*, 7–11 *et passim*. For *Domus* and *Domus Fortis* see Coulson, 'Castellation in Champagne', 353–6; fief-roll material tabulated, Seignorial Fortresses', App. A. 3(c).

[168] Coulson, 'Sanctioning of Fortresses in France', for interaction of style of building, rank of builder, and other factors with seignorial territoriality/lordship.

credit—but highly coloured polemic cannot stand against the dismissive consensus of the record sources. Unfortunately, official silence and indifference take some digging out. The glamorous verdict has been hostile, laying the heaviest emphasis, after the so-called 'castle policy' of punitive demolitions by Henry II, on the actions of Henry III's regency government from 1217, to support the view that non-royal castles were not only somehow anti-social but inherently conducive to anarchy as well.[169] Whether we examine the sanctioning of fortification in France or (especially after 1199) in England, we find that local relationships, not any governmental programme, were decisive. Henry III's early Minority (considered in the next section) was a peculiar episode of pacification, as untypical of normality as were the localized events of 1154–8, 1174–6, and the more widespread crisis of 1208–14. Analytical review of instances of exemplary damaging and of more-or-less complete demolition (which was rare) of fortresses in France,[170] as with searching the much fuller Chancery calendars, does not support the notion that 'private castles' were royal opponents. Still less were they public enemies—unless from a modern 'working-class' perspective.

How the principle tucked into the end of Magna Carta in 1217, that wartime fortifications were *ipso facto* 'purprestures', illicit intrusions, guilty until proved innocent, was in practice selectively and tactfully applied tells us more about the Minority than it does about the position of castles in society. What does very clearly emerge is that there was no general doctrine that 'castles' represented some latent evil which good rulers religiously repressed. This, the 'feudalism-means-castles-equals-anarchy' dogma (even in its benign 'no castles: no feudalism—no good' form) is flatly contradicted by how new fortifications, usually ignoring repairs and rebuilds, were absorbed into the local feudal structure. The conflict model of this process must be discarded in favour of a consensual sanctioning (very clear in France) in which territoriality predominated. There was a right of patronage, recognitory to both tenant and suzerain, and acknowledging ceremonially their relationship, which was exercised by the applying for and according of 'licence'. Much consultation and assent by negotiation undoubtedly took place between the parties—but usually went unrecorded. Another difference was that the superior lord in England was automatically the king, except in the palatinates (*de jure* or *de facto*). But mesne lords might act as petitioning agents, or facilitate application to Chancery, having been first approached. Conversely, the tenant-builder, having genuflected to authority by petitioning (his was almost invariably the initiative—hence the overwhelming proportion of unlicensed sites[171]) could

---

[169] Mild version, Brown, 'List of Castles', esp. 255–8; also *English Castles*, 215–16, 219–21, 223; stronger but modulated, Pounds, *The Medieval Castle*, 27–33, 51–3, 96–101, 141–5, etc.; barely diluted, Bates, *Border Holds*, 6–10; and Armitage, *Early Norman Castles*, esp. 377–8; cautious, Stenton, *First Century*, 63, 191–2, 197, 205–6; doctrinaire, Painter, *Feudalism and Liberty*, 139–43. Cf. Coulson, 'Freedom to Crenellate', *passim*; also for overview of current revisionism, 'Cultural Realities', bibliography.

[170] Coulson, 'Seignorial Fortresses', App. C. 2: 'Punitive and Preventive Destruction of Fortifications in France' (120 cases with reasons 864–1479).

[171] The total of potential English sites is enormous; cf. the 577 actual licences 1200–1578 (including repeats): summary, Emery, *Greater Medieval Houses*, i. 174–80. Also, Coulson, 'Some Analysis of Bodiam', 93–8.

normally expect to be duly honoured—his lord's prerogative was to be notified and to confer, not to refuse, licence.[172] What went wrong over Belet's Marham was ignorance at Westminster in 1271 of the tense local proprietorial situation. In contrast with imparking and new markets, inquisitions *ad quod damnum* to review any objections were not held before non-lucrative grants passed the seal. Wariness as to possible local ructions was common in Gascon practice, but lack of verification of petitioners' claims was general. Town authorities in Britain particularly often very shrewdly exploited licences to crenellate and also the lucrative but no less exemplary granting of murage for walling.[173] These are administrative details primarily, which have been discussed elsewhere—but they contribute to refuting the persistent military-minded idea that the only 'good' castles were royal ones, together with castles which, though 'private', had been (it is imagined) detected and grudgingly approved, so that some supposed inherent maverick tendency was shed. Such notions of the centralized state, as though kings (and palatinates) were Planning Authorities applying (with public-spirited impartiality) statutory building regulations, Green Belt directions, planning and listed-building rules, conservation area legislation, and suchlike bureaucratic red tape, must be jettisoned as anachronisms.

2. Pacification and Fortifications, 1217–c.1226

Letters patent (generally addressed) and close (sealed folded, to individuals) were sedulously enrolled during Henry III's minority (1216–32), with attention to due authorization and to conciliatory procedure. A fortunate consequence is that 'public policy' regarding fortifying is unusually fully illustrated. Among matters clarified is the 1217 addition to Magna Carta. This clause 47 was not a wholesale proscription of even wartime works, but one item in the comprehensive charter, effectively a plank in the pacification manifesto of elderly William Marshal *rector regis et regni*. It was ordered in the king's name to be implemented by all the sheriffs of England in February 1218. The exemplar enrolled was to the sheriff of York, beginning:[174]

We send to you [a copy of] the charter of liberties accorded to all [subjects] of our realm, both regarding the Forest as other matters, instructing you to have them publicly read out

---

[172] See discussion of Henry III's *démarches* in 1260–2 over Leybourne (Kent) and Dudley (Staffs.): Coulson, 'Freedom to Crenellate', 128–31.

[173] Coulson, 'Battlements and the Bourgeoisie', e.g. 184–6 on the Ipswich–Harwich confrontation (1338, 1352–4). In Gascony the *roi duc* licensed more cautiously but strove to uphold his licence to fortify if it was contested (Coulson, 'Sanctioning of Fortresses in France', 71–6). Interregnum in 1271–4, with Henry III's decline and Edward's deferred return to England (Prestwich, *Edward I*, 89–91), may have aggravated Belet's difficulties—but his licence was never cited although a public 'patent', perhaps originally read out in county court.

[174] *Rot Litt Claus*, i. 377: evidently the exemplar. Cf. the Marshal's separate Forest Charter (Nov. 1217), *Stubbs's Select Charters*, 344–8; it reversed territorial extensions of Forest law since 1189 (cl. 1) and since 1154, where injurious to landowners (cl. 3); with quittance for 'purprestures' previously committed, but not future (cl. 4). Castle-lords (*castellanus*; cl. 16) are excluded from holding forest law-courts (*placita*). Cf. Carpenter, *Minority of Henry III*, e.g. 50–1.

in your full [assembled] county [court], having summoned thereto the barons, knights and all free tenants of the county, who shall there swear fealty to us [King Henry]. And, with careful attention to each item (*punctum*) of the charters, you are to have them sworn to and obeyed (*observari*) by all.

These procedures so far were familiar to the assembled county notables, meeting under the elected and appointed sheriff at the regular place, usually the county town. As King John had angrily conceded them in June 1215, Magna Carta's detailed rules for royal–baronial and inter-aristocratic conduct had already been widely published.[175] So the sheriffs were told to emphasize particularly and have sworn and kept:

that which is appended (*appositum*) at the end of Magna Carta concerning the adulterine castles built or rebuilt since the start of the war being demolished, [which] you are to have done, all prevarication (*occasione*) put aside, as is prescribed . . . for it was ordained by the advice of the papal legate and of our faithful men . . . for the great benefit and tranquillity of us and of our realm . . . Witness, the Earl (Marshal) at Sturminster.

Instances which the sheriffs were unable to handle, and had to refer to the Regent for action, are significantly few. Tranquillity was the keynote. Seemingly strict mandates gave scope for local compromise. Only if there were exceptional circumstances of potential local disturbance was anything drastic done.[176] Thus, at Anstey (Herts.), prior to the general mandate, a local spark was promptly stamped out in January 1218.[177] Nicholas de Anstey lacked the means to cause trouble, and seems to have intended none, but the ancient imposing and moated motte-and-bailey castle he apparently reactivated had once belonged to the counts of Boulogne (of King Stephen's family). Early power-centres often left enduring or vestigial castellaries. Nicholas's additions, of which no trace is now visible, can only have been trivial, but he had to be kept in his place. Courteously he was allowed to remove them himself: 'So that nothing of that castle (*castrum*) shall remain but what was long ago (*ab antiquo*) built there and before the war. Anything fortified (*firmatum*) and erected after the war (began) shall be destroyed to the foundations . . . by the middle of Lent next [i.e. about 24 March 1218].' This carefully selective demolition the sheriff of Hertford was not so much to supervise

[175] Bloch, *Feudal Society*, 452, preserves an echo of the traditional 'feudal reaction' interpretation; cf. the old 'Whig view' of Calmette, *Monde féodal*, 342.

[176] Castrophobia so far misled McKechnie, *Magna Carta*, 176, as to misrepresent this 'among the chapters restoring order, next in importance to administrative reforms', as having 'ordered the destruction of the "adulterine" castles, that is, the private strongholds built by barons without the licence of the Crown. These remained in 1217 as . . . in 1154, a result of past civil war, and a menace to peace and good government in the future. It was the aim of every efficient ruler to abolish all fortified castles—practically impregnable in the thirteenth century when artillery was unknown [*sic*]—except those of the King . . .'; similarly A. Thompson, *Military Architecture*, 56–7, 89—perverse, old, but persistent, cf. Eales, 'Castles and Politics in England, 1215–1224', esp. 28–32, 37–40.

[177] *Rot Litt Claus*, i. 350a–459b; *VCH, Herts.*, ii. 112; iv. (1914), 11–12; Eales, 'Castles and Politics in England, 1215–1224', 39–40; Coulson, 'Freedom to Crenellate', 107–9. The case of Nafferton (below) is closely similar: *Rot Litt Claus*, i. 379b; *PatR*, i. 279, 287–8, 291; linked with the special dispute over Harbottle (also Northumb.); Coulson, 'Freedom to Crenellate', 95–6, 99–100; n. 231 below.

as to 'permit', that is, to facilitate. Labourers might have to be found. As a castle, the centre of its castellary, and for the services done thereat to its lord, Anstey was still in full operation in 1377, when noted among the possessions of the late dowager countess of Pembroke, Mary de Saint-Pol.[178] Such powers could not be allowed to a local upstart. Very many 'militarily obsolete', and even residentially antiquated, castles lost little if any of their local administrative virility by structural neglect. Preserving the local power-structure and social hierarchy was also the reason for acting at Hood (Yorks.), apparently an entirely wartime castle. In July 1218 local remedial action was merely verified, made official, and completed, to avoid any cause of conflict.[179] The instance is unique, at least in being centrally recorded. The sheriff was told: 'If the *castrum de Hod*, which has been partly thrown down (*prostratum*) and in part still stands, was erected and fortified within Newburgh fief after the war . . . began, as it is said to have been, then you are to have it fundamentally thrown down (*funditus prosterni*) and destroyed.' Newness and lack of precedent was the objection—a principle enshrined in Henry II's *assize of novel disseisin* (1176).[180] Proven antiquity was *ipso facto* legitimacy. Permanent alteration of the tenurial map by the ambitious promoting of an old *caput*, thus elevating the status of the fief it headed relative to the overlord or to a neighbour, occurred dramatically if an entirely new castellary were created. But any encroachment had to be stopped if it was an unlawful wartime event, either violent or merely surreptitious while the established possessor was unable to assert himself. For this reason, as a French case in 1268 shows, a demonstratively ruined castle building advertised the defeat of a challenge to the lawful status quo and conspicuously upheld legitimacy,[181] just as a usurped intrusion left alone proclaimed successful disregard of the legal process.[182] Hood in 1218 is a rare example not of flaunting the failure to take out a licence (for these were still scarce, and remained optional) but of threat to fragment an established *honor*. Although the fortifying was not apparently accompanied by use of force, it happened during widespread suspension of the peace.

It was also expedient for the work of reconciliation for the Regency, where possible, to affirm the late King John's actions without breaching the spirit of compromise between royalists and former rebels. Kingerby castle (Lincs.), burned by John during hostilities, was officially expunged as a fortress (but not as a *caput*, unlike Hood) by destroying what had remained, in December 1218.[183] It might

[178] *CIPM* xiv. 330–40: 'Anstey, the castle and manor . . .'
[179] *Rot Litt Claus*, i. 366b; Brown, 'List of Castles', 269. A 'naturally strong site on a ridge', apt for wartime fortification: King, *Castellarium Anglicanum, sub.* Yorks. Licensed to be crenellated 1264 by the Montfortian government: *CPR, 1258–66*, 342 (below).
[180] After the 1173–6 disturbances of the Young King's rebellion: Warren, *Henry II*, 338–44.
[181] e.g. the *fortericia* of La Porte, intruded into Méréville castellary (*dép.* Seine-et-Oise) in 1266; in 1268 judicially razed, its archery-loops (*que adhuc sunt signa fortericie*) being 'broken through in such a way that it may clearly be seen that the fortress has been slighted (*dampnata*)': *Les Olim*, i. 226, 730.
[182] e.g. Dudley (Staffs.) in 1218: *Rot Litt Claus*, i. 380a; Coulson, 'Freedom to Crenellate', 107.
[183] *Rot Litt Claus*, i. 383b; *PatR* i. 182; at Kingerby is a wet, rectangular moat with rounded corners: King, *Castellarium Anglicanum, sub* Lincs.

also be judicious to stretch a point for the sake of example, where resistance was
unlikely: in January 1219 the sheriff of Sussex was told to gather his local troops
(*posse comitatus*) to take and destroy the fortifications added to his house, not
during but since the war's end, by Simon de Etchingham.[184] In this case, it may be
that there was consensus among the local gentry class, from which sheriffs were
usually drawn, resenting Simon's arrogance. Local motives lay behind most
apparently central initiatives. It is seldom safe to take at all literally the habitual
protestations of impartial motivation in the wider public interest. Magnate interest is also likely. Power-sharing among the magnates was far too deep and
complex for any simple dichotomy between 'the Crown' (supposedly guardian of
the public welfare) and 'the barons' to be valid. Castles did not occupy some aloof
plane of 'strategic' mysticism but were viscerally involved with local lordly relations.[185] Each lord looked after his own and himself first. The example set by the
Angevin kings (Henry II, Richard I, and John) did not redress, but merely copied
the nobles' own occasionally ruthless individualism. As J. E. A. Jolliffe showed
over thirty years ago, kings' abuses of power too often enshrined not the public
interest but unrestrained partisanship which put royal interests blatantly foremost.[186] During the minority of Henry III the treatment of baronial interests was
necessarily less insensitive. Hubert de Burgh, successor to the Marshal with the
office of justiciar, reflected these fierce undercurrents when forbidding William,
earl of Salisbury, to strengthen (*efforciare*) or cause or permit to be fortified the
castle of Carlton (Lincs.), which was once Robert Bardolf's and was then in the
earl's custody (August 1219). Hubert's aim, probably, was to stop a temporary
bailment from expanding into outright freehold.[187] Fortifying asserted proprietary right, and such a large investment was not easily given up. More relevant to
the public security was the structurally insignificant work at Annesley (Notts.) in
June 1220. The Patent Roll entry reads:

About viewing a certain building (*domus*)—the king to William Bassett . . . [and three
others] sends greetings. We have heard that Reginald Mark is having a certain house made
within the forest of Sherwood at Annesley (*Anelegh*) of such strength (*adeo fortem*) and
built in such a manner that harm could by accident (*casu fortuito*) arise therefrom to the

---

[184] *Rot Litt Claus*, i. 404b: 'quam firmavit post pacem factam . . . sine licentia et precepto nostro
. . .' the latter a useful pretext also exploited by the early Capetians: Coulson, 'Fortress-Policy', 18–22.
Building, not mere stocking and manning, is here meant by *firmare*. On the later Etchinghams and
generally peaceable Sussex gentry politics see Saul, *Scenes from Provincial Life*, 75.

[185] Among general works Norman Pounds's *The Medieval Castle* is a partial exception. Emery,
Greater Medieval Houses, gives much space to social analysis.

[186] Jolliffe, *Angevin Kingship*, e.g. 60; John's slighting of Barnard castle was a *felenie* to the compiler
of the *Histoire des Ducs de Normandie*. John's view (p. 61) was overt that 'it is no more than just that
we should do better by those who are with us than by those who are against us': Jolliffe's indictment
(esp. 50–109, 301–10) is severe. It entirely precludes taking royal conduct as a yardstick of altruism.

[187] *PatR*, i. 201; Brown, 'List of Castles', 265; on William Longspee, Carpenter, *Minority of Henry III*,
index 'Salisbury'. For baronial politics in Lincolnshire, of which William was sheriff, see Eales, 'Castles
and Politics in England, 1215–1224', 32–3; fortifying at Folkingham castle also attempted; ibid. 38, and
Shirley (ed.), *Royal Letters*, i. 64. Major castle-building in the 1220s, not impeded, included Rannulf of
Chester's Bolingbroke (Lincs.), Beeston (Ches.), Chartley (Staffs.): M. Thompson, *Rise of the Castle*,
104–5.

neighbourhood. We instruct you therefore to go to that place and inspect the house, reporting to us by letter under your seal, directed to Hubert de Burgh our justiciar, as to how (*quo modo*) it is constructed, and regarding the nature of the place.[188]

The wording is careful. As the leader of the prolonged defence of Dover castle against Louis le Lion and his English adherents in 1215–16, Hubert, later earl of Kent, put his concerns without overstatement. Reginald Mark was probably one of the brothers of Philip Mark, one of John's foreign henchmen, ordered to be removed from their offices under the original Magna Carta (clause 50), but who was still sheriff of Nottingham and Derby. The encroachments of these former trusties (as at Bedford by de Bréauté) had not ended. Building at Annesley may have infringed Forest Law. Its location might make it a lair of outlaws. Those who 'blew the whistle' to the justiciar are likely to have been watchful neighbours. Bassett and his fellow commissioners may have sent back a reassuring report: at all events, no sequel is enrolled.

Although any sort of aggrandizing fortification might arouse local jealousy, actual usurpation of others' rights beyond mere occupation of the ground might be achieved by peaceful attrition, without armed force. This happened at Hood, its builder stopped (temporarily) from carving a new lordship out of the fief of Newburgh. The possibility of local revenues being seized was part of the concern in Normandy in 1091 to identify potential 'robbers' lairs' (*spelunce latronum* was the stock biblical phrase for occupied or 'incastellated' churches), as we have seen.[189] But action against buildings was purely ancillary to the direct policing of illicit armed assembly. The association of lawbreaking with fortifying was tenuous and the link mostly incidental, even accidental. Virtually all fortifying was done by established authorities, lay and ecclesiastical, and by urban oligarchs. Manning defences for hostile purposes was quite apart. This last case, when fortifying had the aim of resisting law-enforcers, is exemplified by Benhall (Suffolk) in 1225— but the connection with 'castles' becomes remote, even in the wide medieval sense of the word. The Close Roll entry is as follows:

The king [Henry III] to the sheriff of Norfolk and Suffolk, greeting. You have signified to us that since certain [men] of the following (*ex parte*), as you have heard, of Henry le Clavering have forced their way (*intruissent se*) into the buildings (*domos*) of Ralph de Sunderland at *Benhal*, and have fortified those buildings with ditches and palisading (*palo*), maintaining themselves there against our peace by force and arms (*vi et armis*); and you have reported, having gone there, that you found one knight and fourteen lesser armed men (*servientes* or 'sergeants') whose persons you have arrested on the ground that you found those buildings thus fortified. Now, for this diligence we congratulate you and order you to hand over some of them to the constable of our castle of Norwich, and others to our constable of Orford castle, for them to keep securely until further order . . .

[188] *PatR*, i. 238; Coulson, 'Freedom to Crenellate', 108–9. Keen, *Outlaws of Medieval Legend*, examines 'Robin Hood', etc.; Bellamy, *Crime and Public Order*, 83, 88 (Sherwood Forest). Holt, 'Philip Mark', 8–24.

[189] In the *Consuetudines* phrased *et in rupe vel in insula*: Haskins, *Norman Institutions*, 282 (4); e.g. Chibnall, 'Orderic Vitalis on Castles', 52–3.

Counterpart mandates accordingly went to those constables as *ex officio* head-gaolers, one of their many administrative duties.[190] Clavering's people meekly surrendered, in the event, but breach of the peace, aggravated by apparent preparation to defy restraint, made out of a trivial ditch and palisade (in themselves normal and innocuous) combined with armed assembly a quite serious offence—somewhat more emphatic than at Annesley.

Attempts to show from cases of this sort that fortifying was the problem, which had caused a system to be imposed requiring builders first to apply for a licence to fortify (or after *c.*1264 to crenellate) ignore the documentary and archaeological facts as well as the Continental pedigree. Licensing was not a governmental police measure, nor was it even obligatory, but was in fact demand-led; the inverse of its reputation. The licence, as it happens, which inaugurated the regular formula 'to enclose with a wall of stone and lime, and to crenellate and so hold thus crenellated for ever' (but for including the early element 'with a ditch'), was the one granted for the revival of Hood castle in August 1264, to Simon de Montfort's partisan in Yorkshire, John de Eyville.[191] Having lingered in legal (but not functional) limbo since 1219, Hood achieved recognition by this, the sole licence enrolled between the battles of Lewes (at which Henry III was captured) and of Evesham, which freed him from restraint. As normal, not public policy but favour was the cause. A total of twenty-four licences were taken out between the baronial Provisions of Oxford (1258) and the end of the Barons War, effectively in 1266. Turmoil at Court was as influential as the political tensions in the country and ensuing civil war. Afterwards there was no such tidying up of the castellated detritus as had followed 1154, 1176, and 1217, except for inquiries made in 1265–72, some of whose findings are in the Rolls of Edward I's great inquiry begun in 1274. In these, as we have seen, we find only the cases of Barnwell and of Marham to be of any significance. The country-wide 'inquisition' was an opportunity for grievances of all sorts to be aired, but the Hundred Roll inquiry was concerned primarily with 'purprestures' upon the royal domain. A great many were of the pedantic type of one inadvertently committed by Henry III's regency in 1225 over Benhall upon the Liberty of Ely. A week after ordering the miscreants to be taken to Orford and Norwich, 'the king' had them transferred to the bishop of Ely's bailiffs 'to be imprisoned and to be tried to the king's order' in the episcopal prison and lawcourt.[192]

The cases reviewed in this and the previous section may not absolve 'castles' from blame for social injustice due to guilt-by-association, but they do suggest that the habitual picture is seriously wrong. 'Medieval' is not properly a synonym for 'barbaric'; barons were bold but not necessarily bad; 'feudal law' was not a contradiction in terms—nor was 'baronial revolt' a tautology. Castles' traditional

---

[190] *Rot Litt Claus*, ii. 52b. Benhall, by 1369, had graduated to the status of a 'manor . . . including a small park with deer', late of the earl of Suffolk: *CIPM* xii. 408–11 (410).

[191] n. 179 above; on John see *Close Rolls, 1264–68*, 113; *CIM, 1219–1307*, 110 ('one of the king's enemies', implicated in the burning of Sheffield castle, licensed in 1270: *CPR, 1266–72*, 447).

[192] *Rot Litt Claus*, ii. 54b, 56b–57a; after verifying the bishop's claim to have the legal cognizance.

dark reputation is largely the product of perceptions of King Stephen's reign, of clerical propaganda, and of Romance, all inflated by mental inertia.

3. The Angevin Record and 'French' Treaties, 1160–1200

It is now time to adopt a different perspective—to look at these questions from the top downwards. As supposedly the instruments of ('beneficial') conquest, historians have regarded castles until the reign of Stephen (1135), with few exceptions (e.g. Odo of Bayeux's revolt involving Rochester in 1088; the Bellême revolt, 1102), as benign.[193] That after 1135 they turned malignant, even the perceptive Sidney Painter believed. 'Castles', he remarked with unconscious irony, 'were of extreme importance in times of internal confusion. They served as a protection for a baron's own lands and as convenient bases for plundering his neighbors.'[194] Henry II has accordingly been praised (with perhaps a tinge of Anglo-Saxon revanchism) in much the same vein as he was by contemporary Angevin propaganda, for 'razing the new castles which in his grandfather's time never existed' (William of Newburgh), and for 'causing very nasty little fortlets (*munitiunculas pessimas*) to vanish from English ground' (Gervase of Canterbury).[195] To Lewis Warren 'castles' were ambivalent, both Jekyll and Hyde: while they 'sprang for the defence as well as the exploitation of the labouring peasants', their very existence 'seemed for a time to imply the fragmentation of political authority'. (This was not how lords castellan and the aristocracy in general regarded the question). All the same, Warren recognized the vindictive motive behind Henry II's slighting in 1155 of the castles of Bishop Henry of Blois, the late King Stephen's brother, who had opportunely exiled himself.[196] This acknowledgement of Plantagenet vendetta modifies the 'kings embodied the national good' chorus. Allen Brown has justly gone much further. Discussing Henry II's 'ignoring of solemn promises' concerning rights to castles and his ruthless demolitions of others (few or none 'adulterine' by any definition) at the outset of his reign in 1154–8 (seven 'demolitions'; thirty-four seizures documented), and again after the revolt of his eldest son, the young King Henry, in 1174–6 (nineteen 'demolitions'; twenty-one seizures), and also by John in 1203–14 (five 'demolitions'; fifty-four seizures, all the documented minimum), Brown does not exaggerate in describing this 'encroachment upon the preserve of private castles' (itself, to him, 'an achievement of Angevin castle-policy') as seeming 'often to have ridden rough-shod over right and precedent'.[197] The usual complacent statist belief that all this was good

---

[193] For Gallic hostility see Aubenas, 'Les Châteaux-forts', *passim*; Boutruche, *Seigneurie et féodalité*, 31–9, etc.; much the same still in Duby, *France 987–1460*, ch. 6, esp. pp. 55–68.

[194] Painter, *Feudalism and Liberty*, 132; a more sober version of e.g. J. R. Green, *A Short History of the English People*, 194–5, etc.; also Le Patourel, *The Norman Empire*, 304–7, etc.

[195] William of Newburgh, *Historia Rerum Anglicarum*, i. 94. Gervase of Canterbury, Stubbs (ed.), i. 160.

[196] Warren, *Henry II*, 5, 39–40 (cf. Coulson, 'Castles of the Anarchy', esp. 69–70), and generally 60–1, 140–2, 233,368; cf. Eales, 'Royal Power and Castles', esp. 57 (n. 34).

[197] Brown, 'List of Castles', esp. 255–8. Demolitions ordered require caution, especially by John:

kingship and showed 'the smack of firm government', regardless of the reckoning in due course paid by King John (1214–16), Brown rightly resists. Seignorial fortresses, after all, were lawful landed property, albeit in special form, institutionally associated with governmental functions. In this period there was wholesale rebuilding in stone and new 'keep towers' arose everywhere. Resisting it would have been futile, had this ever been a consistent royal aim. Moreover, Brown remarks of John's confiscations—'not infrequently no cause is known, and we seem faced with the brute facts that the king desired certain castles and felt himself strong enough to take them'. It was a counter-productive opportunism. The 'charge of the exercise of mere arbitrary will seems substantiated', in Brown's judgement, when seizure occurred at a baronial succession, as it often did. Had it not been for Henry II's formidable reputation he would be equally indicted.[198] It was no mere form that John, by clause 62 of Magna Carta, was made to promise the restitution of property (expressly including castles) 'seized or taken away by us without lawful judgement of [the victims'] peers'. By accepting that Henry II, quite as much as John, broke the rules of the consensual aristocratic polity more flagrantly than the indulgence customarily given (then and now) to strong lordship allowed, castles as a socio-political institution can be more fairly judged.[199] Rehabilitating them leads to other true inferences.

The fundamental doctrine was that forcible encroachment was aggravated usurpation and should (ideally) be treated as such. In the peace treaty of October 1174 made with Henry the younger's partisans across the Channel, a notably less absolutist and more bipartisan tone is to be found.[200] Thus, King Henry (the father) agreed peace with Henry his eldest son (crowned in anticipation as heir apparent and generally referred to as the Young King) and with Richard (Coeur de Lion) and Geoffrey (of Brittany), who with their supporters were thereby to return to their father's allegiance. The royalists regained 'the lands and castles' which they had had fifteen days before the conflict began, but the three sons' party got back only the lands, their castles being separately provided for. Moreover:

By this treaty (*conventio*) the lord king shall give to the king his son two suitable *castella* in Normandy, with £15,000 of Tours [money] annually; and to his son Richard two suitable

unless backed by expenditure, narrative source corroboration, or structural evidence. Exemplary and punitive slighting seldom terminated a castle's 'military', and more rarely still its real (administrative), existence.

[198] Cf. the relatively punctilious conduct (vindicated by the easy conquest of Normandy in 1203–4) of Philip Augustus: Coulson, 'Fortress-Policy', esp. 17, 22–3, 26–30, 32–8. Even after Philip's triumph (1214) he still acted with restraint: Coulson, 'Impact of Bouvines', *passim*. Scarcely before Philip IV did the Capetians behave so arrogantly towards seignorial fortresses: Coulson, 'Community and Fortress-Politics in France', esp. 82–4, 86–8.

[199] *Stubbs's Select Charters*, 299. Warren, *Henry II*, 141, defends his demolitions of the castles of 'rebels' in 1176 as 'more than an act of reprisal or even of security', making a lord's humiliation an act of state policy; cf. the view of the contemporary author of the *Brut y Tywysogion* that John's opponents in 1215 would make no peace with him 'until there should be restored to each one of them their laws and their power and their castles, which he had taken from them without law or truth or justice': quoted Brown, 'List of Castles', 258.

[200] *Recueil Henri II*, ii. 18–21.

fortresses (*receptacula idonea*), guaranteed harmless [i.e. 'jurable'[201]] to the king, in Poitou, with half the county revenues in cash each year. To Geoffrey, his son, the king concedes half his marital dues from Brittany until he marries Duke Conan's daughter and afterwards all his marriage entitlement.[202]

Here, as usual, castles figure no more and no less prominently than their function of general-purpose instrument and earnest of territorial power demanded—not as though mere keys to military districts.[203] Other matters were also important. Prisoners, including William the Lion, king of Scots, their ransoms, and hostages (in guarantee of payment) are provided for. Henry the Younger promised to observe the charitable payments ('alms') due from his lands, and ratified as heir to the kingdom his father's endowment of the youngest brother, John 'Lackland', with lands and rents in England (Nottingham castle 'and county', Marlborough castle and territory) and likewise in Normandy (*dua castella ad voluntatem patris*), and similarly in Anjou (with a 'castle'), together with a 'castle' in Maine and another in Touraine, all (so that they were not an economic liability) naturally including the attached lands and revenues. John thus had a scatter of castellaries in the family patrimony. Wartime infractions were put under general amnesty, but excluding murder and maiming. Fortresses were restored to peacetime normality, with the familiar proviso: 'but castles which were fortified or munitioned (*inforciata*) after war began shall, at the lord king's discretion, be put back to the state they were in fifteen days before the outbreak.' In the briefer and face-saving summary of the peace terms issued afterwards by Henry II for domestic consumption in England (this version including King Louis VII as a party), he brusquely compressed this item to: 'all the castles which I and my men had at the start of the war are [hereby] returned to me; and those which were fortified against me are to be put back as they were when the war started.'[204] It minimized his concessions; but whatever the propaganda, the fact of rebellion and its debris were erased from the physical record. Even extending the operative date to fifteen days beforehand would bring in no more than emergency works, such as timber hourds to battlements.[205] Other reinforcements or 'fortifications', amounting to mere munitioning (stocking with food, weapons, 'artillery', etc.) would have been practicable in a hurried emergency, not building. There is no questioning of the right of nobles, or of the burgesses of the walled towns, or of prelates with their

[201] Here phrased *unde domino regi non posset damnum provenire*, equivalent to *unde michi nocere non possit* in the popular version: not a specific condition (jurability) but a standard overlordly right less than requisitioning at will (rendability)—Coulson, 'Rendability and Castellation', esp. 60–2. On Richard as count see Baudry, *Fortifications des Plantagenêts en Poitou*, 27–9.

[202] Constance, heiress of Brittany, mother by Geoffrey of Arthur, who died in or before 1203, probably murdered, perhaps to King John's order, having contested his accession after 1199 with Philip Augustus's support.

[203] Conventionally exaggerated, e.g. Warren, *King John*, 57–8, 84; F. Powicke, *Loss of Normandy*, 196–8, 202–4, 252–3 (but with due emphasis on castellaries, administrative role, etc.).

[204] *Recueil Henri II*, ii. 21–2; also nos. 470–1 (two versions of King William's treaty); and source refs. Also printed *Foedera* i, i, 30.

[205] e.g. *Rot Litt Pat*, 10b (Rouen, May 1202); *Rot Litt Claus*, i. 199b (Stafford town, May 1215: a quasi-'licence').

religious precincts, to hold and to maintain, or to renew and replace, their fortresses. Maintenance of seignorial 'plant' was a vested privilege (*de novo* fortifying no less so), which could only voluntarily be renounced and was seldom abrogated.

There was, therefore, no more a political animus against fortresses than against 'feudalism'. Indeed, the archaeological record confirms that castles new and old were proliferating as prosperity rose. The castrophobic myth is no less obsolete than is the notion of a 'feudal anarchy' sustained by selfish barons with nihilistic tendencies, against whom patriotic kings strove with constructive fervour.[206] What passes for the public or the 'national' interest might, however, interfere with fortifying and fortresses on specific, individual occasions. Securing the integrity of major peace treaties and border agreements was one such. Some inter-seignorial examples come later (e.g. Part III, Ch. 1, sec. 4). Another occasion was to preserve the peace if fortifying was truly the *casus belli*; another to punish wrongdoing, but whether really for the public safety or just to exalt the king may often be doubted. The transcendent and general motive of rulers at all levels was to assert the subordination to themselves of fortresses as naturally and properly public assets. In France (and continental western Europe) even lords quite low in the hierarchy utilized the ancient rule and widespread customs of rendability, superfluous in Britain for a variety of reasons. How quasi-national treaties touched the common weal in these special ways now calls for illustration.

Fortresses were affected by the successive Plantagenet–Capetian treaties of 1194–1200. The tendency to modern analogy must be resisted, for example, the Franco-Dutch 'Barrier Fortresses' and frontier *places d'armes*, crucial in the prolonged series of wars of containment fought against Louis XIV (1665–1714). Marcher zones rather than 'frontiers' were involved;[207] and when a place is described in the records as lying *in frontera inimicorum domini regis*, not 'on the frontier' but usually only the vague sense of 'confronting the king's enemies' is intended. Such special-pleading language, commonly of petitioners, uncritically repeated in grants, always requires caution. Moreover, as Sidney Painter argued and R. C. Smail endorsed for even that most supposedly militarized (but still rather different) of settlements, Frankish Palestine, 'from the point of view of national defence against a foreign invader the exact location of a fortress made very little difference'.[208] Castles (lacking long-range artillery) did not 'block'

[206] e.g. E. King, 'Stephen and the Anglo-Norman Aristocracy'; Eales, 'Royal Power and Castles', esp. 72–3, comparing England and Normandy; Hollister, 'The Aristocracy'. Royalism is as grave a problem as is the proper meaning of 'feudalism': Reynolds, *Fiefs and Vassals*, esp. 3–14.

[207] See discussion by Power, 'Frontier of Angevin Normandy', esp. 181–5. Demonstration (by castles) at borders arose primarily out of territoriality: *Château et territoire*, Fillon (ed.), *passim*.

[208] Painter, *Feudalism and Liberty*, 129 (discussion); Smail, *Crusading Warfare*, 204–9 (but see n. 33 above). Cf. Deschamps, *Châteaux des Croisés*, i. 17–42 (somewhat contradicted by pp. 43–57). *Château Gaillard*, 17 (Abergavenny *colloque*, 1994), had as theme 'the role of castles in frontiers'. Tom McNeill concluded: 'if there was a common theme to emerge ... it was not that they were the primary factor in the formation of frontiers. Rather, they would appear to be central to the formation of lordships which then defined their borders around the limits of their power; only later might castles be sited to defend these frontiers': Castle Studies Group *Newsletter*, 8, p. 34; Power, 'Frontier of Angevin

roads, river valleys, or passes; to imagine so is (again in Painter's words) 'to misconstrue the strategic use of these fortresses in medieval war'. Economic geography is a more reliable guide. Similarly, to equate royal fortresses with those of the modern state has exaggerated their peculiarity. At most they were merely 'baronial' castles writ large. Being available for use by the king (or overlord), and being often in his hand by wardship, baronial fortresses were scarcely 'private' in any case. Rendability in former Carolingian parts of Europe, and less formalized co-operation in Britain, made vassals' fortresses in law and in practice as open to rulers' use (in Germany a rendable castle was commonly called *ein offen Haus*[209]) as were their own kept in demesne. Even the most expensive fortresses (Gisors, Niort, Dover, etc.) only took on extra-local importance when subordinated to armies in the field.[210] In the three treaties which ushered in the loss of Normandy to Philip Augustus, fortresses are involved primarily as tenurial entities. With their warlike aspect in 1203–4 this book is not here concerned—but the 'public policy' implications deserve attention. A notable precursor to the 1194–1200 negotiations is the Anglo-French treaty of 1160.

Louis VII (1137–80) and Henry II were then dealing with the perennial friction over the Norman frontier province of the Vexin. This contentious 'waste-land' was omitted from Louis's general release to Henry II of the lands and rights held by his grandfather Henry I at his death—in the standard phrase, 'on the day he was alive and dead' (1 December 1135). Henry II's part of the Vexin was defined as comprising the fiefs of the archbishop of Rouen, of the earl of Leicester in Breteuil fief, and of the count of Evreux.[211] The rest was to go to Henry, but in trust for the future marriage portion of Louis's daughter, contracted to be married to Henry's son within three years. As a face-saver and precaution, 'the castles of the Vexin' were not immediately made over by Louis but were to be kept on Henry's son's behalf (*ad opus filii sui*) by the knightly order of the Temple (already 'international' bankers, as well as crusaders).[212] These *castella*, as mere buildings, were an expensive liability; and since, exceptionally, their appurtenant lands were severed, the treaty laid down, evidently at Louis's insistence, that revenues of the sort habitually attached to castles in Louis's own demesnes should go to the Templars to meet their costs of 'custody'.[213] To denote their peculiar status Louis was, in the interim, to keep his 'justice, homages, and service' in these castellaries. The castle of Etrepagny (*dép.* Eure, near Les Andelys, future neighbour of Richard

---

Normandy', 183; also Kenyon, 'Fluctuating Frontiers: Welsh', 119–26; Eales, 'Royal Power and Castles', 63–9.

[209] Rosentall, *Tractatus et Synopsis Totius Juris Feudalis*, 71. Overview Coulson, ' "National" Requisitioning'.

[210] Mesqui, *Châteaux-forts*, 186–9, 266–7; Brown, 'Royal Castle-Building', 390.

[211] *Recueil Henri II*, i. 251–3; Coulson, 'Fortress-Policy', 30–2. Angevin claims to lordship of Toulouse were postponed but Poitou was fully acquired. F. Powicke, *Loss of Normandy*, endpaper (Stapelton map); Power, 'Frontier of Angevin Normandy', 182 (general map).

[212] M. Barber, *The New Knighthood*, ch. 7 (esp. pp. 267–78).

[213] Viz. 'et habebunt redditus ad castella custodienda quos rex Francie in dominio habebat'. Often translated as 'guarding', *custodia* was usually closer to 'maintaining' or 'keeping'.

I's Château Gaillard) presented insuperable difficulties. Being 'English' but close to the border of the French part of the Vexin, the only way of dealing with a not conveniently divisible *castellaria* was by the drastic solution of demolition: 'Under this *conventio* the *castellum Stripennei* is to be razed (*prosternetur*) by midsummer.'[214] Presumably the lordship was put in limbo (partitioned). It was later reactivated, showing the durability of administrative entities. Military precautions are possible but are not mentioned. Count Simon of Evreux's territory also straddled both districts of the Vexin, and (as was perfectly normal) he served two masters. By the 1160 pact he resumed 'his undisturbed (*quiete*) service in respect of his men and castles', Louis additionally assuring him that 'his castles shall quietly remain his, in like manner as the other barons of France without hindrances hold their *castella quieta*'. These circumspect phrases reflect the constant tension between the elements of territorial *caput*, economic and tenurial focus, centre of forceful control, and prestigious noble palace, which composed the lordly fortress. Etrepagny was unfortunate in its location. Except in *pays de guerre*, fortresses seldom obstructed the peace, because as instruments of civil administration they served it.[215]

Similar quasi *raison-d'état* obtained in 1194 and 1196, when further 'conventions' were made between Richard I and Philip II. Although these settlements turned out to be as impermanent as that of 1160, they do reflect a widespread consensus as to how fortresses ought to be treated, their diplomatic vicissitudes apart. A brief political stalemate is seen, frozen in time, in the Anglo-French one-year truce concluded in July 1194. 'Fortifying' in this pact meant 'munitioning' essentially, since time did not allow much more than extempore structures. Although earthworks might be dug in the winter season, and the long-continuing persistence of timber elements can be underestimated since they are usually only traceable by excavation, the slow and costly procedures of masonry construction, with their long discontinuance in the winter months, did not permit haste.[216] But hostilities, of course, created their own imperatives. 'Fortifying' became a threat—if munitioning, of imminent violence; or if of permanent structures, of colonization and conquest. The 1194 pact was not a *pax* but a truce, and intentionally provisional; and so, on Normandy's borders to the east,

King Philip has granted that the king of England may fortify (*firmare*) if he wish, Le Neubourg [*dép.* Eure; SE near Evreux] and *Drincourt* [Neufchâtel en Bray, *dép.* Seine-Maritime; NE] Conches and Breteuil [*dép.* Eure; SE]. Those other fortifications (*munitiones*), which have been demolished by war, by the king of France or his people (*per suos*), are not to be fortified during this truce, until under a subsequent peace (*pax*). King Philip

---

[214] Perhaps, like Gaillard, an intrusion; approx. 11 miles NNE of Les Andelys, 6 miles W of Gisors.

[215] Cf. Quatremares (*dép.* Eure) begun irregularly by the sire de Blainville, razed 1365 to uphold an Anglo-French truce: *Mandements Charles V*, nos. 209–11. Context Gillingham, *Richard the Lionheart*, 245–74.

[216] Components as hourds, brattices, palisading, etc. (e.g. the *hirsoun*, *hériçon*, or abatis around Colwyn castle, co. Radnor (1315), replaced triennially: *CIPM* v. 401) are to be distinguished from extempore fortifications: e.g. Barker, Higham, *Timber Castles*, 326–47 (Hen Domen, Montgomerys., pp. 361–3); Kenyon, *Medieval Fortifications*, 3–38.

and his side shall in everything remain as they were when the truce was made, including Le Vaudreuil [*dép.* Eure] and its territory as far as La Haie Malherbe and Pont de L'Arche. Beyond them is the king of England's own.

Both warring kings swore (by proxy, as befitted high rank) to induce observance of these terms by the members of their respective coalitions, effectively suspending some lordly freedoms by fiat and imposing various territorial adjustments. Policing and arbitration of infractions were provided for. There was only one breach, and the definitive 'peace' between Richard and Philip followed in January 1196.[217]

Even major fortresses were quite quickly physically demolished, or at least made temporarily untenable, but local dispositions and lordly right were more enduring and had to be conciliated. Defences might come and go but castellaries went on (almost) for ever. The 1194 truce makes clear this ephemeral quality:

In regard to all fortresses (*fortellescis*) which the king of France has (*est saisitus*) on the day of this truce, it shall be thus: that he may, within the truce, strengthen (*infortiare*), demolish, or burn them, if he wish; and do his will with all the land he holds (*tenet*). And the king of England, similarly, with all the fortresses he holds (*est tenens*); but he may fortify (*firmare*) none of those demolished by the king of France or his, apart from the four previously stated.

Le Neubourg, Neufchâtel, Conches, and Breteuil, the four in question (all major settled places) were thus restored to normal status. This pact, 'made between Verneuil and Tillières', was provisional and speaks of 'fortresses', selecting their military aspect; for even in war 'castles' were still territorial entities, a fact which the formal 'peace' concluded 'between Gaillon and Le Vaudreuil' (Treaty of Louviers), in January 1196, duly reflects.[218] Richard Coeur-de-Lion ceded, *inter alia*, Neufmarché, Vernon, Gaillon, Pacy, Ivry, and Nonancourt, all *cum castellaniis eorum*. Among Philip's cessions was the *feodum* (lordship) *castelli Melliantis* (Meulan, *dép.* Seine-et-Oise). Just to assert his full right to Châteauneuf-sur-Cher (in the latin *Villanova*, *dép.* Cher), Philip 'may fortify there should he so wish'; and similarly Richard and the count of Toulouse in all their possessions (hereby acknowledged) 'shall do and shall fortify (*inforciabit*) as they wish there, as their own land (*tanquam de sua*)'. Fortifying, as usual, proved lordship. Tenure of Châteauneuf at Tours and fortifying the castle-proper (expressed as *domus Castelli novi*) were less straightforward: Richard was to act as the archbishop of Reims and Dreu de Mello (Philip's Constable and his negotiating plenipotentiary in 1194) should prescribe. The crucial question of Les Andelys, directly between Richard's capital Rouen and down the Seine from Paris, the manor being a fief of the archbishop of Rouen, was put completely in limbo. Neither king was to claim

[217] *Foedera*, i, i, 64; F. Powicke, *Loss of Normandy*, 104, 107; and pp. 83–4 on the Treaty of Messina, March 1191.
[218] *Recueil Philippe II*, ii. 52–7; recording terms agreed 5 Dec. 1195, 'between Issoudun and Charost' (in Berri), including Toulouse, Périgord, Turenne, etc. previously outstanding. Richard's counterpart printed in *Layettes*, i. no. 431.

lordship, and consequently *ipso facto* it was not to be fortified (*non poterit inforciari*). This point, interestingly, was tagged on, reflecting the location on the river-border of Les Andelys as well as the fact that fortification was a statement as well as potentially a forceful vindication of lordship.[219] How Richard then dispossessed the archbishop to forestall Philip and seized the borough and *roche d'Andely* to build not a mere statement but a bastion of ducal Normandy with appurtenant new town on the river below Château Gaillard, is well known. Richard's famous 'keep', with its machicolated and battered (sloping) keel-like prow, backed onto the chalk precipice, seemingly a place of last resort in the classic image, can be seen by close inspection to have been internally a two-storey hall of audience, with no well. In these respects, despite its bravura, this tower conforms to a long line of *donjons*. The whole complex of castle, outworks, new town, previous water-girt township, manor-house, and flood-plain below the chalk escarpment was an extravagance more than an investment: an act of bravado and defiance. Militarily, as the exceptional six-months siege of 1203–4 showed, it only bought time at a very expensive rate, time which John's political failures prevented him from using.[220] But no fortification by itself ever did more.

Apart from their grand scale and political consequences, these treaties are not abnormal. Their fortress-provisions are standard, typical of seignorial castellation pacts.[221] When the balance of advantage had begun to move decisively against the Plantagenets in May 1200, King John's treaty merely varied the same theme. More territory was conceded in recompense for Richard's encroachments, including the remainder of the Evreçin with Evreux itself, halfway to Neubourg, Conches, and Acquigni, demarcated by Noë abbey and the course of the River Iton. Where there was no such linear marker, precision was a matter of consent. Within this new borderland, on either side, restrictions on fortifying were drastic but reciprocal. According to Philip's charter, dated at Le Goulet:

Neither we nor the king of England may fortify within the bounds defined between Le Neubourg and Evreux [about 15 miles SE], nor at Quitteboeuf [on the 'English' side but allocated to Philip], that is, neither we on our side nor the king of England on his, unless at places now fortified (*nisi ubi firmatum est*). In addition the *fortericie* of Portes [near Conches] and of Les Londes shall be immediately demolished, and no other fortifications (*fortericie*) may be rebuilt there.[222]

[219] *Recueil Philippe II*, Item 21; 17, not numbered: p. 56.

[220] F. Powicke, *Loss of Normandy*, 114–17, 190–6, 204–6 (expenditure: up to £8,000 in three years exceeding Henry II's Dover in 1180–90), 253–6 (siege). For a corrective view showing John's incompetence, Gillingham, *Richard the Lionheart*, 278–82, etc.; Mesqui, *Châteaux forts*, 109–11 ('strategic'). Details of Gaillard 'keep' show Richard's supreme confidence: Coulson, 'Peaceable Power', 84, n. 76.

[221] Early sample in Coulson, 'French Matrix'; more generally, see id., 'Sanctioning of Fortresses in France', e.g. on Champagne–Dreux pacts. Philip II's dealings 1214–23 over fortification(s) in cos. Boulogne, Eu, Flanders, Perche, and Ponthieu discussed in Coulson, 'Impact of Bouvines', 71–80; and see Index.

[222] At Le Goulet Richard's vassalage for Normandy was explicit: *Recueil Philippe II*, ii. 178–85 (5); *Rot Norm*, i. 1–3 (archbishop of Rouen's exchange for Les Andelys manor *cum novo castello de Ruppe* ratified, 1200). F. Powicke, *Loss of Normandy*, 169–72. King John's verbatim counterpart printed in *Layettes*, i. no. 578.

As at Etrepagny, dis-fortified under the 1160 treaty, manorial functions at Portes and Les Londes are likely to have continued. In addition, further consensual adjustments of vassal-holdings were necessary to reduce conflicts of fealty.[223] The marriage agreed between John's niece, Blanche of Castile (later regent), and the young Louis (VIII, 1223–6), and the settlement of Angoulême and Limoges affairs were the banner headlines. Existing castles (if not too sensitively located) were immune, with the usual vested freedom to update them; but not so within a belt of borderland between the two powers—hence this curt fine print, integral but subordinate: 'Now we [King Philip] are not able to fortify beyond Gamaches [E of Château Gaillard] on the Normandy side, nor beyond the bounds of the Forest of Vernon [S of Château Gaillard] but [we may] on our side (*sed infra*). On his part, the king of England cannot fortify beyond the Forest of Les Andelys,[but may] on his side.'

Fortresses of all sorts were caught up like any real estate; but, as administrative centres (naturally sited at towns, economic *foci*, on the routes and crossing-points), as the nuclei of castellaries, as arsenals and bases, and as royal and lordly *points d'appui* they fittingly take their place among the major power-bloc arrangements. All these elements are rather jumbled together in an ad hoc, brief but clear way. Peacetime fortifying under local tenurial sanctions may have been temporarily interrupted in the interests of peace to help stop aggression between rulers, but the encroachment upon feudal continuity was undoubtedly limited in time and extent. War, essentially, was extraneous and superimposed.[224] Obvious though it is, moreover, that troop movements particularly affected the major fortresses far more than the minor fortlets, any capacity to stand siege still depended on manning, munition, and on the moral and political conditions for resistance at least as much as on architectural structures. The human component always came first. Strong defences were costly but economized on manpower; but no cost–benefit analysis was applied to such heavy capital expenditure—even where it might most be expected.[225]

4. Anglo-Scottish Affairs, 1209–1388

The political history of fortresses lies outside the scope of this book—but some further top-down review of some episodes within Britain may be illuminating.

[223] Exceptionally clear in William the Marshal's almost too courteous arrangements with Philip II after his reduction of Normandy in respect of William's castle-lordships of Orbec, Longueville, and Meulers: *Layettes*, i. 250; cf. 486 (1219); Coulson, *Fortress-Policy*, 34–8; n. 323 below. Gillingham, 'Warfare and Chivalry in the History of William the Marshal', argues 'that "pillage and robbery" were central to chivalrous war-making' (p. 263).

[224] Even in early twelfth-century Palestine: 'it is easy to see that there was a military element in such use of fortified buildings, but it was fused with administrative, economic, and social considerations', Smail, *Crusading Warfare*, 215. On 'the pattern of medieval settlement' in the Sharon plain, Pringle, *The Red Tower*, 13, asserts 'the castles' functions were thus not always, if ever, exclusively military'; nn. 25, 33 above.

[225] On Palestine, Marshall, *Warfare in the Latin East*, e.g. 93–4. Fedden and Thomson, *Crusader Castles*, 14–19. Coulson, 'Peaceable Power', 80–1.

Welsh examples have so far been few, but similar political arrangements sanctioning or forgoing the building of particular castles occur in the principality, notably in the Treaty of Montgomery between Llywelyn ap Gruffydd (*inter alia* recognizing him as prince of Wales) and Henry III in 1267.[226] Seignorial competition between their respective partisans is again the keynote. On the Scottish border relations were both more equal, intense, and prolonged. King John accepted William the Lion's destruction of Tweedmouth castle, a joint venture between the Crown and the bishop of Durham, despite Scottish weakness in 1209. This castle had not so much threatened William's burgh of Berwick, on the opposite (northern) bank, as competed for the lucrative tolls on the river.[227] Thinking of states with abundant resources with which to carry out far-flung schemes can be misleading. Exploitation of revenue resources was as much a royal as a baronial aim. Fortresses chased money. Controlling it also established an effective power-presence. This was the object (especially desirable on a border), not Vauban-type frontier defence. The question does not surface again until after the failure of Edward II to maintain the brief English grip on the Lowlands.[228] Even then, bans and demolitions were as much symbolic as precautionary. In 1220 the castle of Harbottle, in the borderlands though deep within Northumberland, had been extolled as a public (English) benefactor. King Robert Bruce picked on it in 1319. Following up his victory at Bannockburn, his two-year truce included refraining from building any new fortresses within the sheriffdoms of Berwick, Roxburgh, and Dumfries, and correspondingly on the English side.[229] Even there power to repress fortifying was slight. Since the earliest War of Independence against Edward I the Scots had destroyed Lowland castles, chiefly their own, to prevent the English exploiting them.[230] Harbottle, south-east of the Cheviot Hills, Bruce had briefly occupied, and from retaken Berwick in December (1319) he recorded Edward II's personal envoy's agreement to destroy it, over the head of Robert de Umfraville, its lord. Harbottle's position, 'over against the great waste', was a significant one, especially as an emblem of Scottish success.[231] The thirteen-

---

[226] *Foedera*, i, i, 474. Roger de Mortimer was to be able to build a castle within a disputed land, but Robert de Montalt was not to do so for 30 years in another. Richter, 'National Identity', 71–84, has 'a cool appraisal'.

[227] Brown *et al.*, *King's Works*, i. 66; ii. 750, 849; Poole, *Domesday Book to Magna Carta*, 282; King, *Castellarium Anglicanum*, *sub*. Northumberland, mentions two towers, one completely destroyed (1209); later revived.

[228] Documents in Stones (ed.and trans.), *Anglo-Scottish Relations 1174–1328*. Goodman, 'Defence of Northumberland', 161–72, focuses on late-14th- and 15th-century social aspects (see Part IV, Ch. 2, sec. 2 below).

[229] *CDScotland* iii. 129–30 (from a fragmentary summary). Negotiated with Aymer de Valence (earl of Pembroke), Bartholomew de Badlesmere (steward of the Household), and the bishop of Ely (chancellor).

[230] e.g. Bothwell, Lanarks, twice; 1314, 1337: Simpson, *Bothwell Castle Guide*, 7–8; the fine cylindrical *donjon* modelled on Coucy remains halved. Brown *et al.*, *King's Works*, i. 409–22.

[231] Richard de Umfraville in 1220, defending its existence against challenge, declared: 'situm est in marchia Scotiae [7½ miles from 'border'] versus Magnam Wastinam [lit. 'uncultivated land'] ad magnam utilitatem regni,tam tempore pacis quam guerrae', Shirley (ed.), *Royal Letters*, i. 140–1; n. 177 above. Harbottle's garrisoning was subsidized in 1316; in 1320 it was to be razed or delivered to Bruce;

year truce concluded in May 1323 renewed and extended the 1319 ban. The whole rather empty demonstration was more a triumphalist gesture against the castle-symbols of English power, which had extravagantly flaunted the subjugation of Wales but had entirely failed in Scotland (partly for lack of money), than it was a practicable measure of restraint. Indeed, it had conspicuously no impact on forti-fying by the magnates of the North.[232] None of the great Border fortresses (Wark, Norham, Alnwick, etc.) was touched, so English humiliation was minor. The suspicion must be that Bruce enjoyed dealing *en prince* with England as the kings of France did. The relevant passage (in French) as printed by the *Foedera*, is:

> Item, that no fortress (*forturesce*) be made nor rebuilt anew (*redresce de nouele*), on one side nor on the other; namely, within the lands contained between Scotland (*Escoce*) and the entering of the Tyne into the sea, and thence along the water of Tyne as far as South Tyne; nor [shall there be fortifying] in the land of south Tyndale, nor in the county of Cumberland, be it within franchises or without; and none on the Scottish side (*devers Escoce*) in the sheriffdoms (*viscountes*) of Berwick, Roxburgh, and Dumfries, within fran-chises and without, except the fortresses which are [now] built or are presently being built (*en fesaunt a ore*).[233]

This (theoretical) buffer zone intruded deeply into England (Cumberland and Northumberland), reflecting the extensive region most subject to Scottish raids after the English disaster at Bannockburn (1314); but it was still reciprocal, apply-ing also to the east (Berwick, Roxburgh) and to the west (Dumfries) Scottish Lowlands. The ban on fortifying seems to have been the ephemeral product of Bruce's triumph and of Edward's broken spirit. Scotland's sovereignty and England's abasement were celebrated. It is not surprising that no follow-up action occurs on the English Rolls.[234] On the Scottish side there was an equal lack of precedent. Neither king could have interfered even had he wished to. In the Marches on both sides, the northern tower-house form of castle rapidly prolifer-ated. Protecting their lords and dependants, architectural analysis shows, mattered less than proclaiming their glory, that universal motive for aristocratic building of all kinds and in all periods. In 1336, following Edward III's resumption of campaigning in the Lowlands (1333), a more realistic truce was formally promulgated which has nothing of the euphoria of Robert Bruce's ruthless counter-attack (he died in 1329) nor the supineness of the English response of 1322

---

in 1321 it was ordered to be razed according to the truce; in 1325 it was a site 'much burned by the Scots': *CPR, 1313–17*, 396; *1317–21*, 416; *1321–4*, 21–2; *CIPM* vi. 379–80.

[232] Emery, *Greater Medieval Houses*, vol. 1; nor was any royal Scottish inhibition on fortifying ever issued: W. Mackenzie, *Castle in Scotland*, 76; cf. Cruden, *Scottish Castle*, 141–2, 145.

[233] *Foedera*, ii, i, 521: by the captive French lord of Sully's mediation, after King Robert's humiliat-ing surprise attack at Old Byland had nearly captured Edward himself: Hutchinson: *Edward II*, 118–19. Scottish passion for sovereignty explored in B. Webster, 'John of Fordun', 85–102.

[234] Scant relevant licences 1323–36 (Bamburgh town, 1332; Eslington, 1335: *CChR* iv. 266–7; *CPR, 1334–8*, 78) are due to quite other factors: Emery, *Greater Medieval Houses*, i. 179. Until 1157, at least, 'the Scots thought of Carlisle and Cumberland as theirs': Barrow, 'The Scots and the North of England'; no 'frontier' even theoretically existed until 1249: J. Holt, *The Northerners*, 209.

and 1323.[235] But a narrowly military picture would still be wrong. Fortresses, though instruments of occupation, were trading places also, as essential continually to the passive and suffering majority in their everyday lives as occasionally to the soldiery. From recaptured Berwick-on-Tweed, still very poorly fortified (the castle especially), Edward III promulgated his unequal terms, including that the Scottish siege-works (*obsessiones*) at Coupar in Fife and at the small island castle of Lochindorb (*Logherindorn* in Moray, now Grampian)[236] must at once be removed and the keepers be free to come out, buy and take in provisions, and munition both *castra* without hindrance during the truce. The agreement (26 January 1336) also insisted:

> that the keepers (*custodes*) of all the other castles, peel-towers (*pelorum*), and fortresses (*fortalitiorum*) in the land of Scotland, and other people within them staying faithful to us, shall not be disturbed at all in going out of them, buying and selling victuals and anything else, exercising their business (*negotia*) throughout that land, namely they and others of their following; coming and going to and from the same castles, peels, and fortresses, and entering them to supply victuals and all things needful, as often and whenever it shall please them and other similar people.

Unrestricted freedom for merchants to trade, as well as to supply the garrisons, basing themselves in walled-towns (as usual, not differentiated from 'castles') was Edward's and King David's regents' aim, seeking to insulate economic life from hostilities. It has a pragmatic tone contrasting with the later truce of 1388 between Richard II and Robert II, when the balance of border strife was again more even. Scottish pride and English passivity resurrected Robert Bruce's symbolic 1323 ban on fortification and refortification within Northumberland and Cumberland, and north of the Border in Berwick, Roxburgh, and Dumfries counties. Under this 1388 revival, except for trade, subjects of each realm were not to 'communicate', and merchants before entering 'any castle or enclosed town' must first obtain official permission. Habituation to endemic raids, reprisals, and lawlessness made fortresses a part of ordinary living for all classes more than ever. Established castle-lords may have allowed the ban as a safeguard against upstarts; certainly, they and the leading families on both sides did not consider that it applied to them. Northern licences, even, are scarce after that for Fenwick in 1378, but not fortifying.[237] The significance was psychological. Originally it had been part of Robert Bruces's campaign to get English recognition of himself as king of Scots, dealing direct with the English king as an equal over the heads of the Border magnates. Scottish sovereign status had become enshrined in the national idea.

Interventions, chiefly hierarchical, ensured that the military freedoms natur-

---

[235] *Foedera*, ii, ii, 930–1, 933 (Mar. 1336 likewise); Nicholson, *Edward III and the Scots*, esp. 45–56, on 'the shameful peace' of 1328.

[236] Fry, *Book of Castles*, 454.

[237] *CPR*, 1377–81, 290. *CDScotland*, iv. 85, (cf. *Foedera*, viii, 35–6). As in 1336, influenced by France (now Charles VI) who nominally attested it as 'mutual (*sic*) friend' (*medne ami*). Successor to the broken truces of *c.*1381 and 1386–7, it was meant to survive the death of either king but was over by 19 June 1388: *CDScotland*, iv. 80–1; McKisack, *Fourteenth Century*, 438–40, 463.

ally vested in an armed aristocracy and operating in a number of spheres seldom went to the length of social irresponsibility. In the previous chapter the privileges of weaponry and their limits were considered. Whether these 'liberties' were arms-bearing or actual forcible self-defence and pre-emptive aggression (or worse), they cannot properly be labelled 'private war'. Examination shows that to modern eyes the less heinous 'fortifying' of noble residences, town-halls, city walls, and burgesses' houses, (as well as religious precincts and such seignoralia as granges and corn-mills) is related to noble privilege but derived its force from public authority. Accountability for that force, imperfect though it was, preserved the powerful notion of an overriding public interest. The architectural forms of conspicuous consumption, natural and proper to the wealthy in a period which made a cult of chivalric display, were naturally and inevitably those of fortification, the architectural simulacrum of force. Despite deep differences, the broad similarities between Britain and 'France' are compelling in these areas which constitute what may be described as the social and moral environment of fortresses.

However coloured by medieval (chiefly ecclesiastical) polemic, and by constitutionalists of a statist cast of mind misapplying the concepts of the modern nation, fortresses ('castles' in the original comprehensive usage) were not so much private force embodied in stone (or earthwork and timber, latterly brick) as, rather, the most conspicuous contemporary and still surviving manifestation of the socially diffusive medieval ruling class. This art, along with the 'religious' architecture to which it is so closely related as to be indistinguishable, was among the most noble achievements of medieval culture. To derive it from violence and to subordinate it to warfare is, at best, to select much less than half the picture, and to distort what remains. However incongruously (and uneasily) art historians have sometimes incorporated 'castles' into their cultural synthesis, that they do not ostracize fortresses entirely is a victory of sympathetic insight over conditioned expectation. Theirs is the lead to follow. It lies closer to elusive aristocratic ultimate reality than does warfare.[238]

---

[238] e.g. Brieger, *English Art, 1216–1307*, 258–70 (with 'military' spasms; pp. 258–61, aesthetically acute); also J. Evans, *English Art, 1307–1461*, ch. 6 (excellent in parts); and Frankl, *Gothic Architecture*, 244–51; also Tulse, *Castles of the Western World* (Teutonic). Heslop, 'Orford', and *Norwich Castle Keep*, *passim* (acute but adventurous); Coulson, 'Cultural Realities' (bibliography). Fernie, *Architecture of Norman England*, seamlessly integrates secular noble buildings with ecclesiastical. Brown, 'Status of the Norman Knight', contrastingly believed that *militaria* have had insufficient insight—'There are not many horsy figures among academics, any more than love of war' (p. 140). Cf. *ANS* 6 (1983), frontispiece. But military history has a large constituency, fully served.

3

Private Property But Public Utility

Considering that they were personal and family residences, the degree of subordination of castles to public priorities is remarkable. Fortresses were not above the law, and more importantly they were not outside it. This chapter begins by examining some sharper consequences of their dual personality—in what circumstances it was acceptable for them to be seized or even demolished (though still not erased from the map). Because war, it may be said, was not so much the vocation of fortresses as their hobby, certainly very seldom their *raison d'être*, it is almost always by ordinary mundane custom, not by any martial law, that they were regulated. The rarity of 'military history' (sieges, storms, and suchlike) at the great majority of sites refutes violent caricatures as well as the notion of a dedicated defensive architecture[239]—unless medieval builders were as one-track-minded as the modern war-gamer. But if being attacked was normally unlikely, interference in the public interest represented by the castellan's superior (*senyor*, *seigneur*, or lord) was a contingent liability of the fortress. Their possession was therefore interruptible (rendability: see sec. 2)—and their very existence as fortresses was terminable. But this degree of subservience to powers above did not mean that castles aroused no resentment on the part of subordinates. In section 3 some notable instances of urban hostility are included. Since the clergy, the *bourgeoisie*, and even the rural populace possessed their own castles, resentments were often those of rivals rather than of victims.

1. Legitimate Sequestration and Improper Demolition

Police action, with growing frequency from the late thirteenth century (but still only occasionally), is recorded as causing the short-term taking over of a fortress to repress armed conflict, actual or incipient. In England early examples are Penros, in the Welsh March (Mons.) in a dispute over possession in 1248–52;[240] and the castle of Chartley (Staffs.) in similar circumstances (1271, 1282).[241]

---

[239] Tabulated in D. King, *Castellarium Anglicanum*, using narrative and record sources to reduce the 'problem of silence'. His own convictions were military-utilitarian: e.g. pp. xv–xvi; cf. pp. xxi–xxii.

[240] *CPR, 1247–58*, 28–9, 97–8, 100, 202; *Close Rolls, 1247–51*, 540–1; *1251–3*, 50, 54: an early motte castle (cf. Caer Penrhos, Cardigan).

[241] *CCR, 1272–9*, 12, 17–18; *CPR, 1281–92*, 39–40, 53. Motte with two baileys, updated with 13th-century masonry.

Comparable measures in France occur even before the marked extension of royal jurisdiction initiated by Philip IV (1285–1314). An instance in 1268, seignorial though quasi-royal, since it was Louis IX's brother Alphonse de Poitiers, who was acting, as count of Toulouse, concerned La Mothe-Cabanac (*dép.* Haute-Garonne). The minor lordly seat (*forcia*) had been taken over by the Paris-based count's local representative. In December 1268 Jordan de L'Isle, its lord, asked to have it back. Count Alphonse's record relates the circumstances, according to Jordan's petition:

It has been shown to us on behalf of our *nobilis et fidelis* knight Jordan, lord of L'Isle, complaining that our dear and faithful P. de Landreville, knight, now deceased, once our seneschal of Toulouse and Albi, took into our hand Jordan's fortress of La Mothe (*Mota*) for the good of the peace, because of the conflict (*guerra*) between Jordan's son and his people with Lord Bernard of Astaffort, knight, and his partisans (*complices*). Now this fortress ought to have been restored and returned to Jordan at the Feast of All Saints [1 November 1268] last passed, but has, he asserts, not yet been restored to him. We therefore direct you [the present seneschal], having fully inquired the truth of the matter, to have the fortress returned to the same (Jordan and his son), unless you should find reasonable cause why the fortress ought not to be handed back (*reddi*); and provided that it was indeed taken and retained by our people. You are first to discuss the matter and take counsel with Sicard Alemann, knight, and the deceased seneschal's people (*gentes*), who know the full truth.[242]

This so-called 'war' against the neighbouring Astaffort party, as so often, was a formal state of declared hostility—what, from its minor nature, might otherwise be called a mere aggravated quarrel, or an affray (were this not also a technical term). *Guerra* grandly flattered and proclaimed the status of these lordlings near the marches of Plantagenet Gascony.[243] Alphonse was right to be wary of possible manipulation by misinformation, relying on his trusted roving lieutenant Alemann. If the facts were as Jordan represented them (and the tone is one of believing him), Alphonse, through his seneschal, had entirely 'reasonably' seized La Mothe-Cabanac, but not quite impartially as it was an apparently one-sided act doubtless intended to check aggression by Jordan's (unnamed) son.[244] This residence itself may have been used as a base; but impounding it temporarily by way of indirect distraint was the sort of salutary shock otherwise solely administered after proper judicial process, culminating in forfeiture as a last resort. 'Confiscation' in the sense of arbitrary seizure was seldom lawful, and was accordingly rare.[245] In contrast, but after due process as a punitive act of derogation and humbling of an offender, damage was quite often inflicted on the residences of

---

[242] *Correspondance A. de Poitiers*, i. 596; probably L'Isle Jourdain (*dép.* Gers, *arr.* Auch). As was usual, Jordan employed an agent (Pons Astoard, knight) and a barrister (Maître Odo de *Montoreria*) at court in Paris.

[243] On 'private' war under the 1339 Gascon liberties see n. 80 above.

[244] On the lord's 'duty of not acting in any way that would injure the life, honour, or property, of the vassal', see Ganshof, *Feudalism*, 85. The ubiquitous test of acting *rationabiliter* and *per rationabilem causam* implemented this general obligation of good lordship (ibid. 85–8); n. 328 below.

[245] Reynolds, *Fiefs and Vassals*, 60–2, 157–8 (Carolingian transition), 319, 344, cf. 'forfeiture'.

culprits regardless of whether they were houses or fortresses, in the records of
Louis IX (1226–70) and especially by verdict of the parlement under Philip IV.[246]
We have met it already, particularly as a tool of condign humiliation of opponents
(with little or no judicial process) used by Henry II and King John in England.[247]
It was most derogating when inflicted on a fortress, of course, because slighting
(truly 'insulting') and demolishing fortresses brands them seemingly as anti-
social (although it was the owner and his pretensions which were the target).
Some examination of cases is needed.

   King John (ultimately disastrously) so often ordered fortresses to be
'destroyed' during the political crises in France of 1202–4[248] and in England of
1212, and in the actual hostilities of 1215–16, that some at least of his later orders
for castles to be demolished can only have been coded 'counter-signs' put in to
authenticate his writs to his henchmen.[249] The fact that often there was no actual
demolition or corroboration (e.g. by record of expenses incurred)—and considering the sheer impossibility of hasty execution in many instances—suggests a
subtler agenda.[250] John's suspicious nature (and suspicion of him) may have initiated the keeping on Rolls of the very copies of writs on which we depend. What
is not plausible is that these were acts of military precaution against some revived
danger from 'private castles'. Individual circumstances seldom support such
interpretations, which give more credence to royalist propaganda and to 'strategic' ideas than either of them deserves.

   Whatever ills John's demolition orders may be imagined to have averted, he
brought more trouble upon himself by actions supported by no baronial consensus as to what constituted good lordship, or even acceptable precaution.[251] It
damaged loyalty in the county of Anjou, in the summer of 1202, to seize lands and

---

[246] e.g. by Abbeville borough custom (1184), as more generally in Picardy: *Recueil Ponthieu*, 160 (8);
also at the Cinque Ports (Kent–Sussex), but noted as 'a strange custom', Round, *Feudal England*,
416–23.

[247] nn. 198, 126, 81 above; nn. 197, 169, etc. above.

[248] n. 82 above. That some of these 'destruction orders' may have been authenticating countersigns
was suggested by Brown in 1953, 'English Castles, 1154–1216', 271, 339–40. On co-operation with the
Crown over castles, ibid. 354–6.

[249] On this habit, 'too clever by half—that was the trouble with John', Warren, *King John*, 190 (also
on his 'unnecessarily underhand or nasty behaviour'). At Cirencester, 1 Sept. 1216, with civil war in the
SE, John instructed the constable of Newark on Trent castle, of the bishop of Lincoln (where he died
11 October), to hand over custody 'by these countersigns (*intersignis*) that we have told you that you
should overthrow the castle to the foundations or commit it to the bishop's seneschal'. The constable
had used *alliis et intersignis* to inform the king that the custody was 'burdensome': *Rot Litt Pat*, 195b.
Also undoubtedly spoof for Richmond (1215–16), ibid. 148b (nothing done), cf. 186b probably likewise
at Sleaford (1216); cf. possibly acted on Tamworth (1215): *Rot Litt Claus*, 279a, 244b. Also Painter, *King
John*, 107–8; Church (ed.), *King John*.

[250] But Malton (Yorks.) in 1213 had expenditure recorded for its razing: n. 263 below. Cf. Painter,
King John, ch. 9 ('The Civil War'), pp. 61, 350–3, 372, etc. Reasons for ascribing the Patent, Close,
Liberate, etc. Rolls personally to John (rather than to Hubert Walter), ibid. 97–106 (esp. 104). But
'much business, especially when of a dubious nature', was not enrolled: Jolliffe, *Angevin Kingship*, 75.

[251] Cf. his supportive subsidies for Parthenay (Poitou: May 1202); to enclose Rouen (Feb. 1203); to
fortify *Bodlamcourt* (June 1200), Chennebrun (June 1202), Tosny (Feb. 1203), and Douville (Apr. 1203),
all in Normandy: *Rot Litt Pat*, 11a, 25a; *Rot Norm*, 26, 52, 74, 87.

castles until their tenants had 'made good security of good and faithful service'—
as John did to the lord of Châteaubriant and to the vicomte de Thouars.[252] Gérard
d'Athies, his mercenary captain watching potential waverers in Anjou at this time,
was backed up by an overweening mandate to the seneschal of the province, dated
by the king on 5 August 1202 at the great Plantagenet depot, treasury, palace, and
fortress of Chinon (*dép.* Indre-et-Loire). Gérard was told to 'keep' William de
Précigni's lands and 'wholly throw down his fortresses (*forteslescias*)'. Before
handing over Torigny in Normandy (*dép.* Manche) to Jean du Bois in May 1203,
John instructed the seneschal to 'have the castle thrown down (*prostratum*)', so
that Jean received only the town and territory.[253] Jean, it is true, had been only the
appointed constable; but naked coercion, thinly justified as pre-emptive precaution, is blatant in the treatment of Geoffroi de Palluau.[254] In August 1203 King
John accepted the advice of Gérard d'Athies that Geoffroi be freed, having given
oaths and hostages and after handing over as agreed his castle of Montrésor (*dép.*
Indre-et-Loire *arr.* Loches). Geoffroi will have thought this was to be a temporary
pledge, in the usual way, but d'Athies (not noted for moderation) was brusquely
told:[255]

when you shall have received that castle of Montrésor you are to have it thrown down
(*prosterni*) at once, because we will that this and other [castles] which could be acquired by
our enemies shall be thrown down, sparing only the castle (*castris*) of Loches and other our
demesnal castles (*dominicis castris*) which are in your area of responsibility (*pertinentiis
vestris*).[256]

Armed with this writ, d'Athies was, no doubt, able to bully more severely—but
rule based on the principles of Caligula showed its defects in the collapse of loyalty
which caused the Plantagenet débâcle in Normandy and to the south.
Unsurprisingly, we find that Geoffroi de Palluau concluded a rendability pact in
July 1205 (one of many by the castellans of Anjou and Touraine) at Chinon itself
with Philip II of France, from whom he could expect punctilious lordship. No less
cunning than John, Philip knew how to behave with politic decency.[257] It was not

---

[252] *Rot Norm*, 55 (14 July 1202); in Oct. 1201 he seized Moncontour castellary (*castrum et pertinentia*)
on his Poitou campaign, without legal process; early in 1202 he made Rannulf of Chester give pledges
to deliver ('render') Semilly castle (*dép.* Manche) at will, released Apr. 1203: *Rot Litt Pat*, 2a, 7b, 28a;
Rot Norm, 96–7.

[253] *Rot Norm*, 59, 95. With Torigny, a major fortress and later granted, perhaps in fact only a 'countersign': F. Powicke, *Loss of Normandy*, 183–4.

[254] By comparison, the razing of buildings encumbering urban defences was costly but is reliably
diagnostic; e.g. 6 May 1216, 'all houses in the ditch and on the walls and barbican' at Exeter: *Rot Litt
Claus*, 270; also at Cherbourg; likewise castles near towns in war, as Le Gard and Montferrand near
Bordeaux in 1294–1303 (n. 11 above).

[255] *Rot Litt Pat*, 33a; Gérard's 'relatives and his whole following' (named) by the Articles of the
Barons (1215) were to be removed from all English office (*ballia*); he is duly first named as proscribed
in Magna Carta: *Stubbs's Select Charters*, 289 (40), 299 (49).

[256] Montrésor's early *donjon*, ascribed to Count Fulk Nerra of Anjou (987–1040), survives: Enaud,
Les Châteaux forts, 220. Palluau was an impressive hexagonal castle in the later 13th century, not to be
confused with Palluau in Berry; Baudry, *Fortifications des Plantagenêts en Poitou*, 209–14.

[257] J. Baldwin, 'La Décennie décisive: les années 1190–1203', anticipates somewhat. *Layettes*, i. 293–4;
with three guarantors, each pledging 250 marks, for due delivery of the *fortericia* to Philip or his

that John really thought that the only good castles were royal: his hubris ended in paranoia once he had alienated his natural supporters. Few insults hurt them more deeply than damage to their castles. Individually fortresses were easily put out of action (for example, by burning), whether penally or as a precaution, however ill-judged, but the institution as a whole and the realities of power which fortresses enshrined were very resilient. The power-balance was not to be changed as easily as Allen Brown believed. More apt was his comment on Henry II's takeover 'of all the castles in England (and Normandy)', by putting royal keepers in them, reported by two chroniclers for the year 1176 (a unique English mass use of rendability), by which he affirmed that 'the private castle survived as triumphantly after 1176 as before'.[258] There was no antithesis between kingly power ('monarchy' it literally was not) and seignorial fortresses beyond what was inherent in the pluralist power-sharing of the medieval polity.[259] Consensus very seldom broke down—when it did, all bets were off. Conditions were far from normal in Normandy, Anjou, and Touraine prior to the seizure of the duchy by the French in 1203–4. Worse still was the acute English crisis on the brink of warfare in 1212–13. But Capetian comparisons show that fortress-law could cope, given a record of decent lordship. Without it 'everything was given over to the power of the sword', as Charles I expressed it on the scaffold (1649). Expediency now ruled. In August 1212 King John sent the following direction to his mercenary captain in west Wales, Fawkes de Bréauté: 'We order you to destroy as much as you can of Strata Florida abbey [Cardiganshire] which, as you inform us, sustains our enemies. And the ruinous (*debilia*) castles of your bailiwick, which cannot be held, you are to have burned; those which are good and tenable you are to munition well and cause to be kept (*custodiri*).'[260] Substantial, especially stone, buildings of any kind might defensively harbour guerrillas. The great Cistercian abbey, consecrated in 1201, may have been 'incastellated', but mere punishment for offending de Bréauté is as likely a reason, although no resultant damage is now apparent.[261] Perhaps Fawkes's warrant was sufficient to intimidate the monks. Eliminating potential enemy lodgements in the lesser castles, most still of earth and timber, made no political sense, whatever the militiary excuse.[262] Putting in royal troops was already standard practice; but Fawkes's *carte blanche* was framed so as to demonstrate his full powers.

'legitimate heir', *ad magnam vim et ad parvam, quociens ab ipso fuero requisitus*. On Chinon (superseded by the stupendous Capetian castle of Angers in the 1230s) and Loches (of Fulk Nerra) see Mesqui, *Châteaux forts*, 18–21, 125–7, 217–20.

[258] Brown 'List of Castles', 253; two authors, in three chronicles (n. 5): n. 289 below.

[259] Reynolds, *Fiefs and Vassals*, 34–40, 475–90, etc.

[260] Warren, *King John*, 199–200 on the aborted 1212 Welsh campaign. *Rot Litt Claus*, i. 122a. Timbered earthwork castles, in the *honor* of Montgomery were still the rule in 1224–5: *Rott Litt Claus*, i. 605a (royal grant of timber to lords *ad fortelicias suas firmandas*); ibid. ii. 42a: order *quod sine dilacione motas suas bonis bretasciis firmari faciant*, for their and local protection.

[261] Butler and Given-Wilson, *Medieval Monasteries*, 347–8; not completed until the 1270s but begun in 1184: Radford, *Strata Florida Abbey Guide*, 1–2. Of Norman foundation, it soon became a Welsh native cultural centre.

[262] Cf. Avent, 'Castles of the Welsh Princes', 11–20.

In May 1213 John's order to another henchman, Philip Oldcoats in Northumberland, 'so to throw down Eustace de Vesci's castle of Alnwick that it cannot henceforth be of use (*necessarium*) to him', was possibly executed, although expenditure on such a considerable task was recorded only for razing Malton castle (Yorks.). The target in both cases was John's bitter enemy.[263] Personal animosity, and a ruthlessness which Henry II had had the power to let loose but which in John was pure recklessness, was worse still for being implemented by outsiders, alien to the English baronage, creatures of his favour. Not only fortresses felt John's spite. With no shadow even of military justification he made an example of Henry de Braybrooke: in May 1215 his lands and chattels were seized and the king ordered that 'his houses be thrown down to the foundations (*funditus prosternere*)', in the stock phrase made callous by repetition. At Runnymede, five weeks later, Henry's restitution was reluctantly ordered;[264] but castle, manor, abbey, or mere *domus* was not so quickly rebuilt, or local reputation restored or compensation made, by the Magna Carta showdown.

Less pressure than was applied at that famous confrontation by concerted baronial indignation had already obtained redress for the bishop of London. His castle of Stortford (Herts.) was dismantled by royal order in 1213, apparently soon after Bishop William's joint embassy to Rome had produced Pope Innocent III's formal deposition of the king.[265] But whether this behaviour was an act of war, of reprisal, precaution, or of mere revenge, spite, and intimidation matters little, since even in war the Crown was bound by custom. It is all too easy in retrospect to slip into amoral *raison d'état*, applying to castles such ideas as 'confiscate', 'requisition', 'commandeer', 'resume', 'eliminate', ' take out', and so on.[266] Bishop William and the Church were better able than most to protect their own property. John issued this conciliatory open letter accordingly in late November 1214, after he had returned from the crushing defeat of his grand alliance on the field of Bouvines at the hands of Philip Augustus. The abbreviated Patent Roll copy gives all but the opening in full: 'The king to all faithful [people] to whom this present writing

[263] *Rot Litt Pat*, 99a. Holt, *The Northerners*, ch. 6 (the 1212 rebellion); pp. 94–5, on Alnwick being in use (again) in the civil war (1215), ibid. 134. Even true 'demolitions' were militarily rarely permanent. Alnwick's rebuilding by the Percies from *c*.1309 has removed traces of any 1213 damage.

[264] *Rot Litt Claus*, i. 200a, 216b. The agent, Geoffrey de Marteny, was proscribed in 1215 by the Articles of the Barons as incorporated in Magna Carta: *Stubbs's Select Charters*, 289 (40), 299(50). Henry was loyal in 1212 as under-sheriff of Northants; sheriff but wavering in 1215, checked by Marteny's appointment as constable of Northampton castle; removed as sheriff, 25 June 1215, two days after his forced restitution: Painter, *King John*, 268, 287, 302, 307, 329.

[265] *Rot Litt Pat*, 101b; King, *Castellarium Anglicanum*, *sub*. Herts. Bishop William was exiled 1208; episcopal refugees' lands suffered after the Interdict published by the bishops of London, Ely, and Worcester; in 1209 they wielded the papal threat of excommunicating John, published in November: Painter, *King John*, 175, 179, 182, 190; Warren, *King John*, 169.

[266] e.g. Painter's picture of John: cynic, mordant humourist, anticlerical, principled defender of 'royal right'(cf. power), suppressor of 'feudal rebellion'; even nationalist as in Shakespeare, but with 1939–45 resonances ('island kingdom', etc.)—is rationalized in his *King John*, ch. 6 ('King or Tyrant'). Despite the 'unhistorical method' of Chief Justice Sir Edward Coke (1552–1634), his remark that 'Magna Charta is such a fellow that he will have no sovereign' (1628) is memorable: McKechnie, *Magna Carta*, 208, 447, etc.; Jolliffe, *Angevin Kingship*, 50–109, 301–10 is corrective.

(*scriptum*) shall come [sends] greeting. Know that we are under obligation (*tenemur*) at the reasonable summons of our venerable father [-in-God], W. bishop of London, to repair the castle of Stortford as well and as strong as it was when the discord began between us and the clergy of England . . .' With the usual pious realism John explicitly provided that if he should die before carrying out his promise, William or his successor would be entitled to require its fulfilment from his heir.[267] That John's motive had been revenge for the papal Interdict (1209) and deposition from the throne is obliquely acknowledged. William was vulnerable in his Hertfordshire lands as he was not in his cathedral city.

Wider issues than defending the reputation of castles are present. Conflict did not obliterate property rights, nor were fortresses a category apart. Special customs reflected their peculiar status—which was more seignorial than strategic—but as residences they were still landed property. No sort of 'martial law' set these principles aside; but warfare inevitably bent them. When conflict resumed after Runnymede, King John not unjustly ordered (December 1215) his forces to go to Tamworth (Staffs.), 'taking to our use' all the prisoners, horses, arms and other armour (*harnasiis*) found in the castle'; but he then overstepped the mark (unless it was an authenticating code) by ordering the buildings to be 'demolished'.[268] In fact, the ancient motte with its shell-keep, and other enclosures, defied rapid destruction. It is not really so strange, in the wider view, that many earthwork castles were militarily ephemeral but institutionally and physically almost ineradicable. Solidity and concentrated weight of masonry, by contrast, were the undoing of Rochester castle. Archbishop Corbeil's magnificent 'great tower' (1127–c.1136) and nearby curtain wall fell to tunnelling, which destroyed the entire southern corner, in October–November 1215. This was a siege where the building itself was an instrument of resistance to King John in person. His summons to surrender it was rejected with contumely; so it was damaged in exemplary style as an example to others. At least the Barnwell chronicler was impressed, commenting: 'Our age has not known a siege so hard pressed nor so strongly resisted . . . Afterwards few cared to put their trust in castles.'[269]

Relying upon castles in that fashion was never prudent. Solving an immediate military problem and achieving psychological impact here were simultaneous. But very often 'slighting' served no 'strategic' or moral purpose, inculcating fear

---

[267] *Rot Litt Pat*, 124a. No royal expenditure on the castle is noted by Brown, 'Royal Castle Building', 394–8; nor (1214–16 or later) by Brown *et al.*, *King's Works*. The surviving structure (oval motte with tower, and bailey) is 'early' and not illuminating. William de Albini's Belvoir (Leics.), possibly slighted in 1201, appears to be a similar case: *RotLib*, 34–5 (May 1203); cf. Painter, *King John*, 48.

[268] *Rot Litt Claus*, i. 244b: *statim illud prosterni faciatis* (a countersign?). Torching floors, roofs, doors, palisades, etc. was quick—but is not indicated.

[269] n. 109 above; 1127 custody grant to archbishop (not 'licence'): *Regesta*, ii. 203, 356; and Coulson, 'Castles of the Anarchy', 79; Brown, *Rochester Castle Guide*, 11–13; Bradbury, *Medieval Siege*, 139–40. It had been in conditional royal custody under archiepiscopal guarantee, 'so that by it no ill or harm shall come to us or our kingdom' (i.e. jurability). John accused Langton of treacherously refusing to hand it over as (diagnostically) demanded 'in our great need' (rendability). Intricacies explored in Rowlands, 'King John, Stephen Langton and Rochester Castle'.

and loathing rather than respect, as John's ruthlessness often did. Fortresses were not public enemies. Ordering demolitions at the royal hunting-lodge castle of Knepp in May 1215 (transferring the troops there to the *domus* and *castrum* of Bramber, Sussex),[270] likewise at Richmond (Yorks.) in July, and elsewhere before he died (19 October 1216),[271] might be defended as frantic necessities (perhaps rationalized as a 'scorched-earth' policy), or discounted as countersigns to re-assure the recipients, but King John was perfectly capable of desiring it done.[272] Additions to his 'favourite' castle of Corfe show a strong aesthetic sense, but others' residential property, besides Braybrooke's, of all kinds indiscriminately drew his venom.[273] On the Close Roll for 10 April 1216, under the heading 'lands seized into the lord king's hand', the royal constable of Norwich's warrant to persecute four named local dissidents instructs him at once to seize their lands . . . 'And if you are able to take their persons (*corpora*), keep them securely until further order. Also you are to root out [the crops] on all of William de Hasting's land, give over his demesnes (*dominica*) to fire and destroy them, and throw down his castle (*castrum*), keeping his land securely'.[274] Actions of this type, not only by John and his father Henry II, but after his majority even occasionally by his son Henry III,[275] do not agree with the royalist scenario of impartial public spirit. Because fortresses expressed pride in wealth, rank, and power they were quite often targeted. Wartime munitioning, countermanded at Bury St Edmunds in 1215, and forcible damage to, and encroachments upon, the property of others must be distinguished, being aspects of the general interruption of the peace.[276] The suspension of vested fortifying rights during truces is a similar peripheral issue, as we have seen. Fortresses belonged to society at large, and particularly to its aristocracy (rulers, prelates, baronage, knighthood, gentry, and burgesses), as one of the warlike appurtenances attached to rank. That religious precincts were crenellated and towered, and that the image of the greater churches themselves

[270] *Rot Litt Pat*, 137b: John, at Freemantle (Forest, Hants.), on 18 May notified R. Bloet that the Londoners had 'of their own pure, spontaneous initiative' gone over the day before to Louis of France. Knepp, 22 May 1215, referred to as still operative; order 'to burn and demolish'; repeated June 1216: *Rot Litt Pat*, 138a, 187a. Knepp and Bramber had been seized from the de Braose; restored to Giles de Braose, Oct. 1215: Brown *et al.*, *King's Works*, ii. 691.

[271] e.g. *Rot Litt Pat*, 148b, 186b, 184b (Bolsover), 186a, 190a (Stogursey), 195b (Newark); *Rot Litt Claus*, i. 279a (Sleaford), 284 (Newark).

[272] Jolliffe, *Angevin Kingship*, 108 etc.; cf. John 'endeavouring to tread the narrow course between the letter of the rigid law and formless equity', and his 'singular strength of character, a genuine *stabilitas*', etc.: D. M. Stenton, 'King John and the Courts of Justice', 108, 111.

[273] esp. the Gloriette chamber-block in the upper ward: Brown *et al.*, *King's Works*, ii. 617, pl. 37.

[274] *Rot Litt Claus*, i. 260a: one of the silent majority not in Brown's documentary 'List of Castles' (327 recorded, England and Wales).

[275] e.g. after the Marshal revolt, 1233, including Inkberrow *domus* or castle (Worcs.): *Close Rolls*, 1231–4, 542–3. A 'manor and park' in 1296: *CIPM* iii. 221.

[276] Dec. 1215: injunction to the prior and sacristan of the abbey not to fortify (*firmare*) Bury town, 'which is situated within the truce area'. They are to destroy any works put up, expelling rebels and excommunicates. In May 1215 the abbey had been helped to get tenants' defence-duties performed: *Rot Litt Pat*, 135a, 161. Fawkes de Bréauté's outbreak (Bedford) in 1224 was presaged by his munitioning of Plympton castle (Devon) in 1221: Shirley (ed.), *Royal Letters*, i. 172–3.

was distinctly (if often more allusively) castellated, demonstrates the fact.[277] The king built in that spirit. His nobles emulated him as their means allowed.

Fortifying was a noble attribute and the subordination of fortresses to the public interest (loosely as this moral concept has to be applied) was also institutional and positively enshrined in medieval law and custom. In a variety of ways the doctrine was asserted that fortification was a public trust. Fortress tenure was conditional, like no other property held in fief. This legal characteristic, fully practised but technically undeveloped in England, was what differentiated them, not any gradation of 'strength'. It is allied with that other peculiarity already mentioned—the whole panoply of castellated buildings, whether (to us) 'seriously fortified' or 'non-functional' (sic) or even 'decorative', were (to contemporaries) true fortresses. Structural solidity, sophistication, size, and siege-potential varied according to the lord's resources and local aims.[278] Magnates built great castles (unless a fortlet was more in keeping with rank in the local hierarchy), and the sub-knightly class (always fluid but ever-growing as knighthood moved up the social scale) built what are usually 'fortified manor-houses' and *manoirs* to us, but to contemporaries were often 'castles' and normally 'fortresses', almost regardless of size.[279] The *mentalité* was not utilitarian, as this northern French case of 1253 demonstrates:

We, brother Gualeran, monk and chamberlain of Saint Germain des Prés, make known to all who shall see this writing (*ces letres*), that because we had begun [to build] an enclosure of walls around our property (*pourpris*) near Couilly [*dép.* Seine-et-Marne], the which had belonged to the late Rigaut, the knight (*le chevalier*); [and since] we had made upon these walls two small turrets (*tourneletes*), the nobleman Gaucher de Châtillon, lord of Crécy [by Meaux], has accorded to us by the advice of his dear brother, the count of Saint-Pol, and of other good people, that we may complete (*parfacom*) the aforesaid walls in the manner (*ordre*) in which they have been started . . .[280]

The touchy situation may be visualized: the wealthy ecclesiastic, out to set himself up, in the timeless way acquires a country seat and decides to dignify it with a turreted curtilage. Since *tourelle* regularly meant 'mural tower', differentiated from *tour* (and *turris*), which still usually meant 'great tower' or donjon ('keep' in post-medieval English[281]), 'two small turrets' need not be diminutive—quite large enough, however understated by Gualeran, to arouse the suspicion of competition in lordly rights in the lord of Crécy-en-Brie. Lordlings, not magnates or

---

[277] n. 238 above. Full treatment in preparation, Coulson, *Castles and Crenellating*.

[278] e.g. the imposing 'gate-house castle' of Bywell (Northumb.), built *c*.1415–25 by Ralph Neville 'as an outpost to protect his tenants in an area under Percy domination . . . [with its] more elegant form and decorative windows': Emery, *Greater Medieval Houses*, i. 62.

[279] By entrenched modern usage eg. Viollet-le-Duc, *Dictionnaire de l'architecture*, art. 'Manoir'. Except by locals and by Scots, northern and Lowland tower-houses are often still denied the style 'castle'.

[280] *Layettes*, iii. 192; Part I, n. 303 above.

[281] Kenyon, Thompson, 'The Origin of the Word "keep" ', 175–6: arguing for corruption of *La Cupe*, at Guisnes (late and unduly technical).

rulers, were naturally the most jealous and watchful for possible encroachment.[282] Lord Gaucher's licence, therefore, restricted the fortifying to the unpretentious 'order' of the work already done. Even so, because the mere emblems of fortification still implied noble authority, Gualeran had to promise that, by virtue of his castellated garden wall, neither he

nor others who come after us may be empowered to request or claim against the lord of Crécy any (right associated with) fortress or defence (*forterece ne deffense*), nor against his people, by virtue of these two turrets or of either of them. Should we, or our successor, do so then we [or he] must have these turrets pulled down (*abatre*) at the lord of Crécy's requisition or to his command.

To the document the abbey chamberlain's seal of Saint German-des-Prés remains attached. 'Fortress or defence' covered a raft of seignorial 'military' prestigious and lucrative powers: future (unlicensed) fortifying, jurisdictional rights, perhaps local guard services (*guet et garde*) and claims to serf-labour, and so on, all of them tending to compete with and reduce the status and revenues of the lord of the fief, cadet of the established but minor comital house of Saint-Pol. An alternative solution would have been to make Couilli rendable to Gaucher de Châtillon and his successors.[283]

2. Lordly Castles in 'Public' Use

The whole hierarchical milieu explains why rendability was so much more than military commandeering or than delivery in proof of loyalty (a commoner occasion). It was an act assertive of lordship, available solely (with rare exceptions) to the immediate lord.[284] The vassal-castellan, by handing over his fortress (for this purpose uniquely severed from its lands and revenues) at his lord's demand, acknowledged ('recognized') his subordination[285]—more than that, the primeval Carolingian public quality attached to fortresses per se[286] was affirmed and extended whenever a fortress was recognized to be or was made rendable anew. The tradition had crossed the Channel to England in 1066, where the public character of fortresses had long been (and remained) inherent.[287] Only a full political history of castles in Britain could sufficiently show to what extent co-operation with the Crown was continuous, occasional perhaps but as normal as lordly participation in the administration of justice and in the functions of 'national' and local govern-

---

[282] Coulson, 'Sanctioning of Fortresses in France'. Licensing sometimes kept the peace between vassals.

[283] Solution frequently adopted in Champagne: Coulson, 'Castellation in Champagne', 357–62.

[284] Summarized in seignorial perspective *c*.1283 by Beaumanoir, the former royal *bailli*, see Coulson, 'Valois Powers', 150–1; n. 124 above.

[285] e.g. compilation process of the 1274 Gascon inquiry, *Recognitiones*, pp. xxvii–xxx; acknowledgements of rendable castles and towns are nos. 38, 209, 291, 324, 332, 401, 485, 487, 528 (1274).

[286] Faithfully echoed in the *c*.1022–8 *Conventum*: Coulson, 'French Matrix', 76–80.

[287] e.g. Radford, 'Later Pre-Conquest Boroughs', 1091, *Consuetudines et Justicie* cl. 4 states finally 'et nulli licuit in Normannia fortitudinem castelli sui vetare domino Normannie si ipse eam in manu sua voluit habere': Haskins, *Norman Institutions*, 282.

ment. According to the chronicler William of Malmesbury, the rendability principle was enunciated by Archbishop Hugh of Rouen in council at Winchester in 1139,
on the eve of the civil war.[288] He gave it a royalist slant, as befitted his position, the
English scene, and the dire occasion: 'as it is a time of suspicion all the chief men,
in accordance with the custom of other peoples, ought to put all the keys of their
fortifications (*munitionum*) at the disposal of the king who has to strive for the
peace of all.' It was no formality. The Empress Mathilda's claim to the throne was
reviving. Offering entry to King Stephen's forces tested the loyalty of Henry I's
former clan of episcopal civil servants and dependants. Unwisely, and contrary to
'French' practice, Stephen resorted to seizing castles instead. As in the Dinan scene
in the Bayeux Tapestry (Duke Conan's surrender), in 1139 keys symbolized repos-
sessory right, which continued with walled towns into modern times. It was exercised (bishops of Salisbury, Lincoln, and Ely) by putting in custodians (which, as
already noted, Henry II did to all English baronial castles in 1176[289]), a normal
Angevin practice in individual cases.[290] Proper garrisons, if need be, could be put in
(not a supervising agent). Alternatively, hoisting the lord's banner, with or without
preliminary vacation of the fortress by its lord and his people, and all the ceremony
of brief but complete resumption of control, effectually asserted the same principle.[291] Certainly, 'public' doctrine with rights of authority in general had become
'feudalized' (nominally delegated), but in England the process left to the Crown a
much larger role than in France, where fortress-duties theoretically owed to the king
had long before 1180 devolved upon magnates[292] (and further down the scale[293]),
along with the right to license fortification (in England after *c*.1200 still not quite a
royal monopoly). This 'privatization' ('usurpation' in French tradition) was only
slowly reduced by Philip II (1180–1223). Although serious inroads upon it began
under Philip IV, centralization was still very incomplete as late as 1789. Rights over
fortresses chart the whole monarchical progress in France, which in England was
telescoped and condensed. In both kingdoms, because gates, towers, battlemented
walls, and the powerful (or merely pompous) display of fortified strength expressed
and made most conspicuous the social pride and class-awareness of seignorial,
ecclesiastical, and *bourgeois* personalities, dynasties, and corporations, so it was at

[288] King (ed.), *William of Malmesbury, Historia Novella*, 59; Coulson, 'Castles of the Anarchy', 74–5.
[289] n. 258 above. Brown, 'List of Castles', 253, citing e.g. *Gesta Henrici Secundi*, i. 127, that he 'sent his
envoys around all the castles of England (*per universa castella Anglie*) and took them into his hand',
and in Normandy likewise—quite possible in the light of rendability (then unknown to Brown), e.g.
by hoisting the king's banner in notional takeover, or even by putting in custodians. Stenton (ed.), *The
Bayeux Tapestry*, pl. 26. Conan holds the keys of Dinan out on his lance (ref. M. Prestwich).
[290] Much unpublished material, widely derived, in Brown, 'English Castles, 1154–1216', esp. ch. 8,
'Baronial Castles and the Crown' (pp. 300–62). Intervention was chiefly by sending one or more
sergeants, not to control (much less to guard) but to restrain 'baronial' constables. From 1199 evidence
of costs (esp. Pipe Roll) is supplemented (with gaps) by enrolled Chancery mandates.
[291] In 1176, according to the *Gesta*, signalized (and effectuated) by first removing the normal keepers—a practice later evidenced esp. in Languedoc: these details await comprehensive treatment.
[292] For reminiscences of early Capetian (claimed) monopoly, Coulson, 'Fortress-Policy', 17–22.
[293] e.g. rendability, etc. pacts within the Tournan-Gallande family over La-Houssaye-en-Brie *domus
fortis*, 1217–41: *Layettes*, i. 450–1, ii. 24–5, 410, 448.

and with their fortifications that their owners' wider accountability was most emphasized. In France rendability was the favourite instrument. That this custom has been almost entirely ignored is one result of the *idée fixe* about 'private' castles.

The liability on demand to hand over 'control' (*potestas* in French Languedoc) was approached by the intermediate and originally separate duty, already mentioned, of swearing that the fortress would not be used in any way harmful to the lord's interest. This 'jurability' was already merged with rendability in the earliest fragment of the Champagne fief rolls of *c*.1172, but sometimes remained distinct.[294] Rendability entailed an even closer tenurial dependence than jurability, which went little beyond benevolent neutrality. The vassal habitually 'swore his fortress' to the lord of whom he held it—a direct feudal bond was to such an extent a prerequisite that if none existed one had to be created, as by granting a money-fief before any fortress-facilities could be offered.[295] Military needs were most often tenurially accommodated. Under jurability the operative pact was often termed an *assecuramentum*. By this 'assurance' (as we have seen) the castellan guaranteed to his lord typically 'that from it [the fortress] no harm to him would arise'. Both the phraseology and practice of rendability and jurability tended constantly to extend their grip as the great rulers' powers grew. The consolidation of centralizing authority in France owed much to fortress-customs. The constituent undertakings can superficially be mistaken for ad hoc 'non-aggression' pacts, seemingly eloquent only of barely restrained violence and devoid of tenurial value.[296] What they really entailed was much more.

First, consider a case of jurability, for the fortress of *Montrond*, made in 1225 to Louis VIII. Like many such cases in areas of Capetian expansion after Bouvines (1214), the contractual element is prominent:

I, Renaud de Montfaucon, make universally known to people present and future, that I have granted (*craantasse*) to my dear Lord Louis, illustrious king of France, that from the fortress (*forteritia*) of *Montis rotundi* no ill shall come (*nullum malum proveniet*) to him or to the kingdom of France—which, should it happen—may it not!—the lord king can, without misconduct (*sine se meffacere*), take anything I hold of him and keep it until the matter is adequately put right as he wills and as his court shall decide.[297]

English castle-pacts surviving and in print as explicit as those deposited (immediately or eventually) in the French Royal *Layettes du Trésor* are very rare—inverting the habitual preponderance of the English published records.[298] Searching the

---

[294] *Documents Champagne* vol. ii, i. 4–63, *passim*. The dedicated list of *c*.1201 ('1181–6', Jubainville, *Histoire de Champagne*, i. pp. xi, xiii–xiv) is entitled: *Hec sunt castella jurabilia et reddibilia et domus similiter*: ibid. 103–4.

[295] e.g. in the war of inheritance *c*.1201–34, Coulson, 'Castellation in Champagne', 358–60.

[296] e.g. Le Neubourg, 1141–2: Coulson, 'French Matrix', 82–3.

[297] *Layettes*, ii. 49; Dated Melun (*dép.* Seine-et-Marne), Feb. '1224'; *Montrond* (a motte?). 'Montfaucon', or 'Gallows-hill', is an apt name-place (however gruesome) for a *seigneur haut-justicier*.

[298] But see 1148–53 Chester–Leicester *conventio*: text in Stenton, *First Century*, 249–52 (trans.), 285–8 (Latin); castle terms discussed in Coulson, 'Castles of the Anarchy', 73–74, and 'French Matrix', *passim*. Origins, etc. of the depot of charters received by the Capetians described in Teulet, *Layettes*, i. pp. v–xxiv; Delaborde, *Layettes*, v. pp. ii–xvii.

Chancery files of letters received might reveal treasures as rich as the *Layettes* (published down to 1270). Allusions in the Rolls are rare, but there is a hint in the precautions which are obviously seen in King John's reign of Continental practice; for example his reseisin terms in respect of the bishop of Lincoln's castles of Newark, Sleaford, and Banbury (1203),[299] and of Hornby castle (Lancs.) in 1205. John's pacts bear the stamp of mistrust, if not of conflict; but comparisons with Continental practice are instructive. Third-party guarantees as required for Hornby's keeping by its lord were conventional, but not the direct 'security' demanded from each of the bishop's custodians. Still less courteous was John's demanding hostages for Hornby.[300] For harshness, 'Angevin castle-policy' (Brown) has few French parallels before Philip IV.[301] After *c.*1226 (Henry III's Minority), and outside the twelfth-century episodes of conflict, English practice became more consensual. Continental ways supported the principle exemplified in the May 1215 arrangement with the bishop of Lincoln, for instance, but not its overtones:

The king to the venerable father-in-Christ Hugh, by the grace of God bishop of Lincoln, and to all his constables to whom this letter shall come [sends] greeting. We order you that whenever our dear and faithful William, Earl Warenne, shall come to your parts you are to permit him, and those he brings with him, to enter the lord bishop of Lincoln's castles, to stay there (*se hospitari et receptari*) while such is our pleasure.

Expedient in emergencies as it may have been, bypassing the bishop as John intended was not correct; nor was treating Newark, Sleaford, and Banbury castles peremptorily, as though they were royal, however drastically customary and formally rendable tenure made them the king's to use.[302] Duke Robert and Rufus had declared in 1091 that 'nobody in Normandy was allowed to deny the fortress of his castellary to the duke should he wish to have it in his own hand'.[303] The rule

---

[299] *Rot Litt Pat*, 31b: episcopal custodians must 'first give good security that they will guard them in our fealty and in that of the bishop elect'.

[300] *Rot Ob et Fin*, 275 (as '1200'). Roger de Montbegon, deprived 14 Dec. 1204 for incipient revolt and his chattels ordered to be sold (cf. Jolliffe, *Angevin Kingship*, e.g. 53), had to supply four hostages to be chosen by the king: 'and Roger shall hold his castle so long as he shall well and faithfully serve the lord king. If he shall do otherwise, he shall give up (*reddebit*) to him his castle of Hornby and have back his hostages.' Holt, *The Northerners*, 205–6. Apparently a motte and bailey (Castlestede): King, *Castellarium Anglicanum*, *sub.* Lancs.

[301] An extreme specimen of the 'kings can do no wrong' genre, outstanding even by the standards of French statism compounded by national sentiment, is Éli Berger's 'introduction' to *Layettes*, iv (pp. iii–lxxv). These attitudes, medieval and modern, came to the fore notably over Gascony 1297–1327; Coulson, 'Community and Fortress-Politics in France', 99–108.

[302] *Rot Litt Pat*, 135a; next entry orders all royal constables to admit Warenne, the earl of Salisbury, and William earl Marshal, with their retinues, in the same terms. Summons under rendability was to the fortress-lord, although delivery was (with rare exceptions) due instantly.

[303] n. 287 above. Eales, 'Royal Power and Castles', 74–7, n. 100; *inter alia* correcting the assertion by David King (*The Castle*, 25) that 'this duty of rendability was enforced in England as a general rule of law . . .'. But Yver, 'Les Châteaux-forts en Normandie', 60, goes much too far in suggesting some ducal 'monopole des fortifications'. Compare his ultra-ducal view (throughout) with Eales's caveat, pp. 72–3 on English royal powers to license castles likely being less than in Normandy, not greater. On Robert of Torigny's double-edged statement that Henry I 'used the fortresses of a great number of his barons as though they were his own', see Yver, 'Les Châteaux-forts', 94–5, 111 (with simplistic comment).

was well established already, but the power represented was not so monopolized by kings in France—nor, generally, did they so abuse it. The scrupulous lordship displayed by Philip Augustus (1180–1223) and by Louis le Lion (1223–6) in this regard contributed materially to their very nearly complete triumph over the Angevins. Among the very numerous rendability charters Philip secured and put in his treasury-chests within the castle-palace of the Louvre (*L'Oeuvre*) in Paris, or had transcribed into his Registers (books, not rolls), a typical example is one accorded in 1212 by Amaury de Craon of Anjou, a former adherent of King John.[304] Two years after Amaury's pact came the great Anglo-Imperial counter-attack, defeated at Bouvines, near Lille, by King Philip (July 1214). Crisis was impending, but the language is feudally conventional and the tone almost urbane:

I, Amaury de Craon, make universally known that I have in good faith promised, and by corporal oath have firmly granted (*creantavi*), that I will do to King Philip good and faithful service with my fortress (*de fortericia mea*) at Chantocé (Anjou; *dép*. Maine-et-Loire) with all my land and my body. The fortress I will hand over (*tradam*) to him [in person] or to [the bearer of] his order, to support himself (*ad se juvandum*) against his enemies, to great force or to small, as often as I shall be required on his behalf. Should I fail to comply, forty days having elapsed since my default, my lord the king can lawfully (*sine interceptione*) take all my land until I shall have regained his good favour with a fine of 3,000 marks.

This has elements of the homage charter in the personal service promised. Otherwise it is routine. By this period phraseology in long use had become standardized—'to great or small force (*ad magnam vim et ad parvam*)' in the provinces north of the Loire is the equivalent of 'be he [the lord] angered or peaceable (*irato seu pacato*, and variants)' in the Languedoc. Both formulae meant that rendering was due on mere demand, irrespective of circumstances or of the size of the lord's following at the time of summoning. Philip Augustus made great use of this old and institutionalized element of fortress-tenure. It was neither a tenurial innovation nor an emergency expedient. The period of grace before the king should resort to distraint, like the fixed penalty, are special variants but do not detract from the principle of instant delivery on summons—but they do show a norm of behaviour in sharp contrast with Angevin *machismo*. Amaury's recent coming over to the Capetians also explains why he persuaded ten other magnates to go bail for him, collectively pledging the sum of £5,300 on top of the penalty he had contractually bound himself to pay to redeem the lands which would be seized on his default.

Even under pressure a certain decorous harmony was the correct tone of fortress-relations: but the rules still had teeth. Especially in southern France, where fortress-law had most fully developed and more perfectly survived into the

---

[304] *Amplissima Collectio*, i. 1099 ('1211'); *Layettes*, i. 375–6, preserving all but two of the guarantors' charters, all dated at Le Mans; viz. Count Robert of Alençon, Juhel de Mayenne, William des Roches (seneschal of Anjou), each for £1,000 Paris; Viscount Raoul of Beaumont-en-Anjou (£500), Bernard de La Ferté (*de Firmitate*) and two others pledging £300, another at £500, and two at £200. In the event (*Layettes*, v. 66–7), Mayenne and des Roches gave a joint guarantee in only £800: final total £4,100 Paris. Each made his whole tenure liable to distraint in case of further default.

period when feudal liens were being tightened or created by magnates and rulers, refusal to render was tantamount to repudiating homage. Denial was *ipso facto* rebellion.[305] Contractual and negotiated penalties, by contrast, are an initial feature of the Capetian expansion into Poitou, Saintonge, and, after 1223, into the vast fissiparous territories of the counts of Toulouse, following the 'Albigensian Crusade.' What stands out from the details of fortress-custom (rendability, takeover, guarantee, and licensing chiefly) is the subordination of vassals' castles.[306] This dependence, quite as much as the far better-known armed attendance on their lord ('military service'), knit together the sub-baronial and baronial class and bound them either directly (as chiefly in England) or indirectly via the great feudatories and tenants-in-chief, to the Crown. Fortresses thereby were continually associated with recognizance of lordship (with special features for walled towns), uniquely at the overlord's discretion, at any time at his will. Through the established central (England) or mainly local (France) procedures for sanctioning or licensing new fortifications, political and social cohesion was promoted.[307] In France they were a major instrument of consolidation.

For the county of Poitou, between 'English' Gascony to the south, and 'French' Anjou and Touraine to the north, a record of 1269 expounds these ties of mutual rights and duties.[308] Fortresses and military affairs were an integral part of the social web, not some specialized *attaché*. Significantly, the section of the declaration by Count Alphonse de Poitiers and fourteen of his chief vassals which deals with fortress-liens is subsidiary to the main aim of the declaration, which was the regulation of the relief (*rachat à merci*; i.e. amount at the lord's discretion) which was payable before the heir could take up his inheritance. Since Poitou had been wrested from Henry III, completed by his reverses at Taillebourg and Saintes (1242), thus making good Alphonse's investiture as count of Poitou by his brother Louis IX in 1229 (with Auvergne in 1241), some 'constitutional' clarification was called for. The distraction of absorbing the vast apanage Alphonse acquired in 1249, on the death of Raymond VII of Toulouse, was formidable.[309] The Poitevin

---

[305] e.g. 1209 grant to Count Raymond-Roger of Foix by King Peter II of Aragon of forfeited fiefs, with two rendable *castra* of B. de Alion, forfeited for refusing to render *castrum de Sono*: *Layettes*, v. 62–4. Same rule in Catalonia and Bigorre. Adopted by Simon de Montfort (1212) in his Albigensian conquests: *Thesaurus Novus*, i. 831–8 (18, p. 833). Also Beaumanoir (*c.*1283), 351.

[306] Fortress-customs figure in Coulson, 'Rendability and Castellation', 'Castellation in Champagne', 'Fortress-Policy', 'Impact of Bouvines', 'French Matrix', 'Community and Fortress-Politics in France', ' "National" Requisitioning', 'Valois Powers and Fortresses'—overall study projected.

[307] Ecclesiastical grantees's viewpoint, Coulson, 'Hierarchism in Conventual Crenellation'; borough view, 'Battlements and the Bourgeoisie'; historiographical and local, 'Freedom to Crenellate'; 'French', primarily seignorial, 'Sanctioning of Fortresses in France'.

[308] *Layettes*, iv. 352–4, cf. 354–5; Reynolds, *Fiefs and Vassals*, 297–300 (relief), 313–17, *passim* (*aides* and A. de Poitiers). Baudry, *Fortifications des Plantagenêts en Poitou*, is a valuable pioneering study, necessarily focusing on royal-comital works, down to 1242.

[309] e.g. by Raymond's treaty of submission, disinheriting any son, in 1229: a detailed and characteristic pacification agreement, with fortresses figuring at length: *Layettes*, ii. 147–53; discussed in Coulson, 'Sanctioning of Fortresses in France', 95–7: Petit-Dutaillis, *Feudal Monarchy*, 222, 293. Alphonse's death, childless by Raymond's daughter Jeanne de Toulouse, in 1271 was a bonus for Capetian centralism (Philip III).

ground-rules of governance laid down in 1269 cover many of the issues spelled out in England's Magna Carta (1215). Just how wide were the powers of lordship over vassal 'property', even in the quasi-autonomous province of Poitou, helps to put the specially conditional tenure of fortresses (itself as far from 'freehold' as it could be) into perspective. The fact must be stressed that fortress-law was much older than the reassertion of monarchy after 1180. Alphonse in 1269 was still doing little more than finding out what his powers were as count, and delimiting them. Thus, it was declared, when any tenant or subtenant dies, the count of Poitou, or the deceased's direct lord, shall hold and exploit his estate for one year plus one day in full discharge of the due relief. During that time the lord receives all the revenues, subject to paying widows' dowries, heirs' maintenance, and other fixed charges. The same rule applied as with fortresses temporarily resumed under rendability—that there must be no 'waste', in effect, depletion of capital (here specified as undue felling of timber or killing of game in preserves and warrens) or deterioration of productivity.[310] As always, good stewardship was expected. 'Asset-stripping', though not infrequent, was unlawful. Since revenues were payable and renders were due by dependants at the administrative offices, the consensual rules provided that the lord's men put into each house, manor, and grange must not disturb the heir, heiress, or widow awaiting assignment of their inheritance or dower-property. An under-age (21 years) boy would be in the lord's wardship; a girl also until with her lord's consent, and arrangement, she married—both under customary safeguards.[311] In all but minor holdings the capital residence might well be by repute a fortress and possess a distinct legal status.[312] The implication (as usual) is that which residences were so distinguished was common knowledge:

Be it known, nevertheless, that if there be a fortress in the fief, he whose it is may not deny it to his superior (*son pardessus*) if the needs of the land require (*par le besoing de la terre*). But, that need passed, the latter must return it undamaged by any act of his or due to his default . . . [detailed provisions for demesne land consisting largely of wood, e.g. for hunting, follow] . . . And our lord the count aforesaid may still take over castles and fortresses, and keep them to himself, in those cases in which he was [previously] able to do by law, custom, or by special compact (*par covenance*).

This final reservation had to be specific, since rendability retained the ancient arbitrary element which Count Alphonse and his fellow overlords were giving up

---

[310] Cf. *Beaumanoir* (1283), 351–2,: 'and if the lord damage the fortress in any way, he must repair it at his own expense. If he alters it to make it stronger (*plus fort*) or better to his purpose, his man is not bound to pay anything since he did not do it; although the advantage (*pourfis*) remains his.' Such refinements added little to the existing body of custom of which they were avowedly declaratory.

[311] Cf. Magna Carta (1215), cl. 4–8 *Stubbs's Select Charters*, 293–4. Part IV below.

[312] The 1216 and 1217 reissues of Magna Carta of the Regency significantly add to clause 7 of 1215 (widows' residence prior to dower allocation for up to 40 days *in domo mariti sui nisi domus illa sit castrum*). She may not (explicitly) be ejected (*et si de castro recesserit*), but if she goes a proper alternative *domus competens in qua possit honeste morari* must be found, until she receives her dower. *Stubbs's Select Charters*, 337, 341 (cl.7). Ganshof, *Feudalism*, 127–9. Cf. 'castle'/'house' quasi-ambivalence, 1313–19, over Ribemont castle (*dép.* Aisne), similarly *Registres du Trésor*, i. 98–9, 423, 438; ii. 554.

in assessing relief.[313] What the fourteen chief magnates agreed to applied also down the hierarchical chain of tenure. Whether for recognitory or emergency purposes, rendering had to be (and expressly always was) at the lord's sole will and discretion (later sometimes defined as more or less subject to 'need' and 'reason'). The constant multiplication of lordships, parcelled out into ever-smaller fiefs (subinfeudation) caused problems if rights over fortresses were not to elude the chief lords. In Champagne, and in Bourbon barony, for example, attempts were made to correct this.[314] Over time the result was to bring more fortresses into the rulers' potential control, constantly extending the powers which in France accrued to the Crown well before the 'Hundred Years War'.[315] The centralization inherent in the tenurial system, far more than warfare, ensured this. In England the king had acquired de facto powers of this kind. In their French possessions the Plantagenets had to proceed more circumspectly, so King John's taking over of Fronsac (*dép*. Gironde) on the northern frontier of Gascony in 1206 was notably punctilious.[316] A letter patent was his envoy's instruction and open authority:

> to go at once to Fronsac and to receive the castle to our use, in your custody. You are not to allow any knight or other [person] to remain in it whom you mistrust, whereby any harm might come to us or to the castle; but you are to keep (*custodire*) it well and safely for us (*ad opus nostrum*) as it is of the castles of the parts of Gascony the one we much regard and deem most necessary to us. Take care that you and yours so behave (*curratis*) in the Fronsadais (*in Frou*) that no harm strikes the castle. Also, when you take possession (*receperitis*), inform us in writing when and in what state (*qualiter*) you found it.

An inventory and survey of the stores and structure enabled the duty to return the fortress 'in as good a state as when rendered' to be observed.

There is less need to illustrate such co-operation where it will be most expected—in the 'English' borderlands; so one example from thirteenth-century Ireland and one from Wales will suffice. How the spirit of 'Norman' joint-enterprise could operate (as it had in the settlement of England) is indicated by this Close Roll reply of July 1236 by Henry III (from Tewkesbury, Gloucs.) to Maurice FitzGerald, his viceroy (justiciar) of Ireland, who had also informed the archbishop of Dublin of the facts:[317]

---

[313] Cf. King John 'promised' (1215) to demand only the *antiquum relevium* (£100 per barony; 100s. 'at the most', for a whole knight's fief) or less 'according to the ancient custom of fiefs'. An heir who had suffered wardship was to pay no relief: *Stubbs's Select Charters*, 293 (2, 3); for previous reality, Jolliffe, *Angevin Kingship*, 57, 70, 76, 78–82, etc. W. Morris, *The Medieval English Sheriff*, 143–66, takes 1199–1216 as 'the culmination of Angevin absolutism'.

[314] Viz. Givry (*dép*. Seine-et-Marne): Mortet and Deschamps, *Recueil*, ii. 233 (1223), declaration by Thibaut IV; *Enquêtes A. de Poitiers*, 203–6 (1265), unsuccessful claim by Bourbon that *omnes domus fortes de novo facte debent esse de feodo domini Borbonii*. Cf. Painter, 'Castellans of the Plain of Poitou', *Feudalism and Liberty*, 17–40.

[315] Brown, *English Castles*, 18, citing Coulson, 'Rendability and Castellation' (1973).

[316] *Rot Litt Pat*, 67b; Gardelles, *Les Châteaux du sud-ouest*, 137. No summons to the *vicomte* is enrolled. On effective control, under rendability, e.g. *Beaumanoir*, 351–2; cf. Keen, *Laws of War*, 70 (ref. of 1363).

[317] *Close Rolls, 1234–7*, 364.

You tell us ... that our dear Rose de Verdun has founded (*firmavit*) a good and strong (*forte*) castle in her own land against the Irish (*super Hibernienses*) which none of her predecessors was able to do; and that she now proposes to fortify a further castle to the great advantage (*securitas*[318]) of our land. Since Rose will not be able to complete this work well without help (*subsidio*), we order you to take counsel and, if it can be done without prejudice to us, to afford her [the proceeds of] our due [military] service of forty days from Meath and Uriel to do the said work.

That royal help was needed is standard petition-form—but it does speak of the relationship. Using the feudal host on a county-basis for 'private' castle-building was quite common in thirteenth-century Ireland. Either armed men or, more likely, cash paid in lieu of personal service ('scutage'), or a combination, would be effective; the cash being the essential element, to pay for diggers, carpenters, and masons (if the new castle was not purely of earthwork and palisading). References, as here, to possible prejudice to the Crown habitually covered possible local objections: the *servitium debitum* might have been committed already; even petitions backed by the justiciar and the archbishop could be manipulative or faction-driven. Rose requested no licence to fortify (in Ireland mostly issued by the justiciar as in Gascony by the seneschal), but might have sought de facto approval, on the pretext of needing help for the new *castrum*, so as to deprive a fellow lord surreptitiously.[319] Remote control always required caution.

Before Edward I's conquest of Wales (1277–95), collaboration between the marcher lords and the king was especially necessary, and ultimately successful. In January 1263, before the severe onset of the Montfortian tensions in England, Henry III took precautions against 'Llywelyn's invasions and infractions of the truce' by individually ordering twenty-six marchers to muster in arms and defend their lands. Special letters went to those magnates (twelve, including Mathilda Longspee) noted on the Close Roll as having a castle (*habet castrum*) or castles. Each letter ended with:

Moreover you are to have your castles munitioned and well kept [still *custodiri* only] for the security of yourself and of those parts, being aware (*scituri*) that if you are negligent in this respect we will be obliged (*omittere non poterimus*) because of your default to resume (*revocemus*) those castles into our hand without delay.[320]

Both the public obligation of self-defence and the sanction (seldom more) were entirely conventional. By the ordinary operations of tenure (and mortality), all lands (and fortresses) returned to the hands of the king or lord of the fief in any

[318] See the numerous *Sauveterre*-type names of castles and bastides in Gascony and other marches: e.g. Gardelles, *Les Châteaux du sud-ouest*, places index.

[319] Castle Roche (co. Louth) 'famous as the only recorded example in Ireland of a major castle being built by a woman' (*pers. comm.* Terry Barry): Leask, *Irish Castles*, 63; McNeill, *Castles in Ireland*, 85–8. A substantial stone promontory castle 'in the English fashion', perhaps with a small township, is attributable to Rose (*Roesia*). Irish land was often granted on condition of 'settling' or 'fortifying' it: Rose, in 1242, got two respites for a year in July and October, *de terra sua hospitanda*: CDIreland, i. 383, 386 (from Bordeaux). See Part III, Ch. 2, sec. 1 below.

[320] *Close Rolls, 1261–4*, 275–6: by sanction of total forfeiture, in (earlier) Angevin style—'et taliter vos habeatis in facto predicto quod vestra fidelitas inde merito debeat commendari'.

case, although at unpredictable intervals (minority and 'escheat'). While 'in the king's hand', any heir's title and due age would be verified and the oath of homage administered. Otherwise all would be kept in wardship for a minor or 'taken back' if there was no lawful heir.[321] Fortresses were held under conditions still more rigorous. Supposing that 'the Englishman's home is his castle and fortress' (Sir Edward Coke, Semayne's case), although it has entered into proverb, is an early-modern 'Whig' misrepresentation. The opposite was the case. Walter Scott (in *Marmion*) more correctly has Douglas declare: 'my castles are my king's alone, from turret to foundation stone.' In truth, at no point was realty less absolute than when it was a fortress, liable to arbitrary interruption of exclusive occupation at any time—but protected by the same right of tenure (as distinct from continual control) as other property, so that title was lawfully terminable (involuntarily) only by due legal process of forfeiture.

Thinking of 'castles' as the apotheosis of embattled, defiant, and irresponsible individualism is fun—but best confined to the fantasy of the theme park or the 'Robin Hood' film. Explaining the roots of this delusion is the province of the psychiatrist. Historiographically it has been a most influential and seductive notion. In reality mere suspicion, if it was 'reasonable', entitled 'strong rulers' to require the castellan to pledge his fortress to the king (or superior) as an earnest of his loyalty. That King John's anxieties, even as early as 1202–3, obliged Earl Rannulf of Chester to hand over his Norman castle of Semilly (*dép.* Manche) in guarantee of good conduct, was the least consequence of John's paranoia.[322] Philip Augustus's pact, in 1204 (in process of seizing Normandy almost unresisted except at Château Gaillard), with one of John's staunchest supporters, his son's future regent William the Marshal, may be referred to again. It sought to resolve the conflict of allegiance regarding William's three castellaries of Orbec (*caput* of his Norman honour), Longueville, and Meulers (May 1204). Under phraseology and conditions deriving precisely from jurability and rendability, the Marshal made the castles themselves over temporarily (*ad presens*), in each case the *castrum et fortericia*, and received a respite (postponement) of his homage to Philip until the situation should be clarified. As the *capita* and symbols of his fiefs in the duchy, the trio of castles represented the Marshal's property which was hostage to war between William's two overlords, John and Philip. Militarily they added negligible weight to either side. By giving reasonable terms, Philip hoped to

---

[321] The records can mislead regarding bureaucratic consistency. Oral testimony of due age is occasionally appended to the inquisitions post mortem. The official local focus on revenues, and lack of interest in buildings, treating 'castles' purely as houses (sometimes partitioned between widow and/or heirs) is invariable. In England, the escheator (royal and palatinate) took possession on a tenant's death (but 'escheat' is strictly resumption for failure of heirs or by forfeiture including all revenues). Subtenants' lands were also repossessed, inspected, and valued, if the immediate lordship was in abeyance. Resumption of temporalities (lay property) in ecclesiastical vacancy was usually more nominal and brief (unless new 'election' of bishop or abbot, etc. was delayed—as often *temp.* John): M. Howell, *Regalian Right, passim*. In France palatinate franchises largely interposed, declining only gradually and patchily.

[322] *Rott Litt Pat, 7b, 28a.*

isolate John. As so often, such fortresses were pawns (not convertible to queens) in the game of power.[323]

3. Class-Conflict and Fortification

Individuals' concerns, such as William the Marshal's dual loyalties, can be under-represented by focusing on the moral questions raised by 'the public interest' which, irreducibly, was an aggregation of class and personal concerns. The subordinate majority have left little in the way of relevant documentation. 'Castles and the common man' would otherwise be a fine subject. What can be done is necessarily more generalized—as attempted in this section and in Chapter 3 of Part III. Most attention has to be given to the social minority, the nobility, prelacy, and *bourgeoisie*. Their disputes over fortresses were territorial and predominantly not violent but litigious.[324] Conflict of another sort cannot be disregarded. Medieval society was far from monolithic; nor, still more obviously, was it uniform over time and place. Dividing this book according to the interest-groups of 'class' attempts to reflect vast diversities which cannot be accommodated otherwise.[325] That class-antagonism was latent, with fortification as a catalyst, is part of the downside of the noble culture. Where there was lordship there was also domination. Relatively privileged merchants keenly resented ecclesiastical 'immunity', which set the clergy on a superior legal (and even moral) plane. The discriminations between the free, rent-paying peasant and the serf, tied to his place of birth and to lifelong hard labour (although gradually, but very variantly, improving), which set apart even the poorest noble from the richest *roturier* and townsman, did not promote social harmony. Given the acute strains of adverse economics, aggravated especially by state-war (especially Anglo-French, c.1337–1453) and the lack of 'social justice', social cohesion to the extent which prevailed might be thought remarkable.[326] This section takes some anecdotal evidence of one fault-line, that between townspeople and rural lordship.

[323] n. 223 above. Orbec (*dép.* Calvados); Philip 'is to (*debet*) send his people there for warring (*guerrando*) or to do what he wish with it'. Château Gaillard had surrendered on 8 Mar. 1204; by May resistance was hopeless. Longueville and Meulers (both near Dieppe) were bailed to a trusted third party who *pro tem*, with William, guaranteed them (*securitatem domino regi quod malum non veniet inde*). After 24 June both are to be fully rendable to Philip. If William makes him liege homage by May 1205, Philip will restore the *castra* and lands (except those conquered by mid-May 1204) 'in the same state in which they were handed over to him'. William pays 500 marks for this respite; if he fails in any respect, the castles become Philip's without any recall *ad faciendum totam voluntatem suam*. The enigmatic *castrum et fortericia*, and variants, usually means (as here) 'the castellary, including the castle proper', *castrum* alone being ambiguous. Although William stayed loyal to King John, his widow (1219) and sons William and Richard (1220) recovered the 'castles' under permanent rendability: *Layettes*, i. 250, 486, 499; Powicke, *Loss of Normandy*, 255, 260, 350 and *Henry III and the Lord Edward*, 126, n. 1 (but with 'surrender' for 'render'); n. 223 above.

[324] For territoriality instead of conflict in fortifying see Coulson, 'Sanctioning of Fortresses in France'. Competition barely affected English licensing (cf. Marham, Barnwell etc, Ch. 2, sec. 1 above), unless between towns: notably Hull and Beverley, 1321–c.1350; Ipswich and Harwich, 1352–4; Poole and Melcombe, 1338–1446 (the victor named first): Coulson, 'Battlements and the Bourgeoisie', 161–5, 184–6, 191–2.   [325] e.g. Barber, *Two Cities*, esp. I, 2, IV, p. 68.

[326] e.g. ibid., esp. I, 1, 3; 'famine was an ever present fear' (p. 13).

The wealthy patrician citizens of Bordeaux (*dép.* Gironde), capital of the 'English' duchy of Gascony (alias Aquitaine or Guyenne) had close familial links with the local minor nobility. In 1244 this did not appease a violent dispute. Count Bernard of Armagnac and Fézensac, in a petition to Henry III on behalf of Arnaud de Blanquefort, presented an aristocratic view of the facts:[327]

The men of your city of Bordeaux have entirely demolished the Lord Arnaud's castle (*castrum*) of Blanquefort [about 7 miles N], his men being there (*cum hominibus suis*), and have burned its precincts (*pertinentiis*), wholly without consideration of reason. As insistently as we are able, we therefore beseech your Highness that it may please your royal majesty to have due satisfaction made to him; otherwise we cannot peaceably refrain from protecting Arnaud in his rights (*justicia*) against those men of your city of Bordeaux. Although we will never withdraw from faithfully serving you, we cannot let him down (*sibi deficere*), faced as he is with their malice, being bound to defend him against all men (*contra omnes homines*) who unjustly aggrieve him.

Mutual support was, indeed, integral to the lord–vassal (and ruler–subject) relationship—but fellow-feeling may have had as much to do with Bernard's intercession. His own English loyalties were affected. The *contra omnes homines* phrase was characteristic of the reciprocal support of fealty.[328] But even so, class solidarity in face of the alleged *bourgeois* outrage against a noble's castle, apparently including spiteful damage to its farmyard, orchards, and gardens, would still have moved him. As Bernard went on to complain:

One thing, however, we must put to your lordship: under nobody else's governance (*potestas*) do burgesses or ignoble yokels (*burgenses seu rustici*) so lord it over noblemen (*nobilibus dominantur*) as they do in those parts subject to your authority. For this reason are barons (*barones*) and other nobles provoked to such indignation (*iracundia*) that they would rather [text defective] die than be in that position any longer; for from day to day they live in fear that this sort of thing could happen to them.

Putting burgesses socially on a par with serfs because both were not noble was a typically arrogant class attitude.[329] It was not a simple town–country clash. Trade links were extensive and burgesses very often possessed extra-mural fields: indeed, 'open' towns might be aggregations of farming hamlets. Merchants and gentry families intermingled; but class antipathy was sometimes strong. So Anseau de Caumont, lord of Saint-Baseille and Landron, was persuaded to petition Westminster in similar terms; 'it is our belief', he said, 'that nowhere else do burgesses have as much power as you allow (*sustinetis*) to these burgesses in the parts of Gascony over your barons and knights; wherefor all Gascony is disturbed

---

[327] Shirley (ed.), *Royal Letters*, ii. 33–4. Not until *temp.* Edward II was Blanquefort an Armagnac fief: Vale, *Origins of the Hundred Years War*, 94.
[328] Ideals enunciated influentially by Fulbert of Chartres *c.*1020: Reynolds, *Fiefs and Vassals*, 20; n. 244 above.
[329] On Gascon commercial wealth in the late 13th century, Bordeaux foremost, see Vale, *Origins of the Hundred Years War*, 141–8.

(*quieta sic*)'.[330] Blanquefort castle was soon rebuilt,[331] but powerful townships constantly resented encroachment on their own jurisdictional circumscriptions or *banlieues*, whether de facto or formally constituted as in twelfth-century Ponthieu. Within those zones of exclusive urban franchise the citizens enjoyed entire lordship, naturally including a monopoly of fortifying.[332] Merchant cities, market towns, and mere royal *bastides* and new plantations produced large profits, but were enclaves which it was the rulers' task to hold in balance with competing interest-groups, however great his natural affinity with his peers and noble vassals.[333] Ducal licensing of fortifying in Gascony (exercised largely unrecorded by the seneschals) under Edward I, showed some concern to pacify noble aspirations in the environs of Dax, Bayonne, Bazas, and elsewhere, as well as in the Bordelais. Since licensing was an act of mutual compliment, it was stimulated by the personal presence of the *roi-duc*, notably during Edward's long stay in the duchy in 1289. Those who held of the duke in-chief (directly) were keen to display this distinction by obtaining his licence to fortify. Otherwise licensing was primarily a baronial perquisite in Gascony, as in other regions of France.[334]

For all that fortifying was a mark of nobility, castellation quite freely crossed the very varyingly permeable class-divide. Serfdom was the substantial barrier: in France generally non-nobles, stigmatized as 'rustics' or *roturiers* (*ruptarii*: 'breakers of the soil'), even if 'free men', could not hold land which was a fief, namely a noble tenure—although the rule was not inflexible.[335] In England, obtaining a licence to crenellate often marked the *arriviste* who had made it into the ranks of the landed aristocracy. Mid-fourteenth-century examples are John de Pulteney (mayor of London) and John de Molyns. Michael de la Pole, of Hull, is a case under Richard II. It is also a Gascon phenomenon, particularly for citizens of Bordeaux.[336] Social mobility jeopardizes any simplistic view of a rigid caste structure, but institutionally 'class' was a fact, although to think of a 'class system' might go too far. Castellation, certainly, was widely diffused. Fortifying was

---

[330] Shirley (ed), *Royal Letters*, ii. 34–5.

[331] Gardelles, *Les Châteaux du sud-ouest*, 102–3, notes expenditure in 1247; much augmented by the de Goth after 1308. Repossessed 1254–15 by Henry III under rendability.

[332] Part I, n. 310 above; e.g. in 1214–15, the townsmen of Rue (Somme) agreed with Count William II what minor fortifications he might build at his manor of Gard-lès-Rue: *Recueil Ponthieu*, 353–4. Coulson, 'Sanctioning of Fortresses in France', 55–6, 64–8. In Ponthieu (largely *dép.* Somme) the right to fortify was explicitly vested in nobles of status below high-justice holder, as upheld in 1272: *Les Olim*, i. 917–18; Coulson, 'Rendability and Castellation', 65–6.

[333] e.g. Beresford, *New Towns*, esp. ch. 3.

[334] Coulson, 'Seignorial Fortresses', App. B (3), Ducal Licences, 1214–1317; *Lettres de Rois*, Champollion-Figeac (ed.), ii. 39–47, cf. *c.*1310 (p. 44, 10); see Coulson, 'Community and Fortresses-Politics in France', 96–8.

[335] e.g. *Rôles Gascons*, iii. 460–1 (1305); *CPR, 1330–4*, 336–7 (Ponthieu); n. 136 above. Waltham Abbey (Essex) in 1366 quashed the aspirations of a former serf (as noted), annexing the land he had acquired as a free man: *CPR, 1364–7*, 309 (licence in mortmain, and to crenellate the abbey belltower). Urban aspects of 'class', Hilton, *French and English Towns*, ch. 6, etc.

[336] n. 334 above; Coulson, 'Freedom to Crenellate by Licence', *passim*. G. Williams, *Medieval London*, e.g. p. 3, ch. 3. Molyns: *CPR, 1330–4*, 226, 493, 521–2; *1338–40*, 62; *CChR, 1327–41*, 453–4. Pulteney: *CPR, 1340–3*, 331. De la Pole: *CPR, 1381–5*, 555. Overview, Du Boulay, *An Age of Ambition*.

scarcely less characteristic of collective *bourgeois* franchises (especially of the *Villes Fermées*) than it was of the corporate lordship of ecclesiastical peculiars, both of which (by various degrees of affinity) borrowed noble character—but these deserve full and separate treatment. In any case, the nub of the conflict between Arnaud de Blanquefort and the citizens of Bordeaux in 1244 was lordship, exacerbated by an element of class-antagonism. Fears of the Capetian advance into Saintonge do not appear to have made any impact. Similarly, twenty years earlier in the Rochellais, north of the Gironde, a bitter quarrel between Hugh de Thouars and the important port-town of La Rochelle (*dép.* Charente Maritime), which surrendered to Louis VIII in 1224,[337] was provoked by a castle which Hugh had 'fortified' nearby. Trouble broke out in about the year 1222. The town authorities had offered Hugh money to stop but, failing to reach agreement, rather imprudently destroyed what he had built. Hugh promptly appealed to the regency council in England. What he alleged against the townspeople was duly reported to La Rochelle by their envoy at Henry III's court, producing this rejoinder addressed to the young king:

Our messenger (*nuntius*), your burgess of La Rochelle, has given us to understand that it has been made out to you (*vobis insinuatum fuerat*) that we attempted to make peace with Hugh de Thouars by (offering him) £80 in defective (*debilis*) local coin; and that we have uprooted his vineyards and gardens (*virgaria*[338]). He who told you such a tale beyond doubt has never liked us: you may take it for a fact that we never uprooted his vines; and we promised to pay him, before we should overthrow his castle (*castrum subverteretur*), £400 of Poitiers (*quatuor centum* [*sic*] *libras Pictavenses*), which he refused to accept.

As to the financial detail, the conversion rate for Poitevin currency (or a defect in the manuscript) seem not to explain the discrepancy; but, citing no legal grounds for their action, the burgesses clearly behaved with extreme arrogance. It was returned with interest: their letter to Henry III then quotes Hugh's response to their offer. It is tense with outrage and fury, an offensive parody of the courtesies of diplomatic:

Hugh de Thouars, lord of Montaigu ... to all the ignoble bumpkins (*omnibus rusticis agrestibus*) of La Rochelle [sends] ill greeting (*malam salutem*). I tell you that not for the king of England or for you will I at all refrain from fortifying my castle (*quin castrum meum firmarem*); and this, be sure, I am ready to back up. If anyone does me any wrong (*injuria*), you shall nowise dare to go outside your gates.

Hugh was not unreasonable in supposing that behind the bold assertion of a sort of *banlieue* round La Rochelle lay some active royal backing, reflecting the strong commercial links with England. Twelve years earlier, in 1206, King John had ordered Savery de Mauléon, his seneschal of Poitou, 'without delay to have

---

[337] Louis sanctioned their fortifications, during good behaviour, as also Saint-Émilion and La Réole: *Ordonnances*, xi. 318; xii. 316–17. On relations of the Thouars and Lusignans with Louis VIII, F. Powicke, *Thirteenth Century*, 87–91. Shirley (ed.), *Royal Letters*, i. 186–9.

[338] *Recte*? '*viridia*'. Latham (ed.), *Revised Word List*, '*virgaria*' gives '1222' (perhaps this text) as 'osier beds'.

destroyed all the small fortresses (*fortes domos*) of Peter and John Bertin and others which are close to La Rochelle and found to be harmful to the town'.[339] In *bourgeois* eyes, any rival fortress or noble pressure on their vicinity constituted 'harm' (*nocumentum*); and the French threat to Poitou, just after the fall of Normandy and Anjou, was a powerful lever. A mere seven months before John's death, with south-eastern England largely in rebel hands, the balance of ever-shifting Poitevin loyalties was apparently stable enough, or Bertin persistent enough in petitioning, to have this order countermanded (March 1216).[340] Allegations of 'damage' or worse often deserve considerable scepticism. Exaggeration amounting to untruth was not confined to ecclesiastical propaganda. Whatever the persuasion, John told the seneschal personally, by close-sealed letter, to allow Peter Bertin (once Richard I's seneschal) 'to fortify and peaceably hold his house of *Puilleset*'. To make the seneschal's protection more effective, the king also directly ordered the mayor and citizens to respect Peter's right (nothing regarding John Bertin). Four years later (*c.*1222), at the time when the quarrel with Hugh de Thouars flared up, the unnamed *castrum* at issue (presumably a seat of somewhat greater dignity as befitted the vicecomital family, since it possessed the established amenities of gardens), is unlikely to have been new, at least as a lordship-site. The burgesses failed to get rid of this rival. Hugh was evidently within his rights; so they resorted to the subterfuge of suggesting they had had royal authority for destroying the place. Having sent to Henry III's council, first Hugh's letter itself and then the transcript (translated above), their report proceeded with bland effrontery to declare: 'Now, as we always observe your honour and advantage (*fructui*), and care for them constantly, having received (*audientes*) such an improper (*indecens*) reply, which gravely angered us, we totally overthrew that castle, in fulfilment of your mandate.'[341]

In fact no such order was (enrolled as) sent; nor is it plausible, or the burgesses would have quoted it. Their pretended respect for public authority, cloaking self-interest more scantily than usual, was, as we shall see, later repeated. Claiming to exercise it in this fashion and instance, went too far. Townsmen were not slow to adopt the polemical tactics of the clergy, or to identify the public interest with their own. In fact, noble prerogative was scarcely less 'public' than theirs—not that Hugh's chosen way of using it was judicious: he and his coterie of nobles made an armed demonstration which obliged the townsmen to give in, thus establishing the castle. To rub in La Rochelle's humiliation, Hugh and company compelled the mayor and burgesses to ask Henry III to pardon their lawless violence. Still with that stance of junior-partnership characteristic of so much of town–king relations (as in the suing and granting

---

[339] *Rot Litt Pat*, 58a, '1207'; enrolled a second time, stating Savary's office.

[340] *Rot Litt Claus*, i. 253a. Peter Bertin was favoured by Richard I; in 1192 he was his seneschal of Poitou: F. Powicke, *Loss of Normandy*, 32 n., 98. La Rochelle was loyal in 1214, Warren, *King John*, pp. 218–24.

[341] Viz. *castrum funditus evertimus, mandatum vestrum adimplentes.*

of fortification-aid[342]), La Rochelle's indignant letter expected Henry's sympathy. The mayor, John Galerna, and burgesses told him (confidentially) that their hand had been forced, asking that their 'letter of intercession' be disregarded. They then presented the sort of partisan gloss on the whole affair which is more typical of unofficial narrative (chronicle) sources:

And you should know that the Lord Hugh de Thouars did not delay constructing and building his castle (*castellum*) near La Rochelle, against your prohibition [*sic*] and order (*summonitionem*), served on him by us on your behalf. We therefore, by your mandate, to which we are obedient and God willing ever shall be; and because we saw the town and region (*patria*) likely to be destroyed before our eyes, proceeded to overthrow that castle.

Whatever concocted 'royal' mandate they presented to Hugh, this protestation is not least deceptive (their surrender to Louis VIII in 1224 was pusillanimous[343]). Their sorry explanation of how they had bought off Hugh's punitive party so as to save their 'vineyards and everything we have outside the town [walls]', promising to pay 500 marks 'ransom' (i.e. protection money) and incurring 200 marks in other losses, was, in usual petition-style, angled to induce Henry III's council to delegate to the town officers the management of La Rochelle's dues to the Crown, payable annually as their 'farm'. Harassment by William Maingot, and helping out successive royal seneschals with ready money in 1220–2, were pleaded to the same end.[344] Manipulative petitioning was a particularly developed *bourgeois* skill—not always successful.

It is always necessary to know the source of accusations that a fortress was injurious to the public good, and the precise nature of that party's interest. In Ireland, Castleknock by Dublin lived a precarious existence from late 1214 until 1225, accused of being a 'danger' not only to the city but to the peace. Repeated (unexecuted) orders for its demolition led eventually to a compromise whereby Hugh de Tyrel, its lord, guaranteed it harmless and promised to deliver Castleknock whenever needed 'for the defence of the country', a rare British instance of formalized, typically phrased (jurability and) rendability.[345] Satisfying the royal Dublin administration, the city clergy and the elite citizenry, and vindicating the quasi-monopoly, judicial and economic, of Dublin's newly built metropolitan castle and recently walled town was the hidden agenda at Castleknock. Such

---

[342] In Britain 'murage' (cf. pavage, pontage, quayage); like licence to crenellate, it had symbolic import: Coulson, 'Battlements and the Bourgeoisie', *passim*; also 'Seignorial Fortresses' App. C(1), Grants for Fortification in France.

[343] *Foedera*, i, i: report by men of Bayonne of their assistance in men ('fully 400 armed men') and ships; accusing Savery de Mauléon and burgesses of treason; requesting defence-aid against Navarre and Louis VIII, for enclosing and munitioning Bayonne. In 1221 they had for this £25 p.a. remission of farm: *Rot Litt Claus*, i. 427b.

[344] William *Maengo*; lords of Surgéres castle nearby: e.g. *Layettes*, ii. 634 (1246). Extortion by Savary de Mauléon is also alleged: Shirley (ed.), *Royal Letters*, i. 188–9 ('about October 1222?').

[345] *CDIreland*, i. 81 (1214); 161 (1222: 'for the security of Ireland'); *Rot Litt Claus*, i. 390b: 1219: Tyrel must give hostages 'et securitatem quod malum vel dampnum nobis sive Civitati Dublin sive aliis terris nostris per castrum . . . non eveniet; [also] quod ipsum castrum. . . . Justiciario nostro Hybernie liberabit si forte opus habuerimus propter guerram vel aliud imminens periculum'.

machinations were routine lobbying. Their standard phraseology of impending, possible, or inherent warlike catastrophe was normal scare-tactics.

4. Communes and Community

Towns fought their own corner as selfishly as any nobleman or prelate. If technically 'communes', legally endowed with corporate 'personality', towns had their own seal and officials and, like religious houses, were undying perpetual corporations. It was not that they had as such 'no soul to be damned and no bottom to be kicked', but they were 'communal' only in the legal sense, mostly ruled by oligarchies composed of the richer citizens, under various forms of democracy. Appealing to the public interest (or to 'the good of the realm', and so on) was a common ploy, often by inflating the possibilities of danger into war-scares, as in England during the 'Hundred Years War'. Propaganda, not paranoia, was the cause. Indeed, municipal aggrandizement is nearly always the chief explanation.[346] The fortification of towns (paving streets, building bridges, and having a guildhall were other aspects of 'improvement' or *melioratio*) was promoted by kings and mesne lords because it enhanced their 'honour', as well as the town's dignity.[347] To judge from the ready response and practical help forthcoming from the king in England and in France, and from subordinate franchisees, such works were emphatically esteemed. Bridge-building and repair was a communal duty (the Anglo-Saxon *brig-baut*) as well as a work of piety, often under urban patronage. Castle-work, *burh baut* or *bot, operationes castellorum* in the post-Conquest Latin, was similar. Works to repair quays, causeways, embankments, and roads (*cheminage*), as well as on town walls were also regularly aided by tolls, as well as by direct grants of cash and materials, continually as natural maintenance and improvement, occasionally supplemented in emergencies.[348] Such 'public' subsidy, rarely given for 'castles', since castellans were presumed to have the means to fulfil their obligations, represented a frequently substantial forgoing of potential royal and lordly revenue, but it was accorded almost automatically on application. The English grant of permission to townspeople to tax themselves, chiefly by levies on goods coming into the town market (in effect, a sales-tax which vendors, mostly of raw materials and foodstuffs,[349] passed on in higher prices to purchasers) effectively tapped the general pool of taxable wealth. But the

---

[346] n. 342 above; Turner, *Town Defences*, esp. App. C, table of murage grants; Coulson, 'Some Analysis of Bodiam', esp. 89–98; cf. e.g. Hughes, 'Fourteenth Century French Raids'.

[347] e.g. *Rôles Gascons*, iii. 578: (1285), six years' wine tax *ad melioracionem ville* for Waben (Ponthieu), on plea of heiress Queen Eleanor. Recent socio-archaeological works are most relevant, e.g. Beresford, *New Towns*; Platt, *English Medieval Town*, esp. ch. 5, 'The Borough Constitution'; Bradley, *Walled Towns in Ireland*; Nicholas, *Later Medieval City*, chs. 6, 10. Also Reynolds, *English Medieval Towns*; Barley (ed.), *European Towns*; Barel, *La Ville Médiévale*; still useful, Rörig, *The Medieval Town*, esp. ch. 8, 'Power and Institutions'.

[348] e.g. nn. 251, 342 above. Sequel on 'The Castles of Communities' (urban, ecclesiastical) envisaged.

[349] e.g. 1315 London chargeable items list, reproduced in Turner, *Town Defences*, 227–30.

results satisfied municipal ambition rather than public safety.[350] In England, murage grants (like market grants) begin systematically soon after the pacification following the death of King John—later than royal licences to fortify or 'crenellate', which were included in the Chancery enrolments from John's accession.[351] Each form of privilege corroborates the other: not only was a murage grant an implicit licence to fortify, but many towns were also (like 'castles') licensed explicitly. Both were acts not of regulation, still less of control, but of patronage properly conferred by a feudal superior on his subordinate. But with towns the public interest was conventionally more explicit. A strengthened town, or a newly planted one, was expressly rated as a work of public benefit, although profit and expansion were aims they had in common with 'castles'.[352] In France likewise, where the *bastides* (Part III, Ch. 2, sec. 3 below) colonizing underpopulated border districts were most usually 'closed' or 'fortified' (i.e. provided with demarcating gates and a *closture* of ditch, bank, palisade, or wall), new towns in general and the enhancement of established settlements or *populaciones* were advocated for similar reasons of local prosperity and lordship-consolidation, alias 'defence'. However existing proprietors were affected, public benefit was the ostensible programme. Motives have been clouded by narrowing down to a modern military definition the very broad sense in which 'defence' was originally understood.[353] A batch of English murage grants, based on the early and apparently experimental exemplar of Shrewsbury (1220), illustrates these various forms, views, and conventions.[354] The standard preamble is:

The king to the sheriff of Shropshire, and to all in the same county, greeting. Know that we have granted to our burgesses of Shrewsbury, in aid of the enclosing of the town and for the safety and protection (*securitatem et tuitionem*) of the adjacent parts, permission to take once every week for four years . . . [specified charges on listed items].

Shrewsbury was near Welsh Wales but this is no marcher formula. Public benefit is ubiquitously expressed as 'security', irrespective of location. If the petition alleged local dangers, such allusions were habitually incorporated in the grant. No myth of aboriginal chaos underlay this cynical harping, but merely genuflection to fashionable convention. Essentially, 'defence' justified privilege. When Shrewsbury's term was extended for one year, in June 1224, this form of words was repeated and it was then used unchanged for grants to Northampton, Scarborough, Lincoln, Worcester, York, Bridgenorth, Winchester, and Hereford

---

[350] Occasional commissions to audit receipts and expenditure responded almost exclusively to local dispute, symptom often of patriciate–proletariat tensions: e.g. Coulson, 'Battlements and the Bourgeoisie', 158–60 (Newcastle).

[351] Britnell, 'King John's Early Grants of Markets and Fairs', 90–6; Masschaele, 'Market Rights in Thirteenth-Century England', 78–89 (refs. due to R. Eales).

[352] e.g. Beresford, *New Towns*, 55–97 (valuable documentary exegesis).

[353] Acutely, for Gascony, distinguished by Trabut-Cussac, 'Bastides ou Fortresses?', 81–135: below Part III, Ch. 2, sec. 3.

[354] *PatR*, i. 238–9: some early peculiarities, e.g. it became habitual to send the writ (patent) direct to the town-petitioners; also, daily not once-a-week tolls became the rule; and terms of 3–10 years.

during the following four years.[355] The bureaucratic affection for standard formulae was doubtless responsible—although the respective town authorities would certainly feel they were guarantors of stability in each region.

Whether clerical laziness or urban self-esteem contributed, patronage and assistance by kings and great magnates[356] for building and maintaining town fortifications was continuous throughout the period, and was on a strongly affirmative and liberal scale, albeit not all of it at the rulers' direct cost. Very many towns, on achieving the somewhat equivocal status in England of 'free borough', or more empirically in France of *ville fermée*, enjoyed the right or were explicitly endowed by charter with power to fortify. Control of the whole defence-apparatus was a cherished distinction. With it went authority to levy tolls, raise taxes, to acquire necessary property by compulsory purchase, and to take materials (timber and stone chiefly) in their vicinity.[357] An explicit licence to fortify gave extra honour. Trust in the expertise, honesty (checked by occasional, but usually reactive, audits of receipts and expenditure), and sense of public responsibility, within inherent limits, of elected or quasi-appointative officials, be they mayors, consuls, *échevins*, bailiffs, or *jurats*, emerges as clearly from the records as does the evident but laissez-faire belief that money so spent (however derived) was applied as effectively as it could be for the general welfare. But social dissent often broke through placid complacency. Political factions and internal conflicts of purpose were compounded by possible infringements of competing vested interests. At York in 1226 this problem surfaced on the Patent Roll:[358]

Concerning taking a custom in York from the archbishop's men—the king to the dean and chapter of York, greeting. We request (*rogamus*) you, for the present, to permit to be taken from your men for the prescribed term, the custom (*consuetudinem*) which we have granted by our writ in the city of York for enclosing (*claudendam*) the city, for the protection and defence of the city and of the parts adjacent, and in addition to save you from harm (*ad indempnitatem vestram*), as also for the common utility of everyone in those parts. Be assured, it is not our will that this custom shall reduce your rights (*cedat vobis in prejudicium*) after its expiry, nor become habitual.

Militarily, of course, the walled towns (if their 'enclosure' was more than legalistic) were potentially capacious havens for peasant refugees—but danger from the Scots was not conceivable at York at that time. Such seemingly ominous allusions were the stock phraseology of public power which war justified and activated. In York and everywhere, defence touched delicate nerves because implementing it

---

[355] *PatR*, i. 445–6, 499–500, 508–9, 518–19, 555–6; ii. 32–3, 116, 189–90, 228; and Worcester's renewal (13 Jan. 1229), 253.

[356] Crown and palatinates in England; e.g. Durham intermittently, including imparking, crenellation, mortmain, forfeitures of war, etc.; asserted by Bishops Bek (1284–1311) and Longley (1406–37): e.g. *CCR, 1327–30*, 144; *1374–7*, 427–8; *CPR, 1330–4*, 360; *1388–92*, 395; *1408–13*, 35, 54–5. Hartlepool had royal murage, e.g. 1315, 1326, but in 1410 another was revoked as prejudicial to the bishop's 'franchises, jurisdication, and royal rights': *CPR, 1313–17*, 347; *1324–7*, 250; *1408–13*, 264.

[357] A notable series is Philip II's borough charters: Coulson, 'Fortress-Policy', 24–30.

[358] *PatR*, ii. 55; evidently, by plea of the mayor, etc. to remove clerical obstruction. General picture Nicholas, *Later Medieval City*, 173, 180–8.

was a franchisal power and symbol of authority. Consequently, actual military precautions took second place to the constant business of reconciling juxtaposed and sometimes overlapping jurisdictions. Archbishop and chapter could not accept any element or implication of subordination to the mayor. Walled towns were particularly liable to such clashes whenever there were (as so often) resident ecclesiastical lords jealous of any *bourgeois* encroachment upon their (usually prior) lordship.[359] Such words as 'security', 'protection', 'defence', 'tranquillity', and so on were a code which requires unpicking.

The paradox that 'castles', while being to some extent 'private' because individual, familial, and dynastic, were at the same time institutionally (and, with varying capacity, also structurally) public places, has its counterpart in the walled boroughs. Towns, seemingly more 'public', were hardly less ambivalent. Although usually greater in area and population (even tiny Cowbridge, Glamorgan), towns were nevertheless in law 'private' collective entities, akin to the great monasteries and ecclesiastical enclaves. (The loose modern analogy might be respectively with family-controlled and 'public' limited corporations.) This, by modern standards mixed, character is faithfully reflected linguistically in medieval 'terminology', and tenurially by rendability most notably and in licensing. There is another similarity in that personal, seignorial fortresses, also combining administrative, territorial, military, and commercial as well as residential purposes, sometimes when necessary received direct grants and subventions. Normally their 'keeping', in all its aspects, was (compulsorily[360]) paid for out of the lord's own revenues, manpower (labour dues—*guet et garde*) and materials (demesnal woods, lime-kilns, quarries) inseparably attached. Towns often had similar resources, though of greater diversity. Castellans' own self-interest was enlightened by tenurially institutionalized co-operation—most conspicuously, but sporadically, in Ireland, Wales, and, continuously from the early fourteenth century (albeit in a 'do-it-yourself' fashion) in the Scottish March, both the east and west districts. The demands on fortresses of all kinds by the wider constituency which they served fluctuated but tended to rise.

In war-torn France, during the episodic 'Hundred Years War', the tincture of traditional co-operation concentrated to the point of crystallizing into royal ordinances, pioneered by that of the regent Charles (V) in 1358.[361] Lack of awareness of feudal precedent embedded in the tenurial infrastructure might allow one to suppose that commandeering, compulsory seignorial and royal garrisoning, and even demolishing fortresses for default of due guard and upkeep (to avert seizure and use by an enemy is the usual reason given) had sprung solely and entirely

---

[359] Urban jurisdictional encroachment was more to be feared by religious enclaves than mere expense of paying toll, see Coulson, 'Battlements and the Bourgeoisie', esp. 128–32 (Canterbury), 133–5 (Salisbury), 150–4 (Carlisle), 161 (Beverley), 161–5 (Hull), 165–9 (York), 170–2 (Coventry), 182–3 (Lynn). Nicholas, *Later Medieval City*, 108–13.

[360] e.g. 1263 in the Welsh march: *Close Rolls, 1261–4*, 275–6 (above); cf. Pembroke's request (1220) for help to fortify two castles: Shirley (ed.), *Royal Letters*, i. 144–5.

[361] Coulson, 'Valois Powers over Fortresses', 148–9; text, *Ordonnances*, iii. 219–32.

from 'military law', *raison d'état*, and the brutal necessities of *force majeure*.[362] Circumstances, of course, concentrated minds which were long adjusted to centralism by established theory and familiar practice, but the process was rather one in which precedents were reactivated and reformed. The triumphs of royal military *dirigisme*, celebrated in Philippe Contamine's great work *Guerre, état et société*, were not a revolution but an accelerated evolution.[363] They could scarcely otherwise have been achieved. In late-medieval France, original public safety purposes were restored and extended by insisting (at least in theory) that no lord should demand labour services or dues from the peasantry of his castellary if the fortress was not adequately munitioned and repaired so as to provide them with secure protection in return. Accordingly, some redrawing of the boundaries ensured that people's services accrued to their place of refuge, not to the trad- itional fortress-*caput* if unfit or less convenient—or ideally so: such 'legislation' set out the principles. Implementation was locally interpreted.[364]

Though in practice little more than an empowering warrant open in the usual fashion to local compromise, the regent's follow-up order in March 1360, issued nearly four years after the galvanizing Valois disaster at Poitiers at the hands of Prince Edward, went out to lieutenants or captains and instructed them to destroy inclusively 'all fortresses, other than royal castles or ancient fortresses tenable, defensible, and advantageous for the country round about and for the kingdom'.[365] The whole tract of country north and west of Paris was covered, between the rivers Lys and Somme. Minor lords and forts would be most affected, major ones and towns least or not at all, then and later as such measures become habitual under Charles V as king (1364–80). Under Charles VI (1380–1422) and successor admin- istrations milder variants of the same measures were promulgated, until revived somewhat in vigour and comprehensiveness after *c*.1445.[366] Although their novelty, as well as efficacy, can be exaggerated, the doctrine was old that a fortress's exis- tence depended on its public utility and accountability.[367] Being amenable to the superior's interests (jurability), open to receive his men and to be taken over entirely in case of need or at will (rendability), liable to pledging to purge 'reason- able' suspicion of disloyalty, subject (increasingly later) to compulsory purchase

[362] e.g. Timbal, *Guerre de Cent Ans*, esp. 106–7, 121–8; cf. Coulson, 'Seignorial Fortresses', ch. 4, 2(a), On the *c*.1285–1337 transition see id., 'Community and Fortress-Politics in France'.
[363] Contamine, *Guerre, état et société*, e.g. 7–11, 34–5, 44–5, 127–31, 204–5, 230–1, etc.; cf. (on 'fortresses', etc.). Contamine, *War in the Middle Ages*, 43–7, 53, 66, 83–5, 101–9, 262–70, etc.
[364] Timbal, *Guerre de Cent Ans*, 149–67 ('le ressort des châteaux', etc.). Note the impartial om- niscience implied (pp. 107–8) by: 'le pouvoir royal doit, au reste, tenir compte de la mentalité des sujets, qui ne discernent pas toujours nettement l'utilité defensive des diverses places . . .'
[365] Summarized in ibid. 107, with further examples.
[366] Reflected, Contamine, *Guerre, état et société*, 277–319, etc.
[367] As Aimeri de Thouars (threatened by the French) had put it to Henry III in 1230—'ego vester sum, et dicta castra mea vestro servitio sunt parata': Shirley (ed.), *Royal Letters*, i. 386. As early as the *Hugo Chiliarchus* debate (*c*.1022–8: Martindale, 'Conventum', 546) the record *inter alia* has Count William of Aquitaine ask: 'how can you establish a castle' (*facias castrum*: i.e. reinstate Gençay); 'Fulk [of Anjou] will thereupon require you to deliver it; and you cannot legitimately hold (*non valebis tenere*) a castle which you have not rendered to him . . .': discussed, Coulson, 'French Matrix', 78–80. Part I, nn. 55, 180, 292 above.

for the kingdom's (or king's) good, and, finally, to be demolished if not defensible or 'profitable', fortress-duties exceeded even the feudo-vassalic ideals enunciated *c.*1020 by Fulbert of Chartres.[368] This is not quite the draconian rule that
'the safety of the people is the supreme law', but it fell not far short of the Roman
principle. Where it did so, socio-political constraints were the cause, not anarchic
individualism. The medieval 'community', as a compelling set of ideas, had its
eventual way with fortresses, as this and the two previous chapters have endeav-
oured to show.[369] Colourful notions of swashbuckling lawlessness, derived from
misplaced romanticism of the 'robber-baron' type, are not the only obstacle here.
The proponents of statism regard any 'private' exercise of public authority as
usurpation, and tend therefore to exonerate kings and to condemn power-
sharing pluralism. The debate has new resonances today over the issue of 'privatization'. Fortresses, conditionally held with other governmental powers from the
Crown under delegated or arrogated franchises and liberties, have had a particularly bad press as the supposed accomplices of 'the over-mighty subject'.[370] This
doctrine is the intellectual ingredient of castrophobia, and has given spurious
respectability to the widely diffused belief that all 'castles' are fundamentally anti-
social—with curious exception usually made for those of the king and some
equivocation on the less-easily pilloried corporate fortress, the castles of communities.

Of the original and authentic strain of antipathy two examples, early and late,
may be quoted in conclusion: the first, a mid-eleventh-century specimen of ecclesiastical invective; and the latter, a war-weary reflection on fortresses in the 'occupied' Lancastrian lands in France, at the time (1430) when the impetus of the
English conquest had expired.[371]

The episcopal cartulary of Châlons-sur-Marne preserves 'the memorial of the
accord (*conventio*) granted by Count Odo (Eudes), son of Count Stephen, to
Bishop Roger' (II, 1048–63). Its flowery and propagandist language notwithstanding, it is clear that Odo did no more than adopt the traditional view of his duties
and of the facts which was presented for his acceptance, in return for the usual
(monetary) consideration:

Odo, by the grace of God, count: as we would wisely provide for the utility and needs of
the churches, and of the clerics worshipping God therein, at the petition of priests
entrusted with their governance (*regendi*) and conforming to our Highness's deeds (*nostre
celsitudinis operibus*), obtaining thereby the more readily not only eternal beatitude but
also indubitably deserving the Divine grace—we make known accordingly to all faithful to
God's holy church and to ourselves, clergy and laity, present and future, that the venerable

---

[368] Reynolds, *Fiefs and Vassals*, 20, 227–8, 253; letter to William of Aquitaine, trans. in Herlihy (ed.),
The History of Feudalism, 96–7; also Bloch, *Feudal Society*, 219–20.

[369] Cf. Coulson, 'Castle and Community', Brown *et al.*, *Castles*, 100–13.

[370] Duby, *France 987–1460*, 56–90, attempts to separate the early popular refuge-*castra* (one manifestation only of 'official' fortifying) from seignorial castles which 'had no continuity [*sic*] with previous practice' (p. 59). He takes clerical propaganda at face value.

[371] Griffiths, *King Henry VI*, 200–30, 443–59.

Bishop Roger coming to our presence (*culminis nostri adiens sublimitatem*)—for he saw how all around, by reason of the insatiable greed of certain Franks (*Francorum*), in malice gradually increasing with mutual conflict, in the constructing of castles to the hurt of the people and rather for plundering them than defending the Holy Church of God, which drunken madness (*bacchante insania*) here and there inflamed their souls one and all—has expressed his fears for the church of Châlons . . .[372]

All this grandiloquent hyperbole, revelling in syntactically strained verbosity, was an admired literary genre, one of whose most vituperative exponents (over a century later) was Saint Bernard of Clairvaux, who was particularly intolerant of fashionable elaborate building.[373] The editor who printed the passage translated (in 1859), took it as objective fact. His gloss-summary declared that 'the scourge of private wars at that time devastated France. Roger II . . . suffered particularly. Several lesser barons had built castles close to the cathedral lands and from them, devastated all the environs, not even respecting ecclesiastical property.'[374] M. d'Arbois de Jubainville's exposition of propaganda as impartial historical narrative is far from unique. No doubt but that Odo's 'feebleness' and 'nullity' did contribute to his expulsion from his county by his uncle Thibaut—but Bishop Roger's over-righteous attempt by moral coercion (habitual resort where no legal right existed) to monopolize the urban pale around his cathedral city of Châlons is quite transparent. Attributing 'insanity' (mindlessness) as well as irreligion to the rivals of the Church was standard polemic. The diatribe foisted (at high cost, typically) by Bishop Roger on the pious but ineffectual Odo continues:

Châlons cathedral, where devoted worship of God proceeds, risked suffering evil; so [Roger] humbly prayed that neither I, Odo, nor my successors (as count), should in future allow any fortification (*municipium*) to be built within the space of eight leagues' radius of the walls of the city of Châlons. This most worthy petition . . . we kindly received, accepted . . . and [now] make known to all, embodying our sublime and unimpeachable assent in writing, in God's name, fortifying them with our own signature (*manu*), and with our men's corroboration—[finally] . . . consigning any diabolically moved offender . . . to ostracism, excommunication, and to eternal damnation.

The pen, truly, is mightier than the sword. Not only these but the whole type of aspiring castle-builders have been damned ever since, whereas the illiterate majority suffered in silence.

Whether their lord was the bishop or a self-promoted castellan would have made little or no difference to the productive peasantry. Their feelings, as in post-Conquest England where, after 1070, the native but no less exploitative aristocracy

[372] Jubainville, *Histoire de Champagne*, i. 486.
[373] Compare the architectural asceticism of his co-founded Order: Aubert, *L'Architecture Cistercienne*, e.g. i. 30–4, ii. 207–13; Cistercian Statues 1134–5, 1157: in Mortet and Deschamps (eds.), *Recueil*, ii. 30–8; on Bernard's 'prophetic style', etc. see Knowles, 'Cistercians and Cluniacs' (with thanks to the author), repr. *The Historian and Character*, 63–4, 66; and 'St Bernard of Clairvaux, 1090–1153', ibid., ch. 3, *passim*.
[374] Jubainville, *Histoire de Champagne*, i. 275–8. Dunbabin, *France in the Making*, 190–6, on the Blois–Chartres–Champagne apanages.

was swept away and their former lords' fortified seats were eclipsed by, and often obliterated under, the alien Normans' castles, can only be guessed at. The great Revolt of 1381, and the *jacqueries* of later-fourteenth- and fifteenth-century France were more expressive.[375] *Château*-burning by rioters was almost unknown in England. But in both kingdoms castellated building, symbol and part-instruments of governance, flourished more luxuriantly than ever at the end of the middle ages, as though to rub in the hauteur of the nobility. The memorandum sent in 1430 to Westminster by the English governors of Henry V's French conquests to his 9-year-old son's council, despite its compassionate tone, was probably motivated most by fear of damaging loss of fortresses to the enemy. But the feeling that castles ought to be a benefit, not a burden, to the unprivileged mass of the population was such an enduring one, and so often reiterated by word and deed, that it must be accepted as, within its obvious limits, entirely sincere. In the original English the relevant paragraph goes:[376]

Item: for as muche as there is grete multitude of walled townes and castell in Normendie and in France, as welle of ye kings as of other mennes, and ye keeping of so many is greet charge to ye land and oppression to ye people, it semeth necessarie to be advised wich shul be kept and whiche shul be disempared [dis-fortified], as well of ye kings as of other mennes; forthough other mennes fortresses be nought kept at ye king's charge, yet thai lyve upon ye povere people and if thei were take with thennemys thei sholde be cause of destruccion of ye king's cuntree.

King Henry VI's councillors in France were not able to shift the responsibility. All they got back (as noted on the manuscript) was an affirmation of the public-good principle as reinforced by hostile conditions of inadequate numbers of troops and shrinking tax resources and popular good-will. They were told: 'It is wel agreed here that fortresses and places be disempared such as shallbe thought to the king, by advis of his counsail there, unbehovefull [unnecessary], parillous or harmfull to be kept or to stand . . .'—That is to say: 'decide for yourselves.'

5. Conclusions: Part II—Castles Were Not Anti-Social

To defend perhaps any great medieval social institution, such as consultative monarchy, the Church, or land and people-management by the strictest standards of social benefit to the majority of the population, would be possible but not easy. With fortresses, this inquiry has done little more than demonstrate the truism that as an institution they were chiefly subservient to aristocracy. As architecture castles were often oppressive as well as impressive, dominating the land-

---

[375] e.g. the Parisian *bourgeois* insurrection and *jacqueries* after Poitiers, with widespread sacking of castles: Perroy, *Hundred Years War*, 132–6; P. Lewis, *Later Medieval France*, 283–5. Manorial buildings and records, gaols and castles, and officials were primary targets in 1381 in Kent; e.g. 'Shoford' in Mote Park, Maidstone, etc.: Coulson, 'Hierarchism in Conventual Crenellation', 84–8; *CPR, 1381–5*, 132, 164, 409; *CCR, 1396–9*, 171–2, etc.; Tout, *Chapters*, iii. 367–9. Coulson, 'Peaceable Power', 92–7.

[376] Printed in Bréquigny (ed.), 'Rôles Normands et Francais', 256 ('1431'); also 256–9; *Rot Parl*, v. 417b ('1429–30').

scape, together with park and church. So much is obvious. But how that domination operated requires clarification. That towns and religious precincts were also fortresses and castles by use, symbolism, and spirit as well as in name, requires some adjustment of perspective and as thorough an investigation as is possible in a cursory overview such as this. Context is vital. Castles do not benefit from being studied purely as monuments, architecturally or aesthetically, or even as social documents, in isolation: for one thing, their medieval image as icons of power was all-embracing, surpassing even the makeshift modern formulation that they were emblems of 'feudal pride'. For another, the moral dimension was seldom far from contemporaries' minds. To exclude it would falsify the subject as seriously (but surreptitiously) as do the popularisms of the 'dungeons', 'boiling-oil', and 'strategic' varieties. Territoriality, in any case, offers a better insight than the 'conflict model' of social interaction.[377]

Much of Part II has unfashionably diminished castles—but only to show how great their true importance was, in a diffuse, rather elusive and socially subordinate, though conspicuous, way as an aspect of upper-class identity and as a crucial interface between privilege and the majority. The debunking part of this process removes some meretricious glamour. Weaponry was a fashionable and ritualized cult. It pervaded architecture, complicating peacekeeping. Maintaining a balance with armed individualism required peculiar but conventional concessions to local power, both jurisdictional and military (Ch. 1). It is a milieu quite unlike any other, difficult to judge (Part I, Ch. 4). Castellation was one of the noble attributes, regulated by rank and wealth, which admitted only the upper *bourgeoisie* to a carefully limited aristocratic fellowship. Only in inverted perspective was fortifying an instrument of state. Military display took many other forms, not so much controlled or tolerated by a supposedly autocratic ruler as used as a channel of patronage by a presidential source of favour (the licensing of fortification being but one example), with obvious differences (put crudely) between 'federal' France and 'monarchical' England. Various degrees of partnership in governing refute the prejudice against 'private castles'. So far as this prejudice is authentic, such factors as ecclesiastical–lay rivalry in clerical propaganda, the flagrancy of 'private' power in royalist eyes, historiographical inertia, and a few overworked atrocity stories largely account for it. They are far from the whole view.

Encroachment of any kind upon another's rights, by fortifying or otherwise, especially when prima facie illegal because occurring as part of or during hostilities, had to be put right afterwards, whether that wrong was largely spurious (Ch. 2, sec. 1) or heavily tinged with political expediency but genuine (Ch. 2, sec. 2). English cases after 1217 and the twelfth century show that principles were far from black and white. Rules were broken most often by Henry II and King John. Public

---

[377] M. Thompson, 'Military Interpretation of Castles', is to be compared with his 'The Green Knight's Castle', 317–25. Much cultural material is presented (with references) by R. K. Morris, 'The Architecture of Arthurian Enthusiasm', 63–81, including commentary on the otiose triple turrets of the Eagle Tower, Caernarfon (p. 72), acknowledgement inadvertently omitted from Coulson, 'Fourteenth-Century Castles', 138, 147, q.v. *passim*.

responsibility seldom motivated their opportunistic 'castle-policy'. Quasi-international treaties were more scrupulous, revealing the compromise between custom and expediency more clearly. Anglo-Scottish affairs, down to 1388 (Ch. 2, sec. 3) tend to confirm this picture.

Property in castles, though severely restricted chiefly by de facto or (in France) formal rendability, was combined with observance of various interpretations of the public good. Examples of how this worked were the concern of Chapter 3. How contemporaries saw things can be approximately deduced by the distinct treatment of justified compared with unjustified infringement of rights of property (Ch. 3, sec. 1). *Raison d'état*, today most often 'national security', had little true recognition, whether in peace, war, or cold war. Social realities were the most enduring. What outlasted all the politics was the noble ethos which imbued often quite lowly castle-holding status. Rendability, in all the guises of conditional fortress-tenure, epitomized the public utility of 'private' castles (Ch. 3, sec. 2); while conversely the class antagonisms, which have been illustrated in south-west France, focused on fortification and displayed the practical limits of social consensus (Ch. 3, sec. 3). The walled towns, apparently more akin to the social rural majority, still pursued their own agenda. All this was less changed in France after 1337 (or 1356) than might be expected: a notionally total subordination of fortresses to 'national' policies was no more than sketched out in the 'Hundred Years War' (Ch. 3, sec. 4). The constructive tension between seignorial ethos and public priorities was barely interrupted, and its focus upon the castellated centres of local lordship and administration was an enduring constant.

PART III

Castellans, Colonization, and Rural Community

Introduction

In the first half of this book modern perspectives on medieval fortresses have loomed large. In this second half, the own-view of contemporaries is foremost (so far as presentation of context allows) instead of being interpolated (e.g. Part I, Ch. 1, sec. 3; Ch. 3, sec. 2) between sections whose aim is chiefly to reconcile our preconceptions with the medieval realities. By now reversing the process, as far as possible, the overall aim of seeing castles as others saw them may be brought closer.[1]

In Part III the protagonists are the secular nobility (Ch. 1) and the largely quiet majority comprising the peasantry (Ch. 3), with some further allusion to town-castles and to the higher clergy, within the theme of colonization (Ch. 2). By devoting Part IV to the involvement of noble women and children with castles as proprietors, a fair but unavoidably selective representation of the three 'estates' of the medieval polity is attempted, within the limitations of the evidence employed.[2] Much has still had to be postponed, notably a more adequate discussion of 'fortified' religious precincts (cathedrals, abbeys, etc.) and of those other 'castles of communities', the walled towns.

---

[1] In this Part and Part IV these notes consist, as before, of source references and subsidiary details. The text, it is hoped, will be self-sufficient, thus reducing the need to refer to the infrastructure set out in my journal articles published since 1973.

[2] Concept and realities of 'kingdoms as communities' (England, Scotland, France, and Germany) discussed in Reynolds, *Kingdoms and Communities*, 262–302. For 'estates' as representative bodies, ibid., e.g. 315–19. Classes or 'estates and conditions of men' (*Book of Common Prayer*) is the sense here.

1

Castle-Lords, Castle-Lordships, and Noble Civilization

Because the lords of castles, small, medium, as well as large, were public figures involved in local and even 'national' government, none of them, down to the one-manor 'esquire' with his castellated home or up to the multi-castle magnate, can be regarded as what today would be a 'private citizen'.[3] Consequently, to move from questions of public policy (Part II) to the preoccupations of the 'gentle' classes is to change the scale, not the subject. It makes little difference that in Britain what we call 'the castle' was not so much introduced in 1066 as more widely and visibly imposed upon the existing pattern of towns and villages with their thegnly seats; whereas in France the castellary developed and multiplied organically, subdividing and budding-off from the first without evolutionary interruption.[4] But any attempt at contrast cannot avoid overstating the differences. Whether or not the British experience of 'castles' was sudden imposition and the French one of gradual evolution, they have in common a third and more general pattern, that of diffusion. This is the theme of Chapter 2, on colonization. In this first chapter first to be discussed are the more personal aspects of noble architectural ambition, previously introduced (Part I Ch. 3, sec. 2), so as to show more of the practical implications and individual vicissitudes. How closely jurisdictional powers were associated with castle-status follows next (sec. 2). The chapter then concludes with a range of case-studies involving relationships between greater lords in which fortresses were crucial. Throughout, the self-view of those who had the documents produced to put their actions, intentions, and aspirations on record is put first, with in second place issues of interpretation and of definition.

1. Some Greater English Castellans: Pride, Responsibility, and Danger

Once a castle-lordship was duly established, the rivalries which its lord may have

---

[3] e.g. in England the builders and occupiers of Little Wenham 'Hall' (Suffolk: Goodall, *Country Life*); Ightham 'Mote' (Kent: Parker, *Domestic Architecture*, ii. 282–4); and Stokesay 'Castle' (Salop: Hall, *Country Life*). In France e.g. Bur (ed.), *La Maison forte au moyen âge*; Pesez and Pipponier, 'Les Maisons fortes bourguignonnes' (bailiwick of Dijon).

[4] Plea for a correspondingly integrated study in Debord, 'Châteaux et résidence', 41–51. His major (unfortunately posthumous) work (*pers. comm.* M.-P. Baudry) will undoubtedly be important.

encountered diminished but did not necessarily disappear. It was a great strength, but also a potential weakness, that the great castellaries possessed large, inherent governmental functions. Private rights and public duties, by more or less enlightened self-interest, became almost inseparable. In this section I consider some thirteenth- and fourteenth-century examples showing that in England, most clearly, the social, tenurial, and economic eminence of the castle conferred power but also imposed responsibilities.

Richard de Umfraville, it was recorded in 1212, 'holds the barony of Prudhoe [Northumberland] in-chief by service of two and a half knights' fees . . . as have all his predecessors from the time of King Henry I' (1100–35). Defence of the castellary of Prudhoe was, for the Umfravilles, defence of the kingdom. Later on we find 'the same Richard, by ancient enfeoffment, holds the valley of Redesdale by the service that he shall guard the valley from robbers'. His successor Gilbert, in 1242–3, is stated simply to 'hold Redesdale by regalian power'. In a later Gilbert's inquisition *post mortem* in 1307, the service was to 'defend the same from wolf and robber'. His castles of Harbottle and Prudhoe both possessed large parks and revenues, but on Robert de Umfraville's death in 1325, Harbottle was a mere 'site of the castle' and the jurors said Prudhoe lordship had been 'wasted by the Scots'.[5] The official prison for Redesdale had to be transferred temporarily 'for ten years' to Prudhoe castle, an arrangement renewed in 1336 and again in 1351, since by treaty Harbottle was not to be rebuilt (Part II, Ch. 2, sec. 4 above).[6] If prisoners kept awaiting trial were convicted on a capital charge by the king's justices, and if their crime occurred within an appropriate liberty, then they would be handed over to be hanged. Barons holding directly from the Crown in Northumberland, it was noted in the Hundred Roll inquiry (1274–5), 'possessed gallows (*furcas*), though by what warrant [authority] the jurors know not'.[7] Barons, in such circumstances, did not 'take the law into their own hands', but they did execute it—not always correctly, particularly in remote areas and when royal authority was slack.

---

[5] *Book of Fees*, i. 201; ii. 1121. *CIPM* iv. 379–80. Appurtenant to Prudhoe in 1307 was 'a park a league in circuit' and another at Birtley. Harbottle castellary included a borough. At Otterburn Gilbert II had 'a capital messuage, free tenants' and a third park 'nearly a league in circuit'. Labour services to maintain the paling would make its length (3 miles?) familiar. Birrell, 'Deer and Deer Farming'; Lasdun, *English Park*, ch. 2 and refs. pp. 204–5.

[6] *CDScotland*, ii. 523 ('1300–7'), Gilbert, earl of Angus, having 'shown that from time beyond memory his ancestors and himself have warded prisoners within their franchise of Redesdale in the prison of their castle of Harbottle, but it is so *abattu* (damaged) by the Scots that prisoners can no longer safety (securely) be warded there'. *Foedera*, ii, ii, 934 (full Latin); *CPR, 1350–4*, 42. The earl was exonerated regarding Harbottle's state of ruin. A prison at the castle of Goodrich (Herefs.) or in its castellary was licensed in 1348: *CPR, 1348–50*, 193–4. In 1359 the earl of March punctiliously got licence to put felons from Ewias Lacy liberty (Longtown, Herefs.) in his prisons at New Radnor or Builth castles, claiming that he had only a prison at Ewias, where there had been a break-out. Prisoners were to be kept 'until delivered [tried, convicted, or released] according to law and custom of those parts': *CPR, 1358–61*, 202.

[7] *Rot Hund*, ii. 20b. Power to arrest (and to pursue) criminals was widely vested: Summerson, 'Structure of Law Enforcement'; Cam, *The Hundred*, 107–27, 137–45, etc.; Bellamy, *Crime and Public Order*, ch. 4.

At the end of his reign, when Henry III was ailing and anxiously awaiting the return from Crusade in the Holy Land of the Lord Edward, the unresolved arrears of 'disturbances' since 1267 had accumulated. Some are meticulously listed in the Hundred Rolls. Most of them were remarkably tame and technical—but game-keepers might turn poacher: Gilbert de Umfraville was said to have harboured outlaws, indicted criminals who had eluded arrest, at Prudhoe and Harbottle, and had even shared their plunder. Gilbert was accused of having:

received Walter de Was with his accomplices . . . when Walter was a notorious brigand (*communis depredator*) into Prudhoe *castellum* and had then had them escorted from the castle (*castrum*) to his liberty of Redesdale and within it, namely to Harbottle. There they lodged for a month. After that to procure from Gilbert letters of safe-conduct, Walter paid him £40 . . . the safe-conduct being made out in their names, requesting that nobody should interfere or harm them. Gilbert provided them with a guide who subsequently was executed by beheading along with that Walter.

A safe-conduct was like a passport, an official act, making Gilbert a clear acces-sory.[8] Less flagrant was the offence alleged against the chief officer or seneschal of Thomas de Furnivall, in his castellary of Sheffield, who was said to have taken bribes to allow escapes from the castle gaol. 'Private' prisons were not meant to be profitable in that way. Thomas, in his lordship of Hallamshire, also used public gallows and had hunting rights of free warren. Sheffield was once a splendid castle, licensed in 1270.[9] Based in their ancient castle of Lewes, with its two mottes and Cluniac priory, the Warenne earls of Surrey, William and John, had also been usually asserting their position, apparently resenting the sheriff, Robert Aguillon, who took the unusual step of getting three licences to crenellate his manor-house of Perching to wave in the earl's face, namely in February and in March 1264, and finally in February 1268. As a Warenne tenant, Robert was vulnerable to pres-sure.[10] At Arundel, the seneschal also overreached himself, or so the monks of

---

[8] *Rot Hund*, ii. 21b. Misuse of liberties was the concern of heads of inquiry nos. 8–11; but among the 34 such items, misconduct of sheriffs and royal officials, not of franchise-holders, predominates: *Rot Hund*; i. 13–14. Complete list (51 heads) in Cam, *The Hundred*, 249–56 (items 35–7, 43–4 also reflect misconduct by franchisees); also *Liberties and Communities*, ch. 13 ('The king's government as admin-istered by the greater abbots of East Anglia').

[9] *Rot Hund*, i. 110a; against Rannulph de Atton (1275/6). Thomas's gallows and hunting rights (free warren) in Hallamshire liberty were perfunctorily queried 1278–81; also his crenellation of Sheffield (*CPR, 1266–72*, 447) with associated judicial powers, penal (gallows, tumbrel) and economic (survey of bread and ale, weights and measures), and exemption from county-court suit (attendance). Thomas's reply is incomplete. Licences to crenellate Braybrooke (Northants., 1304: *CPR, 1301–7*, 209), Bletsoe (Beds. 1327: *CPR, 1327–30*, 130), and Aberystwyth town (borough charter 1277, *CChR* ii. 206) were also incidentally recited under Edward III: *Quo Waranto*, 187a, 75b, 573b, 817a. Cam, *The Hundred*, 233–9 (on 1278–93); Part II, n. 153 above.

[10] Part I, n. 131 above, and n. 316 below. *Rot Hund*, ii. 201a, 209a, 210a, 210b, 213b; *CCR, 1272–9*, 116; *Rot Parl*, i. 6b. To assert the right he claimed to hunt anywhere in his barony, Warenne's 'dogs and huntsmen, with armed force' intruded on Aguillon's and others' land; his men 'followed Robert's men, with horse and arms, to Robert Burnell's house in Chichester liberty, taking and imprisoning them in Lewes castle', so that the sheriff had to enforce the king's writ in person. On Burnell's later career see F. Powicke, *Thirteenth Century*, 225, 335–8, 338–9, etc. Harassment at Perching manor was continuing in March 1274. In 1266 there was serious trouble in Lewes priory (Knowles and Hadcock,

Fécamp asserted on behalf of their daughter house, whose cattle had been wrongfully impounded at, or in, Arundel castle.[11]

These are not the brutal acts sometimes ascribed to castle-lords (Part II, Ch. 1, sec. 2). 'Robber barons' were not numerous. In fact, even a lord with a prestigious and (which was far from usual) a well-maintained castle, when carrying out his normal governmental functions, could suffer violence himself. At the end of Edward III's reign, in August 1375, the duke of Lancaster, John 'of Gaunt' (the rendering of Gand, Gent, or Ghent, his birthplace), had himself put at the head of a commission of four:

> to make inquisition in the county of York touching a complaint by William de Furnyvall that certain evildoers came armed to Sheffield, assaulted . . . his parker, and although he ordered the constables of the town to arrest them, so threatened the latter in life and limb that they dared not do so; whereupon William, as one of the keepers of the peace, was grievously disturbed and came forth from his castle to arrest the evildoers according to the duty of his office: but they chased him back with bows and arrows, besieged him a long time, and lay in wait for him and his servants to kill them or to do them other mischiefs.

Immediately afterwards the affair was transferred to the king's council itself.[12] Unless an inquiry was obtained, or litigation ensued, such incidents (especially minor ones) went unrecorded; but it was very unusual for the protection of a castle to be needed in this, or indeed in any way, even during local outbreaks of civil war such as occurred in 1173–4, 1215–17, 1263–6, 1322, and episodically in the period 1451–85 (the Wars of the Roses).[13] A comparable incident at Wisbech castle—now a minor earthwork site, but never imposing—occurred in 1350. The rioting was against the bishop of Ely's liberty.[14] Even great lords depended for their protection upon the king's peace; but another affray, in 1348 at Tamworth (Staffs.), shows how even unmanned castles could still protect inmates, however powerless they were to prevent interference with the lord's people outside. Baldwin de Frevill, lord of Tamworth, as was usual, accused by name four persons in the *oyer et terminer* commission he obtained (by lobbying and a variable fee)

Religious Houses, 100). Warenne also made excessive collections of murage (three-year grant, 1266: *CPR, 1258–66*, 590) to wall Lewes town.

[11] *Rot Hund*, ii. 214b. The seneschal of Arundel refused to release the cattle despite royal order brought by the sheriff, Matthew de Hastings. Aguillon was nominal keeper of the *honor* from 1273, pending partition between daughters of Roger de Somery's widow. The sheriff had difficulty in obtaining possession of the castle. *CCR, 1272–9*, 85; Sanders, *English Baronies*, 2; *Rot Hund*, ii. 215a.

[12] *Obsedere*, 'besiege', in the calendar often meant only to surround or harass. Burned in 1265, but rebuilt apparently after licence to crenellate in 1270 (worded as though for a new castle), Sheffield was fatally slighted c.1647: *CIM, 1219–1307*, 110; *CPR, 1266–72*, 447; M. Thompson, *Decline of the Castle*, 184.

[13] Events summarized in Mortimer, *Angevin England*, 86–94; Powicke, *Henry III and the Lord Edward*, 456–502; McKisack, *Fourteenth Century*, 62–7; Gillingham, *Wars of the Roses*, 23–4 *et passim*.

[14] *CPR, 1348–50*, 583. Protestors (exaggeratedly) at the bishops' receiving and acting on royal writs, etc., assaulted the bishop's servants and 'besieged his castle of Wysbech and, what is worse, daily threaten the constable and his other servants and ministers within the liberty of the Isle of Ely with loss of life and mutilation of their limbs, so that they are unable to stay there without a great multitude of armed men, and dare not go out to execute the king's mandates or keep the peace within the liberty . . . or levy the bishop's dues and hold his courts . . .' (inquiry obtained by the bishop, to investigate these accusations, paying 2 marks).

from Edward III's chancery. The malefactors, he alleged, 'broke his houses at Tamworth, carried away his goods, assaulted his men and servants, whereby he lost their service for a great time, chased them as far as his castle in the same town and besieged him and them therein so that they could not come out to procure victuals for their sustenance'.[15] Ancient Tamworth perhaps deterred more than it could have resisted attack, but the quite numerous cases of housebreaking on the Rolls do not suggest that mere buildings were much of an obstacle.[16] Getting the overriding commission of inquiry betokened wealth, privilege, and the power to avenge insult. Defence against burglary was evidently more a matter of having a vigilant household than of moats, walls, and ditches. Attack by stealth or at night did occur; but occasions are not rare when it was overt, flagrant, and in some force, almost ritualized in sequence.[17] A commission in 1302 'touching the persons who entered and broke the castle and manor of Lyonshall' (Herefs.) may refer only to extramural properties (as at Tamworth), but at Easebourne manor-house (Sussex) in 1317, 'gates and drawbridge' could not stop entry of 'the dwelling-place' nor avert theft.[18] A place styled 'castle' might be grander and have a larger household (when the lord was in residence), but a group comprising porters, a chaplain perhaps, one or two watchmen, a steward or often-absent constable, with a few stable-hands, kennel-men, and servants could hardly deter thieves such as robbed Manorbier castle (Pembs.) in 1331.[19] In 1322 the seizure of Bowes castle (Yorks., ex-Roman *Lavatrae*) occurred when Scottish invasion was possible and during the rebellion of Thomas of Lancaster which, for a time, threatened Edward II with deposition. Its lord, the Breton earl of Richmond, named twelve suspects (one a knight) whose depredations gravely concerned him. They,

while the earl was coming by the king's command to the parliament at Westminster . . . came to his castle of Boghes, besieged and took it, expelled John Nowell the constable and his men and servants, and held the castle for a long time, not permitting him to receive his toll and other customs and rents . . . levying the same themselves. They partly burned a hall

---

[15] *CPR, 1348–50*, 171; 'By fine of 10s. paid in the hanaper' (Chancery cash-office). Seat of an inferred barony, Tamworth has a large motte with shell keep and bailey: Sanders, *English Baronies*, 145–6.

[16] e.g. Maxstoke (War.), licensed 1345, burgled 1357. John de Clinton's *oyer et terminer* (cost 2 marks) accused a band of eight, all with local or non-noble names. One of the finest English castellated palaces: *CPR, 1343–5*, 431, 444; *1354–8*, 651; Coulson, 'Fourteenth-Century Castles', 142–7; Emery, *Greater Medieval Houses*, ii. 415–21.

[17] e.g. *CPR, 1292–1300*, 545–6: inquiry 'touching the persons who by night and by scaling the walls entered the manor of Middleton, co. Essex', committing assaults and damage. Overview in Coulson, 'Hierarchism in Conventual Crenellation', 84–92; analysis in Kaeuper, 'Special Inquisitions of Oyer and Terminer', e.g. 736, 739–42, 748, 758, 781.

[18] *CPR, 1301–7*, 47; *1313–17*, 698, 701 (enrolled twice, in error), John de Bohun of Midhurst complained that 'the gates and drawbridge of his mansion . . . and the door and windows (*fenestras* i.e. shutters) of his houses' (*domorum* i.e. buildings) were broken and a horse and property stolen. Often the 'close of the house' was 'broken', sometimes specified as 'walls'. 'Breaking' and 'entering' were distinct offences.

[19] *CPR, 1330–4*, 199, 236: 'certain persons besieged' David de Barry's 'castle at Maynerbir, broke the doors and walls, carried away his goods there and at Pennaly, and assaulted his servants', killing one of them. House-breaking was the ancient felony of *husbreche* or *burh-bryce*: Maitland, *Domesday Book and Beyond*, 225–6.

in the castle, consumed four tuns [large barrels] of wine worth £20 and other victuals, and carried away his armour, springalds [large, mounted crossbows], and engines [artillery] and other goods, leaving the castle without guard while the Scots were in those parts, and hunted in his free chase . . . carrying away deer and assaulted the keepers.[20]

Although the aggravating circumstance of the Scots being active on the Border is not left out, it is not emphasized. Whether the earl had left Bowes adequately provided is similarly passed over. What he wanted was compensation and punishment for the contempt done to him. Lost revenues was the main complaint, as it would be at any humbler lordship-seat illegally occupied, though not equipped with Norman 'keep' and bailey like Bowes, but having the ubiquitous moats doubling as fishponds, drawbridges, curtilages with gatehouses, crenellated parapets, and perhaps a turret here and there.[21] Theft of documents of title caused particular concern. Charters, coined money, jewellery, and vessels of gold and silver secured and stored the profits of an estate. Removing documents could make obligations unenforceable at law. Beverstone castle (Gloucs., near Berkeley) was robbed for this reason during the final disturbances of Edward II's reign. The incoming heir evidently checked his inventories:

Commission . . . on complaint by Thomas ap Adam that some persons entered by force his castle of Beverston at the time when it was in the king's hands by reason of his minority; [they] broke the doors and windows [i.e. *fenestras*, 'shutters'] of the houses and the walls and turrets of the castle, and broke also a chest of his there in the king's custody and carried away forty charters and thirty writings obligatory relating to his inheritance.[22]

Massive, iron-bound 'trunk' chests, sometimes with multiple locks with keys in different hands for security, were the safes of the day, sometimes in special, often vaulted, 'treasuries'. Unless the heir was very privileged to get premature *seisin* (possession) of his inheritance (for a 'consideration'), as was Henry de Percy in 1318, giving as reason the need to defend his castle of Alnwick against the Scots, he and his were the lord's responsibility until he was 21. The royal keeper of Beverstone may have been to blame. The facts of burglary are much simpler than its circumstances.[23]

---

[20] *CPR, 1321–4*, 157: the knight is Thomas de Lethum (*Laton*), of a Lancastrian family, with John *de Laton* (Walker, *Lancastrian Affinity*, 29, 161), but other names, and their deeds, suggest local jealousies. John of Brittany was later captured by the Scots and held for two years; McKisack, *Fourteenth Century*, 75 n.

[21] e.g. Aydon, Northumb.; licensed to Robert de Raynes (*Reymes*) to be crenellated with Shortflatt, 1305; styled 'manor', 1324, when 'lying waste'; 'Aydenhall', 1369; 'castle', 1415. Raynes's (*alias* Ramsey) tenure of half of Bolam barony recognized by 1296 (*CPR, 1301–7*, 328; *CIPM* vi. 373; xii. 398–9; Bates, *Border Holds*, 15; Sanders, *English Baronies*, 17. Aydon's architecture seemingly contrasts with Raynes's war record: Emery, *Greater Medieval Houses*, i. 40–1; M. Prestwich, *Three Edwards*, 73.

[22] *CPR, 1324–7*, 237. Shutters holding 'glazed' panes evolved into casement framed 'windows': Viollet-le Duc, *Dictionnaire de l'architecture*, art. 'Fenêtres . . . civile et militaire'. One document at Beverstone may have been the pardon to Maurice de Ghent, of 1229, for technical disregard of licence to crenellate: 'the castle which he has caused to be fortified at his manor of Beverston shall stay there and remain in perpetuity as it is now fortified' (*CPR, 1225–32*, 260). The government was still very sensitive (Part II, Ch. 2, sec. 2 above). It is a towered enclosure with major 14th-century additions.

[23] *CCR, 1323–7*, 102–3; *CFR, 1307–19*, 378–9. See Part IV below. Low-level theft-precautions

One category with motives more complex than theft is the break-in accompanied by abduction of women, to which we will return. From this outrage a living husband might be no protection, for instance, if the validity of the marriage of a wealthy heiress was contested. In 1366 Nicholas de Cantilupe complained that a band led by Sir Ralph Paynel 'broke his castle at Greasley [Notts.] ravished Katherine his wife, and carried her away with his goods and chattels, which they still detain from him'. It could hardly have been expressed more offensively, whether forced marriage, lust, or extortion by kidnapping was the reason.[24] The need to show financial loss as the basis of Nicholas's claim meant treating Katherine just as baggage. For the present, note only that wealth attracted violence which mere buildings (even the intercessory prayers of a monastery in the park) could not avert. Greasley, in fact, had been licensed in 1340 to be crenellated. All that remains is a moated rectangular enclosure with the foundations of a round tower.[25] Any kind of courtyard plan was more open to intrusion than the tower-house favoured in the northern counties, in the lowlands of Scotland, in Ireland, and in the borderlands of south-western France and Gascony.[26] But the defensive potential of the tower design once again, close inspection shows, was seldom fulfilled, being subordinate to the advantages of compact, self-contained, noble, and 'keep'-like accommodation.[27] The southern and midlands fashion is better represented by Greasley, the castle-type of the knightly and sub-baronial class. The Borders did suffer from cattle-raiding, ambushes, and abduction for ransom. Further south, lawlessness by armed gangs, often led by rogue members of the gentry, has justly been emphasized as a serious social problem. But the architectural response is not at all what might be expected, be it in any of the English regions.[28] Apart from the surviving but neglected majority of castellated resi-

---

discussed in Oman, 'Security in English Churches', 90–8. In April 1330, during the Mortimer ascendancy, ap Adam granted Beverstone and its appurtenant manors to Thomas de Berkeley, implicated in the murder of Edward II: *CPR, 1327–30*, 507.

[24] *CPR, 1364–7*, 281; *raptus* covered violent seizure of goods as well as of persons (with or without the carnal motive of 'rape' in the modern sense): Orr, 'Rape Prosecutions, 1194–1222', *passim*. More generally see Hanawalt, 'Violence, Domestic, Late Medieval', 197–214.

[25] *CPR, 1338–40*, 240–1, 449. In February 1339 he had licence 'to found a monastery or house of canons . . . in his park of Greasley and build a church or oratory there' and to endow it, in mortmain: on the trifling site, Speight, 'Early Medieval "Castle" Sites', 65–72. Knowles and Hadcock, *Religious Houses*, note only Greasley (Derbys.), 139, 154. In 1396 it was 'the castle and manor and appurtenances': *CCR, 1396–9*, 6–7.

[26] Gardelles, *Les Châteaux du sud-ouest*, pls. 2–4, 10, 16–17, 39, 41, 49, 78–9, 89–90, 136–7, 153, 161, 170–7 (small 'châteaux à quatre tourrelles du Bordelais'), 178–85 (rectilinear small 'châteaux dits "gascons" '). *Rôles Gascons*, iii. 1305: order to the seneschal of the Agenais not to hinder Pierre de Gontaud, lord of Biron, from heightening his *domus* of Lauzun (*dép*. Lot-et-Garonne) and fortifying (*inforsare*) it *turribus et aliis modis* in the local fashion (*prout alii nobiles de Agenesio consueverunt*) and to repress any objectors.

[27] Kightly, *Strongholds*, 120–7; Emery, *Greater Medieval Houses*, i. 48–50 (Belsay, 61), 68–70 (Chipchase), etc.; Leask, *Irish Castles*, 75–124; Tranter, *Fortalices of Scotland, passim*. English examples are studiedly spectacular, e.g. Nunney (Som., licensed 1373), Old Wardour (Wilts., licensed 1397), Ashby de la Zouche (Leics., licensed 1474), and vanished Hunsdon (Herts., licensed 1447)—*CPR, 1370–4*, 367; *1391–6*, 261; *CChR, 1427–1516*, 243; *CPR, 1446–52*, 77.

[28] This architectural *insouciance* is already conspicuous in post-Conquest England: Coulson,

dences themselves, the enrolled licences to crenellate provide some insight into the actual motives at play.

Normally the wording of licences is purely formulaic and terse in the extreme; but sometimes the wording of the builder's petition is incorporated and preserved in the calendar version. One such licence is that issued by Henry IV in 1403, as duke of Lancaster, to his faithful adherent James de Radcliffe. Licences, similarly, to equip the lordly mansion with parks, jurisdiction, and hunting preserves, and to divert roads to enhance a mansion's dignity and privacy, are seldom much more explicit.[29] But Radcliffe's licence to crenellate, issued from the ducal, now royal, and once splendidly towered castle of Pontefract, gives sparse details:

Licence for the king's esquire (*armiger*) James de Radeclif newly (*de novo*) to enclose his manor-house (*manerium*) of Radeclif, held of the king in-chief as of the duchy of Lancaster, with walls of stone and lime [mortar]) and within these to build a new hall with two towers (*aulam cum duabus turribus*) similarly of stone and lime, and to crenellate the walls, hall, and towers thus made with battlements; and to hold the manor as a fortress.

The standard elements here, applying to licences for the whole period 1200–1500, are building and battlementing 'of stone and lime' (*de petra et calce*); and holding the place thus crenellated like realty without disturbance. The addition 'as a fortress' occurs occasionally. Licence is sometimes 'to build a fortress (*fortalicium*)' or 'a castle', both occurring from the later fourteenth century. In the event, judging from the surviving Radcliffe Tower, James had to modify his ambitions.[30] Official acknowledgement of standing at Court and in regional noble society being recognized by the mere issue of a licence to crenellate, no further action was often taken. Both Radcliffe and John de Stanley—Henry IV's steward of the household, licensed for 'a house newly built in the town of Liverpool' in 1406 and commemorated once by Stanley Tower—did succeed in making their mark.[31] Renown as a builder, especially for lesser men at the family name-place, was an ambition which English kings readily gratified.

'Peaceable Power'. For post-1300, Emery's *Greater Medieval Houses*, vols. 1, 2, and 3 (forthcoming), sheds an incidental flood of new light. Ground-breaking essay, Dixon, 'Hall to Tower', e.g. 87–95 ('Halls').

[29] This large group, mainly on the Charter Roll, extends in time from Kirkoswald (Cumb., 1201: *Rot Chart*, 89) to Oxburgh Hall (Norfolk, 1482: *CPR, 1476–85*, 308) and beyond; cf. urban and conventual licences.

[30] *CPR, 1401–5*, 255: Parker, *Domestic Architecture*, iii. 421; Emery, *Greater Medieval Houses*, i. 243–4 (site and family). Radcliffe Hall was an eventually quadrangular castellated mansion of some dignity. The non-disturbance formula (e.g. Allington, Kent, 1281: *sine occasione vel impedimento nostri vel heredum nostrorum aut ministrorum*: Brown, *English Medieval Castles*, 198, facs. 203, transcript) was formulaic—cf. special exemption 1308 for John de Benstead's 'dwelling-house in Eye near Westminster, called *Rosemont*, from livery of stewards, marshals and other ministers of the king'. The day before John had had licence to crenellate this house: *CPR, 1307–13*, 58, 61; also *1330–4*, 219 (1331), directing officials lodging in houses at Westminster not to be oppressive.

[31] *CPR, 1405–8*, 207. William de Caverswall's self-congratulatory tomb-epitaph (licensed Caverswall castle, Staffs. 1275: *CPR, 1272–81*, 109) quoted with Tudor addition, courtesy of John Blair, in Coulson, 'Some Analysis of Bodiam', 84.

Maxstoke castle, in Warwickshire, exemplifies very well the pride of the new-made earl of Huntingdon and the personal glory he desired to pass down to his family. The public responsibility displayed by the architecture lies purely in its visual upholding of the social hierarchy. Danger receives but the remotest deference. When he was made earl, William de Clinton could not have Huntingdon castle, since the countess of Pembroke possessed it for life. But what he wanted was a palace imbued with the castle aura, not an antiquated, town-centre, lordly business-office, except for the revenues and comital symbolism. His new castle, accordingly, is a large, moated and towered quadrangle, the apartments now on one side only, for which he had licence in 1345 in favour of his heir and nephew, John de Clinton. An imposing priory was founded in 1342, a chantry of atavistic grandeur, and given the buildings of the old Clinton manor-house with its moat in 1344, by which time it would appear that the castle was already fit for occupation. Palatial Maxstoke certainly is, satisfying the Stafford dukes of Buckingham in the next century, but once intruders had crossed the moat and penetrated within the rather thin and low screen of walls, the house itself lay open. As at Bodiam (1385), the chapel window opens through the 'curtain'. None of the four octagonal towers, nor the imposing gatehouse, was capable of independent defence.[32] Such castellated mansions were no less 'castles' for being chivalric architecture. They served an aristocracy which successfully practised warfare, first in Scotland and then throughout France, under the soldierly Edward III. Skilful planning, the integration of 'state' and private spaces, domesticity combined with appropriate grandeur, all within a militant outer envelope, was always for the aristocracy what 'the castle' properly was, whether in the twelfth century, the fifteenth, or in the early Tudor period.[33]

The ostentation of established, secure, historically grounded and legitimate power and wealth, fearing no man, was expected of all grades of nobility. Some of their houses suffered for it. As has been noted, Maxstoke (Part I, n. 315) was burgled in 1357, Sir John de Clinton accusing eight culprits (including one woman), alleging that with others they 'broke the walls of his castle and his houses at Maxstoke, carried away his goods, and assaulted his men and servants'. The law was duly set in motion to vindicate Clinton's pride.

Leeds castle, near Maidstone in Kent, enjoys a similar continuity of occupation. Set on two islands in an artificial lake, held back in the valley basin by sluices and banks, and surrounded still by maturely timbered parkland,[34] Leeds's 'fairy-

---

[32] n. 16 above. In 1341 Clinton was compensated in cash for not receiving *pro tem.* the actual 'site or place of the castle of Huntingdon', 'destroyed' to derogate rebel William of Scotland in 1173/4 but still (as so often) in use: *CCR, 1341–3*, 61; Brown *et al.*, *Kings Works*, ii. 682. Clinton could have had a more militant and defensible palace, such as Bolton in Wensleydale (licensed 1379: *CPR, 1377–81*, 369), for his money.

[33] Coulson, 'Peaceable Power'; Faulkner, 'Domestic Planning' and 'Castle-Planning'; Morley, 'Fourteenth-Century Castle Design', esp. 104–6, 111–13; Platt, *The Castle*, 150–87.

[34] Felling by royal purveyors of timber of 'trees growing around mansions to their great damage, *gast et blemissement*' was forbidden in 1350, emphatically repeated with severe punishment of offenders in 1351: *Rot Parl*, ii. 230, 239. Cf. The 'finely timbered park' of Somerleyton advertised in 1861: Girouard, *Victorian Country House*, front endpaper.

tale castle' satisfies modern romantic expectations. Whereas Bodiam (1385–c.1392) added a strong (but bogus) element of architectural brutality to the 'castle in the valley' look, Leeds almost disclaimed it. Although half post-medieval, its 'genuineness' is still not questioned. How it was regarded at the end of Edward II's reign, in the famous affair of 1321 and its sequel, reveals a 'lifestyle' assessment (Part I, Ch. 3, sec.2) as shrewd as that of a modern estate agent. If the walls of the original *Gloriette*, built like a shell-keep on the smaller motte-like island and rising sheer from the water, were once lime-washed the effect would have been superb. All these various qualities, visual, palatial, and noble, were highly prized by Queen Isabella, daughter of Philip IV of France. Under Edward I, with no need to intimidate a conquered people, as in North Wales with such a panoply as at Caernarfon or Conway, the larger island was still walled with round bastions, similar to those of the outer ward at Harlech, and equipped with a barbican, outer mantlet, and demonstratively 'fortified' corn-mill (with crosslet loops) attached to it, powered by a shallow mill-race next to the main sluice.[35] As 'overkill' Leeds is modest, but still demonstrative. The high estate of this 'prestige property' was accordingly most attractive to the ambitious and influential courtier Bartholomew de Badlesmere, soon to be named seneschal of Edward II's household. Proximity to London and the court, and to the inland route from Dover, added to Leeds's allure. In 1318 Bartholomew was ready to pay for the manor considerably more than its mere revenues justified. The deal was struck directly with the king, as a precaution being entered in full on the roll of Letters Close, but only after consulting 'the prelates, earls, barons, and others of his council'. King Edward II:

agreed to grant to Bartholomew the castle and manor of Leeds, which Margaret, queen [dowager] of England, now deceased, held for life by grant of the late king [Edward I], as of the value of £21. 6s. 8d. yearly [i.e. 32 marks] net of fixed alms [charitable payments], to have and to hold to Bartholomew and his heirs in return for 100 marks [£66] yearly in land to be given to the king. Now, although the manor of Adderley, co. Salop, is worth £99. 19s. 8¼d. p.a., and its church is worth 60 marks (£40) . . . thus greatly exceeding the 100 marks p.a., and the woods of Adderley manor are worth £3,521. 6s. 8d. . . . . Bartholomew has given Adderley manor, with the advowson [presentation to the benefice] of the church, together with the woods of the same, to the king in exchange for the said castle and manor of Leeds and the advowson of the priory of Leeds . . . [36]

It could not have been more deliberately done, probably because it disregarded the expectations Queen Isabella had due to the tenure of Leeds by both Queen

---

[35] Edward I set up a chantry here to his beloved Queen Eleanor (d. 1290). Leeds's supposed lake-water plunge-bath was probably a boat dock: Brown *et al.*, *King's Works*, ii. 695–702; *Leeds Castle*, 10–12. The White Tower of London and its *cingulum* were whitewashed in 1240; Corfe tower was also harled (roughcast), over good ashlar, in 1244. This was customary: *CLibR, 1240–5*, 14, 222; Salzman, *Building in England*, index 'roughcast', 'whitewash'.

[36] *CCR, 1313–18*, 607: witnessed by the archbishop of Canterbury, the bishop of Winchester (chancellor), the earls of Pembroke and Hereford, and the powerful Hugh Despenser, father and son: 20th March, 1318. McKisack, *Fourteenth Century*, 55, 64. The precision of the estate accounts of Leeds and Adderley is typical (e.g. Clare lands, Holmes, *Higher Nobility*, App. 3). Adderley woods will be valued at 'capital', i.e. annual income x 10–20.

Eleanor (d. 1290) and Queen Margaret, Isabella's aunt. Nevertheless, Isabella did not accept losing Leeds. Probably with her vacillating husband's connivance, she presented herself at the castle in the autumn of 1321, demanding admission for herself and her retinue. To open the gates to her and allow her to stay in the castle risked damage to Badlesmere's ownership for which he had agreed to pay over three times the income from Leeds, and had eventually given the king between fourteen and twenty-two times the income-value of the castle-manor. So Lady Badlesmere, in her husband's absence, refused entry.[37] Had the queen proffered an order from Edward II, or had the king been there in person, it is likely that the gates would have been opened, at least as a courtesy, since Leeds was held in-chief. As a French princess, accustomed to fortresses being deliverable ('rendable') at the lord's demand, Queen Isabella may have believed that right was on her side—but being refused admission was an insult to majesty, whatever the legalities. The castle was manned at the time, as it happened. Whoever was in charge allowed a shooting affray to develop outside the barbican, and some of the queen's party were killed or wounded. Edward II, deciding to make an issue of this 'disobedience and contempt', but insisting that it was not an act of war, summoned troops to Leeds so that, put thoroughly in the wrong, Badlesmere's wife and household had to give in.[38] It was not this particular blunder in the complex Court-politics preceding Earl Thomas of Lancaster's party's defeat at Boroughbridge (1322), as much as the ambitions of Isabella's adversaries the Despensers and his opposition to them in 1321 which led to Bartholomew's subsequent fall and execution.

His widow, Margaret de Badlesmere of the family of Clare, was left in a difficult position, deprived of Leeds as well as of Adderley—much more lucrative, though with a poor earthwork castle as its lordship-seat. After the revolution which deposed and murdered Edward II, she petitioned Queen Isabella (nominally 'the king and council') ruling with Mortimer until October 1330, 'to be allowed to enter upon and enjoy her [Margaret's] castle of Leeds', or failing that, to have back Adderley. The councillors who dealt with her request had good reason to know the queen mother's attachment to Leeds. Margaret's petition had their decision noted on the back ('endorsed'): 'it seems to the council that she ought to have the one or the other; and because the castle of Leeds is in the hands of the queen she must be spoken to about this.' William de Clinton, of Maxstoke, duly asked Isabella. In February 1327 he reported that she wished to keep Leeds and have the 1318 exchange for Adderley revoked. As a result, Margaret and her 14-year-old son Giles were much better off financially, though not in point of prestige.[39]

---

[37] Fryde, *Fall of Edward II*, 50–1 (ref. due to M. Prestwich). She was put in the Tower until November 1322. Cf. John Balliol's action in 1267 in suing his own constable of Fotheringhay for delivering the castle to 'the enemy of the king and of John', Baldwin Wake: *CDScotland*, i. 488.

[38] Bartholomew de Burgersh, Thomas de Aldon, and John de Bourn were forfeited (Nov. 1321) for having 'detained of late the castle of Ledes against the king, hindering the king's entrance thereto', they having given themselves up with the castle. Badlesmere's forfeiture, with other 'Lancastrian' rebels, followed: *CFR, 1319–21*, 77, 84. Numerous entries e.g. *CCR, 1318–23*, 504–5 (Oct. 1321), specifying that the 'contempt' was against the queen with Badlesmere's connivance (text, *Foedera*, ii, i, 458–9).

[39] *Rot Parl*, ii. 436–7; recited *CIPM* vii. 89–97 with the 1327/8 findings. Fortunately for Margaret, her

But Leeds was exceptional, pre-eminent among the small group of glamour-castles which fluctuated in composition over time. Most castles were to their lords not the proud seats of major dynasties but, like the headquarters-castles of sheriffs in the county town, administrative offices and (if the lord had several) occasional residences. Their buildings were not so much a source of pride as a charge to revenue. Capital seat of the shrievalty of Rutland, the modest ringwork-castle of Oakham was surveyed in 1340 for amenities and state of repair because it was promised to William de Bohun, newly created earl of Northampton, after the death of Hugh de Audley, earl of Gloucester:

The castle is well walled and within are a hall, four chambers, a chapel, a kitchen, two stables, a grange [barn] for hay, a prison-house, a chamber for the gatekeeper (*janitore*), and a drawbridge with iron chains. Within the walls are two acres of land by estimation. The buildings are of no yearly value beyond outgoings and are likewise called the Manor . . .

Thus dismissed is one of the most elaborate late-twelfth-century aisled halls in England.[40] William de Bohun also received the 'jam-tomorrow' reversion of Fotheringhay castle and manor (Northants.), after the life-tenant Mary, dowager countess of Pembroke. Partial dependency on royal grants was usual, especially for magnates elevated in the king's service. Edward III's exchequer, as in the case of Oakham, needed to know the yield of the castellary and, in general terms, the buildings' state of repair, since the new tenant, if only a life-custodian, as with bailment of any property, would be liable to keep the productive plant (mills, ovens, barns, etc.) 'in as good a state as when received'.[41] In France the same rule applied to castles under rendability, as we have seen.

The castle of Fotheringhay under the dukes of York from the late-fourteenth century, with the famous 'fetterlock' plan of its nucleus, took its place among the foremost; but it was already in 1340 an ancient seat of dignity with motte (*mota*) and two baileys, fragments of which, and of the once-magnificent but truncated Perpendicular castle-church, alone remain. The jurors tersely noted:

title to Adderley was not contested, although a recent (1311/2) acquisition jointly with her late husband. Richard II's courtier, Simon de Burley, tried in 1384–8 to get hold of Leybourne castle nearby, to boost his county standing as seat of a barony. To break a mortmain alienation he alleged that conventual possession was 'to the great weakening of the defences of Kent'. He eventually failed: *CPR, 1381–5*, 367–8, 423; *1385–9*, 37, 96, 468.

[40] *CIM, 1307–49*, 418–20: commission 'on the extent [revenue] of the castle and manor of Okham and the shrievalty [office of sheriff] of Rutland', with report. De Audley, husband of Margaret, one of the Clare heiresses, died in 1347 holding 'the shrievalty . . . for life . . . including a walled castle and a manor house built within the castle, and a fishpond (*vivarium*) . . .'. William de Bohun's inquisition (1360) is fuller: '. . . the castle in which there is a hall with divers chambers, a chapel, kitchen, stable and . . . offices, and a fishery in the moat; meadows called "le Fishpoll" . . . pastures . . . a weekly market and a yearly fair . . . and two parks, one with deer . . . one surrounded by a stone wall and the other by a hedge': *CIPM* ix. 54–65; x. 523–30. Fernie, *Architecture of Norman England*, fig. 69, p. 87, noting that the hall may once have had a clerestory.

[41] Compare the purely fiscal and barely descriptive inquisitions of 1282 on Cottingham and Liddel castles (Yorks.); also of Kenilworth, Lancaster, Pickering, and Tutbury, late of Edmund, earl of Cornwall (held 1297): *CIPM* ii. 258–62; iii. 288–321. Use of the style 'castle' is typically honorific.

The castle is well built, walled and crenellated, and has a stone tower and a moat. There are therein a great hall, two chambers, two chapels, a kitchen and a bakery of stone; a gatehouse with a chamber, underneath which [in the gate passage] is a drawbridge. Outside the castle there is another plot within the walls built over with houses and called the manor, where are a grange . . . cowhouse, dairy and larder, a forge, and a house for the outer gate with a chamber above. The buildings are of no yearly value beyond outgoings.

As usual, 'houses' (*domus*) are discrete buildings of any kind. 'Chambers' are either single rooms or, apparently as here, units of private apartments. Timber mobile bridges were very perishable, so duly noted as in working order.[42] The noble part, or castle proper, was separate from the working farmyard (or *basse cour*) but attached to it (contrast eighteenth-century snobbery). Such residences housed the great peripatetic households and were more like staging-points, as were the king's own castles and manor-houses, than permanent homes, except to their small resident administrative staff and to more-sedentary wives and children. The humbler sub-baronial knight, esquire, and *valettus* may have had fewer houses, often one only, but his class also lived a mobile life, busily travelling about the public affairs of the king or of their lord or on their own behalf, often seeing little of their wives and children. Attendance at Court, particularly in London where lay magnates and bishops had their inns or *hôtels*, left the supervision of estates (in the modern sense of land) to stewards and to *châtelaines* (Part IV).[43] The living centre, most of the time, was not the *Salle d'Apparat* or state ('estate') apartments in the inner bailey, but the home farm and the parts frequented by servants and tenantry. William de Bohun, cadet of the house of the earls of Hereford and Essex, received on his elevation to reward him for his military and administrative expertise a set of castles, houses (and expectations) to match and sustain his dignity as earl of Northampton.

Stamford castle, town, and lordship was also part of his endowment in 1340, but again in reversion only after the death of John de Warenne, earl of Surrey. Expectations were a constant potential asset of landholding. In buildings Stamford was dilapidated. The inspectors reported in April 1340 that: 'The castle is old and the walls decayed. Within are an old tower, a great hall, a chamber with solar (upper retiring room), a chapel, a turret and a prison-house, all of no value beyond outgoings. The site of the castle comprises two acres and is called the manor . . .'[44] When, as at Stamford, there were no strong motives of pride,

[42] Sketch plan, etc. in Mackenzie, *Castles of England*, i. 320–2, 326–7. *CIM, 1307–49*, 419. The lifetenant, Countess Mary of Pembroke, in fact outlived de Bohun, dying in 1377: *CIPM* xiv. 330–40, with details of attached lands including 'a common oven . . . a park with deer . . . and woods'. Fotheringhay then went to Edmund of York, son of Edward III.

[43] On the itinerant household see e.g. Woolgar, *The Great Household*, ch. 9; continuing in the 16th century: Thurley, *Royal Palaces*, 67–83. Schofield, *Medieval London Houses*, ch. 3 (Pulteney's towered inn, fig. 38), *et passim*. In general, Denholm-Young, *Country Gentry*, chs. 1, 2. County study in Saul, *Knights and Esquires*, esp. chs. 2 ('military service') and 4 ('Office Holding and the County Community').

[44] *CIM, 1307–49*, 419. John de Warenne died in 1347. Reversioners could hardly go and 'measure up for the curtains', so these reports were both encouragement and warning. Those who compiled them doubtless enjoyed visiting the homes of the great and inspecting the estate accounts. Stamford (an old

whether on the king's part or of lesser lords, the vastly expensive outlay of keeping fortifications 'up to date' was not indulged in, despite the strong instinct of
medieval stewardship to conserve and to improve resources of all kinds, which
ran counter to the wastefulness of war. Munitions also frequently mouldered into
uselessness. A list compiled in 1348 of the equipment stored in Scarborough castle,
after enumerating various items of body armour (apparently sufficient for over
100 footmen), added the comment: 'the foregoing have been there for thirty-eight
years and more and are rotten and hardly of any value.'[45] The fact bears repetition
that fortresses possessed a total role in medieval England to which the strictly
military contribution was relatively slight.

2. Castellation and Jurisdiction As Insignia of Nobility

Because the ruling classes, both landed and mercantile, were partners in government, having 'rights of justice' was as natural to them as to the eighteenth-century
magnate whose mansion often had its 'justice room' or magistrates' chamber. The
medieval peculiarity was to associate the architectural panoply of fortification so
closely with governmental power that jurisdiction and castellation were almost
inseparable: 'the baronial castle was the expression of ideas which underlay the
custom of the whole French-speaking world.'[46] Despite great regional variation
until the end of the *ancien régime* (1789), this connection in France was particularly strong, and there the *droits seigneuriaux* flourished even as monarchical
centralization advanced. As late as the reign of Louis XI (1461–83) two Normandy
castle-holders, in 1475 and 1477, successfully applied to the Crown for the right to
execute judgements on criminals sentenced to death by the local court. Their
castles, their wealth, and their (quite modest) seignorial status were all the justification they put forward. Another castle-holder, a widow, was licensed to create
the whole package entirely anew.[47] Although this prestigious and lucrative power,
running all the way from using gallows (*fourches*), of types graduated in France
according to rank, to the humdrum assize of bread and ale, was occasionally
refused, *haute justice* and its lesser forms were especially, though not even in
France exclusively, castle-linked. Petitions which failed tend to be unrecorded,
but the powerful abbot of Saint-Denis in 1321, requesting high justice for Soisy-
en-Gâtinais, in conjunction with Philippe de Soisy, on the ground that Soisy 'had

Anglo-Saxon seat) now has only traces of earthworks and of masonry. The town was prosperous: Platt,
English Medieval Town, 40 (plan); Blair and Ramsay (eds.), *English Industries*, 170, 204–5, 348.

[45] *CIM*, 1348–77, 3–4 (detailed). The seizure there in 1312 of Edward II's 'favourite' Piers Gaveston,
who may have laid in these stores, would explain the '38 years': McKisack, *Fourteenth Century*, 23–5.

[46] Stenton, *First Century*, 191. He does not overstate castles' cultural diffusion.

[47] *Ordonnances*, xviii. 83–4, 288–9. Jean de Brosse, lord of L'Aigle in Normandy, held 'une bien
ancienne baronnie, et y a chastel et droit de chastellenie'. William de Villiers declared that at Gournay
he had 'à foy et hommage [i.e. by noble tenure] un chastel fort beau, bourg et village'. At Chavaignes,
Margaret, widow of Louis de Belleville, with her children under age, was licensed 'de faire construire
un château et place forte avec tours, portaux, ponts-levis, fossés etc, avec création de chatellenie, droit
de haute justice', etc. (1474): *Ordonnances*, xviii. 11–12(d). Nobles below *haut-justicier* rank in Ponthieu
fortified without lordly licence; a verdict in 1272: Les Olim, i. 917–18.

all the attributes of a *châtellenie'*, clearly did not expect to be refused. It was not any public principle that held it back, but only encroachment on the royal castellary of Lorris. Similarly in Gascony, Edward I had no hesitation in granting Elias de Caupenne's request to have 'high and low justice within the *honor* and precinct of his castle'.[48] Official control of the trial process, less close in France than in England (sometimes much less close), differentiated 'private justice' from lynch-law; but scarcely acceptably to modern eyes. The right to be hangman would also seem rather a bizarre aspiration.

An active and thoroughly institutionalized class-discrimination was, of course, the corollary of noble privilege. In France explicitly, land which was classed as 'noble' could not officially pass into *bourgeois* possession unless held, somehow, as a fief. In 1305 Edward I was called upon to uphold this principle:

The king to his dear and faithful John de Havering, his seneschal of Gascony, greeting. Vitale de Branne has asked us to have restored to him and to Dulcia, his wife, the castle of Oeyre near the city of Dax [*dép*. Landes] which is a *feudum nobile* and belongs, as he asserts, to Dulcia de Montaulieu, lady of Villenave his wife, by hereditary right. The castle is occupied and kept by John de Mirabelle, citizen of Dax, contrary to the rule once laid down by us [King Edward] about noble fiefs not being transferable to non-noble tenure (*ad manum ignobilem*) . . .

Perhaps they were indebted to John de Mirabelle and had pledged Oeyre, necessarily the land and not only the residence, as security. If he had then foreclosed, the delicacy of Edward's instructions would be fair: 'Now, since we desire to do them justice in this matter, we direct and firmly enjoin you that having summoned the parties to your court (*coram vobis*) and heard the arguments on each side, you shall speedily do them justice as our said statute prescribes, and as the custom is to do in such and similar cases.' It was usual to reward good service by enriching 'new men', or cadets like William de Bohun, endowing them with lands, lucrative offices, and also by steering valuable marriages in their direction. Vitale may have been one such *arriviste*.[49] Getting a licence to fortify, creating a castle lordship, and then a grant of high justice promoted a mere 'gentleman' into the landed aristocracy, however small (within limits) his castle and castellary. William-Arnald de Sescas is an example. He was licensed by Edward I to fortify (subject to rendability) in 1304, soon after the French had handed back the duchy. Ten years later he ambitiously 'besought us [Edward II] that as he has a fortress in the parish of Coimères . . . we should graciously grant him high and low justice' there.[50] The consistency over the centuries of these associations makes it possible

---

[48] *Actes du Parlement*, i, ii, 382; *Rôles Gascons*, ii. 283; in land held of the king-duke in-chief; cautiously *quantum in nobis est*, as quite usual, in view of possible conflicting claims.

[49] *Rôles Gascons*, iii. 57, 460–1. Vitale was to be rewarded in 1292 for good service with the first office of bailiff to become available.

[50] Ibid. 430; iv. 338. In standard form, the new *domus fortis* was to prejudice no others' rights and was under written obligation to be handed over 'nobis vel seneschallo Vasconie, irato vel pacato [i.e. unconditionally] quociens nostre vel seneschalli nostri placuerit voluntati'. It was to have crenellation and loops (*arqueriis*). But the petition for high justice was referred for investigation by the seneschal.

to speak of a noble culture, perhaps even of a 'noble civilization'. Entirely the same underlying ideas are to be found, for instance, in Louis XI's licence to the head of the pantry department of his household in 1472. Patris Valentin, the king's pantler, as lord of Saint-Maixent and Germeville in Poitou, lordships he said both extensive and rich, asked for and received complete jurisdiction over his subjects and tenants there, with power to set up his own hierarchy of officials under the royal seneschals. At each place he was accordingly and duly empowered to construct a *forte maison* equipped 'with towers, machicolation, crenels, draw-bridges, ditches, bulwarks (*boulevars*), and all such appropriate elements of forti-fication'. He did not receive watch-and-ward services or *guet* (Ch. 3, secs. 3, 4 below), despite claiming his lands were *en frontière*, and his lordships were but *châtellenies* in miniature, but perfectly complete nevertheless.[51]

When considering the socio-architectural embellishments of lordship which relate to the buildings and institution of castles, 'late' does not mean 'fake'. Supposedly 'decadent' elements are early, and virile ones endured. Similarly, war and (as we have seen) weaponry (Part II, Ch. 1, secs. 3, 4) did not lose their actu-ality, despite elements of ritualism. The social hierarchy became more subtle, with gradations of status ever more nicely defined (knight, esquire, *valettus*, donzel, *armiger*, gentleman, 'man-at-arms', etc.), but was equally real and enduring.[52] How the very diverse regions of 'France' differed from England in this respect, at what periods and how far, is a morass for the unwary; but it would seem, at least, that had John de Mirabelle been a citizen of London rather than of Dax he would have had no difficulty in legally acquiring a local castle. Certainly, castellan-status in England was less socially exclusive. John de Pulteney, four times lord mayor and (later) financier to Edward III, took over Penshurst in Kent, building a 'baro-nial' hall with which few could compare. He obtained licence to crenellate (as did not a few prominent Gascon citizens for their country residences).[53] In France, as late as 1659 under Cardinal Mazarin, the parlement of Paris, as reported by Salvaing, upheld a baron's order to certain burgesses of Lyon to remove battle-ments from their houses since they were ignoble and not entitled. Although towns were fortified, under formal licence or without, in both kingdoms, as occasionally were burgess-houses, battlements and the like continued to signify communal

[51] *Ordonnances*, xvii. 462–3. In 1566 and 1586 nobles' fortress-rights were vindicated at law. Cardinal Richelieu's occasional exemplary demolitions (1622–42) barely touched them: Salvaing, *De l'Usage des Fiefs*, 258–74. Énaud, *Les Châteaux-forts*, 84–5, on Josselin (Brittany) in 1629.

[52] e.g. Lewis, *Later Medieval France*, 173–201; Given-Wilson, *English Nobility*, 1–83; Crouch, *Image of Aristocracy*, 1–38, 106–73; and 177–251 on 'the outward manifestations'.

[53] For Pulteney's manors of Penshurst and Cheveley (Cambs.), and his great inn on Candlewick Street: *CPR*, *1340–3*, 331; Parker, *Domestic Architecture*, ii. 278–81; n. 43 above. From 1392 (relicensed: *CPR*, *1391–6*, 164) the palace moved rapidly up the social scale, with castellation to match. The Bordeaux patrician Jean Colon was licensed in 1289 (during Edward I's stay) for two 'strong houses'; Doat de Pis, of Bazas, in 1289; and Arnald-Sanx, (presumably a settled merchant) of Lucca, in 1313, likewise. Colon and de Pis had to render on demand; de Pis, additionally, was to claim no jurisdiction by virtue of fortifying. The same applied to the noble Bertrand de Podensac's licence (1289)—so caution not discrimination may be inferred: *Rôles Gascons*, ii. 434, 367–8, 507, 516; iv. 251.

and individual privilege, proximate but not equivalent to that of nobility, with some blurring of the finer distinctions of etiquette.[54]

Closely linked with residence, deer-parks, rabbit and other game preserves, dovecots, mills, ovens, prisons, gallows, chantries, tolls and other charges, mature woodland, and hunting chases all denoted the noble. Most, like dovecots, yielded a profit; but pigeons did not feed only on the produce of the home farm, nor was hunting always so confined. Like the village or *burgus*, and like the church planted outside, these appurtenances of rank simultaneously proclaimed lordship and asserted it as forms of taxation, direct and indirect.[55] Usurping them had to be stopped, not so much for the public benefit as to protect privilege. Thus, in 1297 Philip IV's government sent an order to the royal bailiff of Caen to allow Matthew, lord of Crépon, to rebuild a dovecot of his on a new site. If there were objections it would explain why this was confirmed in 1306, although the condition had been that it must not be built outside the boundary of his lordship. Licences of this kind could be used to check competition between aggressive lordlings and to repress upstarts, operating in very much the same fashion as mill-bans, oven-bans, chapelry licensing, and, of course, licences to crenellate or fortify, elastically on a small or larger scale according to the individual's personal or tenurial rank in the locality.[56]

Where a dovecot might be erected depended, in general, like castellation, on the status of the tenure, as in Normandy for instance, not on the rank of the tenant. But exceptions might be graciously accorded. In 1308 Philip IV's squire Roger Fresney obtained leave to add a dovecot to his house and plot (*pourpris*) at his name-place, although it was not a *fief d'haubert*, held by noble service. In 1310 another royal squire, Peter de Jambville, had an apparently similar dispensation. In 1318 another such grant made this favour to Robert de Verson, *valet du roi*, explicit. Even a minor manor-house, if moated, crenellated, and perhaps turretted (if rank

---

[54] Coulson, 'Battlements and the Bourgeoisie', 'Seignorial Fortresses', App. B. Towns licensed as appendages of castles include Southwold (Suffolk, 1259), Tonbridge (Kent, 1259), and Filongley (War. 1301): *CPR, 1258–66*, 61, 108; *1292–1301*, 564. Murage grants gave less prestige but necessary cash: Turner, *Town Defences*, App. C; 'Seignorial Fortresses', App C.

[55] Detailed case-study with references, Liddiard, 'Castle Rising', 177–80 (deer park), 180–2 (rabbit warren, township, dovecotes), etc.; overview and summary, C. Taylor, 'Medieval Ornamental Landscapes'. *Registres du Trésor* i. 53 (1307), licence to Enguerrand de Marigny, chamberlain, to wall and impark as a warren any part of his lands, forest or open, diverting any public or royal roads; ibid. ii. 116 (1317) permission to Cormery abbey to have a dovecot at their daughter priory of Marchesieux's manor in the Cotentin. Norman custom was restrictive: Salvaing, De L'Usage des Fiefs, 258–65. A large group of English licences to crenellate confer lordly perquisites, e.g. Aston Mullins (1336), Athelhampton (1495), Baconsthorpe (1561), Betchworth (1379), Cestersover (1465), Drayton (1329), Eccleshall (1200), Hatch Beauchamp (1333), Herstmonceux (1441) Kettlewell (1405), Moor End (1347), Rickmansworth (1426), Slingsby (1344); Thatcham (1446, including gallows): *CCh R, 1327–41*, 453–4; *1341–1417*, 13–14, 427, 72; *Rot Chart* 60b; *CPR* (in order as above) *1494–1509*, 43; *1560–3*, 219; *1377–81*, 380; *1461–7*, 542; *1327–30*, 319; *1330–4*, 494; *1345–8*, 270; *1422–9*, 351; *1343–5*, 190. Many more such grants were not incorporated in licences but associated with castles.

[56] e.g. Coulson, 'Castellation in Champagne', 357, 361–2; *Registres du Trésor*, i. 39. In 1318 the Châtelet court for the bailiwick of Paris reasserted the doctrine that new warrens, game preserves and tolls required royal grant 'as they touch the king's majesty and the common people': *Les Olim*, iii. 1157–9 (text); *Actes du Parlement*, ii, i, 190 (calendar).

permitted), with, in the adjacent *cour* or farmyard and stabling, the squat, usually round turret of a dovecot with its conical pyramidal roof, proclaimed noble affinity, more or less remote.[57] Norman custom is particularly well attested. The two large, round dovecots on the river frontage of Stephen de Penchester's Allington castle, near Maidstone in Kent (licensed to be crenellated in 1281), are notable English examples.[58] But the nice feudal proprieties which surface in the French registers of letters close and writs of the last Capetian kings are not so prominent in the very comparable, but much more complete and longer, series of English rolls. This is undoubtedly significant. Very characteristic of France is the arrangement whereby Richard de La Hêtrée in 1318 agreed with his lord, the *écuyer* Ralph de Bosc-le-Hard, that Richard's tenure of the manor of Réel should effectively be ennobled by uniting it with a fief (*membre de haubert*). The most lowly man armed with a mail-coat, hauberk, or *lorica* was by occupation, rank, and perhaps by blood a 'gentle'. The mail-coat long kept its early distinction in France. Castle-ownership was a club with a large associate membership. Applying for the lord's approval—in this case, Philip V's as duke of Normandy—and the lord's reciprocal acknowledgement, even in so simple a matter as establishing a dovecot at Réel, affirmed the gradations of hierarchy.[59]

Service to a great lord, to the king pre-eminently, was always the commoner's route to rank. Two career-officials who had served Philip IV, Louis X, and Philip V received in 1320 the modulated accolade of dovecot-grants. One had been keeper of the king's seal at Carentan, the other a royal sheriff (*vicomte*) at Valognes. Three judgements of the Norman court of the *Echiquier* in 1210, 1223, and 1240 show how closely associated was the *feudum lorice* with castle-status. For the servile inhabitants, living (*se couchant et se levant*) there, custom put them under legally enforceable obligation both to repair old fortifications and to help build new ones. Since the fief-holder was entitled to have his miniature *château*, the building was graded according to his wealth and status, as also were his dress accoutrements, his pillory and tumbrel (if not entitled to gallows), and (in the later period) his armorial 'hatchments' emblazoned on castle-portals and on tombs.[60] Marks separating him from the urban craftsman and merchant, and especially from the tillers of the soil (*ruptarii* or *roturiers*), were jealously defended—but even the right to have gallows could be acquired by long (or not so long) user.[61]

---

[57] *Registres du Trésor*, i. 57, 234; ii. 311. Viollet-le-Duc, *Dictionnaire de l'architecture*, art. 'Colombier'.

[58] *CPR, 1272–81*, 437. In 1344 the omnicompetent Norman exchequer court enforced the ban on dovecots in unfree tenures. None, of any type, were to be allowed there: *Ordonnances de L'Echiquier*, 13.

[59] *Registres du Trésor*, ii. 342–3, 409. Ralph upheld his superiority by reserving wardship in minority. Philip V in 1319 ratified a similar adjustment of sub-fiefs made in 1316.

[60] Part I, n. 255, quoted. *Registres du Trésor*, ii. 672–3. *Rot Hund, passim*; Sumptuary Laws, *Rot Parl*, ii. 278–9 (1363), etc. Also for England, Clayton, *Catalogue of Brasses*, plates. Morganstern, *Gothic Tombs of Kinship*. Militant ambiance, Denholm-Young, *History and Heraldry, passim* (pp. 77–8).

[61] *Les Olim*, ii. 426: order to reinstate the lord of Beaujeu's gallows (*dép*. Rhône) if, when demolished by the bailiff of Mâcon, they had stood for a year and a day. On defining the limit of 'legal memory' (1189), Sutherland, *Quo Warranto Proceedings*, 226–8.

Much of this, no doubt, constitutes noble culture rather than noble civilization, since privilege for the few was degradation for the great majority. Upholding
the monarch's position as the fountainhead of preferment also involved creating
arriviste beggars-on-horseback, who duly lorded it over subordinates more
roughly than established lords might have done. The tendency in France seems to
have increased, not diminished, under 'the princes of the Renaissance'. Louis XI's
1469 grant of castellar rank to his clerk (*notaire*) and secretary Baudes Meurin
illustrates very fully the noble self-view while also, perhaps, suggesting some of its
social defects:

Maistre Baudes Meurin has expounded to us how that he has lately acquired territory,
property, landed income, and hereditaments near Saint-Benôit-sur-Loire, in the bailiwick
of Montargis, in which territory he has a fine earthwork (*une belle mote*) known as Mote-
le-Roy, which is girdled by splendid and great ramparts (*fossés*) and is very well suited to
be the site of a castle and stronghold (*chasteau et place forte*)—And at this 'moat', having
resolved to make his dwelling in that area, Baudes now proposes to have a house erected,
constructed, and fortified (*fortiffier*); but this he would not do without our leave and
licence, the which he humbly requests—We therefore . . . desiring that our good and loyal
servants should be lodged as befits their rank (*estat*), have . . . granted . . . leave and licence,
of especial [*sic*] grace . . . to our said clerk and secretary, who for a great while since his
youth and childhood has continually served us and still does so daily about our person with
great pains and diligence—that he may have a house (*maison*) built, erected, and
constructed within the said King's Moat, and that he may fortify the same with walls,
towers, machicolations, crenels, barbicans, drawbridges, bulwarks (*boullevars*), ditches,
and other things whatsoever proper and necessary to a *place forte*.[62]

Despite the habitual grandiloquence, nothing in this so far might not fit a major
contemporary castle-seat rather than the splendid country retreat Baudes
evidently had in mind. Realism often lay in the non-architectural detail. Lucrative
local impositions, unlike display, were public and collateral costs: so Louis XI
added cautiously: 'provided always that the inhabitants and dwellers thereabouts
be obliged only to do the services of watch and ward (*guet*) as of old.' His instructions otherwise, to his bailiff and *justiciers* of Montargis (to whom the patent
would be shown, as well as proudly to Baudes's neighbours), were to permit the
new work, but no official help is mentioned, nor did Baudes receive any jurisdictional rights, despite the full panoply of late-fifteenth-century castellation which
is authorized. His rank did not justify creating the oppressive public burdens
which were freely transferred in this period, or revived, in favour of great lords in
not dissimilar circumstances.[63] With few exceptions, not much had changed

[62] Mentioned Part I, n. 255, Part II, n. 74 above; *Ordonnances*, xvii. 219; 'de grace especial' (as in
England) is formula. Baudes is *Maître*, i.e. a member of the (future) Noblesse de Robe, insinuating
himself into the landed nobility (Noblesse d'Epée) with an appropriately militant architectural
display.
[63] e.g. *Ordonnances* xvii. 205–6 (1469), authorizing the king's kinsman ('cousin'), Louis, Bastard of
Maine, to re-establish the castellary of Sainte-Neomaye in Poitou, near La Rochelle, alleging value as
a local refuge. It had been razed by Charles VII to punish the previous lord's 'disobedience and rebellion', although 'en pays de frontière' (English expelled from Gascony in 1453). Works specified

towards the end of the fifteenth century, and even later, in France—which makes such late examples hard to leave out.

3. Case-Studies in Seignorial Relations

The borders which concerned inter-seignorial treaties in the central middle ages are not frontiers but rather 'marches', zones of uncertain control and sometimes vague demarcation lines between the territories of magnates, where tenurial liens might be weak, conflicting, or even absent.[64] The *franc fief* problem, of 'alods' free of all but the most nominal subjection, did not apply to England, but the famous *conventio* made in 1148–53, in the latter part of King Stephen's reign, by Rannulf, earl of Chester, and Robert de Beaumont, earl of Leicester, is typical of continental castle-pacts. Rannulf wished to retain some right over Mountsorrel (Leics.), so Robert agreed that he and his retinue (*familia*) should be received into the town and baileys, with nominal freedom to base themselves there for war, 'as of feudal right'. This embryonic rendability was signified by Rannulf in person and alone being entitled to enter the castle itself of Mountsorrel (*in dominico castro*) if deemed 'necessary', under guarantee of good faith (conduct) by Earl Robert. No such compromise—effectively lordship-sharing, with Rannulf's the 'superior' part in law but inferior in possessory right—could cope with the awkwardly placed castle of Ravenstone. This, Robert conceded, should be destroyed unless Rannulf relented, giving to him an effectual lordship over it—as so often with fortresses, one more subtle than the simple lien. If, moreover, any third party attempted to use Ravenstone against Robert of Leicester, Rannulf promised to join forces with him to demolish the castle. Only this last provision appears to relate unequivocally to the possibility of hostilities and not to the militaristic posturing reflected by the phraseology of rendability.[65] The agreement between the earls to respect a tract of country lying in an arc around Leicester as under

---

(perfunctorily) are 'towers, crenels, barbicans, drawbridges, and other fortifications whatever'. No public assistance, beyond *guet*-finance, was granted; cf. Licence to the comte du Maine (1464) to create a castle at Queue-de -Vache, by La Rochelle, with toll, capital justice, noble fief, customs, etc. to resist *nos anciens ennemis les Anglois*: *Ordonnances*, xvi. 188–90.

[64] True also of 'sacred bans' and of urban *banlieues*: Coulson, 'Sanctioning of Fortresses in France', 51–2, 54–6, 62–8, 81–5; Rosenwein, *Negotiating Space*, ch. 8; Power, 'Frontier of Angevin Normandy', *passim*.

[65] Taken at face value by Stenton, *First Century*, 249–54; text pp. 285–8 (ref. Part II, n. 298 above). To discussion, Coulson, 'French Matrix', esp. 66–70; add, Bradbury, 'War of Stephen', esp. 117, 122, 130; Dalton, 'Ranulf of Chester', 39–59; and Cronne, 'Ranulf de Gernons', 103–34; offering the conventional explanation of the 1148–53 *conventio*—cf. E. King, *King Stephen* (forthcoming) and Crouch, *Reign of King Stephen*. Comparable elements, including castellation, e.g. in the 1173 bishop of Le Puy (Auvergne)–*vicomte* de Polignac accord following quarrels (possibly a 'fictive dispute'). By mediation of Louis VII they shared tolls in Le Puy. Polignac would seek episcopal licence for building *nova castra*. Back home they amplified this: Polignac put two of four disputed 'castles' under the bishop's lordship, giving up two others; neither would acquire anything without consent within the other's castellaries (*castris*), unless *terra plana*, nor construct castles there; war-damage to 'castles' to be freely made good: all confirmed 1188, 1192—*Layettes*, i. 105–6; *Recueil Philippe II*, i. 514–15; cf. 1219, *Layettes*, i. 491–2; summary, Coulson, 'French Matrix', 73.

truce, so that neither should claim control by fortifying there, is less complex but
no less typical of 'French' castellation pacts which form the bulk of this section:

Neither the earl of Chester nor the earl of Leicester may establish (*firmare*) any new castle
between Hinckley and Coventry, nor between Hinckley and Hartshill, nor between
Coventry and Donington, nor between Donington and Leicester; nor at Gotham, nor at
Kinoulton nor nearer, nor between Kinoulton and Belvoir, nor between Belvoir and
Oakham, nor between Oakham and Rockingham, nor nearer, except with the joint consent
of both. And if anyone fortifies a castle at those localities or within those bounds, each shall
help the other in good faith (*sine malo ingenio*) until that castle is destroyed.

The resemblance between this and the Anglo-French truces of 1160–1200 (Part II,
Ch. 2, sec. 3 above) is quite close: so close that, but for elements which have
'national' connotations, those truces would belong here—but retrospective 'state'
thinking is inappropriate. It is another reminder of the sometimes fortuitous
process of nation-formation that the states of Hainaut and Flanders are now
(uneasy) components of the kingdom of Belgium, created in 1831–6 and representing the residue of the former Burgundian and then Spanish Netherlands
which was left after the conquests and losses of Louis XIV. In 1176 both of these
counties were in tension between the Emperor Frederick Barbarossa and the kings
of France (Louis VII) and England (Henry II), as well as with each other. The
following treaty struck a temporary balance. It is a pact of mutual support and
solidarity, to concert their foreign policy and to minimize friction:

I, Baldwin, count of Hainaut, and Philip, count of Flanders, my brother-in-law (*sororius*),
make known to all our people, present and future, the confederation made between us in
consultation with our men and sworn by our faithful oath—namely, that I must support
him [Philip] against all men, subject to the fealty I owe to my lord the bishop of Liège; and
Philip shall do likewise, saving the fealty owed to his lord the king of France—Accordingly,
neither of us shall encroach upon the other's county, nor make any fortification (*firmitudo*) there. In the confines of our territories, commonly known as 'the march' (*marcha*),
we may and shall not construct fortifications other than [at] those [fortresses] which now
exist, unless it be by the joint assent and wish of us both. Similarly, neither of us shall take
the other's subject as a retainer nor take in anyone whom the other has banished. Each will
help the other against evil-doers. Thus, no man of mine [Baldwin's] shall be held to
ransom in Flanders, or vice versa.—If any dispute arise, or modification of these terms
seem expedient, it shall be settled by negotiation . . .[66]

It was a chyrograph, written in duplicate, each part sealed by the other party and
divided like an 'indenture' by a wavy or a jagged cut, so that the copies could be
matched up like tally-sticks to check their authenticity. Neither Philip, who held

---

[66] On Flanders 1108–80, and Count Philip 'of Alsace' (1163–91), uncle and after 1180 unwelcome
mentor to Philip II, see Dunbabin, *France in the Making*, 318–23; Petit-Dutaillis, *Feudal Monarchy*,
202–4. Text, *Thesaurus Novus*, i. 585–6. What 'liege homage' meant was largely circumstantial:
Reynolds, *Fiefs and Vassals*, 269, 283 (13th cent.). Technical phrases include *non debemus* [i.e. 'we have
no right'] *nec possumus* ['and are debarred'] *alias construere* ['to build at or repair'] *firmitudines quam
illas quae modo ibi sunt* [i.e. no new castles]. The Reims–Loos pact of 1237 similarly involved magnates
of the Empire and kingdom: *Layettes*, ii. 350.

his county partly from the Empire and partly from France, nor Baldwin, tenant of the Empire via the bishop of Liège, ought overtly or lightly to contravene their obligations to their respective lords in a region which was already a 'cockpit of Europe'. By creating any sort of fortress, a claim to legitimate and effective control of its territory was made. If, as in the March, the lordship was unclear, those who claimed proper authority had to reach agreement. In 1188 Arnald de Saga, in Pyrenean Catalonia (Spain), appeased his feud with the 'viscount' of Castelbon under the same principle. Arnald's 'fortification' of Toloriu was held from an intermediate ('mesne') lord for whose actions Arnald could not be responsible, since 'nothing could be denied to him as the lordship of that castle belongs to him'; but the claims of Castelbon were satisfied by participating directly in the *dominium*. The aspiring viscount was 'assured' that he would suffer no harm from Toloriu (jurability), he received Arnald as his man, directly promising to help him defend the castellary, and agreed that the castle be 'built, adapted, and improved in whatever manner Arnald wishes and is able'.[67]

Overlapping and juxtaposed rights, just as much in the heartland of the Île de France, might also require diplomacy. The Parisian county of Beaumont-sur-Oise in 1206 was no march, but its lords still saw themselves as exercising rights which, if not always castle-based, were still expressed by fortifying within a demarcated territory. Levying tolls on the road between L'Isle-Adam and Nesles, on this occasion, brought matters to a head. Matthew III, count of the squeezed and miniscule county of Beaumont, and Anseau, lord of L'Isle-Adam, agreed that Anseau's men and bona-fide traders at his market should be exempt from the comital toll and that he should try in his court cases of theft of the proceeds. An acquisition of a fief by Matthew, balanced by his promise not to make any fortification (*firmitas*) in an area around Pontoise south of the Oise tributary Sausseron, was reciprocated by Anseau's promise not to fortify on his side of the river 'unless at L'Isle itself, where he will do as he pleases'.[68] The respective zones of lordship were small and located little more than 25 miles from Paris, quite near Montmartre, but Philip Augustus was not asked to intervene. Especially in marcher districts, the extent of seignorial power was almost as much a matter of claim as of fact, as may be seen in the 'Spanish' borders. The reach of the *vicomte* of Béarn, in Pyrenean southern Gascony, may have exceeded his grasp, but Edward I in 1289 nevertheless discouraged encroachment upon his territory by new *bastides*. He was similarly tactful in

---

[67] *Layettes*, v. 32–3. Fortress-control often put mesne lordship under pressure in this way, but *arrière-rendabilité* was rare: Coulson, 'Seignorial Fortresses', Index, 'Subinfeudation', 'Sub-Rendability'. Background and references, Bisson 'War of the Two Arnaus', 95–107 (with acknowledgement): Toloriu is styled *municio*, then *castrum*. Arnald de Castelbon's record vitiated his promise to Arnald de Saga to behave 'as your lord ought to one who is my man'. Rendability was commonplace in this region (e.g. *Layettes*, v. 20–1, 24–5, 28, 31, 33, 34–5—1163–90), but conceding it fully at Toloriu would have eclipsed the mesne lordship and (probably) given up too much.

[68] To do so proved Anseau's plenitude of lordship at his *caput*, but the rank of the fief was crucial: *Layettes*, i. 307. In 1232, at Gueux (*dép.* Marne), Archbishop Henry of Reims needed licence from the count of Champagne (vassal of Reims for other lands) to add to the modest *domus*: *Layettes*, ii. 232. See 'dominants behaving as subordinates', Coulson, 'Sanctioning of Fortresses', 40–56.

1305 regarding the castellaries of Pons and Bergerac in the centre and north of the duchy. There were many internal 'marches' and boundaries were frequently a matter of discretion, both in treatment and on the ground.[69]

Since, for a long time, the extent and depth of overlordship greatly varied, and few territories except in the early period were truly '*francs fiefs*', the impact of 'alods' on these questions does not loom large. Certainly, in the case brought in 1284 by Erard de Dinteville of the Bassigny before the Grand-Jours court of Champagne, the alodial exemption from interference with fortifying which he claimed smacks of special pleading. Freedom to crenellate was, in any case, widely diffused. In this instance it was a further complication that the marriage of the heiress Jeanne in that year to Philip of France, who succeeded as King Philip IV in 1285, meant an accelerated loss of 'autonomy'. Erard's complaint was that 'when he began to build a strong-house on an alod within the county, for which he had newly entered the count of Champagne's homage, the men of the king of France [Philip III], at the instigation of the bishop of Langres [mesne lord] forbade him to build any further at that place'. The issue evidently was which lord had the right to license; but for Erard, it was whether any had, since: 'there are several other strong-houses within the same alod, held of the count in fief.' In view of the tenurial complexities the case was referred to the royal parlement.[70]

Alods, like many marches, can be regarded as internal lordship-voids which were far from being vacuums. Any vacuity did not mean that borderlines might not frequently be precisely defined. Even the rough-and-ready demarcations of the Anglo-French truces of 1160–1200 (Part II, Ch. 2, sec. 3 above) were, in places, very exact. The Sausseron rivulet was the Beaumont–L'Isle-Adam 'border' in 1206.[71] In the 1172 Champagne fief roll a paved road (*calciatam*) was the boundary of a castellary, and the *banlieues* of jurisdictional peculiars developed around towns in Ponthieu were defined by reference to topographical features as small as individual trees.[72] Ecclesiastical 'liberties' were demarcated on the ground, as also,

---

[69] Below Ch. 2, sec. 3. Gaston's *terre vel districtus* were what he deemed them to be, in effect; none of his serfs (*homines questales*) was to be accepted into Edward's *bastides*. He died next year: *Rôles Gascons*, ii. 510. Ducal officials 'exercising jurisdiction or justice in the castles and castellaries of Bergerac, Gensac, and Castelmoron, of our dear kinsman Reginald [IV, died 1308] of Pons' were to 'do him no wrong or aggrieve him by neighbouring *bastides* in cases belonging to our lordship: ibid. iii. 443.

[70] Text quoted Brussel, *Nouvel Examen*, i. 385–6; despite commentary, it seems Erard's *domus fortis* should, as such, have been a full fief. As husband of Blanche d'Artois, Edmund of Lancaster was titular count of Champagne 1275–84: F. Powicke, *Thirteenth Century*, 240–1. In 1206 the great new Dreux castle of Fère-en-Tardenois (*dép*. Aisne) was sanctioned by Countess Blanche to be rendable, converted to a liege-fief: Brussel, *Nouvel Examen*, i. 387.

[71] See above. Reynolds, *Fiefs and Vassals*, e.g. 145–60, 284–9, stresses that circumstantial facts are both very various and crucial regarding 'alods', discrediting previous generalizations.

[72] Jubainville, *Histoire de Champagne*, ii. p. vii: 'talis est consuetudo Pruvini, [Provins, *dép*. Seine-et-Marne] quod si guerra emerserit erga castellum Pruvini omnes milites a chemino calciato usque and nemus Aliotri et a nemore Joiaci [Jouy] usque at Secanam [River Seine] venient stare Pruvinum exceptis illis qui sunt de honore Braii.' Evidently the circumscription of Bray-sur-Seine, like that of Montereau *castellaria*, also mentioned, needed no such exact definition; cf. Ponthieu castellation immunities: Part I, n. 310 above.

necessarily differently, were hunting chases and deer-parks. Territoriality was always the overriding imperative, so that fortresses were prominently set within the landscape. If related to territorial borders, it was as markers (like prehistoric barrows) or to exploit tolls, social-control, and other economic opportunities concentrated at crossroads, passes, river-crossings, and other so-called 'strategic' points.[73] That essentially seignorial aims predominated tends to be affirmed by the virtual irrelevance of 'natural frontiers' such as major rivers (arteries of communication, not barriers) and mountain ranges for most of the middle ages. The concept as propounded by Louis XIV and by Napoleon in 1813–15 was newfangled. Although in 1700 it may have seemed novel that 'there were no more Pyrenees', it had once been a reality.[74] The post-Roman states of Europe were not capable of creating artificial frontiers, like Hadrian's Wall or the *limes* of the Danube, until the partly ephemeral geo-military efforts of Louis XIV in the wars of 1668–1714, seconded by the fortresses associated with Vauban. Not until the 1860s did the Alps become a national frontier with the creation of the kingdom of Italy. Modern frontier fortification has few useful analogies to offer.[75]

Comparisons which have some relevance concern warfare, which falls outside the present subject; but how seignorial society was repaired after breakdown, and the use of fortress-customs to contain conflict, lie within it. Two documents, the 1314 Lorraine–Bar settlement and the Franco-Castilian truce of 1280, provide examples. To take the latter first: containment of the strains of fragmenting old castellaries and proliferating new castles was the normal pattern.[76] Arresting the process by prohibiting fortifying occasionally happened, but usually by agreement (as has been seen). Putting places and areas under a dispensable 'ban' extended the principle of licensing by the feudal superior. Demolition was a last resort,

---

[73] J. Hunt, *Lordship and Landscape* (*honor* of Dudley, 1066–1322); Liddiard, *Landscapes of Lordship* (Norfolk, 1066–1200). Paled or walled parks still denoted major country seats in early-modern maps (e.g. Henry Fricx, Kent, 1709): Part II, n. 208 above. Most frontiers fluctuated: Bauduin, 'Bourgs castraux' (Normandy); Lartigaut, 'Frontière Périgord–Quercy?'; D. Lutz, 'Territoire et frontières' (SW Germany), etc. The later essays in Fillon (ed.), *Château et Territoire*, tend more to the 'strategic'.

[74] Fortress-custom was 'international': by a complex enfeoffment treaty in 1112 the *vicomte* of Béziers resolved the ambiguities of holding the *honor* of Carcassonne from Toulouse, and of Rasez from the count of Barcelona (Aragon). By mediation of the archbishop of Narbonne, Béziers secured 12 *castella*, partly in full propriety (*per alodem*), rendable to Barcelona on demand, for loyal use (*et quod servias illa mihi*). Earlier, *c*.1034, Count Roger of Foix 'swore' to Bishop Peter of Gerona (Catalonia), Carcassonne's 'fortifications, present and future', and the towers and fortifications likewise of Foix (*dép*. Ariège) and two other 'castles', all rendable ('not to be withheld'), guaranteeing all episcopal possessions in Languedoc: *Thesaurus Novus*, i. 250–1, 334–6; Brunel, *Chartes Provençale*, 3–5. Counts of Foix later similarly held Catalan fiefs, e.g. in 1228: *Layettes*, v. 111. Interpenetration of authorities, without geographical demarcation, is conspicuous in the Valois–Plantagenet treaty for Gascony in 1331: *CPR, 1330–4*, 90–5.

[75] Despite e.g. Brice, *Forts and Fortresses*, esp. 34–7, 94–101.

[76] Protecting a castellary against the pretensions of an upstart by securing royal support was demonstrated at Méréville (*dép*. Seine-et-Oise), 1266–8; and Buxy castellary (*dép*. Saône-et-Loire), 1309–10. 'Strong houses' built without licence of the châtelain adjudged to be razed: (texts) *Les Olim*, i. 226, 730; iii. 296, 460–1; *Actes du Parlement*, i, i, 96, 115; i, ii, 52, 69 (calendars). How Denbigh castellary was carved out by amalgamating two cantreds in N. Wales in 1282, and the castle created, was recited in 1360: *CCR, 1360–4*, 32–3.

punitive more often than preventive in purpose.[77] When castellation disputes caused hostilities, the act itself of fortifying was most often only part of long-term expansion. Because castles might be instruments of warfare, if incidentally, and frequently represented its solid gains or losses when fighting stopped, any moratorium affected them.[78]

King Philip III, *Le Hardi*, sought to strengthen his authority in the south (as the imposing Porte Narbonnaise at Carcassonne shows), in Navarre taking advantage of the arrangement of 1275 which gave him control of the kingdom in right of the young heiress Jeanne of Champagne, betrothed to his son Philip. Embroiled with opposition by the king of Castile, a special codicil was arranged to the main indefinite truce of 1280 to cover a group of Navarrese 'exiles and rebels'. Their castles were not to be munitioned (*munire*), 'whether with men, arms, or any other kind of reinforcement (*munitionibus*)'. This was to be checked by inspection by the governor of Navarre, putting in an allowance of victuals every month, so that on expiry of the truce their supplies should be at the same level as when it was proclaimed. Combatants (*bellatores*) could be substituted, but not increased.[79] In these circumstances little in the way of architectural fortification was possible, but it was carefully prescribed, at the end of the document, that: 'They shall not be permitted to build anew in these castles, nor to rebuild or repair any old buildings or ruins; nor to fortify these castles in ditches or earthworks (*fossis sive fossatis*), or with any kind of other munitions or defences; nor may they alter anything outside (*circa ea*) throughout the truce.'

Hostilities imposed their own constraints upon fortresses, as the Hundred Years War (1337–1453) often showed; but the architecture itself does not yield to any monocausal explanation, the military least of all, virtually irrespective of the 'military environment'. Seignorial panache at all times remained a fluctuating but constant ingredient in the mix.[80] Truces effectively show both the instrumental-

---

[77] Cf. Tweedmouth castle to be razed under the 1209 Anglo-Scottish truce: *Regesta Scot*, ii. 445–6; Part II, Ch. 2, sec. 4 and Ch. 3, sec. 1 above. An early French penal demolition is Montbellet (*dép.* Saône-et-Loire, *arr.* Mâcon): during Queen Blanche's regency (1249–52) its lord had allegedly murdered the royal baliff of Mâcon. His fortress was razed by order of the parlement. His son agreed with Peter *Chevrer*, king's sergeant, son of the bailiff, on a mere residence at the site, but proceeded to build what was, after appeal (1266—recounting events), held to be a fortification. Demolition order then issued: *Les Olim*, i. 654; *Actes du Parlement*, i, i, 99. The blend of impartiality and partisanship is typical.

[78] e.g. it was recalled in 1299 that Castle Emlyn (Carmarthen) had been built by Meredith ap Rees in order 'to hold' the commote: *CIM* i. 496–7 (with estate-history). Two famous Welsh castellation disputes were provoked by Earl Gilbert the Red; the Caerfilly affair, 1267–72, and the Morlais intrusion on Brecon, 1289: *Close Rolls, 1268–72*, 546–7; Clark, *Cartae*, i. 123–140; iii. 575; *CCR, 1288–96*, 47, 126, 138, 151–2; *CChR Various*, 334–49. Altschul, *The Clares*, 122–34, 145–53. Sequence of works, Johns, *Caerphilly Castle*, plans 1, 2; n. 178 below.

[79] *Foedera*, i, ii, 581; F. Powicke, *Thirteenth Century*, 238–40. Philip III began to rebuild the town walls of Carcassonne in imperial style (to rival Edward I in Wales), notably the Porte Narbonnaise, his *morceau de prestige*: Mesqui, *Châteaux-forts*, 94.

[80] Although Mesqui, *Châteaux et enceintes*, uses 'defence' and 'residence' conventionally as autonomous mechanisms, he gives considerable space to lordly symbolism and domestic functionalism. His superbly illustrated exposition of generalized detail could be improved only by a closer integration of aesthetic and 'military' motives. The most relevant sections are I (Les Organes de la

ity of fortification in warfare and its limitations. Thus munitioning, not architecture, was the target of the Navarrese truce clause: not to impose a lordly *ban* but temporarily to stop the sort of patching-up and emergency fieldworks which could make a multi-purpose site more defensible.

The Bar–Lorraine alliance of 1255–66 against the count of Luxembourg was nearly wrecked by Thibaud of Bar's refortification of la Motte at Saint-Alairmont (*dép.* Haute Marne), ignoring the right claimed by Duke Ferry of Lorraine to give licence as lord. Proper diplomacy had been neglected, but underlying doubt about whether Saint-Alairmont and Bourmont were Lorraine fiefs was the basic problem, settled by arbitration by Thibaud V of Champagne, Hugh of Burgundy, and Eudo of Nevers in 1261. In 1314 tenurial obscurities endemic to this region, where kingdom and Empire were enmeshed, again put the Lorraine–Blâmont party at odds with the Bar family (Count Edward, his uncles Peter and Erard, Renaud, bishop of Metz, and Count John of Salm). Edward was unfortunate enough to be taken. His captor, Henri de Blâmont, by the mediation of Louis of France as count of Champagne, eventually received ransom, restitution of two villages in fief, a share in a large indemnity, a grant of land or cash at will, and, to signalize his victory further, from Bar also permission to build a fortress in the fief he held of Count Edward of Bar.[81] As usual, this was but one of many tokens in a complex range of adjustments, clarifications of dependency, and accommodation between the individuals involved.

Not war but diplomacy sometimes caused castles to be demolished as well as constructed. Because licensing one affirmed the lord's position while enhancing the status of his vassal, so likewise destroying a castle humiliated and demeaned its owner. The later Capetian and early Valois kings of France were particularly vindictive. Edward III's 'unequal treaty' with Philip VI in March 1331, regulating their feudal relationship and the situation in the fragment of Gascony remaining after the War of Saint Sardos, required parts of four *chasteux* to be *abatuz*.[82] Such treaties, like those between Capetian and Plantagenet in 1160–1200, and with the Scots (Part II, Ch. 2, sec. 4 above), in fact differ chiefly in their scale from the magnatial and 'baronial' relations which are the concern of this section.

With the pact made in 1197 between Count Stephen of Auxonne, near Dijon,

Défense), pp. 81–4 (1350–), 91–6, 176–82 ('*donjons*'), 342–7 (multi-function gatehouses); II (La Résidence et les Eléments d'Architecture), *passim.*

[81] *Layettes*, iv. 4; v. 245 (with variants); *Registres du Trésor*, i. 460; Coulson, 'Sanctioning of Fortresses', 88.

[82] Until then the French siege (blockade) of Saintes would remain, nor meanwhile might '*le chastel et bourc* be supplied (*garni*) otherwise than at present': *CPR, 1330–4*, 90–5. Edward III was playing for time: Vale, *Origins of the Hundred Years War*, 251–6. On derogatory demolitions, Coulson, 'Valois Powers over Fortresses', 159–60; Part II, Ch. 3, sec. 1 above. Tenurial constraints in 1205 even obliged the holder of Villeneuve-aux-Riches-Hommes (*dép* Aube) to promise to raze (the fortifications) if found not to be a Champagne fief, so that he could not lawfully swear (*non possem garantire*) the fortress to Countess Blanche: *Layettes*, i. 566–7. Among the 'trespasses' of William de Cantilupe in 1253 was causing John de Monmouth's castle of Penros 'to be thrown down': *CPR, 1247–58*, 202. The 1322 Marcher attack on the Despenser lands in South Wales was a larger-scale vendetta, involving Caerfilly and other ex-Clare castles: e.g. *CCR, 1318–23*, 541–6.

and Hugh III, duke of Burgundy, we return to issues classically centred upon fortresses by virtue of their cardinal tenurial significance. Already the developing intricacies of lordship imposed multiple and potentially conflicting obligations upon castellans. Ad hoc arrangements were usually cast in permanent form, or by the usual working of legal precedent tended to modify the structures of tenure, altering and refining feudal relationships.[83] In this way fortress-customs were a powerful creative force. In this instance, Duke Hugh desired the support of Auxonne in his contest with Count Otto of the imperial county of Burgundy (Franche-Comté), although Auxonne was a fief of the powerful priory of Vergy (Autun diocese). Achieving this aim required Hugh and Stephen to exploit the loose lien binding Auxonne to the monks. Stephen announced:

that, with the approval (*laude*) and assent of Beatrice, my wife, of my son Stephen, and of my heirs, I have made my town (*villa*) of Auxonne with the castle into a fief (*in feodum et casamentum*) of Duke Hugh (*Odo*) to be jurable and rendable to him and successors as often as he or they shall require, subject to the lordship (*salva fidelitate*) of Saint-Vincent-de-Vergy, so that Auxonne cannot be denied to the duke (*duci . . . deesse non potest*) for anything that the prior or monks may say, short of question of forfeiture, and then only if the duke refuse to satisfy their complaint. Should they reject the duke's amends for the offence, whereby I might incur forfeiture, then Auxonne shall not on this account be with-held from the duke (*non ideo Auxona duci deerit*).

Stephen and Hugh were keeping themselves technically in the right, but sailing close to the wind.[84] Auxonne had not apparently been rendable to Vergy, but there was some danger that Hugh's intrusion might be regarded as transgressing Stephen's fealty to the prior. What compensation Hugh might offer in this eventuality is not stated, nor is the inducement which led Stephen to take the risk. Auxonne, castle and town together, whatever happened, was to be made available: the early phrase using *deesse* (sometimes *vetare*) occurs twice for emphasis.[85] Pressure was being put on Vergy to renounce their rights. The document continues:

---

[83] Notably during the war of inheritance: Coulson, 'Castellation in Champagne', 358–61. Pacts of rendability, of slight direct military use, nevertheless affirmed the liens of comital lordship.

[84] *Layettes*, i. 193–4. Duke Hugh (Eudes) in 1197 also secured the rendability of the 'donjon or castle of Vergy' from Hugh, its lord, under restrictive terms, viz. deliverable on demand, for 14 days only unless the duke's longer need of it should be certified by the abbots of Cîteaux and La Bussière, then returnable in as good a state as when rendered. Hugh de Vergy received concessions including rever-sion of the seneschalcy of Burgundy. Terms recited 1216, excerpted in Du Cange, 'Dissértations' (1668; the sole systematic study of rendability), 492–3, 513, 521: specifying that any consumption of stores during ducal repossession 'beyond hay or straw', and any damage, shall be made good within 40 days of request: Salvaing, *De l'Usage des Fiefs*, 82.

[85] As *vetare*, 1091, *Consuetudines et Justicie*, ch. 4, Haskins, *Norman Institutions*, 282. In Languedoc and throughout Occitanie *auferre* and *tollere* are standard until the late 12th century, e.g. Brunel, *Chartes Provençale*, 11–12 (1103), 13–14 (*c.*1103) etc. Conversion to rendable tenure was often by grant of a money-fief: Lyon, *From Fief to Indenture*, 195–7 *et passim*; n. 83 above (Champagne); *c.*1261, for a money-fief, Henry III made Peter of Savoy's castles in the Val d'Aosta rendable to him, as customary there: Shirley, *Royal Letters*, ii. 200–1; Du Cange 'Dissértations', 498.

But if the duke seek to obtain [lordship of] the fief, I [Stephen] or my successor will both consent to the transfer and promote it; but the duke is not to acquire any further rights at Auxonne town from the priory—And be it known that I and my provost (*prepositus*) of Auxonne [town] and with him four others of the most substantial (*meliorum*) townsmen, have sworn the town–castle complex jurable and rendable (*juravimus Auxonam cum castro jurabilem et reddibilem*) to the duke of Burgundy and to his succcessors against all men, this only excepted that I and mine shall keep our [right of] residence (*mansionem*) in the said castle.

Stephen's wariness about making his lordship over the town too nominal is understandable. If the duke exercised his rendability by putting in troops, or merely his household, Stephen can still lodge in the castle (whether or not in his own apartments is not specified). There then follows one of the most explicit declarations of the facilities which a repossessing lord could enjoy. Custom, here, had to be spelled out because Stephen's position was feudally equivocal, not only with regard to Vergy but also as the tenant (of other lands) from Count Otto, Hugh's opponent, whom Stephen had previously backed:

If the duke shall be in need, the said castle [–town] shall support him (*castrum ducem juvabit*) so that he and his men shall base themselves there.[86] Now, if I decide to return to Count Otto's allegiance (*hominium*) and wish to go [over] to him, then I must [first] deliver the castle and entire town to the duke. If the duke or his people do any damage in the town meanwhile, beyond [consumption of] hay and floor-strewing, he shall make it good within forty days of being summoned; and within seven days after the duke has finished his use (*negotium suum . . . fecerit*) of the castle and town, he shall in good faith restore them to me.

This alternation of *castrum* and *villa* to mean both elements, except where 'castle' or 'town' are specifically meant, is characteristic.[87] The tenor of the pact suggests that Stephen was unlikely to defect to Otto's party. If he did, he bound himself to surrender his home-base, with considerable risk of permanent loss. Otherwise, all the terms intend a lasting new relationship with Hugh, including the final clauses whereby Hugh binds himself to defend Auxonne against Otto and all men, Stephen reciprocally swearing to support Hugh against all men except the king of France. It was a well-balanced arrangement.

The castellan whose *caput* was an interdependent town–castle complex was in a special and sometimes difficult position. Stephen has to ensure that his townsmen of Auxonne did not make their own terms with the duke of Burgundy. So did William of Montpellier, lord of Frontignan (*dép.* Hérault), in dealing with

---

[86] Viz. *in eodem castro receptaculum suum habebunt.* On lordly rights of reception under the 1148–53 Chester–Leicester *conventio* and their Continental parallels see Coulson, 'French Matrix', esp. 82–5.

[87] An exceptional alternative was temporarily to waive rendability or to make rendable castles neutral during lord–vassal conflict: Du Cange, 'Dissértations', 516 (bishop of Clermont, 1199); Brunel, *Chartes Provençale*, 52–3, 72 (bishop of Mende, 1147, 1152). On Vergy see Richard, 'Châteaux, châtelains et vassaux', 436, 442, etc.; wrongly associating rendability with liege homage, p. 446; discusses terminology, pp. 433–4. If a castle was pledged (e.g. for debt) the revenues normally went with it, but under rendability they remained the castellan's: *Rôles Gascons*, iii. 50 (1292); despite Bémont's editorial note (p. cxx), Louvigny was not delivered under rendability.

Count Raymond VI of Toulouse in 1194. Similar complications affected the Champagne–Lorraine arrangements in 1220 for the castle–town of Neufchâteau (*dép*. Vosges), made rendable having formerly been an alod; likewise the count of Foix in his *castrum* of Saverdun (*dép*. Ariège) in 1201. These cases vividly demonstrate the community *castrum* in feudal operation.[88]

A vital matter affecting all seignorial treaties (one frankly addressed in the Auxonne–Burgundy pact of 1197) is the problem of 'enforcement'. If agreements were not honoured they represented aspirations only, however important those might be as ideals of conduct. The changeability of circumstances could never be fully anticipated, despite strenuous efforts. Fortress-pacts, like other solemn engagements, strove to preserve personal honour and the supremacy of law—but to see them as rationalizations of brute force would be very misleading. A full study of rendability would show not only how towns were liable, but demonstrate how common was the rendering of fortresses to 'recognize' the overlord's suzerainty.[89] The force of moral suasion also mattered. Breach of faith, unless plausibly justified (an important qualification), made the perjuror an outcast and one 'forsworn'; and the sanction, frequently invoked, of excommunication was no more to be risked than the financial penalty clauses alternatively relied upon.[90] Enforcement, when no overall judicial power existed, required a range of corroborating sanctions. Thus, in King Stephen's reign (1135–55) the over-maligned Geoffrey de Mandeville, earl of Essex, went to great lengths in 1141 to secure the most emphatic charters alternately from the king and from his rival, the 'Empress' Mathilda, Henry I's daughter, so as to give lawful status to his wartime acquisitions, including new castles.[91] The same principle was applied (see Part II, Ch. 2, sec. 1, 2 above) after the *turbaciones regni* in England of 1215–17 and 1262–9. To show that the same happened in France, where widely varying conditions in place and period obtained, would require evidence of much wider scope than could be used in a book of this length. The basic fact is that magnates were seldom self-made by naked force: the 'brigand today, baron tomorrow' doctrine of the old

---

[88]   *Layettes*, i. 177–8 (Frontignan, *dép*. Hérault detailed rendability enfeoffment); *Thesaurus Novus*, i. 880–1 (castellary and *castrum*, comprising the *forterissia* and *burgus* of Neufchâteau, rendable together as guaranteed by 'all the knights and men of the castle'); *Layettes*, i. 93–4, 225–6; ii. 451 (Saverdun, *dép*. Ariège, 1167–1241: a saga of revealing dealings).

[89]   See Coulson, 'Seignorial Fortresses', Index, 'Recognitory Rendering'. To the future Charles V, on his investment as dauphin of Vienne (1349), Raymond des Baux, prince of Orange, expressed his three castles as held *in feudum francum et nobile, reddibile tamen, quod naturam habeat antiqui feudi reddibilis*, i.e. deliverable on demand in war or reasonable fear of it, tenable by the dauphin for the duration, at his costs; secondly, for recognition of lordship (*pro bono dominio*) on demand, at Raymond's costs; thirdly, at every change of lord or tenant, for three days with the delphinal banner displayed, at the dauphin's cost: Salvaing, *De L'Usage des Fiefs*, 83. These terms are a codification of earlier general practice.

[90]   In the Capetian conquests of Anjou, Maine, and Poitou, etc. 1204–26, reflecting uncertainty legal, political, and military. Catalan custom (13th cent.) made any refusal to render an act of perjury (*car en so que requer fieltat, e par contradir se sequeys bausia, no espresa neguna defensio*): Du Cange, 'Dissértations', (498), 504 (517–19, 520–9). *Beaumanoir*, *c.*1283, said the same for the county of Beauvais, pp. 351–3.

[91]   *Regesta*, iii. 99–103; discussed in Coulson, 'Castles of the Anarchy', esp. 87–8.

anarchie féodale school of historiography has been discredited.[92] Charters of all kinds, whether for rendability, mode of tenure, or the construction of castles, in large numbers witness to a custom and code of lordly (and royal) conduct which, while it was not always binding, was undoubtedly generally compelling.

In this connection, the negotiations in 1220 between Richard de Umfraville and the regent Hubert de Burgh over Harbottle castle have already been referred to, as have some later vicissitudes of the Umfravilles (above sec. 3; Part II, Ch. 2, sec. 4). The texts evince a certain public spirit tempered by self-interest typical of seignorial negotiations. The dialogue began in July 1220, with the justiciar's instruction to the sheriff of Northumberland to take with him twelve knights to inspect and report upon Richard's alleged fortifying at Harbottle contrary to William the Marshal's post-war pacification measures (Part II, Ch. 2, sec. 2 above). He was to be told to stop and to remove any works done since 1215. Richard aborted or intercepted this writ and, following an oral message, sent it back with a letter full of injured innocence and righteous indignation. He had expected more understanding from Hubert, as 'his man'; 'the king' (aged 13) had been 'entirely misled': Harbottle was very useful to the kingdom, confronting the Great Waste towards Scotland, 'as much in time of peace as of war', being over 25 miles ('nine leagues') from Bamburgh castle (on the coast). It had, moreover, been constructed (with studied vagueness) 'a while ago (*dudum*) under (*per*) King Henry II, with the aid of the county forces of Northumberland and of Durham, by royal order'. Richard evidently had no document, or witness, to prove it, but certainly in 1173 the manning of the Umfraville chief seat of Prudhoe had been subsidized. At all events, Richard in 1220 expected the justiciar, as his friend and 'to earn his gratitude', to make the council accept that Harbottle was legitimate (*non sit adulterinum*). He seems to have been successful in fudging the actual issue, which concerned any fortifying done since 1215, when civil war broke out with the failure of the Magna Carta peace.[93]

If the justiciar was not so sure of his own standing as to go beyond demonstrating with a show of impartiality that the ways of the recent civil war must be put aside, Richard on his side is also likely to have had ulterior motives. Rivalries and local ambitions were so habitually cloaked by professions of concern for defence and the public weal that caution is always desirable. In this instance, however, the Harbottle business may well have originated in friction between Richard de Umfraville and an upstart henchman of the late King John.[94] In July 1218 the regent, William the Marshal, had sent this personal letter:

[92] e.g. Richard, 'Châteaux, châtelains et vassaux', 438, 445, amplifying the arguments of Robert Aubenas, 'Les Châteaux-forts'.

[93] *Rot Litt Claus*, i. 436b–437a; Shirley, *Royal Letters*, i. 140–1; Part II, nn. 177, 231; Ch 2, sec. 1, above; *CDScotland*, i. 17–18 (Prudhoe). William the Lion took Harbottle in 1173, initiating its symbolic victimization. The motte-and-bailey type earthworks would be atavistic for *temp.* Henry II.

[94] Cf. Gascony: it was rare for a magnate to be seneschal. Even under Edward I, John de Grailly may have abused his official position in his quarrel (1278–89) with Gaillard de Lalande (provost of Barsac), whose castle of Labrède was demolished: *Rôles Gascons*, ii. 47, 54–5, 196, 239, 242, 265, 267, 286–7, 371, 527. Labrède was close to the *vicomte*'s castle of Benauges: Gardelles, *Châteaux du sud-ouest*, 96–8, 148.

The king to Philip de Ullecotes, greeting. Richard de Umfraville has shown us (*indicavit nobis*) that you are constructing a castle without our permission (*contra licentiam nostram*) at Nafferton where no castle ever used to be, to the detriment of the lands and castle of Prudhoe, which are Richard's. You are to desist . . . and to have what has been built there, to Richard's damage, destroyed without prevarication.

Disclosure of who procured a royal writ is most unusual. The anonymous 'we have been given to understand . . .', or suchlike phrase, is the general rule. Licences to fortify (or crenellate) were still rare, and one without written authority was now of diminished value; but the theoretical regalian right, so much utilized by the counts of Champagne and other Continental magnates, was often a useful pretext for intervention.[95] Nafferton, in fact, now represented by a large rectangular earthwork enclosure, 'where no castle ever used to be', lacks both aura and masonry. The *nouveau-riche* Philip, attempting to establish himself, had no doubt resented the Umfraville power. To riposte by accusing Richard of infringing the Marshal's pacification ban on 'adulterine' (wartime) castles, launched in the 1217 reissue of Magna Carta, and thus (it seems likely) procuring the 1220 challenge to Harbottle's legitimacy, would have been shrewd. Prudhoe, with its extensive, established castellary, could not be impeached. Harbottle was more vulnerable, but Richard's claims on Hubert de Burgh, who succeeded the Marshal, made success doubly unlikely. Philip had died or been forfeited late in 1220 or early in 1221. At all events, 'the land of Nafferton and the house (*domus*) of Nafferton' were committed to a royal custodian in January.[96]

Richard's jealousy had good cause. Mere unchallenged existence and the exercise of lordly rights could create a new and expansive *caput*. Every castle, however small to begin with, was the potential seat of an encroaching dynasty and the embryo of an aggressive lordship. Prevention required swift action at law.[97] Nafferton was unlucky. The justiciar's order, this time final, in May 1221 to the sheriff, replete with objective political correctness, declared that:

---

[95] *Rot Litt Claus*, i. 379b; Richard's allegations were not apparently checked. Local undercurrents tend to be disguised in the Rolls, even of the Minority. In France they are often explicit, e.g. the count of Champagne's insistence in 1239 that any fortifying at Courcemain (*dép.* Marne) must have his licence was procured by a jealous neighbour: Jubainville, *Histoire de Champagne*, v. 372. Many licences were obtained for this reason as well as for self-promotion; e.g. Sedgewick (Sussex twice) in 1258–63: Shirley, *Royal Letters*, ii. 157–8; *CPR, 1258–66*, 1, 206, 269, 273, 279—despite royal favour, to John Mansel.

[96] *PatR*, i. 279; Painter, *King John*, 252, 268–9, 272, 304, 333, 352, 354. Cf. Clare–Winchester competition for the dominant lordship of Portland conducted with rival licences to crenellate: *CPR, 1247–58*, 607; *1258–66*, 11.

[97] Continental pluralism (most conspicuous in Languedoc) makes explicit much that is concealed or undeveloped in England: e.g. Louis VIII's court *c*.1224 upheld the bishop of Auxerre in his castellary of Varzy, forbidding fortifying near Varzy itself: *Amplissima Collectio*, i. 1196. Urban *banlieues* operated in the same way, e.g. Rue (1214–15) and Dax (Gascony, 1305–15): *Recueil Ponthieu*, 353–4; *Rôles Gascons*, iii. 429, 438, 480, 504; iv. 380. Similarly Henry III requested a Welsh lord to allow Kinnersley castle (Herefs.) to be repaired by its lord in 1249: *Close Rolls, 1247–51*, 195. Repairs to Folkingham (Lincs.) in 1219–21 also caused local concern: Shirley, *Historical Letters*, i. 64.

Since it appears to us and to our council that the castle of Nafferton is such that it cannot be defended against our enemies, should we have need, and because it might happen that by it we and our land might quickly suffer harm from the attacks of our enemies, and especially so (*maxime*) our castle upon Tyne [Newcastle] if perchance Nafferton were occupied by our enemies—we order you, on sight of this letter, to cause that castle to be entirely thrown down and destroyed. The larger timbers (*maeremium*), namely the *bretasche* and the planks, and the timbers remaining from the other *bretasches*, you shall have carried to our castle of Bamburgh. The other small timber you are to have carted to our town upon Tyne for making our gaol . . .

A detailed survey of Nafferton's structure was clearly before the economically minded councillors. They subsequently, three weeks later, changed their minds to the extent of having all the timberwork taken to Newcastle. The prefabricated, framed and planked blockhouse or *bretasche* was to be 'put at the gateway with the turning-bridge, to take the place of the turret which has fallen down owing to defective foundations'. It was, in fact, to be a barbican; but the kings *gaiola* was still the destination of some of the remaining timber.[98]

Throughout medieval England, Wales, Ireland and France there were many failed upstarts like Nafferton. Colonization of all kinds was fraught with hazards. Normally peaceful relations between castellans implied some exclusion from their ranks of those who might disturb the sometimes fragile seignorial equilibrium.

---

[98] *PatR*, i. 287–8. This *gaiola* may not be a prison but palisading to the town ditch, often termed *le garrol, jerullium*, etc. The *porta ad pontem turneicum* will not be the Blackgate (built 1247–50) but its predecessor, to which the timber blockhouse or *bretashe* was to be an outwork, replacing the failed stone one: *Rot Litt Claus*, i. 459b; Brown *et al.*, *King's Works*, ii. 747.

2

Colonization and Fortresses

This title is not a semi-tautology—the populating of 'empty' territory, and the more intensive exploitation and settlement of relatively undeveloped land, could be done without fortifying. Settlers, to till new ground and make it productive, and to create new towns as markets, centres of craft production and of trade, were the indispensable material. Of the various 'capital inputs', the human component was much the most important, to be supplied by a natural surplus in one place migrating to where there was a deficit. When 'land-hunger' declined, with the demographic reverses setting in from the earlier fourteenth century, the mainspring of colonization ran down.[99]

Fortifying was closely associated with colonization for reasons more complicated than the stereotype of conquering an indigenous people and forcibly imposing alien rule. This view of the Norman subjugation of England is familiar but open to many objections. What ensured the continual relationship of castles to colonization was not so much the resistance it sometimes had to contend with, but rather the stamp of new lordship which fortresses set upon the whole transformation.[100] In the British Isles, next to Wales, the largest-scale working out of such changes, apart from the Norman Conquest itself, occurred in Ireland from the late twelfth century. Section 1 of this chapter exemplifies this process. Section 2 then adds some comparative illustrations, chiefly drawn from French records. Because castles with dependent townships are so common, entire fortress–town complexes being called 'the castle', or the walled-town itself having the title *castrum* or *castellum*, the plantation of new towns is an essential part of the picture and is accordingly dealt with in the third section of this chapter. The term *bastide*, although naturalized to some extent in English, characterizes town-colonization in south-western France so effectively that it has been retained as a French borrowing from the late Latin *bastida* or 'building'.

---

[99] e.g. Oakley, *Crucial Centuries*, pt. 3: a vast subject with literature both extensive and technical to match.

[100] Italian historians accurately equate *incastellamento* with the formation of settled land-exploitation, based on nucleated villages: e.g. Castillo, *Incastellamento de Luca, passim.* Coulson, 'Peaceable Power', for an architecture-based reappraisal. King Edgar's grant (1097–1107) of land in Lothian to 'a knight of English race', who attempted to build a castle there, is characteristic: *Regesta Scot*, i. 163; context, Cruden, *Scottish Castle*, 6–10; also see R. R. Davies, *March of Wales*, and 'Frontier Arrangements: Ireland and Wales', 77–100.

1. Castle-Building and Colonization: Ireland

Colonization may fitly describe the purely 'internal' process which spread populated, protected lordship into the voids of settled exploitation, in contrast with what has been called 'imperialism' or colonialism. It would go too far to claim that civilization could not exist without some such process; but in practice, this is how it frequently came about. Into the marches fortresses were imported as a package bringing protection and law, settlement and 'order', to the rural community, at the price of various degrees of servitude. The Anglo-Saxon kingdom in 1066 was already relatively populous and socially hierarchical on the ground. Quite otherwise were the sparsely occupied 'wastelands' in parts of France, in the north of England (aggravated by the 'harrowing' of Yorkshire and beyond by William I in 1069–70), and in Ireland. The contrast in Britain between the lands of the 'Celtic fringe' (including Cornwall) and the central, southern, and eastern counties of England was very marked. Cultural differences, of language, race (or more politically correct, of ethnicity), and, in a word, of civilization were profound.[101]

As seen in the English records, the advance of settlement in Ireland, mostly with castles, from the third quarter of the twelfth century presents a contrast between largely orderly 'English' areas and 'waste' allegedly caused by 'the Irish'. Associating the new castellaries with civilization does at least reflect the needs of settled agrarian and mercantile exploitation, but it misrepresents Irish culture as much as it exaggerates the element of alien intrusion, given that 'going native', whether by cultural assimilation or directly by intermarriage, was always continuous and transforming. But this was not always a peaceful process. Fortresses, in these circumstances, were perhaps more often military bases than elsewhere; but as administrative nuclei of cultivation their role is equally clear, as can be seen in the following letter sent to an Irish castellan in 1357 by Edward III's administration (as calendared):

To William de Loundres, lord of Wicklow castle (near Dublin) in Ireland. Order to cause that castle to be repaired, completely [re-]built, ruled and guarded with men and other things necessary for its provision; otherwise the king will cause it to be taken into his hand, severed from William's lordship, repaired, and at his cost kept and furnished against his enemies, as the king has learned that the castle which is situate on the frontier of his enemies of Ireland and is necessary for the repulse of those enemies and as a refuge for the king's lieges of those parts in time of need, is cast to the ground by the said enemies by default of William's good governance.[102]

---

[101] Kapelle, *Conquest of the North*, 117–121; Sweetman, *Castles of Ireland*, 1–2; McNeill, *Castles in Ireland*, esp. 7–8, 75–8, 157–64; Gillingham, 'Foundations of a Disunited Kingdom', on the various nations of Great Britain.

[102] *CCR, 1354–60*, 345. Wicklow castle was royal in 1210 but 'not very impressive': McNeill, *Castles in Ireland*, 233. Frame, 'Military Service in Ireland'; and on interpenetration, Simms, 'Bards and Barons', *passim*.

Since the great majority of writs of this (and every) kind were issued in response to lobbying, usually by petition, motives in this case may not be transparent. Recipients sometimes procured 'orders' addressed to themselves which could then be used to enforce castle-work or other dues. Here a follow-up writ suggests that the Dublin administration had asked for 'Whitehall' backing:

To Thomas de Rokeby, justiciar of Ireland. Order to call before him William de Loundres and to enjoin upon him the speedy repair and furnishing with men and victuals of Wicklow castle, in accordance with the preceding order: and if William neglects or is unable to make such repair then with the assent of the council of Ireland [order] to ordain what reason and necessity demand for the safety of those parts.

Presumably previous pressure by the English viceroy had not worked; but the procedure was still consultative, although lands could quickly go out of cultivation and be abandoned if peasants were not protected and governed. Measures of this kind were adopted in France quite systematically after the defeat (and capture) by Prince Edward of the Valois ruler, Jean le Bon, at Poitiers the year before (1356).[103] In Ireland since Strongbow's 'conquest' began (1169), they had been standard form. Lands were granted on condition that they were occupied, stocked, cultivated, 'built', and fortified upon, failing which the enfeoffment would be revoked.[104] Neglected land was, or quickly became, 'waste'. Loss of resident cultivators by natural decline, by war, or by disease made this permanent. The economic benefits associated with castle-building were so convincing that the Irish king of Connacht, in the north-west, co-operated in the projected colonization of the province. In August 1204 King John's government (at the time of the fall of Normandy) replied to the justiciar of Ireland:

You have by your letters and envoys given us to understand that the king of Connacht is prepared to give up to us two-thirds of Connacht, keeping the rest to hold himself hereditarily from us in fief, paying to us and our heirs annually the sum of 100 marks [£66]. Now, as this proposal seems to us and to our council to be advantageous to us, we instruct you upon the fealty you owe us, yourself agreeing, to implement his offer by choosing for us the two parts most beneficial to us, namely lands which have the best towns and ports with the most useful sites and places for fortifying castles (*fortes domos*).

'Foreign direct investment', as it would now be called, was the Irish ruler's aim, or aid at least from the more anglicized east. Viewed from Westminster, and even from Dublin, the Atlantic provinces promised more, perhaps, than the rather barren reality could fulfil.[105] This optimism is typical of this era of expanding

---

[103] e.g. Timbal, *Guerre de Cent Ans*, 106–8; *Ordonnances*, iii. 219–32 (text, 1358); below Ch. 3. The peasantry were also capable of much self-help, including by fortifying: Wright, *Knights and Peasants*, uses much unpublished record material to great effect.

[104] Examples for John and Henry III: *CDIreland*, i. 19 (1200); 252 (1229); ii. 65–6 (1254: full text C. Bémont (ed.), 'Lettres Closes', 16–7); *Rot Litt Claus*, i. 218b, 224a (1215); 408a (1219); 413b (1220); ii. 138b (1226); 197b (1227). The policy became permanent, see e.g. *CCR, 1327–30*, 148–9. K. O'Conor examines the integration of castles as manor centres in *Rural Settlement in Ireland*, with contrasting Gaelic and Anglo-Irish patterns.

[105] *Foedera*, i, i, 91: *ubi scilicet meliores villae et portus fuerint*, i.e. where the justiciar's officers shall

population and crop-yields, blessed by climatic trends. English doubts concentrated on ensuring that the pact would be secure, as well as on driving a hard bargain. So the justiciar was told to be cautious:

You are to obtain from the king his [written] guarantees and also hostages that he will hold that third part in due loyalty, and will persuade the peasantry (*nativos*) of the other two-thirds to resettle there with their goods and stock. In that share of ours you shall fortify castles, establish towns, and put out properties to rent, duly receiving the revenues, as you consider most profitable to us. When we hear from you again we will issue our charter of grant to the king [of Connacht] according to what you tell us. At Geddington [Northants].

Negotiations were still in progress at the end of 1205 to secure necessary native co-operation. Whereas towns, especially on the coast and on navigable rivers, were readily founded by English settlers (particularly from Bristol), keeping native workers for labour-intensive agriculture on inland lordships was more difficult.[106] The Irish king, of course, had his own agenda. To the new justiciar John's Chancery wrote in December:

... Know that Dermott has explained to us on behalf of the king of Connacht that his master insists that he shall hold (*exiget tenere*) of us his third part as a barony, paying 100 marks annually ... He has in addition made over to us two districts together with their peasantry (*cantredos cum nativis*) for us to fortify therein or do as we please. Accordingly we instruct you, if this seems to you to be in our best interests, to put it into effect for we will most readily follow your advice. But you should carefully consider whether we might get more for agreeing to this [fortifying] since we are informed that he would give at least 400 marks extra in premium to obtain it. Also you are to ensure by negotiation that he will give cows (*vaccae*) and other things annually to supply the castles (*castra*) which we [shall] have built (*firmavimus*) there. Witness myself at Brill [Bucks.].

The Irish king evidently desired baronial rank.[107] English castles were also desirable for the security of settlement and the proof of commitment which they implied. Treaties of 'coparceny', (see sec. 3 below), which this effectively is, often included such fortifying (which also proved the parties' rights), although in this case it is unilateral. John's son Henry III, in turn, actively promoted this Connacht partnership which only turned to 'conquest' after the Irish king's death. There were three 'royal' castles there by 1236 when the justiciar was authorized to found two more, this being 'greatly conducive to the tranquillity of our land of Connacht'.[108] Nothing asserted lordship so visibly or, in case of need, so forcefully; but nothing

---

find such settlements. McNeill, *Castles in Ireland*, 10–11 (question of Irish native 'castles'); 130–7 (de Burgh conquest of Connacht, 1235); 18–20 (successful English colonization of the south-east by *c*.1210: map).

[106] Recent, well-illustrated, brief survey, Bradley, *Walled Towns in Ireland*, 14–41; Coulson, 'Battlements and the Bourgeoisie', 144–6.

[107] *Rot Litt Claus*, i. 62a, as '1206' (20 Dec. an. 7). The O'Connor is styled *Rex Conoc'*, *Conacie*, or *Cunnoc*. For the other two parts of Connacht, the Irish king was to pay 300 marks p.a. but as tribute (*debitum tributum*). On the status of baron, summary, Sanders, *English Baronies*, pp. v–viii.

[108] *Close Rolls, 1234–7*, 510–1. The king profusely thanks the justiciar for his diligence *circa negotia nostra in partibus Connac' expedienda*, giving him full authority to continue. See also ibid. 140–1 (July 1238).

could be achieved without workers on the land. Because castle-building, like founding new towns (usually walled) to promote manufacturing and trade, was expected to yield a profit, the justiciar had authority to do both.[109] He applied to this the commuted cash proceeds of the military service owed by royal tenants, together with other receipts.[110] His wide discretion governed merely the best means of achieving the universal aim of land-development which, all over Europe in the later twelfth and the thirteenth centuries, was bringing marginal land and pasture into cultivation to meet and to exploit the 'land hunger' of an expanding population. With respect to Ireland the English king was only a facilitator, through his magnates and appointed officials.[111] He responsively backed their efforts with grants of cash, rent- and tax-remissions, by assigning to individuals military service in cash or physically performed, depending on whether the need was primarily financial or military. There was much which is strongly reminiscent of modern programmes of capital investment.[112] In the heyday of settlement the true foe was desolation. After the mid-fourteenth century that enemy was widely ascendant.

Conditions—economic, climatic, demographic, and political—had worsened by 1357 when (as has been seen) even Wicklow castle near Dublin was in trouble. The impetus of English expansion fell away or was diverted to Gascony, and then to France in general from the 1340s.[113] Edward I's failure in Scotland (c.1297–1307), after success in Wales, was followed by King Robert Bruce's victory over Edward II (1314) and by Edward Bruce's ultimately unsuccessful but ominous invasion of Ireland. Settled exploitation was so closely associated with fortresses that both declined together. Problems were less than ever susceptible to military solution. Inventories and descriptions made on the Irish lands of deceased tenants-in-chief, from the earlier fourteenth century, tell a sad tale of castles in ruins, farmland laid waste, productive populations reduced or fled, and lordships 'now worth nothing because totally wasted by Irish felons' (sic); or 'worth nothing because all the tenants are destroyed by war', as the 1324 inquisition on the late earl of Pembroke

---

[109] M. Beresford, *New Towns*, ch. 3, e.g. pp. 91–2: 'in . . . 1296 the four planted towns of Newcastle on Tyne, Ludlow, Portsmouth and Lynn paid £200 in tax; this was as much as the whole county of Westmorland.' In 1334 'the plantations were then giving the king almost an extra London (£733) . . . few wars could capture such prizes'.

[110] *CDIreland*, i. 161 (July 1222): 'The king [*sic*] to the barons and others who hold of the king in Munster . . . *Desmonia* [Desmond], and the vale of Dublin. Mandate that when the justiciary goes with an armed force into Ulster . . . or other remote parts to fortify castles, etc., they render in money the service due to the king.' Cf. Frame, 'Military Service in Ireland', e.g. 103–4.

[111] e.g. *CDIreland*, i. 256 (July 1229): 'Mandate to Richard de Burgh to retain as demesne of the king the best land in the cantreds in the king's hand, not built upon or colonized; and to take counsel with Richard Duket and the archdeacon of Dublin as to settling and committing [i.e. farming out] the residue to the king's advantage'; fuller repeat, Sept. 1230, ibid. 275.

[112] e.g. *Rot Lib*, 10 (1200); *Rot Litt Claus*, i. 310a (1217), 427b (1220), 495b (1222); ii. 32a (1225); 127a, 134a (1226); 210b (1227). This policy was long-lasting: e.g. *CDIreland*, v. 59–62 (1302). In Wales and the north such measures were less systematic.

[113] Neglect of Ireland in favour of more glamorous exploits in France (far beyond restoring and defending Gascony) although ephemeral achievements, was a decision quite deliberately made: e.g. *CCR, 1354–60*, 595–6.

put it. The agricultural cycle was easily disrupted and very hard to restore. Local famines could seldom be met by importing foodstuffs. In current language, to 'destroy' an individual or a place was to annihilate the means of subsistence. In some areas of Ireland, taking refuge in the (mostly) 'English' dominated towns increased the relative depopulation of the countryside. Colonial stereotypes are inevitable but misleading, as are 'ethnic' absolutes.[114] The peasants were an underclass, very variously oppressed, throughout medieval Europe. Notions of 'military occupation' of Ireland, even of an alien aristocracy, obscure the economic function of estate-centres, fortified because this was the noble style and frequently not in a manner for effective defence.[115] But in any case, self-sufficiency condemned castles to decline powerlessly along with their agrarian and social infrastructure.

Inquisitions *post mortem* were fiscal reports of landed revenues. When buildings are described it is usually for the purpose of indicating what repairs were required or, in some very detailed inventories, so that rooms and accommodation units could be shared out between a lady dowager and the heir. In Ireland, by contrast, the local jurors often showed a more than financial interest, but it is in the condition of buildings, rather than defensibility. Thus the late earl of Pembroke, Aymer de Valence, held in 1324 'a ruined castle and chapel' at Carrick, and at Wexford 'a stone castle with towers roofed with shingles', an odd but conspicuous detail if the roofs were not concealed by parapets. At Kilkenny, Aymer had had 'a mote upon which are two houses roofed with straw and a grange' (barn).[116] In some places dereliction set in early: in 1292 La Nalle had 'buildings with stone walls of which the timber is of oak, wholly unroofed'. At Ardmays timber buildings were again thatched, and there was a stone tower, 'worth nothing because they are in the march among the Irish and cost much for maintenance', both of these in co. Meath. In this case the jurors were anxious that if the place 'were thrown down it will be to the great damage of the whole country'.[117] It was at best a vestigial symbol of English lordship. In 1306 Carlow was scarcely more, though *caput* of the county: 'a castle badly roofed; a hall opposite to it in which the pleas of the county and assizes are held, wherein there are many defects both in the roof and in the walls which cannot be extended [costed]

[114] *CIPM* vi. 314–40. Settlement by technologically more advanced peoples is examined by contributors to Bartlett and Mackay (eds.), *Medieval Frontier Societies*, e.g. Bartlett, 'Colonial Aristocracies', Knoll, 'Polish–German Frontier'.

[115] McNeill, *Castles in Ireland*, 230–6 (esp. 235). Other than military explanations are preferred throughout, but with some equivocation: M. Johnson, review, *Antiquity*, 72: 276 (1998), 460–1 (with acknowledgement); but see McNeill's 'Hibernia Pacata et Castellata', esp. 268–70 on the 'strategic question'. Sweetman, *Castles of Ireland*, is more traditional; cf. B. Smith's broad-based, *The English in Louth 1170–1330*, as 'a colonial society'. Also important discussion O'Keefe, 'Three castles of *c*.1300 in County Carlow', esp. 194–7.

[116] Part II, n. 321 above; Part IV below; n. 114 above. Pembroke had Ferns castle, co. Wexford, with its famous 'towered keep'. In 1306 the manor-house of Old Ross, Wexford, included 'an old hall without a roof outside [i.e. ?over] the gate, almost razed to the ground, a little hall in which is a chapel and a kitchen in ruins, a sheepfold thatched with straw, all of no value because no one will rent (*conducere*) them'. At Great Island, Wexford, Bigod had also 'a castle without roof': *CIPM* iv. 290–310 (pp. 306–7). The calendars print only extracts but indicate omissions.

[117] *CIPM* iii. 37–8.

because no one will rent it, but it is much in need of roofing and care.'[118] Examples of estate-seats of all types in similar condition might be multiplied. The Clare lands in Ireland left in 1307 by the death of Joan of Acre, daughter of Edward I and widow of Gilbert, earl of Gloucester (d. 1295), seem to have been better kept, but the minor castles appear quite primitive and their lands had suffered large-scale damage.[119] The cadet Thomas de Clare, who died a minor in 1321, had six Irish castellaries, of which Corcomohide (co. Limerick), the jurors reported, had 'the hall, the lord's chamber and the chapel . . . badly roofed, nor are there doors or locks'. Despite these weaknesses, the castle 'is strong and the place is pleasant'.[120] No such optimism appears in the catalogue of 'ruined' castles and seats which is William de Burgh's inquisition (1333) for his earldom of Ulster. Of one of his castles (Ballintubber), the jurors remark that it would be 'of much value for the preservation of the peace of those parts if there were sufficient custody there, but now ruinous'.[121]

The interdependence of fortresses and prosperity was seemingly complete. Of the late Giles de Badlesmere's co. Limerick lands in 1348 the inquisition noted 'a stone tower (in need of much repair), 120 acres of land which used to be under the lord's ploughs, a wood containing 200 acres of wood and moor extended at 12 pence yearly and not more, because it is amongst the Irish and there is nothing but war'.[122] Whether it was Anglo–Irish feuding or 'Irish-Irish' hostilities (or economic decline, which is more evident in historical retrospect), the result was the same; but a few pioneers still came forward. In 1335 Elias de Ashburn was pardoned seven years' 'farm' (rent) in respect of his lands: 'In the march of Leinster . . . on his petition showing that on account of the frequent invasions by the Irish he cannot receive anything from them or answer for the farm unless a fort be built therein to repel the Irish . . . on condition that he and his heirs build such a fort within the said term.' Elias was one of many absentees, resident on their lands in England.[123] His like were less prone to 'go native', but keeping even a basic 'English' presence was still a difficult problem in the sixteenth century,

[118] *CIPM* iv. 304; on Roger de Bigod who also held Wexford etc. (n. 116).
[119] Ibid. 311–31; e.g. at Kilkenny, 'a ruinous stockade (*bretagium*), grange, stable, and a ruinous sheepfold of stakes'. The castle 'has a hall, four towers, a chapel, a mote', and 'a stone market-hall [for tolls and dues] in the town'. Fermaill, 'including a castle surrounded with a stone wall, and a hall with stone walls, both roofed with wooden shingles, a grange of forks [i.e. cruck-built] thatched with straw'; also *Offarclan* (Castletown, co. Leix, Offerlane parish—*per* T. Barry, C. Manning), 'the castle . . . and lands . . . used to be worth £26. 4s. 4d. but because it is in the high march the land now lies waste . . . but the king spends £40 p.a. on its guarding' (pp. 328–30). The inquisition on Gilbert the Last (d. 1314 at Bannockburn) is uninformative on Ireland: *CIPM* v. 325–54.
[120] Ibid. vi. 159–63 (pp. 160–2); Thomond, Quin ('thrown down'), *Ardrahan*, Youghall ('a capital messuage called the castle'), Askeaton.
[121] Ibid. vii. 371–9. The Ormonde (Butler) lands and castellaries were in as bad a state in 1338: ibid. viii. 117–27. 'Nothing can be levied in time of war' is a typical comment: McNeill, *Castles in Ireland*, 101–3.
[122] Namely *et tota guerra: CIPM* ix. 132.
[123] *CPR, 1334–8*, 126. Appointed 'chief justice of the king's bench of Ireland', 1337. Leinster kept him long enough in 1335 to be obliged to empower attorneys to act for him in England (Northants.): ibid. 389, 124.

under the Tudor monarchs.[124] Absentees were continually coerced, by withholding as much as two-thirds of their Irish revenues, to defend their lands in person or by deputy.[125] The pool of potential settlers tended to dry up after the Black Death (1348–9) and its recurrent sub-plagues. After 1337 the French war was more glamorous. Port and coastal towns, such as Dublin, Drogheda, Waterford, and Wexford in the south-east, and Cork and Limerick in the south-west—walled, as was proper to municipalities anywhere—strove to maintain their Englishness and their trading links, which did something to mitigate the shortage of human resources. Even subsidizing the custody of castellaries (by assigning revenues or even by direct grant) might be ineffective, as an order no later than 1341 indicates. Offers of life-leases might attract no takers.[126]

Towns often possessed considerable and contrasting advantages, not the least being a reduced (but often still considerable) dependence on their hinterlands. Waterford in 1375 likened itself modestly to 'a little castle'. Many resembled modern country villages in being agricultural centres as much as merchant emporia and bases of craft guilds.[127] Their relationship to their formal *banlieue* or de facto economic hinterland had many affinities with that of the lordly *caput* to its castellary or manor. In 1244 Henry III sent a letter close 'to the bailiffs and good men' (i.e. substantial burgesses) of the new plantation diagnostically called Kingston, exhorting them to make a physical reality of their privileges by 'building securely on their burgage plots, cultivating the land allotted to them, since the king will grant to them as much in the way of liberties as the good men of other towns of Ireland freely enjoy under the king's lordship'. Official planning might extend to arranging streets, plots, market-place, and church as a grid and to walling in *bastide* style, but organic growth and local initiative were often original. A writ for Cork, by the regent Earl Marshal in 1218, was 'not sent' but is entirely typical:[128]

We have been given to understand by our lieges that it would be a major safeguard (*securitas*) to us and to our land of Ireland if our city of Cork were strengthened (*firmata*); and since we have heard from Thomas Fitz Anthony, our bailiff [of Cork], that it could be

---

[124] e.g. Elton, *England Under the Tudors*, 22–3, 28–9, 30–3, etc.

[125] e.g. CCR, 1343–6, 375; 1346–9, 77; 1349–54, 195, 587–8; 1354–60, 575; CPR, 1385–9, 78–9, 432, 523; 1391–6, 387, 413.

[126] CCR, 1341–3, 312; *Balecyn*, perhaps Ballykine, co. Mayo, where there is a hall-house (Sweetman, *Castles of Ireland*, 95). Nothing was to be given away: the lessee must be 'able and willing to defend it . . . and to maintain it in a suitable state, as the king has learned that several lands pertaining to that castle, because they are upon the march and among the lands of the king's Irish rebels, lie fallow and uncultivated from the time when the castle came into the king's hands owing to the negligence of the keepers, although they receive a reasonable fee for the custody of the castle and lands'.

[127] CPR, 1374–7, 145; n. 106 above. Towns receiving authority to levy tolls for walling ('murage') on the English Rolls 1218–1509 are: *Dublin* (1218–), *Waterford* (1224–), *Limerick* (1237–), *Drogheda* (1243–), *Kilkenny* (1266–), Youghal (co. Cork, 1275), *Cork* (1284–), Tralee, Moyl, Ard (1286), Fethard (1292), Castledermott (1295), Clonmel (1298–), Tipperary (1300), Trim (1308–), Buttevant (co. Cork, 1316), Kells (1326–), Callan (co. Kilkenny, 1339), Galway (1360–), Kinsale (co. Cork, 1378). Italics indicate numerous grants; CPR index.

[128] *Close Rolls*, 1242–7, 201; PatR, i. 160 (8 July 1218).

fortified if he were given the city farm [royal dues] for three years . . . we hereby direct you
to let Thomas have those dues . . . and to assist him in the work in all possible ways.

The Crown or town-lord might not grant a tax-holiday, but instead license (or
have licensed) tolls levied on goods brought for sale. Such 'murage grants'
(*muragium* meaning 'walling' in general) habitually repeat the burgesses' claims
regarding the benefits to be gained by the locality as well as by the town itself.
They are usually expressed, irrespective of the circumstances, in terms of defence.
Thus, typically, Edward I's grant of murage in 1291 to Kilkenny was 'in aid of
enclosing their vill, for improvement thereof and the security of the men of the
parts adjacent'.[129] The protestations of all petitioners pulling levers of the
Chancery fruit-machine require some scepticism. Towns were potentially capacious refuges, of course. In Wales too there were special factors of 'security', but
the word meant peacekeeping and orderly government rather than 'defence'.
Fortifying was so essential to proprietorship, urban as well as seignorial, that any
possible danger gave added point to the habit. The modalities of aristocracy were
military; even bureaucratic language reflected that fact. Danger was the currency
of petition-speak, and townsmen were its most skilled exponents.[130]

Drogheda, on the east coast, was troubled by the risk of indictment for 'fore-
stalling', or putting up prices by intercepting goods on the way to market. If the
statute was enforced, its townsmen petitioned in 1358, 'many burgesses and
merchants propose to leave the town . . . situated by the march of the king's Irish
enemies and by which all the neighbouring country is defended against invasions,
leaving it desolate'. Their problem was that the difficult harbour-entrance
compelled them to buy up ships' cargoes at sea, or merchants would go elsewhere.
Twelve years' dispensation rewarded this conventional piece of judicious exaggeration.[131] Nowhere was far from 'the Irish'—or in the north of England after
1314, from 'the Scots'—both of them wreckers and destroyers, if we are to believe
the propaganda embedded in the Rolls of Chancery.

Early colonization in Ireland lost its impetus.[132] The topic must be left *pro tem.*
(Part IV, Ch. 2 sec. 1) with a reminder of its original aims and methods, again in
the west of Ireland but in the region of the Shannon estuary, not in Connacht.
While Henry III was suppressing disorders in the duchy of Gascony (1254), John

[129] *CDIreland*, iii. 409–10; dated 24 June to run from 1 August; identical form used for Waterford
(28 June), and (2 Jan. 1292) for Fethard (co. Tipperary) 'for the inclosing of their vill and the greater
security of Ireland': ibid. 410–11, 454. Petition (1290) by Waterford for murage and other privileges,
ibid. 309.

[130] Cf. Turner, *Town Defences*, taking protestations at face value (e.g. ch. 5, 'Walls and Wars').
Harvey, *Castles and Walled Towns*, chs. 9, 10, is still useful and includes a few references to Wales.
Enclosure signified exclusive ownership e.g. of parks and warrens, sometimes with locked gates, as at
Coggeshall abbey (Essex): *Rot Chart*, 114b; *CChR, 1226–57*, 81–2, 97; *Rot Litt Claus*, i. 70b.

[131] *CPR, 1358–61*, 114. They also had to pay for a 'lodeman' (pilot) needed to navigate ships into the
harbour of Drogheda.

[132] But 'out of the large total sum of outside money (£22,922) that was poured into the castles of
North Wales between 1284 and 1290, well over half came from Ireland': Edwards, 'Edward I's Castle
Building', 64. His view was that the cost went far beyond what 'insuring N. Wales against fire and
rebellion' could justify (*pers. comm., c.*1967).

Fitz Geoffrey obtained from him, in court at Bordeaux, a charter of regalian franchise comprising the customary raft of powers rarely found in England after the later twelfth century. Along with part of the vast 'cantred of the Isles of Thomond', John's power was sanctioned to appoint clergy, to execute royal orders ('return of writs'), to try civil and criminal cases (as usual in England excepting murder, rape, and arson), all together with the range of other powers proper to such a franchise, namely:

advowsons of churches, return of writs . . . and full rights thereto belonging, without any reservation save . . . pleas which ought to be heard by our justices and are wont to be, and all Crown cases, all for paying 43 marks yearly at the exchequer of Dublin . . . and doing to us and our heirs the service of two knights' fiefs in full satisfaction. And John and his heirs may lawfully and free of impediment, fortify castles, set up markets, fairs, and hunting preserves, wherever they deem expedient within the cantred . . .

This grant was first made in 1253 but was modified and reissued next year. The final clause (above) was not an extra but an afterthought, spelling out what had been taken for granted. In 1252 Robert de Muscegros had backing for exercising similar powers in another part of Thomond.[133]

2. Castles and Colonization, Mainly in France

Thanks to the fullness of the Chancery Rolls (Henry III's fully printed Close Rolls being especially valuable), it is possible to illustrate from Ireland the Europe-wide colonization process based on 'castles' and towns which, by filling in the gaps by settlement and attrition, converted 'empty' territory into populated assets.[134] In central Europe this activity drove the frontier of the German empire eastwards and, everywhere, tidied up the numerous *lacunae* of early medieval civilization. Initiatives were mostly local and uncoordinated. Marcher lords and townships generally, be they in Brandenburg, Bohemia, Hungary and Austria (*Österreich*), or in Wales, northern England, the Scottish lowlands, and Ireland, or in the marches of Gascony, Périgord, Toulouse, and elsewhere—or indeed in Spain as part of the *Reconquista*—enjoyed with their own superiors a somewhat special relationship. These do-it-yourself entrepreneurs, not of capitalism but of castellation, won their lands by their own efforts.[135] Dukes, counts, kings, and emperors used what authority they had to confer legitimacy and to assert some control. King John, in 1199, issued from Poitiers a charter to an anglophile Welsh lord which reflects one aspect of this general situation:

[133] *Rôles Gascons*, i. 508; *CPR*, 1247–58, 330–1; *CDIreland*, ii. 1, 7, 43, 65; *CChR*, 1226–57, 377–8.
[134] For town-plantation see next section. Economic development of northern England figures in the very thorough study by Kapelle, *Conquest of the North*, e.g. 5–11, 50–85, (pre-Conquest), 158–90.
[135] e.g. on the virtual equivalence in Italy of settlement and founding (often on hilltops) of nucleated villages (commonly *castra/castella*) see Rosenwein, *Negotiating Space*, 140–55 ('Carolingian Italy'); Castillo, *Incastellamento de Luca*. Two exemplary syntheses are: Ulmer, *Castles of Friuli*, esp. 12–13, 35–40, 58–79, 108–16, 300–1 (map), giving a radical, superbly illustrated and integrated historical-architectural study of this region of NE Italy; and Meyer, 'Burgenbau und Herrschaftsbildung', studying early-medieval lordship-implantation by *castra* in SW Germany.

... know that we have granted, and by our present charter confirmed, to our dear and faithful Mailgun ap (*filius*) Rees for his homage and loyal service those four cantreds called Cardigan, Cilgerran, and Emlyn, namely what has already been won there as well as powers (*jura*) hereafter to be acquired from our enemies, to hold from us and our heirs ... He shall loyally serve us and be in our fealty against all mortals. He has given up to us ... perpetually ... the castle of Cardigan.[136]

Taking over the existing land-, people-, and resource-management instruments of lordship, where possible extending and intensifying their profitable operation, can be illustrated again as late as 1306, in the Scottish lowlands. When the momentum of Edward I's campaigns had expired in a vain struggle against lack of money, old age, geography, and guerrilla resistance, the old warrior resorted to 'free enterprise'. His trusted companion-in-arms Aymer de Valence was given, in October 1306, extensive powers over the whole Border region of Selkirk and Peebles. At the same time John de Kingston, constable and sheriff *pro tem.* of Edinburgh, received a similar franchise for the Haddington area nearby. Both charters were confirmed by Edward II's administration in 1308.[137] If this was 'privatization', it was not giving away powers belonging to the Crown so much as seeking to create them. With the castellary of Selkirk, the manor of Traquair, and Peebles itself with its mills, Aymer's jurisdiction covered removing the legal status of 'forest' land, creating parks and hunting chases, and renting out and putting areas of forest to the plough. It was a virtual palatinate, so that:

those whom he and his heirs may enfeoff of any lands, with the licence of Aymer and his heirs by letters patent, may build burghs, towns, castles, fortalices, and other strongholds (*munitiones*) and may make and have markets and fairs; moreover, the said Aymer and his heirs in all the places where there are no parish churches may found such churches and present [appoint] fit persons [clergymen] to them; and they shall have free warren [hunting rights] in all the forest [of Selkirk].

It all seems distinctly fantastical in retrospect.[138] The settlement formula of town–castle plantation which had succeeded in impressing English dominion on Wales, eight great royal castles seconded by seignorial Denbigh, Chirk, Holt, and Ruthin, among others, was far too costly to be repeated. But the quasi-royal and not merely regalian franchise, such as was found in Ireland and in Wales even after the Edwardian conquest (1289) as well as in England (only that of Durham began early and remained 'independent'), were full 'delegations' of regal

---

[136] *Rot Chart*, 63a; background e.g. Edwards, 'The Normans and the Welsh March', 155–77.

[137] *CChR, 1300–26*, 69–70, 109. Aymer was to pay £130 p.a. plus the nominal service of a single knight's fee. Charitable payments settled on the lands by previous kings of Scots he was to honour. He and his heirs were to be hereditary sheriffs of Peebles and Selkirk. An afterthought allowed Aymer to impark what he would of Selkirk Forest, 'enclosing it with a dyke and hedge ... as a free chase for their great beasts' (i.e. deer).

[138] John de Kingston's grant was valued at £68. 16s. p.a., but was temporary until given other recompense for £444. 16d. owed to him. John's franchise also included 'power to make castles and fortalices in the said lands, with free warren therein', and *Luffenock* castle (?Luffness tower house: Tranter, *Fortified House*, i. 40–1). Aymer de Valence retrospectively in 1315 claimed the repayment of 200 marks taken from the revenues of 'his Forest of Selkirk': *Rot Parl*, i. 344 (28).

power.[139] As such the comparatively vast and politically amorphous countries of 'France' and 'Germany' were the true homes of the palatinate. The notion that 'barons' were 'little kings' was there occasionally valid.

Colonization in France, using the name geographically, was a process of internal growth rather than one of absorbing extraneous territory. The more compact and effective *neuf château* castellaries broke up the over-large Gallo-Roman, Merovingian, and Carolingian land-units.[140] Since the land was mostly quite well settled and fertile (but with large tracts of forest and 'waste'), such fragmentation and consolidation was an active process and a constructive one. Fortress-customs were of crucial importance in ensuring that, as the old authorities dissolved, they crystalized out into new forms of order. Robert Aubenas, as early as 1938, showed that it was an orderly evolution more than an individualistic scramble tending to anarchy.[141] New fortresses were subordinated to the ancient *capita*. Evidence of jurability, rendability, and of licensing survives from at least the early eleventh century. *Castrum* (as we have seen) designated whole urban, village, conventual, and secular complexes (Fr. *sites castrales*). Reconstruction of the revered late-Roman system caused its architecture to be avidly imitated, so far as means allowed, and generated a drive for land-improvement at every level, from the promoting of castle-towns to monastic schemes of marsh reclamation, down to the mundane development practised in castellaries, lordships, manors, and home-farms.[142]

An arrangement adopted to finance and facilitate schemes of improvement, fully elaborated before the thirteenth century, was the *traité de paréage*, partnership or coparceny pact. By vesting the land to be developed in joint-ownership with a greater lord, both partners or coparcenors benefited. Pressure from a virile upon a senile lordship was often peaceably resolved. Scrupulous care was taken to ensure that the weaker party and original 'owner' (often the initiator) kept his parity or peer-status. Ideally, coparceny was a merger between unequals, not a takeover by the stronger. Idiosyncrasies are as many as the surviving texts, so examples are representative more in their principles than in particulars.[143] Castles

---

[139] Howell, *Regalian Right*, 201–4, only on royal right to the revenues of ecclesiastics during vacancies. Same limited sense, Petit-Dutaillis, *Feudal Monarchy*, 187, 251, 267.

[140] But Duby's term *châtellenie indépendante* requires caution: Richard, 'Châteaux, châtelains et vassaux', 437–9, 445–6.

[141] Aubenas, 'Les Châteaux-forts', e.g. 548–9, 551, 558–60; particularized, Hadju, 'Castles, Castellans in Poitou, e.g. 28–9, 34–5; but on Aquitaine, Debord, 'Castellan Revolution', 142–8 etc.—comital power was also reconstructed, pp. 40–3, etc. Cursente, '*Castrum* et territoire', looks at 'castle-space' in Gascony more from the tenant's angle; also, on lesser sites in Normandy, Le Maho, '*Curtis* au château', 171–83. The great diversity of early sites is duly emphasized by the term *forme castrale*, e.g. Bois *et al.*, 'Formes castrales, Bourgogne–Provence'.

[142] Campbell, *English Seigniorial Agriculture*, summarizes and updates some aspects of a large literature. The 'constructive' economic view (e.g. Gimpel, *Medieval Machine*, pp. vii–xi) is an antidote to, and perhaps a less misleading modernization than, praising the period for appearing to share the questionable amenities of modern warfare.

[143] Commonplace in France, especially for *bastide*-plantation or *novae populationes*: e.g. Beresford, *New Towns*, 30, 99–102: 'nearly half the foundations in English Gascony were by *paréage*, and three quarters of these involved the English king.'

of all kinds naturally figure prominently, because of the lordly authority they symbolized and made effective. Thus in the pact made in about 1220 between Dalmas de Luzy and King Philip II the frequent stipulation occurs that any castle built in the shared township must have joint consent. But since it would not unbalance the meticulously equal participation, the townspeople as a commune were to be able 'to establish and enclose the church and town'.[144] As in King John's arrangement bringing the Irish king of Connacht into fealty, the parties to a *paréage* each made a vital contribution, the technical donor providing the land and his protector the fiscal privileges. In 1243 Count Henry VI of Grandpré, a dependant of Champagne, made a careful treaty with his lord for a new fortified town near Soissons (*dép*. Aisne). The balance here seems somewhat unequal, but Henry initiated it and there may well be undisclosed factors. What is clear is that Henry was anticipating opposition:

I, Henry, count of Grandpré, make known to all who shall see these letters, that I am to make a new castle (*un chastel nouvel*) at Montretemps in land which is mine and held from my lord the King Thibaut of Navarre, count palatine of Champagne and Brie . . . The borough customs of Beaumont [sur-Oise] shall apply to it and I must enclose it with palisading (*de paliz et de bretesches*) within five months of being summoned thereto by my lord the king . . . within six years and five months thereafter I must have the place suitably (*souffisanmant*) walled in stone. If anyone attempts forcibly to stop me, I must in good faith remove that force on my own, with my own people (*genz*) and to [the extent of] my power. Should I fail, then my lord king must aid me with his power. And if it happen that war be moved against my lord for this, I must serve him in person with my people in good faith for as long as the war shall last to ensure the completion of the town (*chastel*). During the first two years I may not begin the *chastel* without the lord king's assent; but after that I may begin to enclose (*fermer*) it when I wish, being helped by the lord king, as he is feudally obliged, if I am forcibly impeded . . . And the said *chastel* shall be jurable and rendable to the king and to his heirs, to all force great or small, and when he is out of his need (*fors de son besoing*) he must within forty days restore it to me stocked (*garni*) as well as he received it.[145]

It does seem that Grandpré was Champagne's catspaw in all this, but in the mutuality of the benefits expected from the new castle-town the arrangements are conventional. Each burgess was to pay one measure of oats and other dues on the feast of Saint-Rémi annually to Champagne (in cash perhaps). Grandpré was not

---

[144] Viz. *ecclesiam et villam poterunt edificare et firmare communio predicte ville*; context suggests *firmare* is 'enclose', not 'fortify'; Luzy is *dép*. Nièvre, *arr*. Château Chinon, probably the area of the *villa de Salornas*. Many plantations failed, perhaps the reason for 'loss' of this site. No serfs from Dalmas's castellary may be taken in (and enfranchised), unless by consent; nor may any of his tenures, unless by consent when they must be jointly held. A market and fair will be founded. Dues receivable in common from owners of plough-teams, and from those without, are specified: *Layettes*, i. 507.

[145] Ibid. ii. 491–2; v. 150. Jubainville, *Histoire de Champagne*, v. 392 (calendar), refers to the place as *Mont-Otran* and as a *château* (*sic*) near Buzancy (*dép*. Aisne). Identified, Mesqui, 'Crécy-en-Brie', 44–5. Lorris customs were to apply at *Salornas* (above), but those of Beaumont were a favourite model. All sorts of 'fortress' were rendable. The emphasis on *bone foi* (in Occitanie, *sans engan*) asserted that the spirit of the pact must be honoured, eschewing (common) technical evasion. Thibaut's duty to support Henry is *comme de son fié*.

to lose any serfs to the new settlement, but he was under severe financial penalties if he defaulted. By offering support, just in case, Champagne acquired a new fortress, as usable as one of Thibaut's own, over which his lordship could be asserted on demand. It was usual to make a first enclosure in timber. Here, in effect, a maximum of seven seasons' work was available to build the stone *enceinte* (correctly *closture/claustura*). Such a plantation intruded more than a simple 'castle' did. Settlers might be attracted from the peasant labour force, and other markets' profitability would be damaged. Development was not a 'zero-sum game'; some of the increase of prosperity was likely to be real, but some resistance was often met with, though not the technical tenurial *injuria* which could, as in this case, possibly cause a declaration of *guerra* upon the count of Champagne.[146]

All normal forms of pressure were primarily economic, whether by 'new populations' (sec. 3, below) or by 'castles' in the modern sense. Both might intensify or even initiate agricultural exploitation; but 'novelty' was prima facie illegal, hence the stock tautology, *indebite novitates*. A new lordly residence might have its home-farm 'demesne', with gardens (*viridia*), game preserves (*vivaria*), fishponds (*stagna*), corn-mills, dovecots, *fours banals* (manorial-monopoly ovens), new arable and 'forest' reserved from cultivation and put under special rules enforced by verderers, as well as extensive hunting rights ('free warren') beyond the seignorial deer-park: all representing a change of land-use. Ecclesiastical impact also was likely if a new church, parish, or chapelry were established as part of the new 'landscape of lordship'. Even when a previously deserted region was colonized, there were many vested interests to conciliate.[147] With the new castle of Le Palu (lit. 'the marsh'), near Maguelone (*dép.* Hérault) in the south of France, overcoming objections required great care, as this agreement shows:

In the name of the Lord . . . and in the year 1140 this amicable concord was made between Bishop Raymond of Maguelone jointly with the canons and William, lord of Montpellier, so as to resolve the points of their dispute with him. Their first complaint was over the territory men call Le Palu and the castle (*castrum*) now built upon it. Thus it is agreed: William and his successors shall perpetually and peaceably hold the territory and the castle which has been established (*constituitur*), together with the improvements (*melioramentis*) made there, in fief from the [cathedral] church of Maguelone without any dispute henceforth. Secondly, so long as the lordships of Montpellier and Le Palu are conjoined, a single homage shall be done to the bishop and church for both. If the lordships are separated each holder severally shall perform the due oath of fealty and act of homage . . . and if it be that the lord of the castle set up a chapel there, the bishop and canons are to provide for its

---

[146] Stipulating commencement within five months of Thibaut's summons would ensure that work could start in the late March to late September building season (Knoop and Jones, *Medieval Mason*, 131–3), and enable the political calculations to be made. The phrase *chacuns bourjois dou chastel et dou bourc* (i.e. castle-town) still (1243) kept its primitive ambivalence. Non-performance by Henry entailed distraint on his revenues and 'chattels' and of up to £500 from his fiefs held of Champagne, but all not incurring any breach of fealty (*sanz meffaire*, also commonly *sine se mesfacere*).

[147] New landscape studies are advancing understanding of the appurtenances of the lordship-seat: e.g. nn. 55, 73 above. The socio-economic repercussions were no less extensive. Hilton, 'Agrarian Development', etc.

consecration and for its services, William paying the priest a suitable stipend out of the money arising from the two new mills now constructed in 'the Marsh'.

This was a major enterprise and proved lasting. The former area of wasteland, bordering the Mediterranean lagoon of the Étang-de-Lates acquired also 'a port and harbour'.[148] Much of the development in this region was done by ecclesiastics, notably the abbots of Villemagne and of Figeac and the bishops of Lodève. Like the bishops of Maguelone, in their tiny littoral diocese, they were in a marcher relationship to the distant king in Paris. Provence was still technically part of the empire but, in practice, they were free to colonize, whether themselves or, as at Le Palu, by proxy. Louis VII and Philip Augustus were always ready to do what they could to strengthen friendly ecclesiastical franchises.[149] They competed with such powerful lay feudatories as the counts of Toulouse and of Foix, in the upland foothills, and with the kings of Aragon, whose possessions straddled the Mediterranean Pyrenees. King Louis VII (1137–80) was mindful of ecclesiastical support when in 1156 he gave the bishops of Maguelone a *pancarte* backing all they claimed to possess. They had been careful, in presenting the king with the list, to include the newly established fief and castellary of Le Palu. Because castellation, whether the implanting of new lordship-seats or of towns of dignity high enough to possess walls, was an automatic ingredient of colonization wherever wealth and human resources permitted, Louis VII like his father and son backed up these prelates' own founding and licensing of fortresses. This last power had been left out the previous year, but in 1156, doubtless responding to Maguelone insistence, it was put in.[150] No doubt the same concern ensured that Philip II's *pancarte* in 1208 extended the bishops' monopoly to build and license fortification so as to apply throughout the diocese as well as in the cathedral demesnes and fiefs.[151]

Conversely, such castellation franchises could be used (as has been seen) to fend off as well as to promote the expansion of lordship. The abbots of Sarlat, over against English Gascony in frontier Périgord, like the abbots of Figeac, could rely on royal support. When, in 1268, Henry III's seneschal began to found the new

[148] *Layettes*, i. 50–1; confirmed 1311. The bishop's and canons' *querimonie* against William VI of Montpellier (1121–49) for receiving serfs (*rusticos*), ditching his town, encroaching on episcopal revenues, etc., and allowing his burgesses to discharge water and sewage (*aqua cum immundiciis*) from and through the walls onto the bishop's (extramural) buildings, printed 'c.1140': Mortet, Deschamps, *Recueil*, ii. 53.

[149] Coulson, 'Fortress-Policy', 20–2. Maguelone cathedral was demonstratively castellated in the 12th century, but scarcely defensively or exceptionally, despite Bonde, *Fortress Churches of Languedoc* (Maguelone, also Agde, Saint-Pons-de-Thomières: with *preuves* and illustrations), 72–83.

[150] *Layettes*, i. 76–7: confirming a charter of 'King Louis' (VI?) and reciting verbiage of typical sub-Carolingian type, for Bishop Raymond: 'et si castrum vel aliquam munitionem per te vel per alium [i.e. by licensing] ibi facere volueris, liceat tibi et successoribus'; with Carolingian-type immunity within the bishopric. This is what Rosenwein has styled 'competitive generosity': *Negotiating Space*, 152–5; also 6–7, 99–101, 137–9.

[151] *Layettes*, i. 321–2, *Recueil Philippe II*, iii. 101–5 (attributing the original, undated and lost *pancarte* to Louis VI; royally confirmed 1271, 1287, 1312). Bonde, *Fortress Churches of Languedoc*, 201–3, cites a (slightly corrupt) 1173 diploma of Louis VII for the bishop of Agde. The (archaic) castellation clause 'licenses' *turres, munitiones, muros, posterlas* [sic] *et portarum tuitiones et valles*, with *novas fortias* and the right *prohibendi facere novas fortias in toto episcopatu Agathensi*, etc.

bastide of Castelréal (*Castrum Regale*) too close to Sarlat, the monks could appeal to the parlement of Louis IX which, with judicious opportunism, decided in their favour. The Gascon outreach continued here, however, and was not stopped until 1281 when Edward I's appeal was rejected.[152] Not often did colonization have such political impact. In 1317–26 it was more serious still. At Saint Sardos the counter-penetration by Sarlat abbey well into Gascony unleashed a conflict (1324–5) which was the curtain-raiser to the Hundred Years War. With the filling of internal voids within borders, economic expansion became 'peaceful penetration' in the modern French colonial sense, inaugurating a new type and degree of competition.[153]

3. Development and Confrontation: Bastides not 'Fortresses'

The habit of regarding fortresses as belonging to 'military architecture', and believing that peculiarly 'strategic' rules operated, has caused acute difficulties when applied to *bastides*. Belief in an overwhelming 'military' character was systematically tackled in a classic article in 1954 by J. P. Trabut-Cussac.[154] Since, in fact, the Latin *firmare* and its variants and synonyms meant essentially 'to establish', and in special contexts 'to enclose', and because any town (especially if it was new) required a demarcating ditch (and wall) with gates where tolls might be collected in order to define its jurisdictional peculiar (just as did a conventual precinct), the problem was actually artificial. *Bastides* were both 'fortress', much as 'castles' were, and also franchised settlements, initially quite small *bourgeois* enclaves and aspiring townships, with their surrounding lands within an aristocratic and peasant countryside to which, however, they were economically wedded and culturally adjusted.

These various aspects were explicitly conjoined in the donation made in 1268 by the abbot and canons of Pimbo (*dép.* Landes) to the Lord Edward, represented

---

[152] A site regarded as well within English Périgord (*dép.* Dordogne): full proceedings, *Les Olim*, i. 723; ii. 179–80; *Actes du Parlement*, i, i, 113, 224 (calendar). In 1281, Edward I's attorney apologized for *quandam parvam inobedientiam* committed in 1268 by his father over Castelréal. Arguments for Edward and for the abbot of Sarlat are not detailed, the court's decision being made simply 'because it is certain that the abbey is in such manner privileged that it cannot be put out of our [Philip III's] hand'. The site being within a castellary of Sarlat, the abbot's *denuncio novi operis*, as lord of the fief, had to be (*sic*) upheld. Royal 'protection' was arbitrary: *Recuil Philippe II*, i. 82–3 (1181 grant of Sarlat castellation-franchise, 'confirming' Louis VI). On a 'strong' site see Beresford, *New Towns*, 580–1; Gardelles, *Châteaux du sud-ouest*, 119.

[153] Vale, *Origins of the Hundred Years War*, esp. 233–4; ch. 7; Coulson, 'Community and Fortress-Politics', 94–108 (on Valois conquest by quasi-judicial attrition).

[154] Trabut-Cussac, 'Bastides ou forteresses?', esp. 81–6 perhaps too flatly denying 'strategic' 'frontier-defence', but rightly sceptical about modernistic motives ascribed to *bastides* since 1948 as an 'hypothèse séduisante dans sa simplicité', both in Toulouse and in Gascony, using documentary as well as topographic analysis. His conclusion (p. 135) 'is that which the texts support: no credit should be given any longer to a military explanation, even an ancillary one (*même partielle*) for the origin of the *bastides*. Essentially they were part of an administrative, political, and, secondarily, of a fiscal policy. They were not in origin fortresses.' Also F. Powicke, *Thirteenth Century*, 280–318 (esp. 308–10). Beresford, *New Towns*, ch. 6, stresses *bourgeois* security as the motive, actual defence (unexpectedly) becoming more prominent during the Valois–Plantagenet conflict after *c.*1337.

by his seneschal for the duchy of Gascony. With an eye to their advantage, they gave Henry III's heir 'a place or site for building a strong-house or *castrum*', and another site for a *bastidam seu populacionem novam*.[155] Inserting a new settlement was potentially disruptive, tending to cause more local disturbance than a mere lordship-seat (and its *districtus*), but the pains of this organic growth were generally eased by co-operation between the lords, ecclesiastics, the Crown, the new townspeople themselves, and the peasants who might achieve emancipation as burgesses, enjoy a new market, or have to live with a powerful new neighbour. Given how many and how seriously existing interests might be affected, a notable harmony usually prevailed. But not all parties equally benefited from the development. Confrontation with existing towns was particularly likely. Thus, in 1306 the burgesses of Tarbes-en-Bigorre (*dép*. Hautes-Pyrénées) protested against the construction of Rabastens *bastide* by King Philip IV's seneschal. The site was only about 10 miles from Tarbes to the north 'in the wood of La Lorre'. The Capetian high court and council of the parlement, in these days more political and less judicial than it had been (as extended textual comparison makes clear), upheld the French seneschal, ruling that Rabestens would be 'useful to us [Philip IV] and to the *communitas* of Bigorre as well as to the entire commonwealth (*reipublice*) of that country (*patrie*)'. Compensation was, however, to be paid to Tarbes for loss of revenue.[156] Intrusion did not have to have such backing to succeed. The townsmen of Grimsby, in Yorkshire, were not able to stop the foundation and expansion of the new port-town of Ravensrod, also on the Humber estuary, in the late thirteenth century. Grimsby had got nearer to the sea trade than Hull, itself a supplanter of Beverley.[157] But urban enterprise, lords seeking partners in development, or the opportunism of rulers were not the only initiators. In 1310 it was the country community (we are told) which began the formation of a new town in the land of Haumont in Périgord.[158]

The doctrine to which at least lip-service was paid was that such development was publicly beneficial: in 1289 the new *bastide* of Hastingues (*dép*. Landes), its name commemorating Edward I's seneschal, which the abbot and convent of Arthous had sponsored, was approved by the king-duke—'considering particularly the quietude and peace of our subjects', that of the monks, 'and also of the other men of religion and peaceable men of those parts, where lately many

---

[155] *Recognitiones*, 139–40. The seneschal was to choose both sites in the abbey lands. Both the *proprietas* and the *dominium* were made over perpetually, retaining only certain specified dues and revenues to be shared. Apparently abortive, as no site is known: Beresford, *New Towns*, 186.

[156] *Les Olim*, iii. 188–9; *Actes du Parlement*, i, ii, 37; a region of Valois encroachment almost unresisted until after 1331; Vale, *Origins of the Hundred Years War*, 252–60.

[157] *Rot Hund*, i. 292a, 380b, 402a; also ii. 18b, 19a, 20a; Beresford, *New Towns*, 286–9; Coulson, 'Battlements and the Bourgeoisie', 161–5, 184–6.

[158] A typical topographical *bastide* and *neuf-château* name; but many sites were low-lying, by rivercrossings, etc. The *homines territorii de Alto-Monte* were exceptionally well organized to be able to brief a lawyer to put their case in Paris; but spurious 'non-origination' by the French seneschal must be expected. As usual he was told to investigate the pros and cons (*commodum vel incommodum*), and reporting no opposition was then told to proceed, *patrie consuetudine observata*, ensuring that the locals contributed as they had promised: *Les Olim*, iii. 478 (as '1309'); *Actes du Parlement*, i, ii, 71.

murders, robberies, and thefts were committed'.[159] Even in the settled and much-governed English 'home counties', fortification and civilization were associated. The Order of the Hospital at Eagle (Lincs.), on the main road from Lincoln to Newark, claimed in 1345 that a new town on Swinderby Moor would promote peacekeeping. A casualty, no doubt, of the Black Death (1348 and sequels), the scheme was revived in 1449 to justify asking for a (duly granted) licence from Henry VI to crenellate and impark the Hospitallers' manor of Eagle itself.[160] This was more seignorial in motive than utilitarian, of course; but justificatory phrases still reflect aspirations, even when they represent no more than genuflexions to political correctness.

Whether or not the *bastide* was more than juridically fortified so as to make a legal point and to serve everyday management purposes, part of its character was that of a fortress. In the regions north of the Pyrenees it was particularly emphatic, irrespective of marches. King Peter II of Aragon, in pledging (1205) for repayment of a loan his rights in the entire counties of Milhau and Gévaudan to Count Raymond VI of Toulouse, assumed and intended that Raymond would develop the area by planting 'new bastides or fortifications (*munitiones*)', Peter meeting up to 400 marks of the cost. The duties of large-scale land-management are very clearly expressed.[161] In 1250 the viscount of Cardona in Catalonia made a pact of similar effect with the count of Foix.[162] Such towns or villages (the texts seldom differentiate), even when not styled 'fortress' in any form, were habitually treated the same, both being self-supporting economic units. Building and repairing them was normal stewardship; but it was also an assertive act. In 1205, when the monks of the powerful Parisian abbey of Saint-Denis were sold the territory of Le Tremblay (*dép.* Seine-et-Oise) to develop, having acquired the town back in 1153, they were precluded from establishing there any new *villa et fortericia*, a phrase

---

[159] *Rôles Gascons*, ii. 438–9; Beresford, *New Towns*, 131, 186, 200, 385.

[160] *CChR, 1341–1417*, 40–1; *1427–1516*, 112–13; Beresford, *New Towns*, 84–5, 306; also p. 305 (table of increasing failures of Gascon *bastides* 1246–1330); Knowles and Hadcock, *Religious Houses*, 293, 303.

[161] This sum was to be added to the principal of 150,000 sols of money of Melgueil lent by Raymond. The territories (*déps.* Gard and Lozère) included Milhau *burgus*, three *castra*, and 21 lesser places, with all appurtenances, rights, and subjects. King Peter agrees to compensate Raymond (additionally) if he terminates the pledge, 'since it was done for our own advantage'. In case that Sancho, Peter's uncle, should remove *aliquod castrum, sive municionem seu villam* from the pledge, Peter will help Raymond and indemnify him for any other losses due to war or to lawsuit (detailed). If Raymond spends more than 400 marks on *bastides* or fortifications, as licensed by Peter (as lord), the excess will not be refundable; but costs of necessary repairs to Peter's 'buildings', without any improvement, will be repayable. Raymond, in return, will defend the territories and 'castles' as his own, releasing them to Peter or heirs on repayment of the loan: *Layettes*, i. 286–8. No explicit prohibition of 'waste' was thought to be necessary.

[162] *Layettes*, v. 182–3; in lieu of a delayed dower settlement, Count Roger (-Bernard III) takes on the management and revenues of Catalan territories so that his costs *in custodia terre vel castrorum vel villarum vel in defensione vel pro constructione vel refectione vel pro guerra nostra* will be repaid with the 230,000 sols Melgueil cash dower. In 1258 (*Layettes*, v. 229–31) Foix granted the pledge back to Raymond of Cardona *in precario* with his former rights, so that Foix can take them back again on three months' notice, the pledge and other terms remaining in force. Raymond, evidently, was unable to find the money. Later-medieval Cardona was a magnificent complex: Monreal y Tejada, *Medieval Castles of Spain*, 48–59.

usually meaning a walled town.[163] In 1211–12, similarly, to avert disruptive pressure
and undue promotion in status, King Philip II attached a ban on town-planting
to his donation of a modest patch of land and wood made to the monks of St-
Mary, Ouville.[164] The land at Le Tremblay was used for hunting, but in both cases
local disturbance, not damage to noble amenities, seems to have been the difficulty. Permission for plantation might, however, be sold, as King John doubtless
sold it to the Templars in Normandy in 1199.[165] Conversely, not founding a town
might also be agreed at a price, as for example Philip II in 1207–8 did in return for
no less a sum than £1,000 Paris, received from the ruling dowager Countess
Blanche of Champagne.[166]

   A convenient original summary of modes of land development is contained in
Bertrand de Panisals's petition of 1297 to Edward I. He had lost everything in
Philip IV's treacherous seizure of a large part of the duchy of Gascony (provoking a desultory war, 1294–1303), and had served Edward in frontier Périgord. By
his efforts, he claimed, devoted to:

the lord king's advantage and honour, the king acquired the *castrum* of Puy Guilhem and
in consequence the land of Bayenès, which he wrested (*extorserat*) from the hand of the
lady of Bergerac, thanks to the findings of a court of inquiry which Bertrand convened . . .
And in that territory he had the *bastide* of Roquépine constructed, and elsewhere nearby
the *bastide* of Molières, close to Cadouin abbey, and another called Montpazier, in which
place many thefts, robberies, and murders were at that time being perpetrated, with killing
of pilgrims, clergy, and others. Bertrand also caused the fishponds of Lalinde to be built,
which nobody previously had ever thought of doing, much to our lord the king's profit and
honour. By reason of all these acts and achievements, which yield revenues of £1,000 annually and have gained the lord king the services of 4,000 sergeants [-at-arms], Bertrand has
several times been put in prison . . . and burdened with heavy costs by the people of the
king of France. He requests of the king compensation only for the losses he can prove that
he has suffered, offering documentary proof of his claims . . .

The endorsement on this petition (*habet litteram*) shows that it was accepted and
Bertrand duly received an order for maintenance in routine form, until he could

---

[163] Tardif, *Mon Hists*, 174–5; the countess of Dammartin's claim to residual lordship in the form of
a right of refuge and reception *in ipsa firmitate* was unresolved; perhaps a factor in 1205 (*Recueil
Philippe II*, ii. 456–7) but the ratified cession by Gaucher de Châtillon was a chase (lit. *gruerie*:
'heronry'). The monks wanted it recorded that they had paid £400 Paris to complete their Le Tremblay
holding.
[164] *Recueil Philippe II*, iii. 331–2; the 83 *acras* could scarcely contain a planted *villa*—but, as at Le
Tremblay (above), other 'development' was not excluded.
[165] *Rot Chart*, 3b; including a weekly market in the new *burgus apud Spinam Reverii* and annual fair,
near Séez (*dép*. Orne); land given to the Temple by Nicholas de Bois-Ivon.
[166] She procured the abandonment of a scheme of settlement Philip had made with the canons of
Sens. He also undertook not to support any such future project within a specified border region
extending about 10 miles south from Sens, on either side of the River Yonne. Since this created a kind
of lordly *banlieue*, the king was careful to reserve his regalian right over the archdiocese: *Recueil
Philippe II*, iii. 65–7; Jubainville, *Histoire de Champagne*, v. 47. Tenurial obscurities could be profitably
exploited indirectly as well as directly.

be reinstated.[167] His vigorous exploitation of every opportunity, including obscurities of legal title, on the edges of the Capetian abbatial lands of Sarlat, was exactly
the (purely peaceful) tactic by which Philip IV and his successors were able to take
advantage of the weaknesses of Edward II. Malcolm Vale has justly assessed the
cost to political stability, both within the duchy and on its amorphous and porous
borders, of not always scrupulous *bastide* plantation.[168] Under Edward I, royal
agents received full support from an acquisitive master very well versed in Gascon
affairs. Bertrand de Panisals was told, with more than perfunctory politeness, 'the
king is well aware of Bertrand's services and is well pleased therewith, so no letters
testimonial need be submitted.'[169]

The purpose of this *bastide*-plantation and other development in the later thirteenth century, as generally in the south after *c.*1209, was to create a *fait accompli*
everywhere of established and remunerative lordship unrelated to 'external'
borders. French designs on Gascony increasingly made the territories of the outer
bastides into an embattled frontier zone extending over the catchment areas of the
upper Dordogne and Garonne rivers as far south as the Pyrenees. Thus, on both
'sides', land development based on the walled *bastides* became an instrument of
defence in the sense of creating firmly exploited peripheral areas. In the duchy, the
seneschals (central and provincial) or other agents frequently had a standing
commission to receive, investigate, and, if acceptable, commit ducal resources to
implementing schemes of 'population'.[170] In the French seneschalcies of Toulouse,
Carcassonne, Beaucaire, Saintonge, Poitou, and Périgord, all representing lands
annexed to the Crown after 1229 (most of them formally on the death of Alphonse
de Poitiers in 1271), special 'masters of the forests of Languedoc' were given systematic powers of investment, including *bastides*, in 1316.[171] Before the period of intensifying direct royal intervention in the Midi and south-west, under Alphonse,
brother of Louis IX, count of Toulouse by his wife Jeanne from 1249, the more
purely economic aspects of new towns are conspicuous, thanks in part to the
survival and publication of Alphonse's acts and letters.[172]

[167] *Rôles Gascons*, iii, app. pp. clxxxv–vi (no. 4 of a batch of petitions dealt with by Edward I at
Plympton, after Easter 1297). On Puy Guilhem, a castle with adjacent town, see Gardelles, *Châteaux
du sud-ouest*, 202. Bergerac was found to have been conferred only temporarily (*in commendam*) by
Earl Richard of Cornwall, brother of Henry III, in 1225–7: F. Powicke, *Henry III and the Lord Edward*,
174–5. For Roquépine, Molières, and Monpazier (*sic*) (*dép.* Dordogne), Beresford, *New Towns*, 583–4,
585–6.
[168] Vale, *Origins of the Hundred Years War*, 152–60. A condensed survey.
[169] *Rôles Gascons*, iii, no. 4475. Henry de Lacy, earl of Lincoln, commander of Anglo-Gascon forces,
was to restore any of Bertrand's lands recaptured. In the meantime he was to be paid enough to keep
himself and his wife, particularly 'as he had been imprisoned for the king's sake': a frequent French
method of intimidating duchy officials by demonstrating that their master could not protect them.
[170] e.g. *Rôles Gascons*, ii. 3 (1274); 67, 93 (1279); 253 (1285).
[171] *Registres du Trésor*, ii. 266. Capetian expansion here was part of the vast takeover of power from
the native dynasty of Toulouse which followed eventually from their defeat in the Albigensian
'Crusade'. *Bastide* building continued earlier repressive fortress-policies: Coulson, 'Sanctioning of
Fortresses in France', 96–8. The 1316 enabling merely consolidated previous grants of authority:
Correspondance A. de Poitiers, i. 155 (1267); 515, 559–60 (1268), etc. Valuable Introduction by Molinier
and Fournier to *Enquêtes A. de Poitiers*.
[172] Discussing Alphonse's actions in the Agenais, claimed by Henry III after the Treaty of Paris

Through his special lieutenant in the Midi, Sicard Alemann, and his regional seneschals, the largely absentee Alphonse stimulated from Paris ecclesiastics, secular lords, minor gentry, and even groups of peasants and villagers to put forward projects for new fortified agrarian centres. Pressure of rising population chiefly, but also 'honour and profit'—that is, extension and glorification of lordship combined with increase of revenues—drove forward the whole process. It began to press upon the Gascon marches of Quercy, Rouergue, Béarn, and on Bigorre in the foothills of the Pyrenees, and upon ('French') Navarre; but the regular procedure in administrative terms was primarily reactive, investigatory, arbitral, facilitating, and judicial. At times the process seems to have been on auto-pilot—an instinctual and conditioned response to local circumstances which only gradually developed any sense of 'strategic' direction. Procedure was routine. Promising sites would be offered, either in outright gift or in joint-tenure (coparceny), to an overlord able to satisfy objectors, to endow the new burgesses with sufficiently attractive privileges, and to put up the necessary capital in its various forms. Unilateral ventures made for trouble: as witness that of Nadillac (*dép.* Lot), founded aggressively in 1267.[173] When the proposal survived the initial stages and came to Count Alphonse's council, an inquisition taking evidence on the ground usually followed. So it was in 1269, with the claim by the monks of Belleperche that their proposed *bastide*-site would be 'advantageous to us and to the whole vicinity and redound to their honour'. Verification with the usual not-too-insincere parade of judicial impartiality (local officials will already have approved) was then followed by a formal assembly of those interested parties who were called in order to ascertain officially 'what profit or detriment would arise to us in the future by the construction of a *bastide* at that place'.[174] The ruler's 'advantage' was weighed together with the local net benefit, but leaned strongly towards 'development' and change.

Legal right was an issue often calling for circumspect handling. No site lay in a tenurial vacuum. The phrase often used by Alphonse de Poitiers's councillors was that 'inquiry be made whether we may or should make a *bastide* there without damage, injury, or wrong to another', to quote from Alphonse's writ of 1267 relating to a town, perhaps already begun, offered by the monks of Le Loc Dieu in

(1259) and eventually (1279) ceded to Edward I, Trabut-Cussac 'Bastides ou forteresses?', 83–6, argues that even in this appendage of Gascony no 'military hypothesis' is sustainable.

[173] Daurd Baras, knight, in 1267 complained that his neighbour Rater *de Castronovo* 'will have built' (*edificaverit*: fut. perf. of reported 'fact') 'a town at a certain place called Nadillac, against Daurd's wish and to his prejudice, the place being said to be his'. Nadillac (*dép.* Lot) survives. Daurd's lordship had also been challenged by a tenant of his who had refused homage and assaulted a mill of Daurd's at Cabrerets: *Correspondance A. de Poitiers*, i. 303. As instruments of lordship, mills (e.g. Leeds, Kent), granges, etc. were often adorned with 'fortifications': Berman, 'Granges in the Rouergue'; Viollet-le-Duc, *Dictionnaire de L'architecture*, art. 'Moulin'; Parker, *Domestic Architecture*, ii, f.p. 151 (Abbot's Barn, Filton, Som.; with cruciform-oillet 'loops'; 14th cent.) Many such examples.

[174] All this from the proceedings leading apparently to Cordes-Tolosanes *bastide* (*dép.* Tarn-et-Garonne): *Correspondance A. de Poitiers*, i. 614. The site offered was significantly called *Granchia nova*, 'which is asserted to belong to our fief and lordship'.

Rouergue, belonging to the colonizing Cistercian order.[175] The place was known as La Salvetat, a name which in various forms often denotes both 'castles' and *bastides*. A name to reassure settlers no doubt highlighted alluring freedoms to be set out in local proclamations.

Great lords of this region, such as the viscounts of Turenne, Lomagne, and Béarn, and the counts of Foix, Comminges, and Armagnac, were often able to develop lands, responding themselves to local initiatives but resisting with increasing difficulty 'French', 'English', and 'Spanish' pressures. Turenne was vulnerable, though the viscount's franchise naturally included 'high justice', the right to use weapons to enforce protections and safe-conducts, cognizance and power to try infractions of the arms-ban (Part II, Ch. 1, sec. 2 above), and also (nominal) immunity from extraneously supported *bastides*, 'French' or 'English'. He failed, nevertheless, before the parlement to stop the building of Tauriac *bastide* in 1279.[176] The conjoined counts of Foix and Comminges strove continually to exclude foreign plantations, chiefly sponsored from Alphonse de Poitiers's territories, royal, not merely Capetian, after 1271. On the whole Alphonse, unlike his successors, seems to have been moderate. The foundation of Gaillac-Toulza was proposed to him by the Cistercian monks of Calers, but his officials' inquest reported that the site was 'on the frontier of the noble man the count of Foix'. As in apparent law it was under Alphonse's lordship work did proceed, but in 1277 the count made a claim on the *bastide* itself and its territory, indicating that the exact boundary was still undefined.[177] Proof of lordship, in the absence of compelling documentation, ultimately depended on actual use: who collected the revenues and who stocked the land.

On the march between Brecon and Glamorgan, in South Wales, this was the issue in the contest between Earl Gilbert de Clare and Earl Humphrey de Bohun, which came to a violent head in 1289, leaving the unfinished ruins of Morlais

---

[175] 'In Gascony the Cistercian contribution to urbanization was immense': Beresford, *New Towns*, 132, referring to Higounet, e.g. 'Bastides et frontières' (1948), a 'military' interpretation heavily criticized by Trabut-Cussac. *Correspondance A. de Poitiers*, i. 91–2. The vernacular site-name was *Garride Salvahucum*. Assurance was technically needed that the monks were duly entitled; that a *bastide* would be *nobis et patrie utilis, valde et necessaria*; and regarding the location and (present) revenues: 'and should we decide *ibidem bastidare*, whether it would be locally expedient, and under what terms and conditions, etc.'

[176] *Les Olim*, ii. 147; *Actes du Parlement*, i, i, 215: a curt entry—the monks of Dalon had 'associated' Philip III in the place of Tauriac for building a *bastide* there. Despite prejudice to them alleged by Garner de Castelnau and by Turenne, 'it was declared that the *bastide* shall be set up there and shall remain'. When the viscounty was transferred to Plantagenet mesne lordship in 1263, under the 1259 Treaty of Paris, Turenne's immunities were laid down: *CPR, 1258–66*, 244–5, 256 (*Foedera*, i, i, 425–6); confirmed 1280–8, 1350, 1373, 1380: *Ordonnances*, vi. 522–6. The rendering of Turenne and Saint Céré castles (*déps*. Corrèze, Lot) was tactfully limited to one banner-placing at will per reign, with giving up of the keys but no evacuation by the *vicomte*'s people.

[177] *Correspondance A. de Poitiers*, i. 131; ii. 83, 105 (1267–9); also i. 500, 580–1 (1268), 559–60 and note (Gaillac-Toulza). Plenitude of resources tended to overbear technicalities. Most decisions were inherently 'political'. For cases involving the *vicomte* of Lomagne (1269) and *vicomte* Gaston VII of Béarn (1285) see ibid. ii. 150–1 and *Rôles Gascons*, ii. 248.

castle as a memorial.[178] Something not dissimilar was happening on the Gascon border in 1281–2, but in that case unequal negotiations between Philip III (1270–85) and Edward I had to resolve the problem. The facts from the Gascon perspective are recounted in a letter to the *roi-duc* from Count Gerald of Armagnac at Péronne in Flanders, he having been arrested by King Philip's agents and taken to Paris.

To his most illustrious and dear lord Edward, by the grace of God king of England, duke of Aquitaine, and lord of Ireland, Gerald, count of Armagnac and Fezensac, presents his greetings and most devoted readiness of service—Know, lord, that Lord Bernard of Astarac has built a new *bastide* within the territory belonging to Auch [city, *dép.* Gers], which *bastide* the last king of France had taken into his protection with the intention that its inhabitants may the more freely and safely occupy our lands and our men's lands. Now, it happened one day whilst we were at Toulouse, having been there the four previous days, that the men of the *bastide* descended upon Auch and stole a great many sheep. They were pursued by the men of Auch and a conflict ensued in which many men on both sides were wounded, and some of those from the *bastide* were actually killed.

Being in Toulouse when the French seneschal heard of the affair was bad luck.[179] Gerald was held responsible, accused in the seneschal's court, and (so he says) refused justice as the injured party. Official partisanship and opportunism then took its course. When Gerald refused to accept the verdict and appealed to the supreme court in Paris, the seneschal had him taken there under escort, using the pretext of the affray to seize the city of Auch itself:

Since the lord king of France has now taken possession of the *castrum* of Auch and is building there (*et operetur ibi*), exercising the jurisdiction which is our right within the city and without; and since the bailiffs of the *bastide* are violently occupying our lands, depriving us of our rights and jurisdiction by armed force, so that nowhere can we get justice—to you yourself do we resort, asking and, indeed, requiring you to do what your honour dictates in this matter, taking our imminent peril into consideration: for, after God, it is in you that we most trust, above all men.

The count of Armagnac had purely legal action in mind. King Philip was Edward's overlord for the duchy of Gascony and had rights which could easily be— and especially 1294–1303 and 1318–28 were to be—severely abused.[180] All Gerald asked was that Edward should 'send to the next judicial session of the Parlement . . . someone to tell me what you think'. He also wanted the seneschal

[178] n. 78 above. See also Rees, *Caerphilly Castle*, 32–8; Pugh (ed.), *Glamorgan County History III*, e.g. 57–9.

[179] On the aggressive activism of the seneschals of Toulouse see Vale, *Origins of the Hundred Years War*, 93; background in detail, pp. 80–112. Count Gerald's cynicism about French motives (*ut liberius et securius habitatores dicte bastite possent terras nostras et nostrorum hominum occupare*) was realistic: *Lettres de Rois*, i. 163–4 ('1273').

[180] Bémont, *Rôles Gascons*, iii, pp. cxxiv–clxxxii. The occasion of French seizure in 1294 was the rendering, in token of Philip IV's suzerainty, of the principal places in the duchy. On the question of original, and the problem of historiographical, nationalism see Vale, *Origins of the Hundred Years War*, foreword (1995), and Coulson, 'Community and Fortress-Politics in France', esp. 102–3.

of Gascony, his fellow magnate John de Grailly, to instruct the attorneys regularly retained in Paris to keep a watching brief over Gascon matters at court, 'to act as my legal advisors and to assist my defence'. Such intervention, until the drive to seize Gascony entirely took over in Paris, generally procured some moderation of the zeal of local officials who, like Bertrand de Panisals on Edward's behalf, could often be more royalist than the king. The tenurial proprieties had to be observed, a view reiterated by John de Grailly writing to King Edward in 1282 about the Armagnac affair. Not only had Count Gerald suffered; so had his brother, the archbishop of Auch. Grailly told the king: 'it seems to me and to many others that if the brothers are thus oppressed they will at length be compelled to submit themselves, through who knows what trumped-up pretext, to the lord king of France; nor do I believe that they can endure these afflictions much longer.'[181]

Development involved some confrontation, since expansion was never into a political void, but economic imperialism only became conquest by assimilation when space ran out and the mechanism of expansion was not reined in. It continued to operate during the partial French occupation of Gascony. In 1305, newly restored to the whole of his duchy after nine years disseisin, Edward I directed the seneschal to act on a petition concerning a coparceny agreed under the Capetian occupation for a *bastide* to be set up at Saint-Julien-de-Colorbisse (*dép.* Lot-et-Garonne). The circumstances of its origin made no difference; the pact was treated as valid, subject to confirmation that it was indeed 'beneficial'.[182] But financial conditions were now not favourable. After 1303 requests for compensation, building grants, and other subventions, previously rubber-stamped, were constantly turned down on the ground that 'the king's debts must be paid'. Financial crisis caused by local war-damage, the showy extravagance of the Welsh castles, constitutional problems in England, and the by-now clearly unsuccessful Scottish war, all meant a shift of advantage in penetration by colonization towards the Capetians. The notorious incompetence of Edward II (1307–27) left Gascony to its own resources. By the time that Edward III had dealt with the Scots and begun his campaign in Picardy (1337) against Philip VI de Valois, with the eventual aim of freeing Gascony entirely from French suzerainty, the tide of buoyant population had begun to ebb. War and then plague severely depleted the motive power of economic development, and productive investment was switched into wasteful and damagingly systematic conflict. It was as though a new ethos, that of the economically hostile *chevauchée*, typified by the Black Prince's Poitiers campaigns of 1355–7, was reversing and perverting the constructive ideals of the *bastide*-building era, which almost died in the 1330s.[183] National antagonism was

---

[181] *Lettres de Rois*, i. 310–12 ('*c.*1283', but referring to the Welsh revolt and dated in the text 31 March). Grailly's phrase is *per aliquem modum excogitatum*. Same spirit in a *c.*1310 petition to Philip IV by Edward II with Philip's replies: ibid. ii. 39–47. John Balliol, Edward I's intended puppet king of Scots, was considerately treated by comparison.

[182] *Rôles Gascons*, iii. 467–8. Jordan de L'Isle, knight, petitioned for his *pariagium* to be confirmed. If not *ad nostrum utilitatem* the local 'agreements and rights' were to be restored to the *status quo ante*.

[183] M. Prestwich, *Edward I*, 521–36, ch. 19 *passim*; Beresford, *New Towns*, 303–6; K. Fowler, *Plantagenet and Valois*, 13–15, 50–5; Hewitt, *Black Prince's Expedition*, 1–13, 46–9.

one factor—the suspicions expressed by Gerald of Armagnac and John de Grailly as early as 1282 were certainly typical of Gascon opinion. The long-term animosities which Malcolm Vale has so fully analysed finally broke out. By the time of the Saint-Sardos affair, which was the most reckless foray by *bastide* intrusion (1318–24) in its long and varied record, economics had become incidental.[184]

For these reasons it is worth emphasizing that, although aggression was an aspect of colonization, encroachment by *bastides* sometimes stretched but did not flout the law. Their names, in the case of descriptive styles, throw much light on the question. We find, for instance, Montségur, Sauveterre, Bonnegarde, and, of course, chastel, castillon, *Grande Castrum*, castillonnès, etc; but also Beaumont, Beauregard, Beauville, Miramont, Monclar, Montaigu, Montfort, Montréal, Roquépine, and Villefranche as names of heartland and 'frontier' towns indifferently.[185] Moreover, as Trabut-Cussac and Maurice Beresford have so fully demonstrated, no conflict model is required. Plantations in England were not part of any civil war. Even in Ireland (Part III, Ch. 2, sec. 1 above) economic and demographic adversity had no 'military' solution, despite the conventional gesture made, for instance, in Edward III's concession of security of tenure and some financial help to the tenants of Crumlin manor (a mere 122 acres) near Dublin. The grant, in 1336, was made on condition that 'they or their heirs enclose and fortify Crumlin town within ten years against invasions by the Irish'. They had, no doubt, ambitiously suggested that this could alleviate their condition, 'wasted and plundered for lack of enclosure and fortification'.[186] Taking this literally would be to succumb to what Trabut-Cussac has called the 'seductive simplicity' of the military hypothesis. Clear thinking is complicated by the medieval vogue for such language.[187]

What mattered far more was that rulers were expected to make at least an affirmative contribution to the battlements. Because 'fortification' had seignorial functions, defence being but one, the standard lord's part was 'to make the first enclosure', consisting usually of a ditch and palisade. His authority and participa-

---

[184] n. 153 above; e.g. *Rôles Gascons*, iv. 578–82; *Les Olim*, iii. 1299–1300; *Actes du Parlement*, i, ii, 248, 386, 483–4 (calendar only). The Gascon charge that *les Franceys se efforcet de faire bastide en millieu du tout Agenays en leu appelle Saint Serdos . . . en duchee* was first (1318) upheld by the parlement. Reopened in 1322, the inquiry reversed this, ignoring Edward II's proctors' protests.

[185] Gardelles, *Châteaux du sud-ouest*, place-name index, shows such titles used indifferently for *bastides*, towns, and 'castles' (in the modern sense). The *bastida de Salvaterra* is Sauveterre-de-Guyenne (*dép*. Gironde); *bastida nostra vocata de Bona Garda* is Bonnegarde-en-Chalosse (*dép*. Landes): *Rôles Gascons*, ii. 144–5, 178–9. Conversely, Sauveterre-la-Lémance (*dép*. Lot-et-Garonne) is a solitary, 'strategically' placed 'castle' in NE Agenais, facing French Périgord and Quercy, built after Edward I's acquisition of the Agenais (1279), with 'strong' compact *enceinte* and *donjon*, but numerous non-defensive ('archaic') features: Gardelles, *Châteaux du sud-ouest*, 220–2. La Sauve Majeure was an abbey (*dép*. Gironde).

[186] *CFR, 1327–37*, 497–8.

[187] Trabut-Cussac, 'Bastides ou forteresses?', 82. But 'strategic' theorizing is not only a modern mode: Gerald of Wales (*Cambrensis*) in 1190 (*Expugnatio Hibernica*) proposed a scheme for the conquest of Ireland relying on castles which, as McNeill has shown, was purely theoretical, quite impracticable, and ignored by the Anglo-Norman invaders themselves: 'Hibernia Pacata et Castellata', 261, 268–70.

tion were necessary to sanction the setting aside of the built area and to support the new burgesses at law. Sometimes the construction of permanent gateways in stone—just as much as enclosure, the mark of a borough—was also paid for, as at Puymirol (alias *Grande Castrum*) with three other Agenais *bastides* in 1283.[188] The burgesses' and new settlers' part was then to complete the circuit, for which permission to take stone, timber, and other materials in the vicinity was accorded. Commercial and jurisdictional privileges were among the benefits to be expected from great-lord sponsorship. Optimism was quite often excessive: in 1276 Luke de Tany, as seneschal of Gascony, had founded Castelnau-sur-Gupie (*bastida castelli novi*; *dép.* Lot-et-Garonne), as well as Miramont (*castrum seu locum*), and also Castetcrabe (*bastida castri Crabe*; both *dép.* Landes). Of these Castetcrabe was noted in 1283 as 'held back owing to lack of privileges, of new population and of building (*bastide*)'. Deficient in all the essentials, it was again promoted but seems not to have prospered.[189]

Créon, a mere 13 miles from Bordeaux, was an emphatic prestige project of the seneschal in 1315. Its 'fortification' was accordingly prominent. The third section of its forty-clause charter laid down that: 'we will and grant that stones, rocks, or quarries, if any be discovered within the territory (*districtus*) of this *bastide*, may be exploited under the supervision of the bailiffs and jurats without paying any dues of the forest.' Seizure of burgess-property for debt did not customarily extend to personal belongings such as clothes and bedding. Such essential items as the tools of a man's trade were often exempt as well. At Créon this immunity extended to 'the weapons which the burgesses will need for the defence of the said town'. Perhaps recollections of the French occupation of Bordeaux in 1294–1303 still rankled. Ten years' exemption from *aides* (taxes) and power to levy contributions towards the cost of 'works of common utility' (meaning streets, walls, market-places, bridges, etc.) were quite normal; but power to 'banish' throughout the peninsular, wine-producing land of Entre-Deux-Mers to punish their convicted offenders, freedom from the cherished and lucrative Bordeaux city toll on wines, and capital jurisdiction were perquisites of the most distinguished of borough liberties. Clause 26 is more conventional: 'Item, we will and grant that the lord king and duke [*sic*] shall make and be bound to have erected the *prima clausura*, namely the gateways (*portalia*)'.[190]

Just as castle-*caput* and castellary were collectively 'the castle', so the built and enclosed area, with market-place, church and 'cemetery', house-plots, common hall, ovens, and other buildings (usually on a grid-plan), combined with its 'district', similarly comprising arable, pasture, wood, and banal area or *banlieue*, collectively comprised 'the *bastide*'.[191] At Puymirol in 1293 *castrum* had the specific

---

[188] *Rôles Gascons*, ii. 13–16 (details), 213–14. Region handed over only in 1279, but due to Edward I since the death of Alphonse de Poitiers (1271).

[189] Ibid. ii. 175–6; iii, p. cxiii (identified as Lacrabe-en-Chalosse).

[190] Ibid. iv. 471–5. The style *dominus rex et dux* is not a formula of the English chancery (which used just *rex*) but it is found in local Gascon use, here clearly derived from the petition.

[191] In *c.*1305 the burgesses of Beaumont-en-Périgord (*dép.* Dordogne) told Edward I that they had

occasional sense of the actual town wall. In that year those inhabitants whose houses adjoined the fortifications (*coherentes castro predicto*) were allowed to put up 'temporary' structures against the walls of the town (also *castrum*).[192] The peasant labour-force of the extra-mural *districtus*, as was customary with other kinds of fortress (Ch. 3, sec. 3 below), could also be called upon. An entry headed 'concerning our castle of Pouillon' on the roll of the Lord Edward's administration in 1254 awarded the inhabitants this help, but from the whole bailiwick of Dax (*dép.* Landes).[193] A number of aspects are here combined:

We have granted to all who come to settle at Pouillon, our castle (*castrum*) which we have recently had enclosed, that since they shall belong to our bailiwick of Dax, they shall do us military service (*exercitum*) in company with the burgesses of Dax, but cavalry-service (*cavalgatam*) they shall do . . . at the discretion of our lieutenants. And to them we have conceded that they may take timber for all the enclosure of the castle in the usual way. For digging out the ditches and carriage of the palisading (*clausuram*) to the castle they may call upon and use (*vocare et habere*) the men of the bailiwick. And all men, wherever they may come from, who wish to settle there the burgesses may duly accept (*recipere*)—all of these points, and every one of them, being subject to doing no detriment to ourselves or to anyone else.

The final proviso is almost universal, express or implied, recognizing that the king-duke shared powers and had to be vigilant. In October 1255 a second charter *pro castro de Polun* safeguarded others' interests by stipulating that settlers must be king's men. A site for a (fortified) dwelling (*domus*) was also reserved and one for the ducal market, banal mills, and ovens. Also kept back by the Gascon treasury, located in the old castle of Bordeaux, were the market dues together with choice cuts of pork and beef from beasts slaughtered at Pouillon for sale. This was an unusually tight leash on which the townspeople were held, but they were able to elect their own bailiff to try cases on the king-duke's behalf. The same formula, whether for convenience or even-handedness, was repeated simultaneously (1255) in favour of 'the castle of Saint George' (Saint-Geours-d'Auribad, *dép.* Landes).[194]

    These village-towns, most of them deeply immersed in the life of the country-

---

lost six parishes of land from their *districtus* on the outbreak of 'the war in Gascony' (i.e. late 1293), unjustly seized by Renaud de Pons, lord of Bergerac. Recovering this by suing in the French royal court had cost them as much as £1,000 Tours. Their request for aid for their walls out of local ducal revenues had to be refused owing to the financial crisis: *Lettres de Rois,* i. 377–9 ('*c.*1290': cf. *Rôles Gascons,* iii, p. clxxviii).

[192] *Rôles Gascons,* iii. 67, 74–5; cf. Beresford, *New Towns,* 625. At this date the king's share of the work had still not been done; cf. Valence d'Agenais (*dép.* Tarn-et-Garonne) where, in 1285, Edward I had ordered *unum portale cum clausura et fortalicio competenti* to be constructed at his expense: *Rôles Gascons,* ii. 252.

[193] *Rôles Gascons,* i, *Supplément,* 3, '*de castro Pelione*' (title on roll), or *Polionis castrum nostrum.* Gardelles, *Châteaux du sud-ouest,* 198, 229, accepts that this 'château' was a township (on terminology, ibid. 13). Where a site comprised a *burgus* and a fort, deciding which is meant requires great care; e.g. at Tournan d'Agenais, a *bastide* chartered in 1283 (*Rôles Gascons,* ii. 213–14, 252: with Puymirol, Monclar, Monflanquin all styled *villa*) Edward I in 1285 ordered 'the buildings of our castle (*castri*) of Tournan to be constructed and completed in the fashion as begun'.

[194] *Rôles Gascons,* i, *Supplément,* 43–4; *pro castro de Polun.* The grant to take timber for enclosing Pouillon was reiterated. The charter *pro castro sancti Georgii,* near Dax city, is almost verbatim.

side more than in trade, were nevertheless, like the great *villes fermées*, dignified
and given honour by their fortifications. Like ordinary 'castles', they were dependent on their territories, though their governance was communal, not personal
and their officials variantly elective. These *bastides* were in nature, as well as
frequently in name, fortresses of a characteristic but typical expansionary and
colonizing sort.

3

Populace and Fortresses:
Protection and Perquisites

The peasantry formed by far the largest social grouping, still outnumbering many times over the combined nobility, clergy, and townspeople, long after the end of the fifteenth century.[195] This preponderant majority deserves at least parity of treatment—peasants were affected by fortresses in some ways more than was any other class. Materials for a social history of castles would be seriously incomplete if they covered only the habits and class-ethos of the secular, ecclesiastical, and urban aristocracies who built and regularly occupied almost all medieval fortresses. Country labourers might gain liberty of a sort, and serfs be enfranchised, by eluding the restrictions on migrating into the castle-community of a *bastide* or of a proud walled town, with the potential of acquiring full citizen-rights. The castellary and its capital 'castle' (of whatever type) impinged on all inhabitants. But a rounded picture is difficult to achieve, not least within the limitations of the sources which have been searched. More than elsewhere, therefore, this treatment must be oblique as well as short on generalization.[196] For the fourteenth and fifteenth centuries mainly, it is possible to illustrate how fortresses operated to protect refugees and their moveables. The duties laid upon the inhabitants of castellaries by the perquisites of their lords and by necessity can also be described, but largely because those obligations and profits entered the aristocratic written record. Villages and rural dwellers did sometimes barricade their churches as emergency refuges, but probably more often than occasional references to the levies of cash and labour involved would lead us to believe.[197]

The expedient resorted to in this Part, (III) to attempt a 'majority-weighting', has been to consider the rural-dweller as an aspect of colonization, by castles and by *bastides* (Ch. 2 above). War also affected him, but its impact on the countryside figures in the examined royal records largely because of the fiscal aspect.

---

[195] Reynolds, *Kingdoms and Communities*, 108–54, examines the nature and extent of collective rural and village community and common activity.

[196] For a conceptual, top-downwards but empathetic, view, see Freedman, *Image of the Peasant*; overall but detailed social conspectus, M. Barber, *Two Cities*, 24–59 (esp. 45–8).

[197] Case of Gonesse church, Timbal (ed.), *Guerre de Cent Ans*, 166–7 (1365); cf. Wright, *Knights and Peasants*, for 1337–1453, more broadly sourced; also Allmand (ed.), *Society at War* (England and France), *passim*.

Protecting subjects was a matter of the ruler's pride. The local integration of peasant and fortress during hostilities and rumours of war was especially intimate, in England after Edward II's defeat by the Scots (1314), in France much more so after the first phase of the Hundred Years War had relapsed into intermittent regional strife, particularly after the calamity of Poitiers (1356).[198]

1. The Refuge-system in England and the Channel Islands

It has been usual to think of fortresses as possessing an 'offensive' function. As bases only this may sometimes be so, but the primary military purpose of a fortress, be it a castle (in the modern sense), a walled town, fortified abbey, church, or other structure, regular or converted ('incastellated'), was to shield inmates and refugees within its enclosure. The protection of the entire circumscription by maintaining a mounted patrolling force was prohibitively costly and seldom possible. Even manning (falling well short of 'garrisoning') at a level to avert surprise seizure was highly abnormal. The economic infrastructure, which was the land and those who made it productive, presented frequently insuperable difficulties. This is the salient conclusion, in particular, from considering the northern counties of England under Scottish counter-attack and raiding in what then were the novel circumstances arising after the expiry of the impetus of Edward I's attempts to subjugate the Lowlands. The long and seemingly traditional peace on the Borders gave way to 200 years of endemic turbulence, despite Edward III's early pre-emptive campaigns.[199]

The early consequences are illustrated by a petition presented in about 1319 to the king in parliament on behalf of three prisoners of the Scots, taken hostage as security for the still-unpaid sum of £400 of 'ransom' money, extorted to spare the land from devastation 'at the last invasion of England . . . from all the people of the Vale of Pickering'. There was very little else that could be done. Honour and public appearances demanded a royal campaign, punitive, if unable to be preventive. Fortresses without an army were almost powerless. The answer by Edward II's council, endorsed on the petition, was pusillanimous but realistic: the facts were to be verified, and then instructions sent to the sheriff of York 'to levy the money from those who assented, and were thereby saved, according to the value of their lands and chattels, sending the money by elected men of the district to Scotland to secure delivery of the prisoners'. All such forms of self-help, including paying protection money, were acceptable.[200]

---

[198] Narrative summaries with further analysis: e.g. Allmand, *Hundred Years War*; Burne, *Crécy War* (pp. 275–321: Battle of Poitiers); Perroy, *Hundred Years War* (trans.); Analytical overview, Curry, *Hundred Years War*; for administration, etc. in detail, Contamine, *Guerre, état et société* (1337–1494). The question is open whether large-scale warfare was an aberration or the apotheosis of medieval culture as *per* Ayton and Price, *Medieval Military Revolution*, introduction (but cf. pp. 5–6).

[199] Nicholson, *Edward III and the Scots*; despite 'the fruits of victory' (pp. 139–62) creating a buffer-zone (map, p. 161); Strickland, 'Securing the North'; Goodman, 'Defence of Northumberland', (social but not architectural). McNamee, *The Wars of the Bruces*, is important but has not been digested for what follows.

[200] *CDScotland*, iii. 134–5 ('*c*.1319–20'); apparently organized and presented by Henry de Percy (of

Towns might be physically secure behind their walls, but their hinterlands were exposed to this patriotic plundering which united Scots in punishing the wealthier English. After 1808, in the Spanish Peninsular War, the guerilla resistance to Napoleon similarly acted on the slogan: 'Long live King Ferdinand and let's go robbing!' In 1318 the men of the town and liberty of Ripon had to promise the Scottish invaders 1,000 marks (£666) to avert destruction by burning. By November 1320 760 marks were still outstanding and the sheriff of York was told to levy this sum on the householders and inhabitants of Ripon itself. In 1324 the balance was still unpaid, as we learn from a petition from 'six poor women of Ripon' (standard self-abasement of petition-speak), the wives of men (likely to have been substantial burgesses) who with their husbands and children had been taken hostage to Scotland for the ransom promised 'when the Scots lately came there and would have burned the town, church, and franchise'. Lord of the Liberty was the archbishop of York, who had been uncooperative: so 'Let a formal letter be sent to the archbishop . . . that, if the complaint be true, he compel the men of the town and Liberty to have the prisoners released according to their agreement.'[201] Such considerable sums, if spent on fortifications, might add to intra-mural security, but could still do little to protect people and cattle unless they came inside. In 1385 Holmcultram abbey in Cumberland yielded to the same method of making war profitable.[202] Destruction was not always, or even usually, an end in itself. To the extent that fortification responded to these dangers, it was to do little more than to mitigate the risks of kidnapping. The murder of wealthy individuals was neither lucrative nor common, and in their castellated tower-houses and halls a defiant show of pride predominated. Refugees and chattels might be sheltered in the small 'barmkin' enclosures and cramped chambers of these 'towers', but to save organized masses of retreating peasants would have required many such extensive bailies as that of Thomas of Lancaster's coastal peninsular castle at Dunstanburgh (Northumb.), licensed retrospectively in 1315.[203]

Alnwick). But Thomas of Lancaster (1322) and his captor Andrew de Harclay (earl of Carlisle, 1322–3) were charged with treason for negotiating with the Scots: McKisack, *Fourteenth Century*, 68, 75.

[201] *CCR, 1318–23*, 274. Only those owning or inhabiting houses within the town, not the Liberty, were to pay despite the endorsement to the petition in parliament: *CDScotland*, iii. 157. The six hostages had been released on parole to raise the ransom, leaving the wives and children prisoner; this 'the king considers unreasonable'. Petitioning in the wives' name was adroit. Kidnapping and 'protection' was 'a highly lucrative system of blackmail': Strickland, 'Conduct in Edward I's Campaigns in Scotland', 47–9.

[202] They paid £200 to the earl of Douglas, 'as ransom to the Scots for their abbey for one year', but were pardoned 'as they did it under necessity': *CDScotland*, ii. 78; *CPR, 1385–9*, 71. Their petition had said that they would not have presumed (*n'ossent*) to pay without royal *congé*, retrospectively asked: *Rot Parl*, iii. 181. Holmcultram's revenues were £40 p.a. in 1319, in 1379 only £11. 5s., having been £206 in 1291, but had recovered to £477 (subject to inflation) in 1535: Knowles and Hadcock, *Religious Houses*, 113, 120.

[203] A rare exception to the general lack of specific correlation with licences to crenellate, but still very doubtful: *CPR, 1313–17*, 71, 237, 344; Simpson, 'Dunstanburgh Castle', esp. 34–5; at 10 acres larger than Bamburgh, also on a coastal promontory like Tynemouth priory-castle, Dunstanburgh, Simpson argued, had great refuge-potential, but circumstances do not suggest that this was a factor (Michael

How ineffectual such mitigation was, the frequent remissions of taxes granted to devastated areas continually confess. It would be gratifying, whether to the humanitarian or to the military-minded, to be able to argue that had there only been enough fortresses of the right type the damage to rural life and productivity could have been reduced; but even curtailing noble privilege on the scale resorted to in France by Charles V could do little to save barns, fields, and crops. In Ireland and in the north of England (Part IV, Ch. 2, sec. 2 below) the consequences of this failure, due primarily to lack of means but also to lack of political will, were socially and economically very serious in some areas and periods. The architectural response was ambiguous. Manning castles like Alnwick, Wark, and Norham chiefly assured them against humiliating seizure. It did not stop invasion.[204] Delegation of defence efforts based on royal and 'baronial' castles and on the walled towns, Carlisle in particular on the West March, was generally the best that could be done—most effective when by the 'forward strategy' of holding the Lowland castle-towns of Berwick, Roxburgh, Perth, and Lochmaben systematized under Edward III.[205] Traditions of self-help and institutionalized co-operation ensured that, as well as the fortresses of the regalian palatinate of Durham, those of lesser lords, for what they were worth, were subordinated to the common defence.[206] Lords-castellan looked to royal leadership, and expected tax help, but generally made do without. But in all this, the peasant cultivator bore the brunt.

The solitary alternative to the composite defence-expedient of counter-raiding, fortress-refuge, and occasional concerted campaigns, was the ignominious but realistic course of particular or wholesale evacuation of the countryside. Withdrawal from the Border counties of unprotected livestock, valuables, and people began as early as Bannockburn (24 June 1314) and soon became an organized, and later an occasional, routine, during the summer especially, when Scottish invasion in force was most likely.[207] Animals needed pasture beyond the

Prestwich *pers. comm.*). All three had a reduced catchment-area owing to seaside location. Emery, *Greater Medieval Houses*, i, *passim*.

[204] e.g. Strickland, 'Securing the North', 209–19, agrees that 'not all castles were deemed to be defensible in a full-scale war'. Many were able to resist only 'the smallest of raiding parties', etc. Architectural study of later 'fortifications' requires more radical conclusions; e.g. Dixon, 'From Hall to Tower', esp. 99–101. Militant embellishment increased rather than 'strength': Coulson, *Castles and Crenellating*.

[205] Large sums were spent on Lowland garrisons, e.g. Berwick 1314–1508: *CDScotland*, iii. 64, 76, 106–7, 124–6, 199, 287; iv. 80–1, 88, 101, 350–1; Lochmaben (Fife), Carlisle and Cockermouth (Cumb.), iii. 64–5, 76–7, 98 (1313–16); Roxburgh, Stirling, Edinburgh, Perth, Lochmaben: iii. 226–7, 232, 258, 261–2, 283; iv. 11–12, 23, 41–2 (1335–70). Costs of works detailed, Brown *et al.*, *King's Works*, i. 409–22 etc.

[206] Examples of co-operation: *CDScotland*, iii. 110–11; iv. 70 (Wark, 1316; Scots' compensation for illicit damage during truce, 1383); iii. 115, 122, 125, 143–6 (Mitford, Norham, 1318–22); iii., 145–6, 163–4 (Bamburgh, Warkworth, Dunstanburgh, Alnwick, and Melmerby tower, 1322–6), etc. In 1314 Norham was lent for three years by the bishop of Durham; a 'peel' or fort was to be built in his manor of Northallerton, 'at the king's expense for the safety of those parts' (*CPR, 1313–17*, 163–4). Hornby castle (Lancs.) was used as a defence centre, 1323–4. In 1322 the Scots vainly besieged it for 13 days (*CCR, 1318–23*, 695; *1323–7*, 84); etc.

[207] e.g. (Aug. 1314): '. . . safe-conduct, for one year, for the men of the abbot of Newminster driving and conveying his animals, stock, and goods towards the south . . . the Scots having wasted a great part of his goods in Northumberland and continue to do so' (*CPR, 1313–17*, 163).

resources of castle parks and demesnes, unless for short periods. But denying supplies and booty to the invaders was as much a priority.[208] The arrangements ordered in May 1323 (as calendared) were particularly thorough. Attack had to be anticipated, not awaited—which involved guesswork:

Mandate to the sheriff of Cumberland to make proclamation that, as the Scots may invade the realm . . . all persons in his bailiwick are . . . to take their animals towards the parts of Yorkshire where they will be safe from the incursions of the enemy; and their victuals, stock, and all other goods to castles and walled towns for safety, so that the enemy if they invade the county may not have any sustenances. The king has also commanded John de Crombwell, keeper of the forest on this side [north] of Trent, and the sheriff of York to permit such persons to come to the forest and depasture the same with their beasts free of charge . . . and all constables of castles and keepers of walled towns . . . are commanded to permit them to bring in their victuals, stock, and goods, and to remain therein.

This was backed up by mandates to the king's constables of Scarborough, Tickhill, Pontefract, and Knaresborough, and to the sheriff of York, to receive the refugees.[209] Moreover, the sheriff was 'to inform the keepers of castles and walled towns within his county that they are to permit such persons to enter and lodge therein'. Next month (8 June 1323), after a truce with the Scots, the precaution was still taken of appointing two commissioners 'to summon before them at Newcastle on Tyne all [sic] constables of castles in the northern parts to inform the commissioners of the state of the said castles and of the victuals therein'.[210] Similar instructions and exhortations to ensure an orderly withdrawal had gone in May to the sheriffs of Northumberland and Westmorland, and to the bishop of Durham and to many other magnates and officials. The rather inert Edward II was not above blaming others.[211] In such exhortations the danger had to be exaggerated, and much guesswork based largely on rumour covered up, in order to get action in time. The scale and direction of attack, whether on the west towards Carlisle or east towards Newcastle, could not be clear until too late.[212] Great disruption of the seasonal tasks of agriculture was caused, quite apart from damage directly inflicted by the passage of 'friendly' forces, and by the foraging and deliberate destruction of the invaders. The famous 'scorched earth policy'

---

[208] e.g. (July, 1322): mustering ordered of armed men from Cumberland, Westmorland, and Lancashire, 'for the repulse of the Scots who are about to invade the Marches'; but also for the inhabitants to drive 'all their animals . . . [southwards] with all speed . . . lest they be captured and taken away . . . or those enemies be thereby supplied or in any fashion sustained'. Recipient counties were to help, charging nothing (sic) for pasturage, '. . . the king having ordered that the like shall be done in his forests, chases and other pastures' (Foedera, ii, i, 489, 496; CPR, 1321–4, 140; CCR, 1318–23, 680).

[209] CPR, 1321–4, 288–9.

[210] The maintenance of sufficient men in each castle was to be ensured by written contract: CPR, 1321–4, 295. Such direct intervention with non-royal fortresses was unusual. Local agents, drawn from the nobility, had perforce considerable discretion.

[211] In Feb. 1323 he told Louis de Beaumont, bishop of Durham, that his 'election' had been favoured because of expectations by his noble backers that he would be effective in defence of the north-east, which he had not been: Foedera, ii, ii, 506; CCR, 1318–23, 697.

[212] For the citizen perspective in Carlisle and often-manipulative alarmism, Coulson, 'Battlements and the Bourgeoisie', 147–56 et passim.

was, in effect, both defensive and aggressive—with great loss of standing crops, barns, houses, and peasant 'fixed assets'. Consequential losses of life, direct or due to malnutrition, caused further depopulation and distress.[213]

It was not to be expected that intensely local patriotisms and failures of altruism would allow the ideals of co-operation to be achieved. Lordly perquisites (and mere desire to extract compensation) tempted constables of castles to levy charges to admit refugees, or to release them and their goods when they left the castellary. In Northumberland an important and capacious refuge was the royal castle of Bamburgh, on the coast. In 1318 the constable was forbidden to augment his pay by charging rent, even from men of the neighbourhood, 'for the pitches (*placeis*) within the castle wherein they constructed lodgings (*logeas*) when they fled there recently on account of the burning of their houses and buildings by the Scotch rebels and on account of their frequent attacks'.[214] Calling them 'rebels' (as in Ireland) preserved the doctrine of English overlordship. Unlike 'enemies', rebellious subjects deserved no clemency.[215] Because lands in Bamburgh castellary had gone uncultivated, the constable was also told not to levy his usual rents; and the inhabitants of the township dependent on the castle had their collective rent or 'farm' (*firma* or 'fixed payment') halved because they could not pay. In 1332 the townsmen obtained a charter of borough rights from Edward III's Chancery. It included fortification, but it would be simplistic to think that this was directly defensive. The terms say the grant was made 'for the betterment of the town which was destroyed [i.e. financially ruined] by the many incursions of the Scots'. By improving their prosperity as 'a free borough and [that of] the men there living [as] the king's free burgesses', it was hoped (with conventional optimism) that Bamburgh town would deserve and be able to pay for the status-enhancement implied by 'fortifying the said borough with a wall of stone and mortar and crenellating the same'.[216] This had no more reality than the privileges granted to them back in 1255: in September 1322 fugitives from the Scots in Bamburgh castle had had to be pardoned for negotiating directly with the harassing Scottish forces 'for the purpose of saving their houses, corn, and other goods'. Fortifying the town was an aspiration which was neither necessary or practicable. They were allowed 'to stay in the castle and to save their bodies, goods, and corn henceforth by the best means, as they have been accustomed to do heretofore'.[217]

[213] The '*chevauchée*' has generated much discussion since Hewitt: n. 184 above.

[214] *CCR, 1318–23*, 39–40. The refugees had petitioned that the constable for their 'lodgement . . . exacts great sums from them'.

[215] A principle traced by Strickland as crucial in 'Conduct in Edward I's Campaigns in Scotland', in contrast with the Scottish view (pp. 41–2, 60–4, etc.); cf. the Albigensian 'crusade' in the south of France where the culture-clash caused 'all the normal conventions of warfare in the early thirteenth century to be abandoned'; M. Barber, 'Wars Like Any Other?', 45 (with acknowledgement).

[216] *CChR, 1226–57*, 449; *1327–41*, 266–7; terms exactly as for 'castles'. Fortification was a normal privilege of free-borough status, as Aberystwyth: *CChR, 1257–1300*, 206; Sutherland, *Quo Warranto Proceedings*, 817a–818b (1277).

[217] *CCR, 1318–23*, 597. Oddly, the townspeople had been admitted into the castle and had then treated with the raiders, 'with the assent of all the others in the castle'; but 'without the king's licence', implying that the constable denied responsibility. Public distress after 1314 was acute, e.g. petitions of

At Bamburgh the royal constable's perquisites of office did not allow him (in theory) to infringe the people's right to take refuge within the walls. In June 1323 he was instructed: 'to permit the men of those parts lately staying in the castle for the protection of their bodies and goods against the attacks of the Scots, to take and carry whither they wish the timber of their lodges, and their goods, chattels, and victuals in the castle and within the ditch and moat of the same.' Because 'castle' often meant 'castellary', this precision was necessary. A royal official under pressure to find his fee from local revenues, or to pay rent to the hard-nosed clerks of the Exchequer, was at least equally harsh to those under him. Bamburgh town's 1332 charter was an abortive bid for freedom. The townsmen were clearly adept at petitioning the Crown, but in 1334–6 they did guard-service in the castle, perhaps on a rota basis. Bamburgh was a pre-Conquest fortress and an ancient, well-organized castellary thereafter.[218]

A few fortified religious houses were able to take part in this refuge-system. The solidity of their curtilage walls more than their sanctity qualified them (unless as safe-deposits). In this first respect few houses in England rivalled Tynemouth priory, on its coastal promontory north of the Tyne estuary. Both St Michael's Mount, in Cornwall, and the refuge-fort belonging to Furness abbey in Lancashire (Cumbria), owed their defensibility mainly to sea-girt isolation, although the latter, called the Peel of Fouldray, was quite solidly built and digni-fied in 1327 by a licence to crenellate.[219] Many ecclesiastical precincts offered a measure of security, but Tynemouth was a veritable *moustier-fort*. Magnates and officials journeying to and from Durham frequently lodged there, which unduly strained the resources of the priory, and of its mother-house St Alban's abbey (Herts). In 1388 lobbying played upon Crown anxiety that 'the priory, being reputed a castle, is likely to be seized by traitors'.[220] In 1390 a subsidy was procured for its fortification, emphasizing its role as a local refuge:

the priory . . . by its situation at the Mouth of the Tyne, has suffered such excessive destruc-tion by the Scots that its great tower and gate, and the greater part of its walls seawards, are

Cumberland and Westmorland 'to allow them to be at war or truce with the Scots, according as they see most for his honour or their own profit'; and 'above all . . . that . . . they have peace either by covenable [suitable] war with haste' or by truce, with 'covenable sustenance for them' meanwhile: *CDScotland*, iii. 135; also 148–9. Border affairs were no better in 1378: ibid. iv. 57.

[218] Kapelle, *Conquest of the North*, 15 (sacked 993 by Danes); *CCR, 1318–23*, 662; *1333–7*, 266, 286, 386, 399, 646.

[219] Fouldray, on Piel Island (Lancs.), possibly founded *temp*. Stephen, licensed *CPR, 1327–30*, 169. Wark on Tweed was repeatedly 'lent' to the king; Tibbers (Dumfries) was built with subsidy (1298, 1300, 1302) etc.: *CDScotland*, i. 398, 425 (1256); ii. 295 (1300, Wark); 257, 291, 331–2 (Tibbers). Bates, *Border Holds*, 57–61, technically interprets 'peel'. In Leland's *Itinerary* (1535–43) it has become the vague 'pile'.

[220] Licensed to be crenellated as a priory 1296, reflecting Edward I's presence at Berwick but not (future) hostilities: *CPR, 1292–1301*, 197; context, Coulson, 'Hierarchism in Conventual Crenellation'. Royal grant of 'protection' for one year (1388) would give some relief from litigation but not from impoverishment due to 'frequent incursions of the Scots and the arrival of magnates and others flock-ing thereto for hospitality': *CPR, 1385–9*, 494.

thrown down, so that the goods of neither [St Alban's] abbey nor priory suffice for its repair, although it has been in time of war the castle and refuge for the whole country.[221]

The prior had already, during the internal crisis of 1322 (Lancaster's revolt), been made responsible for keeping 'a sufficient garrison of fencible men, both men-at-arms and footmen, to be retained in the priory, for the protection thereof'.[222] The Scots were barely involved. The abbot of Furness, on the west coast, was similarly accountable. In 1323 he was directed 'to deliver his peel [of Fouldray] near the abbey to John Darcy, sheriff of Lancaster, when required to do so by him'.[223] Fouldray was, in fact, temporarily made rendable and, like Tynemouth priory, was held in custody as a public trust. The principle applied to all fortresses that the public safety prevailed over private right—but it was seldom so explicit.

Townspeople were like ecclesiastics in controlling corporate fortresses and in being particularly amenable to royal supervision. Both were also good at lobbying the Chancery. By the head of the Solway Firth towards Scotland, the cathedral city of Carlisle was the English outpost on the West March and regional bastion. A large walled borough, coupled with a royal castle, Carlisle combined its everyday commercial business with performing occasionally the threefold task of the fortress in war of protecting its inhabitants, of receiving refugees in emergencies, and of serving as a base of operations for the constable, the bishop, and latterly for the warden of the (West) March. When Edward III, in 1352, confirmed Carlisle's borough privileges, his patent adopted the citizens' own view of the city as the regional English bulwark: 'Situated on the frontier of Scotland to be a defence and refuge of the adjacent parts against the Scots, the king's enemies.' Such language was the common currency of petitioning, but the citizens pleaded also that 'it is now wasted and more than usually depressed as well by the mortal pestilence [the bubonic plague of 1348–9] lately prevalent in those parts as by the frequent attacks of the said enemies . . .' They obviously had good reasons, but keeping control of their own defence-apparatus (walls, ditches, repairs, manning, admissions, etc.) despite pressure from the royal constable, from the cathedral priory, from the bishop, and from the warden, demanded at least as much vigilance as did the Scots. The citizens preserved their liberties (largely lost at Southampton) while keeping one eye on local rivalries and another on the Exchequer, Chancery, and bureaucracy at Westminster, playing one off against another. Carlisle is a pre-eminent example of the defence of borough autonomy deploying a range of tactics, alarmism being chief among them.[224]

---

[221] *CPR, 1388–92*, 194: £500 over two years—a lavish grant backed by John of Gaunt, Thomas of Gloucester, the earl of Huntingdon (Richard II's uncles and half-brother) and the earl of Northumberland: Butler and Given-Wilson, *Medieval Monasteries*, 369–73. It was paid out of the Newcastle customs: *CCR, 1389–92*, 194–5, 401; *1392–6*, 31–2.

[222] The prior must not allow them 'to go outside, as the prior has the keeping of the priory at his peril' (i.e. will be punished for any dereliction): *CCR, 1318–23*, 621–2.

[223] *CCR, 1318–23*, 627. Naming the sheriff indicates that the duty applied while Darcy was 'keeper of the parts of Hornby castle against the Scots' (p. 695).

[224] n. 212 above; Turner, *Town Defences*, 100–2; *CPR, 1350–4*, 232–3. In 1409 a mere £13 p.a. for 10 years was granted for repairs to city and castle. As traditionally, 'the city is situated on the frontier of

But the danger from the Scots, though often exaggerated, was at times severe. If headed south along the Eden valley, the Scots could pass Carlisle with no difficulty. In 1314–15, however, King Robert Bruce himself tried—first for a week, then the next year very actively for three—to retake this sometime Scottish possession.[225] The power which lay around the walls, unless properly equipped for besieging, usually dispersed unsuccessfully, yielding control again of the (devastated) 'open country' (in France the *plat pays*) to the citizens and to the lords of the surrounding castles. But the burgesses must often have feared the inexorable attrition of their vital hinterland. Ill-supported and apparently forgotten by rulers and magnates drawn away to 'the vasty fields of France', their feelings were expressed in a damaged document of petition, in French, of about 1385. It is a plaintive 'appeal from the Front'. Its exaggerations embroider a genuine extremity:

> Petition to the king and council by the mayor and citizens of Carlisle that [note be taken of] the Lords Percy and Clifford, marchers, and of others who were lately there on a March-day [who reported] on the state of their city. Their walls are in part fallen and great part is on the point of failing through weakness; the ditches [filled up? . . . the gates] cannot be shut without difficulty. They have neither drawbridge, portcullis, outworks, nor watch turrets . . . The inhabitants are now so few that they cannot resist the Scottish attacks. The *seigneurs* of the country around, who used to resort to the city in time of war, have now raised castles of their own on account of its weakness. Many knights, esquires, and others no longer come to the city for the same reason. The castle, which is the king's, is unenclosed on the side next to the city and utterly ruined, as the above-named lords can attest. Wherefore they beg the king and council to remedy these defects which have been laid before every parliament these ten years and nothing done.[226]

Moving from the north-west of England to the far south-east, to the Channel Islands, remnants of the duchy of Normandy and lying close to the French coast, we find very various but similar problems and partial solutions. If 'England' provoked the Scottish War of Independence, the prolonged conflict with the

---

La Westmarche of England towards Scotland, for a refuge and salvation of the said marches': *CPR, 1408–13*, 40. The citizens had pleaded that 'lately the gates and a great part of the walls have fallen to the ground and the greater part threatens ruin'. The tiny sum, and supervision of expenditure by the earl of Westmorland, show appropriate scepticism.

[225] Stocks, manning, will to resist, emergency works and demolitions, and good local command were always what mattered most: *CDScotland*, iii. 70, 72, 88, 100—'during the 12 days [*sic*] siege, the Scots attacked by night and day with *berfreys* [*beffrois* i.e. timber siege-towers] and other engines', the citizens reciprocating likewise. On Scottish possession of Cumbria *temp*. Stephen, Barrow, 'The Scots', 243–7.

[226] *CDScotland*, iv. 70. Translated as 'outworks', the French is *barmecan* (i.e. barbican, 'barmkin'), *bretage*, *bareres*: all extempore obstacles, mostly of timber, vanished and archaeologically almost untraceable, but once important. The 'march days' were consultative, judicial, and social assemblies. Despite the number of castles in the region, Cumberland in this decade had licence only for Workington Hall (1380: 'by the march of Scotland'). The bishop had licence in 1336 and 1355 for Rose castle: *CPR, 1377–81*, 447; *1334–8*, 245; *1354–8*, 252, but thereafter the scarcity of northern licences suggests indifference to court patronage. The royal castle of Carlisle, adjoining the city, was no more than adequately maintained: Brown *et al.*, *King's Works*, ii. 595–600. Hewitt, *Organization of War*, 128–30, 'Devastation in Cumberland' (1346).

Valois kings of France was rather forced upon Edward III after 1336, especially owing to Gascony. The islands of Jersey, Guernsey, Sark, and Alderney were easy targets for forays, sponsored or openly piratical. Enemy 'galleys', chiefly from Norman ports, began to harass parts of the south and east coast, even sacking Southampton.[227] Defence by exhortation and delegation was not sufficient for the Channel Islands. Royal 'Keepers' were appointed and paid to co-ordinate measures, including the repairing, manning, and stocking with food and 'artillery' of fortresses of all sorts. Popular protection was necessarily foremost. To maintain their allegiance and to uphold his own 'honour', Edward III repeatedly assured 'the community of the islands' of his support and co-operated readily with the very self-reliant islanders' initiatives in self-defence.[228] Some early examples must suffice.

In 1337 the Keeper was authorized to pay wages 'to forty men of the island of Jersey whom the community of that island placed in Gurry [Gorey] castle for its defence against the attacks of certain galleys lately come against those islands'.[229] On Guernsey the new perils led the island's leaders to have adapted as a popular refuge a large coastal promontory site, a cliff-peninsula ditched across the landward neck and resembling Iron Age coastal forts like Tintagel in Cornwall. This refuge (previously mentioned) became known as Jerbourg castle. Ten years' 'murage' tolls were authorized in April 1337 to enable Matthew de Saumareys to raise cash and loans to complete the work by the ensuing November 'of repairing [sic] his castle or fortification ... to serve as a place of refuge for the king's subjects in time of war or disturbance'.[230] An emergency ditching, embanking, and palisading with some permanent potential, but involving no changes of lordship or legal status, was envisaged.

Given the threats to the allegiance of the Channel Islands to England, tact was essential. The tone of the follow-up mandate to the Keeper was evidently found to be insensitive, not least in combining the Islands in one refuge-system:[231]

---

[227] In 1338. The finest walled town in Britain, including Conway: Turner, *Town Defences*, 165–76; psychological and fiscal analysis, Ormrod, 'Domestic Response', 83–101; Sherborne, *War, Politics and Culture*, ch. 7, 'Defence of the Realm, 1386', 99–117; and Hewitt, *Organization of War*, ch. 1, on coastal defence, compulsory defence-residence, etc. in 1338–62.

[228] All sorts of mechanical equipment was 'artillery', as well as missile 'engines' such as garrison crossbows (*balista ad turnum*, etc.). Examples of royal action are *CCR, 1333–7*, 434, 525, 586–7; *1337–9*, 220–1, 547 (detailed); *1341–3*, 117. Parallels with defence arrangements under the English kings in the Île-de-Ré group of islands off the coast of Poitou near La Rochelle, are close. They included the requisitioning of fortresses, as operative in 1372 when confirmed by Charles V: *Ordonnances*, v. 564–7.

[229] *CCR, 1337–9*, 159. Galleys were specialized Atlantic (coastal) warships, not confined to the Mediterranean: Brooks, *English Naval Forces*, ch. 7; but also standard in propagandist 'invasion scares'. Gorey or Mont Orgueil was the best fortress, continuously rebuilt: D. King, *Castellarium Anglicanum*, 'Jersey'.

[230] *CPR, 1334–8*, 413; *Girburg*, one of several variants.

[231] *CCR, 1341–3*, 375. The keeper and the 'bailiffs, jurats, and men of Jersey' were also told 'to seize all the goods of traitors supporting the French but attempting to return during truces'. This put a doubtless unwelcome slant on traditional trading with mainland France.

Order to assign to the men [i.e. people] of these islands particular places in the castle called *Gerebrok* in Guernsey and to compel them, by imprisonment and seizing their goods and chattels, to defend those places and to provision them in wartime. So that nobody may make any excuse in the matter, he shall cause proclamation to be made throughout the islands that everyone . . . shall go to the castle with all speed and take up his appointed place.

Remote-control, depending on representations sent to Court, often fell foul of local free enterprise. Insular individualism was especially strong. De Saumareys seems to have been tempted, as castellans so often were. The writ continues, somewhat naively, reciting the reason for the order, as was frequently done:

. . . since for the safety of the lieges of those islands and their goods, the king has caused the castle to be repaired at great cost, as he has learned, at the request of the men of the islands against the incursions of the king's enemies of France; and it is just that what is built for the common advantage and defence of those men shall be defended at the common cost in time of war.

Edward III was clearly anxious to justify popular castle-guard and the 'murage' sales-tax. A similar line was taken for Jersey. At Gorey, a month or more after the danger was past, in December 1342, the Keeper was told expressly to release the valuables deposited in the castle by some Jersey refugees, 'and to treat them so as to avoid future complaint'.[232] Something like the French system of *guet et garde* (sec. 4 below) was operating—but dealing with appointed outsiders caused perhaps as much friction as with self-selected leaders like Matthew de Saumareys. In the event, it seems that Jerbourg did not long remain viable. The murage tolls on trade elsewhere, costing the king nothing unless his 'customs' were thereby reduced, cannot have been popular. The Keeper was changed frequently and, though usually English, risked embroilment in inter-island politics. Such remote and normally unfrequented places as Jerbourg, though secure enough, were seldom satisfactory in the long term. Crag-sites look romantic (as on the Rhine), but unless near exploitable resources, such as trade and population, they were socially isolated and lacked proper castle-character. At all events, the burgesses of St Peter Port, Guernsey, in February 1350 won approval for their proposal to fortify the town and obtained, more materially, permission to levy murage tolls explicitly to enable the town to replace Jerbourg as a refuge.[233] In effect, they had trumped Saumareys. But they too ran into opposition. Despite the king's grant,

---

[232] *CCR, 1341–3*, 597. Petition 'by the men of Jersey' accused the Keeper's deputy of holding back 'divers sums of money and . . . victuals, garniture, and goods which they caused to be brought to the castle in that island'. So long as the islanders 'do what they ought for the custody of the castle', no further distraint was to be made.

[233] *CPR, 1348–50*, 478: 'in view of the fact that the castle of Girburgh, wherein in time of war the people used to find refuge, is destroyed and cannot be repaired to the king's advantage, as he is informed'. For one year (cautious by English standards) from April 1350, they were to take 'a custom at the rate of four [pence] *tournois* on every pound ['s worth] of merchandise bought and sold in the island, one half to be paid by the vendor and the other by the buyer'—'to enclose their town with a good and strong wall, and to crenellate such wall'.

doubtless obtained in part to suppress resistance, in August 1350 they had to procure a backup order to the Keeper exhorting him to enforce payment by merchants coming to St Peter Port. He was also to hurry on the work of walling or 'enclosure'. The writ rather bitterly complained that the levy the Crown had been persuaded to sanction 'was for their own defence and preservation and cannot be called a tallage as no part thereof is taken for the king's use'.[234] Any suggestion that the tolls were like an impost levied on unfree serfs would certainly arouse bitter local antagonism.

The contrasts with France, especially after the Valois disasters of Crécy (1346) and Poitiers (1356), should not be understated—and yet the same somewhat theoretical priority of public safety over lordly perquisites was applied, despite much stronger regional autonomy. The Valois kings had much less efficient and more decentralized representative bodies to work with (the Estates-General and regional *États*). English invasion and 'occupation', after 1356 based on Normandy, Brittany, and Gascony, necessitated permanent war taxation.[235] Consensus still mattered (the popular modern legend of an authoritarian medieval kingship still lingers on), but methods still more draconian than those attempted even in Ireland became the rule under King Charles V (1364–80). Subsequently, the power of the princes of the blood and of the great magnates tended to obstruct implementation of the rule of public safety first. In any case, the complex nature of fortresses meant that they were never as amenable to central authority as were assemblies of troops, whether the unpaid levies organized to defend the coastal 'maritime lands' in England, or the stipendiary armies employed on both sides after the first phase of the Hundred Years War.[236] Nevertheless, it is to France that we must look to see the refuge-system based on the castellary in its various forms developed to organizational and tenurial perfection. England, if not exactly 'a fortress built by nature for herself', did enjoy a relative insulation 'from infection and the hand of war'. Laissez-faire methods and exhortation, varied by sporadic royal intervention, were quite inadequate in France.

[234] *CPR, 1348–50*, 559. The ruinous state of Jerbourg was not contested, only that the islands' payment of Royal Aid exempted them from all other charges. To make his point, Edward III's council insisted that the murage should then run for a full year from 24 August. The proceeds ('a grant of £80' in 1357) paid for the Beauregard tower at St Peter Port: Brown *et al.*, *King's Works*, ii. 605. Stimulated by a French attack: *CPR, 1354–8*, 515, 562, 590. Castle Cornet, on the island in St Peter Port Bay, was 'useless as a refuge', and Jerbourg 'enormous'; Vale castle (Guernsey) and Grosnez (Jersey) were also apparently popular refuges: D. King, *Castellarium Anglicanum*.

[235] Contamine, *Guerre, état et société*, 77, 146–7, 207–8, 233; on the 1356–7 crisis, pp. 44–5, 50, 53–5, 73–4, 77, 85, 87–8, 93, 97–8, 103, 108–9, 116, 171, 200; on princely 'mediation' and consent, pp. 43–4, 50, 87, 130, 141, 151, 159, 163–5, 168–9, 172, 174–83, 194, 213, 223; on royal powers and their limitations at the outset of the great war (*c*.1336), pp. 127–31, 204–5. See also, on underestimated pre-war 'feudal' and kingly powers, Coulson, 'Community and Fortress-Politics in France', and 'Valois Powers Over Fortresses', *passim*.

[236] With due allowance for petitioner-initiative and manipulation, English 'home defence', chiefly against coastal raids, was comparatively consensual and non-coercive: e.g. *CPR, 1338–40*, 236, 275, 316, 423; *1350–54*, 323; *1367–70*, 189; *1381–5*, 553–4; *1391–6*, 85; *CCR, 1333–7*, 521, etc.

2. The Refuge-system of Castellaries in France

The effect upon the French countryside of the Plantagenet counter-offensive, initially from Flanders, which relieved the much-reduced duchy of Gascony, only slowly made its full impression.[237] It was for some time not apparent that a lengthy conflict was in preparation, or that systematic protection of the peasantry would become necessary. One battlefield defeat, at Crécy-en-Ponthieu in 1346, and the loss to Edward III by honourably resisted siege of the Channel-port town of Calais, were humiliating, not catastrophic. But a lord, and especially the king, suffered dishonour by being shown to be incapable of protecting his own people. So when rumours of an English attack on the coast of Normandy (from where the assault on Southampton and the south coast of England was mounted a decade earlier) came to the ears of King Philip VI (1328–50) in late autumn 1349, he notified his son and heir John, duke of Normandy, who set in train defence measures of familiar type. As yet these were no more interventionist, and quite as exhortatory, as were (and remained) habitual in England. We find similar arrangements for a coastal watch and preparedness, largely delegated to local leaders.[238] Officials were ordered to visit 'all notable places on the frontiers, especially those most in doubt, warning their people and others expedient . . . to be on their guard so that everyone should prepare himself on his own account'. The *bailli* was himself to be equipped in all ways and ready; works on 'fortresses and walls' were to be hastily completed; beacons were to be set up 'as is usual' at vantage-points along the coast; and the defence-arrangements of towns were to be reviewed. Naming Henry, earl of Lancaster (such exhortations came to cite 'Lancaster' as a hate-figure), as leader of the supposed attack gave some further credibility. Only when an enemy had landed and was at large were public refuge-measures required.

The problem of an enemy foraging and destroying at will over the countryside had been met already in 1347 after Crécy by ordering the people of Picardy to take refuge, without charge, in the fortresses of the region, particularly in Saint-Omer town, bringing their food with them.[239] This pattern of response was to become the norm after c.1356, with the advent of the Anglo-Navarrese 'free companies', piratical bands of soldiers of fortune of vague allegiance, living off the land. The

[237] n. 198 above; K. Fowler, *Plantagenet and Valois*, on most aspects, esp. 165–72, on the extortion of money to refrain from ravaging, termed *appatis*, mainly by the 'Free Companies' (especially after the Treaty of Brétigny, 1360), posing severe problems of people-protection.
[238] The future John the Good (II, 1350–64), prematurely styling himself also 'duke of Guienne', in three letters to the *baillif* (sic) of Caux transmitted the warning from *Monseigneur*, his father, of impending seaborne attack by the earl of Lancaster (Henry of Grosmont, duke from 1351): *Actes Normands*, 409–13. The second letter (10 Oct.), a week after the first, ordered paid troops and beacons at ports (*faire les feus sur les porz*). The third (3 Nov.) ordered a general muster in arms and visitation of *toutes les villes, bours et pors, les hostelz et les personnes d'iceulx*.
[239] With usual royalist gloss, Timbal (ed.), *Guerre de Cent Ans*, 168, n. 177. The editors err also in presuming that fortifying was a royal monopoly (refuted ibid. 112–13, countess of Evreux at Verdey, 1366), but recognize that 'la distinction des châteaux et des villes tient moins au rôle militaire ou au statut juridique qu'aux conditions de peuplement. Villes et châteaux assument la même mission défensive' in acting as refuges (p. 168).

failure of the Treaty of Brétigny (1360), due in good part to 'French' infractions, subjected great areas of the kingdom to ransoming, pillaging, 'slaying and burning' in the constant phrase, which in this uncontrolled, merciless type of war did not spare the supposedly immune peasantry or even the clergy. Partly because food was seized and partly owing to the deliberate 'tactical' devastation of 'scorched earth', denying resources to the enemy, the countryside was targeted.[240] The numerous ordinances responding to this threat may be exemplified by King Charles V's edict in 1367, promulgated after consultation with the Estates-General.[241] The preamble explains that, to prevent troops of 'the companies' from returning to vex and damage his loyal subjects, the king had summoned notable prelates and other clergy, nobles of the blood royal and others, to meet at Chartres, together with town representatives from the *parties et pays* of Champagne, Burgundy, Berry, Auvergne, Bourbonnais, and Nevers (i.e. central and north-eastern France). By their consensus, and by the advice of the king's Great Council, precautions had been resolved so that *gens de compaigne* should not covertly enter the realm to capture any fortresses: namely, that the king's *bailli*, with two suitable knights in each bailiwick as royal commissioners, should:

diligently view and visit all the fortresses of the bailiwick: those which they find to be good and advantageous (*proufitables*) for defending the land and realm they are to have put in the best state of defence, in regard to repairs, 'artillery' equipment, victuals, and other necessities, at the cost of the lords to whom they belong. Should they find, on their tour of inspection, any defensible forts (*fors tenables*), whether on the frontiers or within the country, which it is essential to guard but whose lords lack the means to munition (*emparer*), victual, and equip (*garnir*) them, then the commissioners shall make these lords do what they can—and for what remains, we will provide as they shall recommend.

Nothing quite so emphatic, by way of subordinating 'private' fortresses to the public good, is to be found in 'English' directives, even in Ireland.[242] If fully implemented, very many lesser nobles would have been obliged to leave their lands and join the king's forces. In practice, much was no doubt modified, particularly under the weak rule of Charles VI (1380–1422). But the fact that obstruction by the great magnates was provided for in the 1367 ordinance, and that drastic treatment was to be meted out to fortresses too insubstantial or poorly maintained to be useful, shows the strength of the moral and political high ground of public safety:

[240] Not, of course, new except in extent and duration: e.g. Brown, *English Medieval Castles*, 168, quoting Philip of Flanders' advice to King Philip II—'first destroy the land then one's foes'.
[241] *Recueil Général*, v. 269–76; also *Ordonnances*, v. 14. Valuable detail 1364–80, *Mandements Charles V*, 49–50 (1364, Du Guesclin). Other defence ordinances in this phase of the war are ibid. 102 (1365), 208–9 (1367), 221–2 (1368), 236–7 (1368), 282–3 (1369), 324–6 (1370), 439–42 (1372), 939–40 (1380), 959 (1379).
[242] Although draconian they became routine, e.g. *Ordonnances*, iii. 219–32 (Languedoïl, 1358); vii. 188–9 (1388), 334–5 ('1389'); viii. 61–6 ('1395'), 258 (1398); ix. 360–8 (1408); x. 119–20 (1413), 414–16 (1417); xii. 286 (1420); xiii. 197–9 (1434–5), 306–13 (1439); xiv. 185–7 (1451); xxi, 315–16 (1504). Other examples printed in *Recueil Général*, vi. 842–3 (1399); vii. 144–6 (1407); x. 809–13 (1479); xi. 37–9 (1483). Fortified religious buildings were in no way exempt, but liturgical functions were respected where possible.

Besides this, if there be some forts, whether defensible or untenable, which belong to lords of such power (*si puissans*) that the commissioners dare not interfere with them, then they are to refer such cases to us for action. But all other forts, whosoever they may be, which are not tenable or profitable they shall cause to be demolished as to their defences and disfortified (*abattre quant au fort et desemparer*) in such a way that no harm shall arise therefrom to the country or to our realm.

Judgement must often have been subjective.[243] Other factors would be involved apart from structural condition and defence-potential. The great majority being defensively trivial would be as unattractive to seize as a base for predatory operations as to man defensively. Certainly, it would not appear on the ground that any wholesale *tabula rasa* of minor fortlets resulted, or of militarily antiquated greater castles, whatever happened in individual cases. Tenurial and administrative fundamentals were seldom touched, in any eventuality. But the exceptionally comprehensive, though typical, 1367 edict also prescribed what the local troop-commander should do if any district covered by the ordinance should be approached by one of the 'free companies'. He:

shall at once have all the country [-people] withdraw into the fortresses (*retraire en fors*) and especially their foodstuffs so that the *gens de compaigne* may not be sustained thereby and so be forced to depart the sooner. In order that the people of the countryside (*gens du plat pays*) may be the more inclined to bring in their goods, it is our will and order that they shall take them into fortresses, be they towns or *chasteaulx*, freely and without payment; and that when the companies have left, they may take their possessions out again to the *plat pays*, without paying any entry or exit dues, nor any other charges.

It would appear that such charges (*entrée, issüe, et aultre redevance*) were habitual but officially waived in the current emergency. As only the most capacious fortresses could accommodate sufficient numbers with their carts and cattle, these rules would apply chiefly to the great and ancient castles and, especially, to walled towns.[244] Other provisions of this ordinance regulate finance, namely the allocation of local war-tax and other revenues in part to local defence, and the halving of the arrears leviable on the peasantry of the *aide* for paying the late King John's ransom. He had died eight years after his capture at Poitiers, in 1364, after a dignified captivity. In addition, the war-impost on salt (*gabelle*), which bore heavily on peasant preservers of meat, was halved; and the fortification and repair of all walled towns was ordered to be subsidized by a quarter of the proceeds of the war-taxation collected within them. The crucial role of the *villes fermées* was emphasized, in that

---

[243] e.g. in 1413 Duke Charles of Orléans appealed against demolition by the commissioner of part of his castle of Soissons (*dép.* Aisne) done to facilitate defence of the city: *Pièces Charles VI*, i. 363–4. In 1372 hindrance by great lords and 'princes of the blood' was provided for in the Caen defence ordinances: *Mandements Charles V*, 439–42. Their co-operation was usually obtained in advance, but coercion was the stronger for not publicly exempting them.

[244] Criteria were fluid despite Contamine, *Guerre, état et société*, 5 (1416, 1444); on (quasi-universal) royal defence-control and subvention of fortresses, pp. 8–9, 62, 75, 77, 129, 230; viewing of forts, pp. 9–11, 77–8; troops in garrison, pp. 65, 71, 73, 76–7, 94, 109–10, 122, 125, etc.; refugees into forts and abbeys, pp. 122, 172 n.; 'companies', pp. 161, 166–8, 173, 183, 194, 197 n., 210, etc. And see Wright, *Knights and Peasants*.

their burgesses were to guard them carefully; no force of troops stronger than the town militia was to be admitted or (less practicably) be allowed to pass the town, unless known to be loyal by personal testimony. Finally, no arms were to be sent out of the town or supplied to persons unfamiliar. Towns 'which are at passes and river-crossings' were to have especial care.[245] Moreover, local captains were ordered to make returns showing how many armed men each could muster for service in the field outside their individual command-districts after allowing for 'keeping' the fortresses in their charge. Most of these provisions were or became routine.

The signs sent out were clear, thorough, and full of that executive clarity which delights both the conceptual and the 'strategic' theorist—but there is little of the realities of peasant calculation of their best interests (e.g. to abandon lands or to stay, perhaps barricading the parish church). Their hardships were often acute, as expressed in numerous bitter revolts (the *Jacqueries* of 1358 and later). There is little in these edicts to hint at local entrenched lordly power—but these factors generally determined what happened on the ground, even in the heartland of the Valois kingdom.[246] An attempt to reduce these gaps is made in section 4, below.

The universality, at least, of governmental concern is shown not only by the enduring of such directives until the fall of Bordeaux in 1453, and beyond during the Guerre du Bien Public (1465) and after it in the contest which ended the Burgundian threat to the integrity of 'France', but also by the fact that Henry V in his French conquests, and the 'dual monarchy' under his son (1422–*c.*1445) adopted the same methods.[247] The power to demolish inconvenient fortresses became a regular part of a commander's remit. It may be that in this long period of episodic warfare some enhancement of social responsibility resulted from enforced co-operation—but even the refuge-system eventually fossilized peasant burdens in the form of seignorial perquisites. The procedures of popular protection, which under Charles V were revitalized and made more thorough, so that 'private' fortresses were more effectively subordinated to the public good, did keep their original virtue for some time; but they tended always to be absorbed and digested into the aristocratic system, so that they survived chiefly as peasant obligations. All that remained for the seventeenth-century *feudistes* to record was an exploitative vestigial institution of vested seignorial power.[248] Although aristocratic privilege, particularly in

---

[245] Item 5. Philippe Contamine's, *Guerre, état et société*, despite its statist, teleological, and military slant, is again almost exhaustive. On town defence see pp. 5–9, 75 (1347–60), 127, 131 (subsidies, etc.), 160, 163, 169, 172, 176–7, 198, 208, 231 (garrisons), etc.

[246] P. Lewis, *Later Medieval France*, 281–9, esp. on the great *Jacquerie* of 1358. Timbal (ed.), *Guerre de cent ans*, is an exceptionally closely source-based interpretation for 1337–69, based on the records of the parlement, containing much local detail, thematically presented but from a 'national' viewpoint. In his bibliography 'C' Contamine lists the few local studies then (1972) available, e.g. Bécet on le Chablis, Fournier on Basse-Auvergne (pp. xxix, xxxiii); see also Baudain, Berman, Bois, Cursente, Debord, Lartigaut, Le Maho (Bibliography).

[247] Bréquigny, *Rôles Normands et Français*, 30 (1418), 55 (1419), 142–3 (1420), 159–60 (1421), 256 (1431), 256–9 (1435); also work by Anne Curry, e.g. 'Field Armies in Lancastrian Normandy', 207–33.

[248] e.g. on the Dauphiné, Salvaing, *De L'Usage des Fiefs*, chs. 46, 48, on the *vintain*, originally a tax for fortress-upkeep, citing records 1339–1618. As late as 1536 and 1550 it was ruled that no *guet* (watch-dues) was owed where no protection by refuge was available.

France, tended to become absolute and no longer conditional on the performance of formerly onerous public duties, this development flourished even as the 'Renaissance monarchy' strengthened. France diverged widely from England in this arena. As symbols and instruments of aristocratic authority, fortresses were affected by the bargain which was struck between Crown and nobility. The *château* came to represent the *pouvoir féodal* of the pre-1789 *ancien régime*—whereas in England it dwindled into nostalgia.[249]

So the fact is the more important that, during the Hundred Years War, the extension of royal control took the form of asserting the public weal over the lord castellan's basic interests. However compromised in practice, the principle was politically made correct that castles in danger of enemy seizure and subsequent use as bases of local brigandage, whether by the 'free companies' or peasant bands, should be demolished if, with appropriate subsidy, their lords could not suffi-ciently munition them. Refuge and 'salvation' were their *raison d'être* when their noble persona was temporarily submerged by war. With the return of peace that other self flourished again, most conspicuously in such architectural ebullitions as Vitré, Avignon Tarascon, and Langeais, a style which merged insensibly into the *châteaux* of the Renaissance.[250] Their militant display was not tamed by any supposed ascendancy of gunpowder artillery. Instead, their pride and arrogance shrugged off the ravages of war. When gunports were put in (as at Bodiam) and other up-to-date devices, they were showy even when effective. The utilitarian was sublimated so that romanticism was liberated and allowed to blossom. Glorifying the defensive element of fortresses' ancient personality produced an architectural hyperbole, fantasy even, as is especially conspicuous in many later Spanish castles.[251] These architectural trends are the more emphatic for occurring when the public burden of fortress-tenure, which began with rendability before the eleventh century, was still sporadically severe. They remind us that noble culture dominated and took fresh vigour from even the intermissions of warfare.

Mixed motives often operated when a fortress had, despite precautions, been occupied as a raiding-base and the cost of recapturing it was deemed to be greater even than the damage inflicted on the neighbourhood by the freebooters lodged

[249] For an art historian's view see Girouard, *French Country House*, ch. 1. The notions of such as Beaumarchais on seignorial rights were often influential fiction (e.g. Mackrell, *Feudalism in Eighteenth-Century France*, 1–47 *et passim*). But lords often bore more heavily than previously on the peasantry in France. 'National' attitudes can be a problem: e.g. A. L. Poole (Part II, nn. 128, 129 above) and Conan Doyle, *White Company*, e.g. ch. 7 (on justice 'high, middle and low') or *Sir Nigel* e.g. ch. 20 (castle of 'la Brohinière'). English society was scarcely more just.

[250] Mesqui, *Châteaux-forts*, 207–8, 411–13, 38–43.

[251] Architectural review, Coulson, 'Fourteenth-Century Castles'; France has many comparable to Warwick: e.g. Mesqui, *Châteaux-forts*, 64–6 (Bonaguil); Bourbon-L'Archambault, Clisson, Fougères, Largoët, Pierrefonds, Rambures, Salses, Tarascon, Vincennes (pp. 71–2, 129–31, 171–4, 208–10, 292–3, 314–16, 342–3, 368; also 372–4, 407–11): Monreal y Tejada, *Medieval Castles of Spain*, photographs, e.g. 174, 183, 211, 226–7, 250–1, 279. The great siege with cannon of Saint-Sauveur-le-Vicomte in 1374–5, eventually vacated by purchase, represents the martial aspect: *Mandements Charles V*, 549–51, 554–6, 562–3, 592, 594–5, 600–1, 604, 638–9. A 'ransom' of 53,700 francs (net) was agreed (p. 592). Mesqui, *Châteaux-forts*, 335–6.

there. Soldierly and peasant interests conflicted—but it was customary to negotiate surrender, buying out the nuisance value, raising the 'ransom' by levies on
those who had already suffered but stood to benefit.[252] This even happened in
England, in 1327.[253] Such evacuation-pacts must often have leaned away from fair-
ness and towards favouring the companionship-in-arms of fellow warriors.[254]
Social antagonisms seldom ran more deep—but such circumstances were still
only part of the whole picture. Peace prevailed over long interludes (notably
1396–1415), and in many parts of France continuously. A vivid glimpse of the relations between castle and community as they usually were comes from the illuminations by the Flemish van Limbourg brothers to the devotional *Très Riches
Heures* of John, duke of Berry (d. 1416), brother of Charles V. In these poetically
idealized but carefully accurate scenes, peasant husbandry figures almost as
prominently as do the duke's and the king's castles. There is the landscape of festi-
val (Riom), courtly dalliance (Dourdan), boar-hunting (Vincennes), hawking
(Étampes), the *vendange* (Saumur) and wheat-harvest (Poitiers), ploughing and
gardens at Lusignan, and crop-sowing with the Louvre (Paris) in the background
and a scarecrow dressed as an English longbowman—all painted late in the period
of twenty years of peace before Agincourt (1415), but some left unfinished on the
death of Duke John and completed later.[255] These gems of miniature detail ethe-
realize the fortress and remind us that it was not their usual character to be military posts scowling over the grim carnage of war—nor did Jean de Berry wish to
think of them as such.

Balance also requires it to be emphasized, not only that military functions were
but one aspect of fortresses, even during the Hundred Years War, but also that
war was not their sole precondition or even their basic cause. Popular refuge in
the early middle ages was a factor in the definition of castellaries, as has been seen.
Protection was deeply rooted in lordship and was institutionalized in fortress-
custom. Virtually all later developments of the refuge-system of castellaries in
France were anticipated. Before returning to them, what might be termed the
'community-contract' from which they sprang deserves to be recalled.

The modes of war and of peace permeated the fabric of society, focusing especially on the fortress. In 1215, for instance, when the men of Coudres (*dép.* Eure)
in Normandy decided to merge and form a new 'commune' with those of the

---

[252] e.g. *Mandements Charles V*, 97–8 (Rolleboise, 1365); 127–8 (Livarot, 1365); 132–3 (Saint-Sever, 1365); 429, 472–3 (Sainte-Sévère); 892–4, 913 (Navarrese castles in Normandy).

[253] For the surrender of rebel-held Knaresborough castle, £200 was exacted from the people of Yorkshire: *CPR, 1327–30*, 152: for France see *Mandements Charles V*, 154, 175, 180 (Mantes town, 1366–7); 491–2, 526–7, 569, 628, 775–6, 809 (aid for count of Alençon's fortresses, 1367–78), etc.

[254] Contamine, *Guerre, état et société*, 184–204, 217, 219, 227–8, on chivalric values expressed by Geoffroi de Charny, law of arms, Arthurianism, knightly orders, ransoms, etc.; Keen, *Laws of War*, 63–81, 137–85, etc.; also Gillingham, Part II, n. 223 above.

[255] Meiss, *Painting in the Time of Jean de Berry*, pls. 419–25; Fowler, *Plantagenet and Valois*, 54–5; also pp. 109–16 on the influence of cannon; O'Neil, *Castles and Cannon*, is posthumous and incomplete; cf. Kenyon, 'Coastal Artillery Fortification', 145–9. Mesqui, *Châteaux-forts*, 153–4, 233–6 (Mehun-sur-Yèvre, with plate), 279–82 (Louvre, ditto), 298–9 (Poitiers, ditto), 346–50 (Saumur, ditto).

castellary of Nonancourt, their lord the prior of Bourgueil, and Robert de
Courtenay, lord of Nonancourt, redefined their own relationship accordingly,
rewriting many details of local custom in the process. King Philip II himself,
acting as intermediary, had the issues clarified by a fact-finding jury, resolving the
problems as follows: jurisdiction over Coudres and its territory was kept by
Bourgueil, but Nonancourt was to be the court of appeal, making Courtenay the
superior. Without the prior's consent no man of his was to withdraw from his
obedience; but over his people of Coudres the lord of Nonancourt was to have
their service:

> For the fortification of his castle (*castri*) they shall bring palisading for the outer barriers
> (*palum et le garrol*) and must help to fetch timber (*ramentum*) needed for works on his
> capital seat, whenever reasonably required. In time of war they shall bring in of their crops
> (*de segetibus*) and shall store them where they choose, both to victual the castle, and for
> their own consumption.

Robert de Courtenay had his own *capitale edificium* there, but the place was
hardly the 'private lordly castle' of English stereotype of conquering Normans and
mutinous Saxons. More specifically, war only concentrated minds already set in a
feudal frame. Nonancourt was, in effect, a community facility for all eventualities.[256] Lordly castles were not the only fortresses to act in this way. Eleventh- and
twelfth-century examples, two ecclesiastical precincts and a walled town, will
show what was commonplace.

At Bourges, in central France, the monastery of St Peter and St Ambrose was
closely and originally involved with the neighbourhood, having the guard-
services of people dwelling on both sides of the River Yèvre from the mill of
Mirebeau down to the abbey gates, as we learn from the (allegedly penitent)
vicomte in a charter subscribed by King Robert II and dated 1012.[257] Nor was the
cathedral close itself, adjoining the city wall of Bourges, at all exclusive to the
canons of St Stephens: in 1174 King Louis VII prescribed that the precinct defences
(*munitio claustri*) should never be withheld from the king (i.e. it was to be perpetually rendable), incorporating this into his grant of jurisdictional immunity in the
close and formal approval of its fortification.[258]

Fortified settlements like the *castrum* or *castellum* of Montchauvet (*dép.* Seine-
et-Oise), founded quite early in the twelfth century where Normandy bordered
upon 'France', were perhaps more obviously integrated with the wider commu-

---

[256] *Recueil Philippe II*, iii. 503–4. In 1217 Courtenay swore Nonancourt and Conches rendable to the
king: *Layettes*, i. 453. His promise to obtain licence to refortify them asserted royal lordship over an
ambitious vassal.

[257] *Catalogue Robert II*, 46–8. Among possessions and rights restored to the monks was their right
(as calendared) that 'le guet, pour la garde du monastère et du bourg' should be done by the extramural inhabitants and by those of the dependent *burgus*. Robert the Pious (996–1031) merely ratified
this reversal of lordship expansion by the *vicomte*.

[258] *Ordonnances*, xi. 206–7: content and phraseology (esp. preamble) are strongly atavistic, suggesting late-Carolingian origin. The rendability formulation of 'deny' or 'withhold' (*detinere*) is found in
the Norman *Consuetudines* of 1091 but is most typical of Languedoc: n. 85 above.

nity, but scarcely more intimately. It was a problem often encountered that peasants, having gone to such settlements for refuge, might seek to settle as burgesses and shed their serfdom. The town's gain was another lord's loss, especially if they came from outside the castellary. To cover the case of Montchauvet, King Philip in 1202 ratified a bilateral agreement made in 1167, prompted by a petition from the monks of Saint-Germain-des-Prés by Paris, providing that '. . . of the serfs of Saint-Germain none shall be detained in the castle. Any serfs fleeing there for refuge from war shall return on the restoration of peace; or, if unwilling to go back, must give up all right to whatever lands they hold hereditarily from the abbey'. Montchauvet in 1167 had been founded within living memory. At the hearing before Louis VII the 'castle' was represented by a 'knight' and four 'others', barely differentiated at this period.[259] With deep roots of this kind in their localities, the updating demanded most insistently by war from the mid-fourteenth century of the ancient institution of the castellary merely stimulated its evolution. Refuge circumscriptions had to be revised. Population-patterns had changed. New castle-territories had been inserted and old ones had decayed. Prestigious and extensive early castellaries might be too big. But the principles needed only to be reasserted and systematized: refuge, the rule emerged, was to be made to the nearest practicable fortress, of whatever kind or lordship, only to the administrative *caput* if convenient. Dues and services (sec. 4 below) were owed only to the place of actual refuge.[260] Approximately 12 miles was laid down in decisions by the parlement (Paris) as the normal maximum distance a peasant should have to travel to reach safety. All these refinements of old ideas forged a revived, or closer, or sometimes a new, association between fortress-lord and the rural dwellers within refuge-radius, whether previously his own dependants or not. Innumerable conflicts had to be arbitrated, but some long-term modifications of the tenurial map and new (and onerous) 'liens of dependence' were the result.[261]

The Crown's contribution to this piecemeal adjustment was to encourage, organize, and exhort through royal officials, commissioners, delegated powers, and regional assemblies at all levels, all under the (real or propagandist) urgency of danger. As in England, under similar but slighter stress, 'the salvation of the realm' was a principle which had to be reconciled with (or subordinated to) 'the saving of privilege'.[262] Compromise was normal in the deliberations of the parlement. For the period 1337–69 this has received fortunate attention.

---

[259] *Recueil Philippe II*, ii. 304–6. These peasants were sharecroppers, i.e. rent paid by a proportion of their produce. Two witnesses in 1167 had been present *in prima constitutione castri*: Tardif, *Mon Hist*, 303.

[260] A doctrine strong enough to survive into the 16th century, at least in the border province of the Dauphiné: n. 248 above.

[261] The phrase is that of Marc Bloch, *Feudal Society*, to which seminal study much reference might be made (e.g. Part vi, 'Nobility'), were it not always clear how much should be modified in the light of Reynolds, *Fiefs and Vassals*.

[262] Encapsulated in 1377, *Rot Parl*, iii. 20 (xxxv); the walled boroughs pleaded *cest present necessitee de guerre si bien pur la salvation de eux come de tout le Roialme*, for power to levy murage on all residents including religious: rebuffed with 'Let all be done as heretofore *salvant a chescun son privilege*'.

In 1357, for instance, the royal councillors at law heard an appeal from the men of Lapenne castellary, near the Mediterranean Pyrenees, against a verdict in the court of the seneschal of Carcassonne. They had been sued by their own lord to perform the works on the ditches and walls of the castle which they had contracted to do in return for right of refuge at Lapenne during the panic caused by the *chevauchée* of the Black Prince, which culminated in his hard-fought and decisive victory of Poitiers. The parlement's judgement upheld the lord of Lapenne but softened the refusal by instructing the seneschal to view the castle and decide what works were really necessary.[263] As was now usual, this was technically an interim injunction, preserving defence co-operation, validating contracts but also checking undue exploitation. Prescription, however, quickly converted temporary arrangements into established rights and duties, thus affirming the organic unity of the castellary.

Attempts to organize new refuge zones sometimes affronted parochial conservatism: in 1370 the men of Vernon castellary pleaded that they had for some time past been compelled 'to do guard services at Mantes, in France, whereas Vernon is in Normandy'. Mantes (they said) 'is so far away that in case of peril and necessity they cannot speedily or effectively have refuge or retreat there, but to Vernon castle they have and may'. The old sense of Mantes as the Capetian bastion against Normandy evidently lingered.[264] Their services were accordingly formally redirected to Vernon, with exemption from the special levies imposed within a 7 leagues' radius (an elastic expression) for the fortification of Mantes, castle and town, which had been accorded in 1367 by Charles V.[265] Another case before the parlement (1367) shows what distance was considered practicable to cover in emergencies. The men of a village about 16 kilometres (10 miles) on the far side of the River Aisne from the king's castle with the pioneering name of Passavant-en-Argonne, north of Paris, had been charged with contributing to the costs of guarding it for ten years previously, although at need they always, they said, resorted to La Neuville-au-Bois castle (4½ miles away) or to Épense (under 4 miles distant). To add to the dilemma, they themselves claimed to belong to Vitry. The old, integral castellary, monopolizing all functions, had been thoroughly fragmented. The Vitry link was roundly rejected by the judges as irrelevant, since fiscal and military circumscriptions no longer had to coincide; but the plaintiff's main grievance was thought reasonable. Rather than trim the royal castle's revenues, however, the constable was to make his case for the status quo, Passavant 'being in an endangered part of the March'. Meanwhile no change should be made. Denial by delay was a normal judicial expedient. The parlement's

---

[263] Timbal (ed.), *Guerre de Cent Ans*, 108–9, no. xxxii. Hewitt, *Black Prince's Expedition*, 112–36; 'the history of war is much too serious a thing to be left to military historians' (p. viii).

[264] Mantes (*dép.* Seine-et-Oise) was where the king's siege machines were loaded for shipping down the Seine, and unloaded on return; an old labour-service included in the 1201–2 borough charter: *Recueil Philippe II*, ii. 255–61.

[265] *Ordonnances*, v. 168–70 ('1369'). An enlarged-area hearth-tax was granted in 1366: *Mandements Charles V*, 154, 175–6, 180, etc.; rule not inflexible.

councillors cloaked their more-or-less overt royalism in the language of judicial and social impartiality.[266]

Most decisions were left to local seneschals applying central guidelines, checked mainly by appeals from the influential, as in the case of the monks of Le Parc-en-Charnie in 1369. Peasant interests, if at all, tended to be brought to court in this oblique fashion; here by the monks' complaint that it disrupted their villagers' labours in the parish of Orques if they went for safety to Sainte-Suzanne castle (*dép.* Mayenne), or, alternatively, to the newly fortified abbey of Saint-Évron, these being the *capita* of the joint overlords of Orques and consequently having equal rights. The relative defensibility of either fortress was not mentioned (which is usual), though Maine had been much afflicted by brigandage, as the petition relates. It was left to the local seneschal to provide some *gracieux et convenable remède*: not an easy task, as the monks of Le Parc may well have been trying to weaken the joint overlords, and perhaps to get work services for some fortress of their own.[267] Such cases serve to emphasize that any impression is false that after *c.*1356 some pervasive and overriding martial law prevailed. Public safety and warlike necessity were doctrines both liable to interpretation. The very diversity of the forts accorded fortification subsidies ('castles', towns, abbey precincts, church-forts, etc.) shows the empirical compromises involved in recasting the old castellaries so as to satisfy as many interests as possible, mostly by conciliation.[268]

Whenever men of influence were interested, outcomes were commonly skewed: the fact is scarcely surprising—but clear cases as recorded are few. At the city of Lisieux in Normandy defence was in the hands of the bishop, a member of the king's council in *c.*1364–7. As such he had obtained a proportion of the money collected for King John's ransom. This allocation, one of many, was meant to be spent on fortification and repairs. Because the town was not walled, the bishop applied the proceeds to his fortified cathedral close—but apparently far from diligently, since in November 1367 the townspeople put their dissatisfaction to Charles V.[269] Their complaint was that they had been obliged in times of danger to occupy small lean-to 'lodges', built by themselves in the close of the bishop's fortress, adjoining its walls. Such poor accommodation was the pretext for advancing a project they had previously put forward to wall the town itself—not all of it, but the quarter next to the cathedral-fort, making a unified fortress-complex to which they might 'retreat and lodge'.[270] With typically paraded altruism, they argued that

---

[266] Timbal (ed.), *Guerre de Cent Ans*, 154–5, with text and diagram. Passavant castle had 12 paid watchmen and guards 'permanently'. Boutaric, *Actes du Parlement*, i, i, pp. i–lxxxix; still valuable, Beugnot, *Les Olim*, vols. 1–3, prefaces; cf. J .F. Baldwin, *King's Council in England*, e.g. chs. 2, 5.

[267] *Mandements Charles V*, 304; scope for compromise seems small.

[268] Excluding 'murage' and defence-aid to 30 towns, mostly in Normandy, cases in *Mandements Charles V* are pp. 9, 200–1, 358, 447, 491–2, 526–7, 628, 775, 809, 933, etc. (counts of Alençon–Perche–Étampes), 38 (lord of Torcy castle); 119–20 ('fort' of Laune); precincts of Lisieux, Coutances, Cerisy abbey, bishop of Troyes, Brienon fort, Séez cathedral and town (all below); 601–2, 696 (lord of la Haye-du-Puits, near Saint-Sauveur).

[269] *Mandements Charles V*, 120–1, 167, 207–8, 562, 919 (1365–80).

[270] The bishop of Coutances was less masterful in that he lost control of his fortified close to an appointed captain. As a refuge for the countryside, it received grant aid; but the townspeople preferred

this work would also benefit 'the people of the open country round about'. This was a standard formula (in England also), but getting rural contributions was the usual ulterior motive. Certainly, towns were the preferred popular refuge and they were usually integrated economically with their catchment areas; but municipal autonomy was always defended first.[271] The king's council gave its normal favourable response, however, and the proposal's feasibility was then investigated by experts. Unfortunately (as the petitioners must have expected), these reported that the cost of even partial enclosure would be so high that:

despite all their efforts (*tout leur vaillant*), combined with royal help, they would not be able to accomplish any viable fortification in the town (*aucun enforcement qui vausist ne qui tenir se peust*), and so they must continue to take refuge in their lodges within the [bishop's] fort, which is in several places much dilapidated and in great need of very costly repairs if it is not to remain in ruin and in danger of being taken by our [the king's] enemies should they come to those parts, which as yet has not happened . . .

The townspeople did not directly accuse the bishop of embezzlement, but they did succeed in outmanoeuvring him, in that the 'murage' tax granted for the unrealizable town citadel was then transferred to pay for the necessary works on the bishop's fort. Over these funds the townsmen, as was generally the practice, had substantial control.[272] They, not the bishop, then obtained a number of renewals continuing the levies, thus taking over and severely impairing the episcopal lordship over Lisieux, the command of fortifications and of general defence being a signal and cherished attribute of municipal as well as of lordly status. From junior partners in the cathedral-fort, the townsmen had become managing directors.[273] It is difficult to believe that the precinct which they had used in various (unjustified) alarms over three years prior to 1367, by their own showing, could really have been so ruinous—but effective petitioning was a matter of careful exaggeration through a knowledgeable and well-placed agent with access to the king's council.

to wall the town and were duly subsidized. The project was difficult to finance; most went on troops: *Mandements Charles V*, 168, 210, 359, 890–1 (1366–79).

[271] e.g. the archbishop of Sens (*dép.* Yonne) in 1366, a royal councillor, in proposing to 'make the town and the house of the archbishop within it strong (*fors*) with walls and ditches'. Royal and official support were won; but an unusually piteous tale of enemy sacking and devastation, causing desertion and cessation of agriculture for lack of any 'fort en la dicte ville ouquel ils puissent retraire ou sauver euls et leurs biens', in case of enemy surprise attack, was required: *Mandements Charles V*, 150.

[272] The abbot of Cerisy was more adroit, obtaining royal subsidy for the abbey from the town taxation by arguing that they had spent large sums on fortifying their precinct (as usual expressed as *leur dicte eglise*) and showing that 'en ycelle eglise les habitants de leur ville de Cerisy [dép. Manche] et du pais d'environ ont accoustumé mettre leurs biens à sauvreté, et retraire leurs corps en cas de necessité et toutes foiz qu'il leur plaist': *Mandements Charles V*, 396–7, 463, 498 (1371–2); also 143–4, 262 (1365, 1369: purpose unspecified).

[273] At Séez (*dép.* Orne) the clergy–burgess partnership was closer. Bishop, prior, burgesses, and townspeople 'of the town, city, and fortress of Séez' had together defended it, with local subsidy, despite being *en frontiere de noz ennemis du fort de Saint Sauveur le Vicomte* (n. 251 above), and had suffered a fire by accident of 'the said cathedral and fortress', which destroyed all but two bell-towers; the vaults and walls of *icelle eglise fort*: *Mandements Charles V*, 583. Apparently the precinct constituted the town citadel.

3. *Castle-works and Services, English and Welsh*

Services of a 'military' kind, whether knightly and noble or public and servile, extended much wider social ramifications than any analogy with modern wartime conscription, draft, or territorial reserve duty might suggest. For the ordinary inhabitant of the castellary, the subject of this chapter, regular 'peacetime' obligations went much further because they became regular sources of labour and money, nominally more than actually devoted to the upkeep and guarding of fortifications. It was consequently the policy of rulers, including territorial lords, castellans, and town authorities, to whom these services were owed to multiply pretexts so as to avert any disuse or obsolescence.[274] Far from all *capita* were 'fortified', in the sense of being 'military structures'; but each had what it took to be recognized as noble seats, according to rank, period, and location. Not relevant here are the purely fiscal and tenurial duties owned by almost every man, 'knight' or peasant, free and unfree, to his lord and to the ruler, which are unconnected with a specific fortress or fortresses; but rather with the peasant perspective, or what it is likely to have been.

Crenellated walls and portcullised gateways had very different associations for the extramural populace. War emergencies in England were normally too few for the message of security to prevail over the burdens of economic servitude, which was often a legal, hereditary, and well-nigh immutable condition. Labour services, perhaps willingly performed out of self-interest during transient crises, in course of time entered into law and custom where they had not originally been imposed or revived after the Conquest. The man's duty became his lord's right. So the obligations of the rural community towards the fortress and the seignorial power it expressed, though originally in a sense contractual (for resisting the Danes, under King Alfred, Ethelfleda, and Edward the Elder), became involuntary.[275]

Under Welsh native law, work on the lord's hall (*llys*) and its proper 'fortification' was one of the regular tasks. It compares with Anglo-Saxon bridge-building, host-service, and fortress-work and guard which composed the 'threefold obligation' or *trimoda necessitas* attached to landholding. King Alfred (d. 899) used it to build, maintain, and man his system of permanent refuge-towns, set up 'for all the folk'. The fact of the Norman takeover was rubbed in by enforcing peasant labour which, in unprecedented speed and number, put up earth-and-timber castles in so many of the old and new lordships. *Burh-bot* converted to *operationes castellorum* thereafter fell into disuse, unskilled labour being subsidiary in

---

[274] Coulson, 'Fourteenth-Century Castles', 149–50, on the 1360s use of quasi-manual, inadequate but knightly, castle-duties in the four duchy castles of Cornwall; Reynolds, *Fiefs and Vassals*, 312–14, 364–6, on the fiscal (financial) aspects of noble tenure, distinguishing 'rents' (non-noble) from 'aids' attached to fiefs.

[275] The 'constructive', state-building aspects (e.g. Stephenson, 'Significance of Feudalism') were not such as would appeal to any 'patriotism' on the labourer's part. Lennard, *Rural England*, leaves to the last (ch. 11) discussion of 'the peasants and their holdings'; pp. 364–87 on labour dues; pp. 387–92, on peasant society; concentrating on Domesday Book. H. Bennett, *Life on the English Manor*, is both detailed and empathetic.

masonry construction; but the frequent—especially twelfth-century—exemptions granted to or by lords for their subjects show how widespread it had once been.[276] In Wales the custom survived, as shown by a legal deed of 1278, entered on the Welsh Rolls of Edward I, doubtless for security of record as was usual. The document is a partition by Griffin *ap Wenonwyn* dividing his lands at Welshpool among his six sons. Owen, the eldest, was to be lord of the whole inheritance, his brothers his vassals for their shares doing him homage. Their subordination was signalized in the provision that: 'if Owen or his heirs shall build or rebuild any castle so that his people shall be summoned as a community for this purpose, all the community of the sons' lands shall lend common aid to the work, the same as Owen's tenants do and are bound to do.'[277]

Collective labouring of this sort operated also at Colwyn in Radnor, as shown by the *post mortem* inquisition in 1315 on Guy de Beauchamp, late earl of Warwick. At Colwyn it mentions 'a castle, 120 acres of land, 20 acres of meadow, a water-mill . . . 40 shillings of rent from free tenants who . . . every third year make a *hirsoun* around the castle of Colwyn, and a Welsh house . . .'[278] The wooden *hérisson* ('hedgehog') was comparable to *le garrol* at Nonancourt (above), namely the outermost paling or 'barriers' setting apart a fortress site and needing frequent repair. That the traditional duty of building the lordly *llys* had not fallen into disuse, whereas in England compulsory communal 'work of castles' had almost disappeared, shows the force of tradition in a somewhat isolated society.[279] Anglo-Norman lords in Wales naturally exercised the rights of Welsh princes. Thus William the Marshal junior, who like his father held much of 'Little England beyond Wales' as earl of Pembroke, in the late summer of 1220 complained to the justiciar, Hubert de Burgh, that:

. . . when Llywelyn [ap Iorwerth] had invaded my land of Pembroke and done manifold wrongs there and damage, he demolished my castles of Narberth and Wiston, killing the men taken captive in them—my knights and other people of that province, to avert instant

---

[276] e.g. Smyth, *Alfred the Great*, 115–18; Part I, n. 110 above; Armitage, *Early Norman Castles*, 252; Hollister, *Military Organization*, 138–40. Comparisons with continental *guet et garde* suggest that 1066 altered the popular tradition in England so that peasant guard duties became rare, unlike labourservices: Brown, *English Castles*, 156–7. Impressing paid labourers and also craftsmen is to be distinguished (pp. 163–5). *Regesta*, ii. 9, 140, etc.

[277] *CChR Various*, 171–3, 328–32: 1291 confirmation, repeatedly using the phrase *edifficacione castri et reparacione*, of pact by 'Sir Owen' with each of Griffin, John, William, Llywelyn, and David, his brothers; arbitrated by Edward's trusted Robert Burnell (chancellor), Henry de Lacy (earl of Lincoln, lord of Denbigh), and Otto de Grandison, his right-hand man from Savoy. In 1342 the whole settlement was again 'exemplified': *CPR, 1340–3*, 496–7. Irish, like Welsh, law provided for labouring on the king's *Dun*, e.g. the 8th century *Crith Gablach*: Stout, *Irish Ringfort*, pp. 112–13. (With acknowledgement to B. K. Davison, *pers. comm.* 1969).

[278] *CIPM* v. 401. At Bridgenorth, the men of one manor of the castellary were bound *tempore guerre facere Hirson et commorare in castro ad wardam si necesse fuerit* (1254–5): *Rot Hund*, ii. 59a. This record contains many details of castle-guard, both knightly and otherwise, at royal and seignorial fortresses. Suppe, 'Garrisoning of Oswestry', 66–74, mentions only mercenaries.

[279] But closely similar in England was labour on earthworks demarcating the manor-place, e.g. *ad circumdacionem murorum manerii* of John d'Aubernon, in the detailed Cambs. returns: *Rot Hund*, ii. 583b, 584a.

destruction of all their possessions and preferring hardship to death, promised Llywelyn £100 and that those castles of mine would not be rebuilt (*non reparent*) . . .

Even in remote west Wales it was desirable to have 'the king', in this case the young Henry III's regency council, on your side. Hubert was asked to watch over William's interests (to be *juris mei executio*) in the judicial arbitration fixed for the day after Michaelmas (i.e. 30 September 1220). If Llywelyn (the Great) or his attorneys should put contrary arguments, 'they should not be believed'. But what Earl William most wanted was official encouragement 'to those men of mine to come back and reoccupy their lands and hold them as they did before Llywelyn's invasion. Also, may the king discharge them from their bond to pay the £100; and may he accord me leave (*libera facultas*) at my discretion to rebuild (*aedificandi*) those castles'. The country people had made what terms they could with the prince of North Wales, at that time extending his power far down to the south-west from his base in Snowdonia.[280] Welsh marcher lords at no period asked royal permission to fortify, but William was anxious to be in the right, and to restore his lands' productivity. He also wrote directly to the boy-king at the same time, his letter containing a more general statement of his grievances against Llywelyn.[281] These assertive measures were successful: in October 1220 the justiciar and council at Westminster in the king's name sent an open letter (patent) to all the 'knights and free tenants' of Pembrokeshire requesting this heterogeneous but coherent community 'to afford manful assistance to your lord for rebuilding his castles at Narberth and Wiston which Llywelyn had thrown down, despite the agreement made with him'. To the Welsh prince, somewhat stretching the royal powers, went a request to keep the peace and not to hinder the rebuilding, now under explicit royal sanction.[282] The obligations of tenantry to their lord, it is implied, should not be interfered with.

Communal work on fortification was, however, clearly easier to obtain with royal backing, in such circumstances. Again in 1220 repairs were carried out to the royal border castle of Shrawardine by the sheriff of Shropshire, supported 'by all the king's faithful, knights and others of the county'.[283] In 'English Ireland' such joint action, frequently as has been shown (Ch. 2, sec. 1 above) by grants of the

---

[280] Shirley, *Royal Letters*, i. 144–5; *Castra mea de Netliebert et de Wych demolitus fuisset*. Llywelyn also demanded possession of part of the Marshal lands, to be held nominally (*quasi ex parte regis*) 'in custody' from the king, glossing over his seizure, 'before he agreed to withdraw from those parts'. William reminded Hubert that he had fully co-operated, promising to accept 'the king's' award. Background since 1216, F. Powicke, *Henry III and the Lord Edward*, 622–31, and *Thirteenth Century*, 392–4.

[281] Shirley, *Royal Letters*, i. 143–4, alleging that Llywelyn had broken the truce 'and done me outrageous wrong' (*me laeserit enormiter*), demanding that Henry III show whose side he was on.

[282] *Foedera*, i, i, 164; *PatR*, i. 252–5. 'The king' denied Llywelyn's allegation of royal connivance, annulled pacts made with the prince of North Wales, and summoned him to conclave at Worcester.

[283] *PatR*, i. 226; requesting help for Hugh de Audley, the sheriff. In May 1221 performance was ordered to be done there, not elsewhere, of the castle-guard services (*warda*) found to have been owed *per* knight's fief before the castle was damaged (*prostratum*) probably in 1215 by Llywelyn the Great: *Rot Litt Claus* i, 476a. The infrastructure (fiscal as well as military) had to be maintained; no expenditure is recorded: Brown *et al.*, *King's Works*, ii. 834.

military service of the areas (or cash in lieu) to magnates for the repair of their castles, was regularly co-ordinated by the king's representatives. This sometimes also happened in Wales.[284] Much (indeed, disproportionate) attention has been given to knightly castle-guard, but what matters here is only knights' castle-services when part of a communal and countryside reaction in which they participated not as individual fiefholders but as the leaders of the local populace, as their position in rural society dictated.[285]

Bamburgh, on the Northumberland coast, has merited mention already as a well-organized castellary with a close integration between fortress and community. Being also royal, it figures quite frequently in the central records. Typically, but in a fashion easily overlooked, the castellary worked continually as an economic as well as a defensive unit in emergencies. An entry of 1212 in the *Book of Fees* notes that 'Geoffrey the smith (*faber*) holds . . . land in [the territory of] Bamburg town . . . by sergeanty, namely by forging the ironwork for the ploughs of the castellary (*castelli*) of Bamburg as did all his ancestors by ancient enfeoffment'.[286] Another of these early sergeanty tenures, again of a technical kind, which shows how habitual was castle-building in the Welsh border, required the holder of 17 acres of land in Herefordshire to hold 'the cord to measure the castle when the king wishes to build any new castle in the march of Wales'. Having someone on the other end of the tape (in this case it would be a rope with knots at intervals) is very helpful. The surveying and marking out for digging ditches and foundation trenches, and also for the periodical recutting and clearing out of eroded earthworks, which was the duty of another sergeanty at Hereford castle, involved considerable skill. This last was paid at the rate of a knight and included directing and looking after (*custodire*) the diggers. It was believed to have been instituted following the Conquest.[287] Obsolescence in some other cases did not preclude the survival of castle-sergeanties as money payments; but to find the primitive missile weapon, the sling, still the subject of a sergeanty (of 'providing

[284] Cf. Ireland; *Rot Litt Claus*, i. 310a (1217); 427b, 430b (1220); 495b, 520 (1222): with the Welsh marches—in December 1219 the sheriff of Gloucester. was told to afford speedy help to Reginald de Braose's 'fortifying his castle of Builth, and making there ditches and trenches (*trencheijas*) against our enemies . . . by [coercing] the men of your county nearest to co. Hereford'. The same went to the sheriff of Worcester, and *auxilium de hominibus* of Hereford county was also ordered up by the justiciar himself at Hereford: *Rot Litt Claus*, i. 40a. Earthworking in winter was practised, but Builth, co. Brecon, is on the upper Wye. It had been seized by King John, 1208–15: Brown, 'List of Castles', 263. The 'trenches' may be 'paths through the woods': Brown *et al.*, *King's Works*, ii. 582. Other instances: *Rot Litt Claus*, i. 530b (Hodnet, Salop. 1223); but Knockin (Salop) received a cash grant: ibid. 545a.

[285] 'Castle-guard' has been regarded as an adjunct to knightly host-service, part of the 'military conquest' view of 1066–70 and its sequel: Part I, n. 202 above.

[286] *Book of Fees*, i. 204. On *servientes* (*ad arma*), e.g. Hollister, *Military Organization*, 129–33; in general see Kimball, *Sergeanty Tenure*. Their military character as sub-knightly soldiers can be overdone. It is often ambiguous: e.g. the individuals bound 'to keep the court' of Roger de Somerton (Oxon.) in time of war for 40 days, and the 'court' of Woodstock royal palace 'in wartime': *Rot Hund*, ii. 839a, 872b.

[287] *CCR, 1364–8*, 1; *Book of Fees*, i. 101 (1212), 382 (1226–8). Perhaps the best-known depiction of diggers is that showing the building of a castle at Hastings: Stenton, *Bayeux Tapestry*, pls. 51 *bis*. In pl. 50 (right-hand side), a quarrel is shown between the oppressed labourers.

a slinger for forty days to defend York castle in case of war in the county') takes conservatism to an extreme. By 1347 this holding had, as usual for fiefs in general, become subdivided into fractions as small as a fortieth part, which made even fiscal tax-assessment functions awkward in the extreme. Curiously, the holder of this tiny fraction in 1347 was Ralph 'Le Arblaster', which suggests that the more up-to-date crossbow had been substituted.[288] York castle had several such tenures.[289] Some sergeanties are so specific, even bizarre, that their very peculiarity seems to have been the motive both for instituting and retaining them—but their holders, often of free-peasant status in economic terms, were bound by their distinctive skills to one place and often to a particular castle.[290]

Fortress support by members (albeit specialized) of the local community, other than knightly castle-guard, was also institutionalized by guard-sergeanties. One at Wallingford (Berks.) was to go and stay for forty days in the castle, but only if it should be besieged (or rather, on the point of being so), which in fact occurred in King Stephen's time (1139–54) but not thereafter.[291] At Launceston and Restormel, in Cornwall, the duty was to get ready individual battlements by equipping them with timber 'hourds'; at Trematon (Corn.) it was to man six parapet-embrasures ('crenels') for forty days, again should there be war in the county. All three were castles attached to the royal duchy of Cornwall.[292] Richmond (Yorks.) had similar guard-services for its battlements, but from the free tenants of Mumby Soke, in Lincolnshire, not locally.[293] Such remote services were the most likely to have become fiscal, commuted for a rent—but fall outside the local scope of the present discussion.

Apart from such technical guard- and support-services due from the castle

---

[288] CCR, 1346–9, 313. Loops continued to be designed so specifically for crossbows as to be awkward, or quite often unusable, by (long-)bowmen. Being able to hold the stretched crossbow still on the aim permitted snap shooting. Slowness mattered less walking: Payne-Gallwey, The Crossbow, 3–10, 20–37; Viollet-le-Duc, Dictionnaire du mobilier, pt. 8, 'Arbalète', and Dictionnaire de l'architecture, 'Créneau', 'Meutrière'; Mesqui, Châteaux et enceintes, ii. 251–300 (thorough); summarized, Mesqui, Châteaux-forts, 24–7; Jones and Renn, 'Military Effectiveness of Arrow-Loops' (showing superior performance of the crossbow tested). King John, by Magna Carta, item 51 (Stubbs's Select Charters, 299), agreed to expel 'foreign stipendiary soldiers, crossbowmen, and sergeants'.
[289] e.g. CFR, 1327–37, 305–6 (a one-eighteenth fraction); 1337–47, 429, 477. All relate to Northgeveldale, viz. Great Givendale, Yorks.
[290] e.g. Book of Fees, i. 281 (crossbow-making in Norwich castle), 386; ii. 863, 913, 1254 (making iron-work for doors of Carlisle), 1364, 1391 (carpenter and mason in Lancaster castle): recorded 1219–50. Also CIPM vi, 356: supplying to the king 'whenever he comes by a lane called Goodstreet (Chichester) to make war upon the southern sea, a spindle full of raw thread for making a false cord for [stringing] a crossbow' (1325); vii. 256 (1331) ditto; xiv. 4–5: land at River, by Dover, 'held of the king in chief by service of holding his head [sic] on board ship when he crosses from Dover to Wissant' (dép. Pas-de-Calais: 1374); 92, 209–10 (1375); xv. 191–2 (1381), 211–12 (1382); xvi. 10, 77, 304, 417–18 (1384–90). 'Petty sergeanty' is distinguished in Magna Carta, cl. 37, as 'owing knives, or arrows, or suchlike'.
[291] Rot Hund, ii. 778a.
[292] Launceston: CIPM iv. 277 (1307); v. 211 (1313), 48 (1309, Trematon). At Restormel, in 1361, fief-holders were summoned to put up the hourds or bretasche to their respective (few) battlements; afterwards marking the components, taking them down for the winter, and storing them: Black Prince, ii. 9, 185; n. 274 above. More a chivalric performance than a defence-precaution.
[293] CIPM vii. 425–8; in 1334 valued at 25s. p.a.; Richmond, like Dover, was exceptionally well endowed with far-flung knightly castle-guard.

circumscriptions, scattered allusions in the Chancery Rolls show that in England collective 'watch and ward', akin to the *guet et garde* of France but not institutionalized, did sporadically operate. It was sufficiently established to be revived and extended in cases of special need, if only as a corollary of the more active duty to serve, incumbent upon able-bodied ('defensible') men aged from 16 to 60, which provided the musters for defence of the Maritime Lands from 1336 onwards.[294] But fortress-defence in England did not utilize manpower to the extent achieved by impressment for coastal watch, or by recruitment for the wars overseas. Between 1377 and 1385, for instance, the royal castles of Rising (Norfolk), as well as remote Trematon and distant and inland Launceston, were periodically manned partly by local levies, as were the new castle at Queenborough, in Sheppey (Kent), and refortified Hadleigh, by the Thames estuary (Essex), with forces described as 'adequate garrisons from their counties'. This latter service enjoyed no priority as it fell only on men not otherwise conscripted.[295] At Castle Rising it was explicitly the tenants and men of the castellary and beyond, including all owing vested services, who were summoned to come, bringing their goods and food with them.[296] Pevensey, in Sussex, being in the hands of Queen Philippa, was naturally provided for by her, emergency local impressment being the usual method.[297] Such measures, by comparison with France, have an ad hoc air of expediency nonetheless; of resorting to untrained locals in emergencies only, when paid 'archers and men-at-arms' were not available. The extent to which the Crown took the initiative, except with royal fortresses, is also very questionable. Supporting the efforts of magnates seeking to strengthen their hold on their own dependants often gives the appearance of intervening. This was clearly the reason for King John's order in May 1215 to the knightly tenants of Bury St Edmunds abbey (Suffolk) 'to go there in defence of the town and locality'. It was a time when the abbot wanted all his dependants of the Liberty about him.[298] What

[294] e.g. Hewitt, *Organizaton of War*, 12–21.

[295] *CPR, 1377–81*, 2 (July 1377); Brown *et al.*, *King's Works*, ii. 793–804 (Queenborough; almost unique circular plan, unfortunately completely robbed out), 659–66 (Hadleigh: 'a castle of no mean strength' and 'a fitting royal residence'). Trematon's manning was justified (as usual) by 'the imminent peril of invasion', but also because of its 'nearness to the sea' (Tamar estuary): *CPR, 1377–81*, 271, 455; also 566, 600; *1385–9*, 160; *1388–92*, 95 etc.

[296] *CPR, 1377–81*, 2: the 'tenants' to be compelled and distrained, 'who hold of the castle or owe it services', were those subject to the constable of Rising and to the 'receiver' of the lordship. In 1385 the constable or deputy was 'to compel as he thinks fit the men of the parts near the castle to abide in it upon its safe custody' in case of imminent danger, 'as in times past'—an ad hoc catchment area. The transfer of Rising to the duke of Brittany, 1378–96, in exchange for Brest castle made no difference; but the duke's keepers were told to commit no waste: *CPR, 1381–5*, 566; *1385–9*, 160; *CCR, 1377–81*, 163–4; *1385–9*, 333; *1389–92*, 134, 376; *1392–6*, 155; *Foedera*, iv. 32, 34–5, 149; *Lettres de Rois*, ii. 282–6, 294–5; M. Jones, *Ducal Brittany*, 137–9, etc.; n. 320 and text below.

[297] e.g. *CPR, 1350–4*, 195; *1358–61*, 414; *1364–7*, 9. Edward III ratified the queen's appointment of John de Saham as constable, 'for his long service', for life at 6*d.* a day in war or peace, with profits of the pasture 'within the castle' (e.g. the extensive Roman outer bailey), subject to proper stocking and good behaviour (1351). For delegated powers there in the 1339 emergency see *CPR, 1338–40*, 208, 236–7. For exemplary detail of revenues and costs at Dover see A. Taylor, 'Stephen de Penchester's Account, 1272–4', 114–22.

[298] After Magna Carta, in December 1215, the prior and sacrist (in the abbot's place) were told to

appear to be 'executive orders', even during crises, it is clear, frequently originated in petitions stating just what the recipient expected to be told. Superficially 'military' mandates can be misleading, especially in abbreviated calendar form. Thus, in July 1372 a patent 'order' was sent by Edward III's administration:

to the tenants of Adam, bishop of St Davids [Pembs.], and of his church of St David, to obey the bishop; whom the king has ordered to provide victuals, arms, and armour at his own costs for the munition of all his castles and fortresses in Wales; and to fortify the said castles, etc. with the same and have defects in them repaired. [He has also been ordered] to compel them, the said tenants, to carry the victuals and armour to the castle, likewise at his costs, as shall seem best to him. [He is also] to array all defensible men so that they be ready to repel the malice of the king's enemies, who are now upon the sea in a great fleet of ships of war awaiting a fitting time to invade the lands and lordships of Wales.

The 'order' is strangely isolated.[299] Adam de Houghton was a courtier-bishop appointed to be chancellor in 1377. Military command was the mark of eminent lordship. Exercising it kept authority in repair, especially when tenantry could be told it came from the king for an apparently credible reason. By getting such a commission himself, duly nodded through the council and Chancery, Adam also ingratiated himself at Court and kept out interference. Very many mandates are of this type and with similar ulterior motives. What is more straightforward is that cartage services were performed by St David's tenants, but for pay. One of the episcopal castles was the splendidly ostentatious palace-castle of Llawhaden, which, as so often, offers architectural corroboration.[300] Whenever public spirit is advertised, caution is in order.

This is not to say that in Britain the right of refuge was spurious—although in 1350 it was noted that castle-guard was still being exacted (in cash at the rate of 12s. a year in one case) from the knight-tenants of the castellary of Skipsea (Yorks.), although the castle was ruinous and gave no protection. Even the *caput* of the honour had been transferred, to Burstwick.[301] In genuine emergencies fortresses gave protection within their walls to refugees. Thus in 1407, during the revolt of Owen Glyndwr against Henry IV, many Welshmen fled into Denbigh castle. Some were expelled with their chattels as a precaution against treachery when attack seemed imminent. Among these unfortunates, forced to join Glyndwr as

desist from 'fortifying' the town of Bury (where the opposition barons had convened in autumn 1214) as in breach of the recently concluded truce: *Rot Litt Pat*, 135a, 161; Painter, *King John*, 315.

[299] *CPR, 1370–4*, 238; *1374–7*, 404, 417, 457.

[300] Bishop Bek (1280–93) greatly improved the castle and lordship, making it St David's richest. Bishop Adam (1362–89) added an impressive gatehouse, a chapel, and apartments: R. Turner, *Llawhaden*.

[301] After William de Forz's rebellion in 1221, the castles of Cockermouth (Cumb.), Skipsea ('destroyed in the time of the jurors' ancestors'), and Skipton were ordered to be taken and 'demolished' (*dirutum*) by 'the free tenants and all others' and nobles of the respective counties. The main resistance was at Bytham (Lincs.), taken at an enrolled cost of about £500: *Rot Litt Claus*, i. e.g. 449b, 450a, 452b, 453b, 454b, 456a, 462b, 474b, 475a; *CIM* iii. 18–20; Sanders, *English Baronies*, 24–5. Administratively all survived; as fortresses (unusually) only Cockermouth and Skipton did so, but Skipsea may have done for some time: D. King, *Castellarium Anglicanum*.

he claimed, was Griffin ap Meryth, who excused his seeming complicity by petitioning that as soon as he had 'put his goods in safe-keeping' he at once went to Ruthin castle and gave himself up. He was still in custody there, as an earnest of good faith, when the king's pardon was issued.[302] The business of fortresses was, whenever possible, to admit refugees, not to exclude them. Keeping enemies out was quite rare.

Between the castle and the inhabitants of its territory, formal or de facto, the relationship was one of intricate mutual dependence. Although these bonds tended to be tightened by war and to slacken in peace, they constituted a social institution of transcending scope and permanence.[303] Burdens corresponded to benefits: as King John told the knights and free tenants of the honour of Dunster in Somerset in 1202. His letter patent requested them to afford to Hubert de Burgh all possible help in strengthening Dunster castle, so that John 'might be under obligation of gratitude towards you'; adding, 'and this you should the more readily do since the work is on your behalf, and is being done for your security.'[304] Invoking their supposed self-interest in this way tells us much about the relationship; the more so since assuming such burdens voluntarily risked creating a lasting legal obligation. Letters of non-prejudice were commonly granted to avert this, as by William the Lion, king of Scots (1165–1214), to acknowledge help gratuitously given in 1211 by the subjects of Dunfermline abbey. They had voluntarily worked alongside William's bonded tenantry on building several new castles for him to consolidate the king's presence in the county of Ross.[305] The contribution of massed, unskilled labour was generally to carrying materials, ditching, digging foundations, and to fashioning and erecting wooden defences such as palisading. Skilled, salaried carpenters were needed for 'bratticing' and for hourding wall-tops. As late as 1299, for his Scottish campaign, Edward I called on his liegemen of Annandale to aid construction of the 'peel' or castle of Lochmaben.[306]

No picture of the relationship between rural community and its fortress would be satisfactory if it implied that harmony prevailed. Interests were inherently divergent, though not opposite. The practice of 'prise', namely the taking at fixed prices (in theory the open-market rate) of supplies, mostly of foodstuffs, from the locality for stocking fortresses, remained a grievance, especially over

---

[302] *CPR, 1405–8*, 326. The exceptionally strongly fortified priory of Ewenny (Glam.) suffered 'great losses and destructions . . . in tenements, woods, and other places pertaining to it'. The monks only were compensated: ibid. 264.

[303] Notably so in the Clifford lordships in Westmorland, Cumberland, and Yorkshire. On Lady Anne Clifford's (1590–1676) rebuilding of her family seats, including Skipton, M. Holmes, *Northern Lady*, 167–71, is cursory; Clifford, *The Diaries*, is better but incidental; Worsley, 'Gothic Revival', 109–10, pl. 10, is all too short.

[304] *Rot Litt Pat*, 6b. In 1201–2 £20. 0s. 6d. was spent on Dunster: Brown, 'Royal Castle-Building', 384.

[305] *Regesta Scot*, ii. 454 (c.1211–13). William I granted that 'this act is not to become a precedent to force them to do otherwise than they did in former times'; background, Cruden, *Scottish Castle*, 10.

[306] *CDScotland*, ii. 282; also 282–5 on the Scots' siege under the earl of Carrick; Brown et al., *King's Works*, i. 409–20, including the campaign in Scotland; ibid. 183 for the vast logistical exercise of assembling craftsmen and labourers for North Wales castles in 1282–3.

delays in payment, despite the regulation in Magna Carta (1215) which was often reiterated.[307] In England prise tended to be eclipsed by the similar 'purveying' of supplies for the royal household or for military campaigns. To stop prise or purveyance degenerating into mere commandeering required frequent rules and constant vigilance. Naturally less centralized in France than in England, individual lords-castellan there used the right of prise sometimes with less care.[308] Such abuses, rather than the fortress itself (unless as their symbol and sometimes instrument), caused antagonism (Part II, Ch. 1, secs. 2, 4 above). The castle of Dudley (Staffs.) was used in 1311 in a provocative fashion, as previously noted (see Index). In 1331, when held by John de Charlton of Powys, it was again in trouble, being 'besieged' or harrassed by a band of disgruntled locals who, John alleged, killed two of his Welsh servants, inflicted damage, and stole property.[309] Riotous damage and aggravated burglary, as noted elsewhere (Part I, Ch. 1 above), were no more common with castles than proportionately with ordinary manor-houses. When castles particularly attracted animosity, other than as lordship-seats, the cause was incidental it seems. At Banbury (Oxon.) in 1334 an affray began when a group of tradesmen and townspeople broke up the bishop of Lincoln's lucrative fair at Banbury Cross, a great market he held there annually as lord of Banbury. They pursued his supervising officials, there to enforce regulations and collect dues, who fled into the nearby castle which, says the aggrieved bishop's complaint, the rioters then 'besieged for a long time'.[310] Tenacious ecclesiastical lordship, of abbots and bishops especially, resisted rising municipal liberties and caused increasing resentment.

In 1340 the earl's 'men and servants who were in the castle of Richmond (Yorks.) for the safe-custody thereof', were 'for three days continuously assaulted . . . and wounded . . . so that he lost their service for a great while'. This formula for damage suffered was standard—but that the administrative staff, apparently with some armed men, protected by Richmond's massive walled enclosure and early gatehouse-keep could not avoid physical injury is to be noted. As usual, the details are of the one-sided kind contained in the *oyer et terminer* commission reciting the terms of the earl of Richmond's complaint.

---

[307] *Stubbs's Select Charters*, 296–7 (28, 29, 31). In 1322, during Thomas of Lancaster's rebellion, Barnard castle (co. Durham) was ordered to be . . . kept safely and . . . provisioned, taking victuals, if necessary, from the neighbouring parts according to the tenor of Magna Carta: *CCR, 1318–23*, 418; *1330–3*, 101. An emergency expedient.

[308] e.g. in 1333, before any 'English' pretext, the parlement dismissed an appeal by the commune of Marseillette (*dép.* Aude) alleging improper seizures of their goods by the officials of the lord of Capendu castle. The latter's right of prise for the castle was, however, left open for the burgesses to contest: *Actes du Parlement*, ii, i, 78.

[309] *CPR, 1307–13*, 369; *1330–4*, 126–7. The first-named accused is a woman. Other names ('le Fishere', 'Frebody', 'le Rider') are plebian; not apparently linked with the Despenser usurpation of Dudley, restored in April 1327: *CCR, 1327–30*, 63–4. Those killed (Madoc ap Iorworth, Llywelyn ap Eynon) doubtless came from Charlton's lordship of Welshpool. He paid 20s. for the inquiry. Justice yielded a discretionary profit, despite Magna Carta, cl. 40.

[310] *CPR, 1330–4*, 580; cf. Wisbech, n. 14 above. Background, Nicholas, *Medieval City*, 11–12, etc.

What is not clear, unlike with the assault on Banbury, is the motivation of the assailants and whether (as is likely) they were of the neighbourhood.[311]

Walled towns might also cause local friction. Being, to very varying extent, commercial and manufacturing enclaves within an agricultural countryside, the ambitions of the burgesses (especially for aggrandizement and privilege) tended towards costly municipal projects funded, in part, from levies on produce brought into the town market, itself usually enjoying a local monopoly. In February 1338 Edward III's Chancery, at the request of John de Mowbray, lord of Gower, issued licence for customs to be levied for walling ('murage') and paving ('pavage') John's town of Swansea. Reactions were violent: people outside 'assembled . . . to attack the town by armed force', alleging infringement of exemptions, so that in June the patent, as unusable, was surrendered to be cancelled.[312] A century earlier murage grants were still novel, so the request addressed in 1225 to Exeter's rural neighbours in south Devon was notably conciliatory, namely that they:

> should not distrust the grant which the lord king has made for taking a custom in the city of Exeter for enclosing the city and fortifying it, since such fortification (*firmatio*) is for the general safety and protection of themselves and others of those parts. They are so to conduct themselves that the lord king may not be obliged to act more severely towards them on account of the obstruction and vexation which they have caused.[313]

The Crown wished to uphold the dignity of its grants and tended to favour the *bourgeois* view of the public advantage expressed, as it habitually was, in terms of defence. Hypothetical danger constantly justified all levels of authority. At Exeter symptoms of opposition surfaced in 1307–8, when 'the commonalty of Devon' backed complaints by some of the citizens alleging embezzlement. A special audit was ordered, one of a sprinkling of such checks, but nevertheless support for urban fortification at all times and circumstances (similarly in France) was staunch and trusting.[314] The Hundred Roll jurors in 1274–5 occasionally recorded disquiet about the probity of murage collectors and works-supervisors (at Stamford in detail), but burgesses and non-citizens excluded from the ruling oligarchies, rather than the country-people, were almost always the initiators of investigations.[315] The same great inquiry also reported (as has been seen) that Earl Warenne, of Surrey, had levied contributions 'for enclosing his town of Lewes

---

[311] No gentleman-leader is mentioned, only 'John Wychard, John Garcedale, William de Latoun, Peter his son, and others', who 'assembled an armed multitude'. No 'breaking [in]' is mentioned, curiously: *CPR, 1340–3*, 91.

[312] *CPR, 1338–40*, 6, stating term as five years; *CCR, 1337–9*, 417 (as four years).

[313] *PatR*, i. 514. The walls of Roman *Isca-caster* were the basis of the medieval circuit, but 'to enclose and fortify' is habitual for repairs. H. Turner, *Town Defences*, 191–6, gives an archaeological-documentary summary.

[314] Requests for audits frequently reflect political faction: *CPR, 1301–7*, 544; *1307–13*, 86.

[315] *Rot Hund*, i. 353a, 396b; ii. 51b–52a; Stamford's collectors of murage since 1260 are said to have taken minor sums totalling £3. 17s., under a sixth of the total collected. Other allegations recorded ibid. 105a, 120b, 131a (York city); 108b, 115b (Scarborough); 314b–315a, 327b–328a, 398b–399a, etc. (Lincoln city); ii. 19b (Newcastle). Also e.g. *CCR, 1333–7*, 315–16, 390; and *1327–30*, 82 (Nottingham).

[Sussex] with a stone wall, and this without proper authority (*sine warranto*)', during the Barons War ten years earlier. But it was the knights dependent on Lewes castle, who had been made to pay £5 per knight's fief, not the country-people whom the tax may ultimately have affected, who made the complaint.[316]

4. *Guet et Garde*, *Plat Pays*, and *Forteresse*

The many differences of detail between the communal duties and facilities of fortress-support in England, Wales, and Ireland and the system of *guet et garde*, as it was in France in the fourteenth century, do not extend to the principles. This section offers some final illustrations of their diverse outworking in France. Consensus between potential refugees and castellans (apart from the Alfredian *burhs*) was more thorough and more continuous (perhaps more organic) on the Continent. Admitting peasants and their goods into castles was relatively rare in England, in Wales, or in Ireland. Accepting them as useful, if untrained, but normal members of garrisons was more exceptional still; but in France both were regular practice. Nor was this an expedient imposed by warfare, except in the sense that protection was an attribute of lordship: often invoked, sometimes needed. Anseau de Gallande, lord of Tournan in the Île de France, accordingly laid out in a charter of 1193 the duties owed by his people of the town and liberty, due almost without distinction to town and castle alike. They were bound to do one week's cartage service per year for work on the *castellum*.[317] In addition the burgesses had 'to make the bridge and gates of Tournan', Anseau providing the timber, the burgesses fetching it, but no further than from Paris (about 25 miles) if necessary. The castle-town was the burgesses' responsibility to keep watch in (*Turnomium excubiant*), but 'they shall not guard my tower'. Lordly towers, the *tours maîtresses*, were rarely treated differently, far less often than might be expected.[318] Such exceptions to the symbiotic relationship of community and castellan in France must be set against their close co-operation. At Tournan, on the lord's demand, his ordinary dependants accompanied him as a retinue, at his expense; they worked on fortifying what is worded as 'the castle', but also as 'my castle'; they did him other services and payments (some special for 'the lord's

---

[316] *Rot Hund*, ii. 210a. Lewes castle was antiquated, but the earl's control and lordship were no less boosted by promoting the *burgus*. Making fiefs contribute impugned their noble status; n. 10 above.

[317] *Layettes*, i. 172–3. Closely comparable to contemporary Nonancourt: n. 256 above. Anseau, of a prominent but sub-baronial family of the Parisis, obtained the consent to the borough charter of his wife (heiress?) and brother John (potential heir). After liability to hearth tax comes: 'Each year when I shall fortify the *castellum* of Tournan [*dép.* Seine-et-Marne], everyone of the liberty shall help me fortify my *castellum* for a week with whatever conveyance (*vectura*) he may have. Anyone without, or another in his place, shall help me for the week [by other work].'

[318] Viz.—*turrim meam non custodient*. Beaumanoir (*c.*1283) qualified the vassal's duty to deliver his fortress on demand, otherwise unconditional, by saying the vassal must not be put in danger by complying—*donques en tel cas ne sui je pas tenus a baillier ma tour*—but this is only if the lord is not present in person and if the lord does not protect him while in possession of the castle: *Beaumanoir*, 352. Architecturally and symbolically the *donjon* was quite distinct: Mesqui, *Châteaux-forts*, 383–6; *Châteaux et enceintes*, 89–220 (esp. 176–81).

war'). Jurisdiction was shared between the seignorial and the borough court—
but, most tellingly perhaps, at the accession of every new lord of Tournan, after
the men of the liberty had sworn him fealty, 'the incoming lord shall swear to keep
all these customs'.[319]

How political aims also might be formulated by fortress-customs is illustrated
by the case of Brest castle (*dép*. Finistère), in Brittany in English occupation
1378–97, under Richard II by treaty with the duke, John IV.[320] Here the implicit
social compact between fortress-lord and the people of the castellary became
strained but was honoured. In theory (at least until 1389) Brest castle was meant
to be wholly self-sufficient, drawing nothing from the countryside. The splendid
natural harbour and roadstead made Brest as useful as English Calais, but sever-
ance from its hinterland made problems more severe when wages and supplies
from England fell into arrear.[321] Technically, Edward III's recognition by the
duke, hereditarily earl of Richmond, as rightful king of France had enabled Brest
to be rendered to him, which was also a pledge of Duke John's loyalty. In 1396
Duke John, who had been granted reciprocal and complementary possession of
Castle Rising in Norfolk, asked to have Brest returned, claiming that extortion of
'ransoms' had depopulated and ruined the vicinity. No doubt these were prises,
illegal under the treaty. A lengthy truce had, moreover, been concluded between
Charles VI and Richard II. There was no change of allegiance on Duke John's part,
and he still wanted English support for his independence, so he promised King
Richard that his English and French subjects should contrive to have 'refuge and
succour' at Brest: a not unusual casting in feudal form of a working military
alliance.[322]

Brest's was a long-term, but ultimately unsatisfactory, arrangement. Local
work-services, both labour and watch, maintained Breton fortresses in war, being
habitually replaced by cash payments during truces. Thus, during the truce of 1359

[319] It was thought demeaning for a great magnate like Champagne to make oath to a social inferior:
e.g. Blanche and Thibaut IV in 1216 'caused it to be sworn on their souls' by proxy that a rendability
pact with Gautier de Vignory would be observed: *Layettes*, i. 431. The proxy is sometimes named.
Partners to coparceny treaties swore oaths to each other, despite inequality.

[320] n. 296 above, concerning Castle Rising, Norfolk; structurally obsolete but fulfilling 'the treaty
and concord' of 5 April 1378 whereby King Richard 'was bound to assign to the duke and his wife and
to the heirs of the duke's body a castle and the value of 700 marks a year in lands and rents in England
for the castle of Brest which the duke delivered to him': *CCR, 1377–81*, 163–4. The cash balance was
made up from Boston customs receipts.

[321] Calais and its 'pale', or fortified environs, were supported almost entirely from England for long
periods, 1347–1485 (and until Mary Tudor), and at heavy cost: Brown *et al.*, *King's Works*, i. 423–56. P.
Lewis, *Later Medieval France*, 284, attributes the 1358 *Jacquerie* to popular rage at 'the failure of the
nobility to do its social duty and protect the people from the miseries of warfare'.

[322] Similarly, the Anglo-Breton treaty of Nov. 1371 (negotiated and sworn for Edward III 'on his
soul' by an esquire and a knight of his chamber) was old-style *encountre touz qi pourrant vivre ou
morir*. All Breton *ports de la mier* (*mer*), *villes, chasteux et forteresses* are thrown open (rendable), 12
being put in English custody but sworn to be returned to John on his demand at the war's end. The
proxies were to 'demander et recevoir du dit duc l'ouverture et abaundonance de toutes ses villes et
portus de mer en avancement de noz guerres, refrechement, refut et confort de toutz noz subgiez', etc.:
Foedera, iii, ii, 927; also pp. 1019–20 (1374: order to English captains to 'render' the duke's fortresses
to him at will). Full circumstances, 1342–97, in M. Jones, *Ducal Brittany*, ch. 6; e.g. p. 17, App. C, D, E.

preceding the 'Peace of Brétigny', Edward III instructed his lieutenant to allow the men of Vannes, near Quiberon Bay (*dép.* Morbihan), to collect their usual 'emoluments deriving from the parishes' dependent on the town, to enable masons and carpenters to be employed to repair the walls.[323] Refuge-rights subsisted, of course, and were the recompense due to the extramural community—but emergencies were occasional, often theoretical, whereas levies in cash or kind were always exacted. When danger was feared or a demonstration of servitude was appropriate, physical labour when available was demanded; otherwise, paying craftsmen and soldiers was preferred. As duke of Aquitaine himself, and of Lancaster, John of Gaunt in 1395 accordingly instructed the constable of Dax (*dép.* Landes) 'to enforce the accustomed contributions and services for the defence of the castle [-town] from the people dwelling in the castellary and provostry'.[324] All these local duties were clearly routine in France.

It is worth emphasizing that this nexus was merely reactivated where necessary, not initiated, by the wars of 1337–1453, which had many elements of civil war (especially in 1415–35) and only later of 'international' conflict.[325] Service in cash, like knightly 'scutage' (not so very different), was becoming as usual as personal labour, even in France before 1337, and as subject (like many 'agricultural' burdens) to occasional enforcement in kind. Commuting work to rent enhanced the peasant's status, approximating it to that of the 'free tenant', by removing the taint of servile labour, temporarily at least, and leaving more time for his own holding, especially at crucial times such as ploughing and harvest. The distinctiveness, as a form of military service, of *guet et garde* can thus be overstated. At Épernay in Champagne, the men of the castellary (like those of Tournan in 1193) owed cartage-services (*le charroi*) to take materials to fortify the town and castle. In 1300 cartage was replaced by an annual rent, but should there be war, or to signalize the (now direct) lordship of the king, as count of Champagne, when he was personally present in the locality, the service (whether necessary or not) must be physically performed.[326] Like closing a path arbitrarily for a day each year (and in 1770 keeping only the American colonies' tea-tax) so as to demonstrate the right, the exception preserved the legal duty of the subject. Similarly, the same duty incumbent on the men of the town and castellary of Saint-Louet-sur-Vire (*dép.* Calvados), Normandy was changed to a cash payment, also in 1300; but with the English onset after Crécy (1346) labour service gradually and patchily reasserted its grip, unless, as was often the case, money was available and more useful.[327] In 1379, at Nogent-le-Roi (*dép.* Eure-et-Loir) in Normandy, this still

[323] *Lettres de Rois*, ii. 116–17 (from the French Roll).
[324] As reiterated by Henry IV, his son, in 1405: *CPR, 1405–8*, 98. Dax castle was in the NW angle of the Gallo-Roman city enclosure: Gardelles, *Châteaux du sud-ouest*, 130.
[325] e.g. Allmand, *Hundred Years War*, ch. 6, emphasizing also the role of 'popular' participation and the diversity of loyalties.
[326] *Registres du Trésor* i, 19. Philip IV and his heiress-wife Jeanne confirmed the act of the royal *bailli* in the comital administrative district.
[327] *Actes du Parlement*, I, ii, 1. Universal war-taxation diffused the burden widely; e.g. in 1375–6 the burgesses of Vire had part of the local proceeds for 'murage': *Mandements Charles V*, 610, 659; n. 268 above.

occurred, the inhabitants of the castellary contributing in cash to the town fortifications; as they did also in 1401 at Laon (*dép*. Aîsne) in the north, paying levies
by the town authorities for its fortification.[328]

With established and regular war-taxation, in regions subject to Crown control
or to delegated powers, the taxation function of *guet et garde* tended to be
absorbed—but only temporarily: it revived afterwards. If the liability had previously been regularly commutable this was obviously most likely to happen; but
guet et garde was more than 'watch and ward', in that it variously included cartage,
provisioning, and labour on defences, as well as the more skilled and specially
equipped duty of guard. Turning labour to money and emergency into permanence was a seignorial propensity which the Valois kings continually (but with
questionable zeal and effect) sought to restrict, to ensure (in principle) that labour
was only exacted when and where necessary, whether in cash (at prescribed rates)
or in kind. The productive and taxable capacity of the peasantry was vital at every
level and, as has been shown, consideration for their burdens and safety went
beyond lip-service.[329] Nor were wartime measures (so far as our sources admit)
aimed at militarizing the masses; or, conversely, at keeping 'the profession of
arms' to a select caste. The judgement of the parlement in 1271 which held that the
men of La Ferté-Saint-Aubin (*dép*. Loiret) despite being 'king's men', were liable
to defend that castle (*firmitas*) on the summons of the lord-castellan and had to
bring with them arms (weapons and armour) appropriate to their rank and
means, reminds us that the various grades of *roturier* also owned weapons and
used them. This particular verdict is helpfully explicit. Defence-duty was incurred
by residing (they 'slept and woke') within Renaud de l'Île's castellary, holding of
him land or houses by rent or by customary tenure. This status prevailed over
their noble pretensions as *hommes armés du roi*, even in the eyes of the councillors of the king's court of the parlement.[330]

Justifying the privileges of the few by citing defensive needs and exaggerating
dangers induces a certain wariness over such reiterated expressions as *le pourfit
commun du royaume*. The common weal was not dishonestly invoked, but the
social conscience to be expected of a hierarchical society (even one modified by
Christian ethics) clearly had its limitations. Kings wished to reward noble soldiers
and ennobled domestics, one cherished method (as we have seen) being to
respond favourably to petitions for permission to crenellate or fortify their
dwellings. Doing so accentuated and derived its very purpose from seignorial
status. But it was desirable, at the same time as gratifying ambition, to proclaim
the accountability of power.[331] The results are remarkably clearly mirrored in the
phraseology of the later Valois licences to fortify, fully elaborated under Charles

---

[328] *Mandements Charles V*, 913; Tardif, *Mon Hist*, 426.

[329] nn. 246–8, etc. above.

[330] *Actes du Parlement*, i, i, 164–5: as calendared, they were 'tenus par coutume de venir munis
d'armes que peuvent porter les villains' (i.e. *villani*, serfs or unfree peasants) 'pour aider le seigneur à
défendre son château'.

[331] n. 262 above: Coulson, 'Some Analysis of Bodiam', 105, for Cooling castle inscription (*c*.1385).

VII (1422–61) and Louis XI (1461–83). Public benefit is duly claimed (by petition and the wording of the licence based on it), and the refuge-system which the new fort might supplement (and into which any new refuge-area might have to be inserted) is frequently referred to, unless it was too implausible (as in the case of Baudes Meurin in 1469).[332] Public safety at the close of the middle ages in France was still ostensibly an integral ethic of landholding—but, no less importantly, *guet et garde* was a source of revenue as well as of prestige. Major fortification projects, undertaken by correspondingly important personalities, accordingly were normally accorded it.[333] But that the rights of *guet* granted in 1473 to the nuns of Cusset-en-Bourbonnais (*dép.* Allier), in their licence to build or rebuild a *maison forte*, were genuinely for public, not merely for seignorial, profit is more than doubtful. The protestations of general advantage in the licence of 1474 for the castle and port-town of La Hogue-Saint-Vaast, in Normandy, are somewhat more credible; but desire to create a full seignorial package of lucrative and prestigious rights (including jurisdiction: see Ch. 1, sec. 2 above) was undoubtedly persuasive, regardless of the resultant public burden.[334]

Centralized monarchy in France (in marked contrast with England) advanced towards absolutism in collaboration with the most selfish principles of aristocracy, exaggerating rather than dismantling such ancient tenurial power-structures as these.[335] Many social institutions seem to have became more exploitative of the poor. The perversion of fortress-customs during the supposedly humane 'Renaissance' is but one of the ingredients of the socially malign character commonly associated with *les temps féodaux*. A mandate of 1372 by Charles V at least expresses a more compassionate spirit, despite the harsh demands of local and regional defence:

Charles, king of France, to the *bailli* of Troyes or his deputy, greetings—By the petition of our beloved and loyal councillor, the bishop of Troyes, we learn that he has a good fort (*ung bon fort*) 2 leagues [approx. 8 miles] from Troyes . . . which is strong, well-fortified (*bien emparé*), and in such a state of defence that the inhabitants of the village there and of [fourteen named] hamlets and parishes . . . within 2 leagues' radius can flee to take refuge and lodge there, themselves and their goods, more readily than to any other fortress in the vicinity—Moreover, they owe no *guet* or *garde* by night or by day to any royal castle, nor

---

[332] See Part I, n. 255; and n. 62 above; other examples Part II, n. 337; III, note 47 above.

[333] e.g. to Olivier de Coétivy, chamberlain to Louis XI, lieutenant-general of Guienne and husband of Marguerite, one of the four bastard daughters of Charles VII and Agnès Sorel, in 1467 for the castle of Saint-Georges-de-Didonne (*dép.* Charente-Maritime); on petition that there had once been a *beau chastel et fort où avoient leur retraite les habitans de la châtellerie dudit lieu* at the place, demolished 'at the time of the Prince of Wales' (i.e. pre-1376). Wishing to 'rebuild it' on 'a better and more suitable' site, but fearing objections and difficulty in transferring *guet et garde* there, Olivier duly received licence anywhere for *murs, tours, fossez, pons leveiz et autres fortificacions necessaires*, with the same baronial rights as before and powers of coercion: *Ordonnances*, xvii. 51–2.

[334] *Recueil Général*, x. 658–9, 681–5. Giving *guet* rights in 1468 to St Catherine's abbey, Rouen, in preference to the royal castle suggests only strong influence at Court: *Ordonnances*, xvii. 117–19.

[335] Sir John Fortescue (*c.*1394–*c.*1476) compared the English monarchy favourably with the French: 'the power of a king holding sway simply regally is . . . of less safety for himself and his people . . .': quoted, with discussion, P. Lewis, *Later Medieval France*, 377–80. Which part of 'his people' Fortescue had in mind is not clear.

to any other, but they have all, from the first construction of the bishop's fort, always had refuge within it during the wars for their persons and possessions, fleeing and being withdrawn thereto—Now, these facts you [the *bailli*] are to verify and, if confirmed by your enquiries, you are to constrain the inhabitants in all ways possible to do watch and ward services there, by day and night henceforth, whenever the security, protection (*tuicion*), and defence of the countryside shall demand. For thus we will it shall be done and have granted and do grant to our councillor, any future objections notwithstanding.

Seemingly, the courtier-bishop was manipulating the refuge-system. It would have been a bold *bailli* who would have obstructed him. But the concern expressed for *la seurete, tuicion et deffense de tout le pays d'environ* and its population will be more than a verbal formula.[336]

Because *les Angloys* in France—Henry V, in his campaign following after Agincourt (1415–22) and, by the treaty of Troyes, his son's regents (1422–*c*.1435)— exercised kingship there north of the Loire, especially carefully in the regained duchy of Normandy, the ancient relationship of fortress to countryside was observed.[337] A mandate by Henry V to the *bailli* of the Cotentin in 1421, written in a curiously atavistic and stiff Latin by comparison with the relaxed vernacular of the Valois kings, shows how completely and naturally they did it:

The king to John de Ashton . . . recalls that, since a certain section of the circuit of the defences (*certa quantitas clausarum fortificacionis*) of our town of Coutances [*dép.* Manche] recently needed repair, he had ordered him to compel all the inhabitants of the castellary of that place to contribute to the cost. These expenses the king now believes on trustworthy testimony to be beyond their means, without damage to them and impoverishment of their state. The bailiff is accordingly instructed to summon before him the notable persons of the nearer vicinity and to devise, agree, and arrange with them how the work of repair may be done. In addition to the people of the castellary, those of the whole administrative viscounty [sheriffdom] of Coutances shall contribute, so as to help and subsidize those of the castellary; with proviso that this shall not be a precedent held against those of the outer viscounty. Given at Rouen, 20 January [1421].[338]

One noble who would have been affected was the lord of the great castle of Saint-Sauveur-le-Vicomte—but for his precaution in 1419 of securing exemption for his tenants and people from 'doing any services of ditching, keeping watch (*vigilia*), guarding (*custodias*), or other such burdens or duties elsewhere than within his own castellary (*dominium*)'.[339] Protection and privilege were but opposite sides of the same coin.

---

[336] *Mandements Charles V*, 469–70. The place is probably Saint-Lyé, *dép.* Aube, according to the editor, Léopold Delisle.

[337] Griffiths, *King Henry VI*, chs. 17, 18.

[338] Bréquigny, *Rôles Normands et Français*, 161.

[339] Ibid. 108, 112. The minor castle of La Haye-du-Puits was close to (and so a rival of) Saint-Sauveur; in 1375 its lord, Henri de Colombières, was compensated in 200 gold francs for damage done by the English there during the siege of 1374–5 (n. 251 above) and in aid of repairing La Haye as the 'Admiral' Jean de Vienne (commander of the besiegers) had recommended: n. 268 above. John de Robsart, lord of Saint-Sauveur (styled *fort* in 1373–5), is likely in 1419, in obtaining his exemption, to have wished in part to counter La Haye's proximity.

5. Conclusions: Part III—Noble Rights and Public Advantage

Reconciling the lordly aspects of fortresses with their public nature was never a simple matter for the medieval ruler. Part III surveys the constituent elements from primarily the castellan's viewpoint (Ch. 1), both in relation to the appurtenances of his castellary (sec. 1 and sec. 2) and to its wider 'politics' (sec. 3). Chapter 2 takes a more demographic and economic stance, so far as the chosen sources permit, focusing on the diffusion of lordship where fortresses were instrumental in the processes of developing and settling the land (secs. 1, 2), and on the vital popular contribution of the labouring majority who produced the food and sustained the whole social edifice. New towns (sec. 3) are a closely related part of colonization and one scarcely less intimately wedded to the countryside. They demonstrate a collective lordship, when fully mature, which shares both the interests of the lordly castellan as well as the economic concerns of the peasantry, while adding commercial and institutional elements of such importance as to require extensive treatment elsewhere. Although warfare is the conditioning background to Chapter 3, it merges still as a social force with factors of class, lordship, and hierarchy. To concentrate on sieges, campaigns, and strategic manoeuvre to the exclusion of all else, or to view everything through that lens, is to neglect the unglamorous but normal business of minimizing agricultural disruption which almost monopolizes the records across more than four centuries, in France especially. When war did achieve some ascendancy, it did so by drawing on traditional institutions of communal co-operation in the face (or remote possibility) of danger. The modes of aristocracy, like those of architecture, were military only in being lordly—and sympathetic to the rural mass of the population to the extent that preservation of the whole social order demanded it.

PART IV

Castles and Circumstances of Widows, Guardians, and Heiresses

Introduction

Societies which have attached legal standing primarily to the ownership (or tenure less than freehold) of landed property tend to fall short of the modern ideal regarding civil rights, especially as affecting the poor in town or country. On the other hand, in such a society 'sex-discrimination' will be less likely.[1] The distinctiveness of male and female was, of course, as the large literature of gender studies has stressed, a fundamental view of humanity in the middle-ages—but the perceived impossibility for women to bear arms was almost their only disability relevant to the tenure of fortresses.[2] Clergy, legally debarred in most circumstances from using weapons of war in person, were under a legal and canonical rather than a physical disability in this regard. But being officially a non-combatant was as much a privilege as a handicap. It was an exemption from some personal dangers (but not from those of childbirth) shared, theoretically at least, with the clergy and with males beneath and over military age and, ideally, also by the peasantry whose labours sustained and fed the whole social edifice.[3]

Devoting this fourth and final Part to fortress tenants who were either not male or not adult is called for since they comprised perhaps two-thirds of the lay aristocracy. Modern demography implies a higher infant-survival rate for women, offsetting their apparently lower age on average at death. Moreover, the special adjustments which were made for the legal and physical condition of women and children illustrate the relatively slight impact of warfare upon fortresses, which is a principal theme of this book, as well as having an intrinsic importance. Unlike the involvement of the rural poor with fortresses, that of landowning women and children is not under-recorded: indeed, because they often required special dispensation, detailed records were frequently produced. But if noble women were less involved in war, this was the sole aspect of aristocratic society in which

---

[1] e.g. Power, *Medieval Women*, 19; 'all feudal marriages of convenience were dictated by interests of land. In some ways an heiress—indeed an heir too—was as much a chattel tied to the soil as was the manorial villein.' Fuller version of these essays: Power, 'Position of Women' (1926), 401–33. See Index under 'dower', etc., 'marriage', etc., and 'women', etc. for previous material not repeated in this Part. Nicholas Orme's *Medieval Children* unfortunately appeared too late to be used, as also did Peter Fleming's *Family and Household in Medieval England*.

[2] Illustrated by the trial of Joan of Arc; but in part contradicted by her military career of 1428–30: Griffiths, *King Henry VI*, 188–9, 219–20; De Vries, *Joan of Arc*, chiefly on her campaigns. Activities considered proper to women depended on class, not physical potential, which with labouring women excluded only 'heavy ploughing': Power, *Medieval Women*, 71; in general Mate, *Women in Society*; Leyser, *Medieval Women*.

[3] Principles propounded in the 11th-century Peace of God movement, e.g. Magnou-Nortier, 'Enemies of the Peace', 60–9 (AD 500–1100); Debord, 'Castellan Revolution', 156–64; Goetz, 'Protection of the Church', esp. 264–7.

their role was not central.[4] It is significant that the *châtelaine* was also a lady's girdle to which household and personal keys, but also such accoutrements as jewels, penknife, thimble, and scissors were attached.

Customs differed widely from region to region, though they tended to converge over time. As throughout this book, the aim is to illustrate the particular. All examples are more or less idiosyncratic. One broad impression is that in childhood girls were often better off than boys; certainly better off than younger sons without expectations. Both were customarily sent away to be trained in a noble household. Even with the preference given under primogeniture to the eldest, and to males over females, sisters were usually more equally (and equitably) treated than brothers—but being put in a convent (as still in eighteenth-century France) was the (not always unwelcome) lot of some of them. Control of a woman's property usually passed on marriage to her husband. But it and the wife's marriage-portion (*maritagium*), customarily settled on the bride by her family when her marriage was arranged, and her dowry or dower (usually an assessed third of his property), were her eventual right. Both were part of the contract made 'at the church door' with her prospective husband. Her inheritance usually went to her own heirs, if different, only the dower reverting eventually to the husband's family. The virtual absence of divorce also had the merit of security. Personal incompatibility was seldom serious. Disparities of age and of survival often led to successive marriages, by women especially, leaving very complicated inheritances.[5] These were, of course, also problems that fortress-tenure had to resolve—but it is to those few which were peculiar to castles, and to those which castle-tenure illuminatingly highlights, that Part IV is devoted.

---

[4] Denholm-Young, *Country Gentry*, 34–8, considering 'the homes of the military class' purely from the masculine and architectural angle (with a simplistic view of licences to crenellate derived largely from the antiquary J. H. Parker). Labarge, *A Baronial Household*, ch. 1, gives a fuller view of the castle as a home (pp. 22–6, 32–7); also without specific reference to women, Mesqui, *Châteaux et enceintes*, ii. 77–250 (halls, chapel, kitchen, latrines, etc.) In fact, no part of manor-house or castle was outside the lady's purview, however much romance might associate her with the chamber and herb- (or privy-) garden: cf. Power, *Medieval Women*, 42–3, 45–52; also on the late 14th century equivalent of *Cassells Household Guide* or 'Mrs Beeton', known as *Le Menagier de Paris*, written for his young wife by an elderly and rich citizen, see Crossley-Holland, *Living and Dining*; also Woolgar, *Great Households*, index 'women'.

[5] Leyser, *Medieval Women*, 114–15 (annulment for husband's impotence), 87–8, 106–12 (marriage, could be secular and private), 171–2 (dower, etc.), 168–80 (widows) *et passim*; 315–28, bibliography; G. Holmes, *Higher Nobility*, 42–4 (*maritagium* and jointure).

1

Female Castellans:
Prevision, Not Prejudice

The difficulties inherent in the female tenure of a fortress might appear greater than with an ordinary fief: but any image of darning soldiers' socks must be put aside. Castles were female preserves, not quite as in the *Roman de la Rose*, no doubt, but certainly as long-stay residences and as administrative commitments.[6] In nearly all respects, and in all but exceptional circumstances, they were indistinguishable from manor-houses not dignified with ostentatious fortification nor styled 'castle'. Given their interests, great ladies undoubtedly influenced, where they did not determine and commission, all types of building in fortresses—but the extent of their patronage awaits systematic exploration.[7] More central to present concerns are the elements introduced into castle relations by *châtelaines*. Castles often denoted important lordships which *ipso facto* were of close interest to the superior, who was jealous to maintain his rights and to exploit them to the full. That a female lord was not able—or could not properly ride astride, armed as a knight—to perform the military service which was one of the charges on the income of the fief mattered less than might appear—disabled men, inexpert *milites rustici*, and those with prior commitments frequently sent deputies. Only if the lord, male or female, was under age and in wardship would the superior take over the administration, personally or by proxy—but for chiefly fiscal reasons: wardship was a valuable (and consequently saleable) right, exploited in Tudor times by a special Court of Wards. Resuming direct possession of the fief, whether effectively or merely notionally, signalized the lord's suzerainty and reversionary interest in much the same way as demanding temporary delivery to him of a rendable fortress betokened his *superioritas et dominium* so commonly in continental Europe. Legal status, not gender, mattered most.

The ability of the *châtelaine* efficiently to supervise the keeping of a castle in her lord's interest depended on her own activity, personality, age, residence, and

---

[6] Lewis, *Allegory of Love*, 134; McNeill, *Castles*, 109–10; 'castle of love' images are numerous, e.g. Burke, *Life in the Castle*, 57. Also Part II, n. 377 above. A late-15th-century duchess of Brunswick led a life of luxury, typified by having been 'born in a fortress and bred in castles': quoted, Power, *Medieval Women*, 36; also 45–6, for instances of women defending castles in war, or in a warlike manner.

[7] e.g. Eleanor of Provence and Eleanor of Castile, queens to Henry III and Edward I: Brown *et al.*, *Kings Works*, ii, index.

experience, qualities all required for the normal running of the estate, rarely on the condition of the peace in the locality.[8] Isabella de Vesci was custodian of Bamburgh from 1307 to 1311 when removed for political reasons, being restored the next year. In 1375, in the closing and uncertain years of the reign of Edward III, Anne, widow of John de Hastings, dowager countess of Pembroke, was allowed to retain the traditionally 'marcher' castle (and castellary) of Abergavenny in south Wales, although it was held by the duty of defending it, on the ground that she had been enfeoffed jointly with John and thus held it in her own right.[9] Most usually, however, a widow (Lat. *vidua*) would not expect to remain *femme sole*, especially if importantly landed. When remarried, nominal control at least of her possessions would then be relinquished, although her administrative personnel, under the steward or bailiff, would likely remain unchanged. If a castle was involved, this transfer potentially concerned the overlord (which with great fiefs, especially in Britain, was usually the king) more closely than it might otherwise have done. If (in France) the castle was jurable (subject to being 'assured'), a specific act of recognition of the fact was called for. In October 1249 Odet of Bourbon, in central-eastern France, made such an acknowledgement in Paris by two charters which illustrate the procedure in Poitou, in the south-west:

I Odet, lord of Bourbon, son of the duke of Burgundy, make known to all who shall inspect this document that in right of (*racione*) my wife, and by the death of Archembaud de Bourbon of good memory, certain castles have come to me in the land of the county of Poitou and Auvergne together with other *castra* being of the fief of my lord Alphonse, count of Poitou. Now, since these castles are said to be jurable (*jurabilia*) to the same count and to his heirs, I have promised and made oath that if the lord count, or my Lady Blanche, by God's grace illustrious queen of France, the count's mother, shall find by inquest that those castles ought to be 'sworn' to the count, then I will make such an oath (*juramentum*) in respect of them to the count, or to his heir, or to their order whenever (*quandocumque*) I shall be required to do so.

By pledging himself personally, with his three guarantors and his lands, to fulfil this undertaking Odet removed the legal barrier to his taking control in her name of his heiress-wife's great inheritance. His formal charter of homage, provisionally made until Count Alphonse should return from Crusade, followed immediately. He promised to pay any 'relief' (succession-duty) for his wife's inheritance

---

[8] But much could be delegated to the steward or bailiff, as by an absent or invalid male castellan, including auditing accounts: Denholm-Young, *Seignorial Administration*, 136–7. Elderly Elizabeth de Burgh, in 1360, was allowed to 'keep' her ('obsolete') castle of Clare (Suffolk), 'in defence of the coast' by her cousin the king: *CCR, 1360–4*, 19–20; J. C. Ward, 'Elizabeth de Burgh', 29–46; id., Elizabeth de Burgh and Usk castle, 13-22, for much valuable detail; Coulson, 'Fourteenth-Century Castles', 151 (for 'Edward III's aunt', read 'Edward III's aunt's daughter').

[9] *CCR, 1374–7*, 135. Tenure of 'the castle, town, and lordship' had with royal licence (usually for a quite nominal Chancery fee) been converted to joint-tenancy in survivorship, 'by the service of keeping the said castle in time of war in Wales'. Anne had duly made her fealty. Heirs as well as royal revenue might be prejudiced. On the complexities of conveyances to other than heirs at law see G. Holmes, *Higher Nobility*, ch. 2. On Isabella de Vesci, McKisack, *Fourteenth Century*, 13–14, 24; *CPR, 1307–13*, 300.

and took on her other obligations for it, all in the presence of Blanche of Castile, the queen mother, widow of Louis VIII (d. 1226) and regent for the absent Louis IX from 1249 until her death in 1254.[10]

Odet de Bourbon's wife's unspecified *castra*, that is, her castellaries or lordships whose residential centres were fortresses of some kind, attracted special attention in the homage-process because of their tenurial renown. In the two following sections the relevant peculiarities of that special castle character are examined. Military considerations, which are so prominent in modern retrospection, played some part in it, but seldom more than a very subordinate role. By contrast, the administrative, economic, and everyday work of women of rank, whether as widows, guardians of children, or as supervising household and estate officials during their husbands' often long absences, was of continual importance in and about the fortress-*caput*.[11]

1. Differentiating Fortress-Factors: Mainly in England

What made fortresses special lay quite as much (often more) in details of tenure than in peculiarities of architecture—although the quality of being fortified was basic. It is those differences in treatment which are particularly highlighted by female tenure. They, in turn, help to illuminate the position of female castle-lords. Frequently, even normally, these differentiating factors were almost imperceptible. We find castles figure in the records in much the same way as less distinguished estate-capitals and residences were treated; and moreover, not so differently from any other income-producing (or consuming) real property.[12] Similarly too, lady castellans figure primarily as individuals, not typecast as women in a male-biased society. To the extent that they were separated it was in matters of inheritance most conspicuously.

When customs became established, it was the general practice that when a tenant died his lands were temporarily, and more or less notionally, 'taken back' into the hands of the lord from whom they technically had come by enfeoffment, which was a conferment in fief made under a virtual contract of mutual support

---

[10] *Layettes*, iii. 82–3. Queen Blanche's second period of regency. A 'jurable' fortress had to be guaranteed neutral or beneficial to the lord's interest, by oath renewable on demand; a duty not yet subsumed by rendability in this province (see Index). He gave guarantees totalling £4,000 Tours. In signal of taking possession, Arnald de Caupenne, in Gascony, obtained licence in 1305 to build a rendable strong-house in his wife's inheritance, at Parempuyre (*dép*. Gironde): *Rôles Gascons*, iii. 470–1. He was a trusted official of Edward I.

[11] Estate management has received due attention, e.g. Denholm-Young, *Seignorial Administration* (1937); G. Holmes, *Higher Nobility* (1957); Altschul, *The Clares* (1965), 201–99; McFarlane, *The Nobility* (1953–73), esp. 43–60, 213–27; Saul, *Knights and Esquires* (1981), 205–53; Given-Wilson, *English Nobility* (1987), 104–23—but the specifically female input is elusive, e.g. Leyser, *Medieval Women*, 165–7 ('the aristocracy'); cf. Labarge, *A Baronial Household*, e.g. ch. 2 ('the lady of the house').

[12] Even deer-parks did well to break even economically: Birrell, 'Deer and Deer-Farming', 115, 118–19, 126. Building maintenance was especially costly if neglected. Architecture, as always, was a noble indulgence (e.g. McFarlane, *The Nobility*, 92–7), not to be subjected to cost–benefit analysis. Woolgar, *The Great Household*, ch. 4; incl. pp. 49–59, on the peregrinations 1296–7 of Joan de Valence, and the family residences.

and tenant service, homage, and fealty. In England and beyond an official of the Crown, the escheator or his agents in each county, notified of the death via the family and authorized by what came to be known as a writ of *diem clausit extremum*, duly took the property 'into the king's hand' (or that of the palatinate lord, as in the bishopric of Durham) until the identity and legitimacy by birth, age, and legal title of the heir or heirs could be established by local inquest.[13] Payment of the appropriate 'relief' would be made or instalments agreed and homage be done or arranged. These procedures would all be conducted by the immediate lord if the tenant did not hold 'in chief' from the king directly. Fortresses were treated indiscriminately in the inquisitions *post mortem* as mere estate-seats, as has been seen, with occasional curt descriptions. Any defence potential seldom stands out from the fiscal preoccupations. If fortifications were in need of attention, as in Ireland particularly, the dilapidations and cost of repairs or (rarely) the military consequences might receive notice. The status of the lordly dwelling came first. Any supplementary obligations of fortress-tenure rarely emerge, and any attached to female possession more rarely still.

The partition of the great Clare territories in Suffolk, Kent, south Wales, Ireland, and elsewhere, after the death on the Scottish pikes at Bannockburn in July 1314 of Earl Gilbert, the king's cousin, might be expected to throw up many indications, given that his three sisters were co-heiresses and that many and important castles were involved.[14] Unsurprisingly, those not in the marches (Clare, Hanley, Tonbridge) and most of the Welsh castles (e.g. Cardiff, Llanbleddian, Kenfig, Caerfilly, Coity, Newport, Caerleon, Usk, Llangibby) figure in the inquisition purely as fiscal units. The 'country, castle, borough, etc.' of Neath (Glam.) was reported as mostly 'burned by the Welsh since the earl's death', in explanation of the lowness of its revenues, but the Clares' vast Irish estates are summarized simply as—'Kilkenny. The county with the castles and manors thereto pertaining held of the king in-chief by service [worth] £44. 8s. 10½d. whenever [military] service shall have been proclaimed [summoned].' The language, as usual, is that of the accountant and lawyer.[15] What alarmed the bureaucrats who compiled the inquisition was the pre-emptive seizure, in May

---

[13] Similar procedure in the case of deceased ecclesiastics, bishops, abbots, etc. At a monastery an official would be put in, most often into the gatehouse, to 'take a simple seisin' for the Crown, until the successor was 'elected', royal 'keepers' being appointed meanwhile: Howell, *Regalian Right*, 60–109, etc. (bishoprics only). Innumerable writs on the Close Roll with corollaries in *Inquisitions Post Mortem* and the Fine Roll.

[14] Altschul, *The Clares*, 169–72, App. 2 ('List of estates in the partition of 1317–20'); G. Holmes, *Higher Nobility*, 110–12 (Elizabeth de Burgh, née Clare, accounts 1322–59); Given-Wilson, *English Nobility*, 37–42 (Clare inheritors: 'the great Clare inheritance provided a major (and usually the chief) element in no less than seven comital families' landed endowments, largely as a consequence of a series of carefully arranged marriages'—p. 42).

[15] *CIPM* v. 325–54; cf. iii. 234–51 (on Gilbert de Clare, d. 1295); iv. 311–31 (on his widow, Edward I's daughter, Joan of Acre, d. 1307). In 1314 apparently, Llangibby castle (Mons.; *Tregruk*) was left unfinished. Its empty interior but immense double-towered gatehouse, extraordinary Lord's Tower, great area, and meticulous sanitary provision, show it 'was intended as a principal residence for a great man': D. King, 'Llangibby Castle', 86–132 (p. 128). Llanbleddian (St Quintins, near the tiny walled town of Cowbridge) was also incomplete: Pugh (ed.), *Glamorgan County History III*, 441.

1315, of the honour of Tonbridge (Kent) by Hugh Despenser junior, husband of
Eleanor de Clare, the eldest of the sisters.

Tonbridge castle and its extensive castellary (*leuga* or 'Lowry') was a great prize
(although the jurors mention only 'a rent of eels' payable by the township), held
from the archbishop by the sergeanty of attending his manor court of Otford
twice a year and of 'being steward on the day of his enthronement'. Hugh took
possession, trying to wrest the castellary from his wife's sister Margaret and Hugh
de Audley her husband, to whose third it had been allocated. Also, it had not been
'ascertained whether Maud, late the wife of the earl, is pregnant'.[16] The putative
baby (boy or girl) would have had almost everything except for Maud's life-
dower. Hugh's custodians then, in contempt of the king's escheator who had been
instructed 'to take the castle and honour into the king's hand' (May 1315), refused
to give him 'livery of the castle'. A timber outwork or barbican in front of the very
opulent and princely double-tower-fronted gatehouse built by the previous Earl
Gilbert (d. 1295) may be the site, or the vanished outer-bailey gate, since the
escheator reported that he then, 'in the presence of witnesses, placed his hands on
the wicket-gate by way of taking seisin but they were removed' by the custodians,
who then 'raised the drawbridge so that he could not enter the castle'. (Such a
disrespect to the king was severely punished in contemporary France.) The
escheator had to be satisfied with the most nominal ceremony, reporting that 'in
words he seized the castle, and he took the borough and foreign [outside] lands
of the honour into the king's hand without impediment'.[17] A weak king and
faction at court did not, however, impede execution of the partition finalized in
November 1317.

It was clear quite soon that the pregnancy of Maud, widowed countess of
Gloucester, had been a pretext for delay. Eventually the machinery of inheritance
was set in motion: Eleanor, Margaret, and Elizabeth de Clare were summoned to
be present (i.e. represented by their attorneys) in the court of Chancery, but no
more than perfunctory measures were taken to call the custodians of Tonbridge
to account.[18]

---

[16] *CIPM* V. 351–3; Part I, n. 201 above (the Lowry). Earl Gilbert the Last had married Maud, daughter of Richard de Burgh earl of Ulster, in 1308. She received her dower, including Llangibby, in Dec.
1314 (*CCR, 1313–18*, 132). She died in 1322. Her parents with Gilbert arranged Elizabeth's marriage (her
first of three) to Richard's son John at the same time. He died in 1313. Theobald de Verdun promptly
abducted and married her but then died. Elizabeth's third husband, Roger Damory, was executed in
1322. Hugh Despenser forced her into exchanging away some of her land. She then remained single,
dying in 1360: Altschul, *The Clares*, 41, 173, 208; J. C. Ward, 'Elizabeth de Burgh'. Her marital vicissitudes matched those of Alice de Lacy.

[17] Archbishop Reynolds (1313–27) was overridden. He had been removed from his position of
chancellor in 1314: McKisack, *Fourteenth Century*, 46. The power-struggle ensured (Oct. 1315) that the
chancellor and council passed the buck: 'for the doubt they see in the business they dare not finish it,
nor advise further without the assent of the great men of the realm, because of the strangeness of the
case': exchange of writs and replies reproduced *CIPM* v. 351–3. Renn, 'Tonbridge Gatehouse', 93–103.
It had no drawbridge, in the usual sense, only perhaps a removable span before the entrance.

[18] One of them, John de Haudlo, had licence to crenellate his manor of Boarstall (Bucks.) procured
for him by the elder Despenser in 1312. An ostentatious gatehouse to the moated manor-site resulted:
CPR, 1307–13, 493; Muir, *Castles and Strongholds*, 151 (photograph of Jacobeanized front).

Against the weight of evidence of respect for rights possessed and transmitted by women, and of castles in their hands seldom being differentiated from ordinary noble mansions and property, must be set the revised and amplified clause 7 put into Magna Carta of 1215 when it was first reissued the following year. Under widespread custom in France, a widow was entitled to remain in the (principal) marital dwelling (unless, as became more common, a joint-tenant) until otherwise provided for.[19] In England an interval of forty days was allowed. This was incorporated in Magna Carta:

> After her husband's death a widow shall at once and without prevarication (*sine difficultate*) have her marriage-portion (*maritagium*) and her inheritance; nor shall she have to pay anything to obtain her dower, or her marriage-portion or [her share of] what she and her husband held on his death. She may remain in the house of her husband for forty days after his death, within which time her dower shall be assigned to her . . . (1215) . . . unless it has already been assigned to her, and except if that house is a castle (*nisi domus illa sit castrum*). If so, and should she remove herself from it, a suitable house shall at once be provided for her, such that she may fittingly (*honeste*) live in, until her dowry has been made over to her in the manner set out above . . . (1216)

Which 'houses' were to be regarded as 'castles' was a matter of status and customary appellation, very largely; so even this measure, in the confusion after King John's sudden death (like the ephemeral provision in the 1217 reissue for 'adulterine castles'), was probably no more than a legal pretext in reserve.[20] The issues were seldom simple. Preventing a widow from denying to her husband's heir the status accruing to a castle-seat was very clearly the *ratio decidendi* in a case before the parlement of Paris in 1258.[21] The councillors of Louis IX ruled that, by the customs of the castellary of Poissy in the Parisis, a widow Emmeline Enguelot was entitled to have one of her husband's houses as part of her dower. This could even be his only dwelling (despite the heir, who might then have to cohabit) unless, they declared, that house was a fortress. In that case the heir had to build for the widow a suitable residence (that is, one appropriate to her rank and size of household), she staying in the castle until it was ready.[22] Similar ideas and practices

---

[19] *Stubbs's Select Charters*, 337 (7); Leyser, *Medieval Women*, 171–2 (as 1225); 1215 version, McKechnie, *Magna Carta*, 254–5; modern translation by Harry Rothwell in Warren, *King John*, 265–77 (p. 267). Occasionally spouses obtained licence to crenellate jointly, e.g. in 1281 Stephen and Margaret de Penchester 'for their *domus* of Allington' (Kent: *CPR, 1272–81*, 437); Hubert and Margaret de Burgh, for Hadleigh (Essex: *CPR, 1225–32*, 417, 422), and sometimes the proprietor with his heir. Formal joint-tenure or heiress-property was thus acknowledged. Licences to women as principal also occur e.g. *CPR, 1370–4*, 407 (Harpham belfrey, Yorks.); *CPR, 1385–9*, 42 (house in Carmelites close, London).

[20] The 2nd reissue (1217) added precision as to the widow's life-share of her husband's lands, substantially restating 1216 regarding the case of a castle but substituting 'capital messuage' for 'house'.

[21] English cases of impatience at widows' longevity, or even chicanery, exemplified in Leyser, *Medieval Women*, 170–2; and on getting dower, and avoiding remarriage, pp. 168–75; including some 'formidable matriarchs', anticipating the Tudor, Bess of Hardwick.

[22] *Actes du Parlement*, i, i, 22 (no. 270). In 1340 the count of Auxerre objected in court to joint-tenure by husband and wife of the strong-house of Villefargeau (*dép*. Yonne), apparently as it would postpone or frustrate his wardship: ibid. ii, i, 298. They successfully appealed from the comital court. In 1282 the lady of Mailly was awarded residence in the castle pending assignment of her dower, but

obtained in Britain: for example, in 1344 the virtually coastal castle of Christchurch was in a widow's hands—but there was enough uncertainty about a widow's right to keep a castle for it to be set aside in unfavourable circumstances.[23] Thus, in 1246 Henry III removed control of the late Ralph de Mortimer's castles in Wales, putting in his own trusty Walerand Teutonicus, not only from the widow Gwladys (daughter of Llywelyn the Great and granddaughter of King John) but also displacing Henry de Mortimer. Neither is likely to have been evicted, however. Heirs had similar rights and, if under-age, were as entitled as widows to appropriate lodging and maintenance.[24] Severing the military command of a fortress from its occupancy was rare, and potentially awkward; but dual- and multi-household occupation was regularly allowed for in the provision of status-graduated sets of apartments in castles as in great houses. In the absence on the estate of a designated dower-house, the mother-in-law problem, like an occasionally intruded lord's official with servants and horses, could be accommodated.[25] The complexities of independent suites contrast with, while sharing, the social conventions of the servants' hall and service rooms, separated from the 'family' apartments of the early-modern mansion. Widows were slotted in, but possessed clear rights.

Injustice could still, of course, occur. It was one of the accusations made in 1213 against Guy, late count of Brittany, opponent of King Philip II, that he had encroached upon land which was in his hands only as dower by building the castle of Saint-Aubin-d'Aubigné. He was also said to have withheld her marriage portion from the lady of Dol.[26] When castellaries were acquired from widows by apparently fair exchange, there must sometimes be suspicion of opportunism and

she was to have thereby *nullum jus in dicto castro, in possessione vel proprietate*. In 1289 the heir in possession and companions were punished for an affray (*cavalcata*) by a fine and he by having the castle doors burned, to be replaced with brushwood only (*de spinis*) in signal humiliation until pardoned: *Les Olim*, ii, 208, 291; *Actes du Parlement*, i, i, 262.

[23] *CCR, 1343–6*, 287: order to the escheator 'to leave undisturbed in possession of Christchurch Twynham castle [Hants.] and its appurtenances Katherine, widow of William de Montague, earl of Salisbury, as she was jointly enfeoffed with him with remainder to the king in default of corporal heirs and as her fealty for them has been taken'. In 1339 Magna Carta justified ordering the Exchequer to allow Mary, widow of Edward III's half-uncle Thomas, earl of Norfolk, the sum of £80 'for her quarantine . . . as a widow shall remain in her husband's chief messuage for 40 days after his death, within which time her dower shall be assigned to her'—presumably in lieu of revenues receivable from Framlingham, or for costs: *CCR, 1339–41*, 19.

[24] *Close Rolls, 1242–7*, 450; Sanders, *English Baronies*, 98–9. Roger de Mortimer succeeded to the Wigmore estates in 1247. For his Albigensian wars in 1212, Simon de Montfort ordained (item 44) that 'no widows, magnates nor heirs, or noble women having troops in garrison (*munitiones in castro*) shall presume, without the count's discretionary licence, to marry within 10 years from now any native of the land; but Frenchmen [i.e. northerners] they may freely marry, as also after the 10 years are over': *Thesaurus Novus*, i. 837.

[25] Faulkner, 'Domestic Planning', and 'Castle-Planning'; see Brown, *English Castles*, 142–5 (Bolton, Bodiam); Emery, *Greater Medieval Houses*, vols. 1–3.

[26] *Layettes*, i. 396–7. André de Vitry said Gui had built part of the castle, its fish-ponds, and mills on part of Rennes forest given in dower with his daughter, André's wife, the rest of the castle on André's own land, namely *fossata et barbaquannas*. Lady Eleanor of Dol alleged detinue of her lands since he died—these among other allegations not unwelcome to the king.

of undue pressure.[27] If the belief that it was inadvisable to leave a fortress in the hands of a widow (*ipso facto* an heiress, variously endowed) may sometimes be inferred, any such prejudice was occasional only and the product of a variety of precautions and interests. There was nearly always the overriding uncertainty over loyalty, focusing on the likelihood of remarriage, for which the king's (or the mesne lord's) consent came to be required as a matter of feudal right and propriety, but which might not be an adequate safeguard.[28] Fortresses undoubtedly sharpened the problem of control, but whether merely because the major castles were usually the title-bearing *capita* of great honours, or because in certain regions and eventualities they might be of potential military importance, is seldom possible to decide. Certainly, 'strategic' hypothesizing has gone much too far, whereas broadly seignorial considerations have been neglected in this and other matters affecting fortresses.

Undoubtedly also, no one-size-fits-all explanation can account for the acquisition from women of castle-fiefs by outright purchase, or by exchange for lands elsewhere, which is so characteristic of marcher areas. The attractions are obvious. An assessed capital sum in return for a dowager's life interest or, better still, an alternative residence away from the 'frontier' carrying with it lands and revenues of equivalent rank, might make a very acceptable 'retirement package'. The rigours of maintaining the viability of the territory, sometimes (as in Ireland) against encroachment, could well induce the heirs in reversion to agree to being bought out. In France under Philip IV the compulsory purchase of 'necessary' castles (always, significantly, with their territories) was used as a formally declared right (but by local custom) to consolidate and advance the royal dominions.[29] Otherwise, opportunistic pressure was sufficient; as was very generally the case in Britain, in Ireland especially (Ch. 2, sec. 1 below), an early example being Christina Marsh (*de Marisco*) in 1280.[30] At all periods much depended on circumstances. Isabelle de Meulan, lady of Thieville, was made of sterner stuff. In 1400 she obtained licence from King Charles VI, in the words of her petition, relating that:

---

[27] e.g. Philip IV in 1309 bought from the widow of Thibaut de Lévis all her share in his 'castles, fortresses, and places' in *dép.* Ariège and near the border of Catalonia for their assessed capital value': *Registres du Trésor*, i. 118–19. Other cases examined, Coulson, 'Valois Powers over Fortresses', 152–6. Countess Aveline of Aumâle and her mother (from whom Edward I obtained the Isle of Wight) were defrauded, argued McFarlane, *The Nobility*, 253–67, examining his similar ' "policy" towards the earls'.

[28] e.g. Joan of Acre, on the death of Gilbert de Clare (1295) whose lands had been settled jointly on her and their children (disinheriting those of his first marriage), 'infuriated her father by sharing her good fortune with a penniless young man of her own choice . . . Ralph de Monthermer, earl of Gloucester *jure uxoris* as long as Joan lived' (d. 1307): McFarlane, *The Nobility*, 261. Fines to stay unmarried could be high: Leyser, *Medieval Women*, 171–3; despite Magna Carta (1215), cl. 8.

[29] e.g. in 1308 the parlement upheld the compulsory purchase of two 'castles' in the Carcassais, made 'on the king's behalf and for his convenience (*commodum*)', holding that 'by the custom of the *patria* the castles were *licite . . . retenta*, justly to be kept for ever, once the balance of their valuation was paid over in coined money': *Les Olim*, iii. 312–13; *Actes du Parlement*, i ii, 54. In fact the deal was extortionate, if not fraudulent: 'Valois Powers', n. 27 above.

[30] *CDIreland*, ii. 369: 'surrender to the king and queen of all the castles, fortifications, lands, tenements, advowsons of churches, knights fees, homages and services, villeins and their retinue' (i.e.

... she has in her land and barony of Le Hommet, Normandy, within the castellary and *vicomté* of Carentan, a dwelling (*hostel*) called La Rivière which is an anciently fine and notable place. There . . . for her own and her household's (*hostes*) and subjects' welfare, advantage, and security, she intends to have the dwelling strengthened (*emparer*) and fortified.

The site, near Saint-Lô (*dép*. Manche), though in Normandy could not during the peace of 1396–1415 have faced much danger—but this was a vigorous and self-confident assertion of her status and entitlement to architectural distinction. Nevertheless, the privilege of formal permission was more than perfunctory. Lady Isabelle was significantly not awarded local *guet et garde* services, but La Rivière was to be 'put in such a state that it is and could be (*puist estre*) defensible and be guarded and munitioned (*emparer*) in time of war and otherwise'. With an eye, moreover, to the not-so-remote evils of occupation and plundering by irregulars, which had led to many untenable places being demolished, as well as to usurpation of lordly rights, Lady Isabelle's works were not to cause 'any damage or inconvenience to the king or to the country round about'.[31] There was always this equivocation between lordly quality and military apparatus. They were two sides of the same coin.

As heads of great households, especially when in their own right, not as wives, women assumed virtually all the duties of an active, adult male head, including those of the castellan. But for the widow of a castle-lord to step into her late husband's shoes might not be automatic. In May 1203 King John sent two mandates from near Rouen, capital seat of Normandy, to Geoffrey fitz Peter, his regent in England. The king had been informed of the death of David ap Owen, lord since 1177 of Ellesmere in Shropshire. Being reluctant to leave castle and land in his widow's hands, he ordered Geoffrey to give to her 'land producing £10 a year (*decem libratas terre*) situated as far as possible from the march, or more or less [land] as may seem expedient, in [very inadequate!] exchange for the castle of Ellesmere'.[32] But John may have desired Ellesmere more than the widow's security: he also instructed Geoffrey, three months later, to buy out David's heir. In the abbreviated format of the reference copy on the Roll, it reads: 'The king *et cetera* to Geoffrey fitz Peter, *et cetera*: we order you to make inquiry about Ellesmere castle and its appurtenances as to what they are worth (*quid valeat*) and to let Owen son of David have [lands to] that value elsewhere—for we wish to have that castle in our own hand as it lies in the march . . . Orival, 2 August.'[33] By

---

sequele = 'offspring')—in return for their 'value' in England, for life plus three years only. She bound herself and (deterrently) her heirs in a penalty of £3,000 in case of non-performance.

[31] *Pièces Charles VI*, 32–4.

[32] *Rot Lib*, 36, 56; an incorrectly labelled close roll; on the 'resumption', Brown, 'List of Castles', 250, 267. The final French invasion had begun: F. Powicke, *Loss of Normandy*, 148–50. John gave Ellesmere (the castle a large motte-and-bailey) in dower with his daughter Joan to Llywelyn the Great in 1205, taking it back again in 1208.

[33] *CCR, 1349–54*, iii. Also in 1349, on the death of Eleanor de Clare's son, Hugh Despenser III, his widow Elizabeth received *inter alia* in dower Hanley castle (Worcs.), 'with the adjacent houses . . . for her dwelling place' temporarily; then, definitively the castles, towns, etc. of Neath, Kenfig, Llanbleddian, and Tal-y-Fan, etc., their values reckoned to the farthing: *CCR, 1349–54*, ii, 31–2.

1349 many circumstances had changed when the lordship of Ellesmere was again noted as involved in a question of dower. The *caput* was now antiquated, but still prestigious. Edward III's council ordered that Joan, widow of John Lestrange, should be allocated the usual third share of his lands in Oxfordshire, Berkshire, Rutland, Lincolnshire, and Cambridgeshire, as well as in Shropshire where she was to have 'a third part of the fortalice and hundred of Ellesmere in the said march . . . she having sworn not to marry without the king's licence'. Unlike *castrum/castellum*, the word *fortalicium* meant usually the fortress itself, so she may have shared the apartments, not just the revenues. 'Castle' normally meant both. This is likely since she, or her steward or bailiff, would need a base locally.

Manor-houses were quite customarily partitioned, the escheator allocating sets of rooms for the widow's sole use, with other facilities shared with the heir, often a son or stepson in the simplest cases. Harting, in Sussex, licensed to be crenellated in 1266, was partitioned in this way in 1350. Henry Hussey's widow Katherine received 'a third part of the chief messuage' comprising, *inter alia*, the west gatehouse and chambers, 'all the chambers next to the east gate and over the same except for the prison-house which remains to Henry, the son', both gateways being 'common to both Katherine and Henry with free entry and exit'.[34] Evidently the profits of the gaol and the task of keeping indicted persons awaiting trial went naturally to the major and reversionary heir. Katherine's shares in the gardens, offices, lands, labour of serfs, and other 'profits' are minutely detailed. It was usually a question of dividing the income from the extramural assets (other than specific fields and villeins' services), but domestic planning facilitated the designation of virtually self-sufficient 'granny-flats' within castles and manor-houses. At Rishangles (Suff.), Denise widow of Thomas de Hickling, was allocated 'in the manor[-house], the great chamber at the head [i.e. upper or dais end] of the hall within the moat on the east, the kitchen and chapel within the moat in common with the heir', with free access and a third of the income of the moat and outer fishpond, and so on.[35]

Some distinction was made, it seems, of eminent castles—but an apparent reluctance to share out the buildings seems to have had more to do with preserving the chief heir's status than with avoiding any domestic (or even military) inconvenience. Thus, in 1322 the great Multon coastal castle of Egremont (Cumb.) was itself kept out of the dower of Eleanor, widow of Thomas de Multon. Instead she received other lands of the demesnes for her due third 'of the chief messuage of the manor of Egremound, which is a castle'. No allowance was made to her for

---

[34] *CCR, 1349–54*, 153–5; *CPR, 1258–66*, 580 (licence to crenellate, 'at the instance of Edward, the king's son'; possibly a new site, which is rare). In 1450 Constance, widow of Henry Hussey, had her dower-share, including 'a bakehouse . . . a barn called the Heyberne with the Wryngehous [? laundry] which is thatched with straw, the Estgatehous with chambers', use of the manor-well, etc., a third of the bucks and does from the parks, specified fields, services, share of advowsons, etc.: *CCR, 1447–54*, 560–1.

[35] *CCR, 1318–23*, 709–10. Dean, 'Early Fortified Houses', links documents (misconceiving licences to crenellate) with ground-surveys for several SE Midlands houses, 1275–1350. Excavation has elucidated some elsewhere in great detail, e.g. G. Beresford, 'Penhallam' and 'Goltho Manor'.

its residential amenities, nor for losing the prestige of having it as her home, but only for her share of the revenues receivable there. Egremont was a great *honor*, for all that the castle itself was antiquated. Sixteen years later (1338), when the heir, John de Multon, himself died leaving three sisters, the usual practice was followed of awarding the chief seat to the eldest, Joan (and to her husband), entire and physically undivided in recognition of her seniority, her sisters having otherwise equal shares.[36] That the principle of primogeniture was what prevailed, rather than any indivisibility such as one might suppose would be vested in the archaeologically and juridically elusive category of 'castles', the case of Hornby (Lancs.) in 1285 tends to confirm. Geoffrey de Neville had held the castellary in part in right of his wife Margaret. On his death a distinction was made so that 'the body of the castle of Hornby' was at once put in her provisional possession (*tenancia*), 'until she come to the king and do what she ought to do for the lands which Geoffrey held of her inheritance' (that is, fealty etc.); whereas most of the attached territory ('the castle with appurtenances') which the escheator had in the normal way 'taken into the king's hand', was in regular style 'delivered up' to Margaret as dowager-heiress. Clearly the purpose of this ritual was to assert the special quality of the castle proper and Margaret's subsisting hereditary right to it.[37] It was a correct and courteous gesture, perhaps due to Edward I personally.

That genuflection was to Margaret as lady of Egremont. That her mansion was a castle merely emphasized her quality—but fortress-custom, most developed in France, was also in play. Because fortification was itself ambivalent, both an aristocratic expression and, very variantly, an instrument of physical power, articulated architecturally and in rendability, those customs were infused with the military expression of the prevailing doctrine of public utility. There was an element of political correctness about this—but it was not some medieval version of the spirit of the 1940 Defence of the Realm Act.[38] Not, of course, that defence was irrelevant. In England since about 1336, when the danger of French raids on the south-east began (the north similarly after *c.*1308), castles, towns, and places within the coastal areas or 'maritime lands' were liable to special defence measures. These became routine and perfunctory; so, in November 1400, not long after Henry IV had seized the throne, this pretext was used to take control of the dukes of Norfolk's main seat of Framlingham (Suff.). The castle is about 12 miles from the sea, though less so to the great waterways inland from Orford, and being late November and during the Anglo-French truce there would seem to be no plausible reasons to justify precautions against external threat—nevertheless:

[36] *CCR, 1318–23,* 566–7; *CIPM* vi. 198–201. An old motte-and-bailey site with probably early-14th-century domestic rebuilding: D. King, *Castellarium Anglicanum* (Cumb). Eleanor, for residence, had another 'messuage . . . enclosed with an old ditch', etc. No 'value' was put on the *caput* ('castle' or 'fortress'): *CFR, 1319–27,* 132–3, 312; *1337–47,* 79–81 (detailed partition).

[37] Hornby, Lancs., not Hornby, Yorks. (nor 'Lincs.': Brown, 'List of Castles', 269; cf. *Rot Litt Claus,* i. 129b). Pettifer, *English Castles,* 134–5; the site is entirely rebuilt; *CCR, 1279–88,* 314. The writ was dated at *Bergh* (Yorks.).

[38] Investigated and illustrated from town projects of fortification from the later 13th to the earlier 15th century: Coulson, 'Battlements and the Bourgeoisie'.

Grant in dower to Elizabeth, late the wife of Thomas (de Mowbray), duke of Norfolk, in recompense of the castle and manor of Framelyngham . . . extended [assessed] at £80 per year, which the king assigned to her in dower and now with her assent wishes to remain to himself during the minority of the heir of the duke, because the castle and manor are on the sea-coast and exposed to various perils.

Instead the dowager duchess was given the castellary ('castle and manor') of inland Bretby (Derby.), worth £25 per annum, plus other lands, revenues, rents, and so on, all together worth £79. 17s. 3d. This exactitude did not apply to the cause of the king's change of mind. Thomas de Mowbray had been Henry IV's challenger and accuser when duke of Hereford. Exiled for life by Richard II, he had died the previous year.[39] It was a magnanimous act by Henry to allow his widow to continue to enjoy the stately glories of Framlingham, once chief castle of the Bigod earls and little altered, with its great earthworks and parks, its landscaped lake and many-towered curtain walls (built c.1200). Bretby was more modest, a social *arriviste*'s castle, licensed to be crenellated by John de Segrave in 1301. The income of its lordship was much less, and the bits and pieces cobbled together to make it up to nearly the value of Framlingham were much less secure.[40] All the same, Lady Elizabeth was better off than the widow of William de la Plaunche in 1335, even allowing for her much humbler rank. Haversham manor (Bucks.) had been the sole residence of importance of Lady Hawisia's husband's family. Like Bretby it had been distinguished by licence to crenellate, obtained in 1304 by James de la Plaunche, her father-in-law, but the record does not award it the title of 'castle'. William's heir was nearly 10 years old in 1335, so his little household (Hawisia was not, apparently, his guardian) and, perhaps, a 'farmer' put in by the Crown to manage his two-thirds of the estate, as well as the widow, all had to be accommodated. The familiar solution was an official partition, allocating to Hawisia (one of many vanished forenames):

. . . the great chamber with the chapel at the head of it beyond the door of the hall, the maids' chamber with the gallery (*oriola*) leading from the hall to the great chamber, the said door into the hall to be shut at the will of Hawisia; also the painted chamber next to the great chamber, with a wardrobe [private storeroom], a dairy-house with the space between the dairy and the door into the great kitchen, to be shut at Hawisia's pleasure; the new stable with the house called the cart-house, a barn called the kulnhouse [cowhouse], a third of the [produce of the] dovecot . . . [etc.][41]

[39] *CPR, 1399–1401*, 399; McKisack, *Fourteenth Century*, 487–8.
[40] Emery, *Greater Medieval Houses*, ii. 19–20; C. Taylor, 'Medieval Ornamental Landscapes', 40, 46–7, 50. No other such measures at 'coastal' castles at this time are enrolled. Duchess Elizabeth remarried (Robert Goushill, knight, d. 1403: a *mésalliance*). Bretby now lacks distinct buildings: D. King, *Castellarium Anglicanum*, Derbys.; *CPR, 1292–1301*, 580; *CCR, 1402–5*, 210.
[41] *CIPM* iv. 242: James de la Plaunche, 1306; vi. 425, on John de Olney, d. 1325, joint holder with Maud, his wife, mother of William de la P.; vii. 494–5, on William, with summary of dower assignment; *CPR, 1301–7*, 233 (licence to crenellate, 1304). In 1272 the manor had a dovecot, grange (barn), garden, and vineyard, with the advowson of the church, all worth 30s. p.a. So long associated with the family as to be known in 1424 as *Plankes Manere*: *CCR, 1422–9*, 103. *VCH Bucks IV*, 367–9.

Most of the high-status 'private' rooms went to the widow, with an assured privacy from the 'public' hall and main kitchen, together with a share of the agricultural outbuildings to this typical 'castellated manor', now represented by a quadrangular 'moat' near the parish church, itself originally manorial as was usually the case. There was no manorial mill, but dovecots were objects similarly of prestige as well as of profit. Knightly families on both sides of the Channel prized this symbol of their nobility, all the more for it being relatively lowly.[42]

Since noble women were occasionally married at 14 years (more usually at 17–24), commonly to older men, they often outlived several husbands, acquiring successive dowries and very complex extended-family relationships, despite the hazards of childbirth. Disentangling what they held for life from possessions held in their own right, some of which might be disposable by will (or, technically, by trust), caused frequent litigation. For an heir, married and of full age, getting rid of a resident dowager, with whom there might well be no blood relationship, was a problem not fully solved by partition. In this regard, 'castles' might have more accommodation but shared the same difficulties. In 1311 the lady of Maule went to King Philip IV's parlement claiming that by the customs of the *vicomté* of Paris widows were able to select and keep whichever they preferred of their marital houses. This she asked the court to uphold in respect of the family castle (with the common name of Le Plessis) against the opposition of Jean de L'Île and his brother, probably her stepsons.[43] It might, on the other hand, require a forceful widow who was guardian of her children (and no little good fortune) to make good their rights against a powerful oppressor. Boys were often especially vulnerable—on top of a biologically higher rate of mortality in infancy.[44]

Families of castellar rank were more likely to possess 'spare' dwellings, making partition of the castle itself less necessary. Dual-occupancy did reduce the lord's status, particularly if of an ancient castle like Egremont. Danger, generally, had as little influence on tenure as it did on construction. But the language of the records is often misleading. Female tenure was clearly a relevant factor, in several respects, but the documents seldom produce clear answers. One quite illuminating case is that of Eleanor, widow of Herbert son of John, lord of the castellaries dependent

---

[42] Lady Auda of Tirent, Gascony (*dép.* Gers), even appealed to Philip V's court in 1319 (for 'default of justice') against the refusal of Edward II's seneschal to license her to construct a mill. Bertrand Caillau's *bannum moute* was thus upheld: *Actes du Parlement*, i, ii, 268. These trivial appeals (the bottom of the seignorial scale of aspiration topped by castellation) had become frequent.

[43] *Actes du Parlement*, i, ii, 82; nn. 21, 22 above.

[44] Whereas a girl, once married, had an adult interested protector, boys might have to wait until 21: in 1230 Count Robert III of Dreux, having obtained the strong-house of Sorel Moussel (near Dreux, *dép.* Eure-et-Loir) from Eleanor, his widowed sister, during her son's minority, opportunistically destroyed the 'tower' of the 'house'. On appeal by Eleanor, Louis IX's court somewhat safeguarded the nephew's interests, prohibiting fortifying by Dreux, making the damage repayable and the *domus* rendable, but leaving open vindication of the nephew's rights at law when of age: *Layettes*, ii. 193–4. In a similar lordship-encroachment in 1332, the men of the bishop of Langres razed 'the tower and strong-house' of Pringey (*dép.* Marne?). Isabella, widow of G. de Rémy, knight, for their children got the verdict that the bishop had no legal right, obliging his officials to rebuild what they had demolished: *Actes du Parlement*, ii, i, 60.

on Blaenllyfni and on the mountaintop fortress of Dinas (generic Celtic for 'fortress'), alias Bwlch-y-Dinas (both previously mentioned), in the Welsh marcher district of Brecknock (Brecon). In 1322, after Herbert's death, Edward II had affirmed his rights over them.[45] After 1327 they were held from the new earldom of March, but matters did not come to a head until 1331, after Roger de Mortimer's forfeiture and execution, when the earldom was taken into the king's hands. As was still customary, Eleanor had been dowered by Herbert, just before their marriage in 1290/1 ('at the church door'), with the bride's 'third part' of all his lands for her life. In 1331 these Brecon territories yielded the considerable annual revenue of £60 and traditionally owed the service of two knights' fees (fiefs). In May the virtually automatic mandate issued, in the normal 'course' of routine writs from the Chancery, instructing the escheator to make over her third share to Eleanor, having first received her homage for it in the king's name and taken her promise not to remarry without royal permission.[46] With his knowledge of Welsh customs (and doubtless prompted by the family), the escheator hesitated to put into Eleanor's share the two castles themselves. Failing to get her due, Eleanor appealed to Edward III's council which, with the benefit obviously of a report from the escheator, had an amended mandate sent on 2 October (1331):

> To . . . the escheator . . . Order to cause the value of the bodies of the castles of Blenleveny, Bulkedynas, and a third of the honour . . . to be delivered to Eleanor as she has given the king to understand that the escheator has deferred making assignment to her of a third of the castles, honour, and lands, as ordered by the king, because bodies of castles have not been usually divided and assigned in dower.

There was, in fact, even in Wales scarcely any such rule; but some unmentioned pressure by the heirs had presumably had enough support from local precedent to make the escheator hesitate.[47] At all events, Eleanor did not object and the royal keepers during the interregnum were told to supervise the procedure of valuing, demarcating, and dividing the component units of profit. As an extra precaution the escheator's resulting very detailed settlement was copied onto the Close Roll (18 November). To Eleanor were assigned additional receipts to cover her share in payments (in cash or kind) made by tenants and peasantry at the castles themselves, no doubt to avert the inconvenience of keeping her own receivers at such remote but once-populated and productive places. But the tangible as well as

---

[45] D. King, *Castellarium Anglicanum*, Brecknock: Blaenllyfni—two rudimentary enclosures, outer of earthwork, inner of 'poor masonry'; mentioned 1205, 1233, 1322. Apparently more was left in 1876: Clark, *Medieval Military Architecture*, ii. 504–5. Dinas—a prehistoric hillfort with two probably 12th-century walled wards; inner 'strong' and large with small rectangular towers and ?keep: D. King, ibid.; *CCR, 1318–23*, 415.

[46] *CCR, 1330–3*, 232; noting that Eleanor (doubtless according to her petition) had not renounced her dower rights when Herbert died in year 14 Edw. II (1320/1). In England, by the late 14th century, automatic rights of inheritance were giving way, for the great families, to licensed discretionary trusts: G. Holmes, *Higher Nobility*, 45, 51–2.

[47] *CCR, 1330–3*, 263. What had occurred between Herbert's death and 1331 is not apparent. Given the political crises of the decade and the location, normal procedures are likely to have been in abeyance.

lucrative perquisites of lordship were hers to the extent of 'a dovecot with a curtilage about it and a small fishpond with the plot (*placeam*) of a garden adjoining it', these at Blaenllyfni. Similarly combining usufruct with symbolism, Eleanor also enjoyed 'the easement of the prison of Blenleveny castle when needed for the custody of prisoners attached [arrested] by her ministers', so that her rights of jurisdiction could be exercised. Other normal appurtenances of a greater castle which she was able to share, without demeaning the new lord, included one-third of the profits of the watermill (at which corn was compulsorily ground), the same at the fulling-mill used for felting cloths from the loom before the final manufacturing processes; and for tied labour a number of serfs were assigned to her, identified by name. Apparently she possessed at least one residence of her own inheritance, since none was specifically made over to her, to enable her to live on hand and to participate in the full economic and seignorial activity of a major marcher castellary.[48]

Lifestyle was all-important. Because the *capita* of the greater fiefs were usually castles, most of them dating back to the Norman settlement (at sites frequently of Anglo-Saxon lordship and sometimes with trivial post-Conquest-era development), what differenced fortress-mansions from others was chiefly not the degree or modernity of fortification but the extent of the lordship and its antiquity, especially if the seat of a barony. Female tenure throws into relief their lordly and economic significance, offering only sidelights on their occasional but potential military role. But some degree of defence-capability was itself integral to the aristocratic image: fortification of buildings, as of the other accoutrements of rank, was noble style. So wealthy widows lived in appropriate 'state'—as Lady Joan de Bohun did in 1278–9:[49]

The jurors say that Lady Joanna holds a certain *forcelettum* in Kimbolton and its hamlet [Hunts.] from the domains of Lord Humphrey de Bohun, earl of Hereford, in right of dower. The Lord Humphrey holds that fortress from the king in chief of ancient [enfeoffment]. To the fortress belong 700 acres of arable, a wood called Heywode of 200 acres, a park of 50 acres, a meadow of 20 acres etc. . . .

2. The Distinctiveness of Fortresses Under Châtelaines

One of the less difficult comparisons between England and France lies in the nature of the accessible documentary evidence, which controls and limits a general survey such as this. Particularly in the printed *Layettes* there is a rich treasure of

[48] *CCR, 1330–3*, 403–5. No other heirs are named as present, so she and Herbert may have been childless. Dinas may already have been moribund. Neither it nor Blaenllyfni had more than territorial significance.

[49] *Rot Hund*, ii. 621a; *CIPM* xii. 427 (Humphrey de Bohun, 1353) describes 'Kynebauton manor' as including 'a *fortalicium* with houses inside and outside the enclosure, a park called Brithalmwyk, 300 acres of . . . wood called Le Haywoode', etc. It was once a quadrangular, double-moated castle, now wholly rebuilt. Henry III made a rare grant of timber for 'houses' here in 1226. Edward II as one of 60 castles put men into it in 1322: *Rot Litt Claus*, ii. 134b; *CCR, 1318–23*, 437.

letters and charters made to, or acquired by, the kings of France from individual
lords; whereas very little of the voluminous English Chancery and Exchequer files
of 'letters received' has been published. Conversely, France lacks the great and
continuous series of records of the royal administration from c.1199 (inquisitions
and personal writs most notably), which tends to give such a strong centrist feeling to English historiography; compensated for by scattered but enormous local
archives, which have had to be left out entirely.[50]

Such comparisons as have so far emerged have tended to affirm the strong
generic affinities between the noble culture of France and in England. Where, as
in Ireland (Ch. 2, sec. 1 below), Wales, and in the borderlands of Scotland and of
France (Ch. 2, sec. 2 below), war and the (much manipulated) rumours of war
impinged particularly on female castle-tenure, just how the situation was handled
depended chiefly on individual circumstances. Certain general tenurial principles
applied, but the age, character, influence, and situation of the lady castellan, her
family relationships, and the degree of trust between her and the lord of the fief
also mattered. Abundant evidence of such personal arrangements is preserved
among the great mass of charters kept in the coffers and chests or *layettes* of the
royal treasury, once in Louis IX's Sainte Chapelle attached to the palace and castle
(the Louvre) in Paris. Something of the attitudes and ideas which permeated
those mutual guarantees may be recovered.

Many of the most illuminating charters involving fortresses of all kinds differ
from all but a rare few English documents in that they focus on rendability, which
formulated castellan–overlord co-operation in terms at once more explicit,
demanding, and specific to fortifications than are to be found across the Channel.
In France, indeed, much of the tenurial and legal distinctiveness of fortresses (in
Britain blurred and equivocal) was bound up with rendability. Great castles and
mere *maisons fortes* were equally affected.[51] Less than any other form of real property were fortresses anywhere generally in absolute ownership or freehold, a fact
which puts into perspective the arrangements for minorities, guardianships, and
female-tenure. English parallels were naturally close, but nonetheless emphasize
the contrasts, the more fragmented tenurial structure of the much larger country
being the chief. In 1315–18, for instance, Edward II's administration and the Percy
family to whom it belonged co-operated closely in the use of the then minor
Northumberland castle of Alnwick, later converted into an important base for

---

[50] Editorial introductions to most of the compilations of royal *acta* in the *Chartes et Diplômes* series
are of value; likewise by Beugnot to *Les Olim*, to the *Actes du Parlement* volumes, to *Layettes*, i and v
(but not iv), and by Bémont to *Rôles Gascons, Supplément*, i, iii. Shirley (ed.), *Royal Letters . . . Henry
III* is a rich but tiny sample of the manuscript material in the PRO. Later compilations and 12th-
century charters have not been searched. In France royal writs were not recorded systematically until
Philip IV, one of the last great chanceries to do so: *Registres du Trésor*, i. pp. ix–liv (p. x). Enrolment
in England began in 1199.

[51] As strikingly shown e.g. by the c.1200/1 (46 places), 1222–c.1234 (19), 1249 (14), 1249–52 (37) fief
rolls of the counts of Champagne: *Documents Champagne*, pp. xv–xxiii, 77–194; *Rôles de Champagne*,
passim; Jubainville, *Histoire de Champagne*, ii, pp. xiii–cxxxi: collated lists of 'conditional' and 'unconditional' fortresses, Coulson, 'Seignorial Fortresses', App. A 3; and commentary, 'Castellation in
Champagne'. Even so, the Rolls are incomplete, some fragmentary.

defence of the Border.[52] The Crown did take over control of the fortress, but initially because the death of Henry de Percy senior had put his lands into the king's wardship for his son and namesake who was under age.[53] As soon as the latter was considered able to assume the responsibility, the keeping was provisionally granted to him until his formal majority.

How the Percies' rights were reconciled with resistance to Scottish incursions, following up the triumph of King Robert Bruce at Bannockburn, can be traced. It was the guardian's duty not to damage the heir's inheritance in any way. At Alnwick the man put in was the king's local commander, John de Felton. His appointment, summarized on the Fine Roll (as calendared), states the basics: 'Commitment during pleasure to John de Felton of the keeping of the castle and manor of Alnewyk, late of Henry de Percy tenant in chief, in the king's hand by reason of the minority of Henry his son and heir, to hold without waste, destruction, or ruin of the houses, woods, men, or other things thereof . . .' (December 1315).

So far, this was normal custody. Land was to be cultivated, managed, and conserved in all its resources, human and agricultural. But the circumstances were abnormal. Military mode required a patrolling force of forty men-at-arms and forty mounted archers ('hobelars') to be kept there, the cost being expected to amount to the full year's revenues of the seven named 'manors and towns' comprising the castellary.[54] Next May (1316) a general letter thanked 'the earls, barons, and others of Northumberland . . . for resisting the Scots', asking them to give credence to Felton, 'constable of the castle of Alnewyk', 'in all matters relating to the king's intended movements'. No royal campaign of significance in fact materialized. Late next year (November 1317) John de Felton was captured, apparently aborting an arrangement by which Alnwick was to be restored to Henry the son, made 'at the request of Eleanor, his mother, the king's kinswoman, late the wife of Henry de Percy, although he [the son] is a minor and in the king's custody . . . Alnewyk being of his inheritance and in the king's hands, to keep the said castle in safe custody and not to deliver it to any person other than the king'. Felton was free again by April 1318, and the original intention to give premature repossession to the young Henry was implemented in November.[55] The dowager

[52] Emery, *Greater Medieval Houses*, i. 36–9. Acquired by Percy in 1309, having fallen in to Anthony Bek, bishop of Durham, his landed base then being in Yorkshire (licensed to crenellate Leconfield and Spofforth in 1308) and an outlier in Sussex (licensed, Petworth, 1308: all *CPR, 1307–13*, 144) *1307–13*, 197.

[53] *CIPM* v. 313–24 (Oct. 1314), noting young Henry as 15½ (16 on 2 Feb. 1315); Petworth as 'the manor' with three named parks; Alnwick, 'castle and barony'; Spofforth 'capital messuage'; etc.—and that 'the constable of Alnwick occupies towns [Tughall and Swinhoe] not permitting the escheater to exercise his office there' (i.e. to take nominal possession).

[54] *CFR, 1307–19*, 267–8: an addendum listed the appurtenances. Felton was not expected to account for any surplus, unless his force was reduced to 20. On 'light cavalry' hobelars see M. Prestwich, *Armies and Warfare*, 52, 124, and 'The Garrisoning of English Medieval Castles', 188, on Felton's force at Alnwick. At the wage-rates given for Cockermouth (*CCR, 1307–19*, 496–7) 40 + 40 for a year would cost £1,095; 10 + 10 would cost £271. 5s., so the allowance of 100 marks mentioned took account of other revenue.

[55] *CPR, 1313–17*, 462–3; *1317–21*, 56, 61, 135: Felton had 'been seized by his enemies (*emulos suos*)

lady de Percy may well have been the power behind the scenes: not only is prominence again given to her remote blood-relationship to the king, but she had held
custody of the Percy lands in Yorkshire, which were accordingly not returned to
her son among 'all other lands late of his father in each county of the realm'. In
addition, the young Henry was to pay nothing to the Crown as wardship
revenues, being expected merely to defend Alnwick castellary against the Scots,
like any similar castellan. Aged 19, he was clearly well able to do a man's job.[56]
Boys matured rapidly, and *châtelaines* bore heavy responsibilities on occasion,
often facing sudden bereavement with fortitude.

If a widow was able to obtain the guardianship of her child and heir (potentially rival relatives tended to be less trusted), the family lands were spared excessive or merely insensitive exploitation by the king's or superior lord's appointee,
who was often the highest bidder and keen to recoup (and increase) his investment. Undertakings required to secure the guardianship, apart from offering
more than any competitor, might involve agreeing a suitable payment for custody
of the heir's person and property during 'nonage'; and, in the case of castellans
quite often, to making special guarantees in regard to the fortress itself.
Compensation was the overlord's, reasonably due for the loss of the vassal's
services, but taking possession in wardship also asserted his *dominatio*. Much was
open usually to negotiation and it was understood that 'good lordship' prescribed
moderate, humane, and 'reasonable' (a favourite but elastic criterion) use of
power.[57] To exhibit 'courtesy' was particularly 'noble', and especially when dealing with a bereaved lady. A document which fairly represents this situation is the
charter made to King Louis IX by the Lady Armoda of L'Isle-Bouchard (*dép.*
Indre-et-Loire) in 1235. It shows a rare extreme of precaution on the king's part,
perhaps because the county of Poitou in western France was not yet securely in
French control. Armoda went north to Corbeil near Paris to obtain her pact.[58]
The terms combine the routine mechanics of rendability with her own problems:

> To all to whom these present letters shall come, Armoda, lady of Isle-Bouchard [Touraine]
> and of Rochefort [-sur-Loire, near Angers], gives sincere greeting. May you all take note
> that I have made oath that I will hand over (*juravi me reddituram*) the castle of Rochefort
> [*dép.* Maine-et-Loire] to the Lord Louis, king of France, or to his heirs or known bearer of

whereby he cannot attend to his duties'; *CFR, 1307–19*, 378–9. Similarly, Roger, son of Robert de
Clifford, killed at Bannockburn: the custodians of his four castles were to provide 'for the sustenance
of the heir and the keeping and defence of the castles'. In July 1318, Roger was prematurely given
possession, aged 17–18 holding the Westmorland castles (Appleby, Brougham, Mallerstang) without
payment but paying the value of other lands to the Exchequer: *CFR, 1307–19*, 212, 370–1; *CIPM* v.
300–7. Keeping back a third of Westmorland shrievalty profits only does not seem to represent a
dower. Henry de Percy married Roger's sister Idoine: Sanders, *English Baronies*, 148, n. 4.

[56] In May 1324 he obtained an order to the Exchequer to charge him nothing for Alnwick since his
premature reseisin on 13 Nov. 1318 (*CCR, 1323–7*, 102–3). He was also granted the keeping of the family
Yorkshire lands until his full age should his mother die first: *CFR, 1307–19*, 378–9. Ages given by *post
mortem* jurors, despite circumstantial detail, are not always honest.

[57] On the exploitation of, and resistance to, wardship see Given-Wilson, *English Nobility*, 149–53;
changed attitudes *temp.* Richard II, pp. 169–71.

[58] Probably Corbeil-Essonnes, *dép.* Seine-et-Oise: *Layettes*, ii. 290.

his letters patent, whether there be with them great force or small (*com magna vi vel parva*), as often (*quocienscumque*) as I shall be requested on his behalf to do so, this being the condition on which the king has agreed to give the castle back to me [in fief]'.

Thus far the agreement is conventional, if expressed in unusually poor Latin for the place and date. It seems that Rochefort had not previously been rendable, but stipulating that the fortress should be delivered on mere authenticated demand, irrespective of compulsion is in standard northern French style (Langue d'Oïl).[59] No doubt Armoda went so far in person because assuring the king of her loyalty and negotiating the terms of her guardianship required it. Notifying her husband's death could have been done by envoy. Even her homage could have been performed by proxy: but personality mattered here. She went on:

And I have promised, of my free volition, that I will not enter into any contract of marriage, whether for myself or any of my children (*puerorum*). For their wardship and custody of their lands I have bound myself to pay £800 in money of Tours in three instalments, at next Ascension [17 May 1236] and at the next two Ascensions.—Now, since the king is entitled (*tenere debeat*), if he wish, to have the castle of Rochefort in his own hand for two years, I have promised to pay to him £100 of Tours a year for [the cost of] keeping his soldiers (*municio*) in the castle; after which he would be bound (*debeat*) to restore the castle to me and I would then have to satisfy him that I will faithfully keep it to the best of my power.

King Louis had apparently not yet decided whether to put a (token) force into Rochefort, but Armoda had secured her right to it, to its castellary, and to be guardian. In addition she was recognized in her own lordship and custody of the under-age heir and lands of a fief subordinate to Rochefort. Royal consent to any remarriage appears to have been discretionary, whereas guarantee for loyal tenure of the castle proper was not. Both ensured that Rochefort was not drawn into any pro-English affinity.[60] That Armoda paid any extra for the exemptions she obtained does not appear—the circumstances do not suggest that she was oppressively treated, but rather imply a degree of cautious trust on the part of the Crown.

The different treatment accorded to *châtelaines* was a compound of the differentiating of women and of fortresses. In other circumstances, as has been seen, neither attracted such disabilities as the Lady Armoda had to overcome. But whereas propertied women, liable to marry with not always predictable consequences for the lord, or surviving to the deprivation of other heirs, always

---

[59] Usually *ad magnam vim seu ad parvam*, equivalent to the 'be the lord angered or appeased' (*irato seu pacato*) formula of the south. Stipulating that Rochefort shall be rendered 'however many times' it was demanded, not merely 'whenever' (*quandocumque*), is emphatic but not notably unusual. Both indicated a brief, demonstrative, and exemplary resumption.

[60] Royal power to consent to her remarriage was evidently not established at this place and period. Using *pueri* (lit. 'boys') for children of both sexes is common. Two years' tenure in lieu of relief (succession duty) is here moderated, compounded for a sum to include a royal military presence. After that, formal enfeoffment against promises for due custody, would be made. Dated *apud Corbolium*, 'Wednesday next after Ascension' (23 May 1235).

required precautions (sometimes harsh), only in a hostile environment did fortresses do so. Philip II's severity towards Countess Joanna of Flanders, Countess Mary of Ponthieu, and Countess Alice of Eu, after he had crushed the Anglo-Imperial coalition at Bouvines (1214), is a notable example (see below). In contrast, 'reasonable' suspicion was normally expected before demanding a fortress in pledge of loyalty;[61] but then it was usual for the castellan to pay the custody costs. Under rendability, no costs beyond ordinary consumption of stores fell on the castellan. Even if the lord should improve the fortress while temporarily in his hands 'so as to serve his need better', ruled the ex-royal official Philippe de Beaumanoir in his treatise on the customs of the Beauvaisis (c.1283), 'his man is not bound to pay anything, since it was not done by him, albeit the benefit (li pourfis) may remain his'.[62] Pledging to prove loyalty (or to repress revolt) entailed understandably harsher conditions.

Throughout Beaumanoir's exposition of lordship rights in the county of Beauvais the duties of li sires to 'his man', are emphasized as much as those of vassal to lord. The tenurial bond, from this perspective, was not so much an instrument of government as a signal of social solidarity. So the count and baronial lords could take over the fortresses but must not do so dishonestly, or without need, or out of malice, or, indeed, to pursue evil designs on the vassal's wife, daughter, or other women in his wardship (en sa garde).[63] This spirit of feudal reciprocity was ubiquitous, but at its most crucial it is fully illustrated where fortresses were involved—so handing them over to appease suspicion of disloyalty, actual or incipient, marks an exception. But it was still expected to be exercised 'reasonably' and consensually. King John used it ruthlessly and often in his French and British dominions during the crisis years of the loss of Normandy (1203–4) and in the conditions of wavering allegiance and civil war of his last three years (1212–16).[64] But, even so, the lord's right to be given appropriate guarantees was absolute. Already in the earlier eleventh century, in the Conventum dialogue between Count William of Aquitaine and Hugh de Lusignan, the count is reported to have asked Hugh: 'how does one establish a castle? You are Count Fulk's man—so he would then require it of you: and you could not rightly hold what you have not rendered to him.'[65] Women normally held castles on almost exactly the same basis.

If there was no absolutely compelling political pressure, a châtelaine might satisfy her lord's concerns by the giving of guarantees by an important relative.

[61] e.g. Renaud de Dammartin's castle of Mortain in 1211: Recueil Philippe II, iii. 311–14 (rare memoranda for oral messages).

[62] Beaumanoir, 351–2 (para. 1663); Part II, n. 310 above.

[63] Beaumanoir, 351 (para. 162).

[64] But requiring hostages was barely acceptable. John's seizure of Ranulph of Chester's castle of Semilly (dép. Manche) in 1202 was at best clumsy, at worst ultra vires. It was restored on guarantees by the archbishop of Canterbury and the bishop of Ely that Ranulph would pledge Semilly if demanded, which he duly did, but received no assurance of restitution: Rot Litt Pat, 7b, 28a; Rot Norm, 96–7; F. Powicke, Loss of Normandy, 167.

[65] Martindale, Conventum, 546.

During the threatening buildup of the Anglo-Imperial coalition in 1212, Philip II had to be reassured by Mary de Courbeville that he would be able to use the castle buildings of Lavardin in Maine (*dép.* Sarthe) for his support, as a rendable castle, while they were in the hands of Mary's niece Alice in dower.[66] After King Philip's great victory over the combined forces of the emperor, the rebel count of Boulogne, and of King John, at Bouvines near Lille in July 1214, his treatment of the counts and communes of Flanders, Ponthieu, Boulogne, and of Eu was a nice combination of quite vindictive punishment and of calculated precaution; but also of good lordship, chiefly confined to the wives.[67] Alice of Eu, Joanna of Flanders and Hainaut, and Mary of Ponthieu were all countesses in their own right. Their husbands were life-tenants and to some extent outsiders: Ralph of Exoudun, with his lands in England, died there in 1219; the Portuguese Ferdinand of Flanders suffered twelve years unchivalrous confinement; Simon de Dammartin of Ponthieu (brother of Renaud, forfeited count of Boulogne, animator of the coalition) was exiled for seventeen years.[68] An exemplary punishment was also inflicted on the fortress-rights of the vanquished. Countess Joanna, in October 1214, had to swear to King Philip 'that I will have the fortifications (*fortericias*) of Valenciennes, Ypres, Oudenarde, and of Cassel demolished, as the lord king may wish'. Communes prided themselves on their walls, so this suspended sentence was deeply humiliating. Any walls destroyed were to require royal consent before rebuilding, and a 'fortification-freeze' (or 'ban') was similarly imposed on 'all the other fortresses of Flanders' and on all new fortification.[69] When Alice was restored on her husband's death in 1219 to her diminutive and further diminished coastal county of Eu, she promised that:

I will also give the lord king my own and my men's guarantees that I will not [re-] marry without his consent (*nisi per eum*); and the lord king will not put pressure on me (*me non effortiabit*) to remarry. Neither I nor my heirs shall fortify, nor shall we strengthen any fortresses beyond their present state, unless with his consent.

It was derogatory of her and Joanna's status as great feudatories to have to seek royal licence, even nominally, and to be unable technically to license their own

---

[66] *Layettes*, i. 377. Marie promised, pledging *totam terram meam erga dominum meum Philippum, regem Francie illustrem, quod ipse se juvare poterit de forteritia de Lavardin*. How closely akin to rendability this was is shown by expressing the bond as being *ad magnam vim et ad parvam*. Marie also swore that 'so long as my niece Alice (*Aeles*) has her dower there, I will not allow that *castrum* to be put in another's hand, without the lord king's will and assent'. She went north to Saint-Germain-en-Laye to settle the question with him.

[67] Political context etc., Coulson, 'Impact of Bouvines', 75–80.

[68] In 1221 Philip seized Ponthieu to stop Simon acquiring the county in right of Countess Mary, heiress of William II. Boulogne county was forfeited and bestowed (1223) on the king's son by his second marriage, Philip Hurepel ('shock-haired'). He signified his establishment there with a new polygonal castle (1223–31), one of a group including Fère-en-Tardenois, Montreuil-sur-Mer, and Bolingbroke (Lincs.): *Recueil Ponthieu*, pp. vi–viii; Mesqui, *Châteaux-forts*, 68–71, 168; M. Thompson, *Rise of the Castle*, 104–6.

[69] The 'ban' was still operating in 1255 when Countess Margaret obtained licence from Louis IX for Ruplemonde castle, being 'on this (French) side of the Scheldt': successive forms, *Layettes*, i. 407–8; ii. 53–4, 76–7, 356–7, 565, 637–8; iii. 151, 226.

vassals to fortify. By contrast, the succession-duty or relief which Alice arranged to pay, in three instalments, was routine.[70] She was completely vulnerable. Countess Joanna was not dispossessed of French Flanders, but before Count Ferdinand was reinstated in 1226, and before Simon de Dammartin's children by Mary of Ponthieu were admitted as heirs and he himself reinstated as count in her right in 1231, the same renunciation of fortifying had to be made.[71]

In separation, exile, and other pains, the defeated party at Bouvines all suffered—but the lords who were counts by courtesy much more than their heiress wives. When conciliation was in the ascendant the same assurances were required from *châtelaines* as from their male counterparts. Courtesy and good lordship were most in evidence when the bitterness of death was past—but fortress-custom provided for all conditions. In most cases the lord's interests were sufficiently safeguarded by the normal operation of rendability. An example is the charter made in 1229, on the death of the seneschal of frontier Poitou to Queen Blanche, regent and guardian for her 15-year old son Louis IX. The customs relied upon being so well established, the widow's pact, dated at the then hunting lodge of Vincennes near Paris, was comparatively terse:

I, Valentia de Blazon, widow of Theobald de Blazon, hereby promise and swear that I will not marry any enemy of the king; that I will always be loyal to the Lady Blanche, the queen mother; and that I will hand over, to great force and to small alike, Maussac and all the castles which Theobald, my erstwhile husband, was holding when he died, whether to the queen personally or to her order, however many times (*quoties*) I shall be requested to do so by her accredited envoy (*certio nuntio*).[72]

Offering better lordship was one of the many forms of the competition for Poitou and Saintonge in which the regent Blanche and Henry III of England were engaged at this period.[73] Plantagenet hopes of regaining their ancestral possessions, lost since the aftershocks of the fall of Normandy (1203–25), were not eventually abandoned until after Henry III's discomfiture and retreat in 1242 at Taillebourg and Saintes.[74] Widows like Valentia de Blazon and Armoda of L'Isle-Bouchard were involved in the great contest during sometimes quite prolonged minorities. They might find themselves more than metaphorically 'holding the fort', as well as taking their normal place in the dynastic succession and in manag-

---

[70] She relinquished claims to Neufchâtel (*Drincourt*) and Mortemer: *Layettes*, i. 485, 487–8.

[71] *Amplissima Collectio*, i. 1198–9; Petit-Dutaillis, *Louis VIII*, 396, 496. Ralph satisfied Henry III's regents by pledging his castle of Hastings.

[72] *Layettes*, ii. 165–6; suggesting Maussac, *dép.* Corrèze. In 1228 Theobald, as seneschal of Poitou, was one of two French adjudicators of the Anglo-French truce. Fortifying at Benon-en-Aunis, near La Rochelle, was prohibited. Either side could forcibly respond to any grave infraction, defined as the taking of any *fortericia vel castrum* or the abduction of any nobleman. Henry III's counterpart, *Foedera*, i, i, 186; Richard of Cornwall's, in full, ibid. 186–7; also '1227', F. Powicke, *Henry III and the Lord Edward*, 176 n.

[73] e.g. appeals to Henry III for Élie Rudel, by the townsmen of La Réole, for Fronsac, by William L'Archévêque of Parthenay, by Aimeri of Rochechouart, Reginald de Pons: Shirley (ed.), *Royal Letters*, i. 25–6, 49–50, 155–6, 302–3, 383–4, 386–7.

[74] e.g. Denholm-Young, *Richard of Cornwall*, 46–7. 'Settled' by the 1259 Treaty of Paris: Vale, *Origins of the Hundred Years War*, 48–56; Baudry, *Fortifications des Plantagenêts en Poitou*, 41–3.

ing the politics of their late husbands' estates as well as their administration. This was the position of Eleanor, viscountess-dowager of Thouars, in bas-Poitou (*dép.* Vendée) in 1270.[75] After long wavering between the rival powers, Capetian and Plantagenet, the *vicomtes* had gone over to Alphonse de Poitiers as count.[76] In 1269 Viscount Savary had been the first-named of the barons and nobles of Poitou in settling with Alphonse how 'relief' (*rachat à merci*) or succession-duty should be regulated, specifically leaving unaffected comital and seignorial rendability rights.[77] Eleanor was the widow of Savary's brother Regnaud, and became responsible for the chief Thouars castellary of Tiffauges with its ancient and very large capital fortress. The Thouars had a great position to maintain. Eleanor had gone to Paris, to the court of the largely absentee Count Alphonse. She announces herself as daughter of Count John of Soissons and widow of Viscount Regnaud, promising to deliver to Alphonse whenever requested the castle of Tiffauges, held as her dower (perhaps not in sole tenure), and also (in atavistic style typical of the region) to make good to him any harm which might arise therefrom. As guarantors for this bond (elsewhere 'jurability') she produced her father, her paternal uncle the *vicomte* of Melun, and the Parisian baron Mathieu de Montmorency as well as Savary, the new *vicomte*. Making her wholly responsible in this way testifies to Eleanor's widowhood and to the continuing strength of Poitevin custom.[78] Rendability did distinguish fortresses, but for reasons for the most part tenurial and recognitory. It had some original connection with defence, and always a possible military function like the fortifications themselves. Lacking the formalized institutions of fortress-custom, interactions in Britain were essentially similar but seemingly more dominated by expediency.

The violence latent in medieval society, despite its idealism, broke the surface repeatedly, and might involve castles—but at least as much for being the *capita* of estates as fortresses.[79] The often prolonged interregnum of widowhood, however, might itself attract violence, as seen in an incident in south Wales concerning the castle and lordship of Coity (Glam.) in 1412. It followed some stirring events. This elegant little walled ringwork, with its Norman square keep, its projecting ovoid

[75] *Layettes*, iv. 418: dated 'Friday before St Peters, 1269'. Tiffauges was of 11th-century origin, continuously updated, refortified for cannon in the earlier 15th century: Mesqui, *Châteaux-forts*, 377–8; Baudry, *Fortifications des Plantagenêts en Poitou*, 333–4.

[76] The viscounty was often in fraternal co-tenure. In April 1242 Aymeri VIII and his brother Geoffrey were recognized pro tem. (*ad viagium nostrum*) as *vicomtes*, in succession to their brother Guy whose under-age son Aymeri IX Alphonse accepted as heir. All three, 'out of pure good-will' (*ex mera liberalitate*), will receive Capetian troops *in castris et villis nostris firmatis* for the war with Henry III (terminated at Saintes) under rendability. In 1246 Aymeri IX did homage at Paris, pledging Tiffauges for five years and paying costs of guard, with all his fortresses made rendable: *Layettes*, ii. 471, 642–3. On Thouars see Baudry, *Fortifications des Plantagenêts en Poitou*, 257–70 (history and archaeology).

[77] *Layettes*, iv. 352–4; see above. Alphonse formally became count in 1249.

[78] Indemnifying the lord for any ill-effects of female tenure was not unusual, but novel for the Thouars castles. The text is known only from summary by Dupuy.

[79] K. Nicholas, 'When Feudal Ideals Failed', analyses the interplay of faith and force, 1127–1296, in the Low Countries. Brief but penetrating exploration of 'chivalry' (in warfare): M. Prestwich, *Armies and Warfare*, 219–22.

latrine turret serving the Hall and apartments with Chapel adjacent, and rectilinear thinly walled and turreted *basse cour*, had been under prolonged pressure
during Owen Glyndwr's uprising (1400–6). Henry IV ordered 'wine and other
victuals' to be taken to Coity in September 1405, among 'other castles of the king
in those parts'. Supplies of beans and malt were taken there by a commissioned
merchant of Bristol and landed near Ogmore castle, on the coast 4 miles distant.[80]
But Coity belonged to the Berkerolles family, and in November 1404 Laurence de
Berkerolles had been besieged there by the 'Welsh rebels'. His relief, with forces
costing over £730, was conducted by the future Henry V (1413–22) and by his
brother Thomas of Lancaster. This 'rescue' in the proper style of overlordly and
royal support for a hard-pressed vassal came in response to Laurence's appeal in
parliament, pleading that 'he is, and for a long time has been, *assegez en son
Chastel de Coitif*'. The whole affair was quite leisurely, a matter of harassment
essentially.[81] He was lord of the small castellary in right of his wife, heiress of the
Turbevilles. A disputed succession, not any warlike pressure, caused the incident
in 1412. The king was clearly anxious to proceed cautiously, while repressing resort
to force. Six commissioners were appointed (16 September):

on information that Gilbert Denys, *chivaler* [knight] and William Gamage, with no moderate multitude of armed men, have gone to the castle of Coityf in Wales and besiege it and
propose to expel Joan, late the wife of Richard Vernon, *chivaler*, from her possession of it—
to go as quietly as they can to the castle and raise the siege, causing proclamation to be
made that no one under pain of forfeiture shall besiege it, but those who pretend [claim]
right or title in it shall sue according to law and custom . . .

That Joan de Vernon had been left in possession of Coity lordship, in a lately
rebellious area, is as notable as the desultory nature, very often, of the harassment
described as 'siege'. Rival (English) claimants to the castellary sought to take
advantage of Joan's widowhood and of the likely weakness of her title—nor did
they desist just for the asking: in late October a new commissioner took over, to
be backed 'if necessary' by the sheriffs' *posse* of Hereford and Gloucester, to make
Sir Gilbert Dennis and William Gamage proceed in accordance with the law, they
having 'stopped the commissioners by force'.[82]

   Pursuing themes of this kind crosses regional boundaries and the sometimes
arbitrary divisions of period. The robust circumstances of Joan de Vernon at
Coity in 1412, though far apart in place and time, nevertheless compare quite
closely with widows' experiences in thirteenth-century south-west France. Louis

---

[80] *CPR, 1405–8*, 63, 163. A storm ruined part of the cargo. No armed opposition is mentioned.
Garrisons totalling 3,000 men (500 men at arms; 2,500 archers) were appointed for eight S. Wales
castles in 1405: ibid. 6, 147, 156, etc. On damage done see Pugh, *Glamorgan County History III*, 300–2;
p. 430 on 'Coety' castle.
[81] *CPR, 1401–5*, 470; Clark, *Cartae*, iv. 312–13 (more urgently, 1403), 314–15 (as 'Alexander' de
Berkerolles, 1404, 1406); also *CCR, 1402–5*, 478–9 (1404). Loss of Coity would 'redound to the king's
disgrace (*fiat in nostri scandalum*) and the destruction of our lieges'; Pugh, *Glamorgan County History
III*, 184; *Rot Parl*, iii. 547.
[82] *CPR, 1408–13*, 433, 476; *CCR, 1409–13*, 407.

IX's brother, Alphonse de Poitiers (as has been seen) was busy asserting his position as count of Poitou and endeavouring to have his rights observed in this tumultuous region as they would be in the Capetian homeland of the Île-de-France, ancient *Francia*. His arrangements with Margaret of Rochefort-en-Poitou in 1243, after the death of her husband Geoffrey, are exceptional only in their precision and detail. Count Alphonse, through his officials acting in his name, in the quite regular fashion allowed Margaret to continue to hold Rochefort castle (a common *neufchâteau* name) subject to rendering it symbolically at once, and thereafter whenever demanded, *sanz contredit et sanz delaiement*.[83] As a further safeguard, practical as well as demonstrative, she must get his licence to fortify it in any way. The logic, very often, of such a limitation was complex: not only might fortifying provocatively assert Margaret's only conditional possession, but heavy outlay would be involved of any surplus income (after payment of relief), very possibly borrowing upon security of the castellary to obtain ready cash. Equally, mere munitioning (also 'fortifying' very often) might herald rebellion—and fortifying constantly signalized permanent full possession.[84] Local friction could easily ensue—so Margaret was not forbidden to fortify (a 'ban' was not a prohibition) but had to seek formal licence. This was the year after the Anglo-Gascon rebuff at Saintes (1242), so no occasion could be neglected to assert Capetian control. Being a widow, with the repercussions of female tenure, as well as a castellan, and holder of a more powerful fief and of a fortress, were all factors which demanded precaution.[85] Margaret, therefore, found among her allies nine guarantors, two of them knights, to go bail that she would duly keep her promises, subjecting them to forfeiture in case of her default. This should not be supposed to be some medieval precursor of the contractual disability imposed on women by the post-1789 French Code Napoléon (by which they could not own property or do legal transactions in their own name)—male castellans might do much the same. Guarantees and pledges in many situations spread the responsibility of

[83] For the period, 'early French' is unusual: *Layettes*, ii. 521–2. Expressed in the first person (*Ge Marguarite . . .*).

[84] Therefore Peter Mauclerk, duke (or count) of Brittany, promised the recently widowed regent Queen Blanche (1227) that he would 'not fortify anew or refortify' in the lands provisionally granted to him for the marriage pact between his daughter Yolande and her son, the boy John of France, under which Peter was to hold John's apanage of Anjou and Maine in wardship until he came of age. In fact, John died and his brother Charles in due course received Anjou (with Provence). The town and forest of Le Mans were also promised to Peter (in a vain attempt to keep him out of the English orbit) should Queen Berengaria (dowered widow of Richard Coeur de Lion, d. 1199) die while John was a minor. Conversely, if Peter's son John should predecease him, John of France shall have no claim (by Yolande) on Brittany in Peter's lifetime. Yolande was to be put *pro tem.* in wardship of Count Philip of Boulogne. Though aborted by John of France's death (and formally cancelled in 1238) this detailed pact is exemplary: *Layettes*, ii. 119–21 (March 1226/7), 374–5.

[85] The vernacular formulae are those which the usual Latin translates: Margaret will *rendrai et livrerai le chastel . . . à toz (tous) termes que ge en serai requise de mon seignor le comte ou de son espéciau comandement qui ses lettres pendanz [patentes*: with hanging seal affixed] *m'apportera, à grant force et à petite*. The castle she will not *efforcer*, nor cause to be, *par negune (aucune) manère sanz la volunté de mon seignor le comte*—all sworn on the Evangels (Gospels). A quirk is that she had to deliver Rochefort castle 'in the same state as she had received it'—a Languedocien stipulation. Only one of her nine guarantors was of status sufficient to have his own seal.

compliance, as English oath-helpers or 'compurgators' at the common level routinely did.[86] Margaret's *coterie* of interested supporters, conjoined with her in the charter, were probably (or included) tenants of Rochefort and members of the lord's regular court or council, consulted on tenurial questions as a matter of course. But that was not all. The charter, by which she speaks with such forthright vigour, concludes with a worst-case scenario. Lady Margaret provided that

> . . . should it happen that the seneschal of Poitou of the time be dissatisfied with these *fiances et . . . tenuz*, then it will be my duty to reinforce them so far as I am able by the [oaths of] the men of my land (*a mon poeir des mes homes de ma terre*). And should matters be such that the seneschal is still not satisfied with such guarantees, then I will have to render to him and deliver the said castle . . .[87]

Isabella de Craon, widow of the hereditary seneschal of Anjou, made a harsher but similar pact with Count Alphonse in 1250.[88] Handing over a castle did not mean vacating it, under most regional customs and circumstances. The residence was seldom affected. When it was, the cause was usually to assert demonstrative repossession by the lord. In Languedoc, 'full control' (*plena potestas*) and the seignorial right of the overlord were sometimes otherwise incomplete, so vacation was insisted on.[89] Margaret of Rochefort's widowhood may have made these terms more severe—but the vacillation of a male castellan might require equal precaution.

Heraldry offers some insight, however oblique, into how the differenced equality in the eyes of the law of male and female landowners was respected. The convention of 'impaling' (i.e. combining) the wife's 'coat of arms', juxtaposed with her husband's, expressed their partnership, and the child's parentage. Indeed, when an heiress without brothers married, her 'lozenge' father's coat was put in the centre of her husband's 'arms' as an escutcheon in still more emphatic demonstration. Sons took their father's name usually, but bore their parents' combined 'coat'.[90] As proprietors, women sought and obtained licences to fortify,

---

[86] Maitland, *Constitutional History*, 116–18, on Anglo-Saxon law. Guarantors under monetary bonds, regularly supported rendability, etc. pacts made to Philip II and Louis VIII in their conquests from the Angevins.

[87] This subjection to a seneschal's absolute discretion (if he *ne se tenist à paiez*—twice) is somewhat degrading. It was severe also to require overriding oaths (as by King John occasionally) by sub-tenants to disobey, in case of need, their direct lord. Sub-rendability, i.e. over the head of the direct (mesne) lord, occurs but rarely and with safeguards for mesne rights: e.g. *Layettes*, ii. 527 (Poitou, also in 1243).

[88] *Layettes*, iii. 109. She accepted that Chantocé, Sablé, Dieuzi, and La Roche-aux-Moines castles (*dép.* Maine-et-Loire) should be put in the custody of two of her knights; notifying that they have sworn to render them to the regent, to Louis IX or to Charles, count of Anjou, or to their order, pledging all their property as does Isabella. She gives also three guarantors, two unlimited, one in £1,000, to be discharged when obeyed and 'these letters' returned (not done). But Amaury de Craon, in 1212, swore to render Chantocé, under guarantees totalling £4,100 Paris: *Layettes*, i. 375–6; v. 66–7.

[89] e.g. Clermont l'Hérault, record of repossession by the bishop of Lodève in 1316: Ducange, 'Dissertations', 498, 509 (excerpts). Other allusions, including in Langue d'Oil (e.g. Auxonne, 1197; Beaumanoir, *c.*1283; above), are to exemptions.

[90] The rules became highly elaborate: Boutell, *English Heraldry* (9th edn.), 174–9 ('marshalling'); Moncreiffe, Pottinger, *Simple Heraldry*, 16; Woocock and Robinson, *The Oxford Guide to Heraldry*, *passim*; M. Prestwich, *Armies and Warfare*, 222–4.

singly as well as conjointly with their husbands. For towns in their lordship they obtained tax-powers ('murage' in Britain) to pay for walling, gates, and ditches.[91] Their rights are put in context by the fact that no case has been found of a castle-fief being withdrawn (i.e. forfeited) from male tenure on account of old age or incapacity for military service; but men who led lives of constant outdoor activity may have survived less often than women as elderly invalids, although 'Proofs of Age' were often given by local men said to be over 70 years old. In cases where the constraints of female tenure were enhanced by such restrictions, as were (to very varying extent) inherent in fortress-tenure per se, the resulting package was generally quite mild, as has been seen, even in circumstances of political stress. Male castellans, in any case, were treated very similarly in comparable circumstances.

In 1216, for instance, Count William of Sancerre agreed with his feudal superior Countess Blanche of Champagne (guardian, 1201–21, of Thibaut IV) a set of arrangements for the custody of his title-place castle near Bourges (*dép.* Cher) before he set out on the hazardous venture of going on pilgrimage to the Holy Land.[92] A complication was the Champagne custom which sought to ensure that fortresses were held in-chief.[93] Another, constantly increasing, was multiple allegiance, still remaining after 'liege', or nominally overriding, homage evolved in the later twelfth century. Another difficulty was that Countess Blanche had to face down (and eventually buy off) claims to the Champagne succession from Érard de Brienne in right of his wife Philippa, and from Alice de Lusignan, titular queen of Cyprus. Custody of the castellary by a friendly neutral, Robert de Courtenay, for up to four years, conferred not by William but by Countess Blanche, was the solution.[94] Should Count William die overseas, Robert was to keep Sancerre castellary in trust (*tanquam de ballio*) until William's son Louis 'arrives at the age of holding land'. Personalities as well as principles mattered. Many such arrangements were fudges, deferring to tenurial propriety but dictated by the facts of power. Nevertheless, doctrines of *raison d'état* and *force-majeure* did not displace the duty of the castellan, male or female, to preserve their fortress in their lord's

---

[91] e.g. Lady Mathilda de Mortimer, in 1283, obtained murage for Radnor, a dependency of her castle; in 1339 Elizabeth de Burgh (Clare) likewise for Callan, in Ulster. Licences to women to fortify have already been cited. Notably, in 1348, Mathilda (Maud) de Marmion had a repeat of the licence to crenellate West Tanfield (Yorks.) obtained by her late husband 34 years earlier: *CPR, 1281–92,* 69; *1338–40,* 325; *1313–17,* 177; *1348–50,* 210.

[92] *Thesaurus Novus,* i. 857; not the Fourth Crusade (1202–4) or the Fifth (1219–21), but pilgrimage or 'setting out to Jerusalem' (*Jerosolymam profecturus*) was the origin of the mass-crusades and was continuous: e.g. Runciman, *Crusades,* i. 38–50, 121–33. Stephen of Sancerre, a Blois-Champagne cadet, had gone with Counts Thibaut and Henri on the Third Crusade and died there, 1190 (ibid. iii. 28, 32).

[93] *Omnes fortericie debent teneri de comite Campaniae quocumque modo fiant in supradicto comitatu:* cited as the reason for Thibaut IV's restrictive licence for Givry in 1223: Mortet and Deschamps, *Recueil,* ii. 233; cf. *Thesaurus Novus,* i. 903–4.

[94] Viz. *custodiam Sacricaesaris castri mei cum omnibus appenditiis suis (de quo castro et de pluribus aliis sum homo ligius dictae Comitissae).* William's other castellaries were, it seems, independently settled by him; 'all this,' he says finally, 'my dear Lady Blanche, at my request, has willed and approved'.

interest, upholding his honour (in both the territorial and moral sense) while considering their own personal and family advantage, which their lord was reciprocally obliged (and well advised) to respect.[95]

Ideals, as always, diverged from practice, but the pride generally taken in gracious 'good lordship' tended to strengthen the chivalric courtesy required of the knight towards his lady by 'courtly love' or otherwise, and theoretically also to the weak and defenceless.[96] The practice of exempting women and children from forfeiture (prior to the introduction in England of Acts of Attainder), and also even from blame, benefited them continually. Edward II was not the most magnanimous of rulers, but in January 1326, three years after the 'rebellion' of Roger de Mortimer, later ruler and earl of March (1328–30), despite removing custody of the chief family castle of Wigmore and others from Roger's mother and sending her to the abbey (nunnery) of Elstow (Beds.), Edward still left her with the revenues of the castellary for her maintenance in suitable style.[97]

How powerful individuals wished to be perceived has often put a too-favourable gloss on events. Charters which record legally binding pacts are far from exempt—as the propagandist preambles of many early examples show. Consequently, the narrative charter recording the reception accorded by Count Guy II of Clermont and Auvergne to the widow of Bompard d'Auzon, in 1206, might seem almost too good to be true. Count Guy is shown acting with compassion as she formally sought from him the custody of her late husband's possessions and the guardianship of their children. It was a commonplace episode, at once ceremonial and personal, in which the parties were on their best behaviour (for the tenantry and notaries, not the cameras). Acting up to the images of chivalry frequently enhanced relationships. Christian ideals and familiar biblical moral stories exercised an incalculable influence for good, which it has become the fashion to decry. In the early thirteenth century the south-central mountainous province of Auvergne only nominally recognized the authority of the king in Paris. To those inclined to believe, with Thomas Hobbes, that orderly society could scarcely exist without state government, the customs of feudal lordship are a poor substitute: but the document testifies to an autonomous self-regulation

---

[95] 'Executive mandates' should always be seen in this light: e.g. Philip VI's lieutenant in Poitou 'instructing' the countess of Roucy to put her castle of Mirebeau (*dép*. Vienne) in a state of defence, or have it done by him at her cost (1348): Timbal, *Guerre de Cent Ans*, 107, n. 7. Similarly, 'orders' to Queen Philippa for her castle of Pevensey in 1339 (justifying local levies and tasks after sack of Southampton); and in 1352 (special oath by her constable): *CPR, 1338–40*, 208, 236–7; *1350–4*, 195 (detailed).

[96] The large literature (some already referred to) has tended to divide between realism-cynicism in anti-romantic reaction, and ideas-ambiance-culture studies. Literary sources, cautiously used, are helpful: e.g. contributions to Purdon and Vitto (eds.), *The Rusted Hauberk*, on 'feudal ideals of order'.

[97] *CPR, 1324–7*, 206, 258; *CCR, 1323–7*, 533 (Dec. 1325); justifying this severity by alleging that she 'held meetings of suspected persons' at Radnor castle and at Worcester. Her rebel son had absconded from the Tower to France (1323), where Queen Isabella had joined him, shortly to invade England. Cf. Edward I's exceptional treatment of Mary Bruce and of the countess of Buchan: M. Prestwich, *Edward I*, 508–9. Attainder (after 1459) was 'an act of anarchy and revenge': Maitland, *Constitutional History*, 215–16; Bellamy, *Crime and Public Order*, 24, 192, 202–3. It came to be associated with brutal physical punishment under Henry VIII.

which was typical.[98] It should go without saying that the great parade of procedural correctness and judicial objectivity (as with royal documents) does not have to be taken literally for the force of the routine to be appreciated. Although the phraseology was standard, a notary was probably present in the conclave of tenants, councillors, and dependants to provide the documentation:

Augarda, widow of Bompard d'Auzon, makes known that in October, in the year of our Lord 1206, she sought from Count Guy confirmation of the custody of her sons (*filiorum*) as lawful guardian according to Bompard's testament, which request the count has granted. That done, he required of the lady that she should assure him of (*juraret sibi*) the fort and *munitio* of Reilhac. Augarda replied that she would in all respects comply with what the count should have adjudged and found (*judicari et cognosci*). The count thereupon declared a court (*curiam statuit*), appointing Bertrand Rascher and P. Bolet to preside. . . . Before them Count Guy deposed that the *castrum* of Auzon was of his fief being sworn (*jurabatur*) to him; and that Reilhac was part of the appurtenances and *castellaria* of Auzon . . .

The facts were not in dispute. Guy's lordly rights of wardship went no further than ratifying Bompard's will. But though his lordship was in that respect atavistically weak, there could be no question but that the new place of Reilhac, being part of Auzon held from the count, must similarly be obligated to him.[99] This was the principle of law by which the authority of the great original castellaries had been extended over the proliferating *neufs châteaux*, even in 'lawless' Auvergne. And so:

The count asserted that by right (*de jure*) and by custom, as Auzon was held of him in fief and was sworn to him, equally and likewise the fort and fabric (*forcia et constructio*) of Reilhac ought to be acknowledged and sworn (*cognosci et jurari*) to him. On this question both parties requested a verdict (*sentenciam*). Judgement was made that Reilhac was of the count's fief and that the Lady Augarda was bound to swear it to him . . .

As was still the common practice in the Midi, the words of her oath are in the form of a personal address to Count Guy, incorporated in the third-person narrative of the typical *procès verbal* homage charter:

Hear, O Guy, count of Clermont, son of *Mahalt* [Maud], I Augarda, daughter of *Papabou*, formerly wife of Bompard d'Auzon, as guardian (*tutrix*) of my sons and in their name, do acknowledge (*cognosco*) that I hold of you in fief the *forcia* of Reilhac. For it and my sons' other possessions, I do to you liege homage in their name; promising also, under oath, that

---

[98] Fawtier, *Capetian Kings*, is sadly typical. Count Guy, he says (pp. 118–19), 'had been brought to heel by Louis VIII'. To Petit-Dutaillis (*Feudal Monarchy*, 291), 'Guy II was a shameless brigand: in 1213, the castle of Tournoël which was reckoned impregnable was captured by the royal troops who found an enormous booty stolen from the churches. It was all restored and a "constable of the king in Auvergne" maintained order there henceforward'. This is supported by citing Cartellieri's biography (1899–1922) and *Layettes*, ii. no. 2485, dated 1237.

[99] *Layettes*, v. 59–60; Reilhac or Rilhac is *dép*. Haute-Loire, near Auzon. How a less formal assembly was transformed into a 'court' in the judicial sense, in which the count was (theoretically) litigant, not master, is notable and typical of early practice; the whole phrase is: *et super hoc comes curiam statuit et qui cognoscerent reddidit Bertrandum R. et P.B.*

at your or your people's summons, as often as you shall wish, I will deliver (*reddam*) it to you or to your accredited (*credentibus*) envoys; I will not evade summons, nor contrive secretly or openly to prevent my being summoned. And when the fort of Reilhac is returned to me I will be in the same oath and fealty as before. These things, I say, will I in good faith perform, without device (*sine inganno*) or deception. So help me God and the Holy Evangels—These deeds were done at La Motte, at the count's fireside (*in fornello*), in the presence of *Papabou* and [twelve named witnesses], and many others: October 1206.[100]

The apparent newness and doubtful standing (legal and structural) of Reilhac, in other regions, and generally at a later period, might have been resolved in the assembly at the outset by the lord's position being recognized and exercised, and the tenant's standing affirmed, by the seeking and granting of *ex post facto* licence to fortify.[101] Fortresses were central to vassal–lord relationships. Alternatively, the lord might require the new or equivocal fortification to be at once rendered to him, and be rendable at will thereafter. Any potential new seat or lordship threatened partition of an existing fief. Its exact nature was relatively unimportant. Guy's comital powers were far less in 1206 than, for instance, those of Alphonse de Poitiers even in Poitou, in 1269.[102] Guy could not make good any right of wardship in this case, but asserting the ancient lien on fortresses was basic, even if he awaited a minority to do it.

Auvergne was added to Alphonse's apanage in 1241. In 1249 he acquired in right notionally of his wife, daughter of Raymond VII (but in reality by delayed surrender), the enormous county of Toulouse. The progress the Capetian takeover of Poitou had made since 1229 (when Alphonse was invested as count) may be illustrated by the example of La Roche-sur-Yon and Luçon (*dép.* Vendée) in 1242, when Joan de Thouars inherited. The multifaceted distinctiveness of fortresses was again put in the spotlight. That peculiar seignorial quality (with its military component), which is inconspicuous in the English records, in the French is trumpeted owing to the much fuller articulation on the Continent of lordship in terms of fortress-customs, substantially ancient but also spreading and evolving. Britain's much shorter and idiosyncratic experience of castles set it somewhat apart from European *seigneurie*. Thus, we find in Lady Joan's arrangements with Count Alphonse, which provided for her two castellaries, that castles figure as more than *capita* of lordships and residences of aristocratic dignity.

When Joan received what was, in fact, no more than a share from her father, some doubt had subsisted as to whether La Roche-sur-Yon, put into her (partial)

---

[100] Notable Languedocien elements are verbal elaboration and the emphasis on maternal descent: *Mahalt* or *Mahaud* is Maud or Mathilda, but *Augarda* is obsolete (sample of many, C. Martin, *Record Interpreter*, 451–64). 'Papabou' is curious, with no forename; possibly a diminutive of *pater*. Being open to summons and promising fair play is also a southern element; but the 'fortifications-as-they-now-are-or-shall-be-in-future' phrase is not present.

[101] Occurring even in England, where this licensing had lost much of its Continental significance, in the form of 'pardons'; e.g. (twice) to John le Rous of Ragley (War. 1381): *CPR, 1381–5*, 64; *1391–6*, 46. But the number of English licences (500 +, 1200–1578) contrasts with the non-use of recognitory repossession at will.

[102] Regulations for relief: *Layettes*, iv. 352–4 (above).

possession, was not rightfully the direct demesne of the count. While reserving this claim, her homage was provisionally taken for it, she promising (as was usual at a change of lords) to render the fortress to his summons meanwhile.[103] Joan did not promise to obtain the count's consent to marry, but only not to take a husband who was an enemy of his or of King Louis, an undertaking guaranteed by Aimery (VIII) titular *vicomte* de Thouars, her father. Another member of that powerful clan, her uncle Geoffrey, treasurer of the abbey of Saint-Hilaire, Poitiers, put his seal to authenticate her charter because, as she says, 'I do not have my own seal'.[104] No doubt one was soon so provided (a pointed oval shape was common for women and ecclesiastics) for the administration of her lands.[105] If so, it was only briefly in use since, by November 1246, she had married Maurice de Belleville who did homage for her to Alphonse, but only for Luçon. La Roche was provisionally given up to the king's brother. In addition, Maurice paid £2,000 Tours for relief. He and Joan promised to render one or both castles on demand. The Capetian grip was tightening.[106]

3. Some Vicissitudes of Heiresses and Dowagers

The Lady Joan de Thouars, by virtue of the share received from her father, became a castellan and, at once, interesting to her lord. Such women never lacked suitors, supposed by convention (and by wardship custom) to be of comparable rank, by blood at least, but always attracted by the prospects of status and wealth. If the heiress was of child-bearing age there was the possibility of begetting by her a son who might unite their hereditary lands—but children by a previous husband and other heirs had reversionary rights to her life-holdings.[107] A 'good' marriage

---

[103] *Layettes*, ii. 500–1, at Pontoise in the Parisis. Whether any payment of relief was due to Alphonse on her succession remained also to be elucidated. The rendability is expressed in formulae typical of 'France' (Langue d'Oil). Aimeri and Geoffrey de Thouars ratified all this in a duplicate charter.

[104] See n. 76 above on the intricacies of Thouars vicecomital joint tenure. Baudry, *Fortifications des Plantagenêts en Poitou*, 326–6—summary of descent and archaeology of La Roche-sur-Yon, but without reference to rendability.

[105] Seals (like regalian coins) were important signs and instruments of lordly authority. Bishops, monasteries, and *femmes soles* all used the pointed oval 'mandorla' shape (common in Romanesque art for displaying the figure of Christ in Majesty, especially in the tympanum over church doorways). Lords, including kings, used round seals: Zarnecki *et al.*, *English Romanesque Art*, 298–319 (p. 306, fig. 337: seal of Isabella, countess of Gloucester 1189–1217, cast-off first wife of (King) John. Similarly, seal of Queen Elizabeth, wife of Philip II: Viollet-le-Duc, *Dictionnaire du mobilier français*, iv. 323.

[106] *Layettes*, ii. 643 (at Paris). Joan and Maurice declare that he has done liege homage for Luçon. Her father Aimeri VIII had died, leaving them in sole (?) possession. La Roche-sur-Yon Alphonse was to hold for six years, they paying nominal custody costs (£20 Tours p.a.). Rendability is expressed as due *ad magnam fortiam et parvam, quotiens . . .* etc. In 1255 Aimeri (IX) made homage for his shares in La Roche and another castellary directly to Louis IX, under rendability: *Thesaurus Novus*, i. 1062–3. Intra-familial cohabitation of fortresses was undoubtedly not a Thouars peculiarity. See also *Layettes*, ii. 642–3 (1246): Aimeri IX commits Tiffauges for five years to Alphonse. Thouars and his other castles will be rendered on request.

[107] Customarily, 'by the courtesy of England', a father would keep for life part at least of his children's inheritance from the mother even after a girl married or a boy came of age. Contrast Ralph de Monthermer, risen from a young squire of Joan of Acre, after Gilbert de Clare's death in 1295

contracted too late by a man on the make risked being barren, nullifying property accumulation intended to raise the status of his family. Dying before the heir (preferably male, and more than one for safety, to keep the lands together) had come of age ran the risks of wardship by the lord's appointee, who pocketed at least the surplus income. Custody of the children meant that the lord could choose, or influence, whom they married, frustrating family schemes of territorial aggrandizement. Even with the signal degree of ceremony attached in France to fortresses—in Britain muted, but latent—the fact of having a reputed castle as a dynastic seat was but one aspect of the family's ranking in the local (regional or merely parochial) aristocratic community. Patterns of consumption in general are corroborated often conspicuously by the architectural evidence of mansions and churches. New families had a point to make.[108] Established power was in less need of such advertisement, so that ancient castles were often left with only the minimum of building needed for administrative purposes.

Breaking into the ranks of the privileged has always tempted the excluded. Marriage to a well-dowered noblewoman, be she heiress technically or widow, might be procured by at least a display of violence rather than negotiated for at length. Parties seeking to evade lordly restrictions of fiscal type might thereby disguise a runaway match or elopement. Some of the aggravated burglaries of castles and lesser manor-houses related in the appointments of judicial commissions of inquiry on the Patent Rolls suggest an ulterior motive, beyond mere housebreaking. One which attracts suspicion, but not of any connivance by the lady, was obtained in February 1382:

Commission of *oyer* and *terminer* to . . . [five appointees], on complaint by Lettice, late wife of John de Kiriel, knight, that John Cornwaile, knight with [nine named companions] and others, with ladders scaled by night and entered her castle of Ostrynghangre [Westenhanger, near Folkestone, co. Kent], broke her houses and chambers, searched for her so closely that she was compelled to hide in some water, narrowly escaping death thereby, carried off twelve horses, value £40, besides other goods, and assaulted her servants.[109]

Risking drowning in some cistern, or in the moat itself; knowing that she was the target, not the getaway transport; her swift presence of mind; and, perhaps, the rank and identity of the ringleader, all suggest that Lady Lettice had feared abduction and was forewarned. Nothing more explicit is to be expected and such denunciations almost always name alleged culprits, who would be known; locals seldom seeing strangers. A pardon granted in September 1383 to an accomplice

countess of Gloucester, etc. in her own right in survivorship. By marrying him, Joan raised him to be an earl. As they had no children, on her death he reverted to (almost) his former lowly rank: Altschul, *The Clares*, 38–9, 158–9.

[108] Many recipients of English licences to crenellate, and of French late-medieval licences to fortify, were *arrivistes* or aspirants to social prominence. Very many castles were due to late-medieval new wealth: e.g. Ampthill, Ashby-de-la-Zouche*, Bodiam*, Bolton*, Caister, Fulbrook, Herstmonceux*, Kirby Muxloe*, Latham, Maxstoke*, Mettingham*, Nunney*, Raglan, Sheriff Hutton*, Someries, Sudeley*, Wingfield*, Wressell. Those asterisked had licence to crenellate.

[109] *CPR, 1381–4*, 133. Her widowed daughter-in-law Elizabeth may not have been in residence.

states that the attackers 'besieged' (i.e. stayed around) the castle; suggesting, however, that Cornwaile was recognized—but mere 'common knowledge' is likely.[110] In truth, Westenhanger was not 'her castle'. Lettice (or Leticia) had continued to live there, presumably in her own apartments, along with her son Nicholas (until his death two years previously) and her daughter-in-law Elizabeth, their infant son William de Kiriel (or Crioll) being the eventual heir to the whole scattered estate, held largely from the archbishop.[111]

The quadrangular castle of Westenhanger, much of it apparently rebuilt in the fifteenth century, was a considerable one, reflecting the long-term if modest rank and wealth of the Kiriel family in East Kent. In plan it compares with Maxstoke (War., licensed 1345) and with the smaller, better-known castle of Bodiam (East Sussex, licensed 1385). Like them it had licence to crenellate (1343), and in 1346 John de Kiriel secured mortmain clearance to put some lands into ecclesiastical tenure to endow a small chantry chapel in the park dedicated to St Thomas.[112] Unlike Maxstoke and Bodiam, Westenhanger was added to over a long period, an accretive pattern much more typical of British and French castles. The moated, somewhat irregular rectangle once had round towers at three of the angles, and rectangular turrets at the fourth corner and at the mid-point of each side, one of these in its original form being the gatehouse. Within, at one corner, is a substantial, largely eighteenth-century mansion, testifying to a remarkable (for England) continuity of occupation.

It is not possible in this book to consider, but only to acknowledge occasionally, the surviving architectural background to the noble lifestyle. In France especially it is vast and highly diversified. Westenhanger represents the upper-level sub-baronial gentry, set in its park, with (surviving) barns and basse-cour adjacent—rural mansion, farmhouse, and prestigious château expressing the social, economic, and political realities; while sepulchral monuments, chantry chapel, and prayers for the dead articulated with noble style the aspirations of the living for the next life.[113]

[110] John de Clyfton, one of the accused, was pardoned 'at the supplication of the king's mother' (Joan of Kent), 'for having with others, broken the gates, doors, and windows [shutters] of the Lady de Kiriel's castle of Estynghangre, co. Kent, besieged her there and stolen a coat and hood of one of her servants, value 40d.'. As late as March 1385 another culprit, prisoner in Newgate gaol (London), was pardoned for his part in the attack stated as on 27 Oct. 1381. Goods stolen, 'worth £50', included horses, saddlery, money, jewellery, etc.: CPR, 1381–5, 319, 548.
[111] CIPM xv. 100–1. So no dower-partition is enrolled; but direct family arrangements were undoubtedly normal, especially with lesser tenants for whom amicable settlements without need of legal record sufficed.
[112] CPR, 1343–5, 106; 1345–8, 72. Wadmore, 'Westerhanger Castle', 200 (plans 1648, 1887). Currently being conscientiously conserved by the owner. There are considerable and rare-surviving remains of barns and outbuildings beyond the moat. In late 1339 John de Kiriel was put in charge of the defence of Thanet: CFR, 1337–47, 161.
[113] Emery, Greater Medieval Houses; Cook, Medieval Chantries, avoids 'overloading the pages with footnotes, only to stub the mental toe of the reader' (p. xii), but is still valuable; Rosenthal, Purchase of Paradise, esp. ch. 3. Castle-chantries (e.g. Maxstoke, Tattershall) and estate church tomb-assemblages are an important illustration: M. Thompson, 'Associated Monasteries and Castles'. In 1374 Joan, widow of William St Quintin, had licence to crenellate for a belfrey in Harpham churchyard (Yorks.) as a memorial to her husband: CPR, 1370–4, 407.

None of these emblems of peaceable power could save Lettice de Kiriel from shock and insult. Latent social violence, along with the tendency in societies of this type to treat women as items of property, sometimes combined to inflict great suffering on vulnerable propertied women. Crimes against the person were as common as those against property.[114] In England the peasant uprisings of 1381 did not go so far as the occasional *château*-burnings of the French *Jacqueries*, but noble mansions were inevitably targeted and almost always vulnerable. Ancient renown, fortifications, and deterrence, legal and ostentatious, gave little protection when only a skeleton household and estate staff was present, at best. Even Lewes castle was attacked, by a crowd looking for manorial records of peasant subjugation to destroy.[115] But women of property were at some risk at other times, even when lodged in the grand, but usually spurious, security of a fortress whose chief purpose had always been to advertise wealth, rank, and authority. Thus Alice de Lacy, in her own right countess of Lincoln, dowager countess of Lancaster and Leicester, in 1336 was ostensibly snatched from Bolingbroke castle. Her case is remarkable. In 1317 she had been helped to desert her first husband, Earl Thomas of Lancaster. Widowed by his execution after the collapse of his revolt, at Boroughbridge in 1322, she remarried two years later. Widowed again, she was in residence at the polygonal, towered, and once impressive early-thirteenth-century comital Chester seat of Bolingbroke in Lincolnshire, when she allowed herself to be abducted by Hugh de Fresne. She was then in her fifties, but the affair has every appearance of an 'irregular' love-match. She married Hugh, much beneath her rank, soon afterwards—but it was politic to cover up the social impropriety.[116] She obtained an official commission of inquiry in 1336, and again in May 1337, in which she accused thirty-two alleged intruders of the theft of twenty of her horses. Although remarkable, the incident is only brought within our purview in that a castle (indeed, structurally a formidable one) was involved. No resistance seems to have been offered—unsurprisingly, as there was undoubtedly connivance and

---

[114] Technically 'rape' was abduction (*rapere*) or the seizing of booty of any kind; sometimes narrowed to 'rape of women'. It was not, as now, a synonym for forced sexual intercourse: Part III, n. 24 above; Herlihy, *Medieval Households*, 55, 78, 157, for an anthropological approach, linking forced marriage with an adverse demographic sex-balance. Land, not libido, was the dominant motive: e.g. in 1278 the knight Odo de Sully and his abettors were fined and Odo's 'best house' was razed in that he had 'seized (*rapuerat*) or forcibly abducted' a noble girl (*domicella*), niece of another knight. In 1287 the same penalty was imposed on Philip de Chauvigny, knight, for abducting by force a noble wife 'without her consent', she being still in wardship. He had to guarantee to compensate her guardian and release the girl before being let out of gaol: *Les Olim*, ii. 115–16, 269, 332–3.

[115] In Feb. 1385 Richard, earl of Arundel, complained that, under two leaders from the town, 'insurgents [the habitual term for the 1381 rioters] in the county of Sussex came armed to Lewes, broke his closes and the gates, doors, and windows [*sic*] of his castle there, threw down his buildings and destroyed 10 casks of wine, value £100 [*sic*] and burned his rolls, rentals and other muniments': *CPR*, *1381–5*, 259. In 1381 some Chancery records at Lambeth were burned: McKisack, *Fourteenth Century*, 409.

[116] Cf. Elizabeth I's comment (*c*.1554) when her cousin, the widowed duchess of Suffolk, married the young Adrian Stokes: 'has the woman so far forgotten herself as to marry a common groom!': Strong, *Elizabethan Image*, fig. 33 (caption only). M. Prestwich, *Three Edwards*, 156–7; M. Thompson, 'Bolingbroke Castle'; n. 68 above.

if Countess Alice's domestic household was all the 'power' she had at Bolingbroke.[117]

Curtilage walls, towers, moats, gatehouses, and apartments graded in status and accessibility from 'public' barns, stables, hall, and so on to 'private' chambers, bower, 'wardrobe', chapel, and treasury, were elements of greater rural residences, whether styled 'castle' or not. (The privy garden was an especially female space.[118]) The castellated seat of Beams near Swallowfield (Berks.), from which the remarried widow Margery de la Beche was forcibly abducted in 1347, was not called 'castle', though licensed to be crenellated by Nicholas de la Beche in 1338.[119] He thereby crowned a long and quite successful career in the king's service, a stretch of it spent in the major administrative position of constable of the Tower of London. Beams today is no more than a rectangular earthwork devoid of buildings, one of the very numerous 'homestead moats', mostly of indeterminate later medieval date, listed in the Victoria County History volumes and usually denoted 'moat' by the Ordnance Survey. Such castles-in-miniature satisfied the self-esteem of county gentry, even one like Sir Nicholas who had done well. Alas, in 1345 he died childless, although Margery had the honour in 1347 of housing in her dower-manor Edward III's young son Lionel (later duke of Clarence) and his household. This made the attack during the night of Good Friday still more heinous, since it violated the 'verge' or legally protected proximity of the 9-year-old Lionel, nominally 'guardian of England' during the king's absence on the Crécy–Calais campaign. Margery herself was obliged to 'marry' one of the attackers. Her complaint accused a party of five knights and thirteen others whom she named. Two men of hers were murdered, Margery was 'raped', and goods valued at £1,000 were stolen. She herself died late in 1349. It was the most flagrant castle- or house-breaking of the era, causing a flurry of Chancery activity, but, with its high political overtones, unrepresentative of the normal state of affairs, for all that Beams itself was commonplace.[120]

---

[117] *CPR, 1334–8*, 282, 450. Her list includes three men 'of Knockin' (Salop), two canons (clergy) and a Welsh knight, and John de Lacy. Her husband, Ebulo Lestrange (of Salop), died 1335. She then married Hugh de Fresne (not listed) of Moccas (Heref.), who died Dec. 1336–Jan. 1337. Alice died, without surviving child, in 1348: Sanders, *English Baronies*, 36, 138. In 1346 the insane dowager duchess of Brittany was lodged in antiquated Tickhill castle (Yorks.), being allowed household expenses of £34. 13*s. 4d.* p.a. She was briefly removed therefrom in 1347 by one Warmer de Giston and his men, who 'entered by force': *CPR, 1345–8*, 211, 468; *1350–4*, 177.

[118] e.g. Kenilworth had its 'pleasance' on the far side of the Mere: Brown *et al.*, *King's Works*, i. 245, ii. 685; Philip II's Dourdan in the *Très Riches Heures* 'April' similarly had a castellated lodge or belvedere with a walled, trellised garden: Meiss, *Painting in the Time of Jean de Berry*, pl. 420 (right-hand side cropped); Landsberg, *Medieval Garden* (with DIY guidance). Loveday Gee, 'Artistic Patronage By Women 1216–1377', will be important but has little regarding castles directly: reference and information due to John Goodall jnr. Sekules, 'Women's Patronage', 120–31.

[119] *CPR, 1338–40*, 24 (with Aldworth, Berks., his name-place; and Watlington, Oxon.); Bellamy, *Crime and Public Order*, 58–9 (as 'Wilts'); also, on 'abduction of women', pp. 7, 32 (heiresses; became more frequent), 45 (as a noble crime); sexual rape, pp. 7, 126, 181. Events *CFR, 1347–56*, 35, 41; *CCR, 1346–9*, 251, 261, 271, 306 (attackers 'arrayed in a warlike manner and armed', etc.), 444; *1349–54*, 118 (4 Nov. 1349: refers to Margery's death), etc.; summarized Bellamy, *Crime*, 58–9; also *VCH Berkshire III*, 268–71; Tout, *Chapters*, iv. 130, n. 7.

[120] Despite Edward III's indignation, 'he possessed no machinery capable of capturing abductors

The attack on Thimbelby (Yorks.) in 1315 reveals a relatively ordinary situation, however reprehensible. Young heiresses, liable to be married to a suitably ranking but perhaps impecunious son or ambitious friend or relative of their guardian, were a valuable commodity. Thimbelby was treated exactly as a 'castle' would have been:

Commission of *oyer* and *terminer* . . . on complaint by William de Aslagby [Aislaby] that Ralph de Bulmer . . . [and two named] with others, came to his manor of Thymelby, broke the doors and gates of his manor and threw down the stone walls there, entered the manor, and abducted Cassandra and Juliana, the daughters and heiresses of John de Edgecliffe, deceased, minors in his custody, whose marriages belonged to him because the said John held his lands from him by military [i.e. noble] service; and they carried away his goods found within the manor.

Much personal grief and tragedy often lay behind the routine formulae of 'breaking and entering'. Theft, here, was added for good measure (but not violence to the person).[121] It was greatly to William's dishonour that he had been unable to protect his wards, perhaps from their own family and affinity defined by often quite remote relationships of blood and marriage.

Whatever the abductors hoped to gain by marrying off the two girls themselves, or possibly by extortion from William de Aislaby, the inheritance of a mere sub-tenant could not compare with the enormous and rare chance to leap directly into the ranks of the great magnates which was presented by the death of Gilbert de Clare at Bannockburn. His three sisters' husbands, as has been seen, were catapulted into wide lands, titles, and great power. It was as the result of an elopement, which may have been an abduction—the exact nature of such escapades, whether voluntary or involuntary on the woman's part, is often (deliberately) obscure—that a further chapter was opened in that momentous saga. The third and most famous sister, Elizabeth 'de Burgh', first widowed in 1313, in 1316 took (or was taken by) Theobald de Verdun as her second husband, who died the same year, leaving her seemingly pregnant, and the Crown, as overlord, faced with another complex situation for custom and policy to resolve. As usual with the great, fortresses were involved, but as incidentally as was normal. The heirs were Theobald's three daughters by his first wife (it was also his second marriage) and the anxiously awaited baby.[122] If a boy he would take the major share of the

who had the sympathy of the gentle classes' (Bellamy, *Crime and Public Order*, 59). Nicholas de la Beche died without a son so Aldworth, 'the place called Beche', passed to his brother: *CCR, 1343–6,* 529 (June 1345). His other lands (the motive for the attack) went with Margery: *CIM* iii. 7–8.

[121] *CPR, 1313–17,* 416; on 'ravishment of wards' see Plucknett, *Legislation of Edward I,* 114–18 (1275–85). Cf. the attack 'with a multitude of horse and foot', arrows, and burning, on William de Mortimer's house at Ingoldsby, Lincs.; also on Aymer de Valence's house at Westmill, Herts., by night: ibid. 410, 417. In 1375 the townsmen of Oakham, in an affray against Thomas le Despenser's men, attacked their refuge in Burley church (Rutland) and then Despenser's manor, using shutters and doors as shields, breaking in, and threatening to burn the house: *CIM* iii. 369–71.

[122] At this time, in France, Philip V (1316–22) succeeded Louis X, whose son John died a few days old, while his daughter was ruled out by pretext of the 'Salic Law', used again in 1328 to bar the claims of Edward III of England.

Verdun lands. If a girl, division among the four heiresses, with some slight preference in status for the eldest, would ensue, and eventually Elizabeth's inheritance
would devolve on the baby. Primogeniture reciprocally gave distinction to the
families' castles.

News of Theobald's death having reached the Chancery, the regular inquiry
was ordered, by writ of *diem clausit extremum* to the escheator in each relevant
county. The returns showed that Theobald's possessions had included, in
Staffordshire, Alton 'the castle with its members' (attached lands, etc.); in
Herefordshire, 'the castle and manor' (-lands) of Weobley; and 'in the marches of
Wales', Ewias Lacy castle and a half of its manor. There were many dependent
knights' fiefs also. 'Elizabeth his wife is pregnant of a living child', said the
escheator's report: '. . . his daughters, Joan aged 13, Elizabeth aged 10, and Margery
aged 7, are his next heirs . . .'. Further on again, the report repeats 'Elizabeth his
wife is pregnant', adding, 'but unless it be of a male child, his heirs are his daughters as above'.[123] As it turned out, the baby was a girl, so the male preference
intended to keep patrimonies relatively intact (subject to dower assignments and
daughters' dowries) did not apply. But the sharing out still met with opposition,
especially regarding the castle and castellary of Alton, whose custodians in 1317
refused to allow in the sheriff to take possession. In a rare demonstration they
even closed the gates and raised the drawbridge (*pons turribilis*) against him and
his men, so that he was able to seize only the appurtenant lands. The obstinate
constable had manned the castle for the occasion, and his deputy claimed that
they were acting on behalf of Edward II's rival and cousin, Earl Thomas of
Lancaster. Competing husbands, again, were behind it all.[124]

Joan de Verdun, a child-bride, who was already widowed and remarried to
Thomas de Furnivall *fils*, then demanded her rights. To remove her lands from
royal wardship, Joan's age and married status had to be verified. Matters were
delayed until her infant half-sister's sex had simplified the succession to a fourfold
partition. Her 'proof of age' as now 14 was conducted in June 1318, elderly local
eyewitnesses being the customary form of authentication. As usual, such inquest
'evidence' justified official action more than it proves literal correctness.[125] There
was little to choose between the three castle-lordships: Alton (rebuilt in the nineteenth century by Pugin), with its spectacular clifftop site, perhaps the most prestigious, was awarded to Joan and Thomas; Ewias Lacy (alias Longtown), having
been moved from its early earthwork site, had substantial thirteenth-century

---

[123] *CIPM* vi. 35–41; cf. v. 95–6 (1309) on Theobald de Verdun (*père*). Background in Hagger, *The de Verduns*.

[124] In Jan. 1317 Alton 'and its members' was committed to the keeping of Roger Damory, third husband of Elizabeth de Burgh, with Weobley and Ewias Lacy castles, etc., for paying £160 p.a. though they were 'worth' £132. 13s. 4d. p.a. But, in Nov. 1317, repeated royal attempts to get possession were rebuffed: *CFR, 1307–19,* 316–17, 346–7 (detailed).

[125] Habitually, in 'proofs of age' elderly local jurors (sometimes men said to be in their seventies) certified the time of the heir's birth by citing some memorable event; e.g. in 1335 Philip Staunton's birth in 1314 was recalled as on the day before 'a thunder[bolt] shattered a tower of the castle of Roch', near Wiston (Pembs.): *CIPM* vii. 490–1.

buildings including a round tower on the motte, and made a second natural share; Weobley castle, as a mere ringwork and bailey, was the least distinguished, but made a third; while the baby's share was to consist of two manors with lands in the town of Ludlow, brought up to the same annual income by transferring £9 of free tenants' rent from Weobley castellary plus £10. 9s. from Ewias Lacy castellary.

The Furnivalls, by contrast, did rather well, suffering no deduction of income—too well, in the view of the famous warrior and jouster Bartholomew de Burgherssh, who by June 1320 was husband of Elizabeth de Verdun, the second co-heiress, now about 14 years old. He successfully urged, on her behalf and his own, that Alton castellary had been under-assessed.[126] Like Hugh Despenser (at Tonbridge and in south Wales), an unscrupulous or merely pushing and well-connected husband enjoyed considerable advantages, but by right of his wife, if he could secure an heiress in marriage, and of any children he might beget.

Early matrimony, acquisitive but often short-lived older husbands, successive marriages, litigious inheritances, and even teenage pregnancies (but sometimes dignified retirement) were widespread vicissitudes of female aristocratic life. Surreptitious pressures and legal technicalities often obstructed justice, as did the strong undercurrent of violence, sometimes covered up or merely condoned. Despite outbreaks of often ritualized displays of force, the fact is very compelling in the records that fortresses were so integrated in, and merged with, aristocratic society that they seldom figured as anything other than residential emblems of rank in their localities. They were instruments of a power which was largely peaceable. That this was so in France, as well as in precociously centralized England, thanks in no small part to the practices of good lordship, is suggested by a very long and detailed document of bequest by a dowager in Poitou, dated 1200/1.[127] The calm of repressed expectations and the judicial finality of a 'reading of the will' by the family solicitor, as in a Victorian genre painting, is hardly to be expected. Poitou in the early thirteenth century was virtually self-governing, which both facilitated and required 'private' settlements of succession problems. This example seamlessly weaves in the fortress-capitals of a lesser baronial territory and the right to fortify which went with their possession. The opening allusion to armed conflict (*multarum guerrarum turbacio*) is the only one, and may be formulaic legal fiction. Since the text touches upon a great many of the issues reviewed in this chapter, an extended but interpolated translation will be appropriate:

After the commotion of many wars, eventually the ensuing agreement (*composicio*) was concluded between Pons de Mirebeau and Artaud, sons of Aichard de Clermont, of the one part; and Reginald de Pons and Geoffrey his brother, sons of Geoffrey de Pons, of the other

---

[126] *CIPM* vi. 40–1. The Furnivalls were summoned to Chancery to answer Burgerssh's case, Elizabeth having 'proved her age' (validating her marriage). By decision of the king's council, a new assessment was ordered.

[127] *Layettes*, v. 45–6, 9 Apr. 1200 (o.s.). The editor's note explains that the text is a notarial copy (*collationnée*) of the original charter, to which four double seal-tags of white leather were still attached, made by order of the seneschal's deputy in 1507.

part, who were all born of the one mother, namely the Lady Agnes. These four have now pledged and sworn (*fide et juramento*) to accept the will and testament of the Lady Agnes, their mother.

It was a complex situation. Agnes's successive husbands having both died, her dower from each had to be disentangled, together with her own personal family property, while dividing the Clermont-Mirebeau and Pons inheritances with due respect to the older sons' position as heads of the separating dynasties. Accordingly:

The Lady Agnes has given to Pons [de Mirebeau], her eldest son, and to his heirs, the land [island] of Oléron [Charente estuary], but has kept back from its revenues £10 per annum to be paid to her daughter Mabiria as her bride's portion assigned to her when she married Geoffrey Rudel: if she die without heirs this payment shall cease—this land [of Oléron] being Agnes's inheritance from her father, Geoffrey Martel. To Pons she gave also all that she has at Mirebeau, except for the fiefs held from it (*preter feodales suos*). If Pons die without heirs, Oléron shall devolve on Artaud, his brother. Failing Artaud or his heirs, these possessions shall go, in turn, to their half-brothers.

By these arrangements, Agnes passed her own paternal inheritance virtually intact to her elder son by her first marriage (who also had his father's lands, or most of them), providing (rather scantily) for her married daughter, but not for Artaud except by way of reversion.[128] Disposing her maternal property was less straightforward, and called for some fine-tuning with fortress-rights and other nuances:

Touching the inheritance which the Lady Agnes had from her mother, she wills that Reginald, her elder son by Geoffrey de Pons, shall have the fortress-proper of *Breuil* (*receptum de Bruolio*), that is to say everything within the outer-works together with all the old pleasure-garden (*de barbacanis infra cum toto veteri plaisamento*). These shall pass to his brother Geoffrey if Reginald die without heirs. If both do so, it shall go to Pons de Mirebeau, or failing him or his heirs, to Artaud—All Agnes's other lands, inherited from her father or her mother, namely woods, hunting chases, subjects, serfs, etc., shall be halved between Pons and Artaud de Clermont, and between Reginald and Geoffrey de Pons.[129]

What was to happen in case of failure of heirs to this last partition was then carefully laid down. Agnes's own portion was to be £10 (Tours?), the same as Mabiria's, but taken from Reginald and Geoffrey's share, in scrupulous equity, except that Mabiria was likely to live longer and to get heirs. It is to be supposed that Agnes's dower portions were to provide for her in widowhood, since they are not otherwise referred to.

[128] Intestacy was seldom a problem since most property went to the heirs at law, not depending on any will, a practice adopted after 1800 in countries which adhered to the Code Napoleon but which prescribes equal shares to male and female children: cf. Maitland, *Constitutional History*, 37–8. Pons (near Saintes) was both a 'surname' and a forename. The Rudels were lords of Blaye and Bourg in northern Gascony. Agnes may have retained the sub-fiefs of Mirebeau for life.

[129] *Receptum* (cf. *Receptaculum*) is a local synonym for fortress. The phrase 'from the gate inwards' (*de la porta eninz*) also occurs e.g.: in a vernacular homage-rendability charter of 1165 for the *castellum* (town) of Dourgne (*dép.* Tarn): Brunel, *Chartes Provençale*, 104. Reginald was permitted to fortify *Breuil* unless conditions regarding Archiac (below) were not fulfilled.

So much, then, for the present; but future and potentially unsettling developments might occur: the elder Clermont brother might resent Reginald's having a
fortress:

Now, if Pons should wish to build himself a fortress (*receptum*) in his portion, he may do
so without contradiction but not at the place called Clermont, nor at the township (*burgo*)
of Guetinaires, nor anywhere between them. Should anyone try to stop Pons making such
a fortification (*municio*) then his [half-] brothers Reginald and Geoffrey shall support him
against all men. Moreover, the Lord Aymer, count of Angoulême, in whose *dominio* all this
land is acknowledged to be, shall also be to Pons a protector and helper against all men.[130]

Avoiding fortifying at the Clermont chief seat, but collectively supporting it where
the town would not be prejudiced, in effect asserted the equal status of the branch
of the family headed by Pons—but tactfully. Tensions might have arisen, or the
position of Artaud, the younger brother, have been affected. So, therefore, Agnes's
will stipulated that their half-brothers Reginald and Geoffrey should 'hold their
shares in fief from the lords of the land and from Pons and Artaud'. All were 'to
share the land in the true way and path of fraternal unity'. A complex condo-
minium and future balance were intended:

The serfs (*naturales*) of the whole territory with the pasture-lands shall be held in common.
If they or their men wish to come to their fortresses they shall freely do so without any
destruction of the natural roads and paths.[131] Moreover, if the [four] brothers shall acquire
the whole castellary (*si . . . ad eos devenerit castrum totum*) of Archiac, then the part from
the earthworks inwards (*a fossatis infra*) shall fall to Pons's share if he wishes. In this case,
the whole land of Oléron shall instead be equally divided (*per medium dividetur*) just as is
the other land. But if Pons decides to keep Oléron entirely, the castellary of Archiac shall
be divided in half.[132]

Evidently, the Clermont and Pons families, jointly or severally, had expectations
which could not be allowed to upset their meticulous equality under their
mother's will. The much simpler bequest by William the Conqueror (1087) of his
patrimonial duchy of Normandy to his eldest son Robert, his acquired kingdom
to his second son 'Rufus', and a lump sum in cash to his youngest son Henry, ultimately failed. The Lady Agnes had the count of Angoulême's support, but fraternal jealousy was always to be feared, despite her optimism. She wisely allowed
Pons de Mirebeau-Clermont some latitude over Archiac as well as in the matter
of building himself a fortress to make up for *Breuil* being in Reginald's portion:

---

[130] (Liege) fealty was commonly expressed as *contra omnem hominem* (or plural), sometimes adding
feminam, etc. (Languedoc), or *qui vivere potest/possunt* (*et mori*). Hostilities are not implied.

[131] Viz. 'vie vero et semite naturales tocius istius terre cum pascuis eis et hominibus eorum libere
patebunt, ita tamen quod si ipsi vel homines eorum ad recepta sua venire voluerint, sine impedimento
viarum et semitarum naturalium venire possint'. Right of entry was normally a right of lordship,
which complicates their parity here.

[132] On the *castrum de Auselac* see Gardelles, *Châteaux du sud-ouest*, p. 26, no. 9 as restored to Hugh
de Lusignan in August 1230.

If, however, Pons shall choose to keep the entire castellary (*castrum*) of Archiac, then any fortress (*receptum*) which shall have been made in his share of the land of *Breuil* shall be destroyed; or, if it has not been built as here provided when Archiac is acquired, then it shall not be constructed. Any rights which the Lady Agnes possesses in the extramural castle ['outside the ditches'] of Archiac shall be equally shared, as above.

It could not be helped that Pons might assert his right to the whole castellary of the more prestigious Archiac (Saintonge), but he had to make compensation if he did so, both to his half-brothers and to his own younger brother Artaud (to whose interests Agnes was unusually sensitive, though a younger son). One other threat of disturbance was the Rudel family, powerful in northern Gascony, into which Agnes's daughter Mabiria had married: and so, finally, she provided that:

If the Lord Geoffrey or his wife, or anyone else, should contest these dispositions, then the four brothers shall support each other to uphold them, in peace or in war—Now this settlement (*pax*) was made ... by the good offices (*in manu*) of Count Aymer of Angoulême and of the archdeacon of Saintes, who have appended their seals to it, as also for greater security have Henry, bishop of Saintes, and Abbot Gautier of La Tenaille.

Subsequently twenty other local notables (named, including Reginald de Pons) 'and many others' met and 'ratified' all the arrangements. All in all, the Lady Agnes had done her best to devise an equitable and sensitive partition, and then to make it stick by committing the local Church hierarchy and possible disputants, as well as her secular overlord of Angoulême, to its success. Nullifying possible Rudel opposition was clearly one objective, as well as accommodating Pons de Mirebeau-Clermont. Fortresses played a subsidiary but crucial role in adjusting the delicate scales of social equality and studied inequality. Other settlements, notably the Melgueil–Toulouse marriage pact of 1172,[133] suggest that the void of royal power in southern France at this period (as elsewhere) was not as deleterious to the peace as has been supposed: and that marriage customs, like fortress-law, provided their own autonomous systems of order.[134] Political history is often less relevant to understanding than were these social mechanisms.

The tenure of castles by women, in whatever capacity, required precautions seldom greater, it would appear, than did their holding of other forms of property. These extra measures, occasionally applied to female castellans, constitute barely a ripple in the usual orderly tenor of fortress-ownership. But they do illuminate and throw into relief, even in England, what was distinctive and socially

[133] *Layettes*, i. 102–4. Countess Beatrice settles her little county of Melgueil on Raymond V with her daughter Ermensinda in marriage to young Raymond (VI), with all comital powers, including having *castella, munitiones et fortias* 'sworn' and rendered to him; details amplified by Ermensinda's charter. Raymond V dowers her with his possessions in the city and bishopric of Uzès (*dép.* Gard).

[134] e.g. legitimacy of birth was essential to inheritance. Bastards' lands usually held for life, then reverting to the lord: in 1253 Alphonse de Poitiers sold Ralph de Mauléon's former possessions to Aimeri IX de Thouars, to Aimeri de Rochechouart, and to G. de Talny, saving the life interest of Savary de Mauléons widow and Alphonse's fortress-rights: *Layettes*, iii. 190–1.

elevating about having a residence and estate office which was also a castle. More particularly, if 'the position of women' be taken 'as a test by which the civilization of a country or age may be judged', then a place of some relative distinction must be accorded to that of the middle ages in western Europe.[135]

[135] Power, *Medieval Women*, 9: opening remark—but the conclusion advanced here is no more than implied by Eileen Power.

2

Ladies of Fortresses and Castle Children

Organized anecdote does not offer many easy generalizations. It is probably true that so far as a 'nuclear' medieval family and home existed, it was 'broken' by the death of one parent, most often the father, and by placing the boys as pages in other (usually more elevated) noble households or the children in alien guardianship, seldom if ever by divorce—even disguised as annulment.[136] Fortresses yield as few generalizations once spurious analogies derived from modern preoccupations with war are set aside. The aristocratic, or merely plutocratic, way of life which lasted in Europe as late as the First World War would provide more reliable channels for understanding and empathy; but 'stately homes' are now almost as remote to us today as is the thought-world of the medieval abbey, cathedral, and parish church. If 'religion' has largely become a sociological curiosity, the sort of intense urban patriotism of the great medieval fortress-townships has fared little better, now surviving chiefly in tourist pageants (as at Siena). The real character of 'castles' is doubly elusive because they were deeply enmeshed in a vanished society, noble, *bourgeois*, and peasant, although always significant and occasionally crucial—but chiefly for reasons of hierarchy which may be less than obvious.

Select but representative cases, therefore, continue to offer the most useful insights in this final chapter. Women and (as Nicholas Orme has shown) children should not be regarded so much as an underclass in a male-dominated society; but rather, as a legally protected majority, as fully vested with property and fortresses alike as was possible in their condition—a fact reflected in documents cited in previous parts of this book (see Index: 'dower', etc.).

---

[136] Having reviewed family law in late-thirteenth century England, Plucknett remarks: 'it is not easy to imagine the normal course of family life under a system seemingly so inhuman': *Legislation of Edward I*, 118; cf. Orme, *Medieval Children*. Girls went out 'to service', and boys to apprenticeships or later to boarding school, in working- and middle-class Victorian Britain. Jean-Jacques Rousseau abandoned his successive children to be brought up as foundlings. Eighteenth-century noble sons might be educated by lackeys ... Cf. Power, *Medieval Women*, 76–88, on 'education'. Herlihy, *Medieval Households*, esp. 112–30; loving, good relationships, he argues, were normal in the nuclear family. Orme sees the children as respected and cherished, boys especially.

1. Thirteenth-Century Irish and Other Widows, Wards, and Castles

Like south-west France in the earlier thirteenth century, Ireland's never-finished
and always-fluid English (i.e. Anglo-Irish) settlement was, as has been seen, a
challenging environment. Since charters mention conflict chiefly only for its
settled results, and record the precautions taken to avert or contain strife, warfare
is not naturally prominent in the 'French' material used here. Ireland is different:
despite the almost total loss of records of the Irish administration in Dublin, there
is voluminous evidence—mandates, patents and financial information (Part III,
Ch. 2, sec. 1 above)[137]—to confirm the impression that 'troubles' were habitually
kept at a level below that of war. In France, even when, as in Poitou, Touraine,
Anjou, Saintonge, and in other regions, minor castellans might be proxies in the
wider Capetian–Plantagenet contest, this holds good. Ireland lacks some political
dimension. What is similar, to some extent, is that castle-lords there were also in
competition with each other. But the enemy was what to them were the forces of
unrest and economic adversity, personalized as 'the Irish' or simply as the 'rebels
and enemies of the king'. Other borderlands, in the Scottish march and in many
parts of France, had similar difficulties (sect. 2 below). Female and child-tenure of
fortresses both highlight those problems and are, in turn, illuminated by them.
They are each separately important but, when pulling the same way, produced a
high tide of enhanced attention to fortresses. But wherever 'military' factors can
be imputed the special problems are prone to overemphasis.[138] So as not to exaggerate the peculiarity of Ireland, comparison is useful, particularly with the north
of England.

   Much has been done in the scholarship of gender studies to rectify the former
neglect even of the aristocratic woman in medieval Europe, but not of their role
as *châtelaines*. In truth, castles were their home territory. Minors also deserve
attention in this regard. Boys scarcely men, elderly women like Nicolaa de la Haye
in King John's reign at Lincoln, and, in northern France, her great contemporary
Countess Blanche of Champagne, valiantly upheld their positions and defended
their fortresses.[139] They fitted entirely naturally into a system not at all confined
to the vigorous adult man.[140]

[137] H. S. Sweetman's 5 vols. of the *Calendar of Documents Relating to Ireland* sought to compensate
by combing the English records but also used some Irish Exchequer Rolls: *CDIreland*, i, Preface.
Similarly Joseph Bain's compilation (*CDScotland*, i, Introduction) tackled the loss of royal Scottish
records.

[138] e.g. owners' traditions are reflected in the background given to Anthony Emery's admirable
architectural vignettes in *Greater Medieval Houses*, vol 1 (Northern England), but are often disproved
by his photographs and meticulous site-particulars. Also Neville, *Anglo-Scottish Borderland, passim*.

[139] Count Thibaut III died prematurely in 1201, making Blanche de facto guardian of their daughter and of their unborn son, whom she successfully defended and reared to become count as Thibaut
IV (d. 1253). In 1213–14 only Philip II upheld in her favour the custom that minors' rights could not be
contested until of age, making with her a detailed wardship treaty until 1221 whereby, *inter alia*, she
agreed not to fortify four principal Champagne towns. In 1214 Philip received the boy Thibaut's liege
homage in addition: *Recueil Philippe II*, iii. 453–5, 444, 463–4; *Layettes*, i. 394–6 (with powerful guarantors).

[140] e.g. in Champagne, despite the desultory war of inheritance until 1234, the fief rolls show 68

Irish conditions, fluctuatingly but increasingly as the momentum of English settlement subsided, called forth all the array of supplementary arrangements for fortresses which have been reviewed in the previous chapter. Cultural confrontation aggravated the situation of an originally alien but variantly assimilated class whose grip was seldom entirely confident and sometimes fragile. Already in April 1273 Edward I's council of regency during his absence on Crusade accepted the argument, one unique to Ireland, that on the death of a tenant-in-chief fortresses should be handed over on request (i.e. be temporarily rendable) to the military commander and viceroy, the justiciar.[141] But, as usual, seignorial politics were implicated: Walter de Burgh, earl of Ulster, had died and the late-justiciar with the former escheator of Ireland had (it was alleged):

improperly assigned in dower to Avelina, late the wife of the earl, five of the earl's castles in the march of the county of Ulster which are in a state of war (*de guerra existunt*), together with almost all the homages of the Irish of that county likewise, retaining to the king's use the castle of Carrickfergus only . . .[142]

Pressure was then evidently put on the steward of Ulster to change this, on the ground that Avelina had received too much, particularly the castles and the feudal services of their castellaries due from native feoffees or subjects. At this point Avelina went over the provincial authorities' heads by appealing to the administration located (primarily) at Westminster ('the king') for 'justice'. To defend their action, the steward (apparently) counter-petitioned the royal council, which allowed itself to be persuaded that a new dower assignment should be made because the first 'is not reasonable, especially as castles at war, or even homages or services of military persons, ought not and are not wont to be assigned in dower to women of this kind'.[143] The 'castles' (castellaries), allegiances, and jurisdictions were all to be kept back. The new justiciar and escheator successfully overruled what their predecessors and the steward had done—but on a rarely invoked and perhaps dubious technicality. In September 1273, with Edward I still absent overseas, the escheator's duty to take possession of both heirs and castles was affirmed—but refined:

The king commands the escheator to be intentive and respondent to the justiciar, as well in regard to wards as to castles of wards in his custody when required to deliver the castles

---

fortresses at some time held by dowagers, heiresses, or female guardians of minor heirs, with many probable instances of coparceny or cohabitation by separate feoffees; Coulson, 'Castellation in Champagne', esp. 363.

[141] 'Justiciary' (after *justiciarius*) in the calendars. His large military retinue was paid for out of his fee, e.g. detailed in 1349: CCR, 1349–54, 47–8, 92; also 192; and CPR, 1345–8, 156; 1354–60, 271, 371. All his men were horsed, often supplemented ad hoc.

[142] CPR, 1272–81, 7. Ireland had a single escheator, England had two on either 'side of Trent', all with numerous deputies. The calendar translates 'which are of defence' inadequately. McNeill, 'Castles of Ward', argues that this term designated 'lesser enclosures to be manned by small, temporary garrisons' (p. 127), but emphasizes economic factors as overriding (p. 133). O'Keefe, 'Moated Settlement', also ascribes sub-castellar 'moats' to socio-economic causes and to the colonizers exclusively. Meek and Simms (eds.), *Medieval Irishwomen*, contains a variety of insights.

[143] Calendar, 'castles of defence'; 'women of this kind', i.e. widows in dower as *femmes soles*, not re-married. The exchange, in Chancery-speak, is summarized and otherwise apparently unrecorded.

to him, and to cause him to have all the receipts of his office whether from wards or vacant sees and abbeys. When the king shall be informed of the amount paid over he will give his writ of acquittance or of *allocate* to the escheator.[144]

It made sense in Ireland that the fortress-proper of a minor in wardship should be available to the justiciar, while administration of the lands was still separately provided for, as in England. Largely automatic bureaucratic and consensual procedures still predominated, however.[145] Measures possibly identifiable as militarily defensive are often ambiguous.[146] Ireland was far from unique. In 1242, for instance, after the death of the Yorkshire baron Peter de Maulay, the 'farmer' who took his lands at rent was exceptionally obliged 'to keep the castle of Mulgrave at his own costs', on top of 'finding all the necessities of Peter's mother and maintaining all the buildings (*domos*) of those lands in good state'. When a new custodian was appointed a year later he also had this extra duty laid upon him.[147] Quite often, it seems, fear of relatives contesting wardship or a succession dispute, not 'defence' as it would today be understood, was the cause. If a great magnate was involved, such reasons might be compelling. Thus, on the death of William the Marshal junior, earl of Pembroke and lord of extensive Irish territories, the following mandate (April 1231) went from Westminster to the justiciar. As abbreviated in memorandum style, the entry on the Close Roll is:

Ireland (*Hibernia*)—concerning the castles and lands which were of the earl Marshal: R. de Burgh, justiciar of Ireland, is instructed that if the constables of the castles of the late earl who have been directed by the king to deliver up (*liberare*) those castles to Walerand Teutonicus and failing that to come to England to speak to the king, should nevertheless be reluctant to hand the castles over to Walerand or to come to the king, then jointly with Walerand the justiciar shall devote his best efforts to obtaining (*perquirendum*) the castles and to taking possession (*saisina*) of the late earl's lands in Ireland . . .

Making sure that Henry III's own trusted envoy acted, not an Anglo-Irish official who might have 'gone native', was the most signal assertion of the king's lord-

---

[144] *CDIreland*, ii. 169; asserting the supremacy of the justiciar; note the non-military sense of 'castles of *wards*'. Officials' expenditure, vouched for by producing such writs, was 'allowed' against sums due from them, or was 'calculated' (writs of *computate*) when working out the balance owing.

[145] In 1232 the Irish dower of the countess of Pembroke, widow of William Marshall jnr, was agreed with his brother and successor Richard, 'and other magnates'. How large was the role of family consensus (especially in Ireland) is suggested by the rubric: 'names of the towns (*villarum*) which Earl Richard Marshall gives (*offert*) to the countess of Pembroke for her dower in Ireland.' She received three *ville*, including a *nova villa*, plus three castles/castellaries, including Ferns but 'excepting the outside Irish' (*Hybernensibus forinsecis*), and a 'manor': *Close Rolls, 1231–4* 144–5; nn. 148–9 below. 'Irish' in too loose a tributary relationship are implied.

[146] e.g. in 1298 the dower of Isabella, widow of William de Vesci who had held Kildare castle and another 'ancient castle burned down of old . . . and land now waste owing to war', excluded both. Kildare was a major *caput* but the other was evidently merely unremunerative. *CDIreland*, iv. 224–5. Following 'the law and custom of Ireland' did not exclude local discretion.

[147] As noted, *custodire* is too often translated 'guard': *Ex Rot Fin*, i. 379–80, 409. This was, in effect, a 'full repairing lease'. Sanders, *English Baronies*, 67, on Peter de Maulay III who came of age in 1247. The shortness of the minority, not any special quality in Mulgrave castle, is the likely reason for keeping the farmers on a tight rein.

ship.[148] Given that defensive pretexts, anywhere and at any period, were regularly emphasized as a routine formula if there was any shadow of need, their absence is always significant. So also, in this instance, is the treatment of the widowed countess and of William's heir. It was routine, though not perfunctory. By a *pro forma* mandate in May 1231, she was to receive her 'reasonable dower' from all her late husband's lands, namely 'in demesne lands (*dominicis*) as in homages and services of knights and other free men, and everything else upon which, by the custom of the land, dower ought to be calculated'.[149] Truly, 'with all his worldly goods she was endowed'. Her revenue share was a matter of due valuation being done. The make-up, in castellaries, lands, rents, and houses might take longer and require negotiation—in this case, over a year. In June 1232 Richard Marshal the new earl, William's brother, agreed his widowed sister-in-law's portion with Henry III, according her in Ireland the town and castle of Kildare, two other castellaries, and various manors, towns (*villas*), and lands. Her entitlement was not in question.[150] Due prestige and respect for rank were next in importance to income. The dowager (still styled 'countess of Pembroke', as was usual) had been living since April 1231 in England at the Marshal castle of Inkberrow (Worcs.), one of the numerous class which tends on structural grounds to be dismissed as a 'fortified manor-house' by modern classification.[151] In name and honour it was a 'castle' nonetheless, temporarily allocated as her residence, according to the custom made explicit in Magna Carta.

Three important Irish castellaries were thus put in the widow's hands despite

[148] *Close Rolls, 1227–31*, 496. Walerand was a former trusty of King John, rewarded and employed in difficult matters by Henry III: F. Powicke, *Thirteenth Century*, 40. *Teutonicus* meant Dutchman as well as German. Henry III and Hubert de Burgh were reluctant to accept Richard as earl since he had been a French vassal for the Marshal lands in Normandy. Troubles broke out in May 1233: developing into full-scale war in the Welsh march: ibid. 53–8.

[149] n. 145 above; also *Close Rolls, 1227–31*, 502 (dower in Ireland). Also, in May 1231 Henry III wrote directly to the Marshal constables of Pembroke, Cilgerran, Tenby, and Haverfordwest, quite exceptionally, commending their stance towards the king since Earl William's death and instructing them to hand over their custodies 'meanwhile' to John Marshal and Amauri de Saint-Amand. Tenants of the castellaries were also mandated. Richard received possession by order of 8 Aug. 1231 (ibid. 541).

[150] But the proper procedure had to be observed: in June 1230 Robert Musard was punished for seizing Miserden castle (Gloucs.) and lands belonging to Ralph Musard, his late father, by having even 'what he holds of the dower of his wife Juliana' confiscated. The order went first to the sheriff of Lincolnshire: *Ex Rot Fin*, i. 198–9. It was La Musadere, i.e. 'Musard's place', a small motte-and-bailey with now 'traces of masonry' (D. King, *Castellarium Anglicanum*, Gloucs.), but seat of a baronial family: Sanders, *English Baronies*, 83.

[151] But Inkberrow had its vicissitudes; built c.1174–6, King John seized it c.1210–13; in April 1231 'the king provides that A, countess of Pembroke, shall stay at *Intebergh* and in the castle there until her dower is assigned'; in the 'war' with Richard Marshal, the *castrum* was to be demolished and its park (fencing) sold off, with Richard's other *domus* of Bosham, Hampstead Marshal, Begeworth, and Crendon: Brown, 'List of Castles', 270; *Close Rolls, 1227–31*, 492; 1231–4, 542–3. Shortly after (Nov. 1233), the sheriff of Worcester was told: '[if] you have not yet had thrown down (*prosterni*) the castle of Inkberrow as we ordered you, [whereat] we are moved and amazed; we firmly order you to have this done, and the earl marshal's garden there uprooted (*extirpari*) without further delay', concluding with the threat redolent of King John, *sicut te ipsum et tua diligitis*. But to Richard's brother Gilbert, his successor as earl, in Sept. 1234, Henry III made some amends by giving him '10 oaks to make shingles to roof his buildings at Inkberrow': *Close Rolls, 1234–7*, 144. Such gifts to non-ecclesiastics are rare.

the likelihood that she would be an absentee, living on her dower-lands in England and in Wales and relying by remote control on her stewards and officials in Ireland. In the fourteenth century a special withholding tax had to be applied to lands of absentees, restricting remitting of money out of the country.[152] Much always depended on the lord's personal presence, with his 'civilian' and 'military' household or *familia*. Many questions were involved—but towards dowagers, especially if not expected to remarry, Henry III's administration displayed considerable clemency, which was not always the case. But these instances were exceptional. Normally matters were decided, within the parameters of custom, according to a wide range of factors, among which pressure at court (as Avelina de Burgh's case in 1273 shows) tended to predominate. Nevertheless, in 1245 Mathilda, who was widow of the notorious traitor and outlaw William Marsh (*de Marisco*) who had based himself on Lundy Island in 1235–42, was able to get an order from the Crown for the restoration to her of an Irish castle and its appurtenances, wrongly forfeited from her late husband. She held the castellary in her own right, but guilt-by-association seems seldom to have affected female title. Her petition had been verified and it was eventually accepted that she had personally received the lordship in fief as a marriage portion from a former archbishop of Dublin, her uncle Henry, and had held it prior to her marriage to William Marsh. Although as her husband he had controlled the lands and castle, his forfeiture could not touch her title, which was more secure than a life-tenure of dower property. A simple widow in such circumstances would be dependent on the king's favour to get a 'gracious remedy' not claimable as of right.[153] What stands out from such examples is not the obvious fact that property was vested as fully in women as in men, nor that as *femmes soles* they had an equal legal title, but that fortresses and the *capita* of castellaries were seldom excepted, even when and where they might have been expected to be. A range of cases shows that this was true also in France.[154] In Ireland the following may stand for an extreme of the fortress exception (June 1241):

[152] The other side of compulsory defence-residence: e.g. *CCR, 1327–30*, 149: *1337–9*, 328, 423–4; *CFR, 1356–68*, 224. But exemptions became common.

[153] *Close Rolls, 1242–7*, 322. Castle Blathac, near Limerick, was, if the petition 'facts' were verified, to be handed over to Mathilda 'or to her certain attorney bearing our letters [i.e. issued by the justiciar] together with her letters'. The William Marsh affair is given in detail by F. Powicke, *Henry III and the Lord Edward*, 740–59. Mathilda suffered detention but the delay in getting justice was endemic (pp. 754–5).

[154] e.g. in 1138, Galburga, lady of Bernis *castrum* (*dép*. Gard), converted her allodial tenure to homage 'in life and limb', making the castle rendable at will to Count Alphonse of Toulouse, oaths to be renewed by any husband: *Layettes*, i. 49–50. About 1159 the castellan of Bernis swore (in Provençal) rendability, etc. to the pregnant widow of Bernard Aton V, viscount of Nîmes, and to her unborn child (B.A. VI): *Layettes*, i. 82. In the north, in 1262–3, Joanna, heiress of Vignory (*dép*. Marne), and her new husband jointly swore the castle rendable to Thibaut V of Champagne; *Layettes*, iv. 50–1, 55–6. Also in 1262, Isabella, widow of Gautier de Vignory, made Thibaut liege homage for the *burghs*, castle, fiefs, and half of the castellary of Vignory (in dower-coparceny). At the plea of her father, the count of Sancerre, she swore the castle rendable: *Rôles de Champagne*, 381.

For Margery, who was the wife of Walter de Lacy—M. Fitz Gerald, justiciar of Ireland, is directed that from the lands and tenures late of Walter de Lacy he shall cause Margery to have land producing £100 per annum (*centum libratas terre*) together with the [standing] corn (*cum bladis*) of that land, in places where it may best be made over to her excluding castellaries (*extra castra*) which were once Walter's, to hold provisionally (*in tenanciam*) until her full dower has been assigned to her . . .[155]

A high proportion of the administrative action recorded on the Close and Patent Rolls responded to petitions. For Ireland the preponderance of reactive government was certainly even higher, since the council (mostly) at Westminster was usually applied to so as to circumvent, or to chivvy, the Dublin administration.[156] Which was Margery de Lacy's aim is not apparent, but four months later the justiciar was told to satisfy her petition to be given her full dower, 'doing her speedy justice in the matter' (a standard rebuke of alleged maladministration).[157] Accordingly, Margery again was to receive no castles—but she may not have asked for any, perhaps not having the backing to do so. Without specific evidence that the reason was defensive—and in this case no such assertion (however suspect) was ever made—neither military need nor central *dirigisme* can be presumed. 'Public safety' cloaked a multitude of motives.

When a boy was given possession prematurely it was quite usual to justify abbreviating his wardship by asserting defence advantages. Several such cases have already been considered. The near-man might well be more effective, and he would certainly be less exploitative from the family point of view, than a royal placeman who sought a profit on his investment. When what could be precautions were taken over castles in such circumstances, more than meets the eye must often be suspected. An English instance is the negotiated succession of Hugh d'Aubigny, brother and heir of the earl of Arundel, in 1233. The Aubigny family bought out the king's right until Hugh came of age in 1235, but had to leave named knights in possession of various lands allotted to them by Henry III in reward for their service. Little more than symbolic effect can have been intended by stipulating that, in addition:

---

[155] *Close Rolls, 1237–42*, 309. Similarly, but in definitive dower, Mathilda de Umfraville, widow of Gilbert, received one-third of his lands and for her residence ('capital messuage') his 'houses' in Otterburn, but not his castles (Harbottle, Prudhoe: Northumb.), kept in royal hands during the ensuing minority: *CDScotland*, i. 304–6. Order for valuation, Chippenham, 31 March; survey ('inquisition') dated 30 April; assignment ordered Woodstock, 20 May 1245. The widow's own preferences may well have been considered, although the division of the manor-fields was by strict measurement (*per sortem perticorum*).

[156] e.g. John de Grantset and Alice his wife had Geoffrey de Morton's licence of 1310 to crenellate bridge-tower and buildings at Dublin, issued by John Wogan the justiciar, renewed in 1331 by English patent, presumably to confront objectors. The very detailed 1310 licence had very exceptionally been vetted by an inquisition as to nuisance (*ad quod damnum*): *CPR, 1330–4*, 98; Parker, *Domestic Architecture*, iii. 409 (Latin text). Without the patent enrolment, this grant could scarcely have survived. Another exists for the bridge-tower at Kilkenny, obtained in 1393 by the chaplain of the bridge-chapel, also ratifying the justiciar's licence: *CPR, 1391–6*, 286 (also 304), which pleaded danger to travellers etc., but essentially affirmed the chaplain's 'estate' in Bennet's Bridge.

[157] *Close Rolls, 1237–42*, 338, 373 (English dower lands). The formula—'doing such justice that the king shall not hear again about the matter'—occurs occasionally.

when Hugh shall have received possession (*saisinam*) of his castles of Arundel [Sussex], [New] Buckenham, and Rising [Norfolk] he shall at once hand them over to three of his knights [named] being his tenants to be kept (*custodienda*) by them until he is of age. The three shall make oath to the king that under their keeping no damage shall be caused to the king or to his land from those castles.[158]

It was important not to create a precedent which might weaken the king's right of wardship or allow family control to encroach excessively. Use of the Continental form of guarantee ('jurability') is notable but still perfunctory. The chief aims were economic: of the family, to avoid 'waste', or damage by an intruded 'farmer'; of the king, to get cash down. The extent, not of 'state' but of regalian, control over 'private' property to us today appears very strange—but it continued (in reduced form) until the Civil War and, in France, until 1789. Heirs 'coming into their own' sometimes complained at what they discovered. Satisfaction was more likely if they could get remedial action before then. One petition, involving the fine and surviving castellated manor-house of Yanwath (Westmorland) evoked from Edward II's administration in 1312 an investigation by the escheator north-of-Trent 'of any waste of the houses, wood, and gardens done therein to the disinheriting of Walter, son and heir of the late Adam de Twynham, a minor in the king's ward', in this instance allegedly committed by two agents put in by Henry de Lacy, earl of Lincoln, who had been granted the wardship by Edward I (d. 1307).[159] It was routinely specified in such grants that land and buildings should be properly run and maintained. Castles were not differentiated.[160] In theory, any capital deterioration, or reduction of income-producing potential or of amenities, was 'waste'—excessive felling of timber beyond normal cropping, failing to keep land in cultivation, running down animal stocks, allowing reduction of the 'bond' (serf) or free labour force, lack of due investment, or indeed asset-stripping in any form. Adverse conditions, conflict especially, made this background code of practice protecting the heir rather theoretical. In marcher conditions the custodian's duty might mean defending the property, but war-damage to agriculture was

[158] *Ex Rot Fin*, i. 1250–1; Sanders, *English Baronies*, 2. Hugh died in 1243, leaving as heirs 'his sisters Nichola and Cecily, and the descendants of two elder sisters Maud and Isabel'. For only two years anticipation of possession 2,500 marks (£1,667) was paid. Henry III was himself of age *de facto* in 1227; formally from 1 Oct. 1228: Carpenter, *Minority of Henry III*, 389.

[159] *CFR, 1307–19*, 136; dated at Burstwick (Yorks.). If proved, they would lose the custody (and whatever unrecouped sum paid to get it). Similar entries are not infrequent, but not numerous. Emery, *Greater Medieval Houses*, i. 259–61; 'the finest late-medieval house in Cumbria', with 'some mildly defensive elements'; part 'still used for farm purposes'.

[160] One of Edward II's last writs, 10 Sept. '1327' (?1326), ordered a survey 'of the state of the castle of Warwick, since it came into the king's hands'. Thomas de Beauchamp, son of Earl Guy (d. 1315), was then about 14. To be reported was the condition of 'the lands, houses, walls, and buildings of the castle, and the mills, parks, woods and stews [fish-ponds] belonging', attributable to 'the negligence of the king's keepers': *CPR, 1324–7*, 352; Sanders, *English Baronies*, 76. Long minorities were doubly risky. Wigmore castle and the manors (Heref.: a large motte-and-bailey site, unsystematically rebuilt in stone) were specifically to be 'maintained in state as received' under Bishop Henry of Lincoln's lease in 1333. Countess dowager Joan had had custody of all the lands since her husband Roger was executed for aggravated treason in late 1330: *CFR, 1327–37*, 345. A careful farmer would have a detailed inventory agreed when he took over.

almost inevitable, whether the manorial *caput* was a fortress or not.[161] Preserving revenues was a common interest, of tenant, lord, and peasantry—but their several aims overlapped, rather than coincided.

In the borderlands of the north, and particularly in Ireland, it was often necessary for the Crown to devolve custody of an inheritance on a magnate capable and willing to assume it. Castles then took on especial importance, but when devastation spread and economic decline (aggravated by worsening climate, demography, and peacekeeping) set in, the profits of stewardship might not cover the costs of defence. It became increasingly usual to set very low rents, or none at all. Loss of labour by depopulation was the ultimate catastrophe. In the following mandate of June 1290 the focus is primarily on fortress-maintenance—but it already suggests deeper problems:

To Walter de la Haye, escheator of Ireland. Whereas Walter, after the death of Theobald le Botiller [Butler] lately committed the castle of *Dorch* [?Thurles, co. Tipperary], which belonged to Theobald at his death, to William le Mareschal [Marshal] to be kept in the king's name on condition that if the castle should be hostilely occupied while in his custody, or if it should decay or be thrown down, William would be obliged to repair it at his own expense, he having pledged his lands to comply—and the castle was afterwards occupied and thrown down, so that the escheator accordingly took William's lands in *Tyringlas* into the king's hands and so holds them—Richard de Burgh, earl of Ulster, has given the king to understand that those lands belong to him, because William gave and granted them to him, so Richard has asked the king to hand them over to him—the king, therefore, now orders the escheator to deliver the lands to the earl upon his finding security that he will have that castle repaired and put into as good a state as it was when committed. Otherwise the king will make some agreement about it with Theobald le Botiller's son Theobald.

Edward I was responsible to the under-age heir for his agent's apparent negligence (and, it would seem, deceit), but had no more leverage to compel Richard de Burgh than keeping back lands he claimed were his to which the duty to repair Thurles (?) castle was still attached—unless making an arrangement with the young Theobald was itself a threat. Any such 'agreement' would probably have included ending his wardship prematurely.[162] Marcher castellaries easily fell into decline if their estate-centre lost its lordly *personnel* and became administratively and defensively inactive. Early re-seisin was often a solution. Capable adolescent heirs, men in all but legal status, could often do better for the 'public interest' as well as for themselves in adverse conditions. Among many early terminations of wardship notable examples are those of William de Burgh (1327), heir to Richard

---

[161] e.g. in 1332, 'irregularities' in the threefold partition of the Valence lands were adjusted. Scottish damage to Mitford and Ponteland castellaries was also allowed for, a fall from £91 (pre-1314) to £30. Ponteland in 1324, at Aymer's death, was actually worth only 22s. 4½d. but had revived to £9. 18s. 8¼d. by 1332: *CCR, 1330–3*, 584–6. In 1391 Queen Anne's lease on Richmond and Bowes provided for rent rebates for war-damage: *CPR, 1388–92*, 393 (with valuable detail).

[162] Avoiding royal embroilment. It was left open for de Burgh to put pressure on the young Theobald, apparently nearly of age: *CPR, 1288–96*, 86. '*Dorch* is probably Thurles', from the Irish *Durlas* anglicized to *Dorz*, per C. O'Brien and A. Empey via Terry Barry.

himself, his grandfather, earl of Ulster;[163] similarly of 19-year-old Gilbert de Umfraville of Prudhoe in Northumberland (1328);[164] and of Edmund de Mortimer for his Irish lands, in 1368.[165] Each was responsible for 'border' castles. After 1337 the glamorous and successful war in France drew away royal and baronial interest from the increasingly intractable problems of Ireland, with consequent lack of interest occasionally interrupted by royal initiatives. The state of castles was merely symptomatic. Widows and minors in wardship were particularly vulnerable to this patchily severe environment, unless they had lands in England—but the Crown quite readily waived its rights under pressure. This mandate from Edward II's Chancery (November 1320) already reflects these problems:

... As the king understands on the testimony of Roger de *Mortuo Mari* [Mortimer] of Wigmore [castle, Herefs.], justiciar of Ireland, that the [resources of the] lands and tenements late of Richard de Clare in Ireland, tenant-in-chief, in the king's hands because his son and heir Thomas is a minor, are insufficient [to provide] for their defence against the Irish and other rebels in those parts—Grant to the said heir, as a favour, of all his father's castles, towns, manors, lands and tenements, in Ireland ... and that Maurice son of Thomas, his uncle, and Maurice *de Rupeforti* [Rocheford], his kinsman, shall be his keepers. The revenues of the lands are to be spent on their defence and on the repair of the said castles and manors and to the profit of the heir.

This family arrangement, mediated by the justiciar (later notorious in the downfall of Edward II), was not to last long.[166] Thomas de Clare died aged about 3 years soon afterwards, and his inquisition *post mortem* made in April 1321 was a sorry record of ruin and desolation.[167] Even if all the income was ploughed back with-

[163] CCR, 1327–30, 185; by the Mortimer–Isabella regime, 'at the request of Henry, earl of Lancaster, and out of confidence that he [the king] has of the good service to be rendered to him by William in Ireland and elsewhere'; but Carrickfergus castle was kept back.

[164] CDScotland, iii. 174–5; 'on account of the losses of his ancestors, in *abatement* (demolition) of their castles and destruction of their lands'; except for dower lands and Redesdale liberty. Harbottle (as noted) was to be razed by treaty with Robert Bruce in 1320. This, too, by Mortimer–Isabella; but in 1410 another Gilbert was prematurely reseised, with explicit duty to keep Harbottle: CPR, 1317–21, 416; 1408–13, 156.

[165] CPR, 1367–70, 114; on the usual condition of finding men for defence. Roger, earl of March, his father, died in 1360. Edmund came of age in 1373. He married Philippa, heiress of Lionel, duke of Clarence (d. 1368), whose 'Statutes of Kilkenny' (1366) 'tacitly admitted that the original attempt to colonize the whole of Ireland ... had broken down completely': McKisack, *Fourteenth Century*, 232, 384.

[166] Thomas de Clare was a baby (b. 1318; d. 1321). His father had been 'slain by certain Irish rebels', apparently an act of treachery since the king's military service in Ireland was called out 'to avenge' it: CPR, 1317–21, 523; CCR, 1318–23, 90; Altschul, *The Clares*, table III on the prolific cadet branches. Wardship by a relative who might profit from the heir's death was usually avoided—but high infant mortality is a less sinister explanation for Thomas's demise.

[167] CIPM vi., 159–63; cf. inquisitions on the lands late of Roger Bigod, earl of Norfolk, 1306, including Framlingham, Bungay, Chepstow (*Strugoil*), Castle Troggy (Mons.) and Carlow castles (*Catherlagh*—'a castle badly roofed', etc.); and on Joan of Acre, late countess-dowager of Gloucester and Hertford, including the castles of Tonbridge, Clare, Cardiff, Dinas Powys, Llanbleddian, Talevan, Llantrissant, Kenfig, Caerfilli, Castell Coch, Neath, Newport, Llangibby (*Tregruk*), Caerleon, Kilkenny, Fermaill, 'Offerclan' (Castletown, co. Leix—*pers. comm.* T. Barry and C. Manning), 'now worth nothing; costing £40 p.a. to keep', and Callan: CIPM iv. 311–31; Part III, nn. 116, 119, etc.

out any going to the king, as was becoming common, it fell below the level of lordly subsistence. In co. Limerick, the castle of Corcomohide, held with a mere two acres nearby, owed no service to the king: its hall, the jurors declared, together with 'the lord's chamber and the chapel are badly roofed, nor are there doors or locks; but the castle is strong and the place pleasant . . .'. Such structural details were of peculiar interest to Irish panels of inquiry. Thomas de Clare's inventory then dealt with the western region of Thomond, its county, castle, town, and liberty. All were apparently in fair condition, but regarding the castle of Quin (*Conghi*) in co. Clare they remark: 'the castle was thrown down during the life of the said heir [Thomas] and could not be rebuilt without great cost.' Two other castellaries are mentioned and, in addition, at Youghal (co. Clare) 'the manor and town . . . including a capital messuage called the castle'. As was ubiquitous, the style 'castle' was a matter of repute and lordly dignity (exactly as *château* continued to be in France). In England this habit was damaged by the Civil War (1642–9), and since *c.*1900 by educated misapprehension (but much less so in Scotland, where tower-houses in general are 'castles').[168]

Earl Richard de Clare (d. 1262), the baby Thomas' great-grandfather, had also been lord of Thomond. His son Gilbert, the great castle-builder ('the Red Earl'), was put in royal wardship, became earl in 1263/4, and emerged in 1265 as a major power in the royalist party which defeated Simon de Montfort. In May 1266 he induced the prime mover, King Henry III's son Edward, to grant to the Clare town of Kilkenny power to levy dues for walling ('murage'), an act regularized by the Chancery.[169] Shortly beforehand, in another act of self-assertion, he had set about challenging his mother's dower assignment, alleging that it was erroneous regarding Earl Richard's lands 'beyond the Wye', that is, in south Wales. Henry III guardedly acquiesced but with suitable dignity:

Notification to the tenants of the said lands that whereas it does not befit the king's majesty that in time of wardship any prejudice should arise, especially in these times; the king understands that in the assignment of dower to M[aud], countess of Gloucester, made while Gilbert . . . was in the king's ward, more was given to her than belonged to her, especially of castles, whereby damage might happen to the realm and the present earl.

A revaluation was ordered of these lands and castellaries, taken meanwhile out of the dowager's possession, 'so that the king may cause to be done both to the countess [-dowager] and to the present earl what ought to be done according to the custom of those parts and by right'.[170] It seems that Gilbert had invoked

---

[168] e.g. Part I, n. 79 above. Even the exemplary Jean Mesqui employs the tendentious neologism *château-fort*, basing his definition on current usage: Mesqui, *Château-forts*, 8–9.

[169] *CPR, 1258–66*, 593: 'to the earl's citizens if Kilkenny, that they may take murage for three years to fortify their town as the neighbouring cities of those parts have been accustomed.' Many Irish towns enjoyed locally granted or vested murage powers long before they were granted in England: e.g. *Close Rolls, 1231–34*, 552; cf. *CPR, 1485–94*, 67 (Hereford).

[170] *CPR, 1258–66*, 662–3. She was Maud de Lacy (d. 1289), Earl Richard's second wife, married in 1237; Gilbert was born in 1243. His own first wife, the 'reigning' countess (1254–90) was Alice de Lusignan; his second, who outlived him, Joan of Acre, daughter of Edward I: Altschul, *The Clares*, table II *et passim*.

against his mother the occasional Welsh and Irish prejudice (scarcely precaution) against the female tenure of fortresses, disguising his concern to oppose without interference the threat of Prince Llywelyn to his own lordship of Glamorgan in customarily patriotic and altruistic language.[171]

2. Inheritance and Survival, Chiefly in the March of Scotland

Lordly life in Ireland offers some useful analogies. It may have been sporadically more militant than in England, but it does not follow that castles in the marches conformed structurally to the pattern that might be expected.[172] Their architecture still responded faithfully to noble style (indeed, with frequent stylistic hyperbole), and the position of *châtelaines* and children was scarcely distinguishable from that elsewhere. In the northern counties of England, as in south-western France in the thirteenth century, the range of issues touching fortresses in minorities was overwhelmingly tenurial and personal. Thus, any dilapidation caused by the neglect or malpractice of the custodian or guardian was treated primarily as damage to the heir. Being disinherited was the most feared of wrongs; but public defence was the superficial ideology. The constant interaction between 'private' concerns and 'public' professions and duties was nowhere more vital than in Cumberland, Westmorland, Northumberland, and throughout the north.

Despite the long Anglo-Scottish entente between Henry III and Alexander III (1249–85), and before him with Alexander II (1214–49),[173] the neglected state of the historic Border castles of Appleby and Brougham (Westmorland) received exceptional attention, but probably not before the heir came of age. Both de Vipont castles, in the Eden Valley, south of Carlisle, were substantial and ancient. As so often, a long minority contributed to the problem. John de Vipont died in 1241. Robert II, his son, survived but did not come of age until 1254–6. Poorly supervised guardianship without benevolent family intervention, by a royal appointee mainly interested in maximizing his income, frequently caused damage when the heir's majority and the day of reckoning were remote. In the case of Vipont a special inquiry was held.[174] Guardian of the lands and children was a local ecclesiastic, the prior of Carlisle. He was held to have 'wasted' the woods, cowpastures, and other lands. Both castles had suffered from poor maintenance.

---

[171] Earl Gilbert was particularly concerned about the threat to his Glamorgan capital castle-city of Cardiff posed by Llywelyn and the Welsh lord of Senghenydd. His answer was to seize and fortify the site of Caerffilly, on the north side of the pass via Castell Morgraig to Cardiff and the plain. Llywelyn destroyed Gilbert's first fortification but he persevered: e.g. Rees, *Caerphilly Castle*, 21–8; Pugh, *Glamorgan County History III*, 53–6, 423–6.

[172] See Emery, *Greater Medieval Houses*, i, for the architectural panorama and detail; also still swayed by tradition but sharply analytical, Dixon, 'From Hall to Tower'.

[173] But Alexander II's resumption of traditional Scottish pressure on Cumberland was marked by the siege of Carlisle, damaging the castle. Appeased in 1237 by grant of £200 p.a. of 'land where there are no castles' (i.e. only lesser administrative centres). Long delays ensued: *CDScotland*, i. 215, 250–1, 257, 261, 284. Economies were then ordered at Bamburgh and Newcastle: *Close Rolls, 1234–7*, 498.

[174] *CIM* i. 143–4; Sanders, *English Baronies*, 103–4. John had a minority of about five years. Robert II died 1264, leaving daughters Isabella and Idoine, who divided the *honor* of Appleby (below).

According to the jurors, 'the walls and buildings (*domus*) of Brougham are dete-
riorated for lack of repair of the guttering and roofing (*gutteriorum et cooper-
torerii*)'. More specifically:

touching the manor of Appleby, they say that the *turris* [keep] is badly damaged (*multum
deteriorata*) and the timber much rotted by default of the prior, who has failed to compel
(*noluit distringere plegios*) the carpenters whose task it was to keep the tower in repair and
who had been paid 22 marks [£14. 13*s*. 4*d*.] by the Lord John de Vipont (*de Veteri Ponte*) .
. . to do the work. Of the 50 marks which the lady queen allocated to the repair of the castle
[in custody] not more than £10 was actually spent, they believe.

Leaded gutters behind parapets and in roof-valleys, as on the twelfth-century keep
at Appleby, needed vigilance anywhere, not just in the rainy north-west.[175]

Even before Bannockburn (1314), as the impetus of Edward I's failed invasions
of the Lowlands expired and Scottish retaliatory raids began, the king's financial
straits and the need to reward deserving soldiers might affect heirs indirectly. The
following petition was doubtless typical. Dateable to *c*.1303, it came from Stephen
de Brampton, former constable ('warden') of Bothwell castle south of Glasgow.
Bothwell, he said:

he had defended against the power of Scotland for a year and nine weeks, to his great loss
and misfortune as all his companions died in the castle except himself and those with him
who were taken by famine and by assault. He was then kept in harsh confinement (*dure
prison*) in Scotland for three years, to the abasement of his estate. He prays the king to give
him the ward and marriage of the heir and lands of Sir Philip Paynel, reputed to be worth
£50 [per annum], or to retain him in his household until he gives him some other advance-
ment. He begs the king's grace as one who has painfully served him in all his Scottish wars
without taking anything from him.

The petition was considered at the highest level (*coram rege*) and this instruction
was given on the back ('endorsed'): 'let the chamberlain of Scotland look out for
some wardship or marriage for Stephen's benefit and inform the king. Meanwhile
let him remain in the king's household (*hospicio regis*).'[176] The net profits of
administering an inheritance until the heir was 21, or the right to decide on a
marriageable girl's husband, were valuable. Correct conduct was expected of the
guardian thus intruded *in loco parentis*, but much was left to his discretion.
Edward's ability to deliver a suitably lucrative position in Scotland was vanishing
rapidly, but Stephen did gain temporary maintenance at the king's expense.

Castle-manors as far south as north Lancashire and Yorkshire were to suffer
lasting economic damage. In 1309 Robert de Clifford extensively improved the
apartments and repaired the castle of Brougham, obtaining a licence to crenellate

---

[175] Cf. derelictions by guardians detailed in 1360 at three Lincolnshire manors (one with a 'drawbridge'). In 1382 John de Mowbray, just succeeded as earl of Nottingham, was licensed to sue the
former royal keepers 'in aid of the repair of his ruined castles and manors': *CIM* iii. 150; *CPR, 1381–5*,
182.
[176] *CDScotland*, ii. 498; Simpson, *Bothwell Castle*, 4–7. This was the 1298–9 siege. Retaken in a month
in 1301 by Edward I; then it was surrendered after Bannockburn and half the great donjon was pulled
down (not mined; the base is intact). Brampton seems to have raised his ransom himself.

from Edward II, largely to signify Clifford possession. Robert de Vipont had died in 1264, his lands passing by his elder daughter's marriage to Roger de Clifford, father of Robert, who thus acquired his mother's half of the barony of Appleby, in 1295. The licence survives only as a Privy Seal warrant.[177] It included also Robert's castle of Mallerstang (alias Pendragon), but he was killed at Bannockburn, leaving his son, another Roger, under age. Inquisitions variously declared that he was born 21 January to 2 February 1300. Henry de Percy, the Northumberland magnate, with the courtier Bartholomew de Badlesmere and the earl of Warwick (d. August 1315), were awarded the:

wardship of the castles of Skipton in Craven [Yorks.], Appleby, Brougham, and Pendragon, and of two parts of the lands and profit of the office of sheriff of Westmorland, late of Robert de Clifford, tenant in chief . . . to hold until the full age of Roger his son and heir . . . [providing] for the sustenance of the heir and the keeping and defence of the castles, paying the annual value of . . . the lands.[178]

Nearly four years later, the young Roger was considered fit to take over his father's lands and castles (still not separately administered) on quite generous terms. But whereas the Westmorland lands, valued at no more than £5 p.a., were to be rent-free, meeting only the heir's expenses and the costs 'of the defence of the said castles against the Scots, the king's enemies', the Clifford lands elsewhere were to pay their full assessed income to the Exchequer until Roger was 'of full age'.[179] The 'castle' (castellary) of Skipton was evidently not considered to be in danger. Self-defence was an unusually prominent public duty in the exposed northern counties, so the Clifford fortresses, like those of the Percies and later of the Neville family, bore the brunt along with the king's castle of Carlisle and especially the townsmen, prior, and bishop of the walled city. But it was nonetheless (contrary to expectations, perhaps) a very exceptional measure for the government of Richard II to intervene with direct help, in December 1383. The sheriffs of Cumberland and Westmorland were instructed (until Easter 1384) 'to take stone-cutters, masons, and other labourers for the repair of certain castles and fortlets

---

[177] CChWarr, 291. Disentangling Lady Anne Clifford's spirited restorations at Brougham complicates analysis: see Summerson et al., Brougham Castle.

[178] CFR, 1307–19, 212; the later contradiction, 'except Skipton castle and lands elsewhere than in Westmoreland', and finally that their 'yearly extent' was to be paid over, is confusing. The castle proper seems to have been in separate custody. The lordship's status was equivocal: acquired by Robert in 1311, then his acquisition reversed by the Lords Ordainers, before being restored to him: CPR, 1307–13, 395, 408–9. He was one of that 'reform' group but had 'royalist leanings': McKisack, Fourteenth Century, 10. The composition of the wardship committee in 1314 reflects curial–local tensions.

[179] CFR, 1307–19, 370–1: Percy and Warwick had died, so Badlesmere was instructed (to direct his local agents) to hand over the Clifford lands, but John de Rither was separately appointed as 'keeper of the castle of Skipton'. A dower portion would account for the reserved third of the hereditary shrievalty (revenues). In 1315 Skipton comprised the castle, 'advowson of the free chapel within the castle', two water mills, and a park. Appleby had a park. The Arthurian-named Pendragon (Mallerstang) castle was merely an adjunct of the 'capital messuage' and manor of Kirkby Stephen: CIPM v. 300–7. Roger backed Thomas of Lancaster's revolt, being executed in 1322 after the 'battle' of Boroughbridge: cf. CIPM vii. 41–2 (1327).

[i.e. *fortalicia* or fortresses] of Roger de Clifford, knight, near the march of Scotland'. This royal power of impressment of skilled craftsmen, who normally were peripatetic unless kept on the staffs of the greater religious houses and secular establishments (which might be exempt), must greatly have helped. Roger had clearly some powerful supporters in the king's council—his plea that his castles were 'useful as a refuge for the king's subjects' was repeated in the sheriff's mandates; but he still had to pay these involuntary winter-workers their wages.[180] Unless retained, masons moved wherever their work took them. The period considered suitable for building in masonry comprised the frost-free and drier months from late spring to early autumn, which underlines both the vulnerability to the Scots of the Clifford lands and the importance of adroit pressure at Westminster.

This blending and interplay of dynastic, tenurial, economic, defensive, and local political factors, with occasional but usually incidental Crown intervention, was ubiquitous. By focusing on fortresses in the marches of Scotland (and in Ireland) when subjected to the stresses of adversity exacerbated by minority (which frequently meant female tenure), some disentangling of these strands can be attempted.[181] If, in these circumstances, the defence component was latently pervasive, it was nevertheless (except in propaganda) seldom prominent and hardly, if ever, decisive in practice. Where fortresses are concerned it was diluted by the principal stream of aristocratic life, in that fortification was chiefly an expression of status; and the architectural programme was predominantly residential. A useful term to extend (at any, but especially the later, period) to the fortified apparatus of turrets, bartizans, machicolation, or plain crenellation and so on with which noble houses were embellished in the northern counties (and elsewhere) would be 'Scottish Baronial', Victorian though the concept might appear. 'The Fortified Style' has yet to find its biographer.[182]

An authentic but haphazard selection of these northern buildings is provided by the licences to crenellate. These dignifying patents of architectural nobility were issued on demand, in circumstances which repeatedly show that the recipients sought to assert their position, to mark wealth and success, and to demonstrate their access to court patronage.[183] Many of these castles or 'tower-houses' vividly illuminate the tenurial vicissitudes in which children as heirs were involved, by no means always passively.

[180] *CPR, 1381–5*, 344; Coulson, 'Battlements and the Bourgeoisie', 149–56, for Carlisle. Edward Dallingridge's licence for Bodiam (1385), claiming it was 'to resist the king's enemies', etc., is the classic example of such special pleading and warns against naivety: Coulson, 'Some Analysis of Bodiam', 91–7.
[181] J. Mackenzie, *Castles of England*, compiles much castle-families' history but is hard to use because diffuse, unreferenced, architecturally vague, and conceptually inept. Emery, *Greater Medieval Houses*, shows how architectural biography should be done.
[182] Despite the perceptive work of Mark Girouard (see Bibliography), the nearest approach is still, perhaps, MacGibbon and Ross, *Castellated and Domestic Architecture of Scotland*, though restricted in scope.
[183] Historiographical reappraisal and overview: Coulson, 'Freedom to Crenellate'. Emery, *Greater Medieval Houses*, i. 174–80; regional annotated lists *passim*. Cf. Pounds, *The Medieval Castle*, 102–6, 260–6.

Not far from the Clifford, later Neville, lands in Westmorland, to the north and west in Cumberland, west of Penrith, is Greystoke. Originally quadrangular with four towers but, as is common in the north, much altered by continuous or prolonged later occupation, Greystoke castle is as typical architecturally as it is dynastically. In 1348/9 it is noted as held in chief as seat of a barony, which dated from the early twelfth century. William, *baro de Craystok*, obtained the usual terse and token 'permission' 'to crenellate his dwelling place (*mansum*)' in October 1353, in the decade after the first devastating onset of the Great Plague which greatly reduced demand for such licences. He had come of age in 1342, dying in 1359, the year after securing Edward III's pardon for the Scots' capture of Berwick on Tweed, of which he had been captain. The reason was 'because the king is informed that William left the town to be with him in person . . . and rode at war in his company', evidently accepting William's excuse for yielding to the lure of the French war.[184] His inquisition *post mortem* (July 1359) shows that he had been sharing Greystoke manor with its two separate parks, corn-mill, a fulling-mill for processing woollen cloth off the loom (the castle-proper is not even mentioned), in company with his mother Alice (there was no other dowager).[185] Since William's father Ralph had died in 1323 she had remarried, into the rising family of Neville. This couple had held Alice's dower third of Greystoke barony, but not Morpeth castellary (Westmorland) nor the other lands in Yorkshire, Northumberland, Bedfordshire, and Hertfordshire. After 1359 there was to be another long minority since William's son Ralph was then aged 7. William may have substantially rebuilt both Greystoke and Morpeth castles in the time available to him, perhaps to assert his accession after 1342; but the dowager baroness Alice was the long-term lady of Greystoke.

Triermain (Cumb.) is now an undistinguished ruin, not far from Birdoswald Roman fort, just north of Hadrian's Wall, of what was once a quadrangular castle of some note. Roland de Vaux, cadet of an ancient family, had it licensed to be crenellated as 'his dwelling-place in the march of Scotland', in 1340. In 1362 the inquisition on the death of another Roland *de Vallibus* (dynasties often clung to particular forenames, to the genealogist's confusion) duly noted that the manor was held for one-eighth of a knight's fee from Ranulf de Dacre and also owed attendance at his *caput* of Irthington ('suit of court') every three weeks.[186]

---

[184] *CIPM* ix. 365; Sanders, *English Baronies*, 50; he had a minority of 19 years, so 1353 may represent opportunity for favour or the recovery of his estates' prosperity; he died at 38. *CPR, 1350–4*, 495; *1358–61*, 18; 15 Feb. 1358.

[185] *CIPM* x. 420–7. Calendar omissions can be deceptive, but William's two-thirds of Greystoke manor are detailed (two named parks, a shieling, mills, etc.). Baron Ralph, his father with other magnates, helped to settle Walter de Selby's rebellion, based on Mitford castle, Northumb.: *CCR, 1327–30*, 441, 456. The disturbances associated with Lancaster's revolt in 1322 were not settled until 1329. On fulling mills, Blair and Ramsey (eds.), *English Medieval Industries*, 330–2, 351–2 (rural cloth-manufacture), 394 (water-powered trip-mallets).

[186] *CIPM* xi. 341–3. These regular assemblies of tenants, whether perfunctory or by deputy, have been cast in the 'military' shade. Irthington was the formerly de Vaux chief seat: Sanders, *English Baronies*, 124. Roland senior's licence follows that for Blenkinsopp (Northumb.), adopting the same wording: *CPR, 1338–40*, 417.

Roland's heir was his son Roland, aged 3. Perhaps because the moated rectangle at Triermain was tenurially subordinate, the jurors meeting at Penrith included it in their valuation of the manor as only a '*forcelettum* of stone' along with 'a water-mill worth a *skep* of oatmeal yearly, price 6*s*.'. No Scots' damage is mentioned to this or to Roland's other manor, but in 1384 the baronial Dacre manor, dependent on Naworth castle but with its seat at Irthington, was declared to be 'largely waste owing to the destruction of the Scots', although the Dacre deer-parks of Kirkoswald castle and Irthington are noted as 'with deer', suggesting that they were not affected significantly.[187] The greatest danger to these aristocratic estates was clearly not from raiders but from the manifold risks to the survival of male heirs who could preserve them by single ownership. Lumley, in co. Durham, was particularly unfortunate in this respect. Robert de Lumley 'died a minor in the king's wardship' in 1374, his father Marmaduke having died about four years earlier. The other son, Ralph, survived to full age (1383), inheriting his uncle John's property which was occupied, as guardian, by the powerful John de Neville of Raby, along with the rest of his inheritance from his elder brother Robert. Ralph was then active in Border affairs, marking his emergence by having his name-place of Lumley crenellated by licence in 1392, the form of words at that period typically being 'to build a castle at Lumley and crenellate it'. The splendid surviving towered, quadrangular building has been more fortunate than the family.[188]

A family's fortunes depended, more than on any other factor, on avoiding the perils of wardship or, worse still, having no surviving male heir. In 1379 the ascent of Elslack in Craven (Yorks.) was interrupted especially poignantly. The family there had begun well: Godfrey Dawtry (*de Alta Ripa*) the first got his licence 'to crenellate his chamber' (*camera*, a vanished tower-house) in 1318, with the help at Edward II's court of Bartholomew de Badlesmere.[189] In 1375 an attempt was alleged to have been illegally made by a 'Thomas Dawtrey, son and heir of Godfrey Dawtrey of Eslack', to give all the family lands to the acquisitive John de Neville of Raby. Godfrey, the father, had in fact died in 1369, and Thomas was 'an idiot', aged over 30 in 1379. Being mentally defective, he was in law unable to hold or to transmit title to property. His two younger brothers being dead without heirs, John de Neville accordingly lost possession and the manor-fraction of Elslack with other lands in Gisburn and Rimington reverted to the Crown.[190] But

---

[187] *CIPM* xv. 380–2 (paras. 971–3). The 1375 inquisition is silent on the question of destruction; *CIPM* xiv. 117–19.

[188] Ralph was executed for treason in 1400. Details: *CIPM* xiv. 74–5; xv. 318–19 (paras. 811–12); *CPR*, 1391–6, 188. Emery, *Greater Medieval Houses*, i. 117–21. The hall entrance from the courtyard, in the form of a double-tower gatehouse, has one of the most lavish heraldic displays to survive, (largely) added *c*.1580 by an antiquarian Lord Lumley (pl. 61; n. 3), but comparable to Bodiam (*c*.1385–93) and to Hylton, co. Durham (B. Morley, 'Hylton Castle', reconstruction p. 121b).

[189] The formula 'on the information of . . .' is habitual for a petitioning agent—one who for 'interest', affinity, or favour would have a petition recast in grant-form and put through the Chancery machinery, perhaps paying the Hanaper fee and forwarding the document: *CPR, 1317–21*, 242.

[190] *Cat Anc Deeds* iii. 275 (no. B3940); 'grant . . . of all his lands and tenements in Gisburn and Rimington in Craven. 15 May, 49 Edw III. Seal'; *CIPM* xv. 66 (1379). Geoffrey had done what he could,

Thomas was not quite a non-person: the cost of providing for him would remain attached to his land.

The same rules of inheritance applied to magnates, with their correspondingly greater castles, as to the gentry. John de Neville himself marked his own ascent by obtaining licence in 1382 'to enclose with a wall of stone and lime and crenellate a plot on his own ground at Shirefhoton, co. York, and make a castle thereof'. The result was an irregular but imposing towered quadrangle.[191] It has large, fearless, exterior windows and no 'military history'. The character of 'palace-castle' has now been generally, if reluctantly, accepted. John, known from his chief seat of Raby, had succeeded his father Ralph in 1367 at the age of 38, inheriting Sheriff Hutton manor and Middleham castle ('worth nothing within the walls'), both equipped with deer-parks, together with a scatter of lands concentrated in Yorkshire.[192] His wife Elizabeth was the principal heiress of William de Latimer (d. 1381), whose far-flung interests included houses in Calais and London and, in Yorkshire, Danby castle (despite its status, termed a mere 'peel in ruins'). She survived him in 1383.[193] The castle ('peel') of Danby manor was still ruinous and Bywell (Northumb.) was noted as 'worth 40 marks per annum and no more, because of burning and destruction by the Scots'. In 1389 Elizabeth inherited her mother's lands. The Nevilles were an immensely successful and prolific family. Elizabeth's son Ralph became earl of Westmorland in 1397 but, with greater savoir faire than the rival Percy earl of Northumberland, defected to Henry IV in 1399.[194]

Castles were mere appendages to the lives of the great, annexed to their ambitions, in the north most demonstratively so, displaying and exercising their power in each cluster of lands. Like Elslack, another minor fortress (but still a 'castle') which has not survived is Wilton by Pickering (Yorks.), licensed to be crenellated in 1335 to John de Heslington (*Heslarton*) who died in 'the Great Pestilence' (Black Death) in August 1349, 'Walter, his son and heir being then a minor and unmarried'. It was unclear whether Edward III or the duke of Lancaster was overlord, a

leaving Elslack in turn to his other sons, Henry and Richard, then to Thomas who was the eldest. John de Neville assumed the guardianship of Richard, although Elslack was not held of him (directly). When Richard died he apparently extracted from Thomas, or forged Thomas's seal to a deed of gift from him.

[191] *CPR, 1381–5*, 108; exceptionally, not an existing manor-site to judge from the wording. Platt, *The Castle*, 136–7 (fig. 127: aerial photo showing invasion by the farm buildings); Emery, *Greater Medieval Houses*, i. 390–3.

[192] *CIPM* xii. 133–43. Raby, as within the palatinate of Durham, received licence to crenellate from Bishop Hatfield in 1378, full if not fulsome: transcript (French), e.g. Godwin, *English Archaeologist's Handbook*, 233.

[193] *CIPM* xv. 155–9; xvi. 277–91. Her age is given as 'over 24', 'over 21', and '26'. The Calais properties owed 'two watches for the safe-keeping and garrisoning of the town'. Elizabeth's dower was 'assigned in the presence of Ralph de Neville, knight, son and heir of John'. She made the usual oaths to the prior of Durham as king's proxy (tribute to her rank). In Jan. 1389 she inherited on the death of her mother Elizabeth de Latimer: *CCR, 1385–9*, 544–5; *CIPM* xvi. 273–4. In his wife's right, John held a manor in Norfolk, five in Bedfordshire for a quarter of the barony of Bedford, another in Lincolnshire, two in Cumberland.

[194] Emery, *Greater Medieval Houses*, i. 123–36 (Raby and the Nevilles); 329–33 (Danby: pl. 163, aerial view of the small but fine courtyard, built c.1300; site occupied by farm buildings). Neville genealogy, Griffiths, *Henry VI*, table 5.

question 'still unsettled' in 1356.[195] In 1367 an inquisition revealed that Walter had succeeded irregularly 'by gift of Sir John de Heslerton, his father, without the king's licence', so although 'the custody of the manor and the marriage of the heir belonged to the king', Edward III had 'had nothing from them'. Walter died in the autumn of 1367. The question was resolved by January 1368 when his inquisition *post mortem* was held, showing that seven manors including Wilton were of the duchy of Lancaster's honor or 'manor' of Pickering, four were held from the Percy family, Wharram Percy alone (famous for the long-running archaeological investigation of the deserted village) being held in-chief from the Crown.[196] Walter's heir was his uncle, 'aged 50 years and more'. His childless widow Euphemia duly received her dower-third of the Wilton lands, namely three fields (named 'garths') and 'the whole of the fish-dam [i.e. fish-pond] with free access', substituted for 'her dower of the castle of the manor of Wilton within the ditch'. But she also received, instead of sharing the accommodation of the mansion itself, 'a close adjoining the castle outside the ditch; a third part of the profits of the manor court, of an oven and of a forge there'—evidently what archaeologists might call a 'low-level industrial complex'—with lands at Ilkley. In return, as was customary, Euphemia took the oath 'not to [re-]marry without the king's licence'.

Harewood (W. Yorks.) was already a somewhat grander establishment than Wilton (indeed, one of singular grace and distinction) even before the licence to crenellate of 1366 obtained by Sir William de Aldburgh, perhaps to celebrate his accession.[197] How integrated such transmogrified farmhouses were with the agriculture and stock-raising on which most were economically dependent is shown by the dower third of the manor-house assigned in 1356 to Maud, widow of the late-owner of Harewood, John de Lisle (*de Insula*) of Rougemont. Her share comprised a basic set of components, namely:

Within the chief messuage of the said manor, a chamber with a cellar called Benal Chaumbre; a chamber with a cellar called Risshton Chaumbre; a small chamber by le Garner towards the east; a small stable by the gate of the manor; a chapel, and an old kitchen thereby for a grange of the said dower. . . .

Since the old kitchen (as usual, obviously detached) was to be used as a barn to service the extramural fields, Maud's needs were presumably met out of the main kitchen which would also have fed the household of the heir, 'a minor in the

---

[195] *CPR, 1334–8*, 88. Despite the 'ransoming' of the Vale of Pickering from the Scots in 1319–20 (*CDScotland*, iii. 134–5: above) and later threats, correlation with such licences is hard to find. So as not to prejudice any rights in 1356, Walter was left in possession undisturbed: *CFR, 1356–68*, 3.

[196] *CIPM* xii. 124–6; anomalously held in spring 1367, 18 years in arrear—testimony to the confusion and local initiative resulting from the plague; ibid. 181–4 (writs 20 Jan., 41 Edw III, i.e. 1368). Wilton was a humble socage tenure paying ½ mark (6s. 8d.) p.a. and receiving 36s. p.a. in rent from smallholders (*grissemanni*).

[197] *CPR, 1364–7*, 355. Long-time associate of Edward Balliol, son of the ex-puppet king of Scotland, Anthony Emery suggests de Aldeburgh may have benefited from his will: *Greater Medieval Houses*, i. 339–44, including a thorough accommodation-survey of the largely intact enlarged tower-house, 'many-windowed . . . dramatically sited on the sharply sloping side of an outcrop overlooking the broad vale of the river Wharfe' (p. 339).

king's wardship', or, if not living here, that of the king's administrator.[198] It made no difference that Harewood was not styled 'castle'. It was already indistinguishable from many that were: in the 1439 order for seisin (possession) of the half-share ('moiety') to be given to Sir William Rither on his mother's death, Harewood figures as 'a manor called the manor of Herwod, of which the site [i.e. seat] is a castle called the castle of Herwod'. It is made clear that this meant 'the whole site of the said castle' excluding only a rabbit-yard (*le Coneygarth*). The accommodation was exceptionally well suited to multiple occupancy.[199] But much of its dignity, so far as it was architectural, apparently celebrated William de Aldeburgh's succession, in right of his wife. Among the features mainly to be associated with his 1366 licence are large windows, heraldic displays, arrow-slits, and machicolated parapets, all in the demonstratively 'baronial' style which to medievals was 'fortification'. The castle, to crown it all, was topped by a roof-walk providing high-level views of the garden. Elaborate landscape setting was an authentic medieval feature in many places, as is now being recognized.[200]

How thoroughly the details of castellated architecture confirm the picture of aristocratic lifestyle to be obtained from the central records is not central to the present purpose. But in turning to Northumberland, like Westmorland and Cumberland a genuinely 'border' county, the same fact is no less evident: the grandeur of a castle depended not on its exposure to any danger but on the wealth (and rank) of the family which chose it as their principal seat.[201] Otherwise, the resources expended upon it were, naturally, governed by those of the attached lands—as well as by the good fortune and caprice of the owner. When a castle was the lord's name-place it was somewhat more likely to express his overall standing in the county, or even more widely.[202] What the castle of Ogle originally was, with its unusual (for the north) round-towered quadrangle and double moat, proudly

[198] *CIPM* x., 290–1 ('at York'), 326 (no. 396). The heir, Robert de Lisle, came of age next year but Harewood passed (via his sister Elizabeth) to de Aldeburgh, whose presumed major rebuilding complicates reconciliation with the existing structure, apparently 'of a single build' (Emery). It once had an outer curtilage, secluding it from the vanished medieval settlement.

[199] *CFR, 1437–45*, 124–5; phrases repeated in 1440; ibid. 167–8. From 1391, for 150 years, Harewood was jointly occupied by the Redman and Rither families, descended from de Aldeburgh's co-heiresses (discussed in Dixon and Boure , 'Aydon Castle', 234–8): Emery, *Greater Medieval Houses*, i. 343. William de Aldburgh snr. died 1388, having previously kept back for his life one manor and a secured income from his son and daughter-in-law Margery. William jnr. died early, leaving sisters and heiresses Elizabeth and Sybil: *CIPM* xvi. 194, 442–3. If Margery survived, her dower and accommodation came from the limited estate and the many-chambered, well-provided, tower-house.

[200] C. Taylor, 'Medieval Ornamental Landscapes', 42–3, 47–8, 51, 54. This aspect and the 1356 dower details of the apartments supplement Emery's description.

[201] Horses were also fittingly housed: at Aydon Hall or Castle, 'the stable is remarkable for the total absence of wood in its construction, the mangers being of stone' (Parker, *Domestic Architecture*, i. 148–9). Parker accepts Hutchinson's view that the stables were 'evidently contrived for the preservation of cattle during an assault', although the analogy with e.g. the stone-built stables of Vanbrugh's now ruined Seaton Delaval (1718–) would be more apt: O. Cook, *English Country House*, pl. 161. But isolating stately mansions, often by moving villages completely, was not a medieval practice.

[202] How exceptional it was for scale and cost greatly to exceed manorial needs and resources must be emphasized; places on regular great-lord itineraries were favoured: Succinctly, Pounds, *The Medieval Castle*, 130–41, 145–51.

reflected the glory (albeit only local) of the Ogles. Robert, in 1341, obtained a licence 'to fortify his manse' in the more solemn form of a charter because it included the hunting right of free warren in all his dependent demesne lands. No doubt it was his petition that mentioned his 'good service rendered in the march of Scotland'. By July 1362 the widow Joan of another Robert was holding 'the castle and manor of Ogle' by virtue of a joint-tenure in survivorship,[203] on just the same basis as Peter de Vaux had held for life the 'fortified house' of Aydon Hall in right of his heiress wife.[204] The heir to Ogle, two other manors, half the barony of Hepple, and other lands was under 9 years old. Given the long minority, Joan naturally remarried before 1374 and had made over her wardship of the young Robert by 1367 to John de Hatfield, second husband of Ellen, the Bertram heiress of Bothal, a closely connected family. These Border *châtelaines* were resolute: Ellen de Ogle/Bothal, the young Robert's mother, it was stated in 1372, 'has had possession since the death of Robert, her husband, receiving the revenues, by arrangement with Joan' and her second husband, John.[205] This intricate game of pass-the-parcel only ended in 1372–4 when the young Robert de Ogle came of age, already married to one of the three heiresses of Sir Alan de Heton of Chillingham.[206] The day of his birth was 'remembered', in standard form for a 'proof of age', by the incident that his father heard the news while with his retinue at Newcastle and rewarded the messenger with the gift of a horse, a typically mannered act of munificence. Another witness deposed that he was 'at Bothal with Sir Robert Bertram, his grandfather, when the latter received the news of the birth of the said heir and gave the messenger a husband-land [smallholding] in Stainton for life'.

The complexities of dynastic subinfeudation made it hard enough for the Crown to ensure that the correct inheritance procedures were followed.[207] Keeping any sort of control of a supposed 'strategic network' of defence-fortresses, such as a glance at the map working on the instincts of a 'military man' might suggest, was barely conceivable. Conflict, in any case, was far smaller in

---

[203] *CChR, 1341–1417*, 4; packages of seignorial rights (as noted above) also occur in patent licences occasionally; *CIPM* xi. 315–17.

[204] By *curtasie* or 'by the courtesy of England', the father could not be ejected in favour of his wife's heirs nor, unlike the mother, have custody of the child removed: Plucknett, *Legislation of Edward I*, 118–21. In 1388 Bertram Monboucher had held Horton, 'the manor and fort . . . in right of Christiana his wife, of the courtesy of England . . . worth 5 marks only because of burnings and destruction of the Scots': *CIPM* xvi. 274–6; *Book of Fees*, i. 386.

[205] *CIPM* xiv. 62–3; xii. 185–6, on another Robert de Ogle who had died three years earlier, in May 1364; apparently a cousin but father of the boy Robert, now aged 14 +. This seems to be repeated by *CIPM* xiii. 167–8; Joan ('de Saumford') married John Philpott, alias 'Baunsted'. Complex extended-family deals for guardianship, etc. were still common in 18th-century England.

[206] In 1372 Robert is noted as 'aged 21 years 16 days'. This precision may (as often) be spurious as the jurors said he was born 8 Dec. 1353, which agrees with his being 'near 9' in July 1362.

[207] e.g. the arrangements to put in trust all but a 'chamber in Widdrington manor' (tower, licensed to be crenellated 1341, by Gerard de W., who also had mortmain licence for a chantry: *CPR, 1340–3*, 289), which trust Roger de W. made, in April 1372 on his deathbed, his son being aged 18 months. Inquiry held that it was done 'fraudently and by collusion with members of Roger's council'; *CIPM* xiii. 198–200, 338.

scale. Close interrelationships in a somewhat introverted aristocracy might generate violence, like the seizure of Chillingham in 1387 and the Bothal–Ogle succession dispute in 1409, due to failure to honour a family arrangement.[208] Balancing the claims of co-heiresses was particularly difficult. The death in 1388 of Sir Alan de Heton, lord of the major castellary of Chillingham, with its famous park and ancient breed of wild white cattle, left as heirs a nephew (whose claim was soon dismissed) and daughters Elizabeth, wife of Sir John de Fenwick (tower, the last for some while to be licensed to be crenellated, in 1378); Mary the wife of Sir William de Swynburn (licensed in 1346), and Robert de Ogle's wife Joan, whose share included 'a fort', probably Barmoor tower (licensed 1341). Settling the partition involved many of the county upper-gentry and magnates.[209] Apart from some protection of persons and chattels, such emulous fortlets[210] could do little to avert the fate of three of Heton's manors noted in his inquisition as 'totally devastated because of destruction by the Scots'. Tax remissions and Crown pensions were commonplace but did no more than acknowledge the problem. In January 1344 Thomas de Heton had obtained licence 'to crenellate his dwelling-place of Chevelyngham' and (unusually for the period) 'to make a castle or fortalitium thereof'. The following autumn the parishioners asked for a tax-rebate pleading damage done by Scottish raids in 1340.[211] Recovery took a long time. William Heron of Ford, whose parishioners joined in the October 1344 appeal which Edward III's council instructed the collectors of the wealth-levy of 'one-ninth' to treat 'as equity and reason demand', had anticipated them. In July 1338 he had obtained licence to crenellate 'his dwelling-place of his manor of Ford'; but in April 1340 he went one better, securing from the king a comprehensive charter of lordly rights including a hunting monopoly ('free warren'), a weekly market, spring and autumn commercial fairs, taking (but not pursuing elsewhere) detected criminals (*infangthief*), and quittance of toll, murage, and pavage levies throughout the realm. (This was a warrant which must have had much wear, but parchment was durable.) So that the glory of William's lordship should have the desirable tincture of patriotism, he also obtained that unique elaboration that he should hold Ford, 'which is enclosed with a high embattled wall, by the name of

---

[208] Detailed in Bates, *Border Holds*, 285–6. Cf. list 'of the names of castles and fortresses in the county of Northumberland', compiled (*sic*) *c*.1415 'to inform Henry V in whose hands he would leave the places of strength on the Scottish border previous to his embarking on the expedition that led to the victory of Agincourt' (Bates p. 13, and pp. 12–20). Why, then, is it confined to Northumberland? Strictly 'border' places, and the few of real defensibility are not differentiated; n. 215 below.

[209] *CIPM* xvi. 223–6; *CPR, 1377–81*, 290; n. 211 below.

[210] Crenellation, especially if privileged by suing out a licence, habitually marked dynastic emergence (albeit often abortive); e.g. John de Fenwick snr. to be pensioned 1327 for war service and losses 1321–2; sheriff, 1321; John jnr. sheriff, 1344; licensed for Fenwick, 1378; married an heiress of Chillingham and was involved in its seizure in 1387: *Rot Parl*, ii. 396–7; *CPR, 1321–4*, 37; *CCR, 1385–9*, 391–2. Fenwick reverts to a pattern common in the late 1330s and 1340s.

[211] *CPR, 1343–5*, 191, 409. The 1387 scramble to succeed the elderly Alan de Heton, whom the group of noble intruders 'shut up in a tower there', is set out in detail: *CPR, 1385–9*, 321, 325; *CCR, 1385–9*, 391–2 ('1386'), 432, 457–8. Henry de Heton was the ringleader, apparently fearing his sisters' husbands.

a castle to him and his heirs . . . for the defence of those parts against the attacks of the Scots, the king's enemies'.[212]

Early widowhood, long and anxious minorities, and harsh conditions of life were universal, but exacerbated by 'military' factors in the north compared with the rest of England. Northern castellated architecture had a somewhat more aggressive air, square-towered forms having a brutal aspect compared with southern castles—but the masculinity and peculiarity of Border society can be exaggerated. The impact of the 'Great Pestilence' was felt everywhere from the mid-fourteenth century, with periodical recurrences. The family of de Raymes, holding the castellated manor of Aydon and Shortflatt tower (licensed together in 1305) was one of many which suffered. The first Robert died in 1324 when his half of Bolam barony was 'worth nothing because now lying waste by the Scots'. Robert, his son, died in October 1349, in the first wave of the Black Death, but grandson Robert survived to come of age, and breed.[213] His son, Nicholas, seems again in the confusion to have succeeded without proper formality: belatedly, in 1369, the escheator was instructed 'to enquire as to the lands and heir of the said Robert' (as usual; but also) 'and who has been in possession of his lands since his death and received the issues', namely of 'Aydenhall' manor and 'Le Shortflat'. The escheator explained the lapse as due to Robert's having himself been sheriff and escheator in Northumberland—his widow Agnes had been 'allowed to keep all his lands for six years to discharge his debts', then for seven years Robert de Herley, lord of the fief of Shortflatt, held of Bolam barony for one-and-a-quarter knights fees, had taken it over.[214] Agnes had clearly held her own as executrix. In the lists, compiled in c.1415, of the castles and fortresses of Northumberland, Shortflatt figures with seventy-seven others as a *fortalicium* whereas Aydon is *castrum* rather indiscriminately, along with the ancient, *arriviste*, and greater castles such as Ogle, Alnwick, Eshot, Bamburgh, Wark, Ford, Etal, Chillingham, Prudhoe, Bothal, and twenty-seven others.[215]

Because the northern environment was so harsh and the aristocratic lifestyle perhaps more militant than elsewhere in England, being more akin to that of Ireland, a higher proportion of noble houses was 'fortified' in the ostentatious manner connoted by 'castle', 'fortress', and 'tower'. Their overtly 'baronial', castellated format asserted an aristocratic affinity which extended to the entire

---

[212] *CPR, 1338–40*, 114; *CChR, 1327–41*, 468–9. In 1387–8 William Heron accused Earl Henry de Percy of imprisoning him and plundering Ford *chastell* to punish him for breaking an official truce with the Scots and forcing him to compensate them for cattle, etc. taken; whereas, as he claimed, he had only led a pure reprisal raid, 'taking pound for pound'. Local arbitration was ordered. *Rot Parl*, iii. 255–6. John Heron also had licence to crenellate, for Crawley (Northumb.) in 1343: *CPR, 1343–5*, 143.

[213] *CIPM* vi. 373; ix. 242–3; *CPR, 1301–7*, 328; Sanders, *English Baronies*, 17. Shortflatt has only a later tower, containing solar chambers once serving a hall, now rebuilt: Emery, *Greater Medieval Houses*, i. 137.

[214] *CIPM* xii. 398–9; stating that Nicholas was Robert's due heir, aged 30 +; i.e. in 1349 he was a boy of 10, not coming of age until 1360. If so the lord retained Shortflatt in wardship about two years too long.

[215] Bates, *Border Holds*, 13–19 (p. 16: in the second part of the list of *nomina fortaliciorum*: total 78. Most are styled *turris*); n. 208 above. Many such towers were adjuncts ('chamber blocks' or 'solar towers') to halls, not self-sufficient structures.

gentry class and to those who aspired to belong to it. The women of this class were landowners, as were their children according to age more than sex, and truly *châtelaines* in much the same fashion as their male colleagues. If less than castellans in their military duties, their economic and managerial role was undoubtedly greater, although it is barely hinted at in the class of records I have been examining. Their importance in the fortress-owning family was unquestionably no less than—to take a modern comparison—that of the wives and mothers of Georgian and Victorian 'carriage-folk'.[216]

If the family members of the de Eslingtons (Northumb.) were scarcely part of a fourteenth-century 'country-house set', they were probably not unrepresentative, at least in their misfortunes. Robert de Eslington marked their emergence in 1335, at a period when eyes were directed to the Court, by obtaining from the chancery of Edward III 'licence to crenellate his dwelling-place (*mansum*)'. The result, it seems, was a tower and small enclosure, listed *c*.1415 as the *Turris de Eslington*, then belonging to Thomas de Hesilrige. Eslington manor was to receive a grant of free warren in 1310 and, in 1330, the widow of William de Eslington was still trying to obtain allowance at the Exchequer for manning costs incurred by John de Eslington when constable of Bamburgh in 1312–13. All these associations are common indications of ascendancy.[217] Successive deaths in 1349 (probably due to the plague), survival of widows and division among co-heiresses, with their husbands, of the exiguous family lands, which by 1385 were 'waste and untenanted' owing to Scottish devastation, reflect a not uncommon picture thereafter of economic decline and tenurial complexity.[218] The appropriately modest family castle or 'capital messuage' may have given some protection to family members and dependants, but only a fully manned barrier such as Hadrian's Wall could sustain agricultural productivity and population, whether by excluding raiders or by interfering with the removal of plunder. Roman imperial defence-measures were now impossible, of course: defence consisted of counter-raiding, occasional organized campaigns, and individual inadequate self-help.[219]

Even in such conditions where dynastic pride exercised itself in danger, causing fortresses to proliferate, their social role was still almost the whole of their being. Castles were conspicuous incidentals of the noble way of life, testifying to the complex nexus of aristocratic relationships, tied together especially by the marriages of heiresses and laws of inheritance. These socio-economic factors

---

[216] McAuliffe, 'The Lady in the Tower', on the virtues and vicissitudes of ('native') Irish *châtelaines*; J. C. Ward, 'English Noblewoman', *passim*.

[217] *CPR, 1334–8*, 78; Bates, *Border Holds*, 17; *CChWarr*, 328 (order for a great seal patent); *CCR, 1330–3*, 107–8.

[218] *CIPM* xvi. 92; ix. 354–8; xvi. 47, 94. In 1349 two-thirds of their lands yielded £4 p.a.; 1385, £5; but one third was valued at £6 p.a. in 1382, reduced to 20s. in 1385: mortality, raids, crop-failures, inflation, errors, etc., have all to be allowed for. The 'tower' has vanished.

[219] Cf. centrist perspective, Goodman, 'Defence of Northumberland'; unlike in the 17th-century Netherlands, these institutions were not 'created as a direct response to the requirements of war': Price, 'Dedicated to War?', 183—but such routines were undoubtedly more defensive than was the secular architecture.

continued, after the Edwardian conquest, to operate in the Welsh march. An inquisition made on the death of Fulk Fitz Warin in August 1349 describing the inheritance of his 9-year old heir (also Fulk), centred at Whittington in Shropshire, conforms to a familiar pattern despite the size, antiquity, and architectural distinction of this great marcher castle. There was at Whittington, the jurors reported when convened at Shrewsbury,

the manor ... including a castle (*castellum*), worth nothing after deductions because it needs 40s. yearly for repairs; two water-mills, worth now only 20s. yearly because the tenants are dead in the present pestilence; two ponds with fishery; a park, a chase and rents, etc., greatly diminished on account of the pestilence ... Fulk, his son, aged 9 years is his heir.

It seems Fulk was a little younger, in fact, but he survived to his majority, obtaining a Proof of Age in March 1362 before the escheator. The witnesses sufficiently proved his birth at Whittington and baptism in the church in Edward III's fifteenth year (25 January 1341–24 January 1342). Another juror deposed that he was present at Whittington 'about [employed in] the raising of the belfrey of the church, and saw Fulk brought to be baptized with a great following praising God for his birth'. The birth and the accession of the heir were great occasions for the tenantry—but nothing was apparently done to arrest the decay of the once-grand buildings of the castle which, in 1395, was said to be 'in a very ruinous state'. Henry IV continued Richard II's rent remission in order to pay for repairs, in 1395–9 and 1404 (when unsuccessfully attacked by Glyndwr's supporters), in order to help Ivo Fitz Warin to do his duty.[220]

The *caput* of the castle-fief of Cilgerran in 'West Wales' (Pembs.) was shown in 1275, just two years before Edward I's Welsh campaign began, to have been neglected in abuse of wardship—this being but one aspect of the acts of 'waste' committed. Master Henry de Bray, bailiff of Abergavenny and Cilgerran was instructed to investigate the heir's complaints by writ dated 7 January. The inquiry, convened on 3 April ('Wednesday before Palm Sunday'), reported that:

Sir Nicholas Fitz Martin took £80 and more from the revenues of Kilgarren castellary and of the lands of George de Cantilupe (*Cantelou*), lately deceased ... after (his son and heir) George was of lawful age and after the king had ordered seisin of the premises to be given back to him; and £10 more from the time George [the father's] death [1273] until Sunday 14 January [1274]. Damage to the buildings of the castle during the period of Nicholas's custody by the king's commission is estimated at 100 marks [£66. 13s. 4d.] at least ... Sir Nicholas took timber valued at £40 and more from the forest of Kilgerran to build his own castle of New Town in Kemeys [Mons.].

Given that this was a very short wardship, an embezzlement of £10 seems more likely than that mere neglect over two years could have wrought such harm to the

---

[220] *CIPM* ix. 163; xi. 288–9; *CPR, 1391–6*, 577; *1399–1401*, 126; *1401–5*, 417. Ivo was custodian during the minority of Fulk (the standard family forename). Richard II remitted £40 of the £60 p.a. due, two-thirds by way of his life-retainer, one-third to remedy Whittington's 'ruinous state'. Henry IV's writ states the whole rent as £20, 'for custody of the manor and castle'. Ivo paid £2 to get the writ.

castle. Denoting it vaguely and in marks suggests dubiety; this accusation looks partisan—but the opportunistic felling of timber when about to lose control of the Cantilupe lands was certainly flagrant.[221] As direct lord the Crown was responsible, but shifting the blame was common. Custodians, moreover, frequently accepted wardships in payment of Crown debts but still usually had to pay over the assessed net revenue or 'extent'. Being obliged to maintain residences of all kinds, manorial 'plant' (e.g. mills, barns, fish-ponds) and to keep the heir in accustomed and due state if also in their custody, it was difficult for custodians to make a profit without bending the rules. It rarely made any difference if 'the capital messuage' was a castle. So, unsurprisingly, many expedients were employed to avoid the cost to the family of an imposed keeper. Joint settlements by will, subject to Crown permission, so that a widow could hold for life were one solution. Settlement on trustees 'to the use' of the heir as beneficial owner became quite common.[222]

Such practices mirrored on a small scale the transfers by gift to an heir *inter vivos* by the father which enabled the son to gain administrative experience. They are most notable in France, where the niceties generally came much later. Almost an *apanage* on the royal scale was the marcher region in Pyrenean Catalonia made over in 1260 to his son by Roger-Bernard III, count of Foix and *vicomte* of Castelbon (Andorra).[223] It may be inferred that Roger-Bernard junior was not yet of age since Roger, *vicomte* of Cardona, his uncle, was invested (as supervisor) with the castellaries, valleys, and 'places' of the territory. He was, moreover, forbidden 'to build three places' (specified) without asking permission, suggesting that the right to fortify was withheld to symbolize the father's suzerainty. In all other respects the cession of authority was complete, the count of Foix being 'confident that the son will have heavy costs to meet'. So as to give the young man, his heir-apparent, full discretion to develop and defend this apanage, lying between the kingdoms of Aragon and France, Count Roger-Bernard renounced all rights to the contrary, be they by charter or by local custom. Most significantly, he gave up 'specifically' his right to have the fortresses delivered to him on demand (rendability: i.e. the *jus patrie potestatis*). His son owed him no more than the 'obedience' which was proper. Although under age, Roger-Bernard junior was obviously well able to cope with the governance of his frontier land. When this was not the case, it was necessary to find the heir a guardian. Like lands, the fortresses within them had to be kept, both as nuclei of power and as 'profit-centres'—hence the following pact of 1206, still with the original seal attached, made to King Philip II and then deposited in the Trésor des Chartes:

---

[221] *CIM* i. 302; *CIPM* ii. 16–21 (nothing at Meole Brace, a tower and other very poor buildings, held of Mortimer); Sanders, *English Baronies*, 8.

[222] e.g. by Roger de Widdrington (n. 207 above); G. Holmes, *Higher Nobility*, 41–57; Plucknett, *Legislation of Edward I*, 79–83.

[223] *Layettes*, v. 242–3. In 1254 Henry III made over the duchy of Gascony to Edward, then aged 15, but such royal control as then existed was barely delegated: F. Powicke, *Henry III and the Lord Edward*, 211–26.

I, Amaury de Craon . . . notify to all . . . that I have made oath to the lord king . . . as my liege lord that I will in good faith keep in my custody all the land late of Peter de La Garnache and the fortresses so that no harm shall arise therefrom to the lord king, or to his land or to his people—Now, the keepers (*custodes*) whom I shall place in the fortresses (*fortericiis*) I shall cause to make oath upon Holy relics (*super sacrosancta*) that, to their power, they will not permit harm to arise to the lord king, or to his land or people, be it from the fortresses or from the land; nor will they suffer armed men (*gentes*) to go across that land to do the king any harm, or his, but will do their utmost to stop them.

Anjou, with Maine, Poitou, and the provinces south of now French Normandy, was hanging in the balance between Philip II and King John of England until the decisive French victory at Bouvines in 1214—so this pact is a blend of the feudal and of the empirical.[224] It doubtless suited the La Garnache family meanwhile, and their immediate lord, as well as King Philip, to have a powerful local magnate act as guardian and intermediary in this fashion. Amaury de Craon made himself the king's agent, so far as custom permitted. Using the classic jurability formula to guarantee or 'swear' that both land and fortresses would be innocuous (*quod malum inde non eveniet*) virtually recognized French lordship. But he went beyond promising rather passive support, especially as the constables were made responsible for the neutrality of their castellaries. The charter then continues in cautiously partisan spirit, mindful of the heir's legal rights as well as of the possibility of English power being reasserted by the unpredictable King John and his adherents:

I [Amaury de Craon] will also cause the custodians of the fortresses to swear that they will not hand over those fortresses to the one who ought (*debet*) to have the land if I die (*si de me humanitus accideret*) until he shall have made this same undertaking (*securitatem*) to the lord king [of France] so that he is bound to him as I now am. And every time that I replace the keepers of the fortresses I will make them [the incomers] first swear likewise.

Because the legality of French royal power was undecided still, and as a former supporter of the Angevins[225] Amaury had to tread very carefully—he must not appear to connive at any disinheritance of the heir, but he had to give King Philip the assurances to which he might be entitled by custom or by the developing presumption of Capetian success. Acting in his personal capacity Amaury could be much less inhibited. As King John could no longer defend him in his rights, he was entitled to do so—but he still had to avoid any act of manifest bad faith to either side. So:

if the *vicomte* de Thouars require military service of me [as guardian] I shall afford it to him in respect of the seven knights' fiefs held of him in those [Garnache] lands. Similarly,

[224] *Layettes*, i. 303. The de Craon family of Anjou held the Lincs barony of Freiston, until Guy's daughter took it *c*.1205 to the Longchamps, dying in 1262 having survived three husbands: Sanders, *English Baronies*, 47; cf. F. Powicke, *Henry III and the Lord Edward*, 722, n. 3. M. Jones, 'Les Seigneurs de la Garnache'.
[225] William Marshal himself, future regent of England, adhered to John in 1204 but (as noted) made special arrangements for his castles of Longueville, Meulers, and Orbec in Normandy, later modified: *Layettes*, i. 250, 486, 499.

within four days of receiving King Philip's order, I must hand over the heir of the land to the [French] seneschal of Anjou. Furthermore, I have made oath to the lord king that I will serve him against all men, as my liege lord and for the observance of all this I pledge all my lands and as guarantors give Juhel de Mayenne, Alan fitz Count, and William *de Guerge*, who will be liable to forfeiture (*ad misericordiam regis*) should I fail therein.

The agreement was dated at Amaury's own chief seat, Chantocé castle, perhaps to assert his own status in a province torn between the rising Capetian monarchy and its traditional loyalties.[226] A punctilious legalism combined with political realism often eased the problems of serving two masters as well as themselves which, in particular, faced Viscount Aimeri VII of Thouars, the Lusignan family of the count of La Marche, and the Archévêques of Parthenay. Inheritance having become the central pivot of noble society, preserving it and the interests of heirs, male or female, mattered more at all levels of the hierarchy than any other single consideration.

Through all the changing aspects of aristocratic life, political, economic, and even psychological, property-rights were thus a continuous and strong leitmotif to which castles were subordinate, even in borderlands. Dynastic identity and family renown were expressed architecturally in a style which naturally and explicitly reflected the martial prowess to which the menfolk aspired but which all respected. For these reasons women and children shared castles as fully in the 'marches' as they did elsewhere. The involvement of women and children with that peculiar kind of residential property constituted by fortresses was no less conspicuous in regions and episodes of danger than it habitually was at other times and in other places.

3. Châtelaines *in Prosperity and in Adversity*

It only now remains to conclude this survey of the crucial role of women castellans with six extended examples. Women were, perhaps, less exposed than men to the changeability of life portrayed as part of the medieval *condition humaine* in mural paintings of the 'Wheel of Fortune' (such as that which faces the bishop's throne in Rochester cathedral[227]), but a succession of bereavements ending marriages, and changes of residence, status, and style over an often prolonged life, subject to the hazards especially of childbirth, compounded the Litany's continual perils of 'plague, pestilence, and famine; battle, murder, and sudden death'. Individuals who were lucky and did not succumb, women as well as men, could often make their mark. One lady of clearly forceful nature, who had scope to exer-

---

[226] In 1212, still before Bouvines, Amaury made Chantocé (*dép.* Maine-et-Loire, near Angers) castle rendable on demand to King Philip 'to support himself against his enemies', promising faithful service in respect of the castellary. This pact, more ad hoc than feudal, he backed by 10 guarantors giving bail for the massive total of £5,300 Paris: *Amplissima Collectio*, i. 1099; *Layettes*, i. 375–6; v. 66–7 (eight guarantors' charters).

[227] 'Above the site of the prior's stall', Brieger, *English Art, 1216–1307*, 88, n. 2; also figs. 22a, 88b, p. 130.

cise diversified organizational talents, was Nicolaa de la Haye, hereditary castellan and sheriff of Lincoln under King John and Henry III.[228] She did not affect male dress nor carry weapons (for which, in part, Joan of Arc was to be condemned in 1431), but was evidently a celebrity in her own lifetime and a legend thereafter, living on in local memories. When evidence about Lincoln castle was given to Edward I's great inquiry (1274–5) concerning the legal and tenurial status of the custodian, 'oral tradition' over sixty years old was recalled and fortunately recorded. The jurors for the Hundred (local district) gave particulars that King Richard (1189–99) and then King John (1199–1216) had possessed Lincoln castle as part of the royal demesne, until John

transferred custody of the castle [sic] to a certain man named Gerard de Camville, who married the Lady Nicolaa de la Haye. He held the same during his life by tenure revocable at the king's pleasure. After Gerard's death the Lady Nicolaa held the custody at King John's pleasure (pro voluntate) in time of war and in time of peace. And after the war [1216] it happened that the Lord King John came to Lincoln and the Lady Nicolaa went out to the west side of the castle carrying the keys of the castle in her hand. She met the king and proffered the keys to him as lord (tamquam domino) . . . [229]

For the keeper of a castle to go out humbly to meet the lord and symbolically relinquish control of it was a customary ritual which was elaborated in the late middle ages (and kept into modern times) in the ceremony of the joyeuse entrée. With castles and walled towns it was a gesture of submission made to the lord. Fortresses, of course, were not latchkey flats—the 'keys' were emblems only of the lordly right of entry.[230] Lady Nicolaa played her cards shrewdly. She told the king (probably in 'French' originally):

that she was a woman of great age who had endured much toil and many anxieties (multos labores et anxietates) over the castle which she could bear no longer. The Lord King John

---

[228] On the 'problem' of vested custody of royal castles see Eales, 'Castles and Politics', 30–5. Nicolaa's custody was contested by the earl of Salisbury after he was appointed sheriff in May 1217. She had 'held the castle as hereditary castellan and defended it in the civil war. In October 1217 she seems to have recovered both the castle and the county' (shrievalty), 'but at the end of 1217 she lost the office of sheriff but kept the castle' (p. 32). The Battle of Lincoln was fought to raise the 'French' siege of the castle; 'some damage had been done to the castle by the baronial siege-engines, and the unflinching woman Nicolaa de la Haye . . . had been in sore need of the help which had come': F. Powicke, Henry III and the Lord Edward, 13, 736–9.

[229] Rot Hund, i. 309a (an exceptional and detailed recital). Nicolaa had inherited her father Richard's rights to Lincoln, as one of his three daughters, together with the English family lands. De Camville, died in 1214, was her second husband and had Lincoln as such. She died in 1230: Sanders, English Baronies, 109; cf. Painter, King John, 59, ascribing the hereditary constableship to the 'de Canvilles'; contradicted p. 355. John's meeting with Nicolaa occurred in the autumn 1216 shortly before his death. She had 'held out valiantly against the rebel earl of the county': Warren, King John, 253 (cf. p. 42 on de Camville).

[230] But elements of entry-closure (doors, portcullis winches, etc.) could be (pad-)locked from within; as at Najac town (dép. Aveyron) in 1249 after the troubled accession as count of Toulouse of Alphonse de Poitiers: Layettes, iii. 133–5. Handing over keys was prescribed e.g. 1263, Turenne–Henry III pact (two castles); and at Puiseaux monastic precinct, 1370. It was common with walled towns: Foedera, i, i, 425–6; Ordonnances, v. 335–8; Coulson, 'Seignorial Fortresses', Index, 'Fortress Customs'. Such keys came to be appropriately ornate. The nightly ritual at the Tower of London continues.

replied compassionately (*dulciter*)—'if it please you, bear them yet a while'. Accordingly, she had the keeping of the castle for King John's lifetime and . . . so continued under King Henry until she retired to *Swaneton* where she died.

What had happened between then and Henry de Lacy's current possession (1274–5), as earl of Lincoln, did not interest the jurors. They seem to have thought that Nicolaa's position was due to her succeeding her husband; in fact, he had acquired it in her right by a more than revocable title. She, moreover, then held it through the final phase of the civil war and into Henry III's minority, although a crucial battle was fought around the castle in 1217, when the royalists under William the Marshal relieved it from siege by the adherents of Louis of France, inflicting on them a decisive and effectively final defeat. Much of Nicolaa's role was, as usual, conducted by officials and deputies, not in person. Her functions as sheriff were delegated—but this did not at all diminish the fame of the meeting with King John in 1216, which the jurors in 1274–5 chose to recall. In an age of minority literacy, oral testimony from memory was relied on for a wide range of judicial and administrative purposes—but was naturally fallible.[231] A second account of the interview is still less aware of the tenurial facts but no less impressed by the lady sheriff-castellan's personality. According to this version:

the Lady Nicolaa handed over (*tradidit*) the keys of the castle to King John as lord in that (*eo quod*) his was the right, nor did she claim any, but only to have the custody at his pleasure. At this the Lord King John was pleased, replying to Nicolaa: 'My dear lady (*dilecta mea*), it is my will that you should keep the castle still as you hitherto have done, until I shall give you other instructions'—and the said Nicolaa kept it accordingly.[232]

The language is still that of a constableship terminable without notice, such as had become normal for royal castles by the later thirteenth century—but, even so, the jurors evinced no surprise that a woman should have been in charge of Lincoln castle. Nicolaa's holding her position from her husband's death in 1214 and thereafter suggests again that the clause against widows' tenure of fortresses, put into the 1216 reissue of Magna Carta, was indeed special and ephemeral. Elsewhere,

---

[231] Fief rolls (in England, Exchequer records) are among the administrative written records which, for the higher tenantry, somewhat reduced reliance on oral evidence and might be used to check it. The earliest (surviving) Champagne fief roll is a fragment of *c.*1172. The 1249–52 roll (still partially surviving) was systematic enough for it to be noted: 'the lord of Chassenay [*dép.* Aube] holds the *mota* of Troyes and St Nicholas's gate . . . and the liberty of the motte and castellary (*castelli*) . . . Records (*scripta*) say he owes guard annually, which he denies.' The same is noted of the tenant of the *corpus forterecie* of Bayerne (*dép.* Marne): *Rôles de Champagne*, nos. 1134, 1271. General discussion in Clanchy, *From Memory to Written Record.*

[232] *Rot Hund*, i. 315a–b: 'predicta domina N. claves predicti castri predicto Regi Johanni tradidit tanquam domino eo quod habuit jus nec clamat [domina Nichola] nisi custodiam tam ad voluntatem suam'. Hereditary custody as a fief was not very different from full feudal tenure: e.g. in 1127 Archbishop William de Corbeil and successors were given *custodiam et constabulariam castelli Roffi* [Rochester] *semper in posterum possidendam*; and also granted 'that in the castle they may build for themselves (*sibi faciant*), have and hold for ever, such a *munitio* or tower as they may desire'. Although the knights' castle-guard was to continue as before, they were 'to make to the archbishop regarding the castle assurances (*securitatem*) subject to our [Henry I's] fealty': *Regesta*, ii. 356 (no. 188). Corbeil trusted his position enough to spend lavishly on creating the great palatial tower-donjon.

King John kept his constables on a tight rein, switching custodies of royal castles so as to stop constables 'going native' and becoming entrenched.[233]

Nicolaa de la Haye's position was derived from being heiress of Brattleby, as one of three daughters of Richard de la Haye whose father had held it in right of his wife, along with the constableship and sheriffdom of Lincoln. 'Labours and anxieties' apart, it was quite a plum job: a letter close sent for Edward III in 1331 to the mayor and bailiffs of the city shows that the lord of Lincoln castle, whether vested custodian or castellan in fief, enjoyed privileges both lucrative and prestigious. As usual, the duties were essentially administrative. Edward II had granted the office, by inheritance but nominally for life, to Alice, countess in her own right as heiress-daughter of Henry de Lacy, earl of Lincoln, and famous for her marital adventures. By Edward III's grant, in 1331, Alice's tenure was enlarged to full hereditary custody for herself and her new husband Ebulo Lestrange. Although unlikely to be resident, unless briefly, they were to hold 'the custody and ward [defence-powers] of the castle of Lincoln with the bailey . . . royalties, liberties, and free customs . . . pertaining . . . as fully as Henry de Lacy, late earl, had held them'. The townspeople were informed so as to ensure that the comital rights there were respected, an inquisition held at Alice's and Ebulo's request having shown:

that the castle of Lincoln, with a place adjoining called *la Batailplace* with adjoining ditches, is within the bailey [jurisdictional precinct] of the castle, . . . bounded by the *Westposterna*, *Newportyate*, *Postgatyate*, around to the eastern end of the shrine (*feretri*) of St Hugh, belonging to the cathedral monastery, and along by the messuage called *Becumhous* to *Suthbailyate* and back to the West Postern.[234]

Alice had deserted her husband, Earl Thomas of Lancaster, five years before his revolt, trial, and execution in his own castle-hall of Pontefract (Yorks.) in 1322. He had at least been wise enough not to try to resist siege there. Confusion and slack lordship in the castle at Lincoln had facilitated the expansion of the cathedral precinct and of the bishop's palace, licensed to be raised, crenellated, and towered, with other seignorially expressive privileges, in 1316, 1318, and 1329 respectively.[235] The earl's rights had to be reasserted. Although the castle buildings

---

[233] e.g. the Beauchamps, as hereditary constables of Bedford, regarded themselves as proprietors, strongly objecting to its penal demolition after the great siege of 1224. The cost of creating a first-class fortress there had been high. In 1224 William de Beauchamp wanted to have the materials and tried to stop the stone lining of the ditches being destroyed. He won (as noted already) the concession of having an uncrenellated dwelling on the site: Shirley, *Royal Letters*, i. 236; *Rot Litt Claus*, i. 632a (detailed). Eales, n. 228 above, on 'the recovery of royal castles'; Brown, 'English Castles', chs. 3, 7; *Stubbs's Select Charters*, 337; n. 19 above. Which castles were 'royal' and which 'baronial' was a matter of fact, not of status, to Brown, 'List of Castles' (p. 259). Lincoln (1154–1216) is taken as 'royal' (p. 271).

[234] *CCR, 1330–3*, 255; 'yate' = gate = street; Elliott and Stocker, *Lincoln Castle*, is a referenced, up-to-date, 'military' guide with plans (pp. 3, 35) and reconstructions; but it is inadequate to remark (p. 24) that 'the Castle played no part in military history after 1216 . . . The Castle continued to function but only as a prison and a court of law'.

[235] *CPR, 1313–7*, 436; *1317–21*, 257; *1327–30*, 453–4; Coulson, 'Hierarchism in Conventual Crenellation', 75–7.

had been neglected, its antiquated condition and the numerous encroachments upon its space by the clergy or by the burgesses were not allowed to diminish the castle's rights.[236] The description of the bounds accordingly sums up:

> ... all the gates, walls, and ditches about the bailey, with the houses built in the ditches, are appurtenant to the said bailey and are of the bailey [-jurisdiction], as under ... Henry de Lacy and Thomas, late earl of Lancaster, who held their court within the bailey aforesaid at the gate of the castle on every Tuesday for all pleas [lawsuits] that may be pleaded in court baron.

This was the mundane and routine business of lordship within the castle's jurisdiction which the mayor and bailiffs of Lincoln were told to respect, allowing to 'Alice and Ebulo free enjoyment of all these and ceasing the impediment offered them since the death of Thomas of Lancaster'. The townspeople had clearly taken advantage of nine years' lax assertion of Alice's rights, due to her separation, to Thomas's revolt, and the confusion of Edward II's overthrow (1326–7) and the Mortimer and Isabella 'regency' (1327–30), and to her own equivocal status. Her *mésalliance* with Ebulo Lestrange, until formally sanctioned, gave further opportunity to whittle away her rights as countess and castellan of Lincoln. For this reason, it was decided to spell out in some detail what her petty jurisdiction comprised. Elsewhere the commonplace 'assize of weights, measures, and of bread and ale', which was the medieval equivalent of the modern local authority inspectorate, needed no elaboration. In 1331 Countess Alice was evidently determined to let nothing go by default any longer. She got from the Chancery, in addition to a routine perambulation to mark the castle bounds, the fullest specification of her powers in respect of commercial fraud in Lincoln and its market, namely:

> the assay of measures, to wit of bushels, gallons, pottels, quarts (*quartorum*), ells, and other measures of corn, wine, and ale; and the assay of weights, to wit of pounds, stones, and other weights of all things sold by weight; and forfeitures of measures and weights aforesaid wherever found to be false [i.e. fraudulent], with the amercements and other punishments for the same; and likewise for breach of the assize of bread and ale; together with fines levied in the court baron.

Checking traders' weights and measures and bakers' and brewers' standards and prices may be far removed from the Hollywood castle-image, but it was how the castellan regularly operated.[237] Countess Alice's resident officers also hired out the

---

[236] In 1344 a survey of dilapidations and a report on liabilities for repairs were ordered, 'as the king is informed that the buildings there are at the present time so much out of repair that there is great reason to fear an escape of prisoners from the gaol': *CPR, 1343–5*, 388. Similar mandates, usually obtained to back distraint for work-services, are not uncommon. The sheriff would be particularly concerned about prisoners held awaiting trial.

[237] Courts were often held, in the open air (as was usual e.g. for the Hundred court) at castle-gates (as here—the interface with the urban community), or within castles, especially those which were sheriffs' headquarters: Pounds, *The Medieval Castle* (pp. 98, 201, 204–5), illustrates the involvement of 'castle and community'. Any military aptitude was almost irrelevant: *pace* D. King, *The Castle*, 28–9 (on Lincoln, etc.). Maintaining trade standards was a regular privilege of borough authorities, who

vacant plots within 'the bailey' and the adjacent field known as 'the Battle-place' for cattle pasture, bringing in 13s. 4d. annually. In addition, places for stalls during Lincoln's famous fairs and for the market were temporarily rented out. The burgesses, apparently, had been trying to annex these spaces.

Individualistic highlights of the *châtelaine*'s vicissitudes may be less true to life than is this mundane routine at Lincoln, typical of innumerable castles of all sorts and sizes all over medieval Europe—but anecdote makes easier reading than generalities and may be more instructive.

Between c.1230 and 1272 events at La Roche Derrien, in Brittany, show a rare but different and illuminating face of things, one peculiar to France since they hinged upon the customs of rendability. Whereas Countess Alice of Lincoln had little difficulty, and no great delay, in vindicating her rights as *châtelaine*, the Lady Joan of La Roche Derrien (*dép.* Côtes-du-Nord) had a very prolonged legal battle to obtain justice. Her castle was to become famous in 1347 as the scene of the defeat and capture of Charles of Blois by Sir Thomas Dagworth, in the course of one of the English campaigns in Brittany.[238] The scenario as presented in 1269 to the high court of King Louis IX was very different. Joan's case before the judges of the *parlement* went back to the time of the revolt of Count Peter of Brittany (nicknamed Mauclerk) against the regent, Queen Blanche 'of Castile', in 1230–5. At some stage of the Breton uprising against the Capetian power, ineffectually supported by Henry III of England, Count Peter, in his capacity as overlord of La Roche Derrien, had requisitioned the castle, possibly important to him as a fortress owing to its position in the far north of Brittany. This he was legally justified in doing, under rendability—but he was not entitled to retain the castle indefinitely when his need of it had expired, as he afterwards showed every intention of doing. As Lady Joan alleged, at the war's end (1235) Peter refused to restore the castle buildings to her, and his successor, Count John, also refused. According to the court register, the Lady Joan's advocate (barrister or counsel) first satisfied the judges of her legal standing and then showed how her parents had lost possession. Apparently:

Pleasance, her mother, had held and possessed the *castrum*. Oliver, Joan's father, had been in seisin of the castle in his wife's right, holding all its appurtenances, when Count Peter of Brittany, father of the Count John that now is [1269] from whom the castellary was held in fief, asked for the castle to be made available to him (*peciit sibi concedi*) because of a war which he was then conducting, namely for the protection of himself and his people in the said war. Lady Joan's father and mother lent (*concesserunt*) the castle to the count and he received possession (*saisinam*) of the castle by virtue of that concession. Afterwards, when

would have been jealous of the comital court. London livery companies still apply (a vestige of) such powers: Crawford, *Vintners' Company*, 248: generally, Nicholas, *Later Medieval City*, 229–33.

[238] Burne, *The Crecy War*, 90–6: intervention to support the Montfort cause in the duchy against the Capetian candidate. On Dagworth's conduct see M. Jones, 'Sir Thomas Dagworth', and on context *Ducal Brittany*, 1–21; Curry, *The Hundred Years War*, 60–1; Allmand, *Hundred Years War*, 14. The castle–town complex stands on a lofty spur, sloping down to the River Jaudi, in coastal northern Brittany. A sortie by the English captain of the castle joined with the relieving army to rout the Blois besieging force.

the war was finished, the count was required by Joan's father to restore the castle to him which, however, the count refused to do.

The style of the record is a succinct official summary of the 'proved' facts, that is, those accepted by the court.[239] No prejudice is expressed for the fact that Peter Mauclerk had rebelled, nor that he was subsequently disgraced and forfeited, although the opportunity to assert royal authority was not to be missed. Events after 1235 had merely obscured the obligations to Joan's parents which John, Peter's son, also refused to honour when Pleasance demanded the return of her castle. Over several years, we are told, Count John rejected her claims, so that eventually she appealed (as she was entitled for 'default of justice') to the court of King Louis, effectively overlord of the county (later duchy) of Brittany.[240] She successfully sued out a writ and had Count John summoned to answer her at law. While in Paris prosecuting her case, Pleasance, Joan's mother, subsequently died, causing further delay. Her son Alan, Joan's brother, the record relates, then took up the legal cudgels and three times had Count John summonsed, but to no avail. When eventually he entered an appearance (by proxy or in person) it was merely to request postponement of the hearing—*diem consilii*; strictly, an adjournment for lawyers to confer. While still waiting for the appointed day, Alan also died (*fuit viam universe carnis ingressus*). The family's cause then devolved on his sister Joan, as heiress.

This was a society always prone to resort to violence to resolve disputes—but it was also (and increasingly) intensely litigious, especially over property. The opportunities for rulers to extend their jurisdictions, for lawyers to enrich themselves, and for procedural pretexts, were numerous.[241] Against Joan's persistence her lord the count of Brittany ('duke' in their charters) deployed every procrastination and evasion. One ploy was to refuse to accept service of the summons to court by the hands of Joan's messenger. At last Count John came before the All Saints (November 1269) session of the parlement. Joan then put forward her claim, requiring not only the restoration of the castle proper of La Roche Derrien as her rightful inheritance but also the entire aggregate income of the castellary accumulated during the whole period of dispossession, amounting to the enormous sum of £30,000 (of Paris money). Count John (through his lawyer) cyni-

---

[239] For what follows, *Actes du Parlement*, i, i, 129, 165–6 (brief summaries); *Les Olim*, i, 311–13, 395–6, 904 (full texts). Ducal/comital powers were relatively undeveloped (as in Poitou in 1269: *Layettes*, iv. 352–4; *rachat à merci* regulated but rendability unaffected). In 1235, on Peter's fall, the Breton nobles asserted that his centralization of power, including his use of rights of 'wardship or relief' (*ballum vel rachatum*), was an 'evil' innovation. They claimed freedom to fortify without comital licence, rights over shipwrecks (salvage), to make wills and grant alms, and to appoint guardians of their heirs: *Layettes*, ii. 302. Rendability is not mentioned but was ancient and is to be inferred from the La Roche Derrien pleadings. Peter was count in his wife's right, a member of the Capetian house of Dreux. His 'custody' (*ballum*) of Brittany was 'annulled' in 1230 (*Layettes*, ii. 178–9).

[240] Royal appellate jurisdiction over Brittany was on an ad hoc basis until formalized in 1297, when the count's status as 'duke and peer of France' was recognized. 'Count' rather belittled him in 1230–72: M. Jones, *Ducal Brittany*, 2.

[241] The technique of judicial attrition is exemplified by encroachment over a century later upon the duchy of Gascony and elsewhere: Coulson, 'Community and Fortress-Politics in France', 82–108.

cally, but routinely, alleged that Joan was illegitimate, unable to inherit as a bastard. Alternatively (a true lawyer's tactic), he claimed to have forfeited La Roche Derrien; then, further, he argued that the castellary ought to have descended not to Joan's mother but by reverse male succession to her maternal uncle 'according to the custom of the country'. To substantiate this defence he called witnesses, asserting that he was lawfully in occupation by consent of the rightful heir. Count John's lawyers could not admit that the castle had been repossessed under rendability without destroying the case for the defence. If it had, indeed, been handed over for his warlike need then it had to be restored immediately afterwards—even a possessory title based on over thirty years' occupation could not, or in this case was not allowed to, override this principle.[242] The judges, in fact, whatever their motives, had no patience with these pretexts—but the councillors' propensity to back the underdog, to assert the competence of the royal court wherever possible, and to favour direct but minor tenants, cannot be altogether discounted. By their ruling, the court set aside Count John's pleadings as irrelevant: the decisive issue was whether or not the castle had originally been handed over, in rendability, to Count Peter for his rebellion of 1230–5. An inquisition was ordered to resolve this question. In due course the commissioners, having taken evidence on the spot (as the court record recounts, in the manner of a retrospective law-report):

found in favour of the said Joan, namely that her father and mother had, indeed, delivered to Count Peter for his war (*propter guerram suam*) the castle-proper (*fortericiam castri*) of La Roche Derrien; and that after this handing over (*tradicio*) her parents had dwelt in the hall (*aula*) below the castle for a year approximately, duly holding their land and receiving the revenues—after which time they were wholly disseised and deprived by Count Peter.

The language for this disinheritance is strong (*totaliter ejecti fuerunt et spoliati*), suggesting that Joan (no husband is mentioned) and her family had loyal tenants in the castellary giving evidence to the king's commissioners. Proving that the revenues were collected and lordship exercised as usual during that year or so at 'the hall' below the castle-eminence, showed that the dispossession was not a forfeiture.[243] It would seem also that the troubles of Peter's revolt had been quite

---

[242] At this time 'the king' committed a similar injustice: in 1259 the parlement threw out a plea by the bishop of Mende (*dép*. Lozère) to have back seven 'castles', plus a quarter share in another, etc., as appurtenances of Grèzes castle, the court holding they were not so. Grèzes had been lent to Louis VIII (1223–6) and only recently regained by the bishop. In 1261 another attempt, arguing that three of the castles had been lent to Louis VIII, was also rejected: *Actes du Parlement*, i, i, 51; *Les Olim*, i, 91–2, 507–8. Grèzes and other local castle-towns were anciently rendable: *Layettes*, i. 54–5 (detailed vernacular charter of c.1137).

[243] In 1347 'an old earthwork called the Black Castle' was manned by the Blois besiegers. If '500 yards to the west of the bridge' it could have been a manor-seat and that used by Joan's parents (Burne, *The Crecy War*, 90–1), but a 'hall' in the little township is more likely. Refunding revenues received by the lord during repossession was a custom relied on in 1292 by Arnald de Gaveston, falsely claiming that his castle of Louvigny (*dép*. Basses–Pyrénées) had been repossessed when Luke de Tany was seneschal (1272–8) 'on account of the wars and troubles of those parts'. In fact, it had been pledged for debt, circumstances entitling Edward I 'by the custom of the kingdom of France' to use the revenues to maintain it—in this case, insufficient. The fact that 'a large part of the principal debt for which the

remote, casting some doubt on the original pretext of warlike necessity—but, under rendability, as has been seen, the lord did not have to prove need, only (as custumals and occasional charters spell out) to act in good faith and to hand the place back in at least as good a state as when taken into his hand, after a period universally (but tacitly) expected to be quite short.[244] So, as La Roche Derrien had been rendered to him in 1230–5, regardless that it was for resistance to the Crown, Count Peter had implicitly recognized the title enjoyed by Pleasance, Joan's mother, and Oliver, her father, who had asked to have their castle returned to them in 1235, as the record states. Alan their son, dying childless, passed his rights by blood to Joan who also inherited the protection given by the familiar rules of rendability to the holders of fortresses. Eventually and accordingly (1269) the parlement 'pronounced' that Count John should restore to Joan the whole fortress complex, castle and town, comprising (as worded) the keep(-tower) and fortifications, namely *turrim et fortalicias castri et ville* of La Roche Derrien.

Joan's (probably considerable) legal costs were, as usual, not taken into account and decision was deferred on her claim to be repaid the arrears of income, which a repossessing lord was not entitled to keep if collected during his occupation of the estate-*caput*. This setback was compounded by another as soon as she had entered into possession of her family's principal home, seat, and name-place. Her jubilation must have turned to dismay on seeing the damage done to the buildings by neglect and perhaps vindictive destruction. The castle seems to have become almost uninhabitable. Back she went to Paris to sue for a second judicial investigation, preparatory to an action against Count John for unlawful dilapidation. His tenure had, strictly, been a trust akin to wardship.[245] In order to pay for restoration of the buildings, and to recoup legal costs borne out of what other income she possessed, an award of damages was needed. By determination, and perhaps some undisclosed influence, Joan eventually obtained a favourable 'inquest'. Three years still elapsed before the parlement acted (November 1271). The verdict summarized in the court register (a book, not a roll as usual in England) declares:

castle had been pledged had been pardoned' added to the king's irritation at Arnald's dishonesty (*tales subrepciones*): *Rôles Gascons*, iii. 50; cf. i. 517; iii. 398.

[244] In June–July 1249, the *vicomte* de Lomagne appealed to Louis IX against the demand by Raymond VII of Toulouse to render Auvillers *castrum* (*dép.* Tarn-et-Garonne). But the circumstances were exceptional: e.g. Raymond had only months to live and Capetian takeover of Toulouse was imminent; Lomagne claimed that he feared vengeful dispossession of his *dominium utile*, from having captured Gerald d'Armagnac and kept him against Raymond's order, but obeying Henry III of England; no infringement of Raymond's *dominium directum* was intended, despite his not trying the case properly—etc.: *Layettes*, iii. 70–2. Count Raymond was asserting his right of overlordship (*juris majoris dominii*) to the last: in August 1249 he demanded in regal style that three Templar castles (*munitiones*) be rendered to him *in signum recognitionis dominii nostri*: *Layettes*, iii. 75.

[245] That it was usual for a repossessing lord to have an inventory of stores and a record of condition made, so as to ensure it was kept in due state and to avert such disputes, is suggested by King John's order for the resumption of Fronsac castle (*dép.* Gironde) from the *vicomte* in 1206. Nobody harmful to its security was to be allowed to remain, but John's agent 'and his people were so to conduct themselves locally that no harm arise to the castle'; finally—'when you have received it, inform us in writing when and in what condition (*qualiter*) you have received it': *Rot Litt Pat*, 67b; Gardelles, *Châteaux du sud-ouest*, 137.

It is found proved by the *inquesta* made by order of the court that at the time when the castle of La Roche Derrien was occupied by the count of Brittany there were certain buildings within the castle—namely, a hall (*aula*) roofed with thatch (*stipula*); an annexe (*appendicium*), a kitchen (*coquina*), stables and farriery (*marescalcia*); another attached building (*appendicium*) in which the lord used to lodge; and a chapel covered with thatch—all of which are now entirely cleared away (*ad aream redacta*), except for the said hall which is now in a better state than it was in formerly—Judgement was accordingly given that the count must reinstate the buildings which have been destroyed.[246]

Royalist judges, career-lawyers, and bureaucrats in the king's civil service (the term is no anachronism) doubtless felt satisfaction in bringing the lord of a notoriously separate province to order—but they were only applying the rules, if with exceptional thoroughness. The family's tenants and dependants, going frequently to the castle to pay rents and renders of produce in kind, to perform labour services, to attend judicial sessions, and other routine estate functions, would have been familiar with the castle's condition over the thirty-five years or so during which a comital steward had taken their lord's place. No doubt some as adults knew it as it had been before the usurpation, as the Lady Joan herself probably did. Even if not, 'hearsay' evidence by secondhand repetition was usually acceptable. Count John had not apparently been able to sway or to influence the choice of jurors, but despite the very clear terms (quoted above) of the 1269 award, he still tried to prevaricate, arguing in court that the fortifications of the small walled town, below the castle-rock, were not included. Rendability applied to fortifications of every sort, but his men were still occupying the town walls and gates, gravely impeding the Lady Joan's borough officials. With remarkable fortitude and patience she went back to the parlement and obtained a third full-scale hearing, summarized in the register for November 1272. The 'poverty' ascribed to her may well not, in this case, be the mere humble and conventional formula of the petitioner. It is possible, as no representative is mentioned, that she appeared before the judges in person and put her own case, although expensive legal advice would still have been needed. According to the record:

The poor noble lady, Joan of La Roche Derrien, pleads that the fortifications (*fortalicia*) of the town of La Roche Derrien have not been handed over to her by the count of Brittany, despite the judgement made in her favour by the court that not just the fortifications of the castle but those of the town also must be restored to her. She asks that seisin of the town fortifications be made over to her accordingly and given up, and that the said count be compelled to do this. Against her the count's lawyers (*gentes*) say that seisin of the fortifications of the castle only was adjudged to her, not of the town. Eventually, the court record ... was shown to the parties and ... verdict was entered that seisin of both had been awarded to the lady. And it was expressly declared also in phrasing the award (*in prolacione*

---

[246] An *appendicium*, pentice or penthouse, could be a mere covered corridor attached to a building, or a substantial detached structure: e.g. Salzman, *Building in England*, 400, 427, 542 (texts). A *marescalcia* or 'marshalcy' building could be for shoeing, saddlery, or any business to do with horses; possibly a 'mews' for keeping hawks, etc. Count John was owed nothing for improving the hall, used perhaps for brief visits or courts for which no residential accommodation was needed.

judicii) that the earthworks around the walls (*fossata . . . sub fortalicio*) are included and form part of that fortress; and so the lady is entitled to have them similarly.[247]

This time no wriggle-room was left. The ambiguity of *castrum*, even clarified by the phrase 'the tower and fortifications of the castle and town' (i.e. not the castellary), had left scope for legal subtlety. It was usual for magnates to retain lawyers in Paris to guard their interests. Much of the preservation, consolidation, and acquisition of land and all that went with it, by the lay and ecclesiastical elite, had already by this period come to be achieved by campaigns in the courts. Legalism imbued the cult of arms. Litigation, conversely, was permeated by force as well as by such casuistry as was used by the counts of Brittany, father and son, against the castellans of La Roche Derrien.[248] It would be simplistic to think of opposite methods of war and of peace. Fortresses themselves embody the same ambivalence. Which aspect came out on top varied according to region, period, and personal circumstances. The Lady Joan won back her family castle-town and also full possession of her castellary, but did not apparently recoup the family's losses from over thirty years' unjust deprivation. Although it began in the Mauclerk revolt, the occasion of loss of possession of the castle-proper (*fortelicia castri*) was established as lawful in origin. Proving that La Roche Derrien castle had been rendered, not just seized, was the most effective tactic—but Joan enjoyed the advantages of an undoubtedly favourable court and of a loyal tenantry.

The final examples of the complex *milieu* of fortress-tenure come from the north of England, in the fourteenth century. Although the conditions of noble life in regions exposed to occasionally deep and damaging Scottish raids, with the intensified dynastic rivalries they exacerbated, were not typical of England, France, and Ireland as a whole during the central middle ages, it is striking to see how 'normal' adversity proves to have been. Female tenure and the operation of inheritance highlight this normality. It is notable, for instance, that Edward III in

---

[247] In England 'seisin' (*saisina*, etc.) meant right of ownership (tenure) as well as actual possession, in the sense that proof of sometime possession gave a prima facie claim to proprietary right; as in Henry II's legal procedure or *assize* of Novel Disseisin: Warren, *Henry II*, 338–9. In France seisin kept the meaning of physical possession; e.g. under rendability, seisin was transferred but not possessory right (cf. *dominium utile*, n. 244 above).

[248] e.g. after July 1201 Count Raymond VI of Toulouse brought a case in his own court at Toulouse, before the count of Comminges and 14 other judges, against Count Raymond Roger of Foix over the rendability of the *castrum* of Saverdun (*dép.* Ariège: *Layettes*, i. 230–1). On the strength of a rendability charter made in 1167 and subsequently often implemented between their respective fathers, in standard Languedoc form regarding 'the fortifications which are there now or shall be in the future' (*que hodie ibi sunt aut in antea erunt*: *Layettes*, i. 93), Raymond VI had demanded that Saverdun be handed over, and again that Foix repair its fortifications and duly render the place to him. Foix replied that the castle (fortified township) on the first demand was out of his control in that he was at war with the coparceners his tenants there, the knights of Saverdun, during which the defences had been damaged—a revolt in which Raymond had connived—as is proved by a homage-rendability charter to him by the knights (July 1201: *Layettes*, i. 225–6). He (Foix) was not to blame for the destruction; but his offer to deliver the place in its present state was rejected, the court ruling that he must rebuild the fortifications by 29 November (1202) and the *turris* by 29 August (?1203).—Whatever the facts of this thorough demolition, Raymond VI's authoritarian duplicity is clear: far from the good faith (*sens engan* or *sine malo ingenio*; *sine omni fraude*, etc.) reiterated in the formulae of charters.

1364 readily accepted that Blanche, widow of Robert Bertram of Bothal in Northumberland, closely linked with the de Ogle family, should keep Bothal castle for her life in survivorship. Licence to crenellate it had been obtained in the ambitious 1340s. (After the Black Death numbers fell sharply, but in the north licences became rare.) In addition to a tower-house with an enclosure, Bothal also still has a prestigious twin-towered gatehouse of that period.[249] Robert had served several times in the army invading Scotland and was rewarded in 1347 (1 January) for handing over to Edward III for ransom William Douglas, a companion of King David of Scotland, captured at the surprise of Neville's Cross.[250] Anxiety to evade a minority and wardship was the reason for the succession of Blanche, arranged by a fictitious gift to temporary stooge feoffees, an increasingly common practice. Royal approval had not been purchased, so a formal 'pardon' and 'licence for her to retain . . . the castle and manor' were required for this tax-avoidance transaction.[251] That Bothal was a castle was irrelevant—but it may have some bearing on Blanche's apparent change of mind two years later when, with royal permission for the transfer, she rented out the estate to her late husband's heir Ellen (already mentioned) and her new husband, John de Hatfield, 'citizen of London'.[252] For him the change to a rugged baronial lifestyle in Northumberland is an exceptionally drastic case of the ruralization and ennoblement of mercantile wealth. John's expectations were only anticipated since his wife Ellen had the reversion of Bothal after Blanche's death.[253]

A few further details of this case are significant: Robert de Bertram, Ellen's father, died in London on 21 November 1363. The writ for his inquisition *post mortem* (serving many of the purposes of probate today) was issued by Chancery the very next day, and the inquest itself was held before the Mayor (escheator *ex-officio*) two days later. Clearly John de Hatfield, one of the oligarchic citizens of London, had moved fast. Since the late Robert is noted as having no property in London, it seems likely that he had died while staying with Ellen and John. It is

[249] *CPR, 1343–5*, 30. 'A provincial version of Dunstanburgh . . .': Emery, *Greater Medieval Houses*, i. 54–5.

[250] *CPR, 1345–8*, 225, 314: grant of a pension ('rent') of 100 marks p.a.; known as the battle of (or 'by') Durham (1346). A note says it was later compounded for 800 marks in cash (£533). But in April 1347 his arrest was ordered for letting Malcolm Flemyng, a Scot, 'escape'. Private Anglo-Scottish compacts were normal on 'the Border'.

[251] *CPR, 1361–4*, 493. As no 'fine' is noted as having been paid, the patent was charged only the Hanaper fee.

[252] *CPR, 1364–7*, 255. Again, no 'fine' is noted, perhaps thanks to John of Gaunt (Lancaster) who had the patent put through. In 1367 John de Hatfield bought the wardship of his stepson the de Ogle heir (above). Ellen's first husband had been Robert de Ogle. In the 1363 inquisition she is variously stated as being 22 and 26 years of age. Since the pair were to pay a rent of £100 p.a. to Blanche for a property in 1363 valued at 100 marks, and for the duration of Ellen's life not her own although Ellen was her heir (and younger), Blanche seems to have driven a hard bargain.

[253] In the event, John did not enjoy them for long: in June 1377 Blanche had licence to let Bothal (for £80 p.a.) 'to Elena [Ellen] and David de Holgrave, her [3rd] husband'; but they outlived Blanche, since in 1386 dues of £6. 4s. 6d. p.a. were pardoned to the couple in consideration of damage done by the king's army *en route* on the recent Scottish campaign and by the Scots themselves to Bothal castellary and locality: *CPR, 1377–81*, 1–2; *1385–9*, 148.

also likely that he had come to the City to organize the succession. By the time of his death he had divested himself of all his property in the north excepting only three minor tenures not held of the Crown. It had all been done in great haste, for the trust deed ('charter') transferring Bothal for the benefit of Blanche and produced at the Mayor's inquest was dated 11 November 1363, presumably in Northumberland since the escheator's official declaration, also submitted to the inquest, 'certified' that it had taken effect. The vicars ('parsons') of Bothal and of nearby Shepwash, two minor local clerics, had been duly vested ('enfeoffed') with the barony of Bothal on the understanding, habitual in such transactions, that they would regrant the property to Robert and Blanche jointly so that she would have it after her father's imminently expected death.[254] Curiously, the inquest jury was told (by Ellen or John) that royal licence had been obtained—in fact untrue, as it transpired later. More crucially, time also ran out on the second part of the transfer—Robert died before the trustees could pass on the property. It was then valued at a mere 100 marks net (i.e. £66), 'by reason of the late mortality in those parts', evidently a recurrence of the Black Death. Although the two vicars were thus in law still owners of Bothal, Blanche simply ignored them and took the property over, having the irregularity rectified in May 1364, as has been seen. It seems that she chose to retire in 1366, with an ample jointure.

Although the Scottish March could be seen as very much a man's world, valiant widows were not dismayed. In 1365 the major border fortress of Wark on Tweed, standing at the south end of a ford across the river frontier of Scotland, was put in the custody of Joan, widow of John de Coupland, who had made his name and his fortune in October 1346 by being the man to whom King David Bruce surrendered at Neville's Cross. The terms by which Joan was to hold Wark, a fortress as strikingly neglected in structure as were Norham, Berwick (both visible from Wark), or even Carlisle, display the confidence in her reposed by John de Montague, lord of Wark.[255] Her contract (in French) was copied onto the king's rolls, where castle-custody pacts for royal castles were occasionally entered, probably not on account of Wark's seeming national importance but because Joan gave a financial bond in Chancery (a sort of caution-money IOU) for observance of the conditions.[256] If held to be in breach Joan was to forfeit no less than

---

[254] *CIPM* xi. 369–71. On the increasing tendency for land to become quasi-absolute property by use of wills and trusts, and on the concentration of land in the hands of a decreasing number of magnates, see McKisack, *Fourteenth Century*, 260–2.

[255] On castle-custody by contract and the probable precedent for indentured field-service, see M. Prestwich, 'The Garrisoning of English Medieval Castles', 190, 196–7.

[256] *CCR, 1364–8*, 182–3; *CDScotland*, iv. 25. An early earthwork, motte and two baileys, on the riverside ridge; now fragmentary. As a focus of conflict, in and out of royal hands, whether formally or by borrowing (one of the conspicuous cases of English empirical rendability). Refortified by Henry II 1158–61, 'it successfully resisted a determined attack by [King] William the Lion in 1174'. Finally, in 1329, it was granted to the Montagues, when described as 'ruined and broken': Brown *et al.*, *King's Works*, ii. 853. Despite numerous captures (1136, 1138, 1318, 1385, 1399, 1419, etc.) and many sieges no serious attempt was made 1161–1519 to modernize or strengthen it: D. King *Castellarium Anglicanum*, Northumb. Bates, *Border Holds*, 338–41 repeats the 'countess of Salisbury' legend (derived from Jean le Bel and Froissart).

500 marks. Her 'lease' 'of the castle and barony' with its appurtenances was for seven years or for her life plus one year (a run-on for executors to settle debts and accruals), whichever was the shorter. She was to pay 200 marks a year by halves at Martinmas (10 November) and at Whitsun, to John in London, at his house in St Clement (Danes') parish 'without the Bar of the New Temple'. It was an all-purpose committal to Joan:

The said Joan, her assigns or executors, guarding, maintaining, and defending the premises during the said term against all men, save the king and his eldest son, at their own costs so far as they reasonably may considering the state thereof at present, or when repaired at the cost of the lessor [Montague] without waste of lands or buildings—save that allowance shall be made to the lessees [Coupland] for any destruction arising from public war, as other lords in those parts make to tenants in like case—but as to making and repairing the castle walls, the lessor, his heirs and executors, shall be therewith charged.

John de Montague expected that no other magnate than Edward III or Prince Edward should interfere. It was a full repairing lease subject to Montague responsibility for structural works.[257] It was provided that John should spend 40 marks on the (antiquated) *donjon* (i.e. motte buildings) and 'walls' in the first year. Any war damage to revenues or 'capital plant' would be met by adjusting the rent. Similarly it was agreed to overlook 'waste' (due to Joan's act or negligence) amounting to less than an assessed value of £5. Premature termination was also provided for: Montague could dispose of (i.e. sell, in effect, or exchange) Wark castellary, informing Joan six months in advance; she could give up her lease on a year's notice, allowing for new arrangements to be made. Most notably, the war-damage rebate applied to the lands primarily and was typical (as is stated) of any Border lease. Even the provision for repair of the castle was standard form for estate buildings. Only the final clause, which would penalize Joan by loss of her bonded 500 marks, relates specifically to the defence of Wark castle, giving some incentive to man it in emergencies—but the sanction is mild for such a place, especially compared with the total forfeiture and taint of treason often incurred by salaried custodians of royal marcher castles. This last clause provides:

that in case the said castle be taken or burnt by enemies and they be thence thrust out by the lessee [Joan] or by her procurement without cost to the lessor [Montague] on condition that she shall, as speedily as may be, repair the damage in walls or buildings by such enemies done, she shall not be charged with the 500 marks . . . nor otherwise be accountable for the taking or burning thereof; the lessor binding himself and his executors for performance of his part of all these matters. London 20 June 1365.[258]

---

[257] Cf. the largely fiscal, but not so different, life-tenure contract for Hornby castle (Lancs.) by Duke Henry (of Grosmont) of Lancaster (d. 1361) with Robert de Neville of Hornby. The duke had paid off £185 of Robert's debts (£45 probably due to building costs) in return for cession of the castle to Duke Henry for life. Major building, beyond the replacement of timber 'houses and bridges', was to continue. Robert will repay costs to the duke's executors in order to get his castle back. No 'waste beyond 100s.' will be done meanwhile: *CCR, 1349–54,* 374.

[258] (*CCR, 1364–8,* 182–3). The documents entered on the Close Roll are: (1) 'recognisance' (i.e. IOU or debt-bond: these often occur, many being provisional to be cancelled, as here, if conditions were

Sir John de Montague was still evidently answerable to the Crown for any loss or damage consequential to a Scottish capture of Wark, and he had to accept less rent in case of damage by unspecified general hostilities ('public war'). He would indemnify her, but still expected her to fight off 'enemies' (i.e. Scots) attacking and even breaking into the castle. He, in London, left her nearly all the responsibility. Joan took on a formidable administrative, supervisory, judicial, and even military assignment—all the more serious since she would have to garrison Wark herself while paying over a high proportion of the income to Montague. Wark was still largely the twelfth-century castle, in earthwork and masonry, so it was no more than fair that Joan was only to a 'reasonable' extent responsible, 'considering the state thereof at present or when repaired at the cost of the lessor'.[259]

Wark, however conspicuous, was not an isolated instance of women assuming more than the administrative burdens of a castellany in the north. Isabella de Vesci, at Bamburgh (1307–11), is a famous example, mentioned above. Edward III's council was also persuaded (the all-important cause of favours is, as usual, obscure) to entrust custody in 1368 of Etal castle, also in Northumberland, to another widow in succession to her husband, in this case Joan, widow of Edward de Letham who had been given the onerous but remunerative task of administering the lands of the late Robert de Manners together with his castle. Possessing a dwelling-tower with enclosure and a sturdy gatehouse, licensed to be crenellated in 1341, Etal is typical of the *arriviste* fortresses of the county, combining the numinous quasi-archaic with the modern.[260] Its lord, Robert, had died in October 1355 leaving a widow Aline to whom dower was assigned by John de Coupland as escheator, at Easter 1356, and a son John, a baby of 1 year and three months, or three weeks, variously according to the inquisition and proof of age in 1375.[261] It was a modest estate, held in-chief but for a mere half a knight's fief. There were a fulling-mill and barns, enclosures and coal ('sea-coal') mines attached, but otherwise only 26s. rent annually and a town house ('burgage') in Alnwick held from Henry de Percy. Aline received her third of the manor and, since there was no alternative residence, one-third of the castle also, her accommodation and facilities comprising:

fulfilled) by Joan de Coupland to Montague (18 June) for 500 marks, secured on 'her lands and chattels in Northumberland'; (2) copy of the duplicate 'indenture' (20 June), each party keeping half as a record; (3) 'Memorandum' that both parties came into the Chancery (Strand, London) and acknowledged the deed as correct (25 June). These were all routine procedures. Our debt to Tout's *Chapters* for providing an alternative to 'drum and trumpet history' is inestimable.

[259] What induced her to risk her modest estate is not apparent. Her husband had been killed two years earlier in a gentry affray (M. Prestwich *pers. comm.*), but Wark had last been taken in 1318 (from Edward II) and was not again captured until 1385, so her calculations were doubtless shrewd. John de Coupland was granted £500 p.a. and the status of banneret in lieu of King David's ransom (nominally 100,000 marks or £66,667). Oddly, he built no celebratory fortress nor had licence to crenellate: McKisack, *Fourteenth Century*, 247–8; Bates, *Border Holds*, 34, 54. Had Gilbert de Clare worn a surcoat of his own arms at Bannockburn, he might well have been captured for ransom by the Scots and not killed: Prestwich, *Armies and Warfare*, 223.

[260] *CPR, 1367–70*, 119. Licensed to a Robert de Manners as the *mansum de Othale*: *CPR, 1340–3*, 179; Parker, *Domestic Architecture*, iii. 413. Emery, *Greater Medieval Houses*, i. 91–2 (again, somewhat militaristic in tone).

[261] For what follows see *CIPM* x. 203; xii. 206; xiv. 177–8.

a house [i.e. *domus* = 'building'] called Kilping Tower, a house called Maiden Chamber, and a house called the New Stable, a brewhouse with the space (*area*) of the Gatehouse towards the chapel, which chapel is in common between the [agents of the] king [by wardship] and Aline, the bakehouse yard there, except that the king has ingress and egress . . . at the time of baking (*furnicionis*) and brewing only . . .

Etal may have been just a glorified manor- and farm-house—but that is what (with appropriate adjustments for style and rank) castles nearly always were. Latin prevailed in official records, but the component buildings at Etal are, as usual, given their names in (anglicized) 'French' as the ordinary language of the household.[262] Giving Aline the more private *Maydenchaumbre*, the whole (apparently) of a tower (but not the tower-house), together with stabling, communal brewing and baking facilities, and shared use of the chapel, enabled her household to function, while cohabiting with the king's official's household apparently occupying chiefly the tower-house and the gatehouse. Multi-occupancy became rare only in very recent times, with the demise of the greater noble house. Etal had also (as was normal, but is seldom now apparent) dependent extramural enclosures, gardens, and barnyard. Given the age of the heir, who survived and reached his majority in 1375, Aline may well have had the care of him, although he was in the king's wardship and a royal placeman managed the estate, in person or by deputy. There might be a succession of such supervisory intruders. Edward de Letham died not long before his widow Joan secured the wardship, not only of Robert de Manners' lands and heir but also of her own children (including Edward's heir, aged 5) in May 1368. Thus:

Grant to Joan, late the wife of Edward de Letham, of [remission of] £20 yearly of the 40 marks [£26. 13s. 4d.] a year which she is held to render at the Exchequer as executrix of the will of the said Edward to whom the king lately committed the keeping of the lands late of Robert de Maners . . . by reason of the nonage [minority] of his heir . . . until his full age, in aid of the sustenance of her children by the said Edward. She is to pay . . . the remaining 10 marks and . . . shall keep safely and securely the castle of Ethale, late of the said Robert, in her keeping among other lands, as executrix of the said Edward.

One reason why Joan de Letham was left in charge and secured this rent-reduction is disclosed by her husband's inquisition *post mortem* in February 1368. He had held three manors in Berwickshire, but on his death Patrick, the Scottish earl of March, had 'come in person and seized them' because Edward had been loyal to England. Losses to his (noble) subjects which the king could not avert he was bound to compensate. Joan's tenure ended before October 1375, when John de Manners, Robert's second son and now heir, came of age, since she had remarried and had sold the wardship on to Sir William Heron, castellan of the major nearby seat of Ford.[263] With John de Manners's succession and proof of age, the

---

[262] This 'medieval French' was an intermediate, even a hybrid, language between archaic English, e.g. as in Spenser's *Faerie Queene*, (1589) or in Chaucer's *Canterbury Tales* (but without the Saxonisms), and 'modern' (Parisian) French: see e.g. *Mandements Charles V, passim*.

[263] See above. Such common arrangements made sense since young adolescent boys (and girls) were customarily brought up in other and nobler households—a sort of compromise between fostering and the modern boarding school. Aline, the dowager, is not mentioned so had presumably died.

tenurial cycle which restored Etal castle to the dynasty whole and entire was completed. Noble widows would usually keep their husband's administrative personnel along with the family property, ensuring continuity, but the heir's 'coming into his own', in the original sense of the phrase, was the outstanding event for land, tenantry, and dynasty. A 'proof of age' was consequently as much an act of ceremony, preceding that of homage and the heir's investiture, as it was a function of judicial exactitude. In the case of John de Manners, the 'witnesses' deposed that John was born at Etal and baptized in the church of Ford, of which Roger Heron (a cadet of the lordly family) was rector, Sir John de Clifford being godfather, about the time of the burial of his father Robert at Ford church when John was 1 year and three weeks (*sic*) old. The record adds: 'Robert del Grene, aged 50 years and more, agrees and says that he was of the counsel of John's father and was present in the castle at the time of the birth, and that he remembers the death of the father.' All went smoothly. William de Heron, custodian of John's lands, accepted his succession, offering no objections, the record says, to the proof of age being taken.[264]

3. *Conclusions: Part IV—The Social Matrix*

The simplicities of 'military architecture' must give way to the social and cultural realities. Fortresses were so embedded in medieval society that the input of women, in particular, corresponded to their aristocratic role in being very large. The military hypothesis hitherto dominant in castle-studies has assumed that the secular male virtual monopoly of fighting made castles also an exclusively, or predominantly, adult masculine preserve. In fact, as proprietors and occupiers, women were surely at least as important as men. The continuum of castle life was essentially administrative, tenurial, and female, suspended only when the fortress was directly attacked—a threat generally rare, remote, and brief. The vast majority of castles in England, Wales, Ireland, and France have virtually no 'military history' of sieges or physical conflict across the whole panorama of more than five centuries. Rather than being built for defence, as was once imagined, the majority display a refined aristocratic taste to which noble ladies must have made a powerful contribution as long-stay residents and as patrons of architecture, whether by indirect influence or in their own right. The records combed through for this book (which has presented no more than a sample of what has been found) are not such as reveal much of this aspect, whether it be 'domestic science' applied to facilities like ovens and brewhouses; or concern for comfort and convenience regarding privacy, the grading of 'public', family, and more secluded areas; or for the provision of well-lit window-seats (for sewing and outlook) or of closets, wardrobes, and sanitation. An important hint is that chapels are so prominent in dower assignments. As gardens come to be studied more carefully (like Elizabeth de Burgh's garden at Clare castle, Suffolk) as regular adjuncts to

---

[264] n. 261 above.

medieval houses, whether kitchen-gardens, herb-gardens, or as recreational pleasaunces, more will be known of the private spaces and particular tastes of the *châtelaine*.

Fortresses were a slightly (but significantly) differentiated type of noble residence, whether (especially in France) distinguished by tenurial customs or by the ubiquitous architectural panache which to contemporaries was 'fortification' and, to us more flat-footedly, is crenellation and castellation. That female tenure made so little difference goes far to correct macho obsessions and to reinstate the central position of the nobly appointed residence in medieval society.

Epilogue

Léopold Delisle remarked in 1856, at the end of his introduction to his compilation of documents of Philip Augustus, that 'works of this sort would never see the light of day had they been kept in portfolio so long as they were capable of being perfected'. Undoubtedly, despite the efforts of advisors and colleagues, this book could do with improvement, for all that it has been long in gestation. Essentially, it has sought to do a little, by focusing on the human and social side of 'castle' architecture, to reconcile the civilized with the violent aspects of medieval society, as we perceive them to be today. Specialists in the fields of culture and of war can afford to put each in its own compartment (although the need for an integrated synthesis is acknowledged), but studying fortresses as an institution allows no such evasion. Writing about the glories of late-medieval architecture, Wim Swaan saw the problem as summed up by Johan Huizinga's remark that medieval life 'bore the mixed smell of blood and roses', observing that 'a study of the chronicles and the histories would have emphasized the blood', whereas 'the evidence of the visual arts . . . would alone have created too rosy an impression' (compare e.g. the Octagon of Ely cathedral with Château Gaillard). The solution Swaan offers to this Jekyll-and-Hyde contradiction, one encapsulated in fortification as nowhere else, is that 'it is a characteristic of great art to sublimate even death and suffering into beauty'.[265] Whether this is not too intellectual an explanation; whether the social mechanisms of fortification as an exemplary noble style, rather than as a response to violence, are adequately reflected; and whether the extent itself of medieval violence has not been distorted by disappointed romanticism or by taking war as the most accessible bridge between our age (now that religion no longer serves) and that truly remote era, are difficult questions.[266] Swaan, perhaps wisely, keeps well clear of 'castles', although they also would demonstrate his judgement that the (late) middle ages was a period 'of proud endeavour and superb achievement in the visual arts'. But, perhaps, the main contribution to knowledge to be made by studying castles in proper breadth is to shed some light on the aspirations and adversities of noblemen and ladies, ecclesiastics, townspeople, and of the great rural majority, and on their civilized achievements, institutional as well as architectural, in the western European middle ages.

---

[265] Swaan, *Art and Architecture of the Late Middle Ages*, 22. The paradox has seldom been more succinctly expressed.

[266] It is a bold scholar who can write today that, although 'the history of Christianity has been a history of quarrels and secessions, with their tragic corollaries: intolerance, persecution and war . . . [it is still] hard to believe that our civilization would have been better off without it': Barraclough (ed.), *The Christian World*, prologue.

BIBLIOGRAPHY

Abbreviations (Select)

AH	*Architectural History*
AHR	*Agricultural History Review*
AJLH	*American Journal of Legal History*
AmHR	*American Historical Review*
ANS	*Anglo Norman Studies*
Ant J	*Antiquaries Journal*
Arch Camb	*Archaeologia Cambrensis*
Arch Cant	*Archaeologia Cantiana*
Arch J	*Archaeological Journal*
BAR	British Archaeological Reports
BM	*Bulletin Monumental*
BNJ	*British Numismatic Journal*
BSAN	*Bulletin de la Société des Antiquaires de Normandie*
CBA	Council for British Archaeology
CCM	*Cahiers de Civilisation Médiévale*
CChR	*Calendar of Charter Rolls*
CChRVar	*Calendar of Chancery Rolls Various*
CCR	*Calendar of Close Rolls*
CChWarr	*Calendar of Chancery Warrants*
CDIreland	*Calendar of Documents Relating to Ireland*
CDScotland	*Calendar of Documents Relating to Scotland*
CFR	*Calendar of Fine Rolls*
Château Gaillard	*Château Gaillard études de castellologie médiévale*
CIM	*Calendar of Inquisitions Miscellaneous*
CIPM	*Calendar of Inquisitions Post Mortem*
CLibR	*Calendar of Liberate Rolls*
Close Rolls	*Close Rolls of the Reign of Henry III (1227–72)*
CNRS	Centre National de Recherches Scientifiques
CPR	*Calendar of Patent Rolls*
CSG	Castle Studies Group
EHR	*English Historical Review*
HMSO	Her/His Majesty's Stationery Office
JAH	*Journal of American History*
JBAA	*Journal of the British Archaeological Association*
JGH	*Journal of Garden History*
JMH	*Journal of Medieval History*
LMA	*Le Moyen Âge*
MA	*Medieval Archaeology*

MGH	Monumenta Germaniae Historica
MK	*The Ideals and Practice of Medieval Knighthood*
MP	*Medieval Prosopography*
MSAN	*Mémoires de la Société des Antiquaires de Normandie*
MSRG	Moated Sites/Settlement Research Group
NA	*Norfolk Archaeology*
NMS	*Nottingham Medieval Studies*
PatR	*Patent Rolls of the Reign of Henry III*
PBA	*Proceedings of the British Academy*
PRO	Public Record Office
RA	*Revue Archéologique*
RBPH	*Revue Belge de Philologie et d'Histoire*
RC	Record Commission
Recognitiones	*Recueil d'Actes . . . in Aquitania*
Regesta	*Regesta Regum Anglo-Normannorum*
RH	*Revue Historique*
RHDFE	*Revue Historique de Droit Français et Étranger*
RS	Rolls Series
SAC	*Sussex Archaeological Collections*
SAL	Society of Antiquaries of London
TRHS	*Transactions of the Royal Historical Society*
VCH	Victoria History of the Counties of England
ZAM	*Zeitschrift für Archäologie des Mittelalters*

Sources

Listed below are the main primary sources cited (abbreviations indicated), followed by the footnotes in which they occur (numbered according to part). Sources searched without yielding material are not listed.

Actes du Parlement [*de Paris*], ser. i, *1254–1328*, Boutaric, E. (ed.):
   i, *1254–99* (Paris, 1863).—I, 254; II 124; III, 76, 77, 152, 176, 266, 330; IV, 22, 29, 239, 242.
   ii, *1299–1328* (Paris, 1867).—II, 40–2; III, 48, 76, 156, 158, 184; IV, 42, 43.
   SER. ii, 1328–50, H. Furgeot *et al.* (eds.):
   i, *1328–42* (Paris, 1920).—II, 136.—III, 56, 308; IV, 22, 43, 44.
   iii, *1342–50* (Paris, 1960).—II, 18, 19.
Actes Normands [*de la Chambre des Comptes sous Philippe de Valois (1328–50)*], Delisle, L. (ed.) (Rouen, 1871).—III, 238.
[*Veterum Scriptorum et Monumentorum . . .*] *Amplissima Collectio*, E. Martène and U. Durand (eds.), 9 vols. (Paris 1724–33).—I, 46, 58, 59; II, 48, 304; III, 97; IV, 71, 226.
[*Philippe de*] Beaumanoir [*Coutumes de Beauvaisis*], Salmon, A. (ed.), 2 vols. (Paris, 1899, 1900; repr. 1970).—II, 124, 284, 305, 310, 316; III, 90, 318; IV, 62, 63.
BEMONT, C., 'Introduction' to *Rôles Gascons*, ii, iii.—II, 88; III, 180.
—— (ed.) [Un Rôle Gascon de] Lettres Closes [expédiées par la chancelerie du Prince Edouard . . . (1254–55)'] (Paris, 1916).—III, 104.
—— see *Recuil d'Actes . . . Aquitania.*
[*Register of Edward the*] Black Prince, Stamp, A. (ed.), 4 vols. (London 1930–3).—II, 44; III, 292.

[*The*] *Book of Fees* [*Commonly Called 'Testa de Nevill'*] Maxwell-Lyte, H. (ed.), 3 vols. (London, 1920–31).—I, 212; III 5, 286, 287; IV, 204.

BRÉQUIGNY DE, (ed.), 'Rôles Normands et Français [et autres pièces tirées des archives de Londres par Bréquigny, 1764–6'], *MSAN*, 3 ser. 3, pt. 1 (Paris, 1858).—II, 376; III, 247, 338–9.

—— see *Lettres de Rois*.

BRUNEL, C., [*Les Plus anciennes*] *chartes* [*en Langue*] *Provençale* [: *recueil de pièces originales antérieures au XIIIᵉ siècle*] (Paris, 1926), Supplément (Paris 1952).—III, 74, 85, 86; IV, 129.

BRUSSEL, N., *Nouvel Examen* [*de L'Usage Général des Fiefs en France*], 2 vols. (Paris 1727, repr. 1750).—I, 243, 247, 295; II, 97; III, 70.

C[*alendar of*] *Ch*[*arter*] *R*[*olls, 1226–1516*], 6 vols. (HMSO, 1903–27).—I, 304; II, 153, 234, 336; III, 55, 130, 133, 137, 160, 216; IV, 203, 212.

C[*alendar of*] *Ch*[*ancery*] *R*[*olls*] *Various* [*1277–1326*], (HMSO, 1912).—III, 78, 178, 277.

C[*alendar of*] *Ch*[*ancery*] *Warr*[*ants, 1244–1326*], (HMSO, 1927).—I, 168; IV, 177, 216.

C[*alendar of*] *C*[*lose*] *R*[*olls, 1272–1509*], 46 vols. (HMSO, 1900–63).—*passim*.

C[*alendar of*] *D*[*ocuments Relating to*] *Ireland*, H. Sweetman (ed.), 5 vols. (London, 1875–86).—I, 155, 235; II, 319, 345; III, 104, 110, 111, 129, 133; IV, 30, 137, 144, 146.

C[*alendar of*] *D*[*ocuments Relating to*] *Scotland* [*1108–1509*], J. Bain (ed.), 4 vols. (Edinburgh, 1881–8).—I, 195, 233; II, 219; III, 37, 93, 200, 201, 202, 205, 206, 217, 219, 225, 226; IV, 137, 155, 173, 195, 256.

C[*alendar of*] *F*[*ine*] *R*[*olls, 1272–1509*], 22 vols. (HMSO, 1911–62).—I, 193; III, 289; IV, *Passim*.

C[*alendar of*] *P*[*atent*] *R*[*olls, 1232–1509*], 51 vols. (HMSO, 1892–1916).—*passim*.

Gervase of Canterbury: Historical Works, Stubbs, W. (ed.), RS (London 1879–80).—II, 195.

[*Descriptive Cat*[*alogue of*] *Anc*[*ient*] *Deeds* [*in the PRO*], 6 vols. (HMSO, 1896–1915).—IV, 190.

Catalogue [*des Actes de*] *Robert II*, [*roi de France*], W. Newman (ed.) (Paris, 1937).—III, 257.

CHAMPOLLION-FIGEAC, M. (ed.).—see *Lettres de Rois*.

CHIBNALL, M. (ed.) [*The Ecclesiastical History of*] *Orderic Vitalis*, 6 vols. (Oxford, 1969–80).—I, 17, 147.

Chronicles [*of the Reigns of*] *Stephen*, [*Henry II and Richard I*], R. Howlett (ed.), RS, 4 vols. (London, 1884–9).—II, 195.

C[*alendar of*] *I*[*nquisitions*] *M*[*iscellaneous*], 3 vols. (*1219–1377*), (HMSO 1916–37).—I, 228; II, 160, 191; III, 12, 40, 44, 78, 301; IV, 120, 121, 174, 221.

C[*alendar of*] *I*[*nquisitions*] *P*[*ost*] *M*[*ortem*], vols. 1–16, (HMSO, 1902–74).—*passim*.

CLARK, C. (ed.), *The Peterborough Chronicle* [*1070–1154*] (Oxford, 1970).—II, 101.

CLARK, G., *Cartae* [*et Alia Munimenta que ad Dominium de Glamorgan Pertinent*], 4 vols. (Dowlais, 1885; Cardiff, 1890–93).—I, 231; III, 78; IV, 81.

C[*alendar of the*] *Lib*[*erate*] *R*[*olls of the Reign of Henry III*], 6 vols. (HMSO, 1916–64).—I, 156; II, 155; III, 35.

CLIFFORD, D., *The Diaries of Lady Anne Clifford*, (Stroud, 1990).—III, 303.

Close Rolls [*of the Reign of Henry III (1227–72)*], 14 vols. (HMSO, 1902–38).—I, 184, 229, 317; II, 191, 240, 275, 317, 360; III, 78, 97, 108, 128; IV, 24, 145, 148, 151, 153, 155, 157.

CRONNE, H., (ed.), see *Regesta Regum Anglo-Normannorum*.

DAVIS, H. W. C. (ed.), *Stubbs's Select Charters*, 10th edn. (Oxford, 1921).—II, 15, 64 etc.

—— (ed.), see *Regesta Regum Anglo-Normannorum*.

DELISLE, L. (ed.), see *Mandements Charles V*.

—— see *Recueil Henri II*.

—— see *Jugements de l'Echiquier*.

DESCHAMPS, P. and MORTET, V., see Mortet, *Recueil de Textes*.

Documents [relatifs au comté de] Champagne [et de Brie, 1172–1361], A. Longnon (ed.), 3 vols. (Paris, 1901–14).—II, 294; IV, 51.

DOUËT-D'ARCQ, L. (ed.) see *Pièces Charles VI*.

DU CANGE, C., *Novum Glossarium Mediae et Infimae Latinitatis*, D.P. Carpenter *et al.* (eds.) (Paris, 1840–   ).—I, 100, 254.

—— 'Dissertations ou Refléxions sur L'Histoire de S. Louys, du Sire de Joinville', (1668) repr. *Collection Complète des Mémoires*, M. Petitot (ed.) 1st ser.; t. 3 (Paris, 1819), pp. 490–527 (22ᵉ Dissertation: 'des fiefs jurables et rendables').—III, 84, 85.

Ex[cerpta e] Rot[ulis] Fin[ium . . . Henrico Tertio Rege], i, ii, RC (London, 1835, 1836).—IV, 147, 150, 158.

Foedera, [Conventiones, Litterae et . . . Acta Publica, 1066–1383], T. Rymer, R. Sanderson, A. Clarke, and F. Holbrooke (eds.), 4 vols. RC (London 1816–30, 1869)—then 1st edn. vii, viii, ix, Supplement (London, 1709–   ).—I, 213; II, 39, 204, 217, 226, 233, 237, 343; III, 6, 38, 79, 105, 176, 208, 211, 282, 296, 302; IV, 72, 230.

Gascon Rolls see *Rôles Gascons*.

Gervase of Canterbury, Historical Works, see Stubbs, W. (ed.).

Gesta Francorum, see Hill, R. (ed.).

Giraldi Cambrensis Opera, J. Brewer, J. Dimock, G. Warner (eds.), RS (London, 1861), i, *De Rebus a se Gestis*.—II, 139.

HILL, R. (ed.), *Gesta Francorum [et Aliorum Hierosolamitanorum]* (1962 repr. (Oxford, 1972).—I, 121.

JUBAINVILLE, H. D'ARBOIS DE, *Histoire [des ducs et comtes] de Champagne*, 6 vols. (Paris, 1859–66); vol. vii, A. Longnon (ed.).—I, 43, 295; II, 294, 372, 374; III, 72, 95, 145, 166; IV, 51.

Judgements de L'Echiquier [de Normandie au xiiiᵉ siècle], L. Delisle (ed.), Notices et extraits des manuscrits de la Bibliothèque Impériale . . ., (Paris, 1865), ii. 238–432.—I, 255.

KING, E., *William of Malmesbury, Historia Novella*, trans. K. Potter (Oxford, 1998).—II, 100, 288.

Lambert of Ardres: The History of the Counts of Guines and Lords of Ardres, trans. and ed. L. Shopkow (Philadelphia, 2000).—I, 256, 274.

Layettes [du Trésor des Chartes], 5 vols. (Paris 1863–1909):
    i, *755–1223*, ii, *1223–46*, A. Teulet (ed.).
    iii, *1247–60*, J. de Laborde (ed.).
    iv, *1260–70*, E. Berger (ed.).
    v, *Supplément*, 632–1270, H.-F. Delaborde (ed.).—*Passim*.

LELAND, JOHN, *[The] Itinerary [of John Leland in or about the Years 1535–1543]*, L. T. Smith (ed.), 5 vols. (1907; repr. London, 1964).—I, 5; III, 219.

Les Olim [ou Registres des Arrêts Rendus par la Cour du Roi: 1258–1318], É. Beugnot (ed.), 4 vols. (Paris 1839).—I, 254; II, 124, 181, 332; III, 47, 56, 61, 76, 77, 152, 156, 158, 176, 184, 266; IV, 22, 29, 114, 239, 242.

Lettres de Rois [, Reines et Autres Personnages des Cours de France et de L'Angleterre . . . tirées des archives de Londres par Bréquigny], 2 vols. M. Champollion-Figeac (ed.), 2 vols. (Paris, 1839, 1847).—II, 334; III, 179, 181, 191, 296, 323.

LONGNON, A. (ed.), *Histoire des ducs et des comtes de Champagne*, see Jubainville.

—— see *Rôles des Fiefs du comté de Champagne*.

—— see *Documents Champagne*.

LUCHAIRE, A., *Louis VI le Gros: Annales de sa vie et de son règne (1081–1137)*, (Paris, 1890).—I, 108.

Mandements [*et Actes Divers de*] *Charles V* [*1364–1380*], L. Delisle (ed.), (Paris, 1874).—II, 215; III, 241, 243, 251–3, 264–5, 267–73, 327–8, 336; IV, 262.

MARTINDALE, J., 'Conventum inter Guillelmum Aquitanorum Comitem et Hugonem Chiliarchum', *EHR* 84 (1969), 528–48.

MOLINIER, A. (ed.) see *Poitiers, Correspondence.*

M[*onumenta*] *G*[*ermaniae*] *H*[*istorica*], II, ii, *Capitularia Regum Francorum* ii, Boretius and Krause (eds.), (Berlin, 1897).—I, 35, 144.

MORTET, V. and DESCHAMPS, P., *Recueil* [*de Textes relatifs à l'histoire de l'architecture et à la condition des architectes en France au moyen-âge*], i (Paris, 1911), V. Mortet (ed.); ii (Paris, 1924), V. Mortet and P. Deschamps (eds.).—Introd. 39; I, 143, 256, 258–9, 262, 265, 267–70, 272–3, 279, 309; II, 314, 373; III, 148; IV, 93.

Ordonnances de l'Echiquier [*de Normandie, aux xive et xve siècles*], F. Soudet (ed.), (Rouen-Paris, 1929).—III, 58.

Ordonnances [*des Rois de France de la Troisième Race*], 21 vols., de Laurière, Secousse, Vilevault, Bréquigny, Pastoret, Pardessus (eds.), (Paris, 1723–90; 1811–49).—I, 255, 310; II, 80, 83, 337, 361; III, 47, 51, 62, 63, 176, 228, 241, 242, 265, 332–4; IV, 230.

Pat[*ent*] *R*[*olls of the reign of Henry III, 1216–32*], 2 vols. (HMSO, 1901, 1903).—II, 177, 183, 187–8, 354–5, 358; III, 96, 98, 128, 282–3, 313.

PETIT-DUTAILLIS, C., *Étude sur la Vie et le Règne de Louis VIII* (*1187–1226*) (Paris, 1894); Catalogue des Actes, pp. 449–508.—II, 71.

Pièces [*inédites relatives au règne de Charles VI; choix de*], L. Douët-d'Arcq (ed.), 2 vols. (Paris, 1863–4).—III, 243; IV, 31.

[*Placita de*] *Quo Waranto* [*Temporibus Edwardi I, II et III in Curia Receptae Scaccarii Westm. Asservata*, RC (London, 1818).—II, 153; III, 9, 216.

Poitiers, Correspondance [*administrative d'*]*A*[*lphonse*] *de*, A. Molinier (ed.), 2 vols. (Paris, 1894, 1900).—I, 145; II, 38, 242; III, 171, 173–5, 177.

—— *Enquêtes* [*administratives d'*] *A*[*lphonse*] *de . . . 1249–71*, P. Fournier and P. Guébin (eds.) (Paris, 1959).—II, 36, 38, 314.

[*Recueil d'Actes relatifs à l'administration des rois d'Angleterre en Guyenne au xiiie siècle:*] *Recognitiones* [*Feudorum in Aquitania*], C. Bémont (ed.) (Paris, 1914).—II, 285; III, 155.

Recueil [*des Actes de*] *Charles II* [*le Chauve, roi de France*], A. Giry and M. Prou (eds.), 3 vols. (Paris, 1943–55).—I, 40.

Recueil [*des Actes de*] *Charles III* [*le Simple, roi de France (893–923)*], F. Lot and P. Lauer (eds.), (Paris, 1949).—I, 64, 144, 243.

Recueil [*des Actes des Comtes de*]*Ponthieu* [*(1026–1279)*], C. Brunel (ed.), (Paris, 1930).—I, 310; II, 246, 332; III, 70, 97; IV, 68.

Recueil [*des Chartes de l'Abbaye de*] *Cluny*, A. Bernard and A. Bruel (eds.), 6 vols. (Paris, 1876–1903).—I, 279, 281.

Recueil [*des Actes de*] *Henri II* [*roi d'Angleterre et duc de Normandie, concernants les provinces Françaises et les affaires de France*], L. Delisle and E. Berger (eds.), 3 vols. (Paris, 1916–27).—I, 285; II, 106, 200, 204, 211.

Recueil [*des Actes de*] *Louis IV* [*roi de France (936–954)*], P. Lauer (ed.) (Paris 1914).—I, 41.

Recueil [*des Actes de*] *Philippe I* [*, roi de France (1059–1108)*], M. Prou (ed.), (Paris, 1908).—I, 247; II, 112.

Recueil [*des Actes de*] *Philippe II* [*Auguste, roi de France*], (*1180–1215*), H.-Fr. Delaborde, C. Petit-Dutaillis, J. Monicat and J. Boussard (eds.), 3 vols. (Paris, 1916–66).—II, 218, 222; III, 151–2, 163–4, 166, 256, 264, 269; IV, 64, 139.

Recueil Général [*des anciennes lois françaises*], Jordan, Decrusy, Isambert *et al.* (eds.), 29 vols. (Paris, 1822–33).—I, 40; II, 68, 79; III, 241–2, 334.

Regesta [*Regum Anglo-Normannorum, 1066–1154*] H. Davis, R. Whitwell, C. Johnson, H. Cronne, and R. H. C. Davis (eds.), 3 vols. (Oxford, 1913, 1956, 1968); Additions and Corrections to vol. iii, in R. H. C. Davis, *King Stephen*, 3rd edn. (London, 1990), App. 8.—I, 154; II, 106, 154, 269; III, 91, 276; IV, 232.

Regesta [*Regum*] *Scot*[*torum*], (*1153–1214*), G. Barrow, and W. Scott (eds.), 2 vols. (Edinburgh, 1960, 1971).—III, 77, 100, 305.

Registres du Trésor [*des Chartes*], (*1285–1328*), R. Fawtier (ed.), 2 vols. (Paris, 1958, 1960).— II, 11, 46, 254, 312; III, 55–7, 59, 81, 171, 326; IV, 27.

Rôles [*des Fiefs du comté*] *de Champagne* [*sous le régne de Thibaud le Chansonnier (1249–1252)* . . .], A. Longnon (ed.), (Paris, 1877).—IV, 51, 154, 231.

Rôles Gascons, F. Michel, C. Bémont, and Y. Renouard (eds.), 4 vols. and *Supplément* (Paris, 1885, 1896, 1900, 1906, 1962).—*Passim.*

Rôles Normands et Français', see Bréquigny (ed.).

ROSENTALL, H., *Tractatus et Synopsis Totius Juris Feudalis* . . . (Cologne, 1610).—II, 209.

Rot[*uli*] *Chart*[*arum, 1199–1216*], RC (London, 1837).—I, 167; 311; III, 29, 55, 130, 136, 165.

Rot[*uli de*] *Lib*[*erate ac de Misis et Praestitis Regnante Johanne*], T. D. Hardy (ed.), RC (London, 1844).—II, 267; III, 112; IV, 32.

Rot[*uli de*] *Ob*[*latis*] *et Fin*[*ibus* . . . *Tempore Regis Johannis*], T. D. Hardy (ed.), RC (London, 1835).—II, 300.

Rot[*uli*] *Hund*[*redorum Temporibus Henrici III et Edwardi I in Turri Lond'* . . . *Asservati*], 2 vols. (London, '1812', '1818', 1834).—I, 294; II, 131, 150, 152, 156, 160; III, 7, 9, 10, 60, 157, 278–9, 286, 291, 315–16; IV, 49, 229, 232.

Rot[*uli*] *Litt*[*erarum*] *Claus*[*arum*],(1204–27) RC, 2 vols. (London, 1833, 1844).—*passim.*

Rot[*uli*] *Litt*[*erarum*] *Pat*[*entium*], 'vol. i, i': (*1201–16*), RC (London, 1835).—*passim.*

Rot[*uli*] *Norm*[*anniae in Turri Londonensi Asservati Johanne et Henrico Quinto Regibus*], 'i' (*1200–5, 1417–18*), RC (London, 1835).—II, 222, 251–3; IV, 64.

Rot[*uli*] *Parl*[*iamentorum ut et Petitiones et Placita in Parliamento* . . .], 7 vols. (London, 1783–1832).—I, 166; II, 58–62, 376; III, 34, 60, 138, 202, 262; IV, 81, 210, 212.

SALMON, A. (ed.), see Beaumanoir, *Coutumes de Beauvaisis.*

SALVAING, D. DE, (Denis de Salvaing et de Boissieu), *De L'Usage des Fiefs* [*et autres droits seigneuriaux*], (1668; new edn. Grenoble, 1731).—I, 88, 188, 278, 316, 321; II, 97–8; III, 51, 55, 84, 87, 248.

SEWTER, E. (trans.) *The Alexiad of Anna Comnera* (Harmondsworth, 1969).—I, 22.

SHIRLEY, W. (ed.), *Royal* [*and Other Historical*] *Letters* [*Illustrative of the Reign of Henry III*], 2 vols. (London, 1862, 1866).—I, 323; II, 187, 231, 276, 327, 330, 337, 360, 367; III, 85, 93, 95, 97, 280, 281; IV, 50, 73, 233.

SIBLY, W. and SIBLY, M. (eds.) [*The History of the Albigensian Crusade:*] *Peter of les Vaux-de-Cernay*['*s 'Historia Albigensis'*], (Woodbridge, 1998).—I, 99.

SMITH, L. T. (ed.), *The Itinerary of John Leland*, see Leland, John.

STONES, E. L. G. (ed. and trans.) *Anglo-Scottish Relations, 1174–1328: Some Selected Documents*, (London, 1965).—II, 228.

STUBBS, W., *Stubbs's Select Charters* (1870), 10th edn., H.W.C. Davis (ed.), (Oxford, 1921).— II, 15, 64, 147, 174, 199, 255, 311–13; III, 288, 307; IV, 19, 233.

——— (ed.) *Gervase of Canterbury: Historical Works*, 2 vols. (London, 1879–80).—I, 246; II, 195.

TARDIF, J. (ed.), *Mon*[*uments*] *Hist*[*oriques: Inventaires des Documents*], (Paris, 1866).—III, 163, 259, 328.

TAYLOR, A. 'Stephen de Penchester's Account as Constable of Dover Castle for the Years 1272–(Michaelmas) 1274', in Collectanea Historica, Detsicas (ed.), 114–22.

Thesaurus Novus [*Anecdotorum Complectens Regum ac Principum . . . Epistolas et Diplomata Bene Multa*], É. Martène and U. Durand (eds.), 5 vols. (Paris, 1717).—I, 159, 279, 285; II, 88, 305; III, 66, 74, 88; IV, 24, 92–3, 106.

TIMBAL, P.C. *et al.* (eds.), [*La*] *Guerre de Cent Ans* [*, vue à travers les Registres du Parlement (1337–69)*] CNRS, (Paris, 1961).—II, 11, 362, 364–5; III, 103, 197, 239, 246, 263, 266; IV, 95.

William of Malmesbury, Historia Novella, see King, E. (ed.).

William of Newburgh, [*Historia Rerum Anglicanum, Chronicles of the Reigns of Stephen, Henry II and Richard I*], R. Howlett, 4 vols. (ed.), RS (London, 1884–9).—II, 195.

Secondary Works

AHRENS, C., 'An English Origin for Norwegian Stave Churches?' *Medieval Life* 4 (1996), 3–7.

ALCOCK, L., King, D., see King D.

ALDRED, D., *Castles and Cathedrals: The Architecture of Power 1066–1550* (Cambridge, 1993).

The Alexiad, see Sewter, E. (trans.)

ALLCROFT, A.H., *Earthwork of England* (London, 1908).

ALLMAND, C., *The Hundred Years War: England and France at War c.1300–c.1450* (Cambridge, 1988).

—— *Society at War: the Experience of England and France during the Hundred Years War* (1973; Woodbridge, 1998).

ALTSCHUL, M., *A Baronial Family in Medieval England: The Clares 1217–1314* (Baltimore, 1965).

ANDERSON, W., *Castles of Europe from Charlemagne to the Renaissance* (London, 1970).

ANDRU, O., COLARDELLE, M., MOYNE, J., and VERDEL, É., 'Les Châteaux de la baronnie de Clermont et la marche delphino-savoyarde', *Château Gaillard*, 17 (1996), 25–37.

ARMITAGE, E., *The Early Norman Castles of the British Isles* (London, 1912).

AUBENAS, R., 'Les Châteaux-forts des Xe et Xi^e siècles: contribution à l'étude des origines de la féodalité', *RHDFE*, 4 ser. 17 (1938), 548–86.

AUBERT, M., Marquise de Maillé, *L'Architecture Cistercienne en France*, 2 vols. 2nd edn. (Paris 1947).

AVENT, R., 'Castles of the Welsh Princes', *Château Gaillard* 16 (1992) 11–20.

AYTON, A., 'Introduction', and 'Knights, Esquires and Military Service: the Evidence of the Armorial Cases before the Court of Chivalry', in Ayton and Price (eds.), *Medieval Military Revolution*, 81–104.

—— and PRICE, J. (eds.) *The Medieval Military Revolution: State, Society and Military Change in Medieval and Early Modern Europe]* (London, 1995).

BACHRACH, B., 'Early Medieval Fortifications in the "West" of France: a 'Revised Technical Vocabulary', *Technology and Culture* 16 (1975), 531–69.

—— 'The Cost of Castle-Building: The Case of the Tower at Langeais, 992–994', in *The Medieval Castle: Romance and Reality*, Reyerson and Powe (eds.), 47–62.

BAKER, D., 'Bedford Castle: Some Preliminary Results from Rescue Excavations', *Château Gaillard*, 6 (1973), 15–22.

BALDWIN, F., *Sumptuary Legislation and Personal Regulation in England* (Baltimore, 1926).

BALDWIN, J., 'La Décennie décisive: les années 1190–1203 dans le règne de Philippe Auguste', *RH* 266 (1981), 312–37.

BALDWIN, J. F., *The King's Council in England During the Middle Ages* (Oxford, 1913; repr. 1969).

BARBER, M., *The Two Cities: Medieval Europe, 1050–1320* (London, 1992).

—— *The New Knighthood: a History of the Order of the Temple*, (Cambridge, 1994).

—— 'Frontier Warfare in the Latin Kingdom of Jerusalem: the Campaign of Jacob's Ford 1178–79', *The Crusades and their Sources: Essays Presented to Bernard Hamilton*, J. France and W. Zajac (eds.) (Aldershot, 1998), 9–22.

—— 'The Albigensian Crusade: Wars Like Any Other?' *Gesta Dei Per Francos: Crusade Studies in Honour of Jean Richard*, M. Balard, B. Kedar, J. Riley-Smith (eds.) (Aldershot, 2001).

BARBER, R., *The Knight and Chivalry* (London, 1970).

—— 'When is a Knight not a Knight?', MK 5 (1995), 1–18.

—— and BARKER, J., *Tournaments: Jousts, Chivalry and Pageants in the Middle Ages* (Woodbridge, 1989).

BAREL, Y., *La Ville Médiévale* (Grenoble, 1977).

BARKER, E. (ed.) *J. J. Rousseau: The Social Contract* (Oxford, 1958).

BARKER, P., and HIGHAM, R., *Timber Castles* (London, 1992).

BARLEY, M., *European Towns* (London, 1977).

BARRACLOUGH, G. (ed.) *The Christian World: a Social and Cultural History of Christianity* (London, 1981).

BARRON, C. (ed.) *Medieval London Widows* (London, 1994).

BARROW, G., 'The Scots and the North of England', *Anarchy of King Stephen*, King (ed.), ch. 7.

BARTLETT, R., 'Colonial Aristocracies of the High Middle Ages', in *Medieval Frontier Societies*, ch. 2.

—— and MACKAY, A. (eds.) *Medieval Frontier Societies* (Oxford, 1989).

BATES, C., *The Border Holds of Northumberland*, 1 vol. only (Newcastle, 1891).

BATES, D., *Normandy before 1066* (London 1982).

BAUDRY, M.-P. *Les Fortifications des Plantagenêts en Poitou 1154–1242* (Paris, 2001).

BAUDUIN, P., 'Bourgs castraux et frontière en Normandie aux xie et xiie siècles: l'exemple du département de l'Eure', in *Château et Territoire*, Fillon A. (ed.), 27–42.

BEAUNE, C., *The Birth of an Ideology* (Los Angeles, 1991).

BÉCET, M., 'Les Fortifications de Chablis au xve siècle: (comment on fortifiait une petite ville pendant la guerre de Cent Ans)', *Annales de Bourgogne* 21 (1949), 7–30.

BEECH, G. (ed.) *Le Conventum* (Geneva, 1995).

BEELER, J., *Warfare in England, 1066–1189* (New York, 1966).

BELLAMY, J., *Crime and Public Order in England in the Later Middle Ages* (London, 1973).

BELLESILES, M., 'The Origins of Gun Culture in the United States, 1760 to 1865', JAH (Sept. 1966).

—— *Lethal Imagination* (New York, 1999).

BENNETT, H., *Life on the English Manor: A Study of Peasant Conditions, 1150–1400* (Cambridge, 1960).

BENNETT, M., 'Wace on Warfare', *Anglo-Norman Warfare*, Strickland (ed.), 230–50.

—— 'The Medieval Warhorse Reconsidered', MK 5 (1995), 19–40.

BERESFORD, G., 'The Medieval Manor of Penhallam Jacobstow, Cornwall', *ME* 18 (1974), 90–145.

—— 'Goltho Manor Lincolnshire: the Buildings and their Surrounding Defences 850–1150', *ANS* 4 (1981), 13–36.

BERESFORD, M., *New Towns of the Middle Ages* (London, 1967).

BERGER, E., 'Les Dernières années de Saint Louis', Introduction, *Layettes*, iv, pp. iii–lxxv.

BERMAN, C., 'Fortified Monastic Granges in the Rouergue', in *The Medieval Castle: Romance and Reality*, Reyerson and Powe (eds.), 125–46.

BEUGNOT, E. (ed.) see *Les Olim*.

BINNEY, M., 'The Château d'Olhain, Artois', *Country Life* (15 July 1982), 174–8.

BINSKI, P., 'The Painted Chamber at Westminster', SAL, *Occasional Papers*, NS 9 (London, 1986) 74–5.

BIRRELL, J., 'Deer and Deer-Farming in Medieval England' *AHR* 40 (1992), 112–26.

BISSON, T., 'The War of the Two Arnaus: a Memorial of the Broken Peace in Cerdanya (1188)', in *Miscellània en Homentage al P. Augusti Altisent* (Barcelona, 1991), 95–107.

BLACKBURN, M., 'Coinage and Currency', *Anarchy of King Stephen*, King, E. (ed.), 145–206.

BLAIR, C. J., 'Hall and Chamber: English domestic Planning, 1000–1250', in *Manorial Domestic Buildings* (repr. Liddiard, 2002).

—— and RAMSAY, N., (eds.) *English Medieval Industries* (London, 1991).

BLOCH, M., *Feudal Society*, trans. L. Manyon (London, 1961).

BOASE, T., 'King Death: Judgement, Mortality and Remembrance', in *Flowering of the Middle Ages*, Evans (ed.), 204–44.

BÖHME, H. (ed.) *Burgen der Salierzeit*: I, *In Den Nördlichen Landschaften des Reiches*: II, *In Den Südlichen Landschaften des Reiches* (Sigmaringen, 1991).

BOIS, M., FEUILLET, M.-P., LAFFONT, P.-Y., MAZARD, C., POISSON, J.-M., and SIROT, E., 'Approche des plus anciennes formes castrales dans le royaume de Bourgogne-Provence xᵉ-xiiᵉ siècles', *Château Gaillard*, 16 (1994), 57–63.

BONDE, S., *Fortress Churches of Languedoc: Architecture, Religion and Conflict in the High Middle Ages* (Cambridge, 1994).

BOÜARD, M. DE, 'Les Petites Enceintes circulaires d'origine médievale en Normandie', *Château Gaillard*, 1 (Caen, 1964), 21–36.

—— 'La Salle dite de l'Echiquier au château de Caen', *MA* 9 (1965), 64–81.

BOULTON, D'A., 'Classic Knighthood as a Nobiliary Dignity: the Knighting of Counts' and King's sons', *MK* 5 (1995), 41–100.

BOUTELL, C., *English Heraldry*, revised A. Fox-Davies (London, 1907).

BOUTRUCHE, R., *Seigneurie et Féodalité* (Paris, 1970).

BRADBURY, J., *The Medieval Siege* (Woodbridge, 1992).

—— 'The Civil War of Stephen's Reign: Winners and Losers', in *Arms, Chivalry and Warfare*, Strickland (ed.), 115–32.

BRADLEY, J., *Walled Towns in Ireland* (Dublin, 1995), 48.

BRAUN, H., *The English Castle* (London, 1936).

BREFFNY, B. DE, *Castles of Ireland* (London 1977).

BRICE, M., *Forts and Fortresses* (Oxford, 1990).

BRIEGER, P., *English Art, 1216–1307* (Oxford, 1968).

BRIGGS, A., *Saxons, Normans and Victorians*, Historical Association (Hastings and Bexhill, 1966), 26.

BRITNELL, R., 'King John's Early Grants of Markets and Fairs', *EHR* 94 (1979), 90–6.

BROOKS, F., *The English Naval Forces 1199–1272* (Hull, 1932).

BROWN, E. H. R., 'The Tyranny of a Construct: Feudalism and Historians of Medieval Europe', *AmHR* 79 (1974), 1063–88.

BROWN, R. A., 'The Place of English Castles in the Administrative and Military Organization, 1154–1216. With Special Reference to the Reign of John', unpubl. D.Phil. thesis, University of Oxford, 1953.

—— *English Medieval Castles* (London, 1954; repr. Woodbridge, 2001).

BROWN, R. A., 'Royal Castle-Building in England, 1154–1216', *EHR* 70 (1955), 353–98 (repr. Liddiard, 2002).

—— 'A List of Castles 1154–1216', *EHR* 74 (1959), 249–80.

—— *Dover Castle Guide* (London, 1966).

—— 'The Norman Conquest and the Genesis of English Castles', *Château Gaillard*, 3 (Chichester 1969), 1–14.

—— *Rochester Castle Guide* (London, 1969).

—— *The Normans and the Norman Conquest* (London, 1969).

—— 'An Historian's Approach to the Origins of Castles in England', *Arch J*, 126 (1970), 13–48.

—— *The Origins of English Feudalism* (London, 1973).

—— *English Castles* (London 1976, repr. Phoenix Press, forthcoming).

—— 'Some Observations on the Tower of London', *Arch J*, 136 (1979), 99–108.

—— 'The Status of the Norman Knight', in *War and Government in the Middle Ages*, Gillingham and J. Holt (eds.) (Woodbridge, 1984), 18–32; repr. *Anglo-Norman Warfare*, Strickland (ed.), 128–42.

—— *The Architecture of Castles: A Visual Guide]* (London, 1984).

—— *Studies Presented to*, see Harper-Bill, C., *et al.* (eds.).

—— , COLVIN, H., and TAYLOR, A., *The History of the King's Works*, 2 vols. album (HMSO, 1963).

—— , COULSON, C., PRESTWICH, M., *et al. Castles: A History and Guide* (Poole, 1980).

BROWN, V., 'Bibliography of the Writings of R. Allen Brown', *Studies Presented to R.A. Brown*, Harper-Bill et al. (eds.), 353–7.

BUR, M. (ed.), *La maison forte au moyen âge: actes de la table ronde de Nancy-Pont à Mousson, des 31 Mai–3 Juin, 1984*, CNRS (Paris, 1986).

BURKE, J., *Life in the Castle in Medieval England* (London, 1978).

BURNE, A., *The Crécy War* (London, 1955).

BUTLER, L., and GIVEN-WILSON, C., *Medieval Monasteries of Great Britain* (London, 1979).

BUTLER, R., 'Late-Roman Town Walls in Gaul', *Arch J*, 116 (1959), 25–50.

BUTTIN, F., 'La Lance et l'arrêt de cuirasse', *Archaeologia* 99 (1965), 77–205.

CAIGER-SMITH, A., *English Medieval Mural Paintings* (Oxford, 1963).

CALMETTE, J., *Le Monde féodal* (Paris, 1942).

CAM, H., *The Hundred and the Hundred Rolls* (1930, repr. London, 1963).

—— *Liberties and Communities in Medieval England* (1944, repr. London 1963).

—— *Law-Finders and Law-Makers in Medieval England* (London, 1962).

CAMERON, K., *English Place Names* (London, 1963).

CAMPBELL, B., *English Seigniorial Agriculture 1250–1450* (Cambridge, 2000).

CARPENTER, D., *The Minority of Henry III* (Berkeley and Los Angeles, 1990).

Castillo, J., *El Incastellamento en la Territorio de la Cuidad de Luca*, BAR (London, 1999).

Castle Studies Group Newsletter, 1–15 (Exeter, Daventry, 1987–2001).

CAUMONT, A. DE, *Abécédaire ou Rudiment d'Archéologie*, 3 vols. (Paris, 1868–70).

CHÂTELAIN, A., 'Essai de typologie des donjons romans quadrangulaires de la France de l'ouest'], *Château Gaillard* 6 (1973), 43–57.

CHERRY, J., 'Imago Castelli: the Depiction of Castles on Medieval Seals', *Château Gaillard* 15 (1990), 83–90.

CHIBNALL, M., 'Oderic Vitalis on Castles', in *Studies Presented to R. A. Brown*, Harper-Bill *et al.* (eds.), 45–56 (repr. Liddiard, 2002).

—— 'Normandy', in *Anarchy of King Stephen*, King (ed.).

CHRISTISON, D., *Early Fortifications in Scotland*, (Edinburgh, 1898).

CHURCH, S. (ed.) *King John: New Interpretations* (Woodbridge, 1999).

CLANCHY, M., *From Memory to Written Record* (London 1979).

CLAPHAM, A., *English Romanesque Architecture*: I, *Before the Conquest*; II, *After the Conquest* (Oxford, 1930, 1934).

CLARK, G., *Medieval Military Architecture in England*, 2 vols. (London, 1884).

CLARK, K., *The Gothic Revival: An Essay in the History of Taste* (3rd edn., London 1962).

The Art of Claude Lorrain, Exhibition Catalogue, The Arts Council (London, 1969).

CLAYTON, M., *Catalogue of Rubbings of Brasses and Incised Slabs*, Victoria and Albert Museum (5th edn., London, 1969).

COAD, J., 'Medieval Fortifications and Post-Medieval Artillery Defences: Developments in Post-War Research and Future Trends', *Building on the Past*, B. Vyner (ed.) (London, 1994), 215–27.

COHN, N., *The Pursuit of the Millenium* (London, 1957).

COLVIN, H., see R. A. Brown *et al.*, *King's Works*.

CONTAMINE, P., *Guerre, état et société à la fin du moyen-âge: études sur les armées des rois de France, 1337–1494*, (Paris, 1972).

—— (ed.), *La Noblesse au moyen-âge, XIe–XVe siècles: essais à la mémoire de Robert Boutruche*, (Paris, 1977).

—— *War in the Middle Ages*, M. Jones (ed. and trans.) (Oxford, 1984).

COOK, G., *Medieval Chantries and Chantry Chapels* (London, 1947).

COOK, O., and KIRSTING, A., *The English Country House* (London, 1974).

COULSON, C., 'Seignorial Fortresses in France in Relation to Public Policy, c.864 to c.1483', unpubl. Ph.D thesis in Arts, University of London, Feb. 1972.

—— 'Rendability and Castellation in Medieval France', *Château Gaillard*, 6 (1973), 59–67.

—— 'Fortresses and Social Responsibility in late-Carolingian France', *ZAM* 4 (1976), 29–36.

—— 'Structural Symbolism in Medieval Castle Architecture', *JBAA* 132 (1979), 73–90.

—— 'Castle and Community', in *Castles*, Brown *et al.*, 100–13.

—— 'Castellation in Champagne in the Thirteenth Century', *Château Gaillard*, 9–10 (1982), 347–64.

—— 'Hierarchism in Conventual Crenellation: An Essay in the Sociology and Metaphysics of Medieval Fortification', *MA* 26 (1982), 69–100.

—— 'Fortress-Policy in Capetian Tradition and Angevin Practice: Aspects of the Conquest of Normandy by Philip II', *ANS* 6 (1984), 13–38 (repr. Liddiard, 2002).

—— 'The Impact of Bouvines Upon the Fortress-Policy of Philip Augustus', in *Studies Presented to R. A. Brown*, Harper-Bill *et al.* (eds.), 71–80 (repr. Liddiard, 2002).

—— 'Bodiam Castle: Truth and Tradition', *Fortress*, 10 (Aug. 1991), 3–15.

—— 'Some Analysis of the Castle of Bodiam, East Sussex', *MK* 4 (1992), 51–107.

—— 'Specimens of Freedom to Crenellate by Licence', *Fortress*, 18 (Aug. 1993), 3–15.

—— 'The Castles of the Anarchy', in *Anarchy of King Stephen*, King, E. (ed.), 67–92 (repr. Liddiard, 2002).

—— 'Freedom to Crenellate By Licence; An Historiographical Revision', *NMS* 38 (1994), 86–137.

—— 'Battlements and the Bourgeoisie: Municipal Status and the Apparatus of Urban Defence', *MK*5 (1995), 119–75.

—— 'The French Matrix of the Castle Provisions of the Chester-Leicester Conventio', *ANS* 17 (1995), 65–86.

COULSON, C., 'Community and Fortress-Politics in France in the Lull Before the Hundred Years War, in English Perspective', *NMS* 40 (1996), 80–108.

—— 'Cultural Realities and Reappraisals in English Castle Study', *JMH* 22, no. 2 (1996), 171–208.

—— ' "National" Requisitioning for "Public" Use of "Private" Castles in Pre-National State France', in *Medieval Europeans*, Smyth (ed.), pp. 119–34.

—— 'Valois Powers Over Fortresses on the Eve of the Hundred Years War', in *Armies, Chivalry and Warfare*, Strickland (ed.), 147–60.

—— 'The Sanctioning of Fortresses in France: "Feudal Anarchy" or Seignorial Amity?', *NMS* 41 (1998), 38–104.

—— 'Fourteenth-Century Castles in Context: Apotheosis or Decline?', in *Fourteenth Century England*, Saul, N. (ed.) (Woodbridge, 2000).

—— 'Peaceable Power in English Castles', *ANS* 23 (2001), 71–97.

—— *Castles and Crenellating by Licence: The 'Salvation of the Realm' and 'the Saving of Privilege' in Medieval England* (in preparation).

—— *The Castles of Communities: Ecclesiastical and Urban Fortresses in England, France and Ireland in the Central Middle Ages* (in preparation).

—— , BROWN, R. A., and PRESTWICH, M., see Brown, R. A., *Castles.*

COULTON, G., *Ten Medieval Studies* (Cambridge, 1906).

—— *Life in the Middle Ages* (Cambridge, 1928–30).

—— *Fourscore Years: An Autobiography* (Cambridge, 1944).

COUNIHAN, J., 'Ella Armitage: Castle Studies Pioneer', *Fortress* 6 (Aug. 1990), 51–9.

—— 'Mottes, Norman or Not', *Fortress*, 11 (Nov. 1991), 53–60.

CRAWFORD, A., *A History of the Vintners' Company* (London, 1977).

CRESSWELL, K., *Early Muslim Architecture* (London, 1958).

CRONNE, H., 'Ranulf de Gernons, Earl of Chester, 1129–53', *TRHS*, 4th ser., 20 (1937), 103–34.

CROSSLEY-HOLLAND, N., *Living and Dining in Medieval Paris: The Household of a Fourteenth-Century Knight* (Cardiff, 1997).

CROUCH, D., *The Image of Aristocracy in Britain, 1000 to 1300* (London, 1992).

—— *The Reign of King Stephen, 1135–1154* (London, 2000).

CRUDEN, S., *The Scottish Castle* (London, 1960).

CURRY, A., *The Hundred Years War* (London, 1993).

—— 'The Organization of Field Armies in Lancastrian Normandy', in *Armies, Chivalry and Warfare*, Strickland (ed.), 207–33.

—— and HUGHES, M. (eds.), *Arms, Armies and Fortifications in the Hundred Years War* (Woodbridge, 1994).

CURSENTE, B., '*Castrum* et territoire dans la Gascogne du XIIIᵉ siècle', *Château Gaillard*, 15 (1992), 91–100.

CURTIS, T. (ed.), *Monumental Follies: An Exposition on the Eccentric Edifices of Britain* (Worthing, 1972).

CURZON, G. and TIPPING, H., *Tattershall Castle* (London, 1929).

DALTON, P., '*In Neutro Latere*: The Armed Neutrality of Ranulf II, Earl of Chester in King Stephen's Reign', *ANS* 14 (1991), 39–59.

D'AUVERGNE, E., *The English Castle* (London, 1907).

DAVIES, R. R., *Lordship and Society in the March of Wales 1282–1400* (Oxford, 1978).

—— 'Kings, Lords and Liberties in the March of Wales, 1066–1272', *TRHS* 29 (1979), 41–61.

—— 'Frontier Arrangements in Fragmented Societies: Ireland and Wales', in *Medieval Frontier Societies*, Bartlett and Mackay (eds.), 77–100.

DAVIS, R. H. C., *The Normans and Their Myth* (London, 1976).

DAVISON, B., 'The Origins of the Castle in England: The Institute's Research Project', *Arch J*, 124 (1967), 202–11.

—— 'Reply to R. A. Brown', *Arch J*, 126 (1970), 146–8.

—— 'Excavations at Sulgrave, Northamptonshire 1960–76: An Interim Report', *Arch J*, 134 (1977), 105–14.

—— *Looking at a Castle* (London, 1987).

—— *The Observers' Book of Castles* (London, 1979; 2nd edn. 1988).

DAWSON, C., *The Making of Europe* (London, 1932).

DEBORD, A., '*Castrum* et *castellum* chez Adémar de Chabannes', *Archéologie Médiévale* 9 (1979), 97–113.

—— 'Châteaux et résidence aristocratique: réflexions pour la recherche', *Château Gaillard*, 13 (1987), 41–51.

—— 'The Castellan Revolution and the Peace of God in Aquitaine', *Peace of God*, Head and Landes (eds.), 135–64.

DEAN, M., 'Early Fortified Houses : Defenses and Castle Imagery, 1275–1350, With Evidence From the South-east Midlands', in *The Medieval Castle: Romance and Reality*, Reyerson and Powe (eds.), 47–74.

DENHOLM-YOUNG, N., *Seignorial Administration in England* (London, 1937).

—— *Richard of Cornwall* (Oxford, 1947).

—— *History and Heraldry 1254–1310: A Study of the Historical Value of the Rolls of Arms* (Oxford, 1965).

—— *The Country Gentry in the Fourteenth Century* (Oxford, 1969).

DESCHAMPS, P., *Les Châteaux des Croisés en Terre Sainte*: I, *Le Crac des Chevaliers*, 2 vols. (Paris, 1934); II, *La Défense du royaume de Jérusalem*, 2 vols. (Paris 1939).

DETSICAS, A. (ed.), *Collecteana Historica: Essays in Memory of Stuart Rigold* (Maidstone, 1981).

DE VRIES, K., *Joan of Arc: A Military Leader* (Stroud, 1999).

DIEHL, C., *L'Afrique byzantine* (Paris, 1896; repr. New York, 1965).

DIXON, P., 'The Donjon of Knaresborough: The Castle as Theatre', *Château Gaillard*, 14 (1990), 121–39.

—— 'From Hall to Tower: The Change in Seigneurial Houses on the Anglo-Scottish Border after *c*.1250', in *Thirteenth Century England*, 4, S. Lloyd and P. Coss (eds.) (Woodbridge, 1992), 85–107.

—— 'Design in Castle-Building: The Control of Access to the Lord', *Château Gaillard*, 18 (1998), 47–57.

—— and BOURE, P., 'Coparcenary and Aydon Castle, *Arch J*, 135 (1978), 234–8.

—— and LOTT, B., 'Courtyard and Tower: Context and Symbols in the Development of Late-Medieval Great Houses', *JBAA* 146 (1993), 93–101.

—— MARSHALL, P., 'The Great Tower in the Twelfth Century: The Case of Norham Castle', *Arch J*, 150 (1993) 410–32.

—— —— 'The Great Tower of Hedingham: a Reassessment', *Fortress* 18 (Aug. 1993), 16–23 (repr. Liddiard, 2002).

DOUGLAS, D., *William the Conqueror* (London, 1964).

DOYLE, A. C., *The White Company* (London 1891).

—— *Sir Nigel* (London, 1906).

DU BOULAY, F. R. H., *An Age of Ambition: English Society in the Late Middle Ages* (London, 1970).

DUBY, G., *France in the Middle Ages 987–1460*, J. Vale (trans.) (Oxford, 1991).

DU COLOMBIER, P., *Les Chantiers des cathédrales —ouvriers—architecture—sculpteurs* (1953; Paris, 1973).

DUFFY, C., *Siege Warfare: The Fortress in the Early-Modern World, 1494–1660* (London 1979).

DUMBRECK, W., 'The Lowry of Tonbridge', *Arch Cant* 72 (1958), 138–47.

DUNBABIN, J., *France in the Making 843–1180*, 2nd edn. (Oxford, 2000).

DYER, C., 'The Consumption of Fresh Water Fish in Medieval England', *Everyday Life in Medieval England* (London, 1994), ch. 6.

EALES, R., 'Castles and Politics in England, 1215–24', *Thirteenth Century England*, 2, P. Coss and S. Lloyd (eds.) (Woodbridge, 1988), 23–43 (repr. Liddiard, 2002).

—— 'Royal Power and Castles in Norman England', *MK* 3 (1990), 49–78 (repr. Liddiard, 2002).

EARNSHAW, W., *Discovering Castles* (London, 1953).

EDGE, J. and PADDOCK, J., *Arms and Armour of the Medieval Knight* (London, 1988).

EDINGTON, C., 'The Tournament in Medieval Scotland', *Armies, Chivalry and Warfare*, Strickland (ed.), 46–62.

EDWARDS, J. G., 'Edward I's Castle-Building in Wales', *PBA* 32 (1944), 15–81.

—— 'The Normans and the Welsh March', *PBA* 42 (1956), 155–77.

—— 'The Personnel of the Commons in Parliament under Edward I and Edward II', in *Historical Studies of the English Parliament*, E. Fryde and E. Miller (eds.) (Cambridge, 1970), i. 150–67.

ELLENBLUM, R., *Frankish Rural Settlement in the Latin Kingdom of Jerusalem* (Cambridge, 1998).

ELLIOT, H. and STOCKER, D., *Lincoln Castle Guide* (Lincoln, 1984).

ELTON, G., *England under the Tudors* (London, 1956).

—— (ed.) *The Tudor Constitution* (Cambridge, 1960).

EMDEN, W. VAN, 'The Castle in Some Works of Medieval French Literature', in *The Medieval Castle: Romance and Reality*, Reyerson and Powe (eds.), 1–26.

EMERY, A., *Greater Medieval Houses of England and Wales*: I, *Northern England*; II, *East Anglia, Central England and Wales*; III, *Southern England* (Cambridge, 1996, 2000, 2004).

ÉNAUD, F., *Les Châteaux-forts* (Paris, 1958).

ENGLISH, B., 'Towns, Mottes and Ringworks of the Conquest', in *Medieval Military Revolution*, Ayton and Price (eds.), 43–62.

ENGLISH, E., 'Urban Castles in Medieval Siena', in *The Medieval Castle: Romance and Reality*, Reyerson and Powe (eds.), 175–98.

ERVYNCK, A., 'Medieval Castles as Top Predators of the Feudal System: An Archaeozoological Approach', *Château Gaillard*, 15 (1992), 151–9.

EVANS, J., *English Art, 1307–1461* (Oxford, 1949).

—— *The Flowering of the Middle Ages* (London, 1966).

EVERSON, P., 'Goltho and Bullington', *Lincs. History and Archaeology*, 23 (1988), 93–9.

—— 'Bodiam Castle, East Sussex: Castle and its Designed Landscape', *Château Gaillard*, 17 (1996), 79–84.

——, BROWN, G., and STOCKER, D., 'The Castle Earthworks and Landscape Context', in *Ludgershall Castle*, P. Ellis (ed.) (Devizes, 2000), ch. 15.

FAULKNER, P., 'Domestic Planning From the Twelfth to the Fourteenth Century', *Arch J*, 115 (1958), 150–83.

—— 'Castle-Planning in the Fourteenth Century'], *Arch J*, 120 (1963), 215–35.

FAWTIER, R., *The Capetian Kings of France: Monarchy and Nation, 987–1328*, trans. R. Adams and L. Butler (London, 1960).

FEDDEN, R. and THOMSON, J., *Crusader Castles* (London, 1957).

FERNIE, E., *The Architecture of Norman England* (Oxford, 2000).

FILLON, A. (ed.), *Château et territoire: limites et mouvances*, Ire Rencontre Internationale d'Archéologie et d'Histoire en Périgord à Périgueux (Paris, 1995).

FINÓ, J.-F., *Forteresses de la France Médiévale* (Paris, 1970).

FITCHEN, J., *The Construction of Gothic Cathedrals: A Study of Medieval Vault Erection* (Oxford, 1961).

FIXOT, M., 'Les Fortifications de terre [et la naissance de la féodalité dans le Cinglais', *Château Gaillard*, 3 (1969), 61–6.

FLEMING, P., *Family and Household in Medieval England* (London, 2001).

FLETCHER, B., *A History of Architecture on the Comparative Method*, 17th edn. (London, 1961).

FORDE-JOHNSTON, J., *Castles and Fortifications of Britain and Ireland* (London, 1977).

FOURNIER, G., *Le Château dans la France Médiévale* (Paris, 1978).

FOURNIER, P. FR. and GUÉBIN, P. (eds.), see *Poitiers, Enquêtes administratives*.

FOWLER, G., 'Munitions in 1224', *Bedfordshire Historical Record Society*, 5 (1920), 117–32.

FOWLER, K., *The Age of Plantagenet and Valois: The Struggle for Supremacy, 1328–1498*, (London, 1967).

FRAME, R., 'Military Service in the Lordship of Ireland 1290–1360: Institutions of Society on the Anglo-Gaelic Frontier', in *Medieval Frontier Societies*, Bartlett and Mackay (eds.), ch. 5.

FRANKL, P., *Gothic Architecture* (Harmondsworth, 1962).

FREEDMAN, P., *The Image of the Medieval Peasant as Alien and Exemplary* (Stanford, 1999).

FRY, P. S., *The David and Charles Book of Castles*, (Newton Abbot, 1980).

FRYDE, N. *The Tyranny and Fall of Edward II* (Cambridge, 1979).

GAINES, B., 'Malory's Castles in Text and Illustration', in *The Medical Castle: Romance and Reality*, Reyerson and Powe (eds.), 215–27.

GANSHOF, F., *Feudalism*, trans. P. Grierson (London, 1952).

GARAUD, M., 'La Construction des châteaux et les destinées de la "vicaria" et du "vicarius" Carolingiens en Poitou', *RHDFE*, 4th ser. (1955), 54–78.

GARDELLES, J., *Les Châteaux du moyen-âge dans la France du sud-ouest: la Gascogne anglaise de 1216 à 1327* (Geneva, 1972).

GARDNER, S., 'The Influence of Castle-Building on Ecclesiastical Architecture in the Paris Region, 1130–50', in *The Medieval Castle: Romance and Reality*, Reyerson and Powe (eds.), 97–124.

GEBELIN, F., *The Châteaux of France*, trans. H. Hart (London, 1964).

GEE, L., 'Artistic Patronage by Women in England During the Reigns of Henry III and the Three Edwards, *c.*1216–1377', Ph.D thesis, Courtauld Institute of Art, University of London, 1998 (Woodbridge, forthcoming).

GEM, R., 'An Early Church of the Knights Templars at Shipley, Sussex', *ANS* 6 (1984), 238–46.

GILLINGHAM, J., *Richard the Lionheart* (London, 1978).

—— *The Wars of the Roses: Peace and Conflict in Fifteenth-Century England* (London, 1981).

—— 'Richard I and the Science of War in the Middle Ages', (1984), repr. in Strickland (ed.), *Anglo-Norman Warfare*, 194–207.

—— 'Warfare and Chivalry in the History of William the Marshal' (1988, repr. in *Anglo-Norman Warfare*, Strickland (ed.), 251–63.

—— 'William the Bastard at War' (1989), repr. in Strickland (ed.), *Anglo-Norman Warfare*, 143–60.

—— 'Thegns and Knights in Eleventh Century England: Who Was Then the Gentleman', *TRHS* 6: 5 (1995), 129–53.

—— 'Foundations of a Disunited Kingdom', in *Uniting the Kingdom*, Grant and Stringer (eds.), ch. 4.

GIMPEL, J., *The Medieval Machine: The Industrial Revolution of the Middle Ages* (London, 1976).

—— *The Cathedral Builders* (1980), trans. T. Waugh (Salisbury, 1983).

GIROUARD, M., *Life in the English Country House* (New Haven, 1978).

—— *The Victorian Country House*, enlarged edn. (London, 1979).

—— *The Return to Camelot* (London, 1981).

—— *Life in the French Country House* (London, 2000).

GIVEN-WILSON, C., *The English Nobility in the Late Middle Ages: The Fourteenth Century Community* (London, 1987).

—— and BUTLER, L., *Medieval Monasteries*, see Butler, L.

GODWIN, H., *The English Archaeologist's Handbook* (Oxford, 1867).

GOETZ, H.-W., 'Protection of the Church, Defence of the Law, and Reform: On the Purposes and Character of the Peace of God, 989–1038', in *Peace of God*, Head and Landes (eds.), 259–79.

GOLDING, W., *The Spire* (London, 1964).

GOODALL, J. A., 'When an Englishman's Castle Was His House', and 'The Battle for Bodiam Castle', *Country Life* (6 Apr., 1998), 68–71; (16 Apr. 1998), 58–63.

—— 'Little Wenham Hall, Suffolk', *Country Life* (6 July 2000), 127–31.

GOODMAN, A., 'The Defence of Northumberland: a Preliminary Survey', in *Armies, Chivalry and Warfare*, Strickland (ed.), 161–72.

GRANT, A. and STRINGER, K. (eds.), *Uniting the Kingdom: The Making of British History* (London, 1995).

GRANT, M., *Cities of Vesuvius* (London, 1971).

GREEN, J. A., *The Aristocracy of Norman England* (Cambridge, 1997).

GREEN, J. R., *A Short History of the English People* (1874); K. Norgate (ed.) (London, 1902).

GRIFFITHS, R., *The Reign of King Henry VI: The Exercise of Royal Authority, 1422–61* (London, 1981).

GROSE, F., *Military Antiquities Respecting a History of the British Army*, 2nd edn. (London, 1812), 2 vols.

HACKETT, J., 'Foreword' to Anderson, *Castles of Europe*, pp. 12–13.

HADCOCK, R. N., see Knowles, M. D. and Hadcock, R. N., *Religious Houses*.

HAGGER, M., *The Fortunes of a Norman Family: The de Verduns in England, Ireland and Wales, 1066–1316* (London, 2001).

HAJDU, R., 'Castles, Castellans and the Structure of Politics in Poitou, 1152–1271', *JMH* 4 (1978), 27–54.

HALL, M., 'Stokesay Castle, Shropshire', *Country Life* (31 Mar. 1994), 72–7.

HANAWALT, B., 'Violence in the Domestic Milieu of Late Medieval England', in *Violence in Medieval Society*, Kaeuper (ed.), ch. 11.

HANFMANN, G., *Roman Art* (London, 1964).

HARDY, R., 'The Longbow', in *Arms, Armies and Fortifications*, Curry and Hughes (eds.), 161–82.

HARPER-BILL, C., 'R. Allen Brown: A Personal Appreciation', in Harper-Bill *et al.* (eds.), *Studies Presented to R. A. Brown*, 1–5.

—— , HOLDSWORTH, C., and NELSON, J. (eds.), *Studies in Medieval History Presented to R. Allen Brown* (Woodbridge, 1989).

HARVEY, A., *The Castles and Walled Towns of England* (London, 1911).

HASKINS, C., *The Normans in European History* (1915; repr. New York, 1959).

—— *Norman Institutions* (1918; repr. New York, 1960).

HAY, D., *Europe in the Fourteenth and Fifteenth Centuries* (London, 1966).

HEAD, T. and LANDES, R., *The Peace of God: Social Violence and Religious Response in France Around the Year 1000* (Ithaca, NY, 1992).

HEARSEY, J., *The Tower: Eight Hundred and Eighty Years of English History* (London, 1960).

HÉLIOT, P., 'Le Château de Boulogne-sur-Mer et les châteaux gothiques de plan polygonal', *RA* 6th ser., 27 (1947), 41–59.

—— 'Sur les résidences princières bâties en France du 10ᵉ siècle au 12ᵉ siècle', *LMA* ser. 4, 10 (1955), 27–61, 291–319.

HERGÉ, *Les Aventures de Tintin: Le Sceptre d'Ottokar* (Tournai, 1947).

HERLIHY, D., *Medieval Households* (Cambridg, Mass., 1985).

—— (ed.), *The History of Feudalism* (London, 1970).

HESLOP, T. A., 'Orford Castle: Nostalgia and Sophisticated Living', *AH* 34 (1991), 36–58 (repr. Liddiard, 2002).

—— *Norwich Castle Keep: Romanesque Architecture and Social Context* (Norwich, 1994).

—— and GRLIC, O., *Twelfth-Century Castles and the Architecture of Romance* (in preparation).

HEWITT, H., *The Black Prince's Expedition of 1355–1357* (Manchester, 1958).

—— *The Organization of War Under Edward III* (Manchester, 1966).

HICKS, M., *Bastard Feudalism* (London, 1995).

HIGHAM, N. and JONES, G., 'Frontier Forts and Farmers: Cumbrian Aerial Survey, 1974–5', *Arch J*, 132 (1975), 16–53.

HIGHAM, R., 'Timber Castles: A Reassessment', *Fortress*, 1 (May 1989), 50–60 (repr. Liddiard, 2002).

—— see Barker, P., and Higham, R.

HIGOUNET, C., 'Bastides et frontières', *LMA* (1948), 113–21.

—— 'En Bordelais: "principes castella tenentes" ', in *La Noblesse au moyen-âge*, Contamine (ed.), ch. 3.

HILL, D. and RUMBLE, A. (eds.), *The Defence of Wessex*, (Manchester, 1996).

HILTON, R., 'Agrarian Class Structure and Economic Development', *Past and Present*, 80 (1978).

—— *English and French Towns in Feudal Society: A Comparative Study* (Cambridge, 1992).

HINSLEY, F. H., *Power and the Pursuit of Peace* (Cambridge, 1963).

HOGG, A., *Hill Forts of Britain* (London, 1975).

HOGG, I., *Fortress: A History of Military Defence* (London, 1975).

—— *The History of Forts and Castles* (London, 1981).

HOHLER, R. C., 'Court Life in Peace and War', in *Flowering of the Middle Ages*, Evans (ed.), ch. 4.

HOLLISTER, C. W., *Anglo-Saxon Military Institutions on the Eve of the Norman Conquest* (Oxford, 1962).

—— *The Military Organisation of Norman England* (Oxford, 1965).

—— 'The Campaign of 1102 Against Robert of Bellême', in *Studies Presented to R. A. Brown*, Harper-Bill *et al.* (eds.), 193–202.

HOLLISTER, C. W., 'The Aristocracy', in *Anarchy of King Stephen*, King (ed.), ch. 1.

HOLLYMAN, K., *'Le Développment du vocabulaire féodal en France pendant le haut moyen-âge* (Paris-Geneva, 1957).

HOLMES, G., *The Estates of the Higher Nobility in Fourteenth-Century England* (Cambridge, 1957).

HOLMES, M., *Proud Northern Lady: Lady Anne Clifford, 1590–1676* (1975; repr. Chichester, 1984).

HOLT, J., 'Philip Mark and the Shrievalty of Nottingham and Derbyshire in the Early Thirteenth Century', *Trans. Thoroton Soc. of Notts.*, 66 (1952), 8–24.

—— *The Northerners: A Study of the Reign of King John* (Oxford, 1961).

—— 'The Introduction of Knight Service in England', *ANS* 6 (1984), 89–106.

—— 'The Treaty of Winchester', in *Anarchy of King Stephen*, King (ed.), 291–316.

HOPE, W. ST. J., 'English Fortresses and Castles of the Tenth and Eleventh Centuries', *Arch J*, 60 (1903), 72–90.

—— *Windsor Castle: An Architectural History*, 3 vols. (London, 1913).

HOWARD, M., *The Early Tudor Country House: Architecture and Politics, 1490–1550* (London, 1987).

HOWELL, M., *Regalian Right in Medieval England* (London, 1962).

HUGHES, M., 'The Fourteenth Century French Raids on Hampshire and the Isle of Wight', in *Arms, Armies and Fortifications*, Curry and Hughes (eds.), 121–44.

—— see Curry, A. and Hughes, M. (eds.).

HUGHES, Q., 'Medieval Firepower', *Fortress*, 8 (Feb. 1991), 31–43.

HUNT, J., 'Lordship and Landscape: A Documentary and Archaeological Study of the Honor of Dudley, *c*.1066–1322', *BAR*, ser. 264 (1997).

HUNT, R., PANTIN, W., and SOUTHERN, R. (eds.), *Studies in Medieval History Presented to F. M. Powicke* (1948; rep. Oxford, 1969).

HUTCHINSON, H., *Edward II the Pliant King* (London, 1971).

JOHN, E., *Land Tenure in Early England* (Leicester, 1960).

JOHNS, C., *Criccieth Castle Guide* (London, 1970).

—— *Caerphilly Castle, Castell Caerfilli* (Cardiff, 1978).

JOHNSON, M., review of T. E. McNeill, *Castles in Ireland*, *Antiquity*, 72: 276 (1998), 460–1.

JOHNSON, S., *The Roman Forts of the Saxon Shore* (London, 1979).

JOLLIFFE, J., 'The Chamber and the Castle Treasuries Under King John, in *Studies Presented to F. M. Powicke*, Hunt *et al.* (eds.), 117–42.

—— *Angevin Kingship*, 2nd edn. (London, 1963).

JONES, M., *Ducal Brittany, 1364–1399: Relations With England and France During the Reign of Duke John IV* (Oxford, 1970).

—— 'Sir Thomas Dagworth et la Guerre Civile en Bretagne au xive Siècle: quelques documents inédits', *Annales de Bretagne*, 88 (1980), 621–39.

—— 'War and Fourteenth Century France', *Arms, Armies and Fortifications*, Curry and Hughes (eds.), 103–20.

—— (ed.), *Gentry and Lesser Nobility in Late Medieval France* (Gloucester, 1986).

—— 'Les Seigneurs de la Garnache et la fondation de L'Abbaye de l'Isle Chauvet', *Bulletin de la Société des Historiens du Pays de Retz* (1999), 83–92.

—— , MERION-JONES, G., GUIBAL, F., and PILCHER, J., 'The Seignorial Domestic Buildings of Brittany: A Provisional Assessment', *Ant J*, 69: 1 (1989), 73–110.

—— —— —— —— (eds.) *Manorial Domestic Buildings in England and Northern France*, SAL Occasional Papers 15 (1993).

JONES, P. and RENN, D., 'The Military Effectiveness of Arrow Loops: Some Experiments at White Castle', *Château Gaillard*, 9–10 (1982), 445–56.

JONES, T., *Ashby de la Zouche Castle Guide* (London, 1953).

JOPE, E. (ed.), *Studies in Building History: Essays in Recognition of B. H. St. J. O'Neil* (London, 1961).

KAEUPER, R., 'Law and Order in Fourteenth-Century England: The Evidence of Special Inquisitions of Oyer and Terminer', *Speculum*, 54 (1979), 734–84.

—— *War, Justice and Public Order* (Oxford, 1988).

—— (ed.), *Violence in Medieval Society* (Woodbridge, 2000), 'Introduction'.

KAPELLE, W., *The Norman Conquest of the North: The Region and its Transformation, 1000–1135* (London, 1979).

KEATS-ROHAN, K., 'The Bretons and Normans of England, 1066–1154: The Family, the Fief and the Feudal Monarchy', *NMS* 36 (1992), 42–78.

—— 'The Continental Origins of English Landholders, 1066–1220 Project', *MP* 14: 2 (1993), 121–37.

KEEN, M., *The Laws of War in the Late Middle Ages* (London, 1965).

—— *The Outlaws of Medieval Legend*, rev. edn. (London, 1977).

KENNEDY, H., *Crusader Castles* (Cambridge, 1994).

KENYON, J., *Castles, Town Defences and Artillery Fortifications in Britain and Ireland: A Bibliography*, vol. 3; CBA Research Report no. 72 (London, 1990).

—— *Medieval Fortifications* (Leicester, 1990).

—— 'Coastal Artillery Fortification in England in the Late Fourteenth and Early Fifteenth Centuries', in *Arms, Armies and Fortifications*, Curry and Hughes (eds.), 145–9.

—— 'Fluctuating Frontiers: Normanno-Welsh Castle-Warfare, c.1075 to 1240', *Château Gaillard*, 17 (1996), 119–26.

—— and THOMPSON, M., 'The Origin of the Word "Keep" ', *MA* 38 (1994), 175–6.

KIGHTLY, C., *Strongholds of the Realm* (London, 1979).

KIMBAL, E., *Sergeanty Tenure in Medieval England* (New Haven, 1936).

KING, D., 'The Taking of Le Krak des Chevaliers in 1271', *Antiquity*, 90 (1949), 83–92.

—— 'Llangibby Castle', *Arch Camb* (1956), 96–132.

—— 'The Trébuchet and Other Siege-Engines', *Château Gaillard*, 9–10 (1982), 457–70.

—— *Castellarium Anglicanum: An Index and Bibliography of the Castles in England, Wales and the Islands*, 2 vols. (New York, 1983).

—— *The Castle in England and Wales: An Interpretative History* (London, 1988).

—— and ALCOCK, L., 'Ringworks of England and Wales', *Château Gaillard*, 3 (1969), 90–127.

—— —— 'The Field Archaeology of Mottes in England and Wales', *Château Gaillard*, 5 (1972), 101–17.

KING, E., 'The Abbot of Peterborough as Landlord: A Study in the Thirteenth-Century Land Market', unpubl. diss., 1966, University of Cambridge.

—— 'King Stephen and the Anglo-Norman Aristocracy', *History*, 59 (1974), 180–94.

—— (ed.), *The Anarchy of King Stephen's Reign*, 'Introduction' (Oxford, 1994).

—— *King Stephen* (forthcoming, New Haven).

KNOLL, P., 'Economic and Political Institutions on the Polish–German Frontier in the Middle Ages: Action, Reaction, Interaction', in *Medieval Frontier Societies*, Bartlett and Mackay (eds.), ch. 7.

KNOOP, D. and JONES, G., *The Medieval Mason* (Manchester, 1949).

KNOWLES, M. D., *The Monastic Order in England, 940–1216*, (1940; 2nd edn. Cambridge, 1963).

KNOWLES, M. D., *The Historian and Character and Other Essays* (Cambridge, 1963).

—— and HADCOCK, R. N., *Medieval Religious Houses in England and Wales*, 2nd edn. (London, 1971).

LABARGE, M. W., *A Baronial Household of the Thirteenth Century* (London, 1965).

—— *Gascony: England's First Colony, 1204–1453* (London, 1980).

LADURIE, E. LE R., *Montaillou: Cathars and Catholics in a French Village, 1294–1324*, trans. and ed. B. Hay (London, 1978).

LANDES, R., see Head, T. and Landes, R.

LANDSBERG, S., *The Medieval Garden* (London, 1996).

LANGLOIS, C., *Le Règne de Philippe III Le Hardi* (Paris, 1887).

LARSON, G., *The Far Side Gallery* 2 (London, 1989).

LARTIGAUT, J., 'Entre deux courtines de châteaux: une frontière entre Périgord et Quercy au moyen âge?', *Château et Territoire*, Fillon (ed.), 43–63.

LASDUN, S., *The English Park: Royal, Private and Public* (London, 1991).

LATHAM, R. (ed.), *Revised Medieval Latin Word List* (Oxford, 1965).

LAURENT, C., *L'Atlas des Châteaux-forts en France* (Strasburg, 1977).

LAWRENCE, A., *Greek Aims in Fortification* (Oxford, 1979).

LAWRENCE, T. E., *Crusader Castles*, 2 vols. (London, 1936).

LEAH, M., MATTHEWS, M., and DAVISON, A., 'A survey of the Earthworks at Hills and Holes Plantation, Marham (Norfolk)', *NA* 42 (1997), 506–11.

LEASK, H., *Irish Castles and Castellated Houses* (Dundalk, 1951).

Leeds Castle, Kent (Guide), Leeds Castle Foundation (London, 1994).

LE MAHO, J., 'De la Curtis au château: l'exemple du Pays de Caux', *Château Gaillard*, 8 (1977), 171–83.

—— 'Fortification de siège et "contre-châteaux" en Normandie (xiᵉ–xiiᵉ siècles)', *Château Gaillard*, 19 (2000), 181–7.

LENNARD, R., *Rural England 1086–1135: A Study of Social and Agrarian Conditions* (Oxford, 1959).

LE PATOUREL, H. E. J., 'Fortified and Semi-Fortified Manor Houses', *Château Gaillard*, 9–10 (1982), 187–98.

LE PATOUREL, J., *The Norman Empire* (Oxford, 1976).

LESLIE, M. 'An English Landscape Garden Before "the English Landscape Garden"?', *JGH* 13 (1993), 3–15.

LEWIS, C. S., *The Allegory of Love: A Study in Medieval Tradition* (Oxford, 1938).

LEWIS, N., 'The Organization of Indentured Retainers in Fourteenth-Century England', repr. in *Essays in Medieval History*, Southern (ed.) (London, 1968).

LEWIS, P., *Later Medieval France: The Polity* (London, 1968).

LEYSER, H., *Medieval Women: A Social History of Women in England, 450–1500* (London, 1995).

LIDDIARD, R., 'Castle Rising, Norfolk: A "Landscape of Lordship"?', *ANS* 22 (1999), 169–86.

—— *Landscapes of Lordship: Norman Castles and the Countryside in Medieval Norfolk, 1066–1200*, BAR, no. 309 (2000).

—— (ed.) and Introduction, *Anglo Norman Castles* (reprinted essays), (Woodbridge, 2002).

LOCKE, JOHN, *Two Treatises of Government* (1691), P. Laslett (ed.) (Cambridge, 1960).

LOTT, B., see Dixon, P. and Lott, B.

LUTZ, D., 'Territoire et protection des frontières. Quelques exemples des xivᵉ et xvᵉ siècles dans le sud-ouest de L'Allemagne', *Château et Territoire*, Fillon (ed.), 73–92.

Lyon, B., *From Fief to Indenture: The Transition from Feudal to Non-feudal Contract in Western Europe* (Cambridge, Mass., 1957).

McAuliffe, M., 'The Lady in the Tower: the Social and Political Rôle of Women in Tower Houses', in *Medieval Irishwomen*, Meek and Simms (eds.), 153–62.

Macdonald, D. (ed.) *Hoofed Mammals* (New York, 1984).

McFarlane, K., *The Nobility of Later Medieval England: The Ford Lectures for 1953 and Related Studies* (Oxford, 1973).

MacGibbon, T. and Ross, D., *The Castellated and Domestic Architecture of Scotland From the Twelfth to the Eighteenth Century*, 5 vols. (Edinburgh, 1887–92).

McKechnie, W., *Magna Carta: A Commentary on the Great Charter of King John* (Glasgow, 1905).

Mackenzie, A., 'French Medieval Castles in Gothic Manuscript Painting', in *The Medieval Castle: Romance and Reality*, Reyerson and Powe (eds.), 199–214.

Mackenzie, J., *The Castles of England: Their Story and Structure*, 2 vols. (London, 1897).

Mackenzie, W. M., *The Medieval Castle in Scotland* (London, 1927).

Mackrell, J., *The Attack on 'Feudalism' in Eighteenth-Century France* (London, 1973).

McKisack, M., *The Fourteenth Century 1307–1399* (Oxford, 1959).

MacMullen, R., *Soldier and Civilian in the Later Roman Empire* (Cambridge, Mass., 1963).

McNamee, C., *The Wars of the Bruces* (London, 1997).

McNeill, T., 'Hibernia Paccata et Castellata', *Château Gaillard*, 14 (1990), 261–75 (repr. Liddiard, 2002).

—— *English Heritage Book of Castles* (London, 1992).

—— 'Castles of Ward and the Changing Pattern of Border Conflict in Ireland', *Château Gaillard*, 17 (1996), 127–33.

—— *Castles in Ireland: Feudal Power in a Gaelic World* (London, 1997).

Magnou-Nortier, E., 'The Enemies of the Peace: Reflections on a Vocabulary, 500–1100', in Head and Landes (eds.), *Peace of God*, 58–79.

Maitland, F., *Domesday Book and Beyond* (1897), repr. with introd. by E. Miller (Cambridge, 1960).

—— *The Constitutional History of England* (Cambridge, 1908).

Manning, C., 'Dublin Castle: The Building of a Royal Castle in Ireland', *Château Gaillard*, 18 (1998), 119–22.

Marcus, G., *A Naval History of England*, vols. 1, 2 (London, 1961, 1971).

Marsden, E., *Greek and Roman Artillery*, 2 vols. (Oxford, 1969, 1971).

Marshall, C., *Warfare in the Latin East 1192–1291* (Cambridge, 1992).

Marshall, P., 'Magna Turris: An Enquiry into the Function of the Great Tower in the Territories of the Norman and Angevin Kings during the 11th and 12th Centuries', Ph.D. thesis (forthcoming), University of Nottingham.

—— see Dixon, P. and Marshall P.

—— and Samuels, J., *Guardian of the Trent: The Story of Newark Castle* (Newark, 1997).

Martène, E., and Durand, U. (eds.), see *Amplissima Collectio; Thesaurus Novus*.

Martin, C., *The Record Interpreter*, 2nd edn. (London, 1910).

Martin, D., 'Glottenham Manor, Sussex', *MA* 12 (1968), 195–6; 13 (1969), 273–4; 14 (1970), 194; 16 (1972), 195–6.

Martindale, J., ' "His Special Friend"? The Settlement of Disputes and Political Power in the Kingdom of the French (Tenth to mid-Eleventh Century)', *TRHS*, 6 ser., 5 (1995), 21–57.

Mason, D., 'The Roman Site at Heronbridge Near Chester: Aspects of Civilian Settlement in the Vicinity of Legionary Fortresses in Britain and Beyond', *Arch J*, 145 (1988), 123–57.

MASSCHAELE, J., 'Market Rights in Thirteenth-Century England', *EHR* 107 (1992), 78–89.

MATE, M., *Women in Medieval English Society* (Cambridge, 1999).

MATHIEU, J., 'New Methods on Old Castles: Generating New Ways of Seeing', *MA* 43 (1999), 115–42.

MAYER, H., *The Crusades*, trans. J. Gillingham (Oxford, 1972).

MEEK, C. and SIMMS, K. (eds.), *'The Fragility of Her Sex'? Medieval Irishwomen in their European Context* (Dublin, 1996).

MEIRION-JONES, G. and JONES, M. (eds.), *Manorial Domestic Buildings in England and Northern France* (London, 1993).

MEISS, M., *French Painting in the Time of Jean de Berry*, 2 vols. (London, 1967).

MESQUI, J., 'Les Enceintes de Crécy-en-Brie et la fortification dans l'ouest du comté de Champagne et de Brie au xiiiᵉ siècle', *Mémoires publiés par la Fédération des Sociétés Historiques et Archéologiques de Paris et de l'Ile de France*, 30 (1979) 7–86.

—— 'Maisons, maisons-fortes ou châteaux: les implantations nobles dans le comté de Valois aux xiiiᵉ et xivᵉ siècles', in *La Maison-forte au moyen-âge*, Bur (ed.), pp. 185–214.

—— *Châteaux et enceintes de la France médiévale: de la défense à la résidence*, 2 vols. (Paris, 1992–3).

—— 'Le Château de Crépy-en-Valois: palais comtal, palais royal, palais féodal, *BM* 152: 3 (1994), 257–312.

—— *Châteaux-forts et fortifications en France* (Paris, 1997).

—— and RIBÉRA-PERVILLÉ, C., 'Les Châteaux de Louis d'Orléans et leurs architectes (1391–1407)', *BM* 138: 3 (1980), 293–345.

MEULEMEESTER, J. DE, 'Les *Castra* Carolingiens comme élément de développement urbain: quelques suggestions archéo—topographiques', *Château Gaillard*, 14 (1990), 95–114.

MEYER, W., 'Burgenbau und Herrschaftsbildung zwischen Alpen und Rhein im Zeitalter der salischen Herrscher', in *Burgen der Salierzeit*, Böhme, H. (ed.), ii. 303–30.

MILLER, M., *The Bishop's Palace: Architecture and Authority in Medieval Italy* (Ithaca, NY, 2000).

MILLINGEN, A. VAN, *Byzantine Constantinople: The Walls of the City and Adjoining Historical Sites* (London, 1899).

Moated Sites/Settlements Research Group Reports, National Monuments Record (London, 1973–   ).

MOLIN, K., 'The Non-Military Functions of Crusader Fortifications 1187–c.1380', *JMH* 23: 4 (1997), 367–88.

MONCREIFFE, I. and POTTINGER, D., *Simple Heraldry* (London, 1953).

MONREAL Y TEJADA, L., *Medieval Castles of Spain*, English edn. (Cologne, 1999).

MOORE, J., 'Anglo-Norman Garrisons', *ANS* 22 (2000), 205–59.

MORGANSTERN, A., *Gothic Tombs of Kinship in France, the Low Countries and England* (Philadelphia, 2000).

MORILLO, S., *Warfare Under the Anglo-Norman Kings, 1066–1135* (Woodbridge, 1994).

MORLEY, B., 'Hylton Castle', *Arch J*, 133 (1976), 118–34.

—— 'Aspects of Fourteenth-Century Castle Design', in *Collectanea Historica*, Detsicas (ed.), 104–13.

MORRIS, R., *Cathedrals and Abbeys of England and Wales* (London, 1979).

MORRIS, R. K., 'The Architecture of the Earls of Warwick in the Fourteenth Century', in *England in the Fourteenth Century*, Ormrod, W. (ed.), 161–79.

—— 'The Architecture of Arthurian Enthusiasm: Castle Symbolism in the Reigns of Edward I and his Successors', in *Arms, Chivalry and Warfare*, Strickland (ed.), 63–81.

MORRIS, W., *The Medieval English Sheriff to 1300* (1927; repr. Manchester, 1968).

MORRISON, S. and COMMAGER, H., *The Growth of the American Republic*, 4th edn., 2 vols. (Oxford, 1958).

MORTIMER, R., *Angevin England 1154–1258* (Oxford, 1994).

MOWL, T. and EARNSHAW, B., *Trumpet at a Distant Gate: The Lodge as Prelude to the Country House* (London, 1985).

MUIR, R., *Castles and Strongholds* (London, 1990).

MÜLLER-WIENER, W., *Castles of the Crusaders* (London, 1966).

MUMMENHOF, K., *Wasserburgen in Westfalen* (Berlin/Munich, 1958).

—— *Schlösser und Herrensitze in Westfalen* (Frankfurt-am-Main, 1961).

NEVILLE, C., *The Anglo-Scottish Borderland in the Later Middle Ages* (Edinburgh, 1998).

NICHOLAS, D., *The Later Medieval City* (London, 1997).

NICHOLAS, K., 'When Feudal Ideals Failed', in *The Rusted Hauberk*, Purdon and Vitto (eds.), pp. 201–26.

NICHOLSON, R., *Edward III and the Scots: The Formative Years of a Military Career, 1327–1335* (Oxford, 1965).

OAKLEY, F., *The Crucial Centuries: The Medieval Experience* (London, 1979).

OAKSHOTT, R. E., *The Archaeology of Weapons: Arms and Armour from Prehistory To the Age of Chivalry* (London, 1960).

—— *A Knight and his Castle* (London, 1965).

O'CONOR, K., *The Archaeology of Medieval Rural Settlement in Ireland* (Dublin, 1998).

O'KEEFE, T., 'Ballyloughan, Ballymoon and Clonmore: Three Castles of c.1300 in County Carlow', *ANS* 23 (2001), 167–97.

—— 'Ethnicity and Moated Settlement in Medieval Ireland: A Review of Current Thinking', *MSRG Report*, 15 (2000), 21–5.

OMAN, C., 'Security in English Churches, AD 1000–1548', *Arch J*, 136 (1979), 90–8.

OMAN, C., *The Art of War in the Middle Ages*, 2nd edn., 2 vols. (London, 1924).

—— *Castles* (London, 1926).

O'NEIL, B. *Castles* (London, HMSO, 1954).

—— *Castles and Cannon: A Study of Early Artillery Fortifications in England* (Oxford, 1960).

ORME, N., *Medieval Children* (New Haven, 2001).

ORMROD, W. (ed.), *England in the Fourteenth Century*, Proceedings of the 1985 Harlaxton Symposium (Woodbridge, 1980).

—— 'The Domestic Response to the Hundred Years War', in *Arms, Armies and Fortifications*, Curry and Hughes (eds.), 83–101.

ORR, P., 'Men's Theory and Women's Reality: Rape Prosecutions in the English Royal Courts of Justice, 1194–1222', in *The Rusted Hauberk*, Purdon and Vitto (eds.), ch. 6.

PAINTER, S., *The Reign of King John* (Baltimore, 1949).

—— *Feudalism and Liberty: Articles and Addresses of Sidney Painter* (Baltimore, 1961) (pp. 144–56 repr. Liddiard, 2002).

PARKER, J., *A Glossary of Terms Used in Grecian, Roman and Gothic Architecture*, 5th edn., 3 vols. (Oxford, 1850).

—— and TURNER, T., *Some Account of Domestic Architecture in England . . . From the Conquest to Henry VIII*, 3 vols. in 4 (Oxford, 1851–9).

PARTINGTON, J., *A History of Greek Fire and Gunpowder* (Cambridge, 1960).

PAYNE-GALLWEY, R., *The Crossbow: Medieval and Modern Military and Sporting* (1903; repr. London, 1958).

PERKIN, H., *The Origins of Modern English Society 1780–1880* (London, 1969).

PERROY, E., *The Hundred Years War*, trans. B. Wells (London, 1959).

PESEZ, J-M., PIPPONIER, F., 'Les Maisons-fortes bourguignonnes', *Château Gaillard*, 5 (1972), 143–64.

PETIT-DUTAILLIS, C., *The Feudal Monarchy in France and England*, trans. B. Hart (London, 1936).

PETTIFER, A., *English Castles: A Guide by Counties* (Woodbridge, 1995).

PEVSNER, N., *Pioneers of Modern Design* (London, 1960).

PHILP, B., *The Excavation of the Roman Forts of the Classis Britannica at Dover 1970–77* (Maidstone, 1981).

PIRENNE, H., *Economic and Social History of Medieval Europe*, trans. I. Clegg (London, 1936).

PITTE, D., *Château Gaillard dans la défense de la Normandie orientale, 1196–1204*, ANS 24 (2002, forthcoming).

PLATT, C., *The English Medieval Town* (London, 1976).

—— *Medieval England: A Social History and Archaeology from the Conquest to 1600* (London, 1978).

—— *The Castle in Medieval England and Wales* (London, 1982).

PLUCKNETT, T., *The Legislation of Edward I*, 2nd edn. (Oxford, 1962).

POOLE, A. L., *Obligations of Society in the Twelfth and Thirteenth Centuries* (Oxford, 1945).

—— *From Domesday Book to Magna Carta* (Oxford, 1955).

—— (ed.), *Medieval England*, 2 vols., 2nd edn. (Oxford, 1958).

POUNDS, N., 'The Duchy Palace at Lostwithiel, Cornwall', *Arch J*, 136 (1979), 203–17.

—— *The Medieval Castle in England and Wales: A Social and Political History* (Cambridge, 1990).

—— 'The Chapel in the Castle', *Fortress*, 9 (May 1991), 12–19.

POWER, D., 'What Did the Frontier of Angevin Normandy Comprise?' *ANS* 17 (1995), 181–201.

POWER, E., 'The Position of Women', in *The Legacy of the Middle Ages*, C. Crump and E. Jacob (eds.) (Oxford, 1926), 402–33.

POWICKE, F. *Henry III and the Lord Edward: The Community of the Realm in the Thirteenth Century*, 2 vols. (Oxford, 1947).

—— *The Thirteenth Century*, 2nd edn. (Oxford, 1954).

—— *The Loss of Normandy*, 2nd edn. (Manchester, 1960).

POWICKE, M., *Military Obligation in Medieval England: A Study in Liberty and Duty* (Oxford, 1962).

PRESTWICH, M., *The Three Edwards: War and State in England, 1272–1377* (London, 1980).

—— 'English Castles in the Reign of Edward II', *JMH* 9 (1982), 159–78.

—— *Armies and Warfare in the Middle Ages: The English Experience* (New Haven, 1996).

—— *Edward I*, 2nd edn. (New Haven, 1997).

—— 'The Garrisoning of English Medieval Castles', in *The Normans and Their Adversaries at War*, R. Abels and B. Bachrach (eds.) (Woodbridge, 2001), 180–200.

—— see Brown, R. A., Coulson, C., and Prestwich, M. *et al. Castles.*

PREVITÉ-ORTON, C., *The Shorter Cambridge Medieval History*, 2 vols. (Cambridge, 1962).

PRICE, J., 'A State Dedicated to War? The Dutch Republic in the Seventeenth Century', in *Medieval Military Revolution*, Ayton and Price (eds.), pp. 183–200.

PRINGLE, D., *The Red Tower: Settlement in the Plain of Sharon in the Time of the Crusaders and Mamluks, A.D. 1099–1516*, British School of Archaeology in Jerusalem (London, 1986).

—— 'Crusader Castles: The First Generation', *Fortress*, 1 (May 1989), 14–25.

—— *Secular Buildings in the Crusader Kingdom of Jerusalem* (Cambridge, 1997).

PUGH, R., *Imprisonment in Medieval England* (Cambridge, 1968).

PUGH, T. (ed.), *Glamorgan County History* : III, *The Middle Ages* (Cardiff, 1971).

PURDON, L. and VITTO, C. (eds.), *The Rusted Hauberk: Feudal Ideals of Order and Their Decline* (Gainesville, Fla., 1994).

PURSER, T., 'William Fitz-Osbern, Earl of Hereford: Personality and Power on the Welsh Frontier, 1066–71', in *Armies, Chivalry and Warfare*, Strickland (ed.), 133–46.

RADFORD, C. A. R., *Strata Florida Abbey Guide* (repr. HMSO, 1962).

—— 'The Later Pre-Conquest Boroughs and their Defences', *MA* 14 (1970), 83–103.

RAMM, H., McDOWALL, R., and MERCER, E., *Shielings and Bastles* (HMSO, 1971).

RASKELL, J., CLARK, L., and RAWCLIFFE, C. (eds.), *The House of Commons, 1386–1421* (Stroud, 1993).

REES, W., *Caerphilly Castle and its Place in the Annals of Glamorgan* (1937; rev. edn. Caerphilly, 1971).

RENN, D., *Norman Castles in Britain* (London, 1968).

—— 'The Avranches Traverse at Dover Castle', *Arch Cant*, 84 (1969), 79–92.

—— 'Tonbridge and some other Gatehouses', in *Collectanea Historica*, A. Detsicas (ed.), 93–103.

—— 'Burhgeat and Gonfanon: Two Sidelights from the Bayeux Tapestry', *ANS* 16 (1994), 178–98 (repr. Liddiard, 2002).

—— , see Jones, P. and Renn, D.

REUTER, T., 'The Making of England and Germany 850–1050: Points of Comparison and Difference', in *Medieval Europeans*, Smyth (ed.), ch. 3.

REYERSON, K. and POWE, F. (eds.), *The Medieval Castle: Romance and Reality* (Dubuque, Iowa, 1984).

REYNOLDS, S., *An Introduction to the History of English Medieval Towns* (Oxford, 1977).

—— *Kingdoms and Communities in Western Europe, 900–1300* (1984; 2nd edn. Oxford, 1997).

—— *Fiefs and Vassals: the Medieval Evidence Reinterpreted* (Oxford, 1994).

RICHARD, J., 'Châteaux, châtelains et vassaux en Bourgogne aux xie et xiie siècles', *CCM* 3 (1960), 433–47.

RICHARDSON, H., review of Brown *et al.*, *The History of the King's Works*, EHR 80 (1965), 553–6.

RICHMOND, I., 'Roman Timber Building', in *Studies in Building History*, Jope (ed.), 15–26.

RICHTER, M., 'National Identity in Medieval Wales', in *Medieval Europeans*, Smyth (ed.), 71–84.

RICKERT, M., *Painting in Britain in the Middle Ages* (London, 1965).

RICKMAN, T., *An Attempt to Discriminate the Styles of Architecture in England* (1819; repr. Oxford, 1848).

RIGOLD, S., 'Presidential Address', *BNAJ* 44 (1974), 101–6.

RITTER, R., *Châteaux, donjons et places fortes: l'architecture militaire française* (Paris, 1953).

ROFFE, D., *Domesday: The Inquest and the Book* (Oxford, 2000).

ROGERS, C., 'Edward III and Dialectics of Strategy, 1327–60', *TRHS* 6 ser., 4 (1994), 83–102.

RÖRIG, F., *The Medieval Town* (rev. edn., Göttingen, 1955; trans. London, 1967).

ROSENTAL, J., *The Purchase of Paradise: Gift-Giving and the Aristocracy, 1307–1485* (London, 1972).

ROSENWEIN, B., *Negotiating Space: Power, Restraint and Privileges of Immunity in Early Medieval Europe* (Manchester, 1999).

ROUND, J. H., *Geoffrey de Mandeville* (London, 1892).

—— anon. review of G. T. Clark *Military Architecture, Quarterly Review*, 179 (July, Oct. 1894), 27–57.

—— *Feudal England*, F. Stenton (ed.), (London, 1964).

—— 'The Castles of the Conquest', *Archaeologica*, 58 (1902), 313–40.

ROWLANDS, I., 'King John, Stephen Langton and Rochester Castle 1213–15', in *Studies Presented to R. A. Brown*, Harper-Bill *et al.* (eds.) 267–79.

RUNCIMAN, S., *A History of the Crusades*, 3 vols. (Cambridge, 1951–5).

—— *The Fall of Constantinople 1453* (Cambridge, 1965).

SALZMAN, L., *Building in England Down to 1540*, (1952; 2nd edn. Oxford, 1967).

SAMSON, R., 'Knowledge, Constraint and Power in Inaction: the Defenseless Medieval Wall', *Historical Archaeology*, 26 (1992), 26–44.

SANDERS, I., *English Baronies: A Study of their Origins and Descent, 1086–1327* (Oxford, 1960).

SAUL, N., *Knights and Esquires: The Gloucestershire Gentry in the Fourteenth Century* (Oxford, 1981).

—— *Scenes from Provincial Life: Knightly Families in Sussex, 1280–1400* (Oxford, 1986).

—— 'Bodiam Castle', *History Today*, 45 (Jan. 1995), 16–21.

—— (ed.), *Age of Chivalry: Art and Society in Late Medieval England* (London, 1992).

—— (ed.), *Fourteenth Century England* (Woodbridge, 2000).

SAUNDERS, A., 'Five Castle Excavations: Reports on the Institute's Research Project into the Origins of the Castle in England', *Arch J*, 134 (1977), 1–156.

—— 'Lydford Castle, Devon', *MA* 24 (1980), 123–86.

SCHOFIELD, J., *Medieval London Houses* (New Haven, 1995).

—— and VINCE, A., *Medieval Towns* (Leicester, 1994).

SCOTT, WALTER, *Quentin Durward* (Edinburgh, 1886–7).

SEKULES, V., 'Women's Piety and Patronage', in *Age of Chivalry*, Saul (ed.), 120–31.

SELLAR, W., and YEATMAN, J., *1066 and All That* (London, 1930).

SHELBY, L., *John Rogers: Tudor Military Engineer* (Oxford, 1967).

SHENNAN, J., *The Parlement of Paris* (new edn., London, 1998).

SHERBORNE, J., *War, Politics and Culture in Fourteenth-Century England*, collected essays, A. Tuck (ed.), (London, 1994).

SIMPSON, W. D., 'Dunstanburgh Castle', *Archaeologia Aeliana*, 16 (1939), 31–42.

—— 'The Castles of Dudley and Ashby-de-la-Zouche', *Arch J*, 96 (1939), 142–58.

—— 'Bastard Feudalism and the Later Castles', *Ant J*, 26 (1946) 145–71.

—— *Bothwell Castle Guide* (Edinburgh, 1958).

—— 'The Tower-Houses of Scotland', in *Studies in Building History*, Jope (ed.), 229–42.

SIMMS, K., 'Bards and Barons: The Anglo-Irish Aristocracy and the Native Culture', in *Medieval Frontier Societies*, Bartlett and Mackay (eds.), ch. 8.

—— , see Meek, C. and Simms, K.

SMAIL, R. C., *Crusading Warfare (1097–1199)* (1st edn., Cambridge, 1956).

—— *The Crusaders in Syria and the Holy Land* (London, 1973).

SMITH, B., *Conquest and Colonisation in Medieval Ireland: The English in Louth, 1170–1330*, (Cambridge, 1999).

SMYTH, A., *Alfred the Great* (Oxford, 1996).

—— (ed.) *Medieval Europeans: Studies in Ethnic Identity and National Perspectives in Medieval Europe* (London, 1998).

SOUTHERN, R., *The Making of the Middle Ages* (London, 1958).

SPEIGHT, S., 'Four More English Medieval "Castle" Sites in Nottinghamshire', *Trans. Thoroton Soc. of Notts.*, 99 (1995), 65–72.

—— 'Castle Warfare in the *Gesta Stephani*', *Château Gaillard*, 19 (1998), 269–74.

STALLEY, R., 'A Twelfth-Century Patron of Architecture: A Study of the Buildings Erected by Roger, bishop of Salisbury 1102–39', in *Ireland and Europe in the Middle Ages: Selected Essays on Architecture and Sculpture* (London, 1994).

STEANE, J., *Archaeology of the Medieval English Monarchy* (London, 1993).

—— *The Archaeology of Power* (Stroud, 2001).

STENTON, D., 'King John and the Courts of Justice', *PBA* 44 (1958), 103–28.

STENTON, F., *Anglo-Saxon England* (Oxford, 1947).

—— *The First Century of English Feudalism, 1066–1166* (1932; 3rd edn., Oxford, 1961).

—— (ed.), see Round, J. H., *Feudal England*.

—— (ed.), *The Bayeux Tapestry: A Comprehensive Survey* (rev. edn., London, 1965).

STEPHENSON, C., 'The Origin and Significance of Feudalism', *AmHR* 46 (1941), 788–812.

STOCKER, D., 'The Shadow of the General's Armchair', review, *Arch J*, 149 (1992), 415–20.

—— , see Elliott, H. and Stocker, D.

STONES, E. L. G., 'The Folvilles of Ashby-Folville, Leicestershire and their Associates in Crime, 1326–47', *TRHS* 5 ser., 7 (1957), 117–36.

STOUT, M., *The Irish Ringfort* (Dublin, 1997).

STRAITH, H., *A Treatise on Fortification* (London, 1836).

STRICKLAND, M., 'Securing the North: Invasion and the Strategy of Defence in Twelfth-Century Anglo-Norman Warfare', in *Anglo-Norman Warfare*, 208–29.

—— *War and Chivalry* (Cambridge, 1996).

—— 'A Law of Arms or a Law of Treason? Conduct in War in Edward I's Campaigns in Scotland 1296–1307', in *Violence in Medieval Society*, Kaeuper (ed.), ch. 3.

—— (ed.), *Anglo-Norman Warfare* (Woodbridge, 1992).

—— (ed.), *Armies, Chivalry and Warfare in Medieval Britain and France*, Proceedings of the 1995 Harlaxton Symposium (Stamford, 1998).

STRONG, R., *The Elizabethan Image: Painting in England, 1540–1620*, Exhibition Catalogue, The Tate Gallery (London, 1969).

SUMMERSON, H. R., 'The Structure of Law Enforcement in Thirteenth-Century England', *AJLH* 23 (1979), 313–27.

SUMMERSON, H., TRUEMAN, M., and HARRISON, S., *Brougham Castle, Cumbria* (Kendal, 1998).

SUPPE, F., 'The Garrisoning of Oswestry: A Baronial Castle on the Welsh Marches', in *The Medieval Castle: Romance and Reality*, Reyerson and Powe (eds.), 63–78.

—— , 'The Persistence of Castle-Guard in the Welsh Marches and Wales: Suggestions for a Research Agenda and Methodology', in *The Normans and Their Adversaries at War*, Abels, R. and Bachrach, B. (eds.) (Woodbridge, 2001), 201 ff.

SUTHERLAND, D., *Quo Warranto Proceedings in the Reign of Edward I, 1278–1294* (Oxford, 1963).

SWAAN, W., *Art and Architecture of the Late Middle Ages: 1350 to the Advent of the Renaissance* (London, 1977).

SWEETMAN, D., *The Medieval Castles of Ireland* (Woodbridge, 1999).

TAIT, A.J., *The Medieval English Borough* (Manchester, 1936).

TAWNEY, R., *Religion and the Rise of Capitalism* (London, 1926).

TAYLOR, A., 'Military Architecture', in *Medieval England*, Poole (ed.), 98–127.

—— , see Brown, R. A., Colvin, H., and Taylor, A.

TAYLOR, C., 'Medieval Ornamental Landscapes', *Landscapes*, 1 (2000), 38–55.

THOMPSON, A. H., *Military Architecture in England during the Middle Ages* (Oxford, 1912).

THOMPSON, K., 'The Counts of Perche, c.1066–1217', unpubl. Ph.D thesis, University of Sheffield, 1995.

—— 'Lords, Castellans, Constables and Dowagers: The Rape of Pevensey From the Eleventh to the Thirteenth Century', *SAC* 135 (1997), 209–20.

THOMPSON, M., 'The Origins of Bolingbroke Castle, Lincolnshire', *MA* 10 (1966), 152–6.

—— 'Associated Monasteries and Castles in the Middle Ages: A Tentative List', *Arch J*, 143 (1986), 305–21.

—— *The Decline of the Castle* (Cambridge, 1987).

—— 'The Green Knight's Castle', *Studies Presented to R. A. Brown*, Harper-Bill *et al.* (eds.), 317–25.

—— *The Rise of the Castle* (Cambridge, 1991).

—— 'The Military Interpretation of Castles', *Arch J*, 151 (1994), 439–45.

—— *Cloister, Abbot and Precinct in Medieval Monasteries* (Stroud, 2001).

——, see KENYON, J. and Thompson, M.

THUILLIER, H., *The Principles of Land Defence* (London, 1902).

THURLEY, S., *The Royal Palaces of Tudor England: Architecture and Court Life* (New Haven, 1993).

TIPPING, H., see Curzon, G. and Tipping, H.

TOUT, T., Chapters [in the Administrative History of Medieval England: The Wardrobe, the Chamber and the Small Seals], 6 vols. (Manchester, 1920–33).

TOY, S., *The Castles of Great Britain* (London, 1953).

—— *A History of Fortification from 3000 BC to A.D. 1700* (London, 1955).

—— *The Strongholds of India* (London, 1957).

—— *The Fortified Cities of India* (London, 1965).

TRABUT-CUSSAC, J.-P., 'Bastides ou forteresses? Les bastides de l'Aquitaine anglaise et les intentions de leurs fondateurs', *LMA* ser. 4 9 (1954), 81–135.

TRACY, J. (ed.), *The Urban Enceinte in Global Perspective* (Minneapolis, 2000).

TRANTER, N., *The Fortalices and Early Mansions of Southern Scotland 1400–1650* (Edinburgh, 1935).

—— *The Fortified House in Scotland*, 4 vols. (Edinburgh, 1962–6).

TREHARNE, R., 'The Mise of Amiens, 23 January, 1264', in *Studies Presented to F. M. Powicke*, Hunt *et al.* (eds.), 223–39.

TURNER, H., *Town Defences in England and Wales: An Architectural and Documentary Study, A.D. 900 to 1500* (London, 1970).

TURNER, R., *Lamphrey Bishop's Palace, Llawhaden* (Cardiff, 1991).

TUULSE, A., *Castles of the Western World*, trans. P. Girdwood (London, 1958).

UDERZO, A. and GOSCINNY, R., Le Tour de Gaulle d'Asterix (Neuilly-sur-Seine, 1965).

ULMER, C. and D'AFFARA, G., *The Castles of Friuli: History and Civilization* (Udine-Cologne, 1999).

VALE, M., 'Seigneurial Fortification and Private War in Later Medieval Gascony', in *Gentry and Lesser Nobility*, Jones (ed.), 133–48.

—— *The Origins of the Hundred Years War: The Angevin Legacy, 1250–1340* (1990; repr. Oxford, 1996).

—— 'The War in Aquitaine', in *Arms, Armies and Fortifications*, Curry and Hughes (eds.), 69–82.

VERBRUGGEN, J., 'Note sur le sens des mots "castrum", "castellum" et quelques autres expressions qui désignent des fortifications', *RBPH*, 28 (1950), 147–55.

VINCE, A., see Schofield, J. and Vince A.

VIOLLET-LE-DUC, É. É., *Essai sur l'architecture militaire au moyen-âge* (Paris, 1854).

—— *Dictionnaire raisonné de l'architecture française du xie au xvie siècle*, 10 vols. (Paris, 1854–68).

—— *Dictionnaire raisonné du mobilier français . . .*, 6 vols. (Paris, 1858–75).

VYNER, B. (ed.), *Building on the Past* (London, 1994).

WACHER, J., 'A Survey of Romano-British Town Defences of the Early and Middle Second Century', *Arch J*, 119 (1962) 104–13.

WADMORE, J., 'Westernhanger Castle', *Arch Cant*, 18 (1887), 200 (plan).

WALKER, S., *The Lancastrian Affinity 1361–99* (Oxford, 1990).

WARD, J., *Romano-British Buildings and Earthworks* (London, 1911).

WARD, J. C., 'The Lowry of Tonbridge and the Lands of the Clare Family in Kent, 1066–1217, *Arch Cant*, 96 (1980), 119–31.

—— 'Elizabeth de Burgh, Lady of Clare (d. 1360)', in *Medieval London Widows*, Barron (ed.), 29–46.

—— 'The English Noblewoman and her Family in the Later Middle Ages', in *Medieval Irishwomen*, Meek and Simms (eds.), 119–35.

—— 'Elizabeth de Burgh and Usk Castle', *The Monmouthshire Antiquary*, 18 (2002), 13–22.

WARREN, W. L., *King John* (London, 1961).

—— *Henry II* (London, 1973).

WATSON, F., 'The Expression of Power in a Medieval Kingdom: Thirteenth-Century Scottish Castles', in *Scottish Power Centres*, S. Foster, A. Macinnes, and R. Macinnes (eds.) (Glasgow, 1998), 59–77.

WATSON, G., *The Roman Soldier* (London, 1969).

WEBSTER, B., 'John of Fordun and the Independent Identity of the Scots', in *Medieval Europeans*, Smyth (ed.), 85–102.

WEBSTER, G., *The Roman Imperial Army* (London, 1969).

WEISSMÜLLER, A., *Castles From the Heart of Spain* (London, 1967).

WHITAKER, M., 'Otherworld Castles in Middle English Arthurian Romance', in *The Medieval Castle: Romance and Reality*, Reyerson and Powe (eds.), 27–46.

WHITE, G., 'Continuity in Government', in *Anarchy of King Stephen*, King (ed.), 117–44.

—— *Restoration and Reform, 1153–65: Recovery From Civil War in England* (Cambridge, 2000).

WILDEMAN, T., *Rheinische Wasserburgen und Wasserumwehrte Schlossbauten* (Neuss, 1954).

WILKINSON, F., *The Castles of England* (London, 1973).

WILLIAMS, A., ' "A Bell-House and a Burh-Geat": Lordly Residences in England Before the Norman Conquest', *MK* 4 (1992), 221–40 (repr. Liddiard, 2002).

—— *The English and the Norman Conquest* (Woodbridge, 1997).

WILLIAMS, G., *Medieval London: From Commune to Capital* (London, 1963).

WINTER, F., *Greek Fortifications* (London, 1971).

WOOD, M., *The English Medieval House* (London, 1965).

WOODCOCK, T. and ROBINSON, J., *The Oxford Guide to Heraldry* (Oxford, 2001).

WOOLGAR, C., *The Great Household in late Medieval England* (London, 1999).

WORSLEY, G., 'The Origins of the Gothic Revival: A Reappraisal' *TRHS* 6 ser., 3 (1993), 105–50.

—— 'An Englishman's Castle Is His Home', *The Daily Telegraph*, 1 Aug. 1998; repr. *CSG Newletter*, 12, 43–5.

WRIGHT, N., *Knights and Peasants: The Hundred Years War in the French Countryside* (Woodbridge, 1998).

YADIN, Y., *The Art of Warfare in Biblical Lands*, trans. M. Pearlman (London, 1963).

YOUNG, A., *Tudor and Jacobean Tournaments* (London, 1987).

YVER, J., 'Les Châteaux-forts en Normandie jusqu'au milieu du xiie siècle: contribution à l'étude du pouvoir ducal', *BSAN* 53 (1955–6), 28–115.

ZANCANI, D., 'Lombardy in the Middle Ages', in *Medieval Europeans*, Smyth (ed.), 217–32.

ZARNECKI, G., HOLT, J., and HOLLAND, T. (eds.), *English Romanesque Art*, Catalogue of Exhibition at the Hayward Gallery (London, 1984).

INDEX

Persons, Places, and Subjects
Note: Places unqualified (e.g. by 'town') are 'castles' by medieval usage. French regions are included but not British counties (historic) or geographical features. Authors of older secondary works are selectively indexed, *see also* Bibliography.
'Subjects' include ancillary as well as major references in order to assemble allusions to topics not treated as chapter sections.

Taillebourg, conflict of 168, 318

Talevan (Tal-y-Fan) 305 n 33, 348 n 167

Tamworth 156 n 249, 160, 195–6

Tany, Luke de 249, 373 n 243

    Robert de 60

Tarascon 268

Tarbes-en-Bigorre town 240

Tattershall 329 n 113

Tauriac *bastide* 245

Taylor, A. J. 6, 41 n 132, 280 n 297

Temple, Order of the, Templars 71 n 265, 145,
    242, 374 n 244

Tenby 243 n 149

'terminology', vocabulary, nomenclature 8, 34,
    37, 39, 42, 49 n 165, 51, 59, 61, 62, 64,
    69 n 254, 79, 83, 133, 169, 171 n 318, 182,
    196, 230 n 120, 235 n 141, 240 n 158, 245,
    248, 272, 297, 302, 306, 321, 331, 349, 358

    arx, dunjo, turris, presidium 22, 30 n 76, 39,
        49, 51–3, 67 n 243, 70–1, 73, 75 n 280, 87,
        162, 218 n 84, 238 n 151, 285, 361 n 215,
        362, 374, 376 n 248; *see also* keep,
        motte

    barmecan, barbacana 77 n 285, 260 n 226,
        301, 303 n 26, 335

    bretasche, bretagium, hourds 47, 71 n 263, 75,
        76 n 282, 80, 146 n 216, 158 n 260, 223,
        230 n 119, 237, 260 n 226, 279

    burh, caer, chester, castel, dinas 16, 32, 34, 35,
        39 n 124, 43, 47 n 155, 156, 252, 310

    camera, domus castelli 111, 204, 355, 357,
        359 n 207

    castellum, castrum, chastel e.g. 2, 15–16, 18,
        21 n 43, 25–6, 27, 30, 32–40, 42, 43,
        44 n 142, 45, 51–3, 62, 67, 79, 236,
        237 n 146, 249–50, 299, 306, 337 n 133, 361,
        363; *see also* definition

    castrum et fortericia, et baluum 88, 172,
        173 n 323, 373, 376

    castrum et villa 219, 220, 374

    claudere, includere, clorre, fermer 140, 152,
        156 n 251, 180, 181, 196 n 18, 199, 230 n 119,
        232, 236–7, 248, 263, 284, 290, 356

    domus (defensabilis), forte maison 40, 42, 68
        n 247, 70, 73, 77, 80, 87, 118, 128, 131,
        133 n 167, 138–9, 139, 147, 161, 170 n 314,
        177, 215 n 76, 222, 226, 250, 289, 312,
        343 n 151, 351, 381

    firmitas, ferté, fère 21, 25, 33, 45, 49 n 165, 73,
        167 n 304, 212, 213, 242 n 163, 288

    fortericia, fortalicium, forcellettum, forteresse,
        fortitudo, fortia etc. 2, 15–19, 42, 49 n 167,
        56 n 201, 59–60, 64, 67, 77, 78, 83, 114, 137
        n 181, 147, 148, 151, 155, 157, 199, 206 n 50,
        207, 289–90, 306, 311, 317, 325, 355, 361,
        374, 375; *see also* definition

    haiae, hérisson, garrol 21, 45, 146 n 216, 223,
        270, 276; *see also* earthworks

manerium, mansum, capital-messuage e.g. 54,
    60, 61, 69, 132, 162, 195 n 5, 199, 203, 204,
    270, 302 n 20, 306, 313 n 53, 345 n 155,
    349, 352 n 179, 357, 362, 380 n 260

munire, firmare, infortiare, emparare 136, 138
    n 184, 146–7, 158 n 260, 161 n 276, 171, 212,
    216, 236 n 144, 239, 284, 305

munitio, municipium, oppidum, moenia 26,
    33, 35, 39, 67, 70, 73, 77, 121, 141, 185,
    213 n 67, 234, 241, 270, 315, 325, 336,
    368 n 232, 374 n 244

pelus (peel) 64 n 233, 152, 182, 356

propugnaculum 45 n 144, 67, 68 n 247, 70, 72,
    74, 77, 78

puy, roche, rocca 26

receptaculum, receptum 77, 143, 219 n 86,
    335–7

situm castri, manerii 61–2, 358

villa et fortericia 124 n 124, 241–2

Teutonicus, Walerand 303, 342

Thatcham 208 n 55

Thetford 76

Thimbelby manor-house 332

Thomond, cantred of the Isles in 230 n 120, 233,
    349

Thompson, A. H. I, 35, 84

Thornbury 102

Thouars, castle, viscounts of 157, 327 n 105

    Aimeri, viscount of 90–1, 183 n 367, 365, 366;
        VIII, IX 319 n 76, 327, 337 n 134

    Eleanor, viscountess dowager of, Joan de
        319, 326–7

    Geoffrey, Hugh de 176–8, 327

    Regnaud, Savary, viscounts of 319

Thurles (*Dorch*) 347

Tibbers 64 n 233, 258 n 219

Tickhill 124, 256, 331 n 117

Tiffauges 319, 327 n 105

Tintagel 261

Tipperary town 231 n 127

Tirent, Auda of 309 n 42

Tolorieu (Catalonia) 213

Tonbridge, castle, town, Lowry 47 n 154, 56,
    208 n 54, 300–1, 348 n 167

Torcy 80 n 295, 273 n 268

Torigny 53, 157

    Robert de 53, 166 n 303

Torrington 62 n 229

Tosny 156 n 251

Toucy 70

Toulouse city, county of 79 n 291, 101, 104,
    145 n 211, 168, 215 n 74, 238, 246

    Raymond IV, of Saint-Gilles and Toulouse
        16; V, count of Toulouse 84, 147,
        337 n 133; VI 220, 241, 337 n 133,
        376 n 248; VII, Jeanne dau. of 168, 243,
        326, 374 n 244

    see also Poitiers, Alphonse de